Acknowledgements

We wish to express our gratitude to the following:

The Arts Council, John McColgan and Moya Doherty, Tony Ó Dálaigh, Dr Joseph Long, the staff of IT Sligo, the English Department at NUI Cork, Vincent O'Doherty, Robert Chambers, Emelie FitzGibbon, Marian Jordan, Una Farrelly, Thelma Lynch, Hilary Gow and Alan Bennis.

Theatre Talk
Voices of Irish Theatre Practitioners

Edited by
Lilian Chambers, Ger FitzGibbon, Eamonn Jordan
Dan Farrelly and Cathy Leeney

Carysfort Press
Dublin
An Chomhairle Ealaíon

A Carysfort Press Book
Theatre Talk: The Voices of Irish Theatre Practitioners
First published in Ireland in 2001 as a paperback original by
Carysfort Press, 58 Woodfield, Scholarstown Road, Dublin 16,
Ireland.
© 2001
Copyright remains with the Authors
Typeset by Carysfort Press
Cover design by Alan Bennis

Printed and bound by Leinster Leader Ltd
18/19 South Main Street, Naas, Co. Kildare, Ireland
This book is published with the financial assistance of The Arts
Council (An Chomhairle Ealaíon), Dublin, Ireland.

Contents

Introduction

What do practitioners think about contemporary Irish Theatre? This was the question that inspired everyone who worked on this book.

Irish theatre practitioners have been gaining recognition both nationally and internationally for some time. They are communicating their visions, articulating their perspectives through their creative choices and constantly interrogating the role of art in society. Many have received international accolades. But even the greatest performance of the greatest play vanishes into the ether in the moment in which it is made. Theatre is the most evanescent of arts.

It is precisely this fleeting, ephemeral quality of performance which makes theatre such a potent and authentic reflection of our reality. Some get the opportunity to speak about their work for newspaper articles and some through radio or television. Seldom do they have the opportunity to speak at length about the making and creating of theatre, and seldom are they in conversation with people with a thorough knowledge of their area of engagement.

One of the antidotes to ephemerality is print. Every year there are hundreds of books, essays and articles analyzing the current state or the most recent products of the Irish theatre and its makers. Most of the books and essays focus on the literary product, the printed play text. Academic analysis may be important in shaping our reflections, but the shaping of the future has almost always come from the practitioners.

The modest ambition of this book is to balance the wide and windy acres of critical analysis with some glimpses of the working conditions, the states of mind, the experiences and ideals of those at the front line in the making of Irish theatre. In this volume, our contributors tell the story as it is, not necessarily as we think it should be.

Irish theatre has developed through many phases since the beginning of the twentieth century and we have tried to represent them here, in some form. We have incorporated the thoughts and memories of very many of the people who have shaped what Irish theatre represents today: creativity, vitality, passion, talent, doom and gloom, repression, frustrations, disappointments but, above all joys, accolades and pinnacles.

The central focus of the book is on writers, actors, directors and others who are engaged in professional theatre-based work, but other voices are also heard: those involved in theatre-in-education, in youth theatre, in the amateur theatre movement, in theatre criticism. These accounts show that one of the strengths and delights of Irish theatre is the capacity and opportunity of people to cross over and work in different sectors. A theatre critic takes time off to become a dramaturg; a company does one show with two actors in a hundred-seat venue but also does a massive piece of outdoor spectacle theatre taking over acres of city centre; an actor becomes a writer; a writer becomes a director. What we have is a wide variety of theatre activity and huge variations in working conditions, funding, visions, purposes and expectations. The day to day experience of a professional actor is in very sharp contrast to the working life of a playwright, which is itself in marked contrast to the perspective of an artistic director who runs the company, hustles for funds, plans tours and directs. We are all happy to lay claim to "one of our own" when they enjoy international success, but why are we not always prepared to support the show involved? There are people making huge sacrifices, professionally and personally, and they deserve our support. As a society, we should be asking ourselves how we might recognize the huge contribution that these people make to the phenomenon of Irish culture.

In the interviews we have taken the opportunity to mix and match director and administrator, academic and playwright, playwright and playwright, broadcaster and critic, actor and director and so on, including practitioners from both North and South, and in the process unusual and unique dynamics have emerged.

The interviews took place over a six-month period in the middle of 2001 and what was most striking during the gestation period was the extraordinary generosity of those who contributed. In a profession often maligned for its suspected "bitchiness, its back-stabbing, its competitive and jealous nature", it was illuminating and inspiring to find Irish theatre folk so devoid of the supposed Irish national pastime of begrudgery. Begrudgery was not "alive and well" in the participation of our interviewees and interviewers. Both groups gave of their time and energies unstintingly.

We found that all contributors had a great willingness, even enthusiasm, to be included in this volume and we hope that you, the reader, will enjoy the deep well-spring of energy and creativity that is flowing through Irish theatre today, exemplifying some of the best qualities of the people working in this field.

The result of our quest gained its own momentum as time went by, and we realized that we had to encompass far more than we had initially imagined. The breadth and scope of Irish theatre is only as limited as the globe, and its popularity is certainly not shackled by the restrictions of land mass or population. We had thought that we could produce a comprehensive representation, but it quickly became clear that all we could include, in one volume, was a sample of the views of some of the established figures and the emerging voices in Irish theatre. Inevitably, there are omissions. There were critical constraints of time and space, and availability. Whilst this is regrettable, to be realistic, it was not possible to include all those whom we would have wished.

Again, our thanks to those who gave their time, their stories and their insights to the making of this book, which originally was the brainchild of Eamonn Jordan. It is not a survey; it is a series of frontline reports. If there is anything with which you disagree remember the words of Oliver Goldsmith in *The Vicar of Wakefield* when he said: "A book may be amusing with numerous errors, or it may be very dull without a single absurdity."

Ben Barnes in Conversation with Martin Drury

MD: *We are in the lead-up period to the centenary of the Abbey, which was founded in a crucible where arts and politics mixed in quite a catalytic fashion. Though a "literary" theatre, the conception and practice of drama and literature were much more "engaged" than the word "literary" suggests to our ears. What are your reflections on the role of the National Theatre in the social, political, economic landscape it currently inhabits?*

BB: I remember when I staged the first Abbey production of *Sive* in the mid-1980s, the Kerry babies drama was unfolding and some commentators made connections between the two events. More recently when we staged Tom Murphy's latest play *The House*, connections were made between the story of returning immigrants and the emergence of what was, euphemistically, called a refugee problem in Ireland. These direct links with political or social events are, however, rare. Irish writers have a tendency to interrogate the present through the past or through a metaphorical or allegorical construct.

Look at the work of Marina Carr or Sebastian Barry. Maybe our society, like our economy, caught somewhere between European humanism and American materialism, is evolving at such a dizzying pace that no writer feels equal to attempting to put his finger on that racing pulse. Tom Murphy was asked at the recent public interview in the Abbey what he thought the younger generation of writers should be writing about and he shot back: money and the consequences of money. I have said that through its new work and the re-visiting of its repertoire the Abbey must always aspire to be a voice for the nation and a definition, within the broader church of European states, of what is quintessentially Irish. I believe that people do look to the Abbey to fulfil that role and in many ways it does. The fact that Ernest Blythe rejected *A Whistle in the Dark* forty years ago as a play which portrayed people he did not recognize as having any basis in reality was to totally miss the point.

In 2001 we can produce this play to acclaim and the maturity of our audiences with that distance from the period is that they can be held in the vice grip of the drama while understanding the social and political circumstances that bred that extreme violence and appropriate it as part of what we are and what made us what we are. On the brink of monetary homogenization we struggle with our identity as mid-Atlantic Americans or Western seaboard Europeans and a play like *Translations*, currently touring the cities of Europe in our production, with its striking meditation on language and cultural identity, speaks profoundly to a whole new generation of theatregoers.

Our spare and intense studio production of *The Playboy of the Western World* this summer [2001] speaks volumes for artists and an audience who have the tools to access a canonical work of our repertoire without recourse to red petticoats and sheebeens. This ease with the non-literal comes to us courtesy of the Théâtre de Complicité-inspired *Tarry Flynn* or the work of Patrick Mason and Tom Mac Intyre in the 1980s. So I suppose that what I am trying to say is that the new work of the Abbey and the excursions into its repertoire make deep connections with the theatre-going public of this country even if no one is writing overtly about the background to the Moriarty tribunal or the moral consequences of all this money. That having been said we have two new plays in 2002 which take as their starting point prominent political figures from the recent past!

MD: *You are a history graduate and therefore have both a keenly-developed knowledge of, and respect for, the past. But you are running a national institution whose raison d'etre is an art form that exists in the now. Have you particular reflections on the idea of "tradition?"*

BB: One of my favourite passages in literature is from *The Great Gatsby* by Scott Fitzgerald and ends with the line "So we beat on, boats against the current, borne back ceaselessly into the past…" I am very mindful of the continuum of history and tradition and that what happens in the present is enabled by what has gone before. I have been reflecting on this as I prepare to make some remarks from the Abbey stage on the closing of the Tom Murphy season this weekend and I think that what I want to say is that the purpose of re-visiting the works of our repertoire, which can be characterized as our engagement with our tradition in that sense, is primarily to re-imagine those plays in ways which will resonate with our audiences. But as well as the important matter of making these works live for a whole new generation of theatre-goers we also demonstrate the continuity of the tradition whether that is as an acknowledged influence or as conscious rebellion. Thus O'Casey would acknowledge his debt to Boucicault just as Tom Murphy spoke eloquently about the importance of O'Casey in his evolution as a dramatist and the likes of Declan Hughes, Billy Roche, Conor McPherson and Jim Nolan would in turn say that in some measure what they are doing owes much to the ground broken by the Tuam dramatist. In terms of the theatre, tradition can have a deadening influence if we are overly respectful of it. I think some of the most exciting work can happen when a traditional work is refracted imaginatively through a contemporary sensibility, again I come to Niall Henry's staging of *The Playboy* last summer, and I suppose we have to bring our ever-shifting perspective to bear on works of art which in one sense, the strict literal sense, are frozen in time.

When I staged *Big Maggie* at the Abbey with Brenda Fricker in 1988 I thought it was necessary to tame the excesses of the text and to root it very much in the social reality of a changing Ireland and the second programme for economic expansion. I wanted to show that the tensions between Maggie and her children were generational and that the matriarch's thrift and tenacity had something to do with the undertow of caution that characterizes someone whose grandparents would have personal memories of the great famine handed down to them while her, as she sees it, rebellious children try to reach out and embrace a brave new world. I was partly reacting to the play's reputation as melodrama and burlesque and was determined to show it had a more profound intent if the accretions of careless productions could be stripped away.

It was very interesting for me that Garry Hynes's new production at the Abbey this year released again the visceral power of Maggie and was monolithic and open to its Greek drama parallels. It amazed me that no one picked up on the *Medea* comparison particularly since we had staged the Euripides's tragedy less than twelve months before in Deborah Warner's production. Maybe this coming full circle of *Big Maggie* was in some way enabled by the successful claim for its inclusion as a serious drama of the repertoire staked out by that 1988 production. Maybe Garry Hynes owes me one!

MD: *What are your expectations about the resolution of the issue of the building? Apart from the issue of location, what are the key guiding principles of any new development?*

BB: If I can take the second part of that first I would say that, regardless of location, I think it is vitally important that the theatre, the physical bricks and mortar, which is after all the National Theatre, built and run by the money of the tax payer, should have a dynamic relationship with the public. This must go beyond a visit to one of its auditoria at eight o'clock in the evening. Public access to a bookshop, archive, outreach and education facilities, a restaurant and daytime platform activities will enable that dynamic engagement and help to both de-mystify the theatre as an art form and place the core work in an enlivening context.

From my side of the footlights, as it were, I would like to see stages with good acoustics and workable relationships to their auditoria and I would like to have the electronic and hydraulic capacity to develop the work of the theatre in repertory as most contemporary European theatres do. While one might want to build settings at another location, the administration, rehearsal facilities and all the supporting logistics of the theatre should be housed in this new building and be given the light and space to engage with the creative and administrative tasks which constitute the work of a modern theatre. Needless to say the current Abbey does not get off the starting blocks with fulfilling any of these criteria.

I believe that the current Government is seriously engaged with this issue and there is an acknowledgement that something radical must be done and that tinkering at the edges of the problem, which might have been the only economic option in the 1990s, is no longer acceptable. It was unfortunate that the views of the Abbey and the Government became polarized over the issue of location and to some extent that polarization was unhelpfully orchestrated by the media. I saw one cartoon of the Taoiseach and myself in flight in batman suits above the grey mausoleum of the Abbey facade, trading punches! While we saw the potential to create a landmark, state-of-the-art building at Grand Canal Harbour and expressed that as a preference in the light of limited other options, we were always careful to say that we would not rule out a north inner city solution should one present itself. Our mistake, what some might characterize as our naiveté, was not that we did not say this but perhaps we did not say it loudly enough or insistently enough and got very quickly painted into a corner. My own views on the whole Northside/Southside thing and the definition of what might constitute the city centre in ten or fifteen years time are well documented and don't need to be raked over here, the fact of the matter is that the political consensus seems to be that the Abbey should stay in or around its current location and the democrat in me accepts that, while the pragmatist in me hopes that the acknowledgement of the importance of the Abbey as a national institution and the serious public debate around the issue of a new building that attended the dispute earlier in the year will create the climate for a solution which, to put it at its most basic, will provide the requisite funding and square metres to deliver the building to match our proper artistic goals and ambitions.

MD: *A "core value" has always been that of the Abbey as a "writer's theatre." Yet it seems to me that there is a danger in making almost a "fetish" of newness at the expense sometimes of quality. How do you hope to make the National Theatre really work to support the development of new writing?*

BB: I think that quality in new writing is paramount. I do not subscribe to the idea that putting something half-baked onto the stage can be a positive experience for the writer and can allow him or her to learn from the process of rehearsal and performance to write a better play. That somehow this is preferable to endless workshops or meetings with literary departments. Besides the fact that I think that this policy takes an audience for granted, I do not think it is of any benefit to the fledgling writer.

The developmental aspect of the work is crucial and I have put certain personnel and mechanisms in place at the Abbey to ensure that helpful mediation in the difficult process of writing a play is available to our younger dramatists. Jocelyn Clarke has joined us as our new Commissioning Manager and I have a tremendous respect for his enthusiasm and integrity. We are developing a large portfolio of play commissions and I believe that Jocelyn will steer them in a challenging and constructive way through the various stages of their development. We have created a studio facility called the Abbey Lab in Temple Bar which will be our research and development operation and here I hope the various workshops and readings can take place on the way to creating new work for the stage. Jocelyn, Ali Curran (the new Director of the Peacock) and I have also been talking about ways in which we can test works in progress before an audience without committing them to full productions. We are also considering a mentoring scheme. It sounds very American but what it is in essence is that a young writer might benefit from the informal advice of a more experienced dramatist and we would broker that connection. In the short term you may see less new drama on our stages but hopefully what you will see will be well thought through and without killing its spirit, voice or individuality, as I believe American dramaturgy so often does, produce drama which has been rigorously tested in the developmental phase.

I think that much of the younger writing in Irish theatre is strong on narrative, character and use of language but weak on structure. Last year we invited David Edgar to give some masterclasses to a group of young and not so young writers and that was very valuable. I think Jocelyn will do a lot more of that sort of work and that is unseen but hugely valuable. Can I also say that when you talk about a "fetish" for newness what I take from that is that there is sometimes a preoccupation with style over real content and I do think that this afflicts the British and American perception of Irish drama. I think that we have to be true to ourselves and tell our stories in ways that are meaningful to us and if that resonates beyond these shores then that is a bonus. It is the only way that I can see to proceed. Trying to second guess the coming fashion in London or New York is hopeless and facile.

MD: *Should work be done in supporting existing writers, particularly in terms of their breaking new ground?*

BB: I think that what I have said in answer to your last question is applicable here as well. The rules are the same whether you are constructing a domestic drama or telling old tales in new ways. All plays by their own lights should be well made. I do think, however, that the Peacock needs to positively discriminate towards work which is pushing at the ceiling of what is possible in the theatre. We must, I think, get back to what makes the theatre a unique experience and that has something to do with the suspension of disbelief, the fluidity of the theatre space, the chemistry of the actor/audience relationship, the capacity of the actor to tell the story with words and gestures, with the voice and the body, and an acceptance of a heightened use of language. None of these assets is applicable to the competing media of television and film and anyway we should not be fighting battles we cannot win. It is why a spare, uncluttered *mis-en-scène* is almost invariably preferable in the contemporary theatre. When I staged *Les Liaisons Dangereuses* in 1987 I told a complex story in half a dozen locations with three pieces of furniture, and the audience, whose imagination should not be underestimated, were never confused. As a director the first question I ask about furniture on a set is whether it is necessary. When you invite an audience to look at your frame everything you put in there must earn its keep.

MD: *You have emphasized the European/International dimension of the Abbey's work since you became Artistic Director. Can you comment on some of the more "internal" lessons learned from such international production exchange and interaction?*

BB: Well I do find it strange that our country is very committed to the European idea in economic, social, political and, increasingly, in defence terms and it seems logical that we should attempt a sort of cultural rapprochement as well. There is a focus in the European mainland theatre on *mis-en-scène*, the importance of dramaturgy and a preponderance for the expression of stories in theatre which are more physically vivid and theatrically committed. You can also see the benefits with a company like the Schaubühne of the cumulative value of the ensemble approach and the ongoing training and creation of a group of actors and dancers who work together. Because we work from such a small pool of actors and many of our artists come back again and again to work with us we have, in some ways, a de facto ensemble but it is not the same as an ensemble which constantly works and trains together. I think the need for such a system will become evident as the demands of our repertoire become more rigorous. At the same time our traditions are literary in this country and our real strength is with drama of the spoken word but to be able to ally that to greater physical dexterity and dramaturgical rigour could move our work onto a different plane. The benefits with our European exchange are reciprocal. As I said earlier, *Translations* is currently touring in Europe and being very well received but what I really hope will be possible will be to develop a co-production project with some of our European partners and take advantage of the Culture 2000 protocols to advance that. Some of our associate directors like Deborah Warner, Laszlo Marton and Katie Mitchell have worked extensively on the European mainland and I think a cross-cultural project could be tremendously exciting and beneficial. On an organizational level I have found it very interesting to visit theatres in Prague, Budapest, St. Petersburg, Paris, Berlin and Milan. The repertoire system allows greater flexibility in scheduling, keeps shows fresh and gives audiences greater choice. It is, of course, predicated on some kind of ensemble but this may be possible to establish in the Abbey on a seasonal basis. The recent Tom Murphy retrospective is a case in point.

It also has struck me that most European theatres operate for nine or ten months of the year and use the down time to build their programmes, do maintenance, plan strategically and close their whole operations down for a month. This seems eminently sensible to me to avoid the kind of burn-out that afflicts our artists and institutions. My European colleagues are agog when I tell them that we present sixteen new productions every year where anything up to six of them can be new plays and that we are open fifty-two weeks a year. It is amusing in that context when you see some journalists complain that the Abbey is not good value for money. That's rubbish, it is incredibly good value for money and they don't know what they are talking about. The argument, however, should be about quality and not quantity and if greater quality can be achieved by performing for forty or forty-four weeks instead of fifty-two then we should look at that.

MD: *I'd like to pursue this idea of perceived notions of "value." What are your concerns about definitions of success? Do you sense, for example, that outside of a relatively small committed theatre-going public, Irish audiences have become, or always were, conservative?*

BB: Success, in superficial terms, is defined by good reviews and healthy attendance. Fortunately the presence or absence of the first doesn't always dictate the second. There is nothing wrong with this kind of success and I would argue that any going concern depends to some extent on critical imprimatur and good box office. But there is no doubt from my perspective that *artistic* success which strikes a chord with the theatre-going public is the hardest won success but also the most gratifying. I like to see the theatre full of people but not just because it helps our bank balance, but because I believe that the theatre is a communal experience and that a full theatre is a less inhibited theatre and the quality of attention, of openness and response is enhanced by the full over the half-empty space.

Conversely I believe, at some level, in a house of 630 seats [the Abbey's capacity] that if thirty per cent of the places remain unsold the audience who are in attendance are wondering why the other two hundred people have not shown up. So a full theatre, which I always hope and strive for, is firstly about chemistry and only thereafter about balancing books. The subsidy attached to the Abbey, however, underpins the need and the duty to challenge artistically even if that means a lowering of expectation with regard to audience numbers. Our production of *Iphigenia at Aulis* earlier in the year [2001] was a case in point. The quality of the ensemble work was glittering, the use of the Abbey stage was breathtaking, the design and lighting were boldly theatrical and the fierce intelligence, integrity and commitment of Katie Mitchell's direction, in my view, confirmed why she is regarded as one of the great European directors. The production and choice of play also challenged pre-conceived ideas about what the Abbey should be doing and how it should be doing it. The production never broke fifty percent attendance. *Medea*, on the other hand, also an iconoclastic production but with a star actor (Fiona Shaw) in the leading role was turning people away at matinées and went on to a successful run in London and will open next year in New York. I believe both productions had significant merits and overcame and turned to advantage the limitations of the notoriously difficult Abbey stage. That the one with the star did best is indicative of a conservatism or lack of sagacity in the wider theatre-going public, but I would have to say that that is not unique to our audiences. Maybe the terms of reference for classical work are not as available to this generation as they were to mine and those who went before and maybe it is not enough to simply present these works without contextualizing them in some way. Maybe the success of our Tom Murphy season had something to do with that and why all our American partners are calling for residencies which include lectures, masterclasses, seminars and publications surrounding the theatre event. I don't know; it's a big subject.

MD: *Has theatre criticism to take some responsibility for public attitudes, in this context?*

BB: Well, of course, it has. Like most of my colleagues in the theatre I believe that the standard of criticism in Irish media outlets is, with a few notable exceptions, truly appalling. It is not about good or bad reviews but about criticism which is perceptive and takes the productions on the terms they are offered and deals with them there. Because of lack of space and time newspaper criticism will always be compromised but the real difference can be made in features writing and greater attention on theatre in performance in the academic treatment of drama. I frequently flick through the index of theatre books to find hardly any reference to the actors or directors who create the work. Theatre is not theatre until it is realized on the stage and academia must take that distinction on board more pervasively. We need to build a literature and establish an intellectual tradition of writing around theatre in performance as opposed to theatre as a literary art form. There are some signs of changes in this area. Indeed the very publication, which this interview is for, is a case in point. But to come back to the newspapers and radio for a moment: there is a war of attrition in which the theatre is losing out and is beginning to look like a minority art form. Obviously this is not so during Theatre Festival time and I have to say that the coverage of our Murphy season was exemplary but how often now do you see a play review with a captioned photograph and how long ago is it that any newspaper had a dedicated weekly page or section of a page devoted to theatre?

MD: *You did what might be described as "a very long apprenticeship" before you became Artistic Director of the Abbey. This included a goodly spell as a central figure in Groundwork, a commercially-minded company with a very strong aesthetic. What did that experience teach you and what of it did you bring to the Abbey?*

BB: Dealing with all I deal with now I am very glad of the "long apprenticeship." I do not think you could do a job like this without a vast reservoir of experience. Before coming to the Abbey I directed well over a hundred plays and operas, including many at the Abbey, and ran my own company and an opera company before that and I have learned very many valuable lessons from those experiences. I have learned to consult others but essentially to trust my own judgement. I have a wonderful wife and children and staunch friends, but being the director of an institution like the Abbey is essentially a very lonely place to be. You have to have reserves of self-belief and realize the job is about enacting the vision you laid out before the people who employ you and, while being mindful of the great tradition of this theatre, not to shirk from re-defining it for a new generation. It's not about popularity; it's about integrity. It's not about self-aggrandizement; it's about public service. I think my "apprenticeship" prepared me for all that. At a less heroic level I learnt the need to delegate and the importance of building a team you can trust and delegate to. This means you have to have colleagues who are genuinely sympathetic to what you want to do and are prepared to help you to do it.

It takes time to build that team and when you inherit people from previous administrations that process can be even more drawn out. I also developed a very strong sense during my Groundwork days of the need for effective promotion and I have very strong views about every aspect of the transaction between a theatre and its public. This, I think, was quite a shock to the people in the Abbey when I came in. They were used to a culture of non-interference by the Artistic Director but I simply do not believe that you can divorce what happens on the stage from the way you promote it and sometimes it's as simple as this: if one operation is nine to five and the other is seven to eleven how can you not be asking for trouble. Enthusiasm and passion are among the best qualities for people working in the theatre in whatever capacity and those qualities are even more precious in a big institution like the Abbey.

MD: *As you reflect on the theatre profession over twenty years, how do you think it has changed for people working in it?*

BB: Well as a director the actors are better trained and more disciplined and that is a huge change. I remember directing plays at the beginning of my career where actors would turn up late for rehearsal and be carrying scripts into the fourth week. Both of those things would be inconceivable today. Actors are very hard-working, totally reliable people and I love that.

Design is technically more assured and production management is more streamlined. Lighting is completely computerized and, therefore, plotting has become speedier and the options are legion. I remember sitting with Leslie Scott while cues were laboriously notated across endless dimmer racks. Nobody would dream of suggesting smoking in a rehearsal room which suits me fine. I hate smoking. I do not think that pay rates and commissioning fees have quite kept pace over the years. We pay all national wage agreements at the Abbey and while I do not think that theatre can ever compete with film or television when it comes to remuneration it is certainly desirable that actors should not have to feel the need to do voice-overs, commercials, T.V. and film to "subsidize" their work in the theatre. I think Equity is a weak organization and if it were worth its salt it would be ensuring that there are pension schemes and easy access to mortgage financing available to their members. It is also true that actors are discriminated against when it comes to things like car insurance by virtue of the fact that they work at night. This is ludicrous. Actors are by and large the most responsible people I know and it is scandalous if they are penalized in this way. It might even be unconstitutional. If they have a union that is one of the things it should look into.

MD: *You mentioned that you believe actors are better trained now. Could you elaborate a little more on what that means for you as a director?*

BB: Well, I regard the work of a director as a process of selection and arrangement. The actors present various options in rehearsal and choices are made on the basis of the story you want to tell. The process of trial and error is the most exciting part of rehearsal and also the most creative. I think that actors of my generation and younger understand the value and the need for that exhaustive process of elimination and they are not afraid or cynical of going there. These actors are also more technically assured and to varying degrees understand the need for continuous exploration and training. We conduct voice classes and classes in Alexander and Pilates techniques and many specialist masterclasses at the Abbey and there is always a healthy turnover of actors in attendance. The best actor to have in rehearsal is the one who has a keen acting intelligence, who is vocally and physically attuned to the needs of the material and emotionally open to the roller coaster journey we are all about to embark on. My most recent foray into the rehearsal room was a joy in that regard working with Mark Lambert, Owen Roe and Catherine Walsh on *The Gigli Concert*. With people like Mark and Owen stepping up to the mark for the great roles in Irish theatre the future is very bright. Here are actors with glittering technique matched by a sustained emotional quality in performance. It is dazzling. A director can only be as good as the actors he is working with and I have been largely privileged to work with the best actors of my generation. I think a shared understanding and acceptance of process is vital for the collective act of staging a play. I have been lucky to work in the past with actors like Ray McAnally, Marie Kean, Brenda Fricker, Niall Tóibín, Joan O'Hara and others but I am glad to be beyond that stage where I might have to negotiate the ego of a "great actor" or listen to what I suspect are the rather dubious pearls of wisdom passed on from the likes of Ria Mooney or Frank Dermody.

MD: *You have a four-year contract with the Abbey which you are twenty two months into. Is that enough time to achieve what you want at the National Theatre?*

BB: Well, I think it would be improper for me to discuss the specifics of my contract at the Abbey in this context. I will say, however, that most people, if they are lucky have one or two good ideas and once they have had a chance to put them into practice they should know that it is time to move on. The length of time it takes to put the ideas into practice depends on the quality of the tools you inherit to do the job, the steeliness of your resolve and probably some good luck. For an artistic enterprise like running a theatre the ideal time is probably seven or eight years. We don't have to look far to see directors who have out-stayed their welcome and where the organizations they run have become too closely bound up with their personality and where artistically they become at best repetitive and at worst atrophied. I am not thinking beyond putting our 2002 and 2003 programme together at this moment in time.

MD: *You enjoyed the freedom of being a freelance theatre director working at home and abroad before taking up the role of Artistic Director. How do you negotiate the administrative demands of your artistic direction role with the necessity to maintain your involvement as a director of productions?*

BB: Well it is not easy. You really need one hundred per cent focus when you are directing a play because it is not an easy thing to do and it has the pressure that within five weeks of starting with a jumble of words on the page you have to present a full blown, living breathing production to hundreds of people who come through the doors, plonk themselves down and say "Ok, show us what you have for us." There are very few professions where that kind of public scrutiny is so relentless and so, properly, unforgiving. But while I am in a rehearsal room the rest of the theatre does not stop functioning: forward planning and casting goes on; negotiations continue for the new building; readings and workshops continue to be scheduled; other plays go into rehearsal and preview; international business needs to have decisions made about it; board meetings take place; endless meetings are requested by writers, directors, visiting producers etc. It is an assault course at the best of times but it does become almost impossible when I am in rehearsal as well. I end up coming in at all hours of the morning and also working late at night. This is not good for my health, my sanity or, indeed, my family life.

I am, therefore, planning to restrict myself to one production a year for the foreseeable future but I do believe that when we have completed our management of change in the administration of the theatre that it will be possible to delegate a lot more and hopefully begin to see the wood and not always the trees. I also think that it is important for the Artistic Director of the Abbey to be out and about and seeing the work of up-and-coming individuals and companies. I was very good at all that before I came into this position but now I am simply far too busy to ever get to anything outside of here. I know that is not good and I am determined to change it in the short to medium term. My wife, Julia, says that Artistic Directors are remembered for how they change a theatre and not for the individual productions they direct and I am sure that, as in most things, she is right but I would hate not to direct at all while I am at the Abbey and I also think that it is important not to become remote from the real pulse of what a theatre is about which is putting on plays. My board have been very wise in encouraging me to direct an occasional production outside the Abbey and while I have not, up to now, felt comfortable about being away from the theatre for that length of time (up to five weeks) I have accepted engagements in Montreal, Barcelona and Toronto spread out over the next few years.

MD: *Finally, can I ask you about this "safe pair of hands" tag which seems to have attached itself to you?*

BB: Well, I am very glad you asked that question! It certainly is not meant to be a compliment and is a product of lazy, myopic and sometimes vindictive journalism from people that I do not know and have never met. It goes something like this: the best that can be said about Ben Barnes is that he is a safe pair of hands and that his career has been built on staging boring revivals and the plays of Bernard Farrell and John B. Keane. The first thing to be said about that is that I am very proud of the work I have done on re-habilitating the more serious dramas of John B. Keane and the hard-won success of the theatre of Bernard Farrell needs no apologia from me. Bernard is a superb contemporary dramatist who works in the most difficult of genres and consistently succeeds in connecting with his audience. It is no accident that he is among the most popular dramatists in the country. If this is regarded as safe territory then so be it but it is far from the full picture. I have directed new work by the likes of Graham Reid, Neil Donnelly, Jim

Nolan, Tom Mac Intyre, Aidan Mathews. My work for Opera Theatre Company at the outset, with productions like *Carmen* and *The Turn of the Screw*, was regarded as iconoclastic and I think that it has been acknowledged that I have brought something fresh and truthful to my productions of plays like *Juno and the Paycock* at the Abbey. None of this or the many other examples I could cite suits the thesis of the safe pair of hands, so it is conveniently ignored.

At an institutional level I believe it is important to set your stall out clearly and to literally give a direction to your artistic tenure. The goals I have set myself I have been very explicit about from the outset: increasing the audience in the Peacock and re-focussing it as a theatre which discriminates towards the experimental and formally daring; creating a European context for the work of the Abbey which operates in both directions; ensuring that my generation of writers and those that follow find their voice on the main stage to replace those writers who have been its staple in the last decades of the twentieth century and that they in turn make way for the new wave of writers in the Peacock; creating a sophisticated and effective associate director panel drawn from the ranks of the best Irish and international directors; modernizing the administration of the Abbey and ensuring that its corporate image reflects its artistic aspirations and achievements. It's all out there and while it is difficult, it's not rocket science either. Productions and activity which have delivered on that vision include touring *Translations* into Eastern Europe, bringing the Schaubühne to Dublin, staging *Medea* and *Iphigenia at Aulis* on the main stage within twelve months of each other, bringing Calixto Bieito to Dublin to direct *Barbaric Comedies*, premiering Mark O'Rowe's play *Made in China* at the Peacock, re-imagining *The Playboy of the Western World* in a studio space, staging the Tom Murphy retrospective. None of this could, by any stretch of the imagination, be regarded as safe and I would respectfully suggest that it is not a bad batting average for twenty months.

On the other hand staging *A Life* by Hugh Leonard and having Garry Hynes direct a new production of *Big Maggie* with Marie Mullen in the title role caters for a wide audience who may have, what some regard as, the less lofty ambition of wanting to come to the theatre to be entertained but who are very much part of our constituency as a National Theatre. That is the key to the vertiginous balancing act of running the Abbey Theatre. At some level you need to serve constituencies at both ends of the spectrum and everywhere in between and try to do so with a clear and identifiable artistic direction and aesthetic. It's hard to know how successful that is when you are in the middle of it but while the journey is often frustrating it is also endlessly exciting and exhilarating. As for the safe pair of hands, well, those who know me and know my work know that it is a glib and unsustainable soubriquet. I think that what I have done and continue to do gives a lie to that lazy categorization but ultimately, while I might be mildly irritated, I care little and lose no sleep over the ill-thought-out and selective ruminations of a few faceless journalists.

Ben Barnes was appointed Artistic Director of the National Theatre in 2000. He has directed extensively in the theatre and opera at home and abroad. He has received national and international awards for his productions which have been seen around the world from New York to Moscow and from Adelaide to Tokyo.

Martin Drury graduated from UCD in 1979, having completed an MA thesis on the later plays of Sean O'Casey. Since then he has worked in a wide variety of key positions in the arts. For five years he was Artistic Director of TEAM Educational Theatre (commissioning and directing new plays by Bernard Farrell, Frank McGuinness and Jim Nolan, among others). He was Education and Dance Officer of The Arts Council for five years, followed by a period as a freelance theatre director (including productions for Druid Theatre and Opera Theatre Company) and was Script Editor for Druid for a three-year period. He has written extensively on arts policy, most significantly a decade ago when he researched and wrote the seminal *Dublin Arts Report*. Recently he is most identified with The Ark which is Europe's only custom-designed arts centre for children. He founded The Ark and was its director until March 2001. While there he commissioned and directed many productions and has now returned to the freelance world as a director and arts consultant. He is currently working on a number of theatre projects and, outside the theatre, as Design and Arts Consultant on the new Mater and Children's Hospital Development, scheduled for completion in 2008. For the period 2001-2004, he is Honorary Fellow at the Department of Psychology of University College Dublin.

Sebastian Barry in Conversation with Ger FitzGibbon

GF: *Was there a particular moment when you realised that what you wanted to do was to make theatre?*

SB: Definitely, because there was a definite intention to avoid it. Given the complicated nature of families, I would have avoided theatre as a way of separating myself from my mother's *métier*. Not out of dislike but to break a connection, to be an individual. I was writing prose and poems in the period 1978-1985 and in 1985 I was fed up with me approaching those forms and writing short novel after short novel. Looking back on it, I can see those short novels – of which there were six, a couple were published – were really play length. So, while I was avoiding the theatre, the shape in my mind of a work was play length, whatever that is! In 1986 my wife [Alison Deegan, actress] went away to do a BBC series for a couple of weeks. I had read somewhere that Lorca wrote his plays in ten days – which seemed handy enough – and I wrote *Boss Grady's Boys*. [It was based on] a very personal matter about two men I had lived beside in County Cork and I heard that there were people in Hiace vans going around robbing such people. I had that complicated impulse – very personal and ridiculous – that the act of writing about them could keep them safe. I tried to write a play about Mai Kirwin – who in fact ended up as the sixth play – and got nowhere, didn't know how to do it. And in that useful despair that we all work out of, I sat down and wrote *Boss Grady's Boys*. I was a bit surprised by it because it seemed to me quite clear and lucid in a way that had eluded me in a lot of stuff I had been doing, which tends to get drunk a bit with language. This wasn't like that. In a way it was them authoring themselves, which was an important distinction: the secret authors of the plays are the characters.

My wife read it and she said "that's not too bad, send it off to the Abbey." Christopher FitzSimons [was] caretaker Artistic Director at the time, and then Vincent Dowling came in shortly after that and definitely wanted to do it. [Eamonn Kelly and Jim Norton played the two lead roles.] It was my first experience – plays, novels or otherwise – of something simplifying happening, where I wasn't suspicious of the approbation. I could see that here was an arena where you were actually dependent on people responding, which was against my idea of modernism where you're meant to keep the audience or the readership at a bit of a remove. That was kind of liberating because it was against my stupefying instincts. Crowds of people came, suddenly we were paying the rent – which was, believe me, a major change in our lives – and it seemed like a world, unlike the world of poetry, which is so parsimonious – the elder playwrights were so welcoming. It was like accidentally finding what you wanted to do without ever realising you wanted to do it. There was not an ease involved, but there was a rightness – against the run of things in my life, against my general instincts.

GF: *So that got you started.*

SB: It was when I wrote *Prayers of Sherkin* that I thought it might be possible to make a series of all the things that had concerned me, all the things I had written about various people. I set off to do it and sixteen years later, here I am with the series finished. But still very much a personal matter, always personal. They don't exist for me as plays, as literary constructs, they are always, for me, done for personal reasons of survival.

GF: *What's been the most difficult thing about that?*

SB: If I've had any difficulty with theatre, it's been at the point where theatre stops being personal and disappears out into other realms – of criticism, of academia, of standing, the ups and downs of Irish writers and writing, the horse race of it all. That's where I've had most difficulty because it has a resounding backward impact upon the personal. You have to maintain – not an innocence, but – the fact of it being a personal matter and not a public matter. As soon as it becomes a public matter something else occurs. You can see in other writers: their work becomes more general or larger or political and *loses* its largeness or polity or whatever because the personal has been assaulted in a backward move. Preserving that personal impulse, that's the thing.

GF: *Is that why you guard your privacy?*

SB: I was talking earlier about not doing interviews – [about needing] to take two years away from saying anything. It's really to quench in yourself the endless capacity for claptrap. Especially if you're working with a book and you're out there on the road and you're flogging the little pony that you are yourself, lashing the back of it to get the stuff out of you, that is *claptrap*. That is not good news for that wandering creature inside you that wants to make the next thing.

GF: *You've had a very wide range of international productions, so what's been your experience of critics and criticism?*

SB: I was surprised that they had the same set of responses to a very varied spread of productions. That doesn't mean it's not useful. When someone comes to a production they're coming with their own mindset, but there's a match for that in another city. [It] took away, to some degree, the fear. You have to take it seriously because it has a huge impact. People read a review in the paper and say "Mmm I want to go and see that." That's where we're vulnerable. And there's no use screaming about that because the fact is that 99% of the time it's the author's fault.

GF: *You think it's the author's responsibility? Should the author control the production then?*

SB: Not control: to do the thing asked of you in respect of the first production. It's the author's responsibility not just to be true to the making of the play; you really have to be true to your input into the production, to be absolutely rigorous about it. It's much easier to avoid it and say "I'll come back in a few weeks" or "I don't want to know about the casting." Because it *is* an extra befuddlement. But only on the first production. Therefore the criticism of the first production *must* have a relation to the author. If you have done your job then it should be almost wholly your responsibility.

GF: *That raises an interesting question about the position of the dramatist in the hierarchy of the theatre, the power struggles there can be between actors, directors, designers ...*

SB: In an ideal production people leave their crowns and sceptres behind the door, like gunslingers used to leave their guns, coming in on equal terms and assuming equal terms, and that's an end of it. A troublesome production for me would be people who sneak in their guns under their shirts. You used a phrase earlier about your "best words being cut" – you were just joking – but I don't feel that way any more. I was talking about the characters as the "secret authors" – our words, their words, it doesn't make any difference. I don't see it as "my words", I see it as maybe harvested, or described, or listened for, or heard again, or honoured because it is brief, or caught – like a watercolour – or captured. But authored? No, not really. Because unless you have described well, you will not allow the characters to be their own authors and the actors will not have any chance to make the play and the director will not have any chance to notice the play, to spot it. I suspect [that] before 1986 they were "my words" but after that it was just a question of surrender, of giving up, a sort of act of despair. You can't do it. And so you stop. And then something else happens. You find a queer sort of benediction, the after-life or your ambition. I wonder how we got to that?

GF: *It links with something you were saying earlier, because it's almost the opposite of it ...*

SB: As I often find.

GF: *... when you were talking about the writer's responsibility in relation to the work – the need to make sure the first production is right.*

SB: That's not an *authorial* activity, that's one of the extra responsibilities. My tendency is to say "yes." When someone rings up and says "what do you think of so & so for this particular role?" numerous things happen, but the first feeling is that I mustn't do anything to offend this or that person because they're in a life and it would be offensive and painful. That's *not* helpful. That's a note to myself – because we're now casting *Hinterland* – I need to be more fierce about that. Maybe there's nothing you *can* do and you should just step back and let it happen naturally. After all, if you're dealing with someone of the magnitude of Max [Stafford Clark] there isn't a great deal to worry about. But I have had to let certain things go. Especially after *Steward of Christendom*, I've had to let productions go the way they wanted to. I'm never sure if that's right or wrong. It's probably wrong. But can you create that ideal world that Beckett did? There is another imperative in my life which is three children – feed the critters and all that – so I cannot be as rigorous as I would like to be. Maybe you should be rigorous. It's a question.

GF: *Surely, if a play is going to survive, it has to survive on its own. Having seen it into the world maybe you have to pat it on the backside and say "off you go."*

SB: Yeah. Although it is a curiosity of plays that their destruction can often be implicit in themselves. You take a play like *King Lear*, whose reputation for being un-actable went on for decades and decades. I think some plays want to go to ground. You're right in that they should have their faith [but] part of my anxiety would be that I would not contribute to their self-destructive nature, to aid and abet them, because there is another instinct in a writer to want to blow things up as he goes – certainly I have that.

GF: *What about the function of the director in steering the production?*

SB: For me the director ought not to know. There's no point if the director knows at the beginning of a production what lies ahead of it. The writer should have an instinct for it, but the director should, I think, be almost lost, and find the solid ground. Once they have found that it's too late for the author's influence to have any importance. That confidence is important. If the first production has been done right the others will follow on from that.

GF: *And if the first production hasn't been "done right?"*

SB: Then you're left in eternal disquiet, doubt, pain. The joy of the successfully done production soon fades, but the sorrow of a badly produced production lasts a long time.

GF: *Is that because of a sense of missed opportunity or disappointment about the work?*

SB: It's the doubt, especially writing a series of plays. Because each one takes two or three years, you want to lay it down, you want to say, "that is as complete as I can make it; I was true to that" and move on. If it's a flop, the 99% possibility is that the play is a poor play; the 1% possibility is that it was badly produced. Therefore you don't *know* if you got it right or not, and so you never get that weight off your shoulders. *The Only True History of Lizzie Finn*, my only out-and-out disaster in theatre, still haunts me because I don't know what to think about it. I know what I thought first and when I read it I still think it's good, but I don't *know*.

GF: *Apart from the original Abbey production, have there been other major productions that could have settled the question?*

SB: It's had a few productions. Trevor Nunn fancied it for the Lyttleton at one point but I expressed my concerns about the play itself and I virtually put him off the idea because of that unsureness. That is certainly another responsibility: the responsibility not to allow things if you're not sure. In a way, there is no other way to be sure except by getting it right on the first production.

GF: *What happened with that original production of* Lizzie Finn?

SB: My original conception for the play was actually very small, for The Peacock, almost without costume. But because of [moving to] the big stage it was felt it had to be enlarged and there were a lot of elements that just weren't from me. They might well have worked for the play but I could never be sure because they just weren't from me. And that's another thing you learn: at least to fall by your own opinions, your own standards. So who knows? I would dearly love to find out some day [because] you see it sits there, number four there in that series, and it's not a good place to be doubtful, right in the middle of something.

GF: *That series is clearly important to you. What holds it together?*

SB: Family. The original idea was seven familiar plays – that's what it was called. Even with the brothers in *Boss Grady's Boys*, it is a family play in that it's a kind of secret portrait of two members of my family. And it's also based on Kelsha [Co. Wicklow], the same place as *Steward of Christendom*, just over the hills there. It's set in West Cork of course, but it's based on knowing the inside of that house in Kelsha. The brothers are there at the start of the series and at the end is a play called *Hinterland*, which is being done next year. *Hinterland* is a father play – father of the nation as well. The series started off as a desire to see where I was in the world, to see *what* I was, not being something very particularly Irish, but to say "that's Irish too, this lot of critters is Irish too, unlikely as they may seem."

GF: *That's a recurrent motif in your work isn't it – you can see it in* Eneas McNulty *and* Steward of Christendom *and* Our Lady of Sligo.

SB: Yes it is. *Eneas McNulty* I tried to make a play called "Freedom for Nigeria" which was an old song in the 60s, but I didn't manage it, so it was happier in a book. But it is related; it is the same. I suppose it's what I've been at since 1986, just after I met Ali.

GF: *A striking feature of the plays is the business of creatures who are stuck between two worlds and somehow are looking for a home. Where does that come from?*

SB: The origins of some of the larger concerns are very small. You could find the reason is simply that when I was a small child we changed house about seven times, we moved from here to London and back, [were] left with cousins over here in the summer while they were setting up house. Every place you come to, you don't know where you are until you start to learn not just the accent but the actual *lingo*. Around here, for instance, they say "chaps" for children, that's very important. You find a place inside the use of language, or the possession of language. And sometimes you spoke raggedly in order to fit in and sometimes you spoke completely in order to fit in. I found as a child that the people who had the least amount, their richness was contained in language, their possession was their language. You make that incursion into other people's lingo as an outsider trying to make yourself an insider, and at the heart of that you find that there isn't actually home. You try for survival's sake, as a child, because otherwise you are eaten alive. But home is not there. In the middle there is that bright eye saying "you don't belong here." But this is endemic. Is anyone immune from nostalgia, the pain of wanting to return home, the nostalgia for a place we have not been, an idea? Just as plays are, I think, an ancient form, before writing, before dialect, before language probably, before words certainly, that idea [nostalgia, home] is probably just an ancient remnant that torments us all. That's our lot and that's our engine.

GF: *You've had great success at the Abbey, but you've also had disappointment. What do you think about the Abbey itself, what would you want the National Theatre to be?*

SB: If I had the power, I'd do what Ben [Barnes] wants to do. There are two major problems with the Abbey. The first major problem is most certainly the physical building. It's only by the help of God and a few policemen that you can carry a play successfully on the main stage. Especially a new play people aren't familiar with, a play with no prejudices attached to it. I've been going to the Abbey since it opened and I've been on the Board. I can see that there are always problems, but for me it has to be that theatre – that big space. [It's] a small theatre – 600 seats – that plays like Croke Park with the acoustics of Croke Park, and that's no good for plays. So the simplest thing to do would be to leave it. Don't mess with it, don't try and improve it, just get out of it and move the spirit of the thing over the river. [Regarding the original Abbey] when you look at the documents of the time, the fire did a lot of damage backstage but the theatre itself wasn't that badly damaged. In today's terms it was infinitely recoverable; they could have kept the old building. The old building was the right size in the right place – by total accident. But then theatre is the sum of its accidents, chaos by design literally. The [modern] Abbey was designed as what was conceived to be the new architecture of the sixties, and essentially it *doesn't work*. It's a failure as a physical place. So I would find the happy accident of somewhere else. Because what is the Abbey? It was just Miss Horniman and Yeats wandering around looking for a suitable building to put on a few plays. That's the spirit of beginning that's needed now. And that's what they've done. They've found this site and a bit of money and that's really how theatres make themselves. There's a small professional company in Dublin, the Gate Theatre, that's run by three people virtually. That is a fantastic theatre. Part of the grace of the Gate Theatre is that it's a Stradivarius of an auditorium. It is the ideal instrument. It is the cello of Irish theatres. My feeling about the Abbey is that the instrument presented to the plays, to the playwright, is a poor instrument. In the Gate you are always given this beautiful instrument to sound. You speak as we are speaking now on the Gate stage and you can be heard down at the back wall clear as a bell. That's the only thing that a theatre *must* have and so few of them do have.

GF: *Apart from the building, what about the institution, the question of new writing, of a permanent company?*

SB: The enormous civil service structure? To be able to honour the accent of the time produces great theatre. Think of the Moscow Art's Theatre accidentally finding the force from the situation in Russia, or the early days of the Abbey. If you impose a Civil Service-like structure on a theatre your chances of being able to preserve the instincts, to harvest the accidents, to reach the status of a great theatre are very much limited. Everyone in the building must be fiercely devoted to theatre – that's something you get a taste of in the Royal Court, say, [where] most people in the building read a new play and they all have an opinion. Now [in the Abbey] that is not the case. That is not a criticism of the people: the structure is composed of people but the people did not make the structure. This is something that Garry Hynes found – that it was a sort of immutable structure, that you could have an *intention* to change it but it actually didn't change.

I had four plays produced there, the third one co-produced with the Bush Theatre, and my experiences were generally happy ones. However, if you look at the reigning team of Irish playwrights, or whatever you call it – the Abbey hasn't really worked. I remember going in there with Billy Roche with *A Handful of Stars* and we left it in the foyer and Billy was high with hopes. And it was rejected. It took Mark Lambert to bring it to the Bush later on for it to be produced and that was Billy on his way. Conor McPherson also had his plays rejected there, as far as I know. I don't know if Martin McDonagh ever sent things to the Abbey but they were not produced in the Abbey first. They are the accidental writers, the good ones. The good ones are the accidental writers, who fall into it, sometimes for stupid reasons, sometimes for glorious reasons, it doesn't matter. They have no designs upon the theatre usually, it just happens. There must be something about the Abbey that makes that not possible and it has not been possible there for some years. You're always thinking with a new Artistic Director that it will again be possible but my suspicion is still that there is something about the structure that actually militates against it. What is that? It also has the largeness and the strength of an unstoppable force and that seems fairly frightening. It's not for no reason that you approach the Abbey with infinite caution.

My new play *Hinterland* is being produced by Out of Joint, the Abbey and the English National. The Irish leg of the arrangements is the Abbey and I confess to an unnecessary sense of fear about the Abbey. Maybe it's something going back to *Lizzie Finn*, I don't know – it's just a sense that it's only 10% an arena for theatre and 90% it has other concerns. And I don't just mean the people and the building, I mean the whole coming together of the citizenry of Dublin in all their glory. I have an infinite respect for that. But like all gunfighters – there are certain towns I don't want to go back to unprotected, and Dublin is one of them, and that's where I was born.

GF: *That's a strange experience. You've always had a very warm audience response.*

SB: Part of the playwright's lot is that the group of people who raise you up one week are the same people who next week are ready to chuck you, your mind and every last bit of your soul and body into the river Liffey. That can be quite confusing. If you postulate that the writer has to be in some way flawed, cracked, ill-at-ease in the world in order to make things, in order to complete things or make things whole, well, consider the effects of that on such a person. It isn't good for you. Distance is a good thing in a way. Having had the experience of being an Irish person in London doing a play, where, for better or for worse, you're not really there, there is no doubt that when you're in Dublin you really are in Dublin. I was born within the canals and, somehow or other, if I could move the Abbey to London I'd have a totally different feeling about it.

GF: *Do you see yourself as having "an audience?" Is there anybody you use as a touchstone?*

SB: There are many touchstones. I couldn't use a director as a touchstone because for me a good director will not really know until it's too late. The last few years – in all honesty and speaking very personally – I lost my touchstone, which was Donal [McCann]. In every way a touchstone because he was coming to plays over the years and he'd say "Very short, but great fuckin' play" and to hear those things back was very important. In the last few years I no longer had that dimension and was the less for it, the more lost for it, no matter what people said one way or another, not really *knowing* without that growly message from the back of the room. I think it's a very important thing for a playwright, having a savage voice that essentially is out to keep you alive but doesn't let that get in the way of the business of severe pruning, if required.

But your question was: do I have an audience? And I think the answer is no. I cannot – nor ever was able comfortably to – sit in the theatre when a play of mine is running. I suffer to the point of stupefaction. Rehearsal is a closed shop but it *is* a form of audience because everyone is listening and intense. I don't have a sense of the public. Maybe I should just admit that they [the Abbey audience] are truly my own crowd and that makes me as fearful as I can be. It isn't a fear of the work or the response, it's a physical sensation of being among other people with their concentration on something made by me initially. I take some solace from the fact that other playwrights have finally not been able to attend first nights. Maybe it's the same thing behind it: just terror – a physical distress. Even when we were down in New Zealand in a fish-gutting factory which Donal somehow made into a theatre and even though it [*Steward of Christendom*] was the hit of the festival, I couldn't sit in the theatre. Ten minutes in and I'll be crashing out through the back of the theatre, just couldn't stick it.

GF: *You spoke earlier about the director "finding the play." The prevailing condition of much Irish theatre is jobbing directors, four or five weeks rehearsal and then it's on. That doesn't give a lot of discovery time.*

SB: No. Well, there's chocolate and chocolate. Because it is what I *do* I'm incredibly hard on myself to an almost suicidal degree [so] it isn't wrong of me to expect or desire other people involved to be in the same bad condition. What thrilled me about Sinead Cusack coming to do *Our Lady of Sligo* is when you consider the reasons she *shouldn't* have done it: it was following *Steward of Christendom*; it's a sister play to *Steward*; it's an enormous part; she's a film actor, or has been in recent years. And here's this person coming to do this play. And it turned out that she was as much a desperado as one could wish and her reasons for doing it were powerful, personal reasons. And *that's* interesting to see. So she was perfect for that play. Approaching these plays – my plays, which are just the borderline of plays, one step the wrong way and you're no longer in a play – you've got to be in a pretty mean-hearted state of mind to do it. There has to be a sense of emergency for the people doing it; otherwise it approaches pointlessness, why do it?

As Woody Allen says, "There are very few professions where you are setting yourself up for public abuse to the degree that you get abused when you don't get it right." It's incredibly destructive. Keats thought it had killed him. Because of the danger of that abuse you better have people of like minds. You're all rehearsing there in "the widow's hole" and you're going to ride out sooner or later and try and rob the bank. If you don't get the gold, you're going to get shot dead. So everyone better be in on it and there better be no Judas figures around. And that's what I feel about it. You're riding out on a dangerous thing. So when you talk about jobbing directors and so on, you're talking about a different sort of chocolate. What you're talking about sounds suspiciously like dabbling. We'll call it the theatre and we'll call it a play and we'll call it an audience and we'll call it a writer but in fact they're not really those things. The real thing happens when everyone is in a secret state of broken-heartedness, or whatever is required.

New plays are a very special territory, in Ireland particularly. When Billy Roche started writing there was no such thing – and hadn't been for a while – as new Irish plays. There were things you did out of a sense of piety, commitment to theatre. Now the big difference I have to say is financial. Always leaving aside Friel, in those days the idea that a young writer in his/her twenties could make a million pounds from a play was not within the realms of anyone's thinking. Nowadays a play like *The Weir* would have earned him [McPherson] something like that, grossing God knows what. Or *Dancing at Lughnasa*. That *should* make it safer but it actually makes it more difficult: not to be missing the mark.

GF: *What do you think of the huge changes in the funding and organisation of Irish theatre in the last fifteen or twenty years?*

SB: It's a paradox. What we've seen in the last few years is structures for Irish theatre. The more you heap structures upon this accidental business the more you militate against actually producing theatre. That's the ridiculous paradox: people must have money in order to mount their productions, there must be structures. [But] the Irish Arts Council seems to involve itself almost wholly with structures and administrators and administration. They are very necessary things – but that seems to be the thing the Arts Council understands. The *Arts* Council! Instead of paying homage, almost by a series of weekly religious rites, to the accidental nature, the instinctive nature of the arts! The thing that they can get to grips with – because that's the only thing you can get to grips with – is the physical thing. But nothing is happening in the arts that can be documented, that can be written down: it's all pre-linguistic. This book is the right approach because you're asking the confused and desperate practitioners what they feel. [For the Arts Council the problem is] the more clarity you bring to the post, the less clarity you're likely to bring to the finish line. Before a race the horses must be pushing, and one of them gets away, one of them falls, the jockey is thrown off, they're trying to put order on it and then the power is released and then *whoosh* off they go. There's a fine line.

Confining those horses completely by structure so that they cannot get through the gate, it's too controlled? That has always worried me about the Arts Council. When I was a very young writer I used to think why, at the age of twenty one, am I making three ha'pence a year when I know there's a thing called a Literature Officer who's getting a weekly wage, a thing I knew I would never have?

GF: *Aren't those perennial problems? On the one hand the balance between funding and control, on the other the fact that Arts Council support is always after the fact.*

SB: And yet it [art] keeps happening. It's like lightning. It's happening in another place.

GF: *Finally, with so many new companies and venues, how do you see yourself in relation to Irish theatre and other writers?*

SB: I have a sense of Irish theatre – the theatres you're talking about – being run by young people. I don't feel any connectedness there, and I wonder why that is. I don't see Irish theatre, I don't go out to it, perhaps that's what it is. I notice when a play goes right you meet a lot of people and when a play doesn't go right you meet very few people. For better or for worse I am not that generation of young playwrights – Conor and so on. I'm often lumped in with them, especially in America: the *wunderkinder* of Irish theatre. Well I'm forty-six, I ain't no *kind*, sadly, so I don't feel part of that. I suppose the people I'm interested in – Conor or Martin – have been out there being shot at. It's the veteran feeling, the level of danger you've been through. It's the same for all artists. They have a huge success and the assumption is it will happen again, which is rarely the case. What happens after *Lughnasa*? *Wonderful Tennessee*, a completely different sort of play, was attacked for not being *Lughnasa*. These are sorrows in a writer's life, no doubt about it. They can be very destructive.

GF: *What would you wish for Irish theatre?*

SB: I would like audiences to be as in flight as the people doing it, to be free of their own assumptions, and of their own knowledge, and of their own education: to be made innocent coming in the door. And *then* if they responded badly you really would deserve it. You really would have destroyed their innocence which is the only crime of any magnitude that there is.

Sebastian Barry was primarily a novelist and poet up to 1988 when his first play *Boss Grady's Boys* was produced by the Abbey. His novels include

Engine by Owl-light , and *The Whereabouts of Eneas McNulty*. A new novel, *Annie Dunne*, will be published in 2002. Since 1988 he has written a sequence of plays, including *Prayers of Sherkin* (1990), *White Woman Street* (1991) and the award-winning *Steward of Christendom* (1995) and *Our Lady of Sligo* (1998). The seventh and final play in the sequence, *Hinterland*, is due for production in 2002.

Ger FitzGibbon lectures in the English Department, NUI Cork and is Chair of the University's Board of Drama and Theatre Studies. He has lectured and published on the work of Brian Friel, Tom Murphy, Frank McGuinness and Sebastian Barry. He is a former board-member and director with Cork Theatre Company and a founder of Graffiti Theatre Company, of which he is currently Chair. He has written a number of plays, including *The Rock Station* (1992) and *Sca* (1999). His stage-directing includes *The Birthday Party* (Harold Pinter), *The Shadow of a Gunman* (Sean O'Casey), *Accidental Death of an Anarchist* (Dario Fo) and *Scenes from an Execution* (Howard Barker).

Dermot Bolger in Conversation with Jim O'Hanlon

JO'H: *Dermot you started off, and I suppose you're still best known as, a novelist. Did you find it a huge challenge suddenly having to tell a story entirely through dialogue?*

DB: There are advantages and disadvantages. Technically I found the challenge very interesting and I still find the challenge interesting, because there are a lot of things that you can do in theatre which you can't in the novel and vice-versa. A play like *Arthur Cleary* was relatively easy to imagine because there was no set and you were almost in that world of a novel, insofar as you could move from Dublin to Timbuktu in the space of a single gesture like in the space between two paragraphs. However the more that physical sets come in, the more confined by place you are. *April Bright*, on the other hand, is a bit like a poem; it just floats out there plot-wise with a build of images like in poetry. When we got it working it worked really well – two times out of three it worked – but on the other night it died because its structure of images is such a delicate thing. *April Bright* wouldn't work as a novel and I'm not sure if it would work on film, but in performance, when it came together, there was a certain magic in being able to see two worlds at once.

JO'H: *Many of your plays are remarkable in their theatricality, their fluid use of time and place – they're certainly very far from observing the unities of the well-made play! That would have been one of the things that attracted me to them as a director. There are wonderful spaces there in the text just waiting to be fleshed out in any given production. Is that a conscious decision when you sit down to write a play – are you consciously trying to exploit the theatricality and the things the theatre offers which the novel or the poem do not?*

DB: I don't think that being a novelist really gave me anything for the theatre. But being a poet did. At one stage I had stopped writing poetry and when theatre came along it gave me the chance to use a lot of the techniques of poetry. *The Lament for Arthur Cleary* works like a poem. *April Bright* was my purest piece of theatre because it was basically the images of a poem made flesh. I often discussed this notion with Sebastian Barry when I used to bring him out to play football with my mates and you can see it in some of his plays too. My plays got a lot of criticism because people were looking at them in a strictly realistic way and saying: "People don't talk that way," but I was more concerned with an inner speech because this is theatre with the dream-like possibilities it provides. If you want to write ultra-realistic dialogue go and write films.

JO'H: *It's interesting you mention this, particularly with regard to criticism of your work, because it seems to me that one of the central tensions in your work is that tension between poetry and realism. The language in much of your work for the theatre is resolutely poetic, and yet the plays appear to be set, at least on the surface, in ultra-realistic, everyday settings: a flat in Ballymun, a house in Finglas, a railway station platform. So people don't quite know how to respond to this juxtaposition of styles; they look at, say,* The Passion of Jerome *and say this is a realistic play, set in flats in Ballymun, and here we have a man developing stigmata. You can't have a character with stigmata in a play set in a flat in Ballymun! Do you think that audiences, perhaps, want a play to be either/or – poetry or realism – and they find it difficult that your work very deliberately straddles the two?*

DB: Expectations can be a problem. When *In High Germany* premiered at the Gate theatre, a lot of critics said the most amazing things, like that the character, Eoin, was too articulate and well dressed for his background. Here is an ordinary working class Dublin guy who's had to emigrate, but is obviously holding down a very good job with a good company in Germany. He's living there with a German girl, a sophisticated guy who has moved on in life. Yet one reviewer even claimed he looked too well fed for his background!

JO'H: *Stephen Brennan wasn't put on a diet beforehand, no?*

DB: Reviewers expected "fuck" in every sentence, that a working class person on stage should be drunk and curse and not be articulate about his background. I don't think Eoin was any more articulate than myself or most people I grew up with. Now if the play had been a three-hander (because it is about Eoin and his two friends who have all emigrated) they would talk quite differently because when men get together they talk in code. But *In High Germany* is about one guy thinking aloud. Still, reviewers would have been happier with a particular type of caricature of a working-class Dubliner they could feel superior about – they didn't want an articulate one.

JO'H: *It's interesting to hear that, having directed and performed the play all over the world, practically, except for here. We've done it everywhere from London to Boston via Edinburgh and Romania, and never once got that kind of objection. Surely the whole point of* In High Germany *is that it comes from inside Eoin's head? It's an interior world, which is why, as you say, the character can be much more articulate than he would be, say, talking to his mates in the pub on a Friday night.*

DB: I'm interested in exploring interior worlds. *Jerome* was an interior world too. The funny thing about *Jerome* is that it was actually based on a real flat in Ballymun where certain things – including a boy's suicide – did occur. Very often – in both my plays and novels – the so-called surreal elements have a large element of reality to them. *Jerome* on one level is about the possibility that a force – call it God – may exist outside of us, though in the play it is not necessarily seen as a benevolent force. Because of this, one reviewer thought that it was a deeply anti-intellectual play. Now, I haven't a clue if God exists, but it seems extreme to have reached the stage where any form of belief is anti-intellectual …

JO'H: *Are you an atheist?*

DB: I'm a strict agnostic who falters when encountering turbulence at 27,000 feet. But there seemed a certain liberal fascism in some reactions to the play. Eighty years ago, theatre in Ireland was run by Horse Protestants, forty years ago Horse Catholics ran it and now it's run by Horse Atheists. There is a rigid conformity that every writer now has to be anti-clerical. As a publisher I've published books like Mary Rafferty's highly controversial *Suffer The Little Children* last year and back in 1988, risked every penny I had to publish *The God Squad*, by Paddy Doyle, which was the first exposé of clerical child abuse produced and for which I had problems even finding a printer willing to run it. So I have paid my dues to exposing the truth about how absolute power corrupted religion within Ireland and controlled people's lives in a Stalinist way. But any writer worth their salt kicks against the pricks of received opinion today. If you went to Ballymun at the time I wrote *Jerome* who would you have found actually working for people? Peter McVerrey, the Jesuit, with his hostel for homeless kids. You'd have found few enough mainstream politicians there because the important swings in voting patterns were not going to come in Ballymum. I think the more marginalised the Church becomes, the more abuse priests get, the more people randomly shout "*paedophile*" at them in the street, the more marginalised they become, the more the good ones can begin to speak for marginalised people. As the Church gets over its obsession with men wearing bits of rubber on their dicks you find a good number of highly interesting individuals working within it saying radical things that don't get reported. The possibility of belief is well worth exploring. Because as Francis Stuart said: "Poets and priests have a lot in common. Both deal with emotions beyond the material world, with people dying, people seeing loved ones born or die, people trying to make sense of whether their bodies are a temporary prison or a full stop."

JO'H: *You've mentioned the existence of God in* The Passion of Jerome *– it seems to me that this sense of spirituality, or the loss of spirituality, is a recurring theme in your work, and again, it's something which attracted me to your work as a director. Many of your plays seem to me to be dealing not with religion, or God or whatever you want to call it, but with spirituality in the broadest sense. But dealing with spirituality in an everyday realistic context is fraught with difficulties. How do you find the form with which to discuss or explore the inner workings of human spirituality in a realistic context? How do you explore these issues when what you have onstage is a representation of a world which, in many ways, has itself ceased exploring them, a modern world in which we have lost that sense of spirituality?*

DB: That's a valid question. All my plays have huge flaws in them – they are not well made, may not even be competent plays. But the opposite of competence isn't necessarily incompetence. In the plays I struggle to find a way of doing things. That's why I think they're not particularly fashionable and will never play huge theatres. But so far they keep playing small theatres and there's a surprising (to me) number of people in various countries interested in doing them on a small scale. One of the things in them is that – and this is true of the novels also – the dead are as real to me as the living. I don't think my work has anything in common with say, Roddy Doyle – who is a friend of mine and whose deserved success I applaud. But he would say the same thing about coming from different angles. There is a dark tradition of Dublin writing, with Sheridan Le Fanu and James Clarence Mangan, a whole Gothic mindset I find interesting. That sense of life and death intermingled. If there's any tradition I work in it is that.

Stoker did it but buggered off to Transylvania. I like how Le Fanu did it in a then contemporary Chapelizod. Likewise I've done it, with no apologies, in a flat in Ballymun – my translator actually entitled the published French text *Le Jesus de Ballymun*. Because obviously that incessant dialogue between the living and the dead exists everywhere, even if it's less blatantly obvious today than a hundred years ago, when death stalked the streets. Go down any Dublin street or any city in the world and you will find thousands of stories from thousands of people on extraordinary emotional inner journeys, haunted and fixated by events of their past. Looking out this window here you see the rational world go by, truck drivers and people coming home from work, people behaving rationally. And obviously we're rational people. Yet all of us are also insane at a certain fundamental level. Different sparks make people irrational. It may be sex, which is why sex is important in my work. It may be a fixation with someone's death. It may be people reaching forty or fifty and finding they are losing their youth. Everybody passing this window is going to die and no matter what they do they cannot alter that terrible fact. The more people think about that fact, the more they react irrationally. What interests me is when people begin to react that way. All my plays deal with the irrational side of people's brains.

JO'H: *But again it poses a difficulty, doesn't it, attempting to undergo such a private, interior journey in the most public of all art forms?*

DB: I always admire actors and directors who take on my plays, because they are not easy plays: they lack neat solutions or easy laughs. Most audiences are happier with very simple plays. Maybe some of the issues I explore should be explored in a philosophical thesis somewhere, but the problem is that I'm no bleeding philosopher!

JO'H: *But there has to be room for those kinds of explorations in the theatre, surely? It's just a question of finding the appropriate form.*

DB: Well hopefully that's where my kind of theatre comes in. That's why I am not someone who makes a living primarily from the theatre. My plays make no commercial sense. Whereas you can actually write novels that mix the realistic and surreal which still sell in sufficient quantities for you to knock out a living.

JO'H: *You're saying that since writing plays was never your primary source of making a living, that has freed you up in terms of allowing you to write the kind of plays that you want to write?*

DB: Yeah. I mean each play is a luxury for me, an excursion into another world. It's always a great privilege when people go and do them.

JO'H: *Why do you think that Dublin critics find your plays so problematic then? What interested me about reading reviews of your stuff is not that the critics say this is good or bad or this is good poetry or bad poetry, it's the sort of vitriol that characterises the reviews, and the anger the plays seem to provoke in people — it's extraordinary.*

DB: I think it's probably nice that they react like that. It suggests that some raw nerve has been touched. I saw a small production of my *Consenting Adults* recently and four young women sat in front of me. When the play finished two stood up to give it a standing ovation while the other two (who obviously hated it) refused to clap whatsoever. I knew they would go to the pub and spend the next hour tearing strips off each other about it. That seemed the perfect reaction – I'd sooner that than have a play which everybody loved. That would be a waste of time. It's really nice when a play provokes different reactions. And I've found that ordinary punters' reactions to the plays have been much broader than the critics' discussions. My plays demand that you suspend disbelief. If you're willing to go on an emotional journey with them then that journey may take you somewhere surprising within your own memories. But if you stand totally cold outside it – which is the reviewers' job – they have to be dispassionately objective – it will fall apart. I saw an extraordinarily competent piece of theatre recently in Dublin, finely done, finely directed, ultra-polished and it got a nice ovation at the end. But as we walked out, not one person was discussing the play. It was so well made that it had covered all the angles and tied up all its loose ends, whereas I love loose ends. They allow the audience to own the play. I love people arguing about what happened next. At my ideal play, if a husband and wife went to see it one of them would end up sleeping on the sofa.

JO'H: *It's interesting you say that your plays call for suspension of disbelief. I think Fintan O'Toole makes a similar point in the "Introduction" to your* Dublin Quartet *when he says that they are about the poet finding the poetry in everyday life. The settings, the characters are very realistic, but the treatment of those settings, the events and often the dialogue – are resolutely non-realistic.*

DB: My plays are realistic in the sense that they are the voices inside people's heads. People talk differently at different times, but when pushed into certain situations will talk openly. It's those times when people drop their guard and speak openly about what really bothers them, that interest me.

JO'H: *Like the moment of Eddie's death in* One Last White Horse …

DB: At the end of *One Last White Horse*, Eddie is flying. As four people hold him he goes right down through the graves, past faces in the soil, right into his private hell to confront all these people who he has failed in his life. It's surreal stuff. Yet at the same time, when people close to me have died, they have called out names of dead loved ones with their last breath as if the dead had come to claim them. I've met people who've had near-death experiences of such faces. Maybe it is a hallucinogenic thing with oxygen cut off from their brains. Maybe it really is ghosts coming for them. It doesn't matter if it is a merely chemical hallucination, because those visions are still real in the sense that they have been experienced. I've undergone several operations in recent years and I generally deal with my nerves by telling jokes. The last time as I lay on the operating table I jokingly asked the surgeon *"are we being a bit hasty here?"* By the time I heard myself say *"here."* I was back in the recovery room and all the time in between had vanished. If I had died, that moment would be *my* eternity. Eternity exists whether or not there is a heaven because that one moment can last forever.

JO'H: *You are exploding a moment – which of course is the very essence of poetry, and of the theatre.*

DB: These moments are real. It doesn't matter whether they are hallucinogenic, they happen to us –

JO'H: *In our imaginations?*

DB: Yes. In some ways all we are is our imagination and our memories, these make us who we are.

JO'H: *The nineteenth century German critic Friedrik Scarsale said that theatre is the art of preparation. For me one of the things that worked very well in plays like* Arthur Cleary *or* One Last White Horse, *and perhaps less well in* Jerome, *is the way you succeed in setting up a dream-like environment in which, if you like, anything can happen.* One Last White Horse *takes place inside Eddie's head, at the moment of his death, and in the production I did in the UK we had all the characters on stage throughout, coming forward and back through the recesses of his mind. The challenge seems to me to be in the setting up of a world where we can accept anything that happens onstage, or anything that the characters onstage say.*

DB: I think that worked better, as you say, in *Arthur Cleary*. One problem with *Jerome* was that it was set in a very physical "realistic" location, because the flat needed to be claustrophobic. So you need a physical set that's very claustrophobic but then when you need to switch to other locations it becomes very difficult with this big monstrosity of a flat onstage that won't go away.

JO'H: *But also you set up a world in which the characters talk about going home to watch* Friends *and* ER *or preparing for presentations at work, and that creates a certain set of expectations which are confounded when Jerome starts to develop stigmata from the ghost of a young boy!*

DB: If you look at a film like *Angel Heart*, though, it successfully straddles those things. I didn't know anything about *Angel Heart* when I saw it, and at first I thought that it was a straightforward, realistic, detective type of film. Then halfway through you realise he is actually working for Lucifer. I think the supernatural works in that way, by building a realistic world before bringing in the supernatural.

JO'H: *But can that come out of nowhere? Don't you have to set up a world on the stage where we can believe that the supernatural could intrude?*

DB: Well, *Jerome* actually had its origins in someone I knew, whose sister had a flat with a poltergeist in it. The poltergeist was the ghost of the boy who committed suicide. So these events seemed quite real to me. I came to *Jerome* to write a play about real events – I wasn't deliberately trying to create a supernatural world. Poltergeist activity happens in ordinary homes where people watch *Friends*. I can't explain what it is but I do believe those situations very occasionally occur when there is an energy released that we know very little about. So with *Jerome* people thought that I was trying to marry real and non-real worlds together, but I was simply creating a world that was 100% real for me. So you're left with two interpretations: (a) this flat is haunted by a poltergeist or (b) Jerome is having a nervous breakdown and committing self mutilation because his child died years ago and he could never cope with the buried grief. But even if he is having a nervous breakdown, the ghosts are still "real" for him so the whole experience is still a realistic world for him.

JO'H: *Why do you think that reviewers find it so difficult to accept this on stage in your work?*

DB: I had to talk to a group in All Hallows Seminary who saw the play – about fifty of them, priests, nuns, students of theology, many elderly. We sat around and I thought to myself "Good Jesus", because it's a very explicit play sexually and also language wise. But they seemed able to understand it fully. They could enter into the duality of that world and came at it from really surprising angles. They had discussions about whether the priest in it actually has lost his faith or not, and strongly objected to one particular line in a valid, reasoned way that I liked. But they showed a totally different reaction to the play.

JO'H: *Of course, because the world of the spirit and the supernatural or God is present in their lives, alongside what you might call more prosaic everyday matters. The two co-exist side by side for them. It's no big deal to them to see that kind of spiritual element in an everyday setting.*

DB: That's very valid.

JO'H: *Who else in the theatre is doing the kind of stuff that you would like to do or are attempting to do?*

DB: The only other playwright that I could really be compared with, and yet who is very different from me, is Sebastian Barry, because I think both of us began writing for the Abbey.

JO'H: *You both started as poets really…*

DB: The Abbey was founded by a poet among others and had a whole notion of doing verse drama. Now their verse drama often didn't work. But the notion of *putting* a piece of poetry on stage is very interesting and I find a lot of Sebastian's theatre interesting. I admire a lot of other playwrights but I can't say I would naturally fit in with that many of them. I'm somewhat out on a limb and I think that would go for being a novelist too.

JO'H: *What you do seems easier in a novel though doesn't it? Maybe because the authorial voice can smooth the transition between the real and the supernatural, the utilitarian outside world and the more spiritual, interior world.*

DB: Plus reading is a solo gig, so somebody can go and like a book without their partner having to be dragged along as well. With theatre you generally go with somebody, so often there is a certain amount of compromise involved in actually going out to plays.

JO'H: *It comes back to that problem of having to go on a spiritual journey rather than an emotional or a psychological one. I mean we see plenty of emotional and psychological journeys in contemporary theatre but to go on a spiritual journey in public, in a world which has lost its spirituality …*

DB: It is putting a lot of demands on the audience as well as on the cast. It's telling the audience you are either going to go with this or you're not because if you don't emotionally commit you're in for a boring night.

JO'H: *Theatre audiences seem to like something that they can be a bit detached from, in a way that novel audiences don't. With* Bridget Jones's Diary *and the* Nick Hornby *novels – the reading public seems to have a voracious appetite for those "people like us" novels; it's great to see ourselves there and read about ourselves as long as it's in the privacy of our own home. We don't seem to like it when it's presented on a stage in front of us. We seem to find it very discomfiting, as if we're somehow washing the dirty linen of the tribe in public. Maybe that's why there are so few contemporary plays chronicling the experience of being middle-class in Ireland, for example. After all, let's face it, the theatre-going audience in this country is predominantly middle-class. And yet there's a real dearth of plays which engage with that experience of Ireland among the post-Bernard Farrell or Hugh Leonard generation.*

DB: Joe Dowling said that the Irish on stage have a terror of not being profound.

JO'H: *Can you not be profound having middle class people on stage?*

DB: You tell me, you know the middle class in a way I don't. Audiences do seem happier with the Bog of Allen rather than the Stillorgan bypass. Maybe it's a lack of confidence.

JO'H: *And yet the English, for example with Alan Ayckbourn, love it.*

DB: Maybe they're not as terrified of not being profound. It's funny though that when I started writing in the late 1970s everybody mocked the notion of any work of literature being set in Finglas or Ballymun. Now the same sort of mental opposition seems to exist about Foxrock and Deansgrange. One of the few books I could find about working class Dublin in the mid century was Lee Dunne's *Goodbye to the Hill* which was famous for being banned and for sexual bits that are boring and dated now. I always regarded it as a bit of a joke but when I actually read it I was quite shocked, because the first forty to fifty pages are absolutely brilliant in capturing his ordinary home life as a child. But then you feel that at a certain stage he loses confidence in the ability of a novel to be sustained about his own life and his family – the thing gets dressed up in war paint and bravado about sex and drink to try and make it interesting, whereas it was actually fascinating when working off its own quiet power in the earlier part. When I started to write I kept being told that the world that I came from was not sufficiently interesting. But now even the middle classes keep trying to write working class plays. It can be very embarrassing, when you see them. So maybe they feel themselves that their lives are not sufficiently interesting.

JO'H: *Maybe that is common to all classes? And with middle-class writers, there is a guilt as well. Not only are our lives not sufficiently interesting, but to try and be a chronicler of pain or suffering or unhappiness or spiritual longing when you have a home and a car and a comfortable lifestyle which most people would envy … it seems almost illegitimate.*

DB: Well Bernard Farrell's plays are hugely successful and they do explore middle class issues. I have a lot of time for him, the last play *Stella by Starlight*, is about ghosts in Carrickmines and worked very well. It was a very well made play, it got huge houses and the audience I saw it with seemed to feel something of their own life in it. Why are there not more essays about Bernard Farrell? That might be an interesting question. Why aren't there more Bernard Farrells? Maybe the young middle class authors are too busy trying to be Sam Beckett when there is a lot of material to be mined by being Bernard Farrell?

JO'H: *Maybe because Bernard's plays don't get the same kind of recognition, certainly in international terms. I know his work is popular in Germany, but in London and New York ...*

DB: Well obviously the British prefer Martin McDonagh. Say what you like about the Irish middle-classes but they do lack a certain local colour. Bernard Farrell's plays aren't set in Connaught and lack Irish war paint. It's interesting how Conor McPherson's *The Weir* – a very fine piece of work – is his play that travels most, yet is the least about his own Dublin suburban world. Internationally people prefer a certain type of Irish theatre, which is fair enough, but often the Irish themselves prefer it as well. There is nothing particularly strange about a foreign audience wanting an Irish play awash with local colour, real or imaginary; it just seems strange that an Irish audience would be equally happy with the diet. [Martin McDonagh's] *The Beauty Queen of Leenane* seemed like *Bailegangaire* for slow learners to me and I found it strange to see it take off in a sustained mainstream way that Tom Murphy has rarely reached. Anyway, to finish your middle-class question, there should be loads of plays set in Rathgar and Foxrock but I am not going to write them because it's not my world and doesn't really interest me. But you're right, it is interesting that there are relatively few of them.

JO'H: *Maybe there haven't been enough people who are resolutely middle class through and through? Maybe the Irish middle classes haven't been around long enough yet to have put down the roots which would allow its chroniclers to blossom.*

DB: Someone who could have been a magnificent middle class chronicler of Dublin life and actually wrote several plays but is sadly dead now, is the poet Conleth O'Connor from Dun Laoghaire. He was an accountant who quit work to write at a terrible economic time and he and his family suffered a lot of financial hardship for his courage. But Conleth didn't want to explore that world. He wanted to be Kafka and go to Prague. His poetry is often a retreat from his world. He hated every second of being an accountant and I always felt that if he could have brought himself to describe that world it might have been something quite unique. He did one or two short plays about the emotional cruelty of office life, but that was it. I do think that Joe O'Connor's *Red Roses and Petrol* is a very good play about that world.

JO'H: *And Declan Hughes' Digging for Fire. But beyond those two – I'm not saying there are no other plays about middle-class life out there, but they're* *certainly not vying with* The Weir*'s or* The Beauty Queen of Leenane*'s of this world in terms of either quality or exposure, for whatever reason.*

DB: I believe that every life is interesting, so maybe you people need to fight the battle the working class fought twenty years ago. When I began to write about Finglas there was a huge opposition to what I was doing and a sense from old *Irish Times* types that nothing that came out of Finglas could be interesting. Yet Finglas produced Paula Meehan, a fascinating poet and playwright, and the novelist and poet Michael O'Loughlin who isn't as well known as he should be. Finglas has produced all kinds of interesting people, all at ease with ourselves. What seems interesting now is how a new generation of writers will cope with Ireland's current affluence. My generation had the huge advantage of a deep anger driving us. What will drive the next generation?

JO'H: *There is certainly interesting work to be done on the place and role of spirituality and the life of the spirit in our newly-affluent society...*

DB: No matter what society you live in you have to establish a meaning for your life and at a certain time you're going to sit down and say: "What the fuck am I doing here – what is this about, how do I cope with X number of years and then death?" It will always be that part of the human dilemma I will be exploring, more than class or politics or anything else...

JO'H: *Tell me about your working relationship with David Byrne because like myself, he's directed most of your plays at one point or another!*

DB: I think he is an interesting director and is interested in things that are not particularly fashionable, which is why he doesn't get that much work in Dublin. The most helpful advice I ever got was from David during rehearsals for my first play, *The Lament for Arthur Cleary*. I was from a totally non-theatre background and early on Dave was trying to explain to me a problem with a speech in the play and I couldn't understand what he was saying. Now David's a fairly slight fellow so I picked him up and put him against the wall and as a way of breaking the ice said "You've ten seconds to tell me what the fuck you're taking about before I'll drop you!" So David explained that the speech was beautiful, every word in it perfect; but this point here – and he pointed to the end of the fourth sentence – that was the point where the guy in the third row of the audience wonders if his car is safely parked. That was the best piece of advice I ever got as a playwright. Because when I go to a lot of plays now – particularly with an older generation of playwrights – you can see the moment when everyone in the audience begins to shift; the playwright has had them in the palm of his hands and then has gone and lost them.

JO'H: *It's a very difficult point to judge though!*

DB: It is, yeah. And of course when you write at home you write more than you need, because what you need on the page is different to what you need on the stage. On the page you need to explain certain things, then when you get it up on stage you begin to see shortcuts, as it creates its own dynamic. I think Dave is a very good dramaturg as well – there will be quite a lot of cutting going on when David and I work together. The same was true when I worked with Jim Culleton, we did a lot of cutting too and it was the reverse of the normal relationship because Jim and the cast had to hold me down or I would have cut the whole play! But it's not only the director – I also like to have input from intelligent actors and say to them "where do you think it should be cut?", because when I'm at home with my false teeth in the glass they are the people on stage living out the lines. One of the reasons that first nights are very fraught is because one keeps changing all the time. It's only when you send your cast out on that night that you have made your final cut of the play.

JO'H: *David directed a play of mine last year in Manchester and I was exhausted by the end of the rehearsal period because I was up rewriting stuff at two o'clock in the morning! But there's no doubt he improved the play 200%.*

DB: It is good to have a director who will challenge you and it is good to have the sort of openness David has. I think that one of the reasons that I have chosen to work with David is that you can cut to the quick, very quickly.

JO'H: *Wrapping up, Dermot, what do you think in terms of theatre in Ireland now – where it is, where it is going – is there a place for the kind of work that you want to do? Is there a place for your brand of theatre?*

DB: I'm not sure there is necessarily a place in Irish theatre for me and that realisation has made me focus more on fiction in recent years. Yet I think there is some place in theatre generally for plays like mine and it's nice that they are done occasionally in Ireland. I'm always moved and touched to find a small audience willing to go on those emotional journeys with me, but I don't think my plays fit easily into any of the categories of Irish theatre. One of the differences between someone who writes plays for a living and someone who writes plays occasionally is that someone who writes plays for a living has got to keep writing plays. I only write plays when I am obsessed by a certain thing, and so therefore the play needs to find an audience who are equally obsessed by the same thing. I think that they are unusual plays, yet they will always interest unusual people and thank Christ the world is still full of unusual people.

Dermot Bolger (b. 1959) is the author of eight novels (including *The Journey Home, Father's Music* and most recently *The Valparaiso Voyage*). His eight plays (including *The Lament for Arthur Cleary, April Bright* and *The Passion of Jerome*) have received the Samuel Beckett Award and two Edinburgh Fringe Firsts and have been published in collection form by Penguin (*A Dublin Quartet*) and Methuen (*Plays 1*). A poet, he founded and edited the Raven Arts Press from 1977-1992, and then co-founded New Island Books of which he is executive editor.

Jim O'Hanlon was born in Dublin and is currently resident in London. A writer-director for television and theatre, he is the author of four plays, two of which have been nominated for Manchester Evening News Awards for Best New Play. His latest play, *The Buddhist of Foxrock*, will be presented by Fishamble Theatre Company in 2002. His productions of Dermot Bolger's plays have been seen in London, Edinburgh, Boston and Romania.

Jason Byrne in Conversation with Willie White

WW: *Theatre for you was a distraction from your studies in music. What did theatre offer that was different from music?*

JB: I was more at home. It seemed to me more accessible and more immediate.

WW: *So the rewards appeared more immediate with acting than with music?*

JB: It probably had more to with the level of difficulty that was involved in the music.

WW: *Because of the apparent lack of difficulty acting appealed to you?*

JB: I think that is ironic. What I was running away from at the time was the hard work that was involved in music. Performing was something that seemed very easy and natural and offered quicker gratification.

WW: *And now you have discovered otherwise?*

JB: The irony is that the way I work now, as a director, is more rigorous and more disciplined and more in keeping with what I was running away from ten years ago.

WW: *When we are talking about training in acting we frequently use music as metaphor, having your chops, knowing your scales, performing a score. How useful actually is that metaphor?*

JB: I think that it is possible to apply the metaphor to acting but that depends on your approach to acting. When you talk about a "type" of acting, this pertains to an aesthetic or to a result. However, process is and should always be removed from objective. The means are not always the end.

WW: *I suppose what I am suggesting is that not everybody takes it as seriously as you and I am asking is it necessary to do so?*

JB: No, I don't think it is.

WW: *So we are talking different aesthetics, different goals.*

JB: Well a different need.

WW: *You told me before that Beckett was an influence at an early stage. Taking playwrights first, who else has influenced your work?*

JB: Beckett, Shakespeare, Marlowe, most of the Elizabethan and Jacobean writers.

WW: *When then did you become aware of theatre practitioners or theoreticians of theatre?*

JB: In the beginning.

WW: *For example?*

JB: Grotowski at a very early stage.

WW: *Really. When did you first encounter him?*

JB: A friend gave me photocopies of exercises and photographs from *Towards a Poor Theatre*.

WW: *When was that?*

JB: I think it was in about 1993, at least that far back. I have also always been interested in Stanislavski.

WW: *What did these people signify for you?*

JB: Well, they seemed to represent an equivalent in theatre of what had appealed to me in music and musicianship. Such an approach seemed to be absent in the practice for me, from what I was being exposed to or how people thought around me.

WW: *Was Grotowski an inspiration?*

JB: Absolutely.

WW: *An inspiration to what?*

JB: He was an inspiration to rigour. He represented for me the pinnacle of the potential that acting has as a creative mode of expression.

WW: *However, your experience of Grotowski was a textual one, you had never even seen a tape of one of his productions.*

JB: Yes, but you have to understand that the images in the book of photographs were very strong and there was a resonance in them that provoked me to something that I couldn't quite identify or articulate. Grotowski always represented something that was not attainable, it was not possible. The gauntlet that he and Stanislavski laid down seemed to be very far away from the route I was pursuing at the time or poised to pursue in the professional theatre. It's just not possible to work with the same rigour and over the same extended periods that these people talk about.

WW: *Is this because typically there are four weeks to rehearse a show?*

JB: That's one of the reasons.

WW: *And because you are not working in a culture of ongoing training.*

JB: Actors use their instinct of course and I think they have been conditioned to believe that without a certain type of spontaneity their performances are dead, lifeless or have no fire. My perception would be that this spontaneity that is so sought after manifests itself as shapelessness, as emotional pumping or chaos. It's not the type of spontaneity that you would associate with jazz or other musical forms that are very disciplined. Spontaneity arises from discipline. It's possible only to achieve real spontaneity, as in valuable spontaneity, from form and from structure. This is the paradox in acting but it's not a paradox to musicians or to other artists.

WW: *Who else has influenced your work?*

JB: Eugenio Barba is another influence. It's odd because these people have influenced my work and at the same time I haven't always been able to be loyal to that influence. Many times I have forsaken it in pursuit of something else that was easier or where perhaps my main influence would have been my peers or the audience or the critics.

WW: *Have you really been influenced by critics?*

JB: Certainly by opinion.

WW: *Are you saying that you were afraid of appearing pretentious?*

JB: No, although that may have been the case sometimes. I'd say it was just because what I was trying to achieve was too difficult or too challenging. What I mean is, if you're asking me about influences, and I'm saying well that I could point to whoever as an influence, that influence doesn't seem apparent in certain aspects of my work in the past or even now, perhaps. While I am saying that Grotowski has been an influence there have been other influences that maybe I don't like to discuss because they're not necessarily good influences. I suppose I am admitting that I have been disloyal.

WW: *What were your bad influences?*

JB: That's what I'm saying – popular opinion, the public, the need to be seen to be good, acclaim, adulation, success, all of these things and these points of orientation are crippling. They produce mediocre, shoddy work, by my standards, in my experience of my work.

WW: *Does the rigorous way of working that you propose guarantee good work?*

JB: No. I think the truth is crueller than that. I think that it's possible that the end result is excellence and a good performance but that not many people will like it.

WW: *Why?*

JB: I don't know the answer to that. You only have to look in history to see examples of great works of art that spoke to the spirit of the time, only in hindsight. Van Gogh is the only one I can think of who was dead but Stravinsky, when *The Rite of Spring* was premiered, it was a complete disaster. That's a pretty serious work of art. I'm not comparing myself to Stravinsky, but you can see my point. I'm sure it happens in other disciplines. I think that it's a question of whether you want to make the theatre that you want to make or the theatre that you think the audience will like. This is the argument. Sometimes the audience will like the same things as you and that's great but sometimes that's not the case. I think that if you take them as your main influence you're in trouble. I have done that and probably will do it again. It's a battle.

WW: *How does your interest in the theatre laboratory apply practically to your work?*

JB: What do you mean? Why do we train?

WW: *Yes.*

JB: Training is a way of discovering your expressive potential as an actor, your tools, of stripping away the necessary armour, the necessary veneer that you need daily, so that people don't find out your secrets. I believe that it's imperative when you act, when you go in front of an audience that these "masks', as other practitioners have called them, are removed. If you become concerned with how you are perceived, the masks block sincerity, the masks prevent reality from existing on the stage. The training is about understanding this through practice and not through discussion, through physical rigour and demanding exercises. It's about discovering the nature of these blocks or masks, discovering why they're there so that they can be dropped at will and immediately replaced when you walk back out of the rehearsal room or the training room. The training is also a means for the actor to understand how their organism works so that they can tame it, as it were, to obey their flow of impulses, so that they can override automatic reflexive impulses. They can choose to wilfully stop an impulse from manifesting into action. Training offers a way of learning certain fundamental principles of expression, expressivity, laws of opposition and displacement of balance – all means of energizing the body, giving the muscular structure justification. Every action that the actor performs is imbued with a necessity, with a motivation, which is often very banal. It's private, but the spectator on a subliminal level will perceive that the action is flowing, it's operating within the laws of reality. There's no disruption. The spectators don't feel that they're watching a sham or a stereotype. This is all very esoteric though.

WW: *You are talking about a very particular direction. Irish theatre has traditionally been and substantially still is about writing and for that reason certain types of demands are made on actors.*

JB: Can you elaborate?

WW: *Well, and this is a very crude definition – remember your lines, don't bump into the other actors and give it a naturalistic, psychologically grounded type of performance, which doesn't seem to be the type of acting that you are interested in.*

JB: Hang on, this is really important. Naturalism, naturalistic, these are all aesthetics. I am not against the aesthetic of naturalism, or verisimilitude. The things that I am talking about are present in naturalism, good naturalism. I think that every action on the stage must be real. It must actually happen, there must always be something actually happening and happening consciously. We're getting off the point of your question, though.

WW: *Yours is a type of theatre that is not preoccupied with the text in the same way. I am suggesting that in Irish theatre, because of centrality of the writer and the word, the agenda has been to deliver the text to the audience. We typify a kind of bad acting, irrespective of the aesthetic, as head acting, acting above the shoulders. It revolves mainly around speech.*

JB: I would call that unimaginative acting – leaning on the narrative, hiding behind the words, delivering lines and using stock emotions. This isn't real life; this isn't naturalistic, and it's rubbish. It's a perversion of real behaviour. There's nothing real in it at all. I don't want to sound as if I'm against writers; I'm the complete opposite to that. I may have a different aesthetic but the way that I am working is applicable to all aesthetics in theatre. The refuge of the people who want to remain lazy is to dismiss the work as "physical theatre'.

WW: *What is physical theatre?*

JB: I don't know.

WW: *Is physical theatre what you do?*

JB: I've said it many times that I think that all theatre has to be physical. The act of speaking is physical. There is a huge physical process that goes on inside your body to make a sound. It's not an intellectual process. It's organic and physical. It seems to me that what people mean when they say physical theatre is that there is an overemphasis on the body and a lack of emphasis on the word. In this country it seems to me that it's trying to solve one problem by shamming in another area. It's trying to solve something with inventiveness or originality or gimmickry or trickery. This doesn't really address the root problem. The root problem is that a lot of actors, unfortunately, are ignorant of their own physical expressivity. They deny the responsibility they have to their craft, to hone their bodies, to understand how an organism works, to understand the nature of their vocal apparatus, to understand why impulses happen and how to control these impulses. They are not able to create; they don't know how to consciously compose and structure artificially a sequence of actions into a score. I am generalizing out of necessity but I have a theory that Stanislavski has been wrongfully associated with developing a process or a "system" for actors that enables them to act in a naturalistic way on stage. This is inaccurate because he first started developing his "system" in order to solve problems of a more surrealistic nature. He was trying to work with the plays of Maeterlink, which are really very off the wall in comparison to Chekhov.

One of the things that everybody seems to forget is that when these famous Moscow Art productions of Chekhov were taking place sometimes they were playing to audiences of a thousand at a time. I defy any actor to go on stage and give me television energy in front of a thousand people and reach them. This again is another refuge of the lazy actor, to think that Stanislavki's actors were on stage in front of a thousand people performing in a mumbling American method sort of way. That was not the case. What they had managed to do was to perform in a style that you can call verisimilitude, which is not the way people behave off stage. They managed to create an equivalent external appearance that didn't make people think that it was odd behaviour. This was done with great technique because how else can somebody reach the person in the back row? They must have been using incredible energies. I think that because the camera was beginning to come to the fore around that time there must have been some kind of upset. We know that everyone was getting excited about the film camera because it made it possible to reach a wider audience and was a very exciting medium. We know that when the actors got in front of those cameras in the beginning they looked melodramatic; they were fish out of water. Gradually a new technique had to be developed for the camera. Somehow this is what happened, this technique of reduction for the camera; the skill is more about drawing in whereas on stage it's more about transmitting. It's extroverted energy. It has to be because the lens is huge. An actor who is good enough can energize a finger and pull you in, in the same way as a close up. That's craft, it's not always necessary in film because the director will do that for them and at all costs it's a candid energy that's being sought after. This is OK in film because that type of spontaneity is fine, you only have to get it once and once you get it it's in the can. In theatre you're obliged every night at the same time to hit that mark. How do you do that? You can't do that if you are relying on spontaneity. It's totally off the mark.

WW: *What do you think of the training that is available to actors in this country? Is it adequate?*

JB: I think that you have to relate the training that's available to the profession. The training services the profession; it grooms people for the profession. So I think we have to look at what is being offered. How are people trained? What do they come out with? What are the demands that are made of people in these institutions or courses and how necessary is this training to people who wish to pursue a career in the profession. I would say that it is not necessary.

WW: *Why not?*

JB: Simply by virtue of the amount of actors who work without it.

WW: *Do many actors work without having trained?*

JB: There are a lot of actors who haven't actually gone through that process.

WW: *There is a perception that someone who has not undergone at least some form of training is an amateur.*

JB: Maybe. It is not a distinction that concerns me much. It may have done so in the past, but that was a misplaced snobbery. What the profession requires is talent, that's what it peddles. It is indifferent if that talent is raw because it's only engaging a person for a particular gig. That concerns me but there's not much that I can do about it and possibly it doesn't concern anyone else. It's a very personal belief and observation.

WW: *Surely time spent training is not a waste.*

JB: Not unless actors waste it themselves.

WW: *Does it at least serve a function of teaching them about theatre?*

JB: Yes, when I trained as an actor it certainly opened me up to possibilities and gave me a sense of how much craft there actually is. On the other hand with the way I'm talking about working now with our company it would be immoral to ask anybody to pay a fee to essentially teach themselves. That's what is required. That act is a very difficult thing. It's not as simple as doing a "turn." Any writer who's any good will tell you about the dark times or the anguish of writing. Sometimes we dismiss this as pretentious but I think that it can be very traumatic. If something comes too easy it's probably trivial. The way these courses are constructed they must offer something. They can't just take something from people so they have to be structured in a way that touches on many aspects and styles of theatre, no one approach. This leads to a potpourri effect. Maybe they're good foundation courses but they don't present themselves as such. They present themselves as places of learning while saying that the training goes on all your life. I don't really see how it's possible to plumb the depths that I'm talking about in those establishments. Certainly, at the risk of being extremely offensive, I don't see the results in actors that have trained. What I see is people who had talent when they went in and who have the same talent when they graduate. The ones who had no talent remain mediocre. That's the reality. Even if there's a slight difference, that's just somebody maturing. I'll happily have that argument with anyone.

WW: *Where does Loose Canon fit in to Irish theatre?*

JB: I think you'd have to ask Irish theatre.

WW: *Well, do you make work according to your own preoccupations and sensibilities and then hope that an audience will be interested?*

JB: I think we have to look for an audience. I think that we shouldn't sit back and expect people to come. We should never rely on people coming.

WW: *Do you worry about finding an audience? What are you trying to communicate?*

JB: I think I have to be provocative, in the sense used by Artaud. That is, a provocation of the senses that may also lead to an intellectual provocation but where the first line of communication is through the body, the nervous system. I have to be clear, and this is very important, that I'm not trying to *say* anything. I'm not wilfully trying to say anything.

WW: *Are you describing some form of speaking in tongues?*

JB: No, no. All I can ever *say* is an idea and an idea is useless. What I can do is I can work in a way that begins to recognize certain cultural associations, a certain language that people will understand who are from Ireland, for example. This may not make sense to people from outside of Ireland in the same way. Let's take our immediate audience, first of all. I think that you must be very careful not to go into an audience with a theory or with an idea, unless the idea is a question that you don't have the answer for. Either that or your answer is private; your answer is not anybody's business. It's about them finding their answer. I don't mean to be obscure. This process is equally structured and quite mechanical and methodical. It's about steering clear of meaning or certainly never starting with meaning, never starting to try to make something mean something – forcing meaning. It's about trying to identify then what these associations are on a general level and then, accepting that as your currency, then you can juggle and contradict associations. You can refuse the possibility of that association or turn it into something that nobody foresaw, not even you. I think that's the creative process.

WW: *How does your approach differ from beginning a rehearsal process with a text, which you then go about interpreting with actors?*

JB: When Loose Canon began to do productions of Shakespeare, we hung on the uncluttered presentation of the text, the literal meaning being transmitted clearly, the possibility of a bit of fluid staging and maybe throwing an overcoat on someone. We were dabbling, though we didn't realize it, in the beginning of that process. To just put on Shakespeare, it doesn't do anything; it's a completely dead form. No matter how much I love it personally, it doesn't speak to a wider audience. Moments may speak but it needs to be imbued with something that is contemporary, by which I don't mean the externalizations or the symptoms of the contemporary. I'm not talking about mobile phones. I mean contemporary thought processes so that the autonomy of the piece remains intact but coexists with a twin element, which is the associative process of a collective mind.

WW: *Speaking of an address to the collective, do critics serve a useful function?*

JB: I think they can but I don't think they do. A lot of them just review.

WW: *What do you think they should do?*

JB: They should criticize.

WW: *Can you explain for me you distinction between the two?*

JB: A review tells me what something is about, what time it's on, who's in it and maybe so and so is pretty good here. A critique dissects it and involves some kind of conflict or polemic. There is some attempt to be a devil's advocate, throw it into relief with a different thought process. It's more in depth. Something like that would be useful. Again, it's like the question you asked me about training. Why are our critics so poor? It's not their fault really. It has to do with theatre in general. If our critics are bad and our training is superficial maybe it's because there is no need for either. Maybe all that is necessary is reviewing.

WW: *I thought Irish theatre was flourishing.*

JB: Maybe. I think that it's better to say that our approach is different. The things that I am talking about are excessive. The way I'm talking about approaching acting is excessive. It's excessive because it's not needed. It seems pointless to work that hard. You don't need to work the way I'm talking about in order to work regularly as an actor.

WW: *If it's not necessary then why do it?*

JB: That's why you make your own theatre; you make your own rules. We need to do it but that doesn't mean that others have to.

WW: *Do you think people are interested in theatre any more?*

JB: I don't think theatre is going to die or anything like that. There will always be a few rebels. If you strive towards excellence you will attract spectators who come to the theatre because they do not have the opportunity to do this thing. Their lives are different and their concerns are different. When they come into the theatre they want and should be offered excellence.

WW: *What do you plan to do next?*

JB: Our training structure is now more or less in place as a daily activity. We start with a warm up, which lasts about twenty minutes. It consists of exercises, various different walks, loosening and stretching the spine. We continue with some exercises in contact improvisation, playing with weight, using sticks, working on reflexes. That usually merges into tumbling and balance. We also work with some basic acrobatic and yoga exercises. All this is aimed at overcoming reflexive responses and at unlocking the spine, which is the centre of expressivity in the body and the source of tension in most people. Then we improvise on plastiques. These are exercises taken from Grotowski and consist of manipulations of various joints around the body. This has to do with precisely playing with a particular joint in the space so that it is displacing the balance and causing spontaneous justification of the muscles. We work on the voice for an hour, opening up the various resonators in the body, areas in the skeleton that sound can be directed into. All that takes about three and a half to four hours and then we break. We have developed our structure, the actors understand the vocabulary and the principles and within that they can pursue various individual needs. These needs are usually quite banal but their investigation is not indulgent. Someone might need to work on a particular rhythm, for example.

With the structure in place I feel that it is right to work in the afternoons in a way that is quite different to the morning. In the afternoons we begin the process of gathering information for us to improvise – in terms of finding a show, constructing a performance. The morning is concerned with rigour; each of the actors is confronting the most difficult challenges that they can. In the afternoon we indulge our intellectualisms. This is necessary, and it also leaves us free to have a looser format of exploration in terms of improvising around materials. We can construct sequences and scores, play with language, play with text and just try to find out what the material is that is being suggested. When I talk about trying to find out what the material is I'm not trying to find out what it means – I'm trying to stimulate my own associative process and I'm trying to recognise emblems that are communicating something to a wider audience than just me. We have to then figure out how we want to structure what is being generated, whether we want to tell one story, one play or whether we want to use strands from different plays. The dramaturgy is something that we're going to have to learn as we go along. That's the second stage. Again, it's like the training – it's like a stripping down, trying to get to an essential friction or conflict and then finding a vehicle in which it will sit and give a certain tension to so that we will bring something that is written by a writer to life.

Jason Byrne (b. 1971) is the Artistic Director of Loose Canon Theatre Company, which he co–founded in 1996. He abandoned study of the piano for theatre when he became involved through friends in UCD Dramsoc. Although not a student there he performed in early work by

Conor McPherson and was part of the group that went on to form Fly By Night Theatre Company in 1992. Jason returned to study in the next year and graduated with a Diploma in Acting Studies from the Samuel Beckett Centre in TCD in 1995. He has directed ten productions for Loose Canon, including *The Duchess of Malfi*, *Coriolanus*, and *Hamlet* and most recently a version of *Macbeth*. From 1998–2000 he worked as a Staff Director at the National Theatre where he directed a revival of *Living Quarters* by Brian Friel as well as new plays by Donal O'Kelly and Elizabeth Kuti. In 1999 Jason directed an opera, *The Wall of Cloud*, by Raymond Deane for Opera Theatre Company. For the past year Jason and a small group of actors have been involved in daily training based on models of the theatre laboratory and theories of acting developed by Stanislavski, Grotowski, Eugenio Barba and others.

Willie White is the General Manager of Loose Canon and has produced all the company's work to date.

Marina Carr in Conversation with Melissa Sihra

MS: *You are currently working on a new version of* Iphigenia *which is due to open at the Abbey Theatre in 2002. How do you choose to write about certain myths or classical figures? Do you seek them, or do they seek you?*

MC: I think I seek them. I have always read the Greek plays, on and off, and usually things come to you finally in a very practical way. Judy Friel, at the Abbey, asked me to write the program note for *Iphigenia at Aulis* earlier this year, and that forced me to revisit it. So it was a case of just going back to it and being hungry to write at the same time. I would hardly call my play a "version" of *Iphigenia* because it is so loosely based. It is called *Destiny* and it follows the sensibility of *Iphigenia*. It doesn't follow the plot order but everything that happens in *Iphigenia* happens in *Destiny*.

MS: *Is* Destiny *set in a specifically Irish context like* By the Bog of Cats *– your version of Euripides' tragedy* Medea*?*

MC: Yes. It is my goodbye to the Midlands, I think. For now. I have completed two drafts, and I have another two to do. I feel that the main structure and line of it is there, and that the key speeches are there, but there are other things that I'm still working on. It is not finished yet so I feel strange talking about it. I have never talked about plays that I'm still working on. I think that there is something vulgar in talking about things that aren't finished yet. And I feel threatened because it is so private. Only a few people have read the second draft of *Destiny* and while it is not completed yet, there is a sense that it will never be completed. I may do something entirely different. I may finish it; I may not. And I want that freedom.

MS: *Is a work of art ever complete?*

MC: No, I don't think it ever is. I think that most would agree about the world's inability to finish any work of art. It is by the flaw that we recognize the original. If something was complete and perfect, we wouldn't be able to cope with it. There is a flaw in every work of art.

MS: *And yet we value physical and material perfection in Western society. The ways in which we try to arrest the physical signs of the ageing process, for instance, seem to belie an attempt on some level to resist or deny our mortality and imperfection.*

MC: Yes. I think that desire for perfection is very Greek. I love people who fight death, because that is what it is. I think you can surrender slowly, that's a very different thing. I think sometimes we surrender too quickly here. I like a little battle. I like people who fight, and who take pride in how they look, because it comes into everything – to take pride in how one behaves and to take pride in what one says. It is not even a simple matter of pride, it's about being *aware* of what is going on with yourself, on *every* level, physically and psychologically.

MS: *The process of death and dying is central to your work. What is it about the tragic sensibility that attracts you as a writer?*

MC: On stage there is nothing more beautiful than looking at the arc of a life and the completion of that life. I have spoken before about Tennessee Williams and the tragic impulse, about him saying that the tragic impulse is both within and outside of time. And of how some people are born with it. I would like to quote Eugene O'Neill, and his ideas on death and tragedy. In this interview with O'Neill, the interviewer is curious to know the source of the incisive, inevitably tragic quality in O'Neill's work, and his answer is: "I have an innate feeling for exultance about tragedy, which comes from a great reverence for the Greek feeling for tragedy. The tragedy of man is perhaps the only significant thing about him."

That is beautiful. The fact that we are dying probably *is* the only significant thing for all of us. And *how* we live, and *how* we die. I think that is so important – *how* one dies. I love biography because I love reading about how people die. I think it says everything about how they have lived – it is extraordinary. I love the idea of the tragedy of man and woman. It *is* the only significant thing about us – that we are going to die, and that we all get it so wrong.

MS: *Suicide is a very different kind to other kinds of death.*

MC: Yes. I used to think that suicide was a valid option. I'm not speaking about myself, but in general terms. But I don't think so anymore. I think it curtails what Kierkegaard calls "eternity's claim" on you. He talks about "eternity's claim" and I think part of that is about complete surrender to whatever that claim is, from beyond. And to arrest that journey before its time, while I have sympathy for those who do, my belief now is that you would suffer beyond for that action.

MS: *Because there is something greater than, and beyond, us? And because we owe something to that process, to "eternity", whatever that may be?*

MC: Completely. We are here for a reason. We are of time, but also beyond it. And to forget that we are beyond it is the problem. Everyone forgets that they are also outside of time – that they are both within it *and* outside of it. And actually that the next world has a claim on us, and when we arrive there we must confront that. It may be as simple as the Catholic idea of "What did you do?", "What did you do that was good?" – of having the book of life being opened up before you. But what's wrong with that – opening the book of life? But equally I think you have to open the book of life while you are here, if you can, and say "What have you done?" and "What are you doing?"

MS: *So death is part of a bigger journey?*

MC: I have always thought that death is just a moment, like two seconds. It is just the end of your world here. It is almost like the starting-block of the race; that is all we are supposed to know about it. While I think that we are punished by reason these days and that we are subject to it, I also don't think we give people enough credit for actually encompassing all the worlds. It used to be said that art creates society, and I think, in a strange way, that is changing because people are changing so rapidly. I think that we are trying to play catch-up with people now, in the sense that we are stuck with the old constructs of theatre, of the novel, of the short story. We are stuck in the old machinery of telling the story, when in actual fact, people have moved so far beyond that. All they need now is just a taste, and the outward structure, and within that the writer can go anywhere and they will take that on, and will understand it, and will be with it. I think that people have never been so open since, possibly, the Greek world. There is a hunger now. While we have more than we could ask for, it does nothing. You can only have one dinner, or wear one pair of trousers at a time. And you get beyond that and think well, we are as much *not* of this world, as we are of it. And how to capture that in theatre is the huge challenge, and is becoming the huge challenge for me. I don't know how to do it. It is so difficult, and yet it is so easy if you just bow to it. I haven't found the way to do it yet.

MS: *What happens after death?*

MC: I think we are put here to work out what we were sent back for. That is the only belief that makes sense to me. I believe in the eternal return until we get it right, that we are sent back until we get it right. Plato talks about the soul being of only one age, that it never changes; the soul is one age. That is terrifying, but it is also beautiful. When we think that there is this impenetrable thing within us, that is just there, observing it all. It is almost like we are in battle with it, that we are fighting it to the death. We are trying to go the opposite way, and it is the one wise fabric inside us, that makes us stop and think, when we *do* stop and think. It is the gauge within us. When we are doing something wrong, and we know it, that is the one-age soul speaking to us. We do not pay attention to every emotion, like we should. That pursuit of darkness is linked into not paying attention, and to not paying attention to the pursuit of light. Because once you realize that you are in the darkness, you are kind of scrambling to get out of it. And sometimes you relish the darkness.

MS: *What do you mean by "darkness?"*

MC: Well, tragic darkness is a very different thing. Chekhov talks about the venial sin and the mortal sin. For him, the mortal sin was the stroke of destiny. It was a necessary sin to commit, and therefore necessary for those all around to accommodate as they could, or not, whereas the venial sin was like killing yourself by the spoonful. All the mean, petty things we do. And they are all the things that we *can* sort out in this existence. The big sins – they are almost beyond us, we have to do them, we have to commit them. The small sins we do not have to commit. For Chekhov it was the small sins that destroyed pride and dignity and eroded the sense of oneself as a human being. I believe that the big sins are almost pre-ordained and going to happen anyway. And the only way we can conduct ourselves is around the small sins. But that is a huge thing, to be able to conduct ourselves around the small things.

MS: *How do you feel about the characters in your plays who have taken their own lives?*

MC: What can I say? I would stand by them through thick and thin. You can never forget the individual choice within the journey either, and finally, as a writer, you cannot take responsibility for what you have done. The plays are there, with my name on them, whatever that means. I used to think it meant more than it actually does. The older I get the more I think it doesn't really matter. If people are coming to see the plays, and if they get something out of it, even if it is a very minor character – and very often it is – *that* is what speaks, not necessarily the hero or the heroine. I find that, with plays that I like, very often it is the minor characters. It can be a line just thrown away – that's the thing that really destroys you.

MS: *Do you feel optimistic for humanity at this time?*

MC: I have never been pessimistic about our capacity for understanding and discovery. I am pessimistic about the dark undercurrent that is there, and that always has been there. The Greeks divided the world, and there were the new Gods and the old Gods. The Daimons were the old Gods, the pre-Gods, the Gods of darkness. And there was a belief that a certain portion of us would hold onto the old Gods. I think that makes so much sense. It is not just the Daimons holding on, it is in all of us, holding on to that darkness. And also that desire for the light, for advancement and improvement. That is in everyone also. Everyone wants the light, and yet there is this awful undertow that is going to hold us back, that holds us back everyday. Just even looking at the daily routine – "Will I work, or won't I?" – it is there in all of that, the mundane. That is the battle about whether to make the mark or not. I have the greatest respect for people who make a mark, no matter what it is, just having the courage to do it, do it, do it – to get it done and then move on to the next thing, but just *do it*. There is so much vacillation that will finally mean nothing in eternity. There will be no book of life about our vacillation or our intentions. The book of life will be what you did and how you did it.

MS: *What makes some people go towards the light, and some people move away from it?*

MC: I am inclined to think that it is destiny actually. But I don't know. I asked a friend recently: "Do you get the sense that the earth is over?" And he said: "Yes, I often think it is like a beautiful experiment coming to a close." There are days that I think that, and then there are days when I look at my children and see their innocence and their hunger for discovery and for being busy. I have never seen anyone as busy as my children. And I think, what happened to my "busy-ness?" Children are natural creators. How does that get beaten out of us? What happens?

MS: *What about the ways in which events of the past weigh so heavily on the present in your plays? Are we, in a sense, yoked down by the actions and experiences of those who have gone before us? Or, do we have the agency to act for ourselves?*

MC: I have never believed that time is linear. If you don't believe that time is linear, then it is all up for grabs really, isn't it? I believe so much in the ways in which my parents and grandparents have shaped me. I can almost imagine what my great-grandparents were like because of my grandparents. Once in a blue-moon you will get a maverick, but that is rare. And if you start hunting back, you will find that it is there in the gene-pool, in the blue-print, the hard-wiring. But I also believe in the individual's ability to put their own version on it – their own variation. What I cannot bear is not to be alive when you are living. Being alive and not being there. I can't bear it. It is like removing yourself from yourself. And that is what we do, so much. I don't know why Western society is so much constructed around pretending you are everything except what you are. I find that terrifying.

MS: *In your most recent work,* On Raftery's Hill, *the tragedy is manifested differently, in the sense that nobody dies.*

MC: The cat dies!

MS: *By not bowing to the option of death, the characters are consigned to a kind of purgatorial entrapment and stasis, with no possibility for change or transformation.*

MC: It is worse than death. I always believe that in theatre, because it is heightened realism, no matter what form one chooses – absurdism, farce, tragic realism or whatever – you have to earn your death on the stage. And I don't think that anyone earned their death in that play. If they had, I would have released them. But that, I suppose, is another way of saying that I did not sufficiently care enough about any of them to kill them, or to allow them to die. Finally I was indifferent to the characters after the curtain dropped. That was as far as I could take them.

MS: *As you were writing* On Raftery's Hill *were you aware of the characters' fate?*

MC: No, I had no idea. I never do, with any of my plays. Even *By the Bog of Cats* had different versions where Hester was alive at the end, and she came back. It was done through monologues. It was only in the fourth draft that I killed her.

MS: *Do you think you will ever write monologue plays?*

MC: I can write monologues very easily. I have written them, but I think I would rather write a novel than a monologue for the theatre. There is something intrinsically un-dramatic about the monologue. I love them and they are very easy to write. The only monologue theatre that has ever worked for me is Brian Friel's *Faith Healer*. But that is so dramatic in the way that the monologues are posited. They play off of one another beautifully. And it is very rare for that to work. I have a problem with monologue-driven theatre. It is very seductive and very appealing for the writer. They are easy to write and you can get all the information that you want across. You can indulge your "literary sensibility", you can show "I can write beautiful sentences", but finally, that is not what theatre is about. It is about the spoken word and conflict. It is about people bouncing off of one another. It is about eliciting the beautiful sentence out of the situation. And that is much more difficult, because you are in the "real" world, and your character in the play has to carry the inner and the outer world. To really work, your character has to carry the spoken *and* the unspoken. That charge in your character is the most difficult thing in the world, because you have to carry it and make it seem normal in the course of natural speech. And that is quite difficult to do. But it is a great challenge as well. The monologue is beautiful because it carries all the unspoken. I can see why it is so seductive. There are some extraordinary pieces of monologue theatre. But by and large, I finally find it unsatisfying.

MS: *What about the novel or short story form for you as a writer?*

MC: I love the novel and the short-story; I keep saying it. Yet I am tied to the theatre. It is something I wake-up with everyday. I get up and I say "How am I going to write a scene?" I have not got from the stage all that I want to get out of it yet. I feel that the possibilities are endless. I remember Eugene O'Neill being asked if he would ever write a novel and he replied that it had taken him fifteen years to learn how to write a play. A novel would take him another fifteen – there is just not enough time! Having said that, I don't know yet.

MS: *What is it that keeps you writing?*

MC: Sometimes I don't know. Sometimes it doesn't keep me going, it's the other things. But I get to the point where, if I don't write, then everything just falls apart. That's the same for most people, no matter what they are doing. It is my work. I have to do something. Sometimes it satisfies me; usually it frustrates me. It is painful sometimes; you see your limitations everyday. Every time you sit down you are battling with things that you just do not have the ability to express, all those fine, delicate things, you just can't get. You can approximate them, but you can't get them.

MS: *Do you find it difficult to look back at the plays that you have written?*

MC: I don't like to read what I've written. I hate looking at anything I've written. I hate going to see any of my plays, even on the first night. I just can't bear it. I don't think it is an ego thing; the actors enhance my plays, they make them better than they are. So it is not a judgement on them, or on anyone else. It is a judgement on myself. And it is almost a judgement on how far I have travelled from the time I wrote the play. There is often eighteen months to two years between writing a play to its production. And you come a hell of a long way in two years, and the older you get the faster you move – you're just taking in so much.

MS: *What writer or work do you return to for solace?*

MC: They change every month! There is so much beautiful writing out there. I could happily sit in a corner and read for the rest of my life. Every time I read something, I want to answer it. It sparks off something in me. Unfortunately it is usually something inferior, the feeling that I can't match-up. Ninety per cent of a writer's life is about reading. I read for at least a couple of hours everyday. Then there are periods where I do nothing *but* read, sometimes for six or seven hours a day. As a writer you can be crippled by that – the feeling of "why bother? It's already been said." There is one writer who stays with me. I have been reading the work of the poet Ted Hughes for about ten years now. His poem *October Salmon*, which is about a salmon dying in a river, is one that I find very moving, particularly the last verse:

> All this too,
> Is stitched into the torn richness,
> The epic poise
> That holds him so steady in his wounds,
> So loyal to his doom,
> So patient in the machinery of heaven.

Marina Carr (b.1964) was raised in County Offaly. She graduated from University College Dublin with a degree in English and Philosophy. She has written eight plays to date, including *The Mai* (1994), *Portia Coughlan* (1996), *By the Bog of Cats.* (1998) and *On Raftery's Hill* (2000). She has been Writer-in-Residence at the Abbey Theatre and Trinity College, Dublin, and is a member of Aosdána. She has won many awards for her work including, most recently, the E. M. Forster Award from the American Academy of Arts and Letters. Her first collection of plays is published by Faber & Faber.

Melissa Sihra is currently researching the plays of Marina Carr for a Ph.D at Trinity College. She lectures in Modern Irish Drama at the National University of Ireland, Maynooth, and is a Script Reader for the Abbey Theatre. She has given talks at the University of California, Berkeley, and the University of Pittsburgh and is a contributor to the forthcoming *Oxford Encyclopedia of Theatre and Performance*. In 2001 she worked as Dramaturg on three productions of Carr's plays in the United States: *Portia Coughlan* for the Pittsburgh Irish and Classical Theatre Company, the US premier of *By the Bog of Cats* for Irish Repertory of Chicago and *By the Bog of Cats* for San José Repertory Theatre.

Daragh Carville in Conversation with Glenn Patterson

GP: *Could I start by asking you about your personal influences and what brought you into theatre?*

DC: I became a playwright by luck of the draw. I knew as a child that I wanted to write or make or create things in some way. As Beckett said, as a young man he had nothing to say but had the itch to make and that was exactly me at sixteen or seventeen. When I was about 17, I bought a notebook and I thought, "right, this is what I'm going to do" and I went to the University of Kent at Canterbury to do my degree in film and drama. On that course they had a playwriting module which, I seem to remember, was just about the only one in the country at that time. They had a lot of competition to get onto this module, so rather than evaluating your writing or anything like that, they put us all into a lecture theatre, put all our names into a hat and drew them out randomly and my name was one of the ones that came out of the hat. So I went into this semester-long module on playwriting which was given by a guy called Alan Beck who was, I suppose, a big influence. During that module I started to write what was to become the first play I ever wrote – a thing called *The Grandfather Grave*. There was some sort of association between the university and the Royal Court in London and people from the Royal Court came down occasionally to see what we were doing. They liked what I was doing and so that play was eventually put on at the Royal Court as part of a Young Writers' Festival.

GP: *That was the first play you had written?*

DC: Well, I had tried out a few things before – but I really didn't know what I wanted to do. I remember trying to write really terrible things about – it's just embarrassing to think about – Greenham Common and things like that. This was 1987/8. I was just trying to find a way to do it, to find some way into writing, but

I was also quite political at the time and was surrounded by the whole Socialist Workers gang. On the drama degree we were doing a lot of Brecht, and John McGrath and Trevor Griffith were big figures in this community at the time, so I was thinking about that at the time – all this agit-prop stuff. But the moment when I actually found myself as a writer, when there was this quickening, was the moment when I completely disregarded all of that and just sat down and started to write dialogue in the language of my friends. There was an extra-literary influence. There was a guy called Garth Ennis writing graphic novels – and he'd written this comic strip called *For a Few Troubles More* or something like that. I can't even remember if it was any good, but it was the language I had grown up with. So I thought – that's what I should be writing. So I started writing like that and that turned into *The Grandfather Grave*, which starts with a bunch of kids sitting in a graveyard up behind my house in Armagh. And I knew as I was writing it, I've got something here – this is real, this is real language.

GP: *You mentioned Brecht and John McGrath but that you had worked those influences out of you. Is there any lingering influence in your work now, people you read or watch with interest?*

DC: Yeah, totally. I read Pinter when I was a student and became really passionate about him in the early 1990s, read constantly, and went to see anything I could, and met him on one or two occasions. I'm beyond a fan, I'm a quasi-stalker of Pinter. Pinter has been and continues to be massively important to me, as a writer, in terms of the work on the page and on the stage, but also as the figure of the writer. As someone who is passionate and serious and involved in the world, he's a hero to me I suppose. Later David Mamet was important and continues to be important, not just for the plays: Mamet writes a lot about the process of writing and they are the closest things I've ever read to self-help books, because he writes so honestly and so well about the difficulties of the process but also about the life-and-death importance of it and he's a very big influence. In Irish terms it would be Tom Murphy who is important to me, not Friel to any real extent. And Stewart Parker is important to me.

GP: *The influences you mention first are all non-Irish. Are you very conscious of what's happening in Irish theatre? Do you think of yourself as an Irish playwright?*

DC: I don't think of myself primarily as part of this Irish tradition but it's inescapable at the same time. I don't deliberately go out of the way to avoid it. My stuff is primarily oral, it's not this highly visual pyrotechnic theatre of Robert Lepage or Théâtre de

Complicité. These are very text-based, in some ways old-fashioned, plays so it fits into that tradition of Irish plays being to do with language and how people use language and what they use language for. I say that, but that's exactly what Pinter does as well, that's exactly what Mamet does, so I am and I'm not connected. The real figure who unites all the people I have been speaking about is Beckett. The question of whether Beckett is part of the Irish theatrical tradition or whether he's outside it is an interesting one. Part of what's considered to be characteristic of Irish plays is, to some extent, a debate about what Irishness is. Right from Yeats founding the Irish Literary Theatre as a way of putting on plays about Irish subjects by Irish writers, Irish theatre has been engaged in this debate about Irishness and what Irishness is. You can probably make a case for Beckett having relevance to that but you couldn't say Beckett writes about Irishness. So he's in a different position obviously, because he's writing in another language as well.

GP: *Talking about what it means to be Irish, are there other issues around the fact of living in Northern Ireland, the North of Ireland? Do you feel you are writing in a tradition that is specifically a Northern Irish one?*

DC: You don't deliberately necessarily set out to do that but it's inescapable, the issue of being a writer in this place. That's my own code of Northern Ireland, the North of Ireland, the North, whatever… "this place" seems to do it. Paul Muldoon said that either you deal with this whole issue of the Troubles, in which case you run the risk of exploiting it, or you don't deal with it, in which case you're hiding your head in the sand and being irresponsible in some way. So it's a difficult one.

The way to get around it is to do what Paul Muldoon has done, to confront it head on with your head in the sand in some peculiar way. For he does talk about "this place" and what happens here but he does it in an oblique and playful way. And while I wouldn't suggest that my plays have in any way been Muldoonesque or playfully postmodern, or pastiches, I have tried to write about Northern Ireland. I've tried to write plays about Belfast that haven't been like other plays about Belfast and I've been quite conscious about doing that. The first proper play that I wrote – *Language Roulette* – is set at the time of the first ceasefire but it's certainly not a Troubles play. That play started life as something called *Talks about Talks* because at that time, 1994, what was happening was people talking about the possibility that they might start talking at some point down the line. As somebody who was passionately involved in what was happening here, but also involved in reading Pinter and the Pinter plays at the time, that seemed really exciting to me – this notion of communicating about communicating rather than actually communicating seemed really rich for theatre.

So I started writing about how people use language to do things other than communicate and I wanted to apply that to this place. What I desperately didn't want to do was write one of those "burning balaclava" plays. So there's none of the iconography of the Troubles and even if the language of the Troubles comes up it is in order to have the piss taken out of it. And that was the way the people around me were dealing with it at the time: it was the source of the blackest kind of comedy and I wanted to write in a way that would avoid hand-wringing worthiness.

GP: Language Roulette *seemed to be a spearhead of a generation of new playwrights from this place, so what do you think about the other work coming out of here over the last years, the "burning balaclavas?" Do you feel heartened by what other people are doing in the theatre, or do you feel it's been in any way retrogressive?*

DC: God, a real combination of both. I'm heartened by the fact that there is unquestionably a group of playwrights that has emerged from here in the last five years who are working at a high level, if I may put it like that. Their plays are being seen in London and New York, going into translation and all of that, which I don't really think has happened before. Obviously there have been generations of poets and prose writers coming out of here but usually we have one or two playwrights. Suddenly there is not a movement – because they're a completely disparate bunch of people – but a group of people writing well and all writing very differently. If you think of what Gary Mitchell is doing, compared to what Owen McCafferty is doing, or I'm doing, or Marie Jones or Colin Teevan is doing, these are very different kinds of writers. There is no way to compare the really popular entertainments that Marie Jones writes with the kind of highly stylized, classical plays that Colin Teevan writes. They're just completely at opposite ends of the spectrum. But I sometimes worry. François Truffaut said a great film should tell you something new about life and something new about film. Similarly with a play. I sometimes worry – with my own stuff as well – that some of the writers from this place aren't challenging the formal shape of plays and playwriting. Sometimes it feels as if people are writing what might nebulously be called "drama" rather than theatre, things that could almost be happening on TV. You'd hope that people could stretch further than that. But I'm conscious of this in my own work as well and conscious that where I want to go as a writer is quite far away from that.

GP: *In terms of theatre and theatricality, how do you think your own work has developed?*

DC: It's probably easier to talk about how I'd like it to develop than how it has developed. Looking back over the plays I've written, the most obvious thing is that I have a much surer sense of structure now and a lot of that actually comes out of writing films, which is such a narrative form that you really do need that sense of structure and how it works. I don't particularly want to write well-made plays. I don't mind things being a bit jagged and dissonant, I think that's good. I think my plays will always be essentially language based, so I don't think I am going to suddenly become a totally different kind of writer where it is all visual or highly physical theatre. Basically I feel connected to the language here and I get most excited about writing when I find the texture of the language and the dialogue becoming organic and having the grain of truth to it. But I would like to be able to push that further and to write something that is poetic – not in the verse play way, but in the way that certain of Pinter's plays achieve, that's where you'd like to end up. And that means challenging naturalism and getting away from documentary realism, social realism and pushing the language further and pushing the people further. I'm conscious that I need to do that because I don't want to write plays that could happen on TV. I want to write plays that can only possibly be plays.

GP: *You've been working on a play for the National Youth Theatre,* The Holyland, *and I understand that, while it's still very much in the idiom of this place, it's creating its own intense version of it, so it is creating an imaginative space that isn't documentary realism.*

DC: I certainly don't think that I write documentary or naturalistic plays but they are a kind of heightened naturalism. If you look at *Language Roulette*, the play more or less happens in real time but the play lasts for an hour and a half, and what happens lasts for an entire evening of these characters' lives. So the audience has the experience that it has been with them the whole way through, but actually time has been telescoped or heightened or distorted and concentrated in the play. And I think that's what's happening – I hope that's what's happening – throughout my writing: making a reality but distorting it, making it more intense and strange.

GP: *To shift focus to the business of theatre production, what do you see as the highlights or lowlights of your career so far?*

DC: The clear highlights have been those moments when the process has worked best, when the collaboration with the other members of the team has been really positive and fruitful. That's happened to me on a couple of projects, most significantly on *Language Roulette*. Just everyone working on that play was so completely committed to it: Tim Loane – who directed it – and the cast and everybody absolutely believed in it, and shared a vision of what it was and what it meant and totally understood those characters. That doesn't mean that it was all lovey and jerky – particularly for the actors it was actually quite bruising and exhausting and they were all wrecked by the end of it – but it was an incredibly positive experience. Really that came out of a sense that we all believed in it, we all shared the same vision, so we were all doing the same job. The opposite I've also experienced. I have had the experience of being in a situation where we didn't have that kind of shared idea of the play and that became really horrible and led to all sorts of unpleasantness; it made it very difficult for the play to breathe and develop.

GP: *Which play are you talking about?*

DC: *Observatory*, which happened at the Abbey. Ultimately it was worthwhile because I think the play turned out well but I look back on it as a really difficult experience because the process somehow didn't work. I stress that the people I was working with there were brilliant at their job: we had a great cast, great director and everyone was really positive and focussed. The problem was we didn't share the vision of the piece – and that's absolutely fundamental. If you're all working together and you've all got the same goal in mind and you're all working to help to achieve the play then that's very positive. If there's any disruption or negativity in that, if there are other agendas at work, then it becomes very, very difficult. The play starts being pulled apart between people.

GP: *What's the answer to that? Is it a matter of the writer having more control over what happens to the plays in production or is it a question of having a better partnership with the director and cast?*

DC: I really think it has to be both. Plays start as an incredibly private, intimate affair in a writer's head, as you sit in a room on your own, talking to yourself or talking to a computer screen and working out these ideas. You don't tell anybody about it; it's like you're hatching something. And that process lasts however long it lasts – from ten days to a couple of years – this private moment when you're working the thing out for yourself. And then you give it to [someone] and get feedback and it starts to take that first step into the public world. Then you give it to a theatre company or a director and again you're widening the circle and moving out into the public arena. Next thing you know you're with a bunch of actors in a rehearsal room, and there's maybe a designer there, or a composer or a couple of other people. And finally you move into the most public of public arenas, the theatre itself, and there they are, the general public coming in.

So you move from something that's incredibly private and close to you and intimate towards something that's absolutely public and really no longer quite belongs to you. As a writer you have to have some way of managing that process psychologically, some sort of strategy. Beckett's strategy obviously was to maintain absolute control so the piece wouldn't deviate at any stage. But you have to have some way of dealing with the fact that you're moving from the private world into the public world and for me that's all to do with trust. You've got to trust the people that you're working with. You've just got to be sure that when you're bringing this delicate, private thing into the daylight that you're with people who understand what that process is. It's very peculiar. When it works, it is fantastic; when it doesn't work it's really battering and bruising and your work is put to such harsh scrutiny sometimes that it's really disheartening. But for an actor to take a part and invest something of their own life in it, and suddenly bring something out of that character that hadn't occurred to you, and bring that character to life, that can be thrilling.

GP: *Just wondering about the extremes of experience that you had with* Language Roulette *and* Observatory, *is there something to do with the North-South here?* Language Roulette *seemed to me to open up theatre experiences we hadn't seen here in many years, something people recognized.* Observatory *was different, but it was part of the same enterprise. Is there a difficulty in having that enterprise recognized, that purpose shared, outside Northern Ireland.*

DC: I really hope not. I don't know. All of those plays have been seen outside of Ireland as well. *Observatory* has just been on in Holland in a Dutch translation and *Dumped* went to France, and *Language Roulette*'s on in America and in Germany soon. So they've all gone beyond the North and South of Ireland and seem to have keyed in, in some way, with people there. So I hope they have something that isn't limited by Northern Irishness. But I do know what you mean. What was exciting about *Language Roulette* and *Dumped* was it kind of felt not just that the plays were about younger people living in Belfast and the way they communicate and live, but it also brought those people into the theatre. So in terms of the audience that was being reached, there was something very exciting about that. It used to be extraordinary to go to the Old Museum when *Language Roulette* was on and just see people coming in who probably didn't go to theatre very much because they probably went to movies. It was very exciting and gratifying to see a non-traditional theatre audience coming to see my stuff. And it was probably more difficult to generate that in Dublin, although *Observatory* did quite well.

GP: *I wasn't suggesting the plays wouldn't travel but that sometimes you can be heard better slightly further away. Sometimes between Belfast and Dublin, or Belfast and London there's a failure of empathy at very close quarters.*

DC: There is a very weird prism between Belfast and Dublin and London, where, depending where you're at, your perspective is totally changed. I read an article Conor McPherson wrote for *The Guardian*, within the last year or so, about Irish theatre. It was an extraordinary piece because essentially what he said was that the characteristics of Irish theatre were lyricism, a poetic kind of concern with language, Catholic guilt and the absence of politics. And I just thought that was an extraordinary thing to say. The lyrical poetic thing I can understand to some extent and it does go back to what I was saying at the start of this: it is a text-based, word-based oral tradition. But at the same time, you know, [with] "lyrical-poetic" we're getting into very dodgy territory, we're starting to sound like Matthew Arnold's idea of Irishness and Celtic Twilight and all of that, quite dangerous stereotypes. That perception of Irishness makes me think of that scene in *Titanic* where Kate Winslett is encouraged to get in touch with her inner child by going dancing with the Irish down below decks: it's kind of horrifying.

And it does go back to Arnold and Yeats and those notions of Irishness as opposed to English materialism and pragmatism and stiff-upper-lip and all of that, both of which are very destructive stereotypes. The other thing was Catholic guilt. Certainly, as a collapsed Catholic myself I can testify to the importance of Catholic guilt but what he didn't seem to be dealing with was the fact that (a) most of the great writers of theatre out of Ireland have been Protestant, (b) that there are a million people in the North who don't experience Catholic guilt at all. They may experience the work ethic, but not the guilt. And then this thing about the absence of politics as a characteristic of Irish theatre? What really struck me about that was that this is a writer – and a good writer – living and working and writing in Dublin, who seems to never have glanced Northward, because you couldn't possibly say that if you are taking into consideration what happens here. And that shocked me and worried me. It made me think "is that what it's like when you're living and working and writing in Dublin? Do you essentially not concern yourself with what's happening here [in Belfast]? "There's part of me which thinks I don't blame him at all because look at the state of this place. But you do *need* to look at the state of this place. If you are an Irish writer – whether or not you are living in Dublin – and you are concerned with issues of identity and belonging, or language and culture, then you have to concern yourself with looking Northward.

GP: *To what extent do writers here look Southward? Is there something as a writer to be learnt or to take on board by looking at the rest of the island?*

DC: It's something I would quite like to write about actually. My dad is from Monaghan so when we were growing up we were constantly back and forth over the border, because we lived in Armagh and Dad's people were in Castleblaney. And this notion of "The Free State" you could escape to, was an important one. My parents did at one stage contemplate moving over the border at the height of the Troubles, and then they didn't for work reasons – they had a young family at the time. So this thing about "down South" as being this place of promise was certainly there in my childhood, and I would quite like to write something about that.

GP: *Thinking of cultural contexts and so on, I notice that music – especially the music of the moment – seems very important to your work, not just as a soundtrack in the plays, but also in your life and the formation of you as a writer.*

DC: The plays have tended to use music in the fabric of the event, as it were. But more than that the aesthetic of judgment I bring to my own work is often informed by a musical sense. I love pop music. I love the classic three-minute, guitar-bass-and-drums-driven song by the Undertones or The Beatles or The Supremes – all the great, three-minute-love-song people. More than that, I love songs that are melodic and to the point and don't faff around with big guitar solos and bombast and pomposity like U2, but also have something dissonant and strange going on – like Velvet Underground, where you've got classic, melodic, love songs but you've also got weird dissonant aspects like John Cale's viola going through it. Or you may have a wonderful pop song but it's not very well recorded so you might just have a crack or buzz on it. I love those things that are a bit wrong. And that, in a weird way, is what I want to do with the plays. I do want them to be well shaped and economical and snappy, but I also want something discordant or dissonant in them, something that leaves you slightly uneasy in some way. But also there are other examples.

At the moment I'm writing a screenplay called *Middletown*, set in a rural town in Northern Ireland, and it's a story about someone who's been away from home for many, many years, comes home as the preacher and proceeds initially to try and save this place because he sees it as corrupt and sinful. But ultimately, because he fails to do that, he ends up destroying it. In writing for film you're told to think about genre, and this isn't any genre – this is so not a comedy or an action movie – so what is this? A gothic thriller? And finally I realized it was a country song, the kind of pre-Tammy Wynette country music of Hank Williams and Johnny Cash which is all blood and death and drink and all of that. Really rooted, Biblical stuff! And when I made that discovery, then the writing was really freed up and it totally changed the language of the piece concerned, pushed it all much further. What I'm really talking about is the way influence can and does work. You make a discovery and you follow it up and keep your nose to the ground and you find things transformed organically.

GP: *And in* The Holyland *you have a* Velvet Underground *tribute band.*

DC: A very bad Velvet Underground tribute band.

GP: *Thinking more broadly about theatre and the position of the playwright, are there things at a policy level that would qualitatively improve theatre in Ireland, increase audiences, or improve the lot of the writer?*

DC: It often seems that in Ireland the playwrights are the Cinderellas of the process. There are lots of literary festivals where you have poets and novelists but they tend not to invite playwrights. I can understand why. It is to do with the strange nature of the process, the role of the playwright as someone who writes and then gives the work to somebody else who interprets it. So it seems slightly odd to ask a playwright to read from their work or to engage in that kind of literary forum. As Writer-in-Residence here in Queens I've been able to ask a bunch of writers to come here to do talks and readings for students and I've been really consciously trying to bring playwrights into that. We've had Gary Mitchell and Anne Devlin. John McGrath and Trevor Griffiths both came last year and I'm hoping we'll get some other playwrights next year. And that's just about giving playwrights their proper dues.

GP: *Given that you are Writer-in-Residence and teaching an M.A. in Creative Writing here, to what extent do you think there needs to be an increasing professionalization of the writing process or training for playwrights?*

DC: That's something I feel very strongly about. I've been very lucky in that I've written four plays but I've also written a couple of screen plays, and I've got involved with producers and they've enabled me to go off on extended trips to these intensive seminars and conferences about story and story-telling and narrative structure, that kind of thing. It is fantastic to be in an environment where you're with other writers, talking about the actual nuts and bolts of what you do and thinking about it as a craft. I mentioned Mamet earlier and he's brilliant on the craftsmanlike elements of writing, the technique. And it is very important for writers to learn that. Obviously you learn as you write, but there are many things I wish I had known when I started out, that I know now, and that are quite simple things to communicate – to do with how story works, what character is, how that role functions within a story and all of that.

I'm very committed to communicating all of that. A lot of writers are less keen to talk about how it happens, or they talk about it in such a way as to make it very mysterious. And there is a mysterious aspect to it: you're trying to write and you're not getting anywhere and you go and make yourself a cup of tea and suddenly the problem is solved; or you wake up in the morning and there's a line of dialogue, or a story idea that wasn't there when you went to bed. That does happen but it happens very, very rarely and you can't rely on it to happen because, if you did, you wouldn't get anything written. So you need to find ways of making it happen and that means you need to develop certain technical skills. So I am passionate about communicating all of that, and creative writing courses and writing groups have a role to play – I'm not snobbish about it. A hundred years ago Yeats would have gone to some aristocratic lady's salon and sat around with poets reading their work and taking hashish.

Really there's not a very great deal of difference between that – apart from the hashish – and coming to a writers' group in a university and sitting down with your peers and talking about stuff. Right here in this building in Queen's [University] "The Group" as they were called – Seamus Heaney and his friends, including Stewart Parker – used to meet in the 1960s and some extraordinary writing came out of that. That can happen. I think actually it's particularly useful for playwrights because the experience of being in a writers' group is not dissimilar to the experience of being in rehearsal for a play. And it can go either way. If everybody is trusting and up for the good of the work then it can be positive; if people aren't trusting and if there are egos being shoved around then it can be a negative thing.

GP: *A final question. If you had one gift you could give to Irish theatre, what would it be?*

DC: I just want to write a really great play. That's always been what it's about. If I have a motto as a writer – and I don't – it would be "I want to be better." I think that's a healthy way to approach your own work. It's not a healthy thing to think I want to be more successful, or as successful as this other writer, or I want to *be* this other writer who is my role model, because these are destructive and meaningless things. Whereas, being in competition with yourself, wanting to grow and develop and become a better writer, is achievable, it's not too unrealistic. And if, ultimately, having written a dozen or twenty plays, I can write something that's great and that will last and that I will be proud of, then that's my gift. Aren't I good?

Daragh Carville is a playwright. He is currently Writer-in-Residence at Queen's University Belfast and teaches part of the M.A. in Creative Writing. His plays include the award-winning *Language Roulette* (1996), *Dumped* (1997), *Observatory* (1999), and *Holy Land* (2001). He is currently working on a number of screen-plays.

Glenn Patterson is a novelist, a former member of the Arts Council of Northern Ireland, has also worked as a TV arts show presenter and film maker. He currently teaches on the M.A. in Creative Writing in Queen's University Belfast. His published fiction includes the novels *Burning Your Own* (1988), *Fat Lad* (1992), *Black Night on Big Thunder Mountain* (1995) and *The International* (1999). He is currently working on a new novel, *No.5*, due for publication in 2002.

Michael Colgan in Conversation with Jeananne Crowley

JC: *Do you remember all those years ago walking me down O'Connell Street and saying, "in two years time O'Connell Street will no longer end at the Gresham Hotel?"*

MC: Yes. When Orson Welles was given a theatre to run at twenty-three he said he'd been given a magic toy box and couldn't believe that everybody wasn't jealous. When I got the job at the Gate, I went on the RTE News at six o'clock and the man interviewing me said, "Congratulations, or should it be commiserations?"

JC: *He didn't!*

MC: He did and that's on record. The idea being that no one was going to the theatre anymore and it was going to be difficult. But of course there are two ways of looking at a job like that. You say, "How am I going to do it?" You're always doubtful of your own training and essentially your training is taste and your ability to persuade. It's not like being asked to perform a piece of surgery when you've spent seven or ten years training to do it. For me I just thought the greatest gift of all was to be given the Gate. It's a beautiful theatre.

JC: *Weren't you intimidated that at that stage of its life the Gate had almost died?*

MC: I was, a little. But, when I took on the Dublin Theatre Festival I knew it had a greater potential than it was achieving and I felt the same about the Gate. I often wonder if I was asked to take over something that was a going concern and very successful, would I have been able to do it. I might easily have failed. I was asked to take over the St. Patrick's Day Festival but that was the same situation. You see something that has essentially an extraordinary potential that's not being used and you go for it! You go in, sort of like a Red Adair, and say "I can do this" – crisis management or something. The things I have tended to take on didn't worry me as much as maybe they should because they could really, more or less, only go up! I think The Gate was at a really bad time when I took over in 1983 and had been for ten years or maybe more and so I didn't have a problem with that in terms of where it would go. I often consoled myself by saying there's certain things you can do like paint the walls and people say that's change, and you can do obvious things like make the sets better. In retrospect I have at times seen the job differently than I did then.

JC: *Is your great skill then in management first?*

MC: I actually think, and I'm not being modest here, that I'm not particularly skilful in terms of the normal skills and I think that when you're born without gifts… I mean I can't play the piano, I can't speak other languages, I can't cook and I can't put up a shelf; there's a long list of things I can't do. If the car breaks down I say, "It's stopped" and can't say anything else; and when you're not necessarily gifted, you do compensate by making sure you can survive and the way you do that is by developing compensatory skills and the compensatory skill for not being particularly talented is to be persuasive: to be persuasive and to be able to spot talent. So that's what you do. You say, "I can't do that very well but she can. She'll become my friend and then she'll help me out."

If the car breaks down I'm quite happy to go up to the only light on the side of the mountain, knock at the door and ask the man to come down and fix it and know that he will… and if he mentions money I'd probably say, "You've done enough for me already, I'm OK for money!" It's that sort of sense, to know that people are happy to do the things they do well.

JC: *But you are being modest because you obviously had a great understanding of theatre. Where did that come from?*

MC: What I'm good at is knowing the things I can do. If I'm on a ship and we have to land at an island run by a malign dictator and ask him for diesel, with six hundred people on the ship I'd be the one to go and ask him even if he is a renowned beheader. I wouldn't be any good at fixing the engines or rationing the food, so I suppose you end up trying to be persuasive and if you don't particularly come from a background where you are an actor, what you do is go in as a punter. For instance, my great "love" is music. When I go to concerts and meet people at the intermission I say, "Isn't it fabulous", but people who are themselves musicians may say, "Well it was quite good." If I were like that with the theatre…if I *loved* it and there are people, who shall remain nameless, who *love* the theatre and they shouldn't be let anywhere near running a theatre because their love and their passion for it, amateur in the real meaning of the word, the real *love* of it, in some way blinkers their judgement.

Where I think I earn my money (if I do earn it) is to sit at that dress-rehearsal and those four previews and say "I've paid my sixteen quid and I've come to see it. What's wrong with it?" And then to be persuasive enough and powerful enough in the position of artistic director to be able to say "There's a big dip in the middle of the second act, we're dropping the ball. I was bored and the audience was bored." Sometimes you present the problem and not the solution. If you're with good directors and good actors they can give you the solution. Sometimes you can give it and sometimes it works, sometimes it doesn't. If somebody wants to be a producer, the particular ability (not saying I have it) is that you have to have a sense of looking at the play as the audience looks at it and ask if it is working for them — not to be too close — and that's a real difficulty.

You need to be able to see something four nights in a row and still try to see it for the first time. The other skill you need to have as a producer is to be a persuader. To persuade people that this is the show they ought to be doing and then to persuade people to come and see it. And then sometimes if you're really smart you can persuade people that what they've seen is really good! So it's essentially being a persuader and on top of that being an organizer. So when I talk about not being skilful, well I've always had a talent for organization. I've always had a talent for knowing that if you have to get home/change/get your hair cut/go shopping/-whatever…to know instinctively the order in which you do these things. So I can turn three hours work into an hour and a half very easily.

JC: *So you didn't set out with a blueprint of what the Gate should be, the plays it should produce and the sort of audience it would want to have?*

MC: Well I did in some ways. One of the things though where my blueprint was wrong is that I thought I was taking over! The interesting thing about the Gate is that in 1928 when it was founded by Hilton [Edwards] and Michael [MacLiammóir] they constituted one Artistic Directorship and now, seventy-three years on, there's only been me and them. Only two Artistic Directors of *The Gate* in nearly eighty years and that's a record. Well not a record but a fact, and it hasn't been copied anywhere else in the world that I know of.

We've now learnt that they were both English and that they were "gay." I was a Dublin working class boy and not "gay" and I believed that my sensibilities would have been different to theirs; however, as it turns out, when you look back, and I'm not a great theatre historian, but when you *do* look back at what they were doing and then at what I've been doing, well we went in very similar directions which is an extraordinary thing.

Their life in the theatre was greatly helped by the work of Oscar Wilde and we made a lot of money and were helped to survive by Oscar Wilde, and it wasn't because they did it that I did it – I thought I hit on that myself! They went to America with a Brian Friel play and I went with *Molly Sweeney* and you'd have thought *Philadelphia, Here I Come!* would be more Abbey fare and yet it was Hilton who directed that.

We had our first big success in New York with *Juno and The Paycock* which was also non-traditional Gate fare. They went around the world and were the first Irish company to go to Egypt; we were the first to go to Jerusalem; their design element was a huge feature in their work and certainly in my early years and even now I would say that I've tried to keep design in the Gate at a very high standard.

So I did set out with some sort of plan. I didn't say I was going to be different from those people, but I thought I would be. However much you may think you're the High Priest and can do what you want, the reality is that there is another force at work and that's the dynamic of the space itself. The georgian building and those chandeliers in themselves have an aesthetic. Pilasters and a rococo ceiling lead you into a type of thing on stage that's going to suit the space. You're less likely to be doing plays about glue-sniffing in Donaghmede for instance. The size, feel and atmosphere of the place led me in a way that was much more similar to Michael and Hilton than I ever thought would happen.

Another thing is that I knew there are certain things you cannot control. You can't entirely control how an audience will react to a play for instance. What you can control is that when they do come in (and I learned this from Tomás Mac Anna) there are things that shouldn't go wrong. You turn on a light and it will come on – it should always come on. You begin with a model and create a set. You don't go in on the opening night and say "Oh God, that pink looks dreadful beside that orange." You have previews and time so there's no excuse for a bad set. So what I tried to do first was to keep that high design element and the second thing in my blueprint was to surround myself with the most talented people I could find, and if you surround yourself with talent – well then the batting average is a little better. Another thing I've discovered about the theatre in the seventeen years working here at the Gate and I think it holds true for most theatres is…and how do I put this… the strength of women in the theatre…I don't mean to be provocative here but I think generally it's a woman's art form.

JC: *Are you saying that because it's mostly women who buy tickets for the theatre? Are you talking about the audience or women-in-theatre?*

MC: I'm certainly thinking that there is an extraordinary imbalance in terms of women directors and writers, but I don't think there's an imbalance in the audience. I did coin that phrase "Women go to the theatre, men are brought", but I think that essentially if you look at the plays that do well they are often about a woman's plight.

JC: *Isn't that because theatre deals with emotion and women are more inclined to be interested in things to do with feelings than perhaps men are?*

MC: What I have discovered is that there is a sense in which we have to look at our imaginations and see what is being changed. Two imaginations have to be in line with each other, the giving imagination which is the imagination of the writers, actors and directors and the receiving imagination of the audience and critics; because there might be a piece of greatness that comes along and is ignored. Mark Twain said, "it doesn't matter what you see if your imagination is out of focus."

There is never going to be a failure of the imagination amongst artists, they are always going to produce something and people like me have got to have the imagination to be ready to see what's happening. For me the most fundamental change in the last ten years, more than anything else that was said to be a threat to the theatre, is the change in the imagination. It is the most potent force in the arts today.

For instance, I recently went to see *L.A. Confidential* with my sixteen-year-old daughter and my mother. It starts with cross-cutting, cameras flashing, simultaneous sounds, half-sentences, over-lapping dialogue, American slang, characters talking in unison, everything topping everything. I was giving it my best just to hold on to it, not helped by my mother who was giving it her complete best but was hopelessly lost and my daughter said, "What's wrong?" I said, "Nana doesn't understand it" and Sophie said, "Doesn't understand what?" She had time to talk to us and she understood every single thing that was going on. The speed, the density was perfect for her. Her world is an entirely different world from ours. It's not a failure of the imagination to say it would be easier for my mother to sit through three and a half hours of *King*

Lear than it would be for my daughter. My daughter would be bored. Maybe the failure is mine in not recognizing that, like technology or maybe because of technology, our imaginations are also rapidly changing.

JC: *So the parameters for receiving have changed?*

MC: Completely. And that's why it's no accident that our new movies are on MTV. Our new movies are ads.

JC: *Where does that leave the theatre we love?*

MC: The theatre you and I love is going to have to adjust to that, because if you are a giver in the shape of a David Mamet say or a Harold Pinter you are also a receiver. You also go and see things. In other words you yourself are subject to this change. If you look at the work of Mamet and Pinter, they're not writing two and a half hour plays any more, nor indeed was the genius who understood this turn before any of us did. Sam Beckett could write a play that was twenty-two minutes long because an audience need was not on his agenda. Pinter and Beckett both had a route into their own subconscious and they could do what they needed to do.

It's not that they didn't care and were putting two fingers up to the audience, I don't believe that for a second; it's just that they weren't writing for an audience. What worries me is that so many playwrights who are "artists" and many of them are, all happen to write plays that are two hours and fifteen minutes long with a fifteen minute interval and usually with one set if they can do it, because it's very producer-friendly and on top of that maybe a cast of eight that's manageable and give it a sexy title. Well there's nothing sexy about a play called *Act Without Words 2* that is twenty-two minutes long. It's not exactly producer-friendly but Beckett, who had a route into his own subconscious, could go in and do what he felt was right. It wasn't that he didn't care about the audience…it's that they weren't on his agenda, he wasn't writing for them. And now we are all experiencing this shift. The ads on telly ten, or fifteen years ago would be intolerable now. Ads are now thirty seconds and they are a complete story with a beginning, middle and end. They are funny, clever, witty and there is characterization – look at MTV. I think it's one of the most extraordinary art forms. I watch MTV all the time.

JC: *There are very few Becketts in the world. Are you saying theatre is going to have to accept and understand a new form? Can it not survive as it is, demanding in a way, or at least asking its audience to sit there for two hours?*

MC: I don't think audiences will sit down for two hours anymore unless you give them a reward. And the reward you give them is by telling them that they have been to an *Event*. When you *Event* something you've a much better chance of getting them to sit through even five hours. They can get together, make it a communal event, have supper and sandwiches and they're all happy doing the marathon. I had no difficulty in getting people to come and see the Becketts in 1991 in London and in New York.

Similarly the *Event* in this year's Dublin Theatre Festival was the Tom Murphy plays because they were *Evented*. And we will continue to event with a capital E. When you event with a small e you really do have to make sure you have an Anthony Hopkins doing King Lear, so you event in a different way. In other words you don't do Lear with an ordinary cast and if you do, you depend on the schools. That's the tragedy. So when you ask if there's a new form, of course there is. It's changing as we speak. Theatre is getting shorter. I've had arguments with people who feel that our imaginations are in some way failing and we can't sustain it; that we don't have that sort of strength of the imagination anymore. But I disagree with that entirely. I think we have new imaginations, different imaginations.

JC: *We have new demands on our imagination maybe but we still need theatre to explain ourselves to ourselves.*

MC: We need it to explain ourselves to us but we need to have ourselves explained too in a form we understand, and there are many plays being written where you say "I've got the point."

JC: *In the first ten minutes?*

MC: Yes. In fact I've even gone as far as to stop putting photographs outside the theatre because I think people can come along and see ten photographs of different scenes and think they've seen the play. They can clone the play from the photos outside the Gate. I know I can. I look at photos outside a theatre at five to eight and think I've seen this now and that's because our imaginations go so quickly.

JC: *Isn't that denying what the actor, and of course I would say this, but isn't it denying what the actor brings to the play?*

MC: It is denying it, unless what is written is dense. And a lot of what is written now is loose and we used to have a greater tolerance of loose than we have now. So *Arcadia*, for instance, is a very satisfying evening in the theatre because it is very dense. In fact it took me four times seeing *Arcadia* before I really began to understand how clever it was.

JC: *Yet the audience loved it because you ran it for three months and didn't have an empty seat in the house.*

MC: It's no accident that the people who are writing this very dense work are attractive to young people. When we did the Pinter and Beckett festivals we got a much younger audience than we normally do for the three-act play. It's not so much that they're interested in nihilism or whatever the play is about, it's that they are interested in getting the information and getting it quickly. Their minds are going faster and that is why it was no problem to me to get Neil Jordan, Conor McPherson and Brian Friel to write plays of thirty minutes and they in turn are different than the one-act plays that were written in the fifties which usually only had one theme. Whether it's good or bad, when you take what is actually *in* the twenty-seven minutes of *Come On Over*, McPherson's play, there is a full-length play there, but he actually condenses it.

JC: *In condensing it, don't you think perhaps you might lose an audience?*

MC: Yes, we do lose an audience.

JC: *That's a problem, isn't it?*

MC: That is a problem, but then again Beckett wasn't concerned. He lost his audiences and so did Pinter. They lost their audiences at the beginning because they did something that was different. Indeed so did Schubert and Beethoven and many other people. You have to believe in the integrity of the work and I believe in both Beckett and Pinter. There are still people today who'll say it's boring and bleak and they don't understand it and what is it saying? But these writers have a great integrity and you have to reward and serve that integrity.

JC: *But you can't serve that integrity at the expense of an empty house.*

MC: No. But I'm glad to say that when we did the Pinters we were full and when we did the Becketts we were full and these three present plays are playing to good houses too. If I did *Waiting For Godot* fifteen years ago, people would have said I was being brave; if I put it on now people would say I was playing safe. *Waiting for Godot* is being done in the West End with Peter Hall at the moment as a commercial run of a hit play.

JC: *Is there no room anymore then for the Ayckbournes of the world?*

MC: Of course there is, but I think the problem is, as we and the theatre develop in the area of serving this new different hunger –

simultaneously in a lot of other areas – that we are going backwards and marginalizing ourselves. There was a time when the theatre had a much more vibrant and potent role in society.

JC: *Because there was no MTV?*

MC: I think we've dropped the ball. For instance Jane Brennan got sick a few months ago and didn't go on in a play at the Peacock and I remember a time when, if an actress got sick and couldn't go on, it would have been on the front page of the newspaper. I'm looking here at an arc of eighteen years and I can see the difference. When I did *Hedda Gabler* in the early days I put a display ad in *The Irish Times* which was the size of my thumb and it was the one and only display ad. The rest was lineage like the death columns. That was 1984 and I took out an ad. Well, what a brave, extraordinary thing to do, can you believe it?

JC: *I think what we're missing is an audience queuing around the block saying, "I've just got to see this play because this play is relevant to me and my life."*

MC: I don't think we've properly provided a career path for talent. There should be a way, if you wake up at sixteen and decide you want to be an actor or director, that you could go into a situation where that desire is tested in some way.

JC: *Testing is important because there are bad actors, bad writers and bad directors.*

MC: I remember once suggesting an actress to Brian Friel and I thought his question would be "is she the right age" or "what does she look like", that's what others would have said. But what he asked me was "Is she skilful?"

It was a phrase that seemed so obvious but it isn't. I do think the Arts Council has a responsibility here, as we do, because there is no proper training and there hasn't been for a long time. If it was Medicine or the Law or even Art School ... our failure is that we haven't given people who want to work in theatre a career path. There is no training for directors. If you wake up in Athy and want to be a theatre director, God help you, what are you going to do? There's no one to tell you what way to go.

JC: *Well in the good old days you were like an apprentice, you became a general dogsbody to start with and worked your way up.*

MC: And you know something, you did it and you were good *enough* but you were never great. But then again you weren't in competition with the movies and the restaurants.

JC: *Restaurants?*

MC: Yeah. The new competition now to the theatre is restaurants. Everybody is now a performer; everybody is an actor. Twenty or thirty years ago if you put a microphone in front of someone, they'd shrivel. Now people go on *Who Wants To Be A Millionaire* and they don't even want to win, they just want to be witty. Everybody is a performer and the best way for them to perform is in restaurants. They want to tell their stories and they want to be funny. They're no longer shy, no longer self-effacing. There's a new confidence about so everybody thinks they can act, and that has been fostered by the belief, wherever it comes from, that anybody can do it. And they *can't*. There's a big difference between being able to act and being a member of Equity and that difference has got to be understood. We've got to realize that when Friel asks "Is she skilful", there are very few who can go out and be so. Actors are often vilified and accused of being "luvvies', a word I detest, and of being undisciplined because of some idiot misbehaving. Actors, when they are doing their work, are extraordinarily disciplined people. They put two alarm clocks on if they're going for a nap in the afternoon before a show, they don't take late planes, don't take a glass of wine at lunch. It is the most disciplined way of life.

JC: *So why did actors get a bad name then?*

MC: Because we have made ourselves a separate community. We must not set ourselves apart too much from other professions. We should start recognizing talent and when we do, start paying that talent properly. The notion that came out of England and is now widespread, that the man playing *Lear* and the person carrying the spear should get the same money, is just ridiculous. Everything that we're doing, in saying we don't need training and don't need to be especially skilled and we can pay people badly, it mitigates against us. When you start paying people properly – my new hobbyhorse – in tandem with that comes a new discipline, one that begins before you take the part.

There are still actors turning up on day one who have read the play once, which is just enough to decide if they want to do it. Really great professionals come to their place of work prepared. Eleven months before he did *King Lear*, Ian Holm had already learned the play off by heart. When Beckett decided to direct *Waiting for Godot* in Germany he needed an extra year to learn enough German, because he wondered how he could be looking at the text and looking at the stage at the same time? When we did *The Homecoming*, Lia Williams and John Kavanagh knew their lines before starting rehearsal. I would like people to work harder beforehand and I would like them to be paid for that and to be paid properly when they're performing. Then they have a responsibility to be so good that people want to see it and will pay extra to do so.

I think the future lies in making theatre *more* special and making a clear division between those who can and those who can't. And not everybody can. It's not like it used to be in the old days, when people would announce a season and say they're doing a *St Joan* or a *Hamlet* and *Macbeth*; and then decide, when they've issued the press release, to go looking for their leading actors. If you can't cast it you shouldn't do it. If it's not properly written you shouldn't put it on. What I'm paid to do is to be the pain in the ass for the people who pay for their tickets and sometimes that's not an easy job to do and you don't always succeed – you can't always succeed. It is much better – if people talk about the theatre being an experimental place – to let it experiment like this!

JC: *I've never quite understood what an Arts Council's role or responsibility to the artists is in all this, or have they any responsibility?*

MC: They have a huge responsibility and it is a very difficult job, I did it for five years.

JC: *Why is it so difficult?*

MC: Because it's very hard to measure. How are you to pick people who can say this is good or this is bad? It's very hard to measure "is that painting good?" It's much easier to measure that the heart operation worked because the patient lived for fourteen years after it was done.

JC: *It's obviously well-meant having an Arts Council but unless it's doing something valuable I don't see the point of it.*

MC: Well, I've had my problems with this Arts Council. We don't always see eye to eye but taking the idea of a Council generally, I think one of the good things a council could do would be to help build career paths for people who wake up to the belief that they want to be a writer or a violinist or a painter or actor or whatever. If I do auditions and find three young actors aged twenty or so – and all three are talented and come out head and shoulders above the others – I have a problem. If I give *A* a part in one play and *B* a part in the next and *C* a role in the third, then the first actor has a long wait to practise his or her craft again because, as you know, they learn by doing it. So in order to do it right, I'm going to have to give *A* the three parts and I have to say to the other two, "This is sad but because of the way we are presently constituted, if I give the three of you equal parts over the next eighteen months, none of you is going to do it." But if I give one of them all the plays then we might be getting an actor. At the moment there is no system. But, if you came out of drama school and there were to be four or five Project type theatres, 200/500 seaters, in this city for the independent companies, that is where a system could be beneficial. The energy in the theatres around the world now is a different energy than the pursuit of excellence. Nor do I think the level of criticism is good enough to be able to say, "Hang on, this is a great piece of work. It's not very well acted, not well directed, but this is an extraordinary piece of work." I don't think the critics are properly paid either, they don't have the space and I don't think they're respected. To be a critic is a job, it's not a sideline.

JC: *Have we ever understood critics in this country? For instance the medical correspondent in one newspaper may become a critic or you might be assigned to cover football one week and theatre the next.*

MC: What's happening for instance now is that someone like Conor McPherson will write a play and will give me that play, but he'll say he's not going to put up with the level of criticism in this country. I'm not saying that the English are smarter, I'm just saying that the English newspapers give more to the theatre than Irish newspapers, so he'll let me produce the play but wants to open it in London. We did open *Port Authority* in London and got great reviews, better than if he had opened it here, it was more thought out, the play studied and given more space. I got half a page in the New York Times for *The Homecoming* – you won't get that here.

I think the media has a bit of a problem. Small example; Jerry Seinfeld is making a million dollars an episode and Oprah is making two million and the Gate actor is making a few hundred quid a week, yet the newspapers will give a free ad to Oprah and Jerry. Every single day they will put in the listings, free, what's on the telly. If you want the same size listing to say what's on in your theatre, you pay. We're not for profit but we're the ones who pay! I would love the newspapers to help the theatre more and give more to it. I sometimes wonder what people are doing for the Arts and for their own culture. I think at times it's a bit taken for granted. They're paying very little to get into high quality work.

JC: *Maybe we have to bite the bullet and admit that theatre isn't mainstream anymore. If you can get in to see a movie for less than a fiver, why go to the theatre?*

MC: The reason should be that it is a more communal event. There is a greater sharing going on. You do get more value for money if it's good. The theatres are the new cathedrals. People do need to rub shoulders together. They need what that theatre company with the great name *Shared Experience* gives – they need to share an experience. But we're having a shift at the moment and this is why I'm enjoying running the Gate more than I ever have, because I'm dealing with the most extraordinary shifts that are going on: the shift of the imagination, the shift towards shorter and denser.

JC: *So you're happy at the Gate and don't intend leaving us for foreign parts?*

MC: I'm happy. I love working in the Gate and there's a fire in my stomach now that's as great or greater than it's ever been in terms of the work. I'm excited by the work, by what I want to do and what I'm going to do.

JC: *You must get asked to work in America and I know you've often been asked to take what we'd call high profile high-paying jobs in London. Is it a commitment to the Gate or to the country that keeps you here?*

MC: You don't work in the Gate for your wage packet that's for sure. It sounds too awful to say it but there is an effort to make the place you live in a better place to live in. That is a great attraction. You get a great buzz out of being able to do something like that.

Michael Colgan was born in 1950 and educated at Trinity College where he became chairman of Trinity Players. He has been the Artistic Director of the Gate Theatre since 1983. Before then he was a director of the Abbey Theatre, manager of the Irish Theatre Company and Artistic Director of the Dublin Theatre Festival. He has produced many award-winning productions at the Gate which have toured to over twenty countries. He has also produced two Pinter Festivals and three Beckett Festivals.

The Theatre presented all nineteen of Samuel Beckett's stage plays in Dublin over a three-week period in 1991. This Festival was presented again at the Lincoln Centre New York in 1996 and at the Barbican in London in 1999. His productions of Beckett plays have also been seen in many cities throughout the world and at many Festivals, notably Chicago, Toronto and Melbourne. In 1999 he formed Blue Angel Films with Alan Moloney specifically to produce the Beckett canon on film. All nineteen of Beckett's plays were filmed using internationally renowned directors and actors.

He is a Board Member of the Gate Theatre, the Dublin Theatre Festival, Millennium Festivals Ltd, the Laura Pels Foundation, New York and the Governing Authority of Dublin City University. From 1989-94 he was a member of the Irish Arts Council and he was Chairman of the St. Patrick's Festival from 1996–99. In 1996 he received the Eamonn Andrews Award for excellence in the National Entertainment Awards and in 1999 he won the People of the Year Award. In 1985 and 1987 he was a recipient of a Sunday Independent Arts Award. In July 2000 Michael Colgan received the degree of Doctor in Laws *honoris causa* from Trinity College, Dublin.

Jeananne Crowley is Dublin-born and was educated at UCD where she began acting with Dramsoc. First professional appearances were with Four In One Players, a company founded by the late Chris O'Neill. After a stint with the Abbey Theatre, she then joined the National Theatre in London during Sir Peter Hall's tenure as Artistic Director. During the 1980s she performed extensively in film and television in Britain whilst also working as a journalist. She returned to live in Ireland in 1989. She appeared in the opening production of the Andrew's Lane Theatre and wrote a short play *Goodnight Siobhán* for the Royal Court. Her role as The Real Charlotte earned her a *Sunday Independent* Arts Award in 1991. She has frequently appeared at the Gate, most recently in *Arcadia* and *An Ideal Husband*.

Frank Conway in Conversation with John Kavanagh

JK: *Was design a career that sort of thrust itself upon you or was it a process you came to through illumination or elimination?*

FC: I passionately wanted to be an actor and was involved with acting here in Sligo with Sligo Drama Circle, and loved it. Absolutely loved it. Felt at home and really didn't want to do anything else. I had also been painting at the time. I went to Dublin to Art College and at some stage at the Art College I got involved with the Abbey – as an actor. I appeared as an extra in a couple of productions. That's how I lost courage ... I had been very unhappy at college. I had been advised to do the design course rather than the painting course – because there were a lot of student occupations going on in the painting course at the time – all sorts of strikes and stuff – and somebody said to me "Look there's not a lot of difference between the Design and Painting Schools blah, blah, blah it was much more suitable." In fact it wasn't. It was hell. So I had this idea at the time that I would combine these two very strong interests – painting and theatre and did theatre design. Really, a very arbitrary decision.

JK: *Why was it hell do you remember?*

FC: Because at the time I was doing the Design course it was very much geared toward commercial advertising and the graphic world and so I was having to do projects that had to do with designing tea towels and packages for ladies tights and all this kind of stuff and I was coming from being a painter – a landscape painter effectively. So it was a nightmare scenario that I found myself in and I wanted to get out of it. Really theatre design was a way to get out of that.

JK: *I presume from the very first play you worked on, you set about the way you wanted to design and I don't know whether this process has changed over the years ... but what I want to ask you is that when a text is presented to you ... what's the first thing you look for in it?*

FC: Feeling.

JK: *Feeling?*

FC: Absolutely, yeah. At least that's what I can say now. I don't know if I would have started with it. Now I would look for feeling. I would look for something that touches something in me that I would recognize. And I would sit with it for a long time. Now in the past you know, what I would do is to start researching ... go off and start looking at books ... kind of try to find some ideas and so on. But now I'll sit with a play. I'll read it once, then read it a couple of times but then I'll let it simmer. And I find that in the simmering process, anything I can come up with – that's the best way I can come up with it.

JK: *And would that period of time vary much?*

FC: Oh, yeah. I mean sometimes it can happen very quickly and other times you just have to trust that it'll come. And I haven't always done that and I sometimes panicked and said I've come up with something because there was nothing happening.

JK: *You know the way actors are sometimes accused of looking at the size of their part – of flicking through the text from page one to the end to see if they're there and so on ... it isn't then a question of looking at the problems presented by the play from a design point of view before you read it?*

FC: No.

JK: *So if it speaks to you – you solve the problems presented by it.*

FC: Yes. If I get a feeling with it ... if it touches something ... then I'm absolutely ready. The problems come afterwards as far as the technical stuff is concerned and all of the demands that a play has. But that's the crucial one. Because if you're not somehow able to express the feeling of the play you're kind of groping in the dark really.

JK: *And you find then for example the stage directions the writers put in are helpful in this process as a general rule. For example, playwrights in the past like Shaw or O'Casey, who we'll come to later, would have been quite specific about the settings and even the appearance of people, how they spoke and dressed – do you disregard these templates from the writer?*

FC: Oh, no, I wouldn't disregard them and there are some that contain fantastic information – some that you can trust completely and others that you have to ignore. There's no law or rule about it. The classic person is Chekhov. His stage directions are, you know, so absolutely essential to what the play is about: his description of sound effects etc., etc. There are others who might write stage directions, but might write them as if they are mounting a production of it and that's always hard because they say that "such and such a scene takes place downstage of the main action." That to me is one of the most difficult things you can read with stage directions because ...

JK: *It locks you in?*

FC: It locks you in. If it takes place on the "moon" – you can do something with that.

JK: *In a sense then the way in which the screenplay format has evolved with its headings like "Interior", "Room", "Day", etc., it gives the designer more freedoms?*

FC: Oh, yes, locate it in the imaginative place, not think about the stage in that sense, absolutely.

JK: *What about the time or period setting; is this a hindrance or an aid in terms of the designer?*

FC: Depends. Obviously life goes on and times change and contexts change. And I think you always have to take on board the context in which a play was written and performed, and that might be a gap of five hundred years. Both of those things are hugely relevant and to look at a play that was written four hundred years ago and to put it on totally faithful to that time only is to lose something.

JK: *We can return to this later in our discussion on your approaches to* The Plough and the Stars. *I presume there must be a play that no matter how famous it is, or who has written it, in your case, given your methods, you have to say no to that play?*

FC: Oh, I do, yeah, absolutely. There were times when I didn't and got into terrible trouble with it, but now, if I don't get a feeling from it I will say no.

JK: *Do you feel that this serves you well in your relationships with directors who commission you, those say who you've worked with before and have to turn down. Has that been difficult for you or do they respect this "artistic" decision?*

FC: In any collaborative situation, who you work with is really what it's about. I've been in situations where you don't have a rapport with the director and that's just as difficult as not having a rapport with the play because equally that jarring will emerge on the stage at some level. It mightn't be obvious, but it'll be there on some level. Whereas if you're working with someone you have a really good rapport with, and I mean a rapport with someone who is on the same wavelength with maybe the landscape of the play, or maybe the same landscape as the person you're working with, is fantastic. It's a very rare thing. I've had it a couple of times down through the years. I've equally lost it. There are directors I've worked closely with that I don't now, or who don't ask me any more. It's tough, but that element is crucial – to be on the same wavelength and having a feeling about the play.

JK: *After the initial stages, do you take out a pen and draw? I mean at what stage do you get to the model? Is that very late in the process for you?*

FC: Oh, yeah and I wouldn't take out a pen now. Again this is more in the last five or six years and I haven't been doing a huge amount of theatre – I won't take out a pen now until I have something clearly formed in my head. I find that once you put it on paper, the paper starts to dictate – you erase what's in your head or what might be beginning to form in your mind. In fact I picked that up from something I read about Brian Friel's approach to writing.

JK: *You mentioned that you haven't done much theatre in the last five years, but of course interwoven with your theatrical designs down the last ten, fifteen years have been designs for the world of film and television and even documentary with music and musicians as subjects: is the process of putting pen to paper different for film and television than it would be for the theatre?*

FC: Oh, it is. Theatre is – for me anyway – a far more imaginative world, whereas in film, you are inevitably dealing with a world of reality. I mean that from my point of view. I don't mean that film isn't dealing in all sorts of extraordinary worlds but for me it tends to be about locations and finding locations and then how you can treat those and how you can heighten them. Very rarely would you get a chance to create an imaginative world on film.

JK: *In terms of interiors, – I'm thinking of a film you designed –* Frankie Starlight. *There is a scene where the character is lying on the roof of a house looking up at the stars, did that sort of tie in somewhat with your theatrical experience? Would you draw that early, for example?*

FC: Well that was a set that we actually built. No, film is movement. And how I would approach them now is I think about them as movement, moving on to one set, and then another set – it's all about a movement from a beginning of a film through to its end and what happens in kind of colours and moods and how things are shifting, what came before and what comes after – a totally different process.

JK: *For a scene that's shifting for example – I remember a memorable visit to see you working on a rain lashed day on the set of* The Field *at Leenane ...*

FC: Oh, God yeah!

JK: *In a place like Leenane, with the rain, the colours would change dramatically. That would colour your design I presume?*

FC: It's a very moody landscape and for me a very dark landscape. I remember thinking it was stunning when I went there first to explore it, but after about three or four weeks, I started to get very oppressed by it.

JK: *So it was then an appropriate setting?*

FC: Incredibly appropriate. It's the highest – apparently – rainfall in Ireland anyway and this was like the worst rain they've ever had. And actually what happened was that you had this fantastic moody landscape all the time, but the weather was so bad we were always having to run for cover. We couldn't shoot the weather as it was. We couldn't shoot that atmosphere because it was so wet, it was just so impossible. So while a lot of the film has sun in it – you would grab the light or the dryness when it was there.

JK: *And the particular "field" itself, that must have been a major design element of the film, to find a pristine field that would look different from any other field that people would believe, somewhere in the back of their minds, that there could have been a patch of ground that was worth a man dying for. That had to be suggested visually. Can you tell us something about such an important factor of film like that?*

FC: Well, you think you'd find a field in the West of Ireland! We scoured the countryside and thought we found a really great field – sort of had this Celtic feel to it – had this big stone wall and we were all getting very excited about it. We were up on some hilltop looking down on it and we brought Noel Pearson to have a look at it and he couldn't see what we were on about at all. He looked literally to his left and said "What about that one down there?" And he, I have to say, found the field! It was just a patch – the one that ended up in the film. We put some fertilizer into it, and some rocks and stone in the nearby fields around it, just to show it up a little bit more. But it was Noel's discovery.

JK: *The producer obviously had an input. In terms of collaboration the director is presumably very much to the forefront? Is that a difficult process – I mean do you get left alone, waiting for him/her to come back and then a cat-fight starts, or do you liaise throughout the process of your design?*

FC: Oh ideally you liaise and collaborate all the time. That's the ideal situation, I mean sometimes you end up where that doesn't happen and that is difficult, it's awful, but if you have the right people, the right mix then it just means that anything is possible.

JK: *I imagine sometimes the writer has certain difficulties with his design but that nine times out of ten they're more pleased with the outcome than with what they imagined as they put it on the page, but back to the director — some of them must feel constricted by what you do — has there been a case for example where directors won't begin rehearsals till the set is finished or certainly until they have a mock up to work with?*

FC: Oh, that would be the standard. People are not always sure that that's necessarily a good thing but the standard procedure would be that you have it all designed for the first day of rehearsal. Some people would say that that's a problem because the actors come into a space, you know that there's been a whole process going on for weeks and weeks before they even come on board. They have to find, obviously, what the play means to them within a certain stage ... there's been a state of development without their involvement and its just because of the sheer practicalities of it. Usually rehearsals are for about four weeks and that's the amount of time you have to build the set. A lot of decisions will have been made. I come from a school where it was ingrained in us as students that we designed space, and more than that, we design action. And that still is really not something I could get rid of even if I wanted. It's where you're very careful in reading about what the action of the play is and particularly the key moments and what's got to happen in that action and so you focus on how do you design and where you put a piece of furniture, where you put a table, how you put a door in relation to a table in relation to a scene. All that was drummed into me in the school that I went to in London. I went to a course designed by a group of designers called, Motley, which was attached to the English National Opera in London. And Motley were big designers around in the 1940s and 1950s who would have done all the John Gielgud and Lawrence Olivier productions and were innovative designers at that time in world theatre. They were at the centre in all of that and Percy (Margaret Harris) who was in her seventies when I was there and only died in fact last year, was a great proponent of that — that you didn't pervert the play by doing something that didn't allow the action to happen. But really I came from the school that said you were designing action, designing space.

JK: *Well how does it work then? Is it for example your relationship with the lighting designer, is it a case that you boldly and baldly present a design and say, "Well this design will give you challenges and problems, you solve them" or is there a collaborative element with the lighting designer also?*

FC: Oh, all is collaborative. I mean in a dream situation you have a lighting designer and a costume designer who are feeling a response, with a director who is feeling a response all coming together. That's the dream situation because then you can create something extraordinary – above all true, with a truth to it where nobody is showing off, none of that ego kind of thing. Sometimes you can be lucky and work with someone who is completely plugged into the same thing as you're plugged into and you can take off, and other times the opposite happens and it can be a horrible nightmare.

JK: *Do you find there is a lot of compromise?*

FC: Yeah, I do. Completely. What I do is the art of compromise.

JK: *In your experience as a director which is considerable in the last ten years, if not longer, have you discovered anything about those compromises? For example that the director has different compromises to make than say the designer?*

FC: I would have been a bit of a control freak at the time so I don't know if I would have liked having to work with me as a designer. At the time it was out of frustration too and was out of a sort of a large ego. Directing is an extraordinary role, an extraordinary thing to do and I tried it and would love to do it more, but at the end of the day I just didn't feel I had the vocation for it.

JK: *Do you think you are easier to work with for directors now as a result of going through that particular process and realizing perhaps how responsible and how potentially overwhelming it is?*

FC: I don't know John, I really don't know. I suppose I was very difficult to work with actually. I'm beginning to feel that I was, in that sense, and because now I very rarely do it, "I don't know is the answer." I really don't know.

JK: *The Shakespearean theatre seemed to allow for a lot of imaginative completion by the audience – "Scene – A heath" or whatever. Can you say something about Shakespearean or Greek theatre as to whether they are easy or difficult plays to design for.*

FC: Hard to say easy or difficult, but there are plays that are more exciting to design for. One of the frustrations I would have in my life for example is that I have designed two Shakespearean plays in twenty five years of being involved and of course it's the most fantastically exciting journey to go down the Shakespearean road. It's challenging and it's hard work and it really puts you to the pin of your collar in terms of your resources and all of those kind of things, but hard/easy, I don't know.

JK: *But you were involved with a more exciting Shakespeare than most, the Shakespeare in the Park with Joe Papp and if I remember correctly it would have had Christopher Walken and Raul Julia?*

FC: Yes.

JK: *A production like that would have presented you with massive resources on the one hand, but obviously a massive challenge to pull off – an outdoor setting, probably limited in what you were able to do. Do you have any special recollections of it?*

FC: It was one of the best times I ever had, I have to say, and all that had to do with being in Manhattan and watching this set creep up over Central Park, I mean that was the personal magic I had with it.

JK: *Do you remember the dominant feature used in the set?*

FC: A huge set of double doors and a fairly big transformation between Venice and Cyprus. I can't say it was the most exciting thing I've ever done, but it was the most exciting experience I've ever had.

JK: *You were working with actors who had enormous status within the business, especially in terms of film. How were they as stage performers did you feel?*

FC: Radically different from each other – like from two different planets. From what I remember Raul Julia was somewhat hammy on stage. I thought he was way over the top, in a wonderful kind of way, in what one imagines as a sort of 19th century ...

JK: *Actor Manager type?*

FC: Exactly. And Christopher Walken was very sharp, very incisive and gave a very incisive performance I thought. And different people liked both of them in their ways.

JK: *Was your own contribution given the recognition it deserved at the time or was it overshadowed somewhat by the gloss of these stars?*

FC: No, it was a new experience to be designing outdoors – a whole number of new things. Worrying about rain was a major factor which I'd never in my life come across before in theatre, working in a whole new environment – the Public Theatre was the last production, insofar as I know, that Joe Papp was involved in, because he had wanted to do the whole canon of the Shakespeare plays but he died very, very shortly after that. So all of those elements were exciting and challenging for me.

JK: *I presume it was done mainly at night.*

FC: It was, but it was daylight going into night-time.

JK: *Obviously this factor of the diminishing natural light and increasing stage or artificial light must have presented more unusual challenges.*

FC: Well it did, because you wanted the opposite – you wanted Venice to be all night-time and Cyprus to be all daylight.

JK: *Were there certain techniques you could draw on or did you have to invent some?*

FC: I don't remember what we did in terms of the lighting that well – but somewhere a third of the way through Cyprus it started to get dark which was good for the play as the play was doing its own journey. And so by the time we got to the final scene and they were dying on the bed it was very appropriate. And obviously any references to the Moon and Pluto were perfect.

JK: *Just to go back a bit on the design – the double doors is a design convention in Greek tragedy – were you trying to place the idea somehow in the audience's mind that they were going to be in the presence of tragedy, that there was a classical play about to unfold, or a classical treatment of it?*

FC: Probably, in that respect. It was probably shaped by the theatre itself which was an amphitheatre with very much that feel to it.

JK: *It was homage in a way?*

FC: It probably was. I mean I wasn't even that conscious at the time. I wasn't doing great work at the time and in terms of Shakespeare *The Hamlet Project* for instance was a radically different role and route and so on and so forth.

JK: *I'm glad you brought that up because it must present one of the most demanding challenges seen for a long time in Irish theatre because you basically took the play on the road, you used ambient settings, so depending on what each location threw up or at you, you more or less had to evolve a design. It must have been a fraught time as a designer?*

FC: It was. A completely and utterly mad idea. I don't know how we didn't realize what a difficult idea that was going to be. I mean we were going to places like Boyle Abbey and then to the disused Mental Hospital down in Cork. They were radically different spaces and we had no crew or resources, or technicians or money or anything. We just went out on the road with this thing.

JK: *You were like a group of medieval players.*

FC: In a way, but even medieval players would have had their stock bits and pieces and caravans and gone to their own spaces.

JK: *It was directed by Fiona Shaw and featured people like Jane Brennan and John Lynch, all seasoned campaigners but there must have been times when you thought, "This is fine for students prepared to live in garrets but I've come on a bit from this?"*

FC: No I didn't feel that at all. It was very exciting. I probably went to more rehearsals for that than almost any other play. I just stayed at rehearsals as much as I possibly could right from beginning to end. It was one of the most extraordinary learning experiences, an experience that I would say changed my whole approach to theatre.

JK: *How was that?*

FC: Because it was like there was no set going into it and we all went along on day one with no preconceived notions and saw what evolved. I mean the Designer is completely dispensable within the theatre. Peter Brook – I'm a huge fan – is someone who's an influence on my work. What he writes about theatre has had a huge impact on me. You have the actor and the space and the light and that was really all we had and so that's how we approached *The Hamlet Project*. It was a major learning curve. I would have been coming to it from the point of one tradition, but that opened my eyes completely to the possibilities of theatre and what theatre is and what everybody's role in that is. I found with Fiona, and with Stephen Rea as well in *The Plough and the Stars*, that actors who direct are a different breed to directors who direct. I don't know why that is, or what that is, or what that chemistry is, but there's a sort of a commitment to something that I can't define, something intangible that they are achieving with the mix of people around them. Both experiences were real learning experiences, *The Hamlet Project* in particular, by the nature of it. It's a bit like you read about Peter Brook going off into Africa. We were going off into these places rehearsing, going into factories or tents around Ireland and the productions had to adapt very quickly to these places, whereas normally we worry about taking sets to various places and keeping it the same in each space; this was one day going into this hospital down in Cork, a mental institution an incredibly derelict, huge space, it must have been a couple of hundred feet long. We adapted the play to that space and did it for two performances and then came back to somewhere like Boyle Abbey or a place up here in Sligo which was some kind of a disused factory and adapted it again. There was nothing consistent. There was no given thing.

JK: *And you were one day ahead of the posse?*

FC: We were all the posse in a way. We opened up in Galway, from then on we literally hadn't a clue what to expect; we had to clean potatoes off the floor on the day of the performance. And the actors were doing it – they were incredibly committed you know. They were quite extraordinary, the cast of that particular project.

JK: *There's got to be a playwright's work, indeed there may not be one that you have a special relationships with, from which you get that feel we talked about earlier.*

FC: Tom Murphy without a shadow of a doubt. Completely. I don't know – imagination, landscape, world whatever you want to call it. I just read his plays and it's an immediate recognition of the landscape, I know it well, feel it very powerfully and so on. *Famine* in particular. I remember bawling my eyes out when I read it and it would still be a highlight of my own work, the work I did on that one.

JK: *You have been involved in four productions of* The Plough and the Stars. *So like it or not, one can say that you have a special relationship with O'Casey or certainly with that play. What fascinates me about this is that over a period of 25 years and four designs, it's the last two that prove controversial or have aroused a greater portion of media comment than would normally be the case. By a coincidence the first time I was ever in the Abbey myself was at* The Plough and the Stars *which you were involved in, directed by Tomás Mac Anna with the great Philip O'Flynn as Fluther. To get into the Abbey so young must have been an awesome experience.*

FC: Yes.

JK: *And Tomás Mac Anna was the leading director of that era.*

FC: He was hugely instrumental in my career at the time and was very generous. He brought me in, literally off the street at the time, I was trying to get into theatre. The big thing I remember was sticking polystyrene bricks on flats that seemed to go up forever. It was very exciting for me coming out of college and being on the Abbey stage; I mean I started off in Sligo and there I was at the absolute centre of the world when I was working on that.

JK: *When you look back at it was it a conventional project in terms of the design?*

FC: It was, I suppose, a kind of naturalistic scenery, sort of painted, realistic scenery with all the elements. Traditional is some ways for its time.

JK: *The play poses problems for the designer. I mean it's a large play, four acts, epic qualities and so on, moments of great intimacy, public and private spaces used. It starts in the Clitheroe's tenement, then it moves to, as he calls it, a "commodious public house", back to the tenement and not only back to the* *tenement but to the steps outside, then back into the almost claustrophobic space of Burgess's room with the corpse. It seems an insurmountable design to someone unprepared or unskilled?*

FC: The first time I designed it for Joe Dowling the main thing that concerned me was how to get across the poverty and then to crack the scene changes and that's what the first production I did was hugely about and quite successful at the time. I mean successful in terms of the scene changes, and you know trying to get them done where the curtain came down and up again maybe thirty seconds later.

JK: *We're talking about the late 1970s with the first one, you would have been using, by today's standards, rather primitive technologies and design techniques in the sense that it was done with the idea of the curtain rising and falling and audiences then would have expected a certain delay, maybe of up to a couple of minutes. But audiences today are in mind of the quick cut and expect things to move a little more fluidly. Do you feel that you can't present that play that way anymore for example?*

FC: Oh, I couldn't present the play that way anymore I must say. Well first of all in my mind at the time that's what the concerns would have been. I wouldn't have been coming at the play very deeply, I would have been coming from the space elements that I talked about.

JK: *Now you would tackle it differently and the first of the controversial productions was the Garry Hynes production, the "shaved heads" production. It seemed a production, from what I understand about it, that was removed from the anchored context of 1916 and set in a more modern industrialized and alienated setting than that text would suggest. Can you remember why you approached it that way with Garry Hynes, or whose idea was it?*

FC: Fintan O'Toole was there in the Abbey at the time.

JK: *He was literary advisor.*

FC: And I remember he had an input into it. He came up with some absolutely extraordinary material and descriptions of Dublin at the time, the degree and extent of the poverty, that it was like Calcutta ... . and really that we had no idea, certainly I had no idea of what Dublin was like, very graphic descriptions, really wonderful stuff and I found it really, really firing. And he was great to talk about the play, fantastically intelligent and that was obviously a major part of the journey, and it did get this name, such as the "shaved heads" production, but I think O'Casey was writing a play that was saying that there's a great big myth about 1916. It's like looking at the reality behind that mythology. And I think you find the same thing about the production of O'Casey plays which have in turn become myths in themselves. Everybody knows all the characters and has expectations of exactly what they're going to do and about Juno and Fluther… Neither I nor Garry had any interest in just providing a repeat of that because it seemed to pervert what O'Casey himself was saying about 1916.

JK: *When you look back on that shaved heads production, did you feel that you could really call it the GUBU production, that the Ireland of the time was going through a very deprived time. It was not a successful nation, the self image was poor, the economic performance was poor, people's expectations were poor, definitely an air of psychic and economic gloom seemed to hang over the place when you compare it with now? Were you conscious of that at the time?*

FC: No, not in terms of the production.

JK: *Would you think that is fair comment or not?*

FC: I don't think so. I don't think any of us were looking at that. We would have been very focused on the play and trying to dust it off, to challenge the mythology that had grown around it and was making it a cosy caricature of itself; thereby subverting O'Casey's original subversion of the mythology that had grown up around 1916 and see it as the play that it is.

JK: *So you were going for a much more social-realist look?*

FC: Yeah, so if you're going to put in a prostitute like Rosie Redmond – I mean child prostitution was rampant in Dublin at the time.

JK: *So you took the age down.*

FC: Absolutely, like a child and the shaved heads thing came solely out of the fact that the … what do you call it the …?

JK: *The lice.*

FC: Lice were rampant and we were being extremely authentic to that element of it.

JK: *Now after your first engagement with the play under Tomás Mac Anna and a second subsequent one with Joe Dowling, both classical approaches in a sense, the elaborate stage directions of O'Casey had no doubt exhausted themselves for you?*

FC: Absolutely.

JK: *And left it ripe for re-imagining? The first of those was with Garry Hynes and, the second, and maybe by far the most controversial, was the recent production directed by Stephen Rea. Now I presume from what we talked of* *earlier, the seeds of the* Hamlet Project *were beginning to sprout, you had completely, radically re-imagined the space ... could you talk a little bit about the approach?*

FC: Well I had a meeting with Stephen at which he said he wanted to do it very barely and minimally and without scenery – complete music to my ears. He had this notion of a screen hanging in space and it would serve certain functions in the play.

JK: *When you say screen, the purpose of the screen being to?*

FC: A projection screen. It became a way of showing Dublin at the time and a way of showing Pearse. I mean Pearse is always the big problem with the Plough, he really is and I've seen him lots of different ways, this was an attempt, in terms of a contemporary audience, to make it more ...

JK: *It's a kind of Brechtian device?*

FC: It is. There was a great reality: there was Pearse shouting, I don't mean shouting his head off – but there's this figure outside the window of the pub, orating publically, to what are meant to be thousands of people around him, coming out with these lines: meanwhile the interior of the pub is meant to be an almost empty space. It's hard to get that. In Garry's production what we did was put him in the audience and we had this massive big mirror. We hoped to reflect an audience of six or seven hundred people surrounding Pearse back up on the mirror on stage. In the Gaiety with Stephen it was just that we had this idea of having Pearse filmed. We filmed in Kilmainham jail, where the signatories to the Proclamation were executed and he spoke the lines quietly, like a voice from the grave. And to me anyway, it had this extraordinary resonance and power that I hadn't heard before.

JK: *Do you feel, if it's a fair question, that Stephen Rea's political background, or his knowledge of the conflict in Northern Ireland somehow dominated this vision of the play?*

FC: I don't know if you can say dominated and Stephen obviously has political opinions like all of us, but he is first and foremost an artist and, while I can't speak for him, I would think that his main mission would be to somehow express the truth of that play and I kept coming up against that again and again and again.

JK: *So what was the truth for you?*

FC: Looking at the whole last scene in the play when the British Army comes in and they're all up in the attic cowering and there's all that stuff going on. I never looked at that myself at what that in reality must be like, to have an invasion in your house and the absolute terror of it in the middle of the night and helicopters flying around and searchlights and being pulled out of your bed and that's what we were investing that scene with. Again it is revealing the play to be more than just cosy with the British soldiers coming in singing *Keep the Home Fires Burning*. It's meaningless to us now, absolutely meaningless to us.

JK: *In human terms of course this violation or oppression is very shocking but did it strike you at the time that there is an equation being made that Northern Ireland now is equal to 1916 Dublin then. There have to be lots of questions arising from that sort of association? I mean were you aware of this at the time? This is one of the criticisms lobbed at such an interpretation?*

FC: But of course one had to do that play in the context of where we are now. There's a direct link, a direct line from what O'Casey was writing about to the present day situation in the North. I don't see how you can do the play without having some sense of relevance of where we're at, at the moment. An audience relates to a play about war, in the context of their own experience of war. Most of us have watched war on television and that was the idea of using the television at the end where they put on the television and watch the city burning ...

JK: *One of the more obvious tropes of change as I understand it in this production for you was the figure of Bessie Burgess, compared say to the more classically mounted productions you would have started out with?*

FC: Bessie clearly has a far different resonance for me now than she would have in earlier productions. I think what Stephen was great at, and what O'Casey was great at, was pulling the humanity out of people between those extreme opposites and at the end of the day Bessie is the one that gives her life for Nora.

JK: *In terms of the design and the scene changes, I mean how were you able to suggest these in the very minimalist approach?*

FC: Well the basic way I approached it was that I didn't want anyone to think it was anywhere. Stephen said that acting embarrassed him sometimes. I find that scenery does the same for me. It's like the stage became a place to let the play live in, potentially, in the sense that if you put the play on and don't pretend that it's happening anywhere else except on stage, which is maybe very Brechtian, and handled well can be powerful. I mean I would see that Beckett is like that; some of his plays can only take place where they are performed. I love that notion and, maybe in a sense, that is what Peter Brook is saying as well.

JK: *You recently worked on the Beckett Project and you designed one of the films, was it essentially a much different experience then, designing a Beckett piece for film as opposed to theatre?*

FC: I don't know. I've never designed a Beckett for the stage and I would love to. I was working with the theatre director John Crowley in a studio; it was all done in a matter of days and the text was treated very faithfully. John and I tried to be fairly exact about what Beckett's requirements were.

JK: *The play was* Come and Go *and Beckett is sometimes difficult for the average reader and viewer to take anything from at all. Given that what starts you off is feeling, can you remember what feeling was coming to you off this script?*

FC: Memory and haunting. I remember a feeling of three ghosts in a graveyard. Fading and merging. I think theatre is a little bit like that in itself anyway, it's all about a sense of evocation and memory. I think sometimes it's like trying to create a sense of memory on stage.

JK: *So when you see the film, what sort of things would you say to the viewer that in design would support the text?*

FC: I haven't seen the thing myself and as I said, it was very, very rushed ... it didn't evolve quite in that way and evolved quite magically in that sense ... obviously in film most of what happens, happens in the editing room and as I haven't seen the finished piece, I wouldn't like to comment.

JK: *But you'd like to work on Beckett again?*

FC: Oh, God yes. I mean that man is absolutely extraordinary.

JK: *OK Frank Conway, thank you very much.*

FC: Thank you.

Frank Conway is best known as a designer for theatre, television and film, but he has also directed for Druid and Sevenwoods theatre companies. Film design credits include *The Field*, *The Mapmaker*, *Trojan Eddie*, *The Last of the High Kings*, *This is My Father*, and *Pigs*. He has been Head of Design at the Abbey and Resident Designer at Druid Theatre and he has worked at the Gate, Project Arts Centre and Gaiety Theatres and internationally in England, Canada and America. Theatre design work includes *Famine*, *Conversations on a Homecoming*, *Bailegangaire*, *The Playboy of the Western World*, *The Plough and the Stars*, *Sharon's Grave*, *The Hamlet Project*, *The*

Bird Sanctuary, Moving, Philadelphia, Here I Come!, Cavalcaders, The Death and Resurrection of Mr. Roche, She Stoops to Conquer and *The Power of Darkness*.

John Kavanagh is a poet, playwright, musician and broadcaster. His plays include *No Comet Seen, Bella Donna* and *The Ballynemid Business*. His collections of poetry, *Etching* and *Half-Day Warriors*, are published by Salmon Publishing.

Anne Devlin in Conversation with Enrica Cerquoni

EC: *You started your career as a writer of prose, television scripts and radio drama before writing for the theatre. What brought you into theatre? Why did you decide to change and how did it happen?*

AD: I like going to the theatre, it's a public conversation. A short story is a private one. As for TV – well, I am currently writing for television, I haven't given up on it. I went into the theatre for the same reason I'll go back to it – there is less censorship. It is Literature. When you create a character in the theatre you are adding to the literary canon, e.g. Mother Courage. She lives on and on. That doesn't happen in TV plays. My best work for TV has disappeared and so have the characters.

As for radio – I started off writing prose and a play for radio at the same time. The TV commission followed because of the success of the radio play *The Long March*. The hierarchy in those days was you don't get to write for TV until you can write for radio. And also my agent at the time - the late Peggy Ramsay - thought that radio was good practice for theatre. It trained the ear.

EC: *Who has influenced your work? And your theatre work? What playwrights do you admire?*

AD: I wish I could say that the playwrights I admire influenced my work – with the exception of Sean O'Casey, they didn't.

EC: *Has Joyce influenced your work?*

AD: If Joyce has influenced me it's unconscious – like "the wings and eyes of light" at the end of *After Easter* is reminiscent of snow falling at the end of 'The Dead' in *Dubliners*.

EC: *During one of your recent talks you mentioned Sartre. Has he been another possible influence?*

AD: Yes, I was twenty-two when I came across Sartre. He was an extraordinary revelation to me: I was going from what I had inherited, what I naturally knew about, and the reading of European literature, and Sartre was so phenomenally interesting to me at that time. I didn't know his work as a dramatist; but I knew he was a Marxist and a Catholic as well. This thing about Sartre really impressed me: he says that you can get rid of the Almighty but not of the Holy Ghost. I find that very understandable. I really loved that idea. Yes, he has been an influence.

Another dramatist who has been influential in my stage work – and I can realize this now from a later perspective – is Beckett. His influence has more to do with dreaming: "I dreamt I danced with him – so I knew I was going to be a playwright." When I had that image of the dance I had no idea that Beckett was the great dramatist who challenged Aristotelian principles and twentieth century drama by writing a play in which "nothing" happens. That is not how he appealed to me. I associate Beckett's work with the unconscious, which is what I am trying to put on stage. The image of purgatory, which Anthony Minghella achieves in *Play* is so wonderful a translation of this territory.

EC: *What theatrical traditions are you most interested in?*

AD: In terms of theatrical traditions I inherited a kind of word-culture, which was about arguments and debates in plays. I find that very hard to get out of – the person who speaks the most is the person who wins the argument – and that's a kind of very old traditional form of theatre. It's very much like Shaw and I had to shed that. I found prose helped me to do that because it was very economical.

EC: *Your most recent stage writing,* After Easter, *is non-naturalistic, whereas* Ourselves Alone *seemed to be more rooted in the naturalistic tradition. How do you explain that?*

AD: Yes, *Ourselves Alone* is quite naturalistic, there are moments which surface with it, but if I am trying to do anything it is to struggle out of that naturalism. When I got to *After Easter* I was grateful for the layers of non-naturalism in that piece. I would describe this as wanting to say goodbye to the room, because I see naturalism as contained in rooms. In *Ourselves Alone* everything happened in a room and I was also aware of criticism being levelled at writers like me: there was all this big drama happening on the streets in Northern Ireland and we were all in rooms. What I was doing was bringing the drama indoors rather than going outside, and then the army, the police, the stranger, they are all coming into the women's room, they are invading the women's space. The progress of the journey of *Ourselves Alone* gets to a moment where Frieda describes a night before the Troubles started when the three women were swimming: "We swam in the night sky and cupped the stars between our cool fingers." Frieda was describing an extraordinary moment of possibility, which is where my optimism comes from: that moment of possibility is just lived through memory, the memory of it is all they have got to stay in.

The staging of the play, and certainly my own technical abilities in imagining it, don't reveal that element of possibility. I have only ever known how to do that through language. It is when language shocks you into another register, from realistic to poetic in the case of certain parts in *Ourselves Alone*, that you feel that sense of transcendence. I have moved more in that direction after *Ourselves Alone*: since then my language has become more musical and muscular – less wordy.

EC: *As a multi-media writer how much have those experiences as a writer of prose and television script informed your playwriting? Are your short stories a kind of rehearsal process for your following plays, a kind of "way-paver" for theatre?*

AD: This is interesting, but first of all I don't want to misjudge the stories. They weren't written as a rehearsal process although there is no question that I ended up bringing the voices I had already in mind and discovered in my prose into the play. I wasn't aware I was doing it in the beginning with *Ourselves Alone*. I became intensely conscious of doing it while I was writing *Ourselves Alone*, but I had already written *Five Notes After A Visit* and what I was doing with *Ourselves Alone* was a development of it. What is happening in the leading characters' relationship becomes the basis for Frieda and John McDermot in *Ourselves Alone*. It was as if I wanted to take something out of it. The thing about the short stories is that they tend to be isolated lives, the thing about the plays is that you put people together.

Because I had already done the biographies in prose, I was then able to move the characters farther on in their relationships. So it becomes an expansion. And I think it is a very positive way of looking at it.

EC: *Does your work for cinema, radio and television make you a different playwright? Do you think of multimedia experience as an important requirement for a good playwright today?*

AD: Oh yes, absolutely. Recently I was particularly impressed by the fact that even traditional dramatists are putting large cinematic techniques behind their works. In the contemporary theatrical scene, I was stunned by Théâtre de Complicité and their play *Mnemonic*, which was technically extremely skilful. They use every form of theatre: they deploy music, sounds and screens; they draw plastic curtains right across the front of the set so that you look at performers right through this plastic curtain; they also use a tape recorder: one of the actors starts off talking to the audience, then he lets the tape recorder run on and you don't realize that the person that has been talking to you has been taped and you are listening to a tape. Such a representation opens up so many different dimensions for the audience.

I was always very grateful for starting off in radio, because radio made me so sounds conscious. I think sounds without pictures are terrifying and terror is part of my experience – you would expect that, given where I have grown up during a particular period – so yes, I do think of multimedia as an essential experience for playwrights.

EC: Wh*at is the ideal relationship between theatre and the other media? Has television killed the theatre-going interest?*

AD: My instinctive response to that is no. While at the beginning it certainly challenged theatre,– there is no question of that in the early 1980s when I was starting to write for television and trying to get to the theatre – the Royal Court were in agony and distress over the fact that all the writers were working in television. A lot of writers still are working in television, because it is an income, it is a way of supporting your artwork. I was never cynical about television, I always felt good about writing for it.

The thing about theatre is that unlike the other media, it really stands up to scrutiny: a group of actors have to spend at least four weeks together and then they are testing it every night before a live audience. Theatre is not a one-night stand. It is sustained. It seems to me that television doesn't always do that. The real problem about film and television and their impact on the theatre and on acting is that it is all on the face and the use of the body and that means that there is no interest in works about people who are older. It all has to be about beauty and fashion, and that is a real disadvantage to your material as a writer. I know a number of women actors who say that the late thirties are a crisis point for them as actresses, because they will simply go absent from movies for about ten years until they have made the transition and then reappear as grandmothers in television characters. It is a terrible dilemma and something that makes me really angry; I was thinking about theatre roots in the eighteenth century when a pregnant woman played Juliet at sixteen, and nobody had a problem with that. It was all based on the voice, and the audience had to use their imagination. This is to me the greatest problem in the relationship between theatre and the other media.

EC: *When you first start writing a play, where do you begin? What's the initial inspiration that starts the creative process? Do you plan the structure of the play before you start writing? Are your characters quite shaped before you sit down to write?*

AD: No, I never plan the structure of a play before I start writing. I do not have shaped characters before I sit down to write. I have a line of thought and it is insistent. I then write the thought down and if it is in prose it's a story, and if it is in dialogue it's a play; however that doesn't mean that I won't translate the line of prose into dialogue at a later stage. It is literally a thought out of nowhere, it just arrives and it's the beginning of thinking about a play. I do not plan the structure before I start because first I try to grow the characters out of the process of the play so that I have some ideas of where I want to go. For me it is all a very slow process and I have to let the play grow. After that there is a real rewriting process that goes on with structure for me and I will have to carefully consider what I am going to do with that scene or the other.

I do know playwrights who start off with a structure and it is just a different process. For me it weakens the journey that the characters will undertake as I do not know what comes: I do know what they are up against, and I do know what the question is; but I do not know what the answer is. If I plan everything beforehand I know that some essential transformation will get missed, as, instead of allowing the language to lead me, I will lead the language, and I shouldn't be doing that.

EC: *You have said in an interview that "all the writing is an act of repossession." Can you expand a bit on that?*

AD: Yes, it is very true for me though I am also embarrassed by that statement because it sounds so aggressive. It has to do with loss and absence. It is not that I suddenly decided to go and live out of Ireland, out of Belfast, and from the safety of somewhere a refugee in the South West of England decided to write about the North of Ireland. I did not do that. I was sort of driven away. There were levels of violence that caused me to be afraid. I could no longer endure that, so I moved. The very first casualty of the journey was that I was no longer hearing the acoustic landscape I had grown up with, and I became intensely sensitive when hearing them again – somebody would phone up from home and I would suddenly be very sensitive to the sound of that tone more than to what was being said. So that was a kind of metaphysical loss. There are also personal losses that you accumulate as you keep travelling. So on one level through writing you try and repossess a happy time – and it's not that I write happy plays – but you try and repossess happy moments in a relationship that you had sustained before. You would like to re-visit them not just for indulgence, but to get over them and find a way out of them the second time.

There were also seriously physical reasons why I found it necessary to leave Northern Ireland. I have referred to this violent phone conversation in *Five Notes After A Visit* where someone is threatened on the telephone. Those things are maybe the last straw because the things that make you leave are really much more powerful.

I am not entirely saying that because of what happened in Ulster I just left. I probably would have gone anyway – I always had this great desire to go to London in 1969, – "swinging London" – and I am someone who has always been interested in travelling around the world. However, there are traumatic events that prepare you for that.

I would like to think that I chose to leave for positive reasons rather than for negative ones, and to reclaim the territory through writing is a way of saying "Yes, it is ok now, I can go back there and I can deal with that. I wasn't pushed out, it wasn't a violent separation."

EC: *Dreams as visions seems to be a recurrent feature in your work. Talking about the main character's closing speech, in your last play,* After Easter, *you said you "had that dream." What part do dreams play in your creative process and why is the subconscious so important to you? How do they blend with the disguised biography in your work?*

AD: I think dreams are terribly important to me because they are so totally original, as they are not influenced by anyone or anything other than me. I am the only person who is owned by them. If you had grown up with that sense of watching your tongue in any situation to avoid certain difficulties, if you feel under public surveillance and you want to keep some space where nobody knows what you are thinking and where you are not being scrutinized for your opinions, then the area that would be prolific in your mind is going to be dreams and that certainly happened to me.

What I feel is that dreams are the most free form of imaginative work – I am not mystical about my dreams. My dreams are how my imagination works when it feels like it. It is just mine. I am not under surveillance. I am not under scrutiny. There is no censorship. It is the free zone and therefore it is ridiculous for me not to use it. I am just amazed that nobody else has gone down to this with his or her own dreams.

EC: *What is the difference in your creative approach to an adaptation and to your original writing?*

AD: There is a great difference but there are also points of contact. *Titanic Town*, my last adaptation, is a special case - when I first read the novel I discovered that Costello had lived around the corner from me in Andersonstown.

I left in 1970 to go to University and she stayed on. It was as if a younger sister was telling me her story. Mary's first response to the script was that I'd stayed true to the spirit of the novel. The main difference between us is that her story is more grassroots than my own. All the same it's easier to adapt than to write an original screenplay because simply some of the creative thinking has already been done for you - like Costello's comic tone.

EC: *What was your journey as a writer in creating the screenplay for* Titanic Town?

AD: The journey for me as a writer was to take a woman who was politically inarticulate and make her more articulate; also to try to understand the relationship between the mother and the daughter so that both of them would grow up. This whole process of bringing the mother and the daughter together allowed me to revisit a character in myself because I had come from a father who was in politics. So in a sense I watched him going from political inarticulacy to articulacy – and also the effects of his politics on our family. Another part of the journey was that I was older and trying to come to terms with the fact that I wasn't thirty-five any more. In that respect I was dealing with a very unpopular subject-matter: I was writing about a middle-aged woman and as you know, nobody is going to make films about that. I also introduced a love-story in the film, which was absent from Mary's novel: nobody is going to make a film that doesn't have love stories in it. It also felt the right thing to do: the love story in the film fails, thus replicating that impossibility of love and relationships which in Mary's book is marked by the absence of them. Though following a different path, I still dramatized that sense of loss, of frustration, and that felt terribly close.

EC: *To what extent do you think text is central to theatre? How do you see the different roles of writer, director, actor and designer in the making of the* *theatre? Who do you think is the ultimate authority, the playwright or the director?*

AD: Yes, first of all I do think that the text is central. I would say that because I am a writer, but even theatre groups like Théâtre de Complicité come up with a text. It does not matter how they do it, what matters is that they eventually come up with a text, even if there is no one single writer. This is the other area outside of prose where the writer's voice is dominant. The play is the product of the single writer's voice. When I go to see Frank McGuinness's work I expect to see how Frank's voice deals with these new sets of circumstances. I want to see his journey, his progress as a writer. Once I have seen the plays in performance I go and revisit the texts. I never read a text before I see a play, because I find I do not like doing that.

With regard to the roles of writers, directors, actors in the making of theatre I will say this: when a play is being done for the first time it is absolutely crucial not to get a director who overwhelms the text and overwhelms the writer. You have to be matched some way. I found that the most generous directors are the ones who have confidence enough to allow the play to emerge and are not trying to impose their vision on it. Especially if it is a first-time production, you need somebody more cautious. Particularly with my work, because it is always an investigation, I do not know what it is going to look like or sound like. It is like journeying through the play again, there has to be collaboration between playwrights and directors.

To answer the last part of your question, to me there is no ultimate authority; the play is the thing. It is a growing process and it requires everybody to be completely focussed and committed to it.

EC: *When you sit in rehearsals, what are your feelings the first time you see your work coming to life, the first time you hear the words spoken by actors?*

AD: It is always a surprise because it is so physical. Writing on a page isn't so directly physical and it is also much safer. Going into a rehearsal room is a terrifying experience. It has made me hugely conscious of what the actors are able to do, how people's voices come to life and how their tones are different from what you had imagined from the physical silence of the page. I feel completely and immediately surprised at first, and it doesn't always feel familiar, it feels as if it has been taken away. And of course it has to be. It is not an easy process, it is often very joyful when you get to the end of it, but the first time it does not always look familiar to me. That is because it is the first time you stand outside and look in. So it is also very exciting.

EC: *Do you tend to go to opening nights?*

AD: I used to, but I now tend to avoid this because I really think that everything that happens in the theatre audience is in the bar, in the arena around the theatre with the critics. I find that the best times in the theatre are those first previews because until you do the first preview you really don't know what you have got. The audience with the play is the experience. I remember the shock, the complete amazement when we got an audience in the Liverpool Playhouse at the first preview to *Ourselves Alone*. I was amazed at what people laughed at, I was amazed at what the presence of an audience did to the play. That still amazes me. I have no idea, until I go in for the first preview, of how much the play is going to change. I have no idea how that is going to happen until I am in the room with them and I find that extraordinary. The final addition is audience to actors. It is so amazing what it does.

EC: *Are audiences a conservative force in Irish/English theatre? What do you think?*

AD: Audiences are forces to be reckoned with. There is also the question of how different audiences are from one country to another and how that tends to transform what is being performed. I have noticed for example in London that the thing that I worried about was a scene in *Ourselves Alone* where Josie says she left a bomb once and it didn't go off, and I remember sitting in the audience thinking, "Oh my God", suddenly realising that I was sitting in this theatre in Sloane Square and I must say that they laughed, and I was very much taken aback by the things they were laughing at. In Derry, it was completely different: there was laughter at things against the Irish. It is extraordinary how each audience opens up different levels of humour in the play. It nearly becomes another play to the point that sometimes it is uncomfortable for me as a writer to be sitting in the audience. Because I am between these two shores, between these two places, I am very aware of the differences between audiences in Ireland and audiences in England.

In Derry, during the interval of *Ourselves Alone*, a man came up to me saying that Frieda's father was right to hit her as she was so provocative. The good thing about audiences is that they are not all united, they are not monoliths, they are coming in as a completely different unruly bunch, which is great. So they are not coming in as a group and if they do, that is interesting too. There are choices to be made. I think audiences go to the theatre to be challenged, or because they expect something. They are not going just to have a good time. So you really have to get hold of them. And so in a way that is interesting too.

EC: Ourselves Alone *has also been produced in the States. What kind of reaction did it get from American audiences? Can you make out some differences?*

AD: It is quite hard for me to say; I found it amazing how terribly unpopular Josie was as a character in Washington, and how much they loved Frieda. Whereas when the play was produced in Chicago, the spectators were completely at home with that play: when Frieda appears in the club they were not looking at Republicans, they were looking at Prohibition, they were looking at gangsters. Audiences from different places unlock different meanings in the play. There was also a German production of *Ourselves Alone*, which was directed by Peter Palitzsch, a German director who trained with Brecht at the Berliner Ensemble. I remember being completely taken aback by the fact that as soon as Frieda appeared onstage from the club she was wearing an Irish dancing costume, and I remember thinking "She wouldn't wear that, the whole point with Frieda was that there is no way she would have been in a club in an Irish dancing costume." She'll be there in a mini skirt or whatever was fashionable at the time. That scene was quite funny for me but for the Germans it would say something else. For someone coming from a completely different cultural perspective that was a cert for a cultural clash.

EC: *How do you think of your earlier work from your present perspective?*

AD: I am very proud of *Ourselves Alone*, I really regard it as a major piece of work but obviously I could never write like that now as I am a completely different writer now. And if I think of my first radio work I think of how terribly naturalistic it all seems to me now. It just does not feel familiar to me any more. But I think that as a writer I do revise what I have done. I think for instance that *Titanic Town* was a revision of *The Long March*. There are works that are revisions of previous ones. When I looked at my prose in *Naming the Names*, which I adapted for TV and regard as one of my seminal pieces of work, I know that was a product of a particular period. I am just not that writer any more. I have moved from a preoccupation with individual love stories to a preoccupation with bigger questions. It does not mean that love isn't important, but that it is part of a bigger picture and I think that I still have a long way to go and I still want to get there.

EC: *Has the political situation in the North shaped the plays coming out of the North?*

AD: Yes, it certainly has. The theatre in the North hasn't always been particularly respectful towards its writers or at least encouraging, and they had to go elsewhere to get their work done. I think women dramatists have particularly suffered in the North. There are obviously people like Marie Jones with the Charabanc Theatre Company who worked in a community. I have never worked in that area. I have done a community play in Birmingham, *Heartlanders*, but that was a different process. Marie was actually part of a group of writers and in a way they were filling a gap, because the plays before Charabanc came along were Ulster comedies.

Someone like Christina Reid and myself went to England to get our work done. It seems to be so obvious now that because of the different stages in the political situation, different plays have been written. It is interesting that a young writer has come through now, Gary Mitchell. He is from the working class. He is writing about things I need to know about.

However, one of the major problems of writing about politics in the North is that if you haven't lived there throughout the Troubles, they feel you have no right to write about them. You shouldn't be coming back to them with plays, and so there is a resistance to where you have chosen to live. This kind of attitude is more prevalent among the journalists there, who actually resent you for going away and coming back and telling them what is happening. I think that happened very much with *After Easter*.

EC: *Is the importance of history in Irish theatre changing?*

AD: There is a big word there, that is "changing", and it is undeniable that the situation has changed, that there has been a real shift. There is no question that it has freed up a lot of things because during the period when I was writing *Ourselves Alone* and writing about political issues, however elliptically, history was a big huge character. Because of the violence in the political situation you got a real sense of responsibility. I do not think that history is a nightmare from which I am trying to awake, I think that it is part of what I call memory and forgetting: before I can forget I have to remember and before we can put down this particular burden that is our history we have to recall certain things that have not been visible during a certain period. Because of the dominance of the ideological conflict between the particular political groups there have been lots of things that haven't been visible and have become almost part of the collective psyche. I think we have got to identify those areas, that is why we are not finished with history: we have buried the body and we have seen the shape of their life, and now we have got to go back and explain. One of the huge changes about the importance of history in Irish theatre is a real shift from what I call the warrior's sword to the scholarly pen: once you come back into the land of the conversation, the word and the pen, there is a chance to see somebody else, somebody else makes an appearance onstage. You can see that in terms of the Peace Process, and the emergence of the Women's Coalition is very important in it. In a time of less violent clashes, in a time of social healing, women do become visible and come back into the frame again. They never actually left the frame for me; I kept telling what was happening to me and to my female characters. And history also changes because women were there and they were there at the end of the Peace Process, they were there as part of the agreement, and they have emerged in a completely different way than they were before.

EC: *I know you have said you don't write political plays, that you never work from the basis of an ideology. You said "always I write about the personality, the self; I never write about politics; I only look as if I do." There are nonetheless strong political implications in your plays. All your work reflects the complexity of women's lives and also the complexities of issues about life in Ireland, in the North and in England. Can you expand a bit on that?*

AD: I think I am changing again. I know that *After Easter* is an interrogation, it is about the personality. I know that in my earlier prose I was always trying to understand facets of the personality and the mysteries of it. Obviously the politics affect that, but my interest is now shifting from personality towards temperament and that shows in *After Easter* where I was trying to reconcile the two things. I think it is Louis Le Brocquy who says that all Irish art is an expression not of personality, but of temperament. It seems to me that while the beginning of *After Easter* is about personality, about how a personality unravels through a course of time, the ending of it is about temperament. In the closure it is the mythical story that dominates: that story of mythical elements, the flight of the stag – the antlered creature that appears from the cold north – represents the link between my two stage plays. Indeed, *Ourselves Alone*, like *After Easter*, ends with a mythical element, which represents temperament. But I know that I am changing again.

EC: *How much is the image of the frozen stag really "defrozen" today? And how much are the potentials for creative powers and self-expression acknowledged in today's Ireland?*

AD: I have controversial feelings about that image today. When I talk about the image of "thaw" in the play I do feel particularly positive about it. However, I think there are other problems too. When I wrote *After Easter* I was very aware of the state of change in Ireland and in Europe, but now there are huge changes occurring especially in terms of population. There is a sense of people not belonging to a territory anymore, but belonging to a state of mind. People would make their home less in terms of territories now. In that respect the world has become a particularly difficult place to be. Therefore, there is more to do, and the positive side of this, in terms of theatre, is that theatre is much more relevant than before.

EC: *Fintan O'Toole has described the committed writer as someone who "has faith in politics, in history and above all in the power of language not merely to communicate things but also to change things." Do you think it is still possible to doubt politics, history and language and still be a committed writer? What is it to be a political writer today?*

AD: I will take the first part of the question, which is to have faith in politics, history and the power of language to change things, because I do believe that writing can change people. I do believe that if you make comments you do not allow yourself to be swept away by shallowness or prevailing cynicism. Certain political stances have enormous seductive power for different generations and I feel obliged as a writer to tackle these matters, and to look for the antidote to things that I regard as dangerous in the culture. Yes, I certainly agree with Fintan O'Toole but I also believe in the need to question politics, history and language. If you believe in certain ideals it doesn't necessarily mean that you trust everything that comes from a culture. The writer is like a prophet (and I do not mean this in a religious sense): he/she has to anticipate where everything is going. I feel quite strongly about this: there are so many things that I don't like, and there are so many views of history that are dominant, and so many political stances.

The writer's task is to reinterpret all the time: I am always very interested in plays that either give me an alternative perspective and bring humour into tough subjects – subjects that are about political icons that are not challenged. But they have to be. The use of humour is seminal for me to achieve that. It becomes a political weapon. I have a character, Frieda, who continually surfaces in my work, obviously in different ways: she is a kind of comic voice that plays jokes at things that are regarded as very sacred in political terms. I would use humour as a political weapon in that way. That is why Frieda in *Ourselves Alone* was terribly popular at the Liverpool Playhouse with younger people in the audience and younger women, but very frowned upon as a character by male members of the audience. I told you about the man in Derry saying that her father was right to hit her because she was so provocative. In the past I have always found it very interesting to put a traditional iconic point of view in one character and then bring another character to question that stance. I think that is really exciting.

EC: *And is there a difference in being a committed woman writer?*

AD: Yes, definitely. It is a completely different experience for women. I mean, it is marginal for a start. And also women are still expected to carry the domestic story, and men are expected to carry the epic story, and I do not believe in that. I think there is a way of rewriting this epic, which in my view belongs more to women: they are the creators of life and I think that is very significant.

EC: *Some say that women are under-represented in the theatre. What do you think? A recent question on Rattlebag: "Why are there so few women writing for theatre?" What is your opinion?*

AD: When I think of theatre in both Ireland and England I immediately think of Marina Carr in Ireland and Caryl Churchill, Sarah Daniels, Timberlake Wertenbaker, Winsome Pinnock, Sharman MacDonald, Judy Upton and Sarah Kane in England – just to mention a few names. But in the North something else has happened: I am thinking of Marie Jones and Christina Reid and myself and maybe I am completely deaf here, but I cannot hear who the other women dramatists are in the North at the moment. There's been a lack of support in the North for women in theatre: I mean the theatre has not supported them. Obviously Marie Jones has represented a breakthrough with her play in the West End, but she had been writing for a long time and what she's got is well-deserved. One possible reason for me is that theatre critics are mostly men and so are the people running the theatres. An example of this: in *Heartlanders*, the play I co-wrote with David Edgar and Stephen Bill in 1989, one of my very favourite scenes was the one where the woman character, who is an instructor, is teaching pregnant women their breathing exercises: I filled the Birmingham Rep Stage with fifty pregnant women lying on their backs doing leg exercises and one of the critics simply couldn't stand it anymore. He said, "This script is full of pregnant women", because there were women at the bus station who were pregnant, there was pregnancy everywhere. A pregnant woman in the audience, however, was sitting there feeling so pleased and at home. And it is one of my favourite scenes, because it is rather beautiful.

EC: *Since* Passages *up to* After Easter, *most of your female characters are storytellers: why is storytelling so vital and central in your work?*

AD: Storytelling is an oral tradition, and of course it is an Irish oral tradition and not an Anglo-Saxon one. Besides, I always wanted to tell stories. My instinctive reaction to this question would be to answer it by telling a story. Storytelling for me is a way of solving a mystery. I had a very insistent storytelling voice when I knew I was going to write *After Easter*. I had this large monologue where the voice was speaking, and I didn't actually know to whom the voice was speaking. So I had to find that out.

Before I started writing for the theatre, what I was trying to do was to find an experience which could satisfy me creatively. What I needed to do was to take that storytelling, that spellbinding thing that I have, and use it in the theatre. I knew that I had found the first impetus for this in that woman's voice: I really wanted to take that woman into the theatre as I knew that if I took her into the theatre, I knew what she looked like. I also wanted to create the first experience of oral storytelling, which is a group of people sitting around listening to someone telling a story. I wanted to put my oral tradition into a dramatic situation which wouldn't be an argument but a story. It may well spark off responses to it as people try to interpret the story: that story comes from a real mystery that I wanted to unravel at the time, the mystery of Greta's visions.

EC: *You wrote the screen play for* The Rainbow *in 1988 and* Wuthering Heights *in 1993. In your other works you seem to be charting a map which is quite time and site specific, growing more out of your personal and public experience in Belfast and England. How do* The Rainbow *and* Wuthering Heights *relate to the rest of your work? What attracted you to both?*

AD: I did *The Rainbow* first. D. H. Lawrence was an English working-class man and that experience of class was very important to me. He was an influence when I began studying literature. I had read *Sons and Lovers* and there was a religious quality to sexuality that was extremely captivating for me. It was also a great change for me as I had never written outside Ireland before. I was also scared to death as I had never done an adaptation before. But in fact it turned out to be incredibly important to me to do *The Rainbow*.

Wuthering Heights was an extraordinary experience: I was living in Sweden at the time, it was one of my journeys away again. It is part of the experience of *Wuthering Heights* to have been in Sweden. I was surrounded by megalithic stones and a very ancient culture and in a most inhospitable climate – I was there in the winter – and all this was imaginatively bringing me somewhere else. I also had a tremendous longing for home, not home in England but in Ireland. When Paramount asked me to adapt this novel, I immediately said yes, because I thought of Heathcliff as that native culture, that ancient native force that I was very aware was there in those stones. And it felt to me as if there was a sort of a polished civilized society operating, and in order for civilization to advance you have to protect your children and your offspring from those ancient stones, from the power of them, and from the people who were rather like those ancient stones. It definitely influenced what came next, having done *Wuthering Heights*.

EC: *Talking about critics: how much effect do you think they have on the success or failure of plays?*

AD: They have a huge effect; I think there are too many men as critics. And they have far too much power.

EC: *How do you see yourself in the context of contemporary theatre?*

AD: I am definitely in between Britain and Ireland, between these two shores. I also see myself very much in women's terms: I am interested in whatever they are doing, whatever nationality they are. I am also seriously considering whether I am writing about the community or not. I am also very attentive to what women are writing: I see something quite unique about myself as a woman writer who is travelling between two zones: I would call this "the fault line." I do feel that this is absolutely major to me, and I do not see it translating to a number of other women, but I do think it is me.

EC: *What in Irish theatre has excited you over the last ten years?*

AD: I really admire Marina Carr and Frank McGuinness. If Frank has something on, I'll definitely be there. Because Marina is newer to me and I have only sometimes managed to catch her, if I haven't seen her works, I have read them. The other playwright I really like is Conor McPherson. I love *The Weir* and the use of storytelling in it. I love Billy Roche's *The Wexford Trilogy*. Those are the ones that immediately come to my mind. The reason why Marina is so important is because she is the child of the Republic, if we can put it like that. She is home-grown here and she hasn't had all this other stuff. Hers has been the society that has got on with it. Imaginatively it takes a lot of pressure off her and it is really wonderful to see what she is up to. Obviously I am very close to Frank McGuinness, I have always been, from *Observe the Sons of Ulster* onwards. I saw *Dolly West's Kitchen* after the death of my father and I thought it was wonderful. I was so grateful to him for that play.

EC: *Which media do you see yourself working more in in the future?*

AD: Well, I do want to devote more time to prose. I know I have to write the third play to match what I have written before for the theatre. I never felt *Ourselves Alone* and *After Easter* were the complete story, I know there is a third play.

Anne Devlin was born in Belfast in 1951. She has lived in England since 1976. She now lives in London with her husband and son.

Anne Devlin has extensively written and adapted plays for theatre, television, radio and cinema. In 1986 she also published a collection of short stories, *The Way-Paver*, some of which have been adapted for television. Television credits include *A Woman Calling* (1984) *The Long March* (1984), *Naming the Names* (1987), *Venus de Milo Instead* (1987), and *The Rainbow* (1988).

Her stage debut was in 1985, when *Ourselves Alone* was co-produced at the Liverpool Playhouse Studio and at the Royal Court Theatre Upstairs in 1985. *Ourselves Alone* has since then also been widely produced in the United States (Washington and Chicago), and in Europe (Ireland, Britain, Holland and Germany). The play won the Susan Smith Blackburn Prize and the George Devine Award, both in 1985. Her second stage play, *After Easter*, was first produced by The Royal Shakespeare Company at the Other Place in Stratford. The play was also produced in Belfast in the same year. In 1989, she co-wrote *Heartlanders* with Stephen Bill and David Edgar. The play premiered at the Birmingham Repertory Theatre in 1989.

Anne Devlin's film credits include: *Wuthering Heights* (1993), *Vigo* (1997) and *Titanic Town* (1998).

Enrica Cequoni

Enrica Cerquoni holds a Masters Degree in Modern Drama Studies from NUI Dublin. She teaches at the Drama Studies Centre at University College Dublin, where she is currently researching the plays of Anne Devlin and Marina Carr for a Ph.D thesis. She has published articles on Augusta Gregory, John Millington Synge and Anne Devlin in *PaGes*.

Joe Dowling in Conversation with Tony Ó Dálaigh

TÓD: *Joe Dowling, can I ask you first, what brought you into the theatre? What started you?*

JD: I think I always knew from about the age of six. My grandmother was the one who started me because, watching me playing games, she thought that this was more than just children playing: there's something here, there's a talent or something. So she started me going to drama classes, first with Ursula White and very shortly after that to Ena Burke.

TÓD: *The famous Ena Burke?*

JD: The famous Ena Mary Burke who trained so many including Brenda Fricker and Milo O'Shea. She trained Maureen O'Hara and so many others, all these names we heard when we were kids. Brenda Fricker and I were there at the same time. So, from the moment I walked into that classroom and started working on what she used to call group mimes, which were actually improvised drama, as well as the poetry and the extracts from plays, I knew straight away that this was what I wanted to do. It was like a total epiphany – I just knew that was it and I've never done anything else.

TÓD: *What then was your route to the professional theatre? Was it through the Feiseanna originally?*

JD: The Father Matthew Feis, with others including Nuala Hayes and John O'Conor. He and I used to be competing, along with Nuala and Brenda Fricker, Ann Kavanagh and many others who have gone on to do other things in the business. Then, when I left school and went to University College Dublin. I very quickly realized that university drama wasn't for me. It wasn't what I wanted to do.

TÓD: *Did you get involved in it at all?*

JD: I began with Dramsoc, very, very briefly, and then realized I couldn't take the casualness of people not turning up for rehearsals. I knew I didn't want to do this – this has to be professional. I met John Kavanagh on the street and I had known him very very briefly through doing stuff at the Lantern Theatre. I knew him very vaguely. John and I walked home as we lived almost in the same place and he said to me, "You know that the Abbey Theatre are setting up a school" and I've applied. He showed me the ad from the paper, which I hadn't seen and I went home and straightaway wrote a letter to the Abbey Theatre for an audition for the school. I joined the school in February 1967, the same time as John Kavanagh, and by the end of that year, I had been asked to join the Company, well not quite to join the Company but to take part in a Gaeltacht tour which was their first time out in the Gaeltacht. That was how I started.

TÓD: *Was the Abbey School a two-year course or was it open-ended?*

JD: My memory of it is that it was sort of open-ended – a number of classes. I think people were then invited to join the company, become apprentices, trainees with the company. Many of us did, John Kavanagh, Niall Buggy, Nuala Hayes, myself, Fedelma Cullen. Several people did join around that time. I actually joined towards the end of 1968 when Phil O'Kelly, then manager, asked me to become an actor of the company.

TÓD: *That must have been a great thrill.*

JD: Well, I'll never forget it! I was twenty years of age, I was still in U.C.D. I hadn't given up the university because that was always seen as the thing to fall back on. Thank God, I never fell back on it. So, the idea of actually becoming an Abbey actor was something that I would never, ever, have imagined. I was very pleased that my grandmother lived to see me actually on the Abbey stage, which was something amazing.

TO'D: *Who were your mentors in the Abbey when you began to act there? Actors often talk about the influence of older people on them.*

JD: Well, when I think back on it now, when I went into the Abbey, it was a very unhappy place, extremely unhappy. They had moved from the Queen's Theatre in 1966, they had moved into the new building. There really was no plan or vision at the time of how were they going to use this new building. It was Tomás Mac Anna who took hold of that place when he became Artistic Director there in 1967/1968. He left and went to America towards the end of 1969. He was pulling it all together by bringing all these young people in.

TÓD: *Was that his first time as Artistic Director or artistic advisor?*

JD: He was artistic advisor but he had a vision. He knew that he had to get a new company and so there was a very distinct split between those of us who were new and young and ambitious and energetic, and those who had been around for a while who had grown into what we might term "the Abbey habit." There were a lot of really fine actors, I mean really, really good actors, who had become discouraged, disenchanted with the theatre and it was a time of great conflict. I remember there were certain people whom I personally admired and they included Philip O'Flynn and Pat Layde, both of them I thought great actors. Philip was one of the greatest comic actors I ever worked with and indeed, ever saw. His ability to make a line feel just absolutely right and get the biggest laughs, was extraordinary. Pat Layde had a kind of depth and a sensitivity. Pat died young, Philip died only very recently, having retired early but neither of them really achieved the kind of status, the importance that they deserved. Look at that whole generation of Abbey actors, whether it be Eddie Golden, Geoffrey Golden, Micheál Ó hAonghusa, Bill Foley, all fine, fine actors, Máire Ní Dhomhnaill probably one of the best actresses ever in this country.

They all were burned out by the experience: they were all disaffected by the way in which the Abbey treated them. It really was a shame, in many ways, that that generation did not have the opportunities which subsequent generations of Abbey actors have had, to really explore the work in some kind of depth. Things were thrown on, in a hurry. I remember one of the first plays I did was *An Cailín Bán*, we did it on the Gaeltacht tour and then brought it back to the Abbey. Proinsias MacDiarmada, who you will remember well, was directing and he never got to Act 3, we never actually rehearsed Act 3. The first bit of direction I ever gave was when Máire Ní Néill and myself, who were playing opposite each other in a scene, were in the top corridor of the Abbey on opening night, never having rehearsed the scene, and I said, "When we go on stage you move left, I'll move right, you move down, I'll move up, we'll turn around, round the table etc." What I said to her was the only direction she got and the only direction I got. Included in that, I was supposed to sing a song and I can't sing. Nobody ever said, "You can't sing, so you can't sing this song." So, Eamonn Ó Gallchoir was on piano and I sang – to my eternal shame I actually went on and sang on the Abbey stage. I am in horror when I think about it now.

TÓD: *Was that perhaps the seed that led you to say, "I'm going to direct?"*

JD: No. I had no concept of it, nor did it ever occur to me. Hugh Hunt, who was the first Artistic Director of the Abbey, as such, – he followed Alan Simpson who was also an Artistic Advisor. Then Hugh Hunt came in and I had by then finished university, had done my degree and I was now full-time in the Abbey, very frustrated (as a lot of us were) about the way in which that company and this new theatre were run. What was the kind of work we were going to do and how were we going to engage young audiences and young playwrights? I went to Hugh Hunt and I talked to him about this. At that stage, I was all of twenty-two years of age and extremely arrogant. I said, "We've got to do something about young people" and he said, "Well, do it!" I said: "Right" and we set up the Young Abbey, which was the first ever theatre-in-education company. He sent me to Manchester, where of course he had been, and was still, professor at Manchester University, to view some of the theatre-in-education companies working in the north of England. I saw those and came back absolutely fired up with the idea that theatre, as an art form, could actually have an impact on education and that young people could actually be affected by what they saw and how they saw it. It was a life-changing experience because, of course, I have been involved in theatre and in education ever since. So, we set up the Young Abbey and it was Hugh Hunt who really encouraged me to think about directing.

TO'D: *There were very few years between your first professional job as an actor and actually directing.*

JD: Well, I first directed a children's play in 1971. I directed *The Serpent Prince* and *The Blue Demon*, both written by a young English playwright, Lynn Forde. That was the first time the Peacock had done any children's work and had actually engaged in children's theatre. When I directed that first play, I really enjoyed doing it and I thought, "Hmmm." I remember Phil O'Kelly asking me about doing it and I said "Well, I really want to act, I came into the theatre to act" and he said, "What you've got to remember is that there are a lot of actors and very few directors and so, you have more of a chance of getting on if you become a director!" Ambitious to the last, I took him at his word! Then, my first time to direct an adult play was when Tomás Mac Anna was to direct *Deirdre of the Sorrows* for the Synge centenary in 1971 and he got a job teaching in a college in America for a semester. He had already cast the play and as I had been his assistant a couple of times on different shows, he said "Why don't you do it?" So, I did. *The Irish Times* reviewer Seamus Kelly, the famous Quidnunc, wrote a review which said, "If the Abbey really wants to celebrate John Millington Synge's centenary, they will take this play away from this man who clearly can't direct and give it to somebody who can." That was my first review as a serious theatre director.

TÓD: *I can remember* The Happy Go Likeable Man *and I think that was the first time I ever saw Barry McGovern on stage.*

JD: *The Happy Go Likeable Man* was much later, that was 1974 when in fact I was running the Peacock. Tomás was back then as Artistic Director of the Abbey. Lelia Doolan had come in, but left in 1973. She was the first woman Artistic Director and in my view, a great, great director and someone who made a significant difference by the way in which she introduced voice coaching to the Abbey. In fact, that first voice coach was Patrick Mason. She supported the idea of an out-reach programme, way before her time. She introduced some really interesting writing onto the stage but, again, it was a very difficult time because that company was so rooted in their own style and method of working. So, when Lelia left and Tomás returned, it felt to them and to a lot of us that it had all been restored but of course, nothing ever changes back – time moves on. I became director of the Peacock then and that was when I put together my first company, which included people like Barry McGovern, John Olohan, Emmet Bergin and several others, Catherine Byrne came later.

TÓD: *It is interesting that when you left that for the Irish Theatre Company and were later appointed Artistic Director of the Abbey, your view was that the Abbey and Peacock should be run by one person – unlike when you were running the Peacock and Tomás was running the Abbey. Interestingly, I think Ben Barnes is now thinking of going back to the model of having a separate director of the Peacock. Is it difficult to have two theatres with possibly independent artistic visions?*

JD: I think the Abbey and the Peacock are part of one overall artistic mission and they should be different reflections of what a national theatre does. I became Artistic Director of the Peacock, while Tomás was Artistic Director of the Abbey, from the end of 1973 until 1976 when you and I started working together in the Irish Theatre Company. It was very clear to me that we could only make "so much" progress down there without some conflict going on, like someone being taken away by the Artistic Director of the Abbey to do something upstairs. So, that whole sense of second-class theatre took hold of the Peacock and when I became Artistic Director of the Abbey in 1978, I decided that I would programme both houses and therefore they would have a very real sense that the work in the Peacock was as important as the work in the Abbey. I think it worked, because with the first full-time script editor, Sean McCarthy, we actually introduced a lot of new writers to the theatre, including Bernard Farrell, Graham Reid, Neil Donnelly and subsequently, Frank McGuinness. So, a lot of really important work was done as a result of saying, "Let's upgrade the Peacock to having the same director, not being a second class citizen, not being a trial place." For instance, early in my time as Artistic Director, people like Ray McAnally were directing in the Peacock and that was a big change, a shift.

TÓD: *Well, Joe, to jump from then to now. You have been in the States for five years now.*

JD: Yes, five years permanently there but I have been back and forth since 1988.

TÓD: *I know that you have just renewed your contract.*

JD: Yes, I will be another five years there, so it'll be over ten years.

TÓD: *What are the basic differences, though I'm sure there must be a million, which would be most central to running the Abbey Theatre as opposed to running the Tyrone Guthrie Centre in Minneapolis?*

JD: There are massive differences. If I said "Board of Directors", it might seem like I'm still carrying chips on shoulders, which I'm not. I have long buried all of that, but the Board of Directors of the Guthrie are people whose involvement and connection with community, be they C.E.O's of large companies, be they people who have a big philanthropic interest in the arts, or wherever they come from, their reason for being on the board of the Guthrie is to support the theatre in the community. That means fund-raising, that means being advocates for the theatre. There is no sense in which they run the theatre or have a say over any artistic policy. That is entirely the responsibility of the Artistic Director. Now, that difference obviously is huge, as opposed to my time in the Abbey, where the Abbey Board (at the time even much smaller than it is now) was and is a very political one, both with a big P and a small p. People appointed by An Taoiseach, or people appointed by the Minister have a very different sense of guardianship over an organization than those who are selected by a committee, as we have in the Guthrie, which is headed by me.

So, my influence over how the board is shaped and what the board does is very different. So, you have a situation at the Guthrie where the board approves the budget that supports the season but they do not approve the season. They have no right to say, "You may not do this play." That's a huge difference, psychologically. It makes for a very different feel to the relationship between board and executive. There's a much more open, much more supportive response. The second and probably most important thing is the difference in funding. Here in Ireland the funding all comes through the Arts Council, or 70% of it. In the States, we have to go out and fund-raise. Our annual campaign, which brings in five or six million dollars, is about me going out and talking to people and raising money. Once we're into what we are at the moment, which is a capital campaign in order to build a new theatre, we will have to raise 60 million and that means going out in a way that I've never done before and actually soliciting that money.

TO'D: *Does the State over there, or the City, give support in any way?*

JD: Yes, in a very modest way, the State does support us. The state of Minnesota is one of the few states in the United States that actually does take its arts funding seriously. I think people are very proud of that. Of course, we now have a Governor who thinks that the arts are not of any value whatsoever. He is a former wrestler, Jesse Ventura. He says, "Well, if I fund the arts, why I'd have to fund stock-car racing or other things people do as entertainment." We keep trying to point out to him that the arts do have a rather different profile than stock-car racing or anything else, but he's not interested and that's it.

TO'D: *Has his election impinged on you in any way?*

JD: No. Interestingly enough, while he's not in favour of state money going to capital expenditure in the arts, he hasn't actually cut the arts budget and it's to his credit that he hasn't done that. However, the money we get from the state is very small. Our money largely comes from private donors.

TO'D: *What would be the total budget for the theatre for a year, including box-office and your funding?*

JD: It would be seventeen-eighteen million, yes, a large budget. We are the second largest budget in the United States. Outside of *The Roundabout* in New York, we have the largest number of subscribers of any theatre in the United States.

TO'D: *Again, that's a huge difference, the whole business of subscribers. In Ireland, I think its not part of our thing that we would book a whole series of plays for eight or nine months ahead.*

JD: Can you imagine the Abbey having subscriptions and people actually sitting down with a brochure and filling it in and saying, "I'll go on Tuesday, 14th to this play and Wednesday 15th to the next play." It happens that people would always just know that they can get in. That whole system of subscribers is coming under some pressure in the United States as well and there are a lot of theatres whose subscriptions are falling. But, it is a way of people actually expressing their own commitment to an organization. We have 32,000 subscribers now. When I went there, there were 15,000, so we have more than doubled the number of subscribers.

TO'D: *Surely all of those would not be going to everything?*

JD: No. There are different packages. We have six plays, so you can buy a six-play package, a four-play package, a three-play package but after that, you're not a subscriber. Three is the minimum. What's been interesting about the last couple of years is that the number going from four-play to six-play has actually increased quite significantly.

TO'D: *Joe, in your career to date, obviously there are playwrights that loom larger than others. Are there playwrights, living or dead, that you feel a particular affinity with or that you have worked more with, than others?*

JD: Brian Friel. I have probably worked more with him than with any other playwright, living or dead.

TO'D: *You have done a number of premieres, maybe three or four.*

JD: Yes, premieres and revivals. I did *Living Quarters*, *The Communication Cord*, *Aristocrats*, *Fathers and Sons* [*A Month in the Country*]. Those were the premieres of his that I have done. But, I have done *Philadelphia Here I Come!* a number of times. I have worked with Friel and on his work a lot, even most recently doing a tour of *Molly Sweeney* in the States. For me it is quite fascinating to have worked with him as much as I have because, when I was sixteen and saw *Philadelphia, Here I Come!*, it absolutely confirmed that I wanted to be in the theatre. It seemed to me to say so much about Ireland, about growing up in Ireland, about how theatre works, as in his use of the two characters.

TO'D: *It is an extraordinary early play.*

JD: Really extraordinary. To think that he was in his early thirties when he wrote it and how mature it is and yet, how it stands up now. I mean, we did it in the Guthrie in my first season there and of all the plays we've done in the five years that I've been there, it is the one that continually I get letters about, people talk to me about. It made an impact way beyond anything else we've done. So for me, it has been really one of the true highlights of my life to get to know and to work with Brian Friel.

Of the great dead playwrights, Sean O'Casey clearly is the one because Sean O'Casey changed my life! Once I did that production of *Juno and The Paycock* in the Gate in 1986 and it went to Broadway

in 1988 – that was really what launched me on an American career.
Without that launching pad, my American career wouldn't have
happened. So, *Juno and The Paycock* obviously has a very close place
in my heart, both as a play and that particular production, because
of Donal McCann, John Kavanagh, Geraldine Plunkett and
Maureen Potter. That first cast was just phenomenal and I think
one of the real reasons why that play was so successful, apart from
that great cast, was Frank Hallinan Flood's great set, which really
redefined the idea of what that house was like and how those
people lived, so closely on top of each other. I think it's often
underestimated how important that set actually was.

TO'D: *You have had a great relationship with Frank and I'm sure you've
lost count of the number of productions that he has designed for you.*

JD: Yes, we've worked together now for nearly twenty years, all
over the States. He has most recently been working in the Guthrie.

TÓD: *So, in a way, the Guthrie was a culmination;* Juno *going to Broadway,
you then doing quite a lot of work around the States for a number of years.*

JD: Yes, I worked in Washington quite a bit at the Arena Stage, the
Shakespeare Theatre there, and I worked in Boston at the
American Repertory Theatre and I worked in New York at the
Roundabout. I did a lot of work in Canada also in the mid-1980s,
working in Montreal and the Stratford Festival in Canada and in
Banff. So, in some kind of way, interestingly for me, the most
obvious route when people decide not to work exclusively in
Ireland is to work in London. That never happened for me. I have
done a couple of shows in London but nothing of any value or
importance in terms of indigenous British theatre, rather than
bringing shows there. A lot of people took that route. Mine seemed
to take me across the Atlantic. I felt almost immediately
comfortable there, I felt very much at home there and felt that I
wanted to be there. Now, I am.

TÓD: *Are there American playwrights that you feel an affinity with?*

JD: Arthur Miller, whom I had the great joy of meeting and getting
to know. He is a true genius and a delightful man, with tremendous
ease and tremendous understanding of how actors work. I did a
production of his play, *The Price*, at Arena Stage a couple of years
ago and just fell in love with that play and his whole style of
writing. More recently, I have got to meet and work with Edward
Albee and I really admire his work too.

TÓD: *Can I ask what the standard of criticism is in Minneapolis, as against
Dublin?*

JD: It's dull to non-existent in Minneapolis. There is one major newspaper in the city and the writer there is a good writer but not always terribly perceptive about theatre. There is one paper in St Paul and the writer there is not a good writer. He is also one of those critics who decided that the big theatres are the ones he is going to make his name on the back of, by bring critical of them, and admiring of smaller theatres. So, you get that same thing, that same tension that we get here all the time. I always remember the day before I took over as Artistic Director of the Abbey, John Boland wrote in the now defunct *Irish Press*. It was a big picture of me, with the headline, "This man will fail" saying very clearly "this is a job he can't do, he doesn't have the skill for it and he's not the person for it." The day before I took over! I remember thinking at the time, there is malice involved here. Why would you do that, why not wait until I was at least a while there? Then, of course, when I was a while there, he said the same thing!

TÓD: *It is extraordinary with the Abbey, unlike any other theatre in the world, that everybody in Ireland seems to feel that they can run it, that it's of huge interest. I think that's a good thing in a way. The current controversy about where it should go involves everybody and people are really interested.*

JD: I think that's really great. The Abbey deserves that and I think it has earned it. For all that I talk about the confusion of the late 1960s when I went in there, when you look at the history of the last fifty years in Irish theatre, how many of the highlights of that period have come from the Abbey Theatre? The number of writers it has produced, actors, directors, the way in which it is constantly reforming itself and changing itself, so that it reflects the differences that happen in Ireland. I think it is a remarkable institution, certainly now that it has become more settled. There were some years when that battle between the executive and the board was a dispiriting and truly negative thing in the theatre. That is all settled now and Patrick Mason deserves enormous credit for the way in which he handled the board and the way in which that board, with James Hickey as Chairman, handled the transition. Now, Ben Barnes is in a very good position where, first of all, there is more money around than there was when I ran it. We were always talking about cut-backs, how we dealt with deficits, how we overcame the limitations financially and that is no longer the case with the Arts Council and with the Celtic Tiger. Now they have the opportunity, it seems to me, to really take hold of a dramatic tradition and to transform it and to continue it, so this debate to me is a great one. Personally, I think the Abbey should move.

TÓD: *South side or north side?*

JD: I just think it should move. That building never worked. With great respect to Michael Scott and to all of those who were involved in it; when we moved in there in the late 1960s it was quite clear that nobody had really thought through how a theatre might need to operate backstage; the size of the scene dock and workshop, the distance between the rehearsal room and the stage, a whole series of things about which the original architect clearly didn't talk to people who were involved in the theatre, and the building doesn't work. Apart from that, it is now nearly forty years old and didn't have the sort of maintenance that it needed over the years.

TÓD: *The site is really constrictive, isn't it? There is talk that one of the options is to go three stories up or to buy right out towards the river where clearly, with a time-frame of 2004 for the centenary, that is just not on.*

JD: The site is constrictive and I think that the move to the south side makes sense. It is an open space, it would allow people to park and the infrastructure could be built round there. It is quite fascinating – I e-mailed Ben Barnes recently because when I read the reports in the paper, it was almost as though we were reading each other's scripts. The Guthrie is going through exactly the same situation. We're more advanced than the Abbey in that we are now searching for an architect and we're in the middle of a capital campaign to raise the money. We have a wonderful site, right on the banks of the Mississippi river, right downtown. It is a site that the city has made available to us. We had to buy it at market value but it was originally earmarked to be a site for a football stadium and they have given it to the Guthrie instead. The big controversy and debate was whether we should leave a building that had become extremely popular within the city, and what was now going to happen to that building? We just knew that to do what we wanted, which was to expand and have a second space and to have proper educational and rehearsal facilities, we had to move. So, we just continued to do that. I think if the Abbey keep making that case, then I believe that people will begin to see the potential of a move.

TÓD: *When do you expect to open that new theatre?*

JD: We'll also open in 2004. It is an absolutely extraordinary coincidence because the Abbey figure is IR£100,000,000 and our figure is US$100,000,000 and we will have a new building. Our building will be forty years old in 2003.

TÓD: *Almost the same as the Abbey.*

JD: Yes. As I said to Ben, it is almost as though we are writing each other's scripts.

TÓD: *There's a good article there or even a good television programme! Joe, you mentioned earlier about Brian Friel and Donal McCann and of course, they came together in your remarkable production of* Faith Healer, *which was almost a premiere in that it had only just opened in the United States.*

JD: It opened in 1979 on Broadway, with James Mason and Donal Donnelly and James Mason's wife, Clarissa Kaye, and while it is quite clear from what Brian told me, because I didn't see the production, that James Mason was a really hard-working, dedicated actor and that he potentially could have been a great Faith Healer, the problem was that they put it into the wrong theatre. They put it into a huge barn of a theatre and so it didn't succeed. I read the script and at one point we thought we should put it into the Peacock – three people, monologues. I remember thinking then that it can only work if it is this very compressed thing in a large space, in the sense of those large halls that are mentioned in the script, that whole sense of compression that the play had, which you can only get in a larger theatre. So, we decided to do it in the Abbey.

Donal McCann was an obvious choice on one level, because of who Donal was, but on another level it was not at all obvious that he should play a role like that because at that time, as has become very clear since he died, Donal was going through the most appalling time with alcoholism and his own demons torturing him. When we cast him, it was very clear that we were taking a terrible risk, because here was a play that depended almost entirely on his ability to hold this together. The other two parts were important but that's *the* part. If you don't have the *Faith Healer* right, you don't have a play. In those first early rehearsals, Donal would arrive with drink taken, he would be extremely difficult. Brian and I sat down one night and we both said, "Unless he stops drinking he can't do this, that's all there is about it." I said this to Donal. Of course, various things hit various fans and there was an absolute nightmare. Brian and I agreed that it was not going to happen. The following morning Donal came in and he didn't refer to the conversation, he simply said, "I take your point." He didn't drink at all after that and he focused. I still miss him terribly and to my mind, Donal McCann was the epitome of a great actor. He never said a line on stage that he didn't completely and utterly believe. Whenever he did a play that he didn't believe in, you knew it. He was uneasy, unhappy.

With *Faith Healer*, he so admired the writing, he so admired Brian, he was able to find that terrible loneliness that is at the heart of that character, the man who does not know from day to day whether or not the gift, the talent he has, will reveal itself. Well, any great actor has that constant feeling that even as the applause happens on a particular night, he'll never be able to recreate it. That is the *Faith Healer*. Donal just found it, absolutely perfectly. It was a tremendous experience. We did it in the Abbey first, then it went out of the repertoire for some time. Then, Noel Pearson, when he was Artistic Director, decided that he wanted to do it again. At that point, we did it with Donal again, Judy Geeson and Ron Cook. When we took it to the Royal Court in London, Sinead Cusack played the part of Grace. That, for me, was the best production that we did.

TÓD: *I saw the first preview of that and it was extraordinary.*

JD: Extraordinary. Donal was almost ten years older, he had come through a great deal in that ten years, including single-handedly defeating the alcoholism, finding a very deep spirituality that went way, way beyond any kind of conventional re-born Christian religion. He was very Christian but he found a spirituality that played right into the role. Sinead was perfection as Grace, she found exactly the right levels of frustration and she was the beauty that the Faith Healer and Teddy described. Ron Cook is a master actor, a truly great character actor. I remember sitting there one night, towards the end of the run, with literally the tears streaming down my face. Somehow we had achieved a kind of theatrical greatness. It wasn't me, though I was a part of it, but it was a coming together of so many different things and there are few times in your life when you can stand back and say, "That's it, that's it, there's no better." Now, we subsequently did it at the Long Wharf Theatre in Connecticut and Judy came back into it. Judy was fine, there was no problem with her but she didn't just quite have what Sinead has, which is that Irish quality as well. When we did it at the Long Wharf, interestingly enough, it was not well received by the local critics. " A Cure for insomnia" was one of the headlines. People were walking out and it was a kind of an ugly time. Then Ben Brantley, who was the second string critic of the *New York Times*, came to see it after about a week of playing. He wrote a review in the *New York Times* which, if one had written it oneself one would be embarrassed. It was absolutely one of the greatest raves. The end of it was, "If you have any interest in theatre, you will make your way straight away to New Haven and see this play and this performance."

Of course, from then on the place was packed, there were standing ovations and everybody was heaping this love on top of the cast.

Now, Donal McCann was a man who had no time for any of that, so when there were producers saying, "We want to take this into New York, to take it onto Broadway", he just said "No." He stepped back from it and said, "That's it, I've done it, I'm not doing it again. I know what we can achieve with this but I don't want to do it again." So, it ended there. Very interestingly, I recently met with Horton Foot, the American writer who has done many movies and films and plays. He said to me, "Didn't you direct that *Faith Healer* that I saw at Long Wharf" and I said "Yes." He said "You know, it was one of the greatest experiences of my life seeing that. It was just great." He has subsequently written three plays that have taken the monologue form, so he got courage as a writer from seeing the way Brian was able to handle that script.

TÓD: *When we talk about Donal McCann – most Dubliners, if you were to ask them what are the ten great experiences of their career, there would be three Donal McCanns – Juno, Faith Healer and finally, The Steward of Christendom. It was a wonderful end for him really.*

JD: Well, who could have thought it – like Siobhán McKenna playing in *Bailegangaire* as her last stage performance. Who could have thought that these great actors would go out with that kind of statement of who they are as people and what they are able to do. Siobhán McKenna transformed herself. I adored Siobhán, I thought she was a most wonderful actor and a wonderful human being. A few years before, when she did *A Long Day's Journey into Night* with us at the Abbey, when she was doing her one person show, when she was being heavily criticized by the younger critics, particularly Fintan O'Toole, I found it very hard to watch all that because she was a great actor, no question about that. But, she seemed to have lost her time, her time seemed to slip by and suddenly Tom Murphy and Garry Hynes gave her this epiphany, this jewel. She was magnificent.

That opening night in Galway was for me one of the great nights of Irish theatre. She was magnificent and then she died. Donal went through a very bad period, as you'll remember, all of those years when people said he was unemployable, when he was doing things like "Elvis" at the Olympia and really bad work. Then he found these three great roles and then he died. It's almost as if the spirit and the instinct of the actor is to know: "I've got to make some mark, because it won't last." For me that is one of the joys of theatre but also its real terror is that everything is ephemeral, it never lasts, it goes. But Donal will last forever because of *The Dead*. That was a great performance in the John Huston film. I watched it the other day and it's a great film, just to see what Donal was able to do, in a movie form. He was not I believe a great movie actor, but he was a great stage actor.

TO'D: *Yes, there was something about him that was The Stage, whereas there are faces that the camera immediately loves, but it's very different.*

JD: Well, remember that Stephen Rea was also a fine stage actor but has become a really great film actor, Liam Neeson the same. Brendan Gleeson is terrific and it's wonderful that there is now a whole new generation of young guys like Stuart Townsend, winning awards.

TÓD: *Joe, thank you very much and good luck with the new building and the next five years. Hopefully we will also see you back here.*

JD: Well, both the Abbey and the Gate have invited me and I would love to come back and do something in Dublin but time, time ...

TÓD: *Do you have time to do just one production a year outside Minneapolis?*

JD: Yes, that's what I try to do, but this year I don't think I'll be able to. Next year I think I may be doing something in New York.

TÓD: *Joe Dowling, thank you very much.*

JD: Thank you

Joe Dowling is the Artistic Director of the prestigious Tyrone Guthrie Theatre in Minneapolis. His career in theatre began – while he was still a student – as an actor at the Abbey Theatre. After directing a number of productions there and founding The Young Abbey, he became Director of the Abbey's second space – The Peacock – from 1974 to 1976. After a further two years as Artistic Director of the Irish Theatre Company he became, at 29, the youngest-ever Artistic Director of Ireland's National Theatre (Abbey and Peacock). He held this position for seven years (1978–1985), after which he combined a career as an international director of plays and Artistic Director of the Gaiety Theatre, Dublin.

His production of *Juno and the Paycock* for the Gate Theatre, which played in festivals throughout the world, won him international acclaim. He has been closely associated with the work of Brian Friel and has directed the world premieres of a number of his plays, including *Living Quarters, Aristocrats, The Communication Cord* and *A Month in the Country.*

Tony Ó Dálaigh is a free-lance arts consultant. He was Director of the Dublin Theatre Festival for ten years from 1990–1999. Previously, he was Director of the National Centre for the Arts (now Irish Museum of Modern Art) at the Royal Hospital, Kilmainham (1986–1990), General

Administrator of the first State-funded touring company, the Irish Theatre Company (1974–1978), Manager of the Irish-speaking professional theatre, An Damer (1963–1965) and Director of Irish National Opera (1964–1985). He is a board member of the Gate Theatre, Dublin, of St. Patrick's Festival and a number of other arts organizations.

Bernard Farrell in Conversation with Jim Nolan

JN: *As you know, writing is by definition a solitary and private pursuit and it seems to me there is some unspoken agreement amongst writers not to invade each other's space. Well, today I get the chance to break that agreement and I'd like this interview to concentrate less on some kind of overview about Irish theatre and your place in it and more on the nuts and bolts of your writing life. For many years, your programme biography usually began with the statement that you were born in Co. Dublin and that following the success of your first play* I Do Not Like Thee, Doctor Fell, *you resigned your job in Sealink to pursue a full-time career as a playwright. Before we discuss that career, can you tell me a little about growing up. You were born in Sandycove?*

BF: Sandycove, yes. Father, mother, two sisters – one older, one younger. Our family was actually quite literary without knowing it. I mean, my friends would not have been literary people at all. My father worked as a foreman for Sealink – or British Rail as it was known then. My mother raised the family. But they were bookish in a very natural, very normal sort of way. Always literature in the house – and as a family, we were often taken to see a play in either the Abbey, or the Queens as it was then, or the Gaiety or the Gate or up to the Garrick Theatre….

JN: *Where's that?*

BF: I think it was up in Parnell Square. A lovely little theatre. It was all made very exciting for us, these trips to the theatre – and, when we were very young, it could also be hilarious because they used to pack sandwiches and flasks of tea and all the paraphernalia for a theatrical picnic.

JN: *So you'd go on Saturday afternoon, Saturday evening?*

BF: Saturday evening. But I think when we were very young we used to go to matinees – if the matinees were there, as they were at the Queens. And then, of course, when we grew up to about thirteen or fourteen in the way that children do, we wouldn't go anywhere with our parents! But I was still going to the theatre – with friends who were interested or with girlfriends and, at the same time, in the privacy of the house, I was writing short stories and poetry and, you might think that with those two parallels in place – theatre and writing – I would consider writing a play? Never crossed my mind!

JN: *But clearly these were great influences, having gone to the theatre as a child with your parents – can you remember particular performances of plays, do any of them stand out?*

BF: I can remember a lot of bad plays – I remember thinking how awful many of them were! But one that made an impact on me was a production in the Gaiety I think, of *Who's Afraid Of Virginia Wolfe?*. T.P. McKenna was in it, if I remember correctly.

JN: *Which year would that have been?*

BF: I don't know, the early 70s I think, at a guess. And a sort of pivotal play I saw was a production of *The Birthday Party* in the Peacock, the Pinter. That had a great impact on me. Those plays kind of hang in the memory.

JN: *So can you remember a day when you said "I've written stories, I've written poetry, I'm going to try a play?"*

BF: Oh I do indeed and it was sparked off by a pal of mine, in a writers' workshop at The People's College. One day he said to me "There's a theatre workshop in the Lantern Theatre on Merrion Square and I'm going to it, because I'm thinking of writing a play."

JN: *This was Liam Miller's place?*

BF: Paddy Funge. I think Liam Miller was associated with it as well. It was a lovely space. And I went along just to keep this guy company and I stayed for about a year – but the funny thing about it, Jim, and I don't know if you were the same, but I was always deeply embarrassed about being exposed as a writer. When I wrote the short stories and the poetry, I always wrote under the name of Michael Farrell and nobody knew it was me. And when I was working at Sealink, I did a lot of freelance journalism and I used to write regular features for the Evening Press, all under the name Michael Farrell. And the guys I worked with never made the association. I remember one of them saying to me : "Did you see that article in the Evening Press last night – it was all about the very thing we were discussing only last week."

JN: *And it was Michael Farrell who had written it?*

BF: Exactly. Don't know if you started that way, did you? Did you hide?

JN: *Well, I'd be shy as well maybe, yes.*

BF: Did you tell your pals?

JN: *Don't you start asking the questions!*

BF: I'm only asking because I'm interested – this is my opportunity!

JN: *I can remember the first poem that I had published. I was writing poetry in school and there was one published in the local paper and it's a curious mixture of pride and deep shame that somehow one's inner thoughts have been exposed to the world and you had no business doing it!*

BF: Did you put your name on it?

JN: *I did of course.*

BF: You didn't hide?

JN: *No, I wasn't bright enough to get away with putting someone else's name on it.*

BF: I wanted to be subversive, I think. I wanted to hide – I wanted to be able to mix around and listen, without anyone knowing I was there.

JN: *There's a sort of double life involved – the private person who's the writer and this other life you live.*

BF: Very much – but I think that, with the theatre, you can't have a private life because the whole thing is so socially-based.

JN: *It's a very public medium.*

BF: Very – and although I revel in the successes and endure the downsides, there is always part of me that screams that I really want to get out of the public side of it altogether. Very difficult though.

JN: *Talking about success, your first play, your first professionally produced play was* I Do Not Like Thee, Doctor Fell *– am I right about that?*

BF: It's the first play I wrote.

JN: *It's actually the first one you wrote?*

BF: Well, I wrote a thirty-minute sketch when I was at the Lantern workshop. It was called *Goodbye Smiler, It's Been Nice*. It was a terrible load of rubbish!

JN: *But a good title.*

BF: A case of "Nice title, shame about the play"! When I came out of that, I thought I could write a play and that I would write a play and it came to me just like that. I just wrote it, and wrote it all for myself…and had a great time writing it because I thought it would never be seen anywhere.

JN: *A great innocence about those first ones.*

BF: Terrific. You get all the tensions as you go on later in life. Then I sent it to Joe Dowling. I remember thinking "What will I do with it now? I'll give it to the Abbey – the worst they can do is send it back."

JN: *Start at the top.*

BF: And work down – to a telephone box!

JN: *And Joe was the Artistic Director.*

BF: He had just come in the year before and that was a lucky break.

JN: *And who was the Literary Manager?*

BF: Tom Kilroy – and he was the first one I met. I was amazed when they asked me to come in and I remember the nice things Tom said about the play and then he said "Would you think of changing this bit of it or that bit of it" and a did a short re-write for him and brought it back and he said "No, I think the other way was better."

JN: *And they decided to do it?*

BF: And they did it. It was an amazing night, you know. The 15th March 1979 and it was snowing.

JN: *Never looked back?*

BF: Oh, I've looked back a lot of times.

JN: *But it was a terrific start, wasn't it?*

BF: It was great – but I didn't realize the pressure that was there at the time because I thought it was all a big joke and just another, more wonderful aspect of my life to be enjoyed. But then suddenly it began to get very serious as the reviews came in – because they were all so good! Then Joe asked me to write another play and I wrote *Canaries*.

JN: *He commissioned that play, did he?*

BF: He did. And when *Canaries* opened at the Abbey in the 1980 Dublin Theatre Festival, a lot of people had a go at me because they wanted another *Doctor Fell* – "Son of Fell" – and I just thought it was lovely the way Joe stood by me through all of that. I remember he took me out to dinner at the Shelbourne Hotel, just as a particularly nasty review came in and told me that the play was "packing" and that he wanted to commission a third play from me. It was so encouraging. So much so, that I then handed in my resignation to Sealink!

JN: *How did you feel? Obviously you were committed to the decision you were making.*

BF: Well the funny thing about it – and maybe it's like the way you're able to handle the monumental things in life like births, marriages and deaths – but a calmness comes over you, a feeling of surety and you don't know where that strength comes from. I felt absolutely relaxed about it. I felt I was doing the right thing. Okay, I wasn't married, I didn't have the responsibility of a wife, kids, mortgages or anything like that, but I did go very untroubled into the decision.

JN: *Can I ask were both your parents still alive at that stage?*

BF: My father had died. My father died in 1978.

JN: *Just before* Doctor Fell.

BF: He knew I was writing *Doctor Fell* and I often wonder what he would have thought because he just idolized the Abbey – he used to almost speak about it in hushed tones. He would have been delighted. My mother was still alive and was suitably astonished, as everyone was astonished.

JN: *Was she at the opening night?*

BF: She wasn't, no. She didn't actually go until it transferred upstairs to the main Abbey stage because of her arthritis and she just couldn't get down the stairs to the Peacock. She was always terribly proud of what I was doing and always ready to gut any critic who ever gutted me! I think, deep inside, she was gob-smacked by the whole thing – didn't know where it all came from. Neither did I, for that matter.

JN: *You say she was astounded about where it came from. Can you identify where it came from? I'm not saying you ought to – personally, for myself, I can't – but is it possible for you, as a writer, to identify what it is, what kink in your metabolism, has you writing?*

BF: It's really very difficult. I sometimes think that writers are flawed people in many ways – that instead of being out there dealing with the confusion of life and all the complex situations, they are creating an artificial world in which they conveniently have total control. And then there are the inner and outer lives, aren't there? The inner that holds the anger and the outer that wants to get onto a soapbox. For whatever reason, a common thread seems to be the need to hide all the feelings and then just turn them loose onto the page.

JN: *And speaking of things coming onto the page, I'm fascinated by how people, other writers, put plays together and I've a feeling it's a subject that may be of some interest to readers. Just for instance – you take a commission from the Abbey, then what? – can you take us along that journey?*

BF: I think there is a moment first, when you think "what is this play going to be about?" There is a spark, just a kind of lift-off, it lights a fuse somewhere and I think, by and large, that I would have that before I would accept any commission.

JN: *So, before the commission, you already have something.*

BF: Could be the tiniest idea. And I may also have an idea where it is all going to be housed. Then you're wondering what will work on the stage; is it possible to tell this story in a theatrical way and will it be exciting for me? And if the spark looks good, then I would start taking notes on bits of paper during the day, shoving them into my back pocket to bring home and compile them – and then all the superstitions kick in, the notebooks all have to be the same red-covered, spiral kind and the pen has to be the right kind of pen, all that stuff. Then I would put a date on the thing, on the little idea, and then I would go back to the Artistic Director and say "were you thinking of commissioning a play – because I think I have one" – and then the serious work would begin.

JN: *But you don't present them with an outline?*

BF: Well, I wouldn't at that stage because I wouldn't have one.

JN: *So it's all for your own security, the sense of "Now I can go back to them, now I have a plan?"*

BF: Exactly – but I think if you are a novice playwright, you wouldn't find yourself in this somewhat privileged position. What artistic directors are thinking is that you have a good record, you can be trusted and, hopefully, this tiny idea of yours will someday blossom as a play. And if I thought too much about that aspect, the panic would really set in.

JN: *But all of this is before you've written "Act One, Scene One?"*

BF: Before a word has been written.

JN: *But there's a structure in your head…*

BF: Well, you're taking notes....

JN: *Making characters and story-lines?*

BF: Exactly – and then, at a certain point you say to yourself that you can actually start.

JN: *So the subject matter usually, or always, comes before character?*

BF: Yes it does.

JN: *Have you ever been in a situation where this character arrives in the head and doesn't go away and then there's a story – or is it always "I'm going to write a play about such-and-such a thing?"*

BF: I have to say, without thinking back over the various plays, that I don't think there is a hard and fast rule and the scenario I have just given you is probably the most common one. I'm sure that a play that has a very strong character up-front – I suppose like Kevin in *Kevin's Bed* or Joe in *Doctor Fell*...

JN: *I was thinking particularly about Joe Fell.*

BF: Yes, I expect, without being able to accurately remember, that those plays may have developed differently.

JN: *So you're armed with structure, some kind of subject matter – where do you go from there?*

BF: Then I would take notes on the characters who are going to inhabit this play – and not about how they necessarily will be in the play – more likely about their background, their childhood, what happened to them when they were young, were they happy, were they contented, were they at ease with themselves, were they popular with the girls or the fellows or whatever, did they play games, why are they quirky, why are they unusual, why are they carrying baggage? I suppose they all have to carry some baggage to be interesting – and these notes would try to place that, to see where they were before they came into the play.

JN: *And to what extent, when you are assembling these identikit pictures of characters, are you pulling from your own world, from the people you know?*

BF: Well not just from the people I know, but also myself – and I suppose we all went through traumas when we were young and growing up with a sense of unease in strange and new places. I think a pivotal area of my life was when I went to Monkstown Park, which is a rugby-playing fee-paying school, while all my previous friends, if you take social levels, stayed a slightly lower level to the one I was moving into, and I found that very difficult for a time. But I assimilated and I played rugby and made great friends at school – but I didn't enjoy school, and I have a feeling that school didn't enjoy me! And I think, like most people, that sense of being uncomfortable in a certain place or with certain people, inevitably leaves some scars.

JN: *Yes, and it seems to me that this kind of transplantation crops up again and again in your work – people moving from one social division to another.*

BF: Yes, being ill at ease and perhaps that's why, in all the plays, there are various kinds of humour at varying levels. Sometimes great dollops and some, I hope, suitably barbed and subtle. But I think, personally, I was always able to joke my way out of situations and to become more acceptable in social situations by being humorous, by being able to see the funny side and turn the circumstance around.

JN: *Comedy was your defence.*

BF: Yes it was – and socially probably still is – how I present myself – but it's not always how I feel most comfortable, having to crack jokes when I don't feel like doing that most of the time.

JN: *So you're saying that the characters then are a kind of assembly of elements of your own life?*

BF: Yes and those borrowed from people I know – parents, family, friends, the lot.

JN: *So the day comes when you can't put it off any longer, you have the notes, and it's time to write it. I know I put that day off as long as I possibly can.*

BF: Why do you put it off? Because you're afraid of making a mistake?

JN: *No, because I know that once I start, there's no hiding, it's every day then.*

BF: That's right.

JN: *You can go round forever – and I do! – I go hiding on a play where I take the notes and I have this idea and I put that note there and assemble this kind of thought here – but the day comes when you can't avoid the desk anymore in terms of "Act One Scene One, someone comes in ... "*

BF: I know – but are you also afraid, quite apart from the commitment, that what you have in your head is never going to match what you put on paper?

JN: *Well, it never does, does it? It never quite gets there.*

BF: That's true.

JN: *There's always the dream and then there's the reality which is as close as you can get to that first spark. But when you do begin — can we talk a bit about the routine then? As I said, I tend to avoid starting — it seems to me, you may go calmly into that dark night.*

BF: Well, not exactly! I'm always afraid of it, I hate it — but then there is a morning when you wake up and maybe it's because the sky is blue or something and you suddenly feel brave and you go up to the room and, exactly as you say, you start to write. From then on, its terribly disciplined — boringly so. In that time, I hate being interrupted, hate being invited out. I really, angrily resent all interruptions of any kind. I don't know if you're in a great humour when you're writing a play, are you?

JN: *Well, just for personal reasons, I move away out of my conventional environment and go to a place where I don't have to relate. So, there's no socializing at all. I'm just locked away.*

BF: And would you do a lot over a short period?

JN: *I tend to, yes, and I think there are positives and negatives to that. Sometimes I yearn for the possibility of having a writing space and a space in my own head that says "you can go into a room in your own home, do a working day and come out of it again" whereas I tend to lock myself away in rented places down at Dunmore East for very concentrated periods of time where you're writing for all hours of the clock and I think there are big disadvantages to that — the sense of "I have to finish it within that very concentrated period of time." But it's just curious how different people work.*

BF: Its different strokes, isn't it?

JN: *Sure. So, as your play is progressing, do you edit, re-write as you go along — or do you sort of throw it all up and say, "There it is and now I'm going to go back and re-work it?"*

BF: I don't think I can keep going if it's not right. I often go back and rip out pages galore until I find the spot where it started going wrong. Then I'm freed up again, then I can go on another little bit until I hit another brick wall and then I backtrack again. So it's backwards and forwards in varying moods of hope and despair…until, eventually, The End.

JN: *Having had some experience, as Artistic Director of Red Kettle, of receiving new plays of yours, I had a very clear sense, shared I'm sure by people like Ben Barnes at the Abbey, of the work being very finished by the time we first see it. Apart from refinements that may occur within rehearsal, there is a sense of when you hand them over, they are damn well finished.*

BF: I always think they are, because they will have gone through four drafts – the first hand-written ones and then nowadays, each corrected, amended, rewritten onto a computer. So by the time I hand it in, I would have this silly pride that it is totally right, that it will not disappoint anyone, that I will not hear someone say "this is not right." I would never put the words "first draft" on any submitted play – I would assume that everyone knows that this is the "last draft." But that is not to say that when you come along, or Ben, or any artistic director and say, "I don't think this part works" that I will not agree…if I sincerely see the point.

JN: *These would be minor adjustments?*

BF: Yes – more in confidence than with arrogance, I would think it should all be in place.

JN: *Sure. Before we leave the writing room, I want to ask you – do you absolutely refuse to talk about a play in progress?*

BF: Absolutely.

JN: *We had an encounter where, I think, on the first or second preview of* Happy Birthday, Dear Alice, *we were driving to the theatre in Waterford and I spat out the plot-line of* The Salvage Shop *at least three years before I wrote it and you were astonished.*

BF: I was.

JN: *You said "Well that's very interesting but why did you tell me – don't ever do that again to anybody." And it was very good advice, but I tend to feed off people, I like to get some sense of where the story is going and there are one or two people that I may be able to talk to.*

BF: I remember that night very well. I think I was amazed that you could see the play so clearly in your mind – that was the first thing. And the second thing was, I thought it was such a great idea – I mean I was just fired-up listening. And I suppose, in many ways, because of that *The Salvage Shop* is very close to me and also because I knew your father well and it has all those resonances – but I was astounded that you were telling me – I would never do that.

JN: *Because you'd have a fear of talking the play out of existence?*

BF: That is the fear.

JN: *Not that somebody might steal the idea?*

BF: No – more a fear for myself – that I wouldn't be interested any more. Once you tell somebody, I fear that the piece could be diminished.

JN: *I have to say I've been a lot more careful. I did try to take the advice – I wouldn't be as good at implementing it – but it does make sense that you can talk it out of existence.*

BF: Yes, the fire should be within you and only released onto the page.

JN: *Do you go to your rehearsals for first productions?*

BF: Oh absolutely, having started off in the Abbey where, as you know, they actually pay the playwright his expenses to be there. And I love the process and I think I have good rehearsal-room manners – I would never talk directly to the actor, always to the director and I would never be critical of directors or actors trying new things, trying something a different way, I would always go for that, see what happens.

JN: *You've been lucky too in working consistently with a small number of directors, most notably with Ben Barnes at the Abbey and, indeed, at the Gate when your plays were premiered there.*

BF: That's right – and Paul Brennan.

JN: *Of course. So there's a lot of trust between you and the director – there is a good working relationship.*

BF: That's right, absolutely.

JN: *But are there also dangers in having a sort of consensus between director and writer at a time when it should be challenged?*

BF: Yes, I know what you mean. I do think that with each play, everybody is on the line – each play throws up its own risks, problems; things that have not been encountered before. And with all of that – for my plays – there is the expectation that lots of people will come to them…and there's another layer of panic. So, in one way or another, it can never become cosy because we are all on a knife-edge.

JN: *And opening nights?*

BF: I hate them – although, having said that, a strange calmness comes over me on opening nights. Well, not entirely – I never remember things like driving to the theatre, going through traffic lights, where I put my coat – but I am very good at going around to the actors, wishing them well, meeting friends – but I'm always so glad when the night is over…. and I only have to wait for the reviews!

JN: *My recent experience of having my first play at the Abbey would tell me that this kind of pressure, the pressure attached to any opening night, is hugely* *magnified, and understandably so, by being at the National Theatre. Would you go along with that?*

BF: I would indeed. I have always felt – and not because it's yourself – that going down to one of my play-openings in Waterford was such a relief – you were out of the city, away from the spotlights, Dublin can be like a pressure-cooker.

JN: *I suppose the National Theatre brings its own demands. I want to ask you, in relation to writing comedy, about a perception that's out there, not just from critics and outsiders but from within the industry itself, that playwrights who write comedy are some kind of lesser species. Is this still the case?*

BF: It is indeed – it's an awful snobbery.

JN: *I think your plays are deadly serious and use comedy as a way of saying something that comes from a source that is driven, very often, by anger.*

BF: Indeed, and I know that you are aware of that Jim, and we have discussed that often in relation to the plays I've written for Red Kettle. But you know, people then come up to you afterwards and say "That was a great belly-laugh we had at your play last night" and you think: "Well, they got fifteen per cent of it anyway – they got the jokes." It can be annoying but I don't worry about it because I am what I am and I do what I do and I have to live with that and I'm not able to do it any other way, nor do I want to.

JN: *Right. May I ask, Bernard – and it's not really your function to answer – but can you identify an overall thematic kind of unity to your work? Quite rightly, it's the function of critics, analysts and university professors to come up with that kind of analysis, but do you have any sense of an overview about your work? You've now had perhaps twenty plays produced professionally, if not more?*

BF: I think it's eighteen. No, it's less. Seventeen. I'm writing the eighteenth.

JN: *I'm sure there will be twenty!*

BF: Thanks very much!

JN: *But is there a theme, a common thread running through them?*

BF: I'm not certain. I think there's often an outsider somewhere in them, someone trying to make his/her way through the morass of pretension and one-up-man-ship. Perhaps some downtrodden people trying hard against the odds…and I suppose, usually, a fair few self-centred, egotists who are also trying to keep their insecure masks in place. Hard to know.

JN: *I'm going to quote you something I wrote about the 1985 premier of* Happy Birthday, Dear Alice. *I said in the programme note that "whilst your plays represent a relentless and often ruthless attack on the pretensions, cruelties and deceits of contemporary Irish society, their collective rage is tempered by a quiet, if impassioned defence of the dignity of those who have been marginalized by that society" and I go on to say that you manage to do the attack and the defence through the medium of uproarious comedy and that's what makes the plays so special. These tragic figures, marginalized by society, turn up pretty regularly in your plays*

BF: Yes they do – perhaps more so these days, these people become the victims, the overlooked, the neglected as the great Celtic Tiger prowls on. Sometimes, I try to do my best for them, give them a chance to assert themselves, often against all the odds.

JN: *Ben Barnes would say – we keep coming back to him because he has worked so often with you – that the plays have got darker as the years have gone by.*

BF: I think that's probably true. I don't think I would write a play like *All In Favour Said No!* these days – although it is a play that I hold great affection for, one that delivers all its comedy on cue…I think I can say that at this remove. More recent plays like *Kevin's Bed* and *The Last Apache Reunion* are more about people in terrible entrapments, facing serious consequences and I think this concern comes with age. I think they have got darker – and I don't think the play I'm writing now is exactly a knockabout farce either!

JN: *We talked earlier about the sense in which plays that speak to the audience through comedy can be somewhat underrated in relation to what is called straight drama. Whatever the truth of this, your work has been recognized at the highest level by both your fellow artists through your membership of Aosdána and by a serious of theatre awards from the theatre industry through the eighties and nineties. I want to ask you about the importance of that kind of recognition – does it help validate your work, does it keep the buzz going?*

BF: Oh yes. But its value lies in the encouragement – in the same way that you may remember, in your dark moments, something someone has said or some piece that someone has written. The negative things last a long time – you often feel that every bad review is printed on your forehead for all to see. So awards, recognition, kind words, Aosdána allow you to get up and start the damn thing all over again – I think that's their real value.

JN: *So you won't be turning them down?*

BF: I won't be turning them down at all.

JN: *In terms of recognition though, isn't it the audience who confer the ultimate recognition?*

BF: Always, always.

JN: *And speaking of audience – and I say this with great envy – your very large and loyal following is not just here in Dublin but throughout the country and indeed overseas.*

BF: And that's nice and it's nice that they seem to know the work so well.

JN: *Do you know them, your audience? I mean in the sense of the person sitting in Row F. Do you have a sense of who they are?*

BF: Well, I used to think that they were a kind of South County Dublin, middle-class type of people…

JN: *The very people you were writing about?*

BF: Exactly! – but then I'm always delighted to see very young people in, as well as our more senior citizens. But I do think that my core audience is somewhere in the middle. I think my groupies are all between thirty and fifty years of age somehow. I could be wrong.

JN: *Lastly, I want to turn to the future! I know your latest play is nearing completion and I'm not going to ask you about it, but I know that, hopefully, it will be premiered at the Abbey next year. I also know that you have bestowed an enormous legacy of work to the Irish theatre and that you'll continue to do so. I get the sense that you are at ease with these achievements but also, as a writer, you are still hungry and not going to go away. Can you tell us where you see the next ten years for Bernard Farrell?*

BF: I don't really know. I would not look beyond the next play – and hope that there may be another lurking somewhere after that. I suppose if I can get this one off the pad, up and running, I'd be perfectly happy. And I always like the early ones being revived and being revived well – I'm always chuffed that a play that was done many years ago, comes around again and does not show its age. That really makes me happy.

JN: *Bernard, thanks very much.*

BF: Jim, thank you very much.

Bernard Farrell is most associated with the Abbey Theatre, where eight of his seventeen plays have been premiered and where he currently serves on the Board of Directors. He has also written commissioned plays for

Dublin's Gate Theatre and Red Kettle Theatre in Waterford. His work includes one of the most performed Irish plays of the past twenty years, *I Do Not Like Thee, Doctor Fell*. His other plays include *The Last Apache Reunion*, *Happy Birthday Dear Alice*, *Forty-Four Sycamore* (Sunday Tribune Comedy of the Year Award), *Stella By Starlight* (Best Irish Production Award in 1996 Dublin Theatre Festival), and *Kevin's Bed* (Best Irish Play nomination in the 1998 ESB/Irish Times Theatre Awards). He has also written drama for both RTE and BBC television and his radio plays have represented Ireland at the Prix Italia. He is a recipient of The Rooney Prize For Irish Literature and is a member of Aosdána.

Jim Nolan is a founder member and former Artistic Director of Red Kettle Theatre Company. His plays for the company include *Moonshine, The Guernica Hotel* and *The Salvage Shop*. *Blackwater Angel* was presented at the Abbey Theatre in May, 2001. *Moonshine, The Salvage Shop* and *Blackwater Angel* are published by Gallery Press. Jim is a member of Aosdána and is currently Writer-in-Association at the Abbey Theatre.

Olwen Fouéré in Conversation with Melissa Sihra

MS: *Why did you choose a career in the theatre?*

OF: It sounds like a cliché, but it probably chose me. I was fairly clear that it was going to be the arts, though I was very interested in medicine. The most obvious place for me to go would have been into the visual arts, which is where I started. I would have probably ended up as a sculptor, or would have gone in the direction of performance art. I'm not sure, but my interest was very much in the non-verbal aspect of art. And of course I ended up in the theatre which, in this country was pretty text-based. But what fascinated me about the theatre was what was underneath the text; the whole thing about presence and performance and the whole non-verbal world, which is so extremely active within the theatre space.

The other reason was probably a product of my upbringing. I was brought up bilingual, my parents being Breton, and I was born in the West of Ireland. I experienced a kind of a linguistic identity crisis when I was quite young – three or four years old, where I found it difficult to decide between speaking French or speaking English. Speaking French was associated with the inside world, and speaking English was associated with the outside world, and I felt I had to make a choice, that I couldn't be in this "middle-place." And that middle-place, I think, is the place that is articulated by my choice to go into the theatre.

MS: *And how has that choice impacted on your life?*

OF: My choice to go into the theatre has created my own sense of personal identity. In other words, it is through the theatre that I feel I function in relation to the outside world, that I can make statements, that I can push the boundaries of communication, of understanding. I think it's been extremely difficult for me to find my place within the theatre, but that difficulty is what has helped me to articulate why I'm in it, for myself, and hopefully for an audience as well.

MS: *You speak about how you feel about the non-verbal aspects of theatre. How did you find being in a theatrical tradition that was and still is so language-based? Was that difficult for you as a performer? How did you feel you could express yourself apart from through language?*

OF: The answer to that quite simply, is presence, bodily presence. If you think of the mind and the body as simply being aspects of the same thing, or the spirit and the body as simply being aspects of the same thing, that's very much the performer's being, I think. It is not simply about being in a space, it's about multi-faceted being in a space. I'm fascinated by language, but I don't believe that theatre has got anything to do with the primacy of the text, so that did present certain difficulties. But I also saw the text as a framework really, within which you could operate all these other powers, if you like.

A turning-point in my career was doing my first physically-based piece of theatre – Stephen Berkoff's version of *The Fall of the House of Ussher* at the Project in 1978, which Peter Sheridan directed. We workshopped it for two months, using all kinds of physical work. It turned out to be an extraordinary piece, and really, Ireland's first "physical theatre" production. While I already had an understanding of what it was to be present on stage, it was only after this piece that I developed a sense of physical grounding, which I can only describe as a sort of umbilical connection to the ground – where you are very rooted, and are using the ground in a more complex way than just simply *standing* on it.

I think that there is a confusion about the idea of being physically present on-stage. It's not so much about "doing" as about finding your stillness so that movement can come out of that stillness. I think that a lot of directors are more concerned with broad-strokes to do with character, delivery and interpretation. However, is this necessarily the director's job? If I was a director I would probably feel that the actors should know all this already. To a certain extent it's the director's job, but the most important directorial task, I think, is to facilitate the creation of a world for the actor to inhabit, and to collectively define and refine the theatrical vocabulary that is being employed. There isn't a huge amount of experimentation or big development in theatrical form happening. I don't quite know why that is. It's something to do with what theatre means in this country.

MS: *How important is formal training in the theatre?*

OF: It's a difficult question, because I was so hungry for training when I started, but could only get full-time training abroad, and funding was a huge issue too. I was getting a lot of work at home, so that meant that I could learn through doing; but it was extremely hard and very, very painful at times because you're exposing yourself so much; you're learning through doing, and you're doing it in front of an audience and you're working with very experienced people. And sometimes it would take me weeks to discover something that I felt someone could have told me in a day. However, that said, I think the organic nature of my training and my search meant that I had to look very deep within myself to see why I was doing it and what were the areas that I wanted to pursue.

I do feel that very often training can block people – I've seen it happen. I'm so wary of it because I think you're dealing with such sensitive areas of a person's psyche, that a lot of blocks can be set-up. On the other hand that's not to say that I'm against training – it's a very, very difficult question. I think there are probably too many schools in Ireland for the size of the theatrical community. I think also, the whole theatre scene, what theatre is within this society, needs to be opened up in a big way before it can cope with the amount of people coming into the business, because it is a business at the moment. Maybe if it was more central to people's lives, it would be another thing.

MS: *You say that the theatre in Ireland is like a business at the moment. What are the implications of this?*

OF: I think there are fantastic energies there still, as there have always been within the Irish theatre. However, I think that it is commerce-driven right now. I think it's getting more like London. I think that the old "bums on seats" or "get a star thing" is more important than the quality of the work. I think it is too expensive, I don't think people should be paying any more to go to the theatre than they pay to go to the cinema. I would like to see something pretty radical happening. I go to see so many shows now where I think "why are we doing this?" – "So what?" kind of theatre. I think we need a war! We need a war for the value of theatre to really become apparent again.

MS: *Is it too comfortable?*

OF: Much too comfortable! I'm not against entertainment. I think entertainment is important, but even as a huge populist thing, the theatre isn't vibrating at the moment and we're somewhere in this place where only certain people can afford it. I don't have a problem with it being writer-driven – we have fantastic writers so why shouldn't it be writer-driven? It's not the writers' fault that it's become so text-based. And there's already a whole move away from text-based theatre. I went to see a show recently, and here was the primacy of physical theatre, but there really wasn't a reason for why it was happening, and I thought, "give us a good play!"

Theatre's place in society has become problematic. I still regard it as my church, if you like, and regard myself as a priest of that church. But it is too elitist at the moment, not in its practice, but in its position in society, partly because people have to pay so much to go. And if the theatre feels it has to spoon-feed the audience, then the audience starts to get used to being spoon-fed, and they start to want only that. Then management starts to lose their nerve, unless they are the type who *really* want to challenge. It depends what yardstick is used as a measurement of success. There are a number of managements in this city who measure success according to box-office. Once you start to measure success like that, you are playing to the lowest common denominator. That's the big problem for theatre.

MS: *Is it all negative – is theatre losing the power to affect us now?*

OF: I don't think it has lost the power, but it's not doing that at the moment because of the kind of stuff being produced and the level that it's going on with – where you get a fantastic play maybe, but produced really badly. I think the power is still there, lying in wait, particularly amongst the acting community. If I was to really pursue this question or problem, I would say that I would try to set up a core-group to work together within their own space, the way directors like Peter Brook, Grotowski and Lepage did. Just to see if you can really push things in some sort of way.

MS: *Who do you admire now, in the theatre?*

OF: I need to travel more, but I very much like Robert Lepage's work, especially his earlier work. I love the way he works with a community of actors, and they lead the process as much as he does. I have done a workshop with Anne Bogart at SITI. She's extraordinary – a great facilitator with a self-effacing way of working. Part of her system has evolved from modern dance principles, which I can relate to immediately. I am particularly interested in many aspects of Japanese theatre also.

MS: *In 1980 you co-founded Operating Theatre company with composer Roger Doyle. The kind of work that you have created together has pushed and broadened the boundaries of theatrical representation in this country. What were your motivations for setting up the company, and why do you think this kind of experimental theatre is important?*

OF: The artistic policy of the company was to create original work with music as a core element, combining my interest in performance generally with Roger's interest in music-theatre, and looking at how most of the music in theatre is just added-on at the end, as an after-thought, or used for background, underscoring or scene-changes. I think music is an incredibly powerful force in the theatrical environment, so the aim of the company was to use music as a core element to it.

MS: *You mentioned* Chair, *a piece you are working on at the moment. Two years ago the company produced a piece called* Angel/Babel. *Can you tell me about what you are trying to do with these pieces?*

OF: With *Angel/Babel* we wanted to work with music leading the text and allowing the text to move around the music. Roger Doyle had been working on *Babel* for a number of years. So I came in with another element which was "angel"; angel being the representation of Babel, or the idea of a being, some sort of energetic being, growing out of the criss-cross of information within the new inner-space of information technology. And that fascinated me: this whole new space that had been created, which is sort of no-where. So it became a semi-science-fiction kind of thing, but very much just working from my physical sense of this being, and all the music that Roger had been working on up until then. And the text just started to grow around these ideas. So it seemed like a slightly reverse way of working; allowing the musical ideas and the performing ideas to lead the process, as opposed to allowing the text to lead the process.

I think it's important that this sort of theatre happens. I wouldn't stand up on a box and say "this is what *has* to happen", but I feel if you work on that level, a lot of deeper things come through, and it probably gets a little bit closer to the Artaudian notion of some sort of shift without the intellect, in a way, being able to get involved, to filter or articulate it. So, for all the shows we've done, that's the one I'm proudest of in terms of what we wanted to do. There was a mixed critical response, but the audiences' response in general was quite powerful – people were a bit disturbed by it – send them home disturbed!

MS: *In* Angel/Babel *language seemed to be taken-apart, and then put back together in a new way. The textual signs were broken down and manipulated by the musical sounds and your bodily movements as you lay on stage as a kind of floating, cyber-body. The effect was quite haunting, with all the elements of performance (lighting being very important also) working together to create a sense of space that was like an infinite void, or vacuum. There was a sense of immense loneliness and humanity in the piece. It seemed to articulate the irony* *of modern communication – about how the more technologically sophisticated we are, the more alienated we become.*

OF: You are quite right to say that language was totally broken-down; in the script there were words broken-down and repeated, and that happened even more when I started working with the interactive elements of light and sound. The text was more like a map that came through a kind of creature which was trying to articulate itself through a flow of information that was sustaining and, in a sense, creating it. So we would start with certain words and begin to understand, and start to connect certain words. So it's still text-based, but I don't know if anybody could really make sense of it just by reading it off the page. What would you call that? Would you call that text or would you call that something else? A verbal map? It's difficult to define. The text never made a complete sentence, but "text" probably isn't the right word because text implies a kind of context, coherence or framework.

The new piece will have a lot of complete sentences and "found" text. It is still in its infancy. It's called *Chair* and it's based on Andy Warhol's lithographs of the electric chair, which I've always found very powerful. I've done mini-performances of this idea of the electric chair. We are looking now, very much at the subtext, the idea and its shadow, the idea of text being shadowed musically through a pitch to midi system, where the musical shadows take over from the speech and then the speech is completely obscured, but still being triggered, so you know that somewhere, behind this musical shadow, which is to the fore, there is somebody speaking, but all you hear is the shadow, and the shadow goes back behind and the speech comes forward. While we are working with the image of the electric chair, the piece is not really about execution; death-row will come into it, execution will come into it, but it's more about the image and the shadow of the image. Warhol was working constantly with the shadow of images, like Marilyn Monroe, the shadow of her fame, where her fame is her shadow, but it has come to the fore, and in a way, is *in front* of her. So it became about construct and organism; construct being the shadow, and organism being the original thing. The construct is created by other people. We're playing with the repetition of images; what happens when one image is repeated? And does that create another kind of shadow?

So we're going to have a central spine which will deal with this idea, and then around it will be woven the image of Prometheus, of him being bound, because he gave mankind a secret – secret knowledge for which he's being punished. This seems to me to be a very eloquent underpinning of the electric chair. The harnessing of natural energy, electricity, for execution, actually goes against the creator or humanity, if you like.

MS: *How do you respond to the critics?*

OF: I think the standard of criticism in this country isn't great. I do read them, because they don't bother me one way or another. I know a lot of people who won't read them, and I say "why not?", because you are allowing them too much power. If I feel pleased with my work, then negative criticism doesn't bother me.

MS: *How do you feel about critics abroad compared with Irish critics?*

OF: Not that much different. The only difference I find is that English critics tend to be more positive about Irish work that we don't really see very clearly here. For instance, Marina Carr's work, *By the Bog of Cats*, which got brilliantly reviewed by the English critics, got mixed reviews here. So it's very interesting. And I think that's because of two things. One is a negative one, which is that Irish theatre is "fashionable", and the second, and positive aspect is that it's taken out of its context. We're so used to very rich work happening here that we're initially not all that impressed by it. But when it's removed from its own context, we suddenly see that it's very powerful writing, compared to some of the other stuff that's happening in, say, London. I can't speak for American critics, but British critics do not seem to have any impact on what's happening. The only person in Ireland whom I felt had any kind of impact in that way, was Fintan O'Toole, because he always came from a very informed basis. I always read him, and have often disagreed with him, but because he has such a wide-reaching interest in other things, and everything seems connected, I feel that there is a follow-through in some sort of way, in how he views theatre. And I don't see that anywhere else, and I think it should be there, whether it be just looking at something from a different point of view, or asking questions from a different angle. I don't think it's about reading the paper to see whether you want to go to a show or not. That's a review, it's not a critique to just say "you'll enjoy this!" or "don't miss it!"

MS: *You have played the lead role in two of Marina Carr's plays, Mai in* The Mai *and Hester Swane in* By the Bog of Cats. *Both roles were written for you. Tell me about your experiences working on these plays, and in her early work* Ullaloo.

OF: With *Ullaloo*, which was produced at the Peacock in 1990, Marina was still experimenting very much with form, and a lot of her influences were more to the fore than her own voice at that point. There was still something extraordinary going on, but there was a layer that needed peeling back. This was a strange time for me as I had had a baby who had died in the womb. I remember carrying the baby for the first two weeks of rehearsals, but it is still a very cloudy time. Working during a time of personal tragedy, and trying to perform, is very difficult. It's very difficult unless you're actually working in a piece which allows that to be channelled out. But if I go to the theatre and see an actor working out their own stuff as opposed to working *with* their own stuff ... well, they are two *very* different things. I hope it hasn't happened to me.

When I was given the script of *The Mai* I had very mixed feelings about it. I thought – brilliant writing – because Marina is a wonderful writer, but I wasn't sure about the character particularly. I couldn't stand her – The Mai! She drove me mad, and I thought, "who would want to play a woman like that?" I was on Robert's side! And it was that very contradiction, and the fact that Marina had written it with me in mind, *and* that she was such a contrary character to the kinds of characters that I would normally expect to be asked to play, that made me intrigued enough to decide to do it. And it was an absolutely fascinating journey.

Whatever connection Marina and I may have, either as people, or as artists, when I mix with her work, something else happens. And this has created something else, alchemical. *The Mai* was an extraordinary journey. What fascinated me was that there was no morality involved in the play, of any kind. It was about going deep into some primal kind of energy and need. The Mai, from this sort of housewife, teacher character, became this "seeker after" everything that was exotic and unattainable. She had a belief in the transcendental nature of sexuality. I think the sexual relationship between her and Robert was probably extraordinary. And this connection that the Mai has made with this desperately errant husband is the thing that brings out the artist in her, and brings out the death-wish. All of this fantastically creative woman's energies have been so narrow all her life, and this is the portal to the otherworld – through this man. I've always found something incredibly powerful about that through-line, which carried me through that play, in a way that I didn't expect at all. I found it very releasing to be in as well. With Hester it was a different story. I had a totally immediate connection with that character. I think that's the best role I've ever been given to play, in terms of me as an actor, rather than as a creator of the work. As an actor, that's been my best one.

MS: *Was that because Hester is an outsider, also straddling two worlds, the inside and the outside?*

OF: Yes, very much so. It was something that I could relate right back to my childhood, even down to the physical landscape of where we were, the bogs. For me, that was very much the West of Ireland, where I was brought up. The connection with her need to stay there. It articulated a lot of things for me, in a way.

MS: *Of being in a dual world?*

OF: A dual world, yes. And the bleak landscape. I've always loved a vast stretch of bog.

MS: *How involved was Marina in your creation of the roles?*

OF: Very much, yes. I don't think I would have discovered what I discovered in *The Mai* without her being around. She made one very key comment which was probably then how Hester Swane was later created. During the rehearsals for *The Mai*, when we were just starting to run it, Marina said; "whatever she is, a teacher, or whatever, she's more of a tinker." And that immediately unleashed the darker side of her, the more primal passions. That was a real trigger, and made me connect with all the things I've been talking about in relation to *The Mai*, where she's kind of, an artist.

With *By the Bog of Cats* it was fantastic – short rehearsals – four weeks and we just worked very hard, very quickly. In week three Marina and I went out together and talked through everything and she gave me a couple of key things – very simple – key things which were not really to do with the character or anything like that, just about rhythms, and taking time. Working within a company as opposed to working on my own, I tend to be quite resistant to just demanding space around me, but with Hester Swane, Marina planted it in me that this was Hester's world – so *take it*, and don't let anyone else intrude on it, in a way. And that was a thing that was planted mentally, and was actually very good. Marina is invaluable to have around at rehearsals. She is also probably the only writer who sees rehearsals as a voyage of discovery for herself, as much as anything – that fantastic thing of being delightedly surprised at what comes out. She sees what she has given as being something to come to life through performance. I have worked with some writers who keep it within the play they have written, all the time. She loves when it explodes *out* of there.

MS: *It can be precarious with, essentially, three voices – the director, the playwright and the performer, all informing the process.*

OF: Very much so. I'm all for the presence of the writer in the rehearsal room – as much as possible, and I feel the best directors are there as facilitators to that exchange between the writer and the performer. Tom Murphy for instance, is very, very precise about aspects of rhythm, language and character. Some people can find that constricting, but I love being in that sort of situation where you have to push against something that's clearly very strong. He's an extraordinary person and I've always had a very productive working relationship with him. Patrick Mason is one director who has a great ability to create the space for that kind of exchange between the performer and the playwright. He very gently guided both Marina and me through our own journeys during *By the Bog of Cats*.

MS: *Do you think that women are under-represented in the theatre in this country? Who are the female voices in Irish theatre?*

OF: Well, we only really have one female playwright in this country, one *really* significant female voice – there are others coming through obviously, but not yet into the mainstream. And I've only worked with one or two female directors. It's something that I don't think about that often and maybe I should; I've only worked with one or two female directors in my entire twenty-something years – they've all been male! And I've really started to think about that recently, because it's not a question that bothers me in any kind of way, but I saw something emerge – I thought, isn't it interesting, that when I did Marina's plays I felt an extraordinary kind of connection and release – and was that connected to gender, or not, who knows? As for being under-represented – I don't feel that there's anything *stopping* women from coming through. If anything, it's probably the opposite – we're almost on the verge of positive discrimination – which I don't agree with anyway. But there aren't that many women out there – that's for sure. But I don't think it's a question of representation necessarily, it's just that they aren't coming through.

MS: *Why aren't more women in Ireland writing and directing for the theatre?*

OF: I'm glad you brought this up, because I always refrain from thinking that these things are gender specific, but I think that they probably are – and there is a need for something to change. I don't quite know why it is. Is there something, do you think, in that whole gender thing which is about the woman being able to keep things fluid, and that things don't have to become fixed? And therefore, the whole kind of massive operation of bringing a show in is a more complex one for a woman, or whatever, if you really take on *all* the aspects that are there, as opposed to saying "I'm going to get this show up?" So, maybe it has something to do with that need to take on all the aspects of what you want to be dealing with – there's this necessity to keep things fluid, and that can be very disastrous within the theatre environment, because so many people have to be brought along in the ship at the same time. I'm very interested in directing, but that aspect of it does scare me, and it's possibly significant, that with my own work, I always have to have a third person, like a co-director or co-writer, because I don't trust my own ability to bring it in.

MS: *Would you say that this tendency indicates an inherent of lack in confidence in women?*

OF: I suppose it *is* a lack of confidence ultimately. Even with me, it's not that I lack confidence, but I lack organizational confidence.

MS: *Have you ever been terribly interested in getting into film and television, or do you resist that?*

OF: Resisted, or it's resisted me, I'm not sure which way around it is. But it's never something I've actively pursued, no. The kind of fame and recognition that comes with film and television is of no real value to me, other than in terms of money! In film I miss the sense of being able to map any kind of path through it. You've no control over the arc, so your artistic involvement is entirely to do with the moment of shooting. The *moment* is the entire context – nothing else.

MS: *How important do you think a grounding in or knowledge of theatre history is to practitioners? Have you systematically studied the history of theatre and its traditions?*

OF: Not at all, and I would very much like to. I've tended just to pick up things as I get interested. I would have said that I didn't think it was that important, but I think it *is* important now because, I don't think there's enough out there at the moment for people to actually realize just how radically differently you can look at what theatre is, and what it's about. When I started I wasn't particularly aware either, but because I worked with the Stanislavsky system at the Focus Theatre, it was very much connected to personal belief. Then working with the Sheridan brothers at the Project Arts Centre, it evolved very much around social, political kinds of issues. It was also very much based on personal belief, and giving voice to that belief. There's an awful lot to discover out there, in the theatre of the world. It is important for us all to start realizing *where* it can be and where it has come from.

Olwen Fouéré was born in West Galway of Breton parents. Initially orientated towards the visual arts, she became an actor twenty-five years ago and has been based mainly in Ireland. She has performed and toured internationally with many theatre companies in Ireland and the UK including the Abbey, the Gate, The Royal National Theatre, the Royal Shakespeare Company and the English Stage Company. Highlights include creating the title role in Steven Berkoff's production of Wilde's *Salomé* at the Gate and her role as Hester Swane in Marina Carr's *By the Bog of Cats*. She has created and performed her own work in *Angel/Babel* and *Chair* with Operating Theatre, a music-based theatre company which she co-founded with composer Roger Doyle in 1980. She has also performed several pieces by artist James Coleman which continue to be exhibited internationally.

Melissa Sihra is currently researching the plays of Marina Carr for a Ph.D at Trinity College. She lectures in Modern Irish Drama at the National University of Ireland, Maynooth, and is a Script Reader for the Abbey Theatre. She has given talks at the University of California, Berkeley, and the University of Pittsburgh and is a contributor to the forthcoming *Oxford Encyclopedia of Theatre and Performance*. In 2001 she worked as Dramaturg on three productions of Carr's plays in the United States: *Portia Coughlan* for the Pittsburgh Irish and Classical Theatre Company, the US premiere of *By the Bog of Cats* for Irish Repertory of Chicago and *By the Bog of Cats* for San José Repertory Theatre.

Ben Hennessy, Pat Kiernan and Ger FitzGibbon
in Conversation

PK: *Red Kettle's most recent production,* The Queen and the Peacock *by Loughlin Deegan, is still out on the road at the moment but what's happening next for the company?*

BH: Our next play is a new play by Tony Guerin. How do you describe Tony Guerin? He's a sixty-two-year-old, ex-Kerry footballer, ex-Garda, who began writing later in life. He's from Listowel and *Hummin'* is the name of the play. We get nearly a hundred unsolicited scripts every year [but] we're in the middle of a three year cycle of work with three-year funding with the Arts Council so I pretty much had a programme in place. I wrote back a positive letter about this script and what I liked about it but that really I didn't have a place for it in the programme. And so I got a letter in return asking could he meet me. He had a play called *Cuckoo Blue* that was put on down in Listowel by the Lartigue Players and played to great success. Anyway, we met. He told me story after story after story – he has such a rich imagination – and he got up and acted stuff out and swore he knew all the characters that he was telling me about. And I just felt at the end of it that here was a man who deserved a go, that had so many stories to tell. Part of the three-year programme had in it a revival of something from the Irish canon – something like a John B. Keane – so we dropped that one in favour of Tony's. We're going into rehearsal in March and I'm going to have a go at directing it.

PK: *So what has happened to the play from the time he submitted it to now, and what will happen between now and the start of rehearsals?*

BH: We have a bunch of readers and one of them came back with a recommendation that I read this one. That's rare enough in itself. So I read it and I liked it a lot. So when we did decided to do it I met him a couple of times more and we talked about the play [and]

I spoke to him about possible changes that I thought might help the dramatic pace of it really. We're at that stage and I think that will go on until quite close to rehearsals.

PK: *And would it just be you? It will just be the two of you before it's cast and actors come into rehearsal?*

BH: Perhaps. There are couple of people that read plays for me and there's a couple on our board of directors: Jim Daly – who's our chairman and is also our lighting designer – and Brian Doherty who's an actor. They're very involved in the actual business of the plays so generally they would be reading anything we were going to do.

GF: *It's very different from the way you work in Corcadorca, Pat, where you workshop scripts and go through different development processes.*

PK: Yeah, but I think that we may have rushed it before. Sometimes we would set the date of production and book ourselves into the theatre and work back from there. For the first time now with Eamonn Sweeney's play [*Lord MacDonald*] we actually said "No, it's not ready," even though we had the theatre booked.

BH: I think that's probably a healthy thing. *The Queen and the Peacock* went through about eight drafts. Jim Nolan was Artistic Director before me and as director he and Loughlin did those drafts. One of the big concerns I have in relation to our new writing is just the physical workload. We don't have a dedicated literary manager and it is something I intend to address in the next three year programme – we don't have the money to employ someone at present – to fulfil that in a real way and give a decent level of response to writers so every play that we read, we send a critical response whether we're doing it or not. I have about five people reading plays and they give me back synopses, critiques and recommendations but the ones they recommend that I read are still sitting on my desk. There's a pile of them, I have at least fifteen now that I have to get to once *The Queen and the Peacock* is doing its own thing. Some of those scripts we would have got nine months ago and the writer would only now be getting a response. That's something the company needs to address.

PK: *There's a year and a bit now left of your three year funding. Was a lot of the programming done by Jim for these three years before you stepped in?*

BH: We knew a good few months before Jim left that I was going to take over, so we did it together. *The Queen and the Peacock* and the *Kings of the Kilburn Highroad* were plays Jim would have initiated. On occasion, when the Board's working really well, we get to talk about plays as distinct from money. They're rare enough but they remind us what it's all about. When *Kings* came along, Jim offered us five scripts and said "We're going to do one of these" and looked for feedback. While Jim, as Artistic Director, selected five that he offered to us, there was a Board consensus or at least a Board input into the making of decisions.

PK: *So the emphasis would be primarily on new writing?*

BH: That came about perhaps because Jim is a writer himself. In our early years we did a lot of plays from the world repertoire – plays like *Equus* and *Bent* – and Irish plays like *Translations* and *Talbot's Box* and *Observe the Sons of Ulster Marching Towards the Somme*. Since 1991 the emphasis has been pretty squarely on new plays. In fact we have produced nineteen new plays in ten years.

GF: *When did the company actually start?*

BH: In 1985 we formed Red Kettle. We were the Waterford Arts For All Project theatre company before that, started around 1979. 1981 was our first production. It was called *When Elephants Walk on the Moon*.

PK: *Were they touring to schools?*

BH: That was a children's play. Every summer we put on plays in every housing estate green in Waterford and every festival that came along in the summer. And then we started to bring small plays into pubs. We did Tom Murphy's *On the Outside* [and] we toured every pub in Waterford. And in 1985 – four years later – we went into a theatre with Jim's play *The Gods are Angry, Miss Kerr*. This was our first play. And the people we were bringing the plays to, now came with us. The play was set in Waterford and about Waterford people and that obviously played a role in bringing people in. I think it's a bit of a cliché about bringing theatre out to the masses but, while we hadn't a plan, it did work that people who had seen the plays in pubs came to see them in the theatre.

GF: *In Corcadorca you've been going the opposite way, Pat, moving out from theatres and playing in public spaces.*

PK: That would be the two strands of our thing – the new writing and the site-specific work. For those reasons too, of audience development. A first time goer might find it easier to go down to FitzGerald's Park [where Corcadorca played *A Midsummer Night's Dream*] or out to Sir Henry's night-club [where they played *A Clockwork Orange*] because there's still that chocolate-box image that can inhibit a first-time theatre-goer.

BH: Absolutely. At the start we played three nights in the Theatre Royal – a 600 seater venue – and we gradually move on to play a week in that venue or three weeks in Garter Lane which seats 180. We've been there ten years now and we've reached a plateau of audience numbers but there's definitely scope for bringing more people in. There's a new venue in Waterford which might help us – a 300 seater, The Forum. The Theatre Royal is a people's theatre. Everyone in Waterford has performed there. A large proportion of the population would still see Garter Lane as "arty" and even the type of play we do there – the new work – would be seen as "not for them," whereas if we put something on at the Theatre Royal nobody has those inhibitions about going in there.

PK: *Going down to Garter Lane in the early nineties I was struck by the fact that it did seem as if it was everyone and anyone was going to see the shows. But the last time, with Conal Creedon's play, it did seem like an older or more settled audience. Perhaps that was just opening night?*

BH: That could be. That was in the Forum, the newer place.

GF: *Do you think you keep your own faithful audience all the time?*

BH: Well, no, as we've found to our costs. *Catalpa*, Donal O'Kelly's one-man-show, garnered Red Kettle its best reviews ever and played to the smallest houses we've ever had. It's gone all around the world, and went to Edinburgh and won Fringe Firsts. We brought it right around some small venues and, maybe because it was a one-man-show, people just didn't come out to see it. Even in Waterford we would play the likes of *Catalpa* for two weeks, whereas *The Crucible* you would run for three weeks. So in some ways you could say they're not sticking with us.

PK: Catalpa *would probably be my favourite Red Kettle show, regardless of the critics or the audiences. It was stimulating new work, as opposed to, say, a Bernard Farrell.*

BH: I loved *Catalpa*. It had a great narrative to it, it told a great story in a way that was very theatrical and very physical. The invention that the actor, Donal, brought to telling the story, but also the imaginative leap the audience were required to make to go with it was exciting. That would definitely be a direction that I would like over the next few years to develop a bit more.

PK: *When I see the kids' shows I see that. And at the same time the first show you've directed as Artistic Director was basically naturalism. And the next show, Tony's, what style is that?*

BH: Tony's is quite traditional. It does have physical possibilities but it's not a *Catalpa* in style. The first show I did when I was

Artistic Director was Liam Meagher's play *All in the Head* and that was great in terms of opportunities: it was huge, massive, physical theatre with a huge cast and all that. In some ways the children's work, while it's an obvious outlet for the children, I also find it a good creative challenge. It's an opportunity to do stuff you couldn't dream of doing using a professional cast.

PK: *But why? I don't get that.*

BH: Well for one, you'd have a cast of fifty. You just couldn't afford to do that. Now with *All in the Head* I managed to do it with a cast of thirty. Of that thirty, four were full-time professional actors, five were making a break-through, semi-professional, and the rest were children or youth drama people. And that break-up of the cast did allow us to do that. Little Red Kettle is the children's wing. Since that first one in 1981 we've always had a children's aspect to Red Kettle's work. We now write stuff for children to perform. I hear what you're saying Pat, and it's something I'd like to do more of. The play after Tony Guerin's play is a two-hander with a walk-on at the end – actually a kind of climb-out-of-a-bag part. It's a new Brian Foster play called *Momma, Jim and Elvis*. When I read it I got a real buzz off it. It's like that story of *Psycho* – very dark, very black humour, set in the basement of a motel.

GF: *You're giving the game away now.*

BH: It's hugely theatrical and ... . I won't give the game away but there is some puppetry required: the actor is required to play numerous parts even though they're all in his head and there is scope for a very good physical way of telling the story. It's demanded from the script that it be visual and physical so it's one that I'm looking forward to a lot and one that would be more natural that I would direct – as opposed to *Hummin'*. One of the reasons I'm doing *Hummin'* – maybe it's not a good reason – is because of the relationship I've built up with Tony.

PK: *That's a very good reason.*

BH: I'm still learning the trade, being a director, but it's something that I make no apologies for. I'm Artistic Director of Red Kettle and as Artistic Director I have to stand over the work that we do, but I also have to be courageous enough to make the mistakes. I don't think I can be Artistic Director of a company like Red Kettle and not direct. It's one of the reasons I was excited when I got the job – the opportunity to go and direct.

PK: *I was very excited when you got the job, knowing you as a visual artist. I suppose that for us, with the site-specific work, they are established texts. I find* *that allows an awful lot more time and thought to go into the actual visual presentation of the production. Whereas, when you're developing a play or working with a playwright closely over a long period of time, it becomes all about the play and the word. If you have a text that's a given you're just saying: "What can we do with this?"*

BH: If you have a script that's already fully refined perhaps that does allow you more freedom to think about other stuff. In developing new work – I was going to say new writing there and I stopped – the theatre that I'm interested in has to be about more than just writing. One of the strengths of Tony's plays is his characters – they're very well drawn, very funny – but there are physical possibilities in the plays. And in some of the dialogue I've been having with Tony, they're the things that I'm trying to get him to develop a bit more.

Likewise with Brian Foster's play, what excites me is that there are those physical possibilities in his way of telling the story. The guy eventually ends up with the skull of his father and the skull of a dead Japanese tourist that he killed. He takes on the persona of his father through the skull and the persona of a Japanese girl through her skull. That kind of theatricality is something that really attracted me. He told me he showed the play to lots of other people and was told that it was too difficult for an actor to do. He rewrote it so that the theatrical puppetry was taken away and he had actors playing the skulls. That seriously compromised what I had read originally and so he has put those things back in, and he's been happy to do that insofar as that's what he wrote. So in terms of answering your question, here's a new piece that we would influence in a positive way towards physicalizing it, making it theatrical as a way of telling a story.

PK: *When I was in London, there was a series of interviews with theatre practitioners, and this guy was saying that all the productions of new plays are so dull and so traditional. It was a director was saying this and someone said back to him "Actually, that's your fault, y'know." It's something that interests me.*

BH: [Yet] your production of *Disco Pigs* was one of the great productions over the last few years. Directors that I would like, like Conal Morrison, the type of plays I'd ask them to do are the type of plays I'd like to do myself. [Laughs] For instance, I've been interested in working with Enda for a long time and I've approached him with a view to commissioning new work. You would obviously be a natural person to ask to direct it but, selfish me here, [that's] the type of play I'd want to do myself. I have plans to do a *King Lear*, a really physical Irish version, hopefully with

Mick Lally who has expressed an interest. So here am I – a relatively inexperienced director – taking on one of the great plays.

GF: *The Glenroe version?*

BH: [Laughs] Certainly not. I was thinking of the likes of Brendan Conroy playing the Fool and John Hewitt playing Gloucester and being a really physical, raw, Irish kind of thing, and the scope for huge drama, huge theatricality in a production like that. I know I was talking to you, Pat, for years about doing *Ridley Walker* [by Russel Hoban]. *Ridley Walker* is a play that I had in this three-year plan and we had to scupper it because of our economic situation. Red Kettle got a lot of money in this three-year plan and had a massively ambitious programme. Our programme came in at £1,100,000. We got £900,000 and everyone was saying "fantastic," but we were £200,000 down on what we wanted to do. It was great to have that security going from one year to the next but, nonetheless, it did catch up on us. We're doing two new plays next year, one with a cast of four and one with a cast of three, and that's all we can afford to do.

PK: *You had an incredibly busy year the first year.*

BH: Yeah. We did a lot of new stuff. One of those was Loughlin's play, *The Queen and the Peacock*. We did that originally in 1999. We had modest hopes for it, based on the subject matter and the minority interest. In some ways the production and the final script Loughlin came up with transcended those things and made for a very accessible and very good, stimulating theatre that audiences have responded to.

PK: *You have said that you wanted to do a popular play – a John B. Keane or something – and that you had modest hopes for* The Queen and the Peacock *because of its minority interest. So what is a successful production for you? Is it the number of people who see it?*

BH: Well, I'm having this conversation with the Arts Council as well, about quantitative analysis and qualitative analysis of your work. And again I would use *Catalpa* as an example. *Catalpa* I would consider artistically right up there as one of the best things we've ever done. Historically that has always been the measure. We lose money hand over fist because we have chosen to do that type of work over the years. We've tried not to be foolish about it either: there's no point in doing plays that nobody wants to see. [But] how do you measure success? *Catalpa* was definitely a success. *The Queen and the Peacock* is a success: whether it's a success box-office-wise or not, is a different question.

PK: *But you do think that from time to time you'll do one that is going to be popular, regardless of its quality?*

BH: It wasn't so much to do with box office, it was more to do with serving the Waterford audience. That's something that has been central to us from the beginning. That's a funny balance to get. We'd do a play like *Bent* next to *Translations*. They're two fantastic plays and as it happened both of them did very well at the box office but one of them, you could see, might attract a different type of audience from the other. We've done three Bernard Farrell plays: commissioned him to do two. *Happy Birthday Dear Alice* is probably our most successful play in terms of box office – it's a new play that has popular appeal. It's been part of a vision of ourselves within a community.

We started as a kind of company made up of actors, directors, designers, and moved to a company that is essentially a production company. But within all of that we've grown with the Waterford audience and the community we're from. Like we didn't go off and do what we wanted to do. There are some plays that, as Artistic Director or as a writer, Jim would have liked more than others. Likewise with myself.

PK: *Would there ever be a play that you wouldn't actually like, that you've done yourselves?*

BH: There're plays that in retrospect I'm sorry we did. Absolutely.

PK: *But say there's a play that commercially does really, really well. Would you say "That's important for us to do but I mightn't necessarily like it?"*

BH: Yes, but as a company providing theatre for Waterford, we've tried over the years to have a kind of balance in the programme: to have a play like *Chickadee* [by Tom Mac Intyre] next to a play by Bernard Farrell. I was hoping to commission Bernard Farrell and Enda in the same year. A new Bernard Farrell play is always exciting; Alice in *Happy Birthday Dear Alice* is a great creation. While it's not the kind of theatre that would excite me as a theatre worker, it's offering a variety of different types of work. And it has been central to our policy over the years.

PK: *This is something I'm curious about as well because we're in a similar situation. I know it's offering a choice, but is there any consistency there?*

BH: I would love the people who go and see *Happy Birthday Dear Alice* to go in and see *Catalpa* and, in some ways, a way of bringing them into that kind of play is to bring them into the Bernard Farrell play. There are also theatre production values that you want people to see. We work hard at having good production values. When someone goes to see *Happy Birthday Dear Alice*, they're going to have a good night out at the theatre and that might attract them to come back and see the next Red Kettle production, even if it be a play called *Choke My Heart* by Celia McBride – a seriously warped vision but a fantastic piece of theatre that explored issues that were not going to make it a popular night out.

GF: *How do you deal with that in Corcadorca, Pat? Reconciling the artistic policy and company identity with the need to reach and retain an audience? Is that an issue?*

PK: It is I think. In terms of the site-specific work, I'm very happy that – having the text ready, and the site – they're overtly theatrical I think. In trying to develop new writing, Eamonn [Sweeney] is the first commission outside of Enda. There were three or four plays we did with [Enda] and he was an overtly theatrical writer anyway. So I suppose that it is commissioning writers that will fit in with the type of work we want to do. Eamonn's play is very demanding already in terms of its staging. The other strand is the Playwright's Award, which is like getting the hundred unsolicited scripts in. The majority of them are formulaic and I suppose [it's] just trying to find plays that allow us to be consistent in our presentation, really ...

GF: *But there have been big contrasts in your work.* Disco Pigs *was very contained: it's a theatre piece, two actors, two characters. And then* The Passion *took over half of Cork city with a cast of thousands.*

PK: I think the consistency would be that both plays would be very much an experience. There isn't a fourth wall there for starters. For *Disco Pigs* they enter through the audience. In terms of sound, it's coming from behind you as well as in front of you. Any production is attempting to create a whole experience, whether it's in a theatre or a site other than a theatre.

BH: *How did you find the Playwright's Award one that you did in the Opera House,* The Banshee Makers?

PK: That was a weird one. It actually came down to two plays. One was a completely off-the-wall play called *Noose* and the other was *The Banshee Makers* [by Ger Bourke]. We spent a lot of time debating – I wanted to do the other one – and the panel of readers and the Board were saying this might be an interesting challenge for the company to do. And I suppose I wasn't very comfortable with that, doing that type of work. Now, it was great time for the writer and he's a great writer, but I don't think there was enough time in developing the play. We had set the date: we were going into the theatre in August, after selecting the play in March and doing a quick workshop for a week. It just wasn't enough time. With Eamonn Sweeney's play it is evolving: more time, to allow more theatricality in the production and the staging. That's why I want six actors, and musicians, for two weeks, with the writer, away ahead of the actual production time so that it allows both Eamonn and me to develop it as a piece of theatre as opposed to a play.

BH: It's certainly something that's been occupying my mind. I was listening to Malcolm Hamilton recently in relation to Blue Raincoats saying "We do what we like to do and people come to see it if they want to" and it was really pure. He spoke as an artist, in the way that you're speaking as a director. Blue Raincoats is a company of actors and directors and writers and they *are* artists. Red Kettle aren't artists as such: we employ artists, as most companies do – a director and actors and a designer. So it moves a little bit from what *you* want to do. [To] programme the stuff that I want to do because it's creatively exciting for me and therefore I would expect that it would be creatively exciting for an audience, that's very valid. But also there are plays that I know that Waterford people would like but that would not provide the same creative buzz for me. And therefore should I *not* do them? I think we have evolved into a different kind of thing. Whether that's good or not, it's who we are.

PK: *But ultimately, you certainly will be picking the directors – or in a lot of cases you will be the director – so you can influence the type of designer as well.*

BH: As a painter, you start from scratch and you finish up with a thing that you're in charge of. And while the theatre is a very collaborative thing, sometimes I feel that as a designer you design something and someone else gets to colour it in. I would like to have a go. A play I might pick for visual or physical reasons I'm obviously going to want to have an influence on the physical and visual look of it.

PK: *Have many practitioners started out with you, like the ones, say, coming out of the Granary [U.C.C. Theatre Cork] now? Do you see it as important to offer accessibility to up and coming practitioners in Waterford?*

BH: Most people who choose to make a living out of it have to go outside. 98% of actors live in Dublin now and likewise with directors. You can occasionally offer a taste of it but you can never really provide a living or even a serious, sustained period of time where they're working at it. There are some like Joe Meagher, who has acted in Corcadorca shows and in Red Kettle shows, he still lives in Waterford. But essentially there is no way Joe can make a living as an actor in Waterford. He'll have to go where the work is.

GF: *Some regional companies complain bitterly about actors based in Dublin not wanting to move out, even for a decent contract, because the actors, or their agents, are dreaming of a nice film role or an ad.*

BH: I'd say it's true. Red Kettle would have a very good reputation nationally among actors. However, I've found in recent years that the plays we're doing, unless they're getting a Dublin run, they're certainly not as attractive.

PK: *Speaking about Dublin, what do you think about Abbey and its role?*

BH: I thought that last year's programme in the Abbey was brilliant: *Barbaric Comedies* and *Translations* and new stuff going on in the Peacock. We've tried to offer a variety of programme. I thought that Ben Barnes did that last year: seriously adventurous stuff, his production of *Translations*, the quality of new writing [like] *Eden* [by Eugene O'Brien]. Sure, they have the budgets to do it [but] I was impressed I have to say.

I would love to see them out and around more. The Abbey's production of *The Great Hunger* [by Tom Mac Intyre], with Tom Hickey, directed by Patrick Mason, came to the Theatre Royal in Waterford and I remember going in to see it a couple of times. I was in College at the time and going to see a play twice was unheard of but I just thought it was really fantastic, a great example of physical theatre. It was great to see that calibre of play being brought out. It gave real sense to the words "The National Theatre." It was great to see *Eden* out on the road, but *Eden* is easy. It's obviously a budgetary thing but I do think it would be a great thing to see the National Theatre going ...

PK: *Going national?*

BH: [Laughs] Going national, yeah. Going national with the stuff from the *main* stage. The Peacock is great but to take that stuff on the road – while it's great – it's a cheap option. But it would be fantastic to see *The Gigli Concert* down in Waterford. A few years ago I saw a production of *The Gigli Concert* in Waterford. It wasn't a great production and Waterford audiences saw that play. So their first experience of Tom Murphy would have been through a poor version of *The Gigli Concert*. That colours their view of Tom Murphy. In Red Kettle we had actors and designers and directors, and we came to a play that we couldn't get good enough in our own heads with the company that we had, so we chose to hire in a professional actor from out of town. That was a turning point. It wasn't for us just to be doing the play, it was to render the play as well as we could for a Waterford audience. That made the shift from us doing our thing to bringing this theatre to Waterford.

GF: *Just to wrap up, is there any particularly exciting piece of theatre you were involved with yourself or encountered that had an effect on your work?*

PK: For me, *Carmen Funèbre*, performed by that Polish company.

BH: Definitely. We saw them in Edinburgh and on the back of it we invited them to Waterford.

GF: *I found the use of darkness and public space and sound and fire was very impressive. What struck you about it?*

PK: And I suppose it was an influence as well. It was just pure theatre. I loved seeing the open mechanisms of it. The audience was such an important part of it. They were active in it. It was incredibly clear. The language was irrelevant.

BH: One of the best story-telling things I ever saw – I was involved in it myself – was Siamsa Tíre's *Clann Lir*, a production of the story of the children of Lir, told through dance and singing – the singing was in Irish – really visual theatre, really strong visual and physical stuff. Essentially it was a dance piece. You could say *Carmen Funèbre* was choreography with its stilt-walking and all the rest. I'm just interested when you say it's a complete theatre piece, yet it essentially doesn't use the spoken word.

PK: I wouldn't even have noticed that now, looking back on it. For us I think the most important piece would be *Clockwork Orange* in Sir Henry's [Night Club]. It was incredibly exciting in terms of the audience, and it was a different experience again.

GF: *Was the audience brought in by* Clockwork Orange *or because it was in Sir Henry's?*

PK: It was a combination I would say.

GF: *Did* Carmen Funèbre *influence your promenade production of* Phaedra's Love *[by Sarah Kane] where you used an old building and a street?*

PK: Well yeah, in terms of what it was possible to do outside of a theatre. Rough and ready. Because it was rough and ready, not comfortable. So you can work outdoors. And actually that was the production directly after it as well, which had fire in it. I nicked loads of ideas off them.

GF: *Did you have low points – moments that almost made you give up?*

PK: The ones that don't work well are the ones you learn from. There was one year where we just devised shows. They were terrible actually. We had four actors on schemes and it was going into the rehearsal room, booking the Triskel [Arts Centre] for a certain date and saying: "We'll all do it together. We'll all write and we'll all direct." It became the lowest common denominator in everything. After that, when we approached a text – *Greek* by Stephen Berkoff – it was liberating. We could play around with that.

BH: Creativity is not really a democratic business. The nature of putting a play on is close to dictatorship. I suppose the great directors are the ones that have the power to give the power away, to give people around them their head.

GF: *And what would make the theatre scene or your working life better?*

BH: I think the biggest thing in Ireland at the moment is the poor wages – primarily for actors. It's changing a bit. I was talking to two actors recently, both of them in work a good bit, both of them married recently, and for them to get a mortgage was impossible. No fixed employment, no security once you're finished your job, and the rates of pay don't really compensate. Even well-known actors are poorly paid. So if I was Santa Claus ...

PK: Something for us that would be a huge help in Cork is a venue that's dedicated to drama. There are lots of venues but none of them has a policy really. You have the Triskel, but that's film so many nights a week; you have the Granary, but that's largely student drama; the CAT Club is largely amateur; and then you have the Opera House and the Everyman, which take in everything and anything – a hypnotist one week, an amateur drama company the next week and the Abbey the week after that. There's no consistency.

GF: *So decent wages and a devoted three hundred seat theatre. No problem. Thank you both.*

Ben Hennessy is Artistic Director of Red Kettle Theatre Company, which he helped to found with Jim Nolan in the early eighties. He is principally known as a visual artist and designer, having designed over forty productions for Red Kettle, the most recent being *The Kings of the Kilburn High Road* by Jimmy Murphy and *The Grainne Stone*. This last play he co-authored with Liam Meagher; it is the fifth play he has co-written and directed for Little Red Kettle – the attached youth theatre. His directing includes *All in the Head* by Liam Meagher and *Glory Be To The Father* by Conal Creedon. He has also worked with Corcadorca on *A Clockwork Orange* and *Animal Farm* and with Meridian Theatre Company on *The Rock Station*. He currently has on tour an exhibition of paintings called

Chimaera with fellow-artists Ger Sweeney and Debi O'Hehir and is planning to direct *Hummin'* by Tony Guerin in the new year.

Pat Kiernan is Artistic Director and one of the founders of Corcadorca, a Cork-based theatre company. He has directed twenty-two productions for the company. His theatre-based work for the company includes *Leonce and Lena* (Georg Büchner), *Greek* (Stephen Berkoff), *The Ginger Ale Boy* (Enda Walsh) and *Disco Pigs* (Enda Walsh). His site-interactive work for Corcadorca includes *The Clockwork Orange* (Anthony Burgess), *Phaedra's Love* (Sarah Kane), *The Trial of Jesus* (Conal Creedon) and *A Midsummer Night's Dream* (Shakespeare).

Ger FitzGibbon lectures in the English Department, U.C.C. and is Chair of the University's Board of Drama and Theatre Studies. He has lectured and published on the work of Brian Friel, Tom Murphy, Frank McGuinness and Sebastian Barry. He is a former board-member and director with Cork Theatre Company and a founder of Graffiti Theatre Company, of which he is currently Chair. He has written a number of plays, including *The Rock Station* (1992) and *Sca* (1999). His stage-directing includes *The Birthday Party* (Harold Pinter), *The Shadow of a Gunman* (Sean O'Casey), *Accidental Death of an Anarchist* (Dario Fo) and *Scenes from an Execution* (Howard Barker).

Declan Hughes in Conversation with Ryan Tubridy

RT: *Declan Hughes, the one thing that strikes me about reading in and around you and the work that you do is that you have a particular feeling or attitude towards Irish theatre. Describe that attitude to me – Irish theatre as we know it.*

DH: Well, on the one hand I don't want to wave a flag in particular. I find myself that when I express opinions very strongly, as I sometimes do, about a week later I tend to disagree with them and then find myself arguing against people who have agreed with me. It's fairly weird.

RT: *What does that say about you?*

DH: It says – well I think it was Oscar Wilde who said that a playwright is someone who can see both sides of the same question and agree forcefully with each of them. Although, doubtless, Oscar put it a great deal more elegantly than that. I suppose I write about an Ireland that up until maybe ten or even five years ago people thought either didn't really exist or wasn't worthy of chronicling, which is I guess the suburban or Dublin 4 or middle class – the Ireland that is the same as pretty much everywhere else in the world. It seemed to me important to say that that was the case – that what was important about Ireland, it seemed to me, was what we had in common with other countries rather than what set us apart. The rural, the pastoral increasingly didn't seem to me to actually exist any more.

RT: *You have referred to this sort of Paddywhackery theatre and very often you might see something in the National Theatre which is people stomping around the stage, kind of shouting at each other with thick rural accents. Then you come along with your plays and you juxtapose them or compare them at least to someone like Martin McDonagh, who is not that much younger than you, as it were. He seems to revert to type, if you like.*

DH: Well, I am not in the business of caricaturing anybody and I think you can be very glib about it and make points, essentially journalistic points, which are not the points I try to make, so in no way would I deride other writers or other ways of seeing the world theatrically. Where I came from, there was a sense that there is a gap here, there is something that isn't being said. Its absence seemed to suggest that it doesn't exist. I think most writers write from a very primitive urge, artists of any kind, to make your mark. Bruce Springsteen talks brilliantly about the worry for people in life is that they are going to disappear because nobody listens to them and nobody is aware of their existence. So, on a very general level that is why I do what I do.

RT: *You talk about where you come from, let's talk about that for a moment because you are a Dubliner, you were born in the early 60s. Where were you born and what sort of family life did you have?*

DH: Well, I grew up in a semi-detached house in Dalkey, I had two elder sisters.

RT: *What did Mum and Dad do?*

DH: My father is from Glasgow and he worked as a marine engineer in Fairfield's Shipbuilders in Glasgow. He was away a lot because basically he worked there so he was more absent than the usual absent father. So I grew up in a house largely with my mother and two sisters. I went to the local national school, was very ordinary, was obsessed with football, read a lot.

RT: *Who were you following?*

DH: Oh, Glasgow Celtic, because my cousin Jim Craig played for the Lisbon Lions in 1967.

RT: *Your father being away all that time – did that affect your writing in later years?*

DH: I really don't know. I think most people's memory of their childhood is that their fathers were a shadowy presence around the house. You see them very, very late at night if at all or at weekends or whatever. I don't know.

RT: *Would it be fair to say that you come from the quintessential middle class village of Dalkey? – everybody points to Dalkey as middle class.*

DH: Well, "millionaires row" didn't quite exist in the same way then as now and I'd say the circumstances we grew up in were lower middle class – I went to the local national school. Obviously there are tougher places to grow up in, than Dalkey. But there was a chipper you could get beaten up outside in Dalkey just the same as anywhere else.

RT: *No village would be complete without it! You then went to Trinity College and that's when, I gather, the theatrics entered your life. Or was it a secondary school thing too?*

DH: Well, there was a little bit at secondary school but I got the sense then, that there was something that I wanted to pursue. I went to Trinity, taking a degree in English and Philosophy, but I went as much to get involved with Players and the drama society there. I suppose my goals were that I either wanted to be a writer or an actor, or some blend of the two. When I got to Players, I realized pretty soon that I couldn't act.

RT: *What did you act in there, can you remember? Were you truly awful?*

DH: No, I could survive. I was in *The Island* with Martin Murphy, who now runs TEAM Theatre, and *Angel City* a Sam Shepherd play but by and large I realized, early on. Also, I was there with a bunch of people who were just so talented and so obviously better than me, Stanley Townsend, Darragh Kelly, Pauline McLynn and I felt: "These people can really do it and I'm not as good as they are."

RT: *Is there still an actor in you struggling to get out?*

DH: No, but I think most dramatists have a sense of performance. I really do think if you haven't gotten yourself out there in some shape or form it is hard to understand what actors go through. Obviously you write in a study or a room alone but you do, more than any other writing I think, need a practical connection to the theatre. If you have acted, I think it helps. It is also useful if calamity occurs like for instance the first preview of *Twenty Grand*. In appalling circumstances, one of the actors was injured and I had to go on for four performances.

RT: *You had to go on and perform the part?*

DH: Yes, well, I kept the book in my hand because I didn't think it would be useful in the previews for me to be dropping cues I wouldn't need to pick up anyway. That was rather hair-raising for me, though not as hair raising as it was for the actor who was injured.

RT: *Was that a tough decision? Let's take that particular incident for a moment. There you are, probably one of the most nervous men in the country as I'm sure any writer is when his play is about to go on the stage, and you get the call to say: "Your actor is injured, what will we do?" Did you not flinch and go for it or did you say: "Oh my God, what do you do?"*

DH: I suppose your adrenaline kicks in. It was down to either me or the Director and he was from Armagh and I was from Dublin. The character was from Bray and I was considerably closer geographically. Also, the more useful thing is for the director to be watching the performances and at least helping the other actors along. You could say "Oh, you must have been very brave" but I suppose you really don't think about it. I was heartily relieved to get out of it and happily the actor concerned was fine and came back. He was in for the last preview and did the show.

RT: *One often hears about screenwriters who talk about watching their work up on the big screen or in the process of being made if they come to set (which I'm told they shouldn't do). Do you ever feel, watching your plays say in rehearsals, that somebody is just not doing it right and as someone who was an aspirant actor, do you ever feel "I'd love to go in and just do it properly?"*

DH: Oh no. I have no nostalgia about it. I just have the greatest admiration mixed with a sense of fascination or even incomprehension about what actors do, how they can do it and how they can do it every night. So, however much I might feel it is not quite working, I would never think I would be better suited to do it.

RT: *Presumably you have great respect for actors and actresses, (if I'm allowed use that expression any more) and I presume that you think these are tremendous people who are probably grossly underpaid.*

DH: I think we are all underpaid really.

RT: *On all sides?*

DH: Yes, in the theatre, but I wouldn't necessarily go on about that. What excited me when I was in Trinity: because that's when I first started to think that I don't think acting is the thing for me, but what I really want to do is work with these people, and so I started to direct.

RT: *Who do you like acting-wise in Irish theatre, even going back to say Siobhán McKenna? Who do you like, or is that an unfair question?*

DH: They're all, without exception, absolutely wonderful. And no, I'm not going to single anybody out.

RT: *Okay. But you do single out and you have written about him – you might contradict this now, you do change your opinion as you admitted earlier on – you refer to Laurence Olivier and the time you watched him playing in Othello and you called him a blacked-up ham. You really didn't like him in that performance, you seemed aghast watching that. Can you describe it?*

DH: Well, the point about theatre is that it's there and it's gone and I think the point I was trying to make there is that it's written on the wind. When everybody has been at a party but you and they're all telling you "Ah, you missed it" and they tell you what happened and you're thinking "Well, that doesn't sound so great to me." In a way that's what theatre is like. You record or film a performance and twenty years later you watch it and you've heard it chronicled as a legendary show. That's very much what I felt with that *Othello*. I had read that this is the definitive – it just looked ridiculous. But I think that is the brilliant thing as well about theatre, it is so vital and so of the moment that when it works, when it happens, nothing can come close to it.

RT: *Players in Trinity has an equivalent group, Dramsoc, in U.C.D. I read about a particular singer recently who went to study architecture in U.C.D, just to get involved in Dramsoc. These places are very necessary incubators for talent.*

DH: Absolutely. Certainly I went to Trinity in 1980 and that was before there was any formal drama training. There wasn't the Gaiety School and there wasn't the Drama Diploma in Trinity at the time so you didn't really have anywhere else unless you were going to go as an actor to RADA. There wasn't anywhere to get started, to make your mistakes. So, Trinity was the place to do it. I know a lot of people, like my long-time colleague in Rough Magic, Lynne Parker, who would describe themselves as people who had gone to Players and occasionally we would manage to duck into the odd lecture. It seemed to us that we were working full time in the theatre.

RT: *What did you do when you left Players?*

DH: Directly after that – I left in 1984 – Lynne and I founded Rough Magic and we had a core company of actors who joined us and we did a season in Players for the summer. The intention basically was to form an independent theatre company that would do the work. I suppose it had two goals, one was to do the work we thought was missing in the Irish theatre which was largely, at that time, productions of contemporary plays from England and America in particular; secondly of course to give us something to do, to gainfully employ us. I think that the Abbey in the past few years has been terrific in getting in younger directors, but at that time it just didn't happen, or didn't seem to happen to us anyway.

RT: *Why was that?*

DH: I don't know. Maybe it was because the Abbey had a reputation of being quite difficult in terms of the permanent company who had been there a long time. Younger directors might go in and get a show and there would be a lot of unhappy experiences and I think what is called "hazing" in another context and they'd disappear. They'd be seen later in Bangkok, gibbering wrecks, so it wasn't really somewhere that you wanted necessarily to go. It's what the Abbey is there for. Somehow I think, if you're twenty-one, and you don't think that the Abbey is just way too institutionalized, way too conservative and way too – just *The Man*, then perhaps there's something wrong with you. Perhaps you should be working in financial services or something.

RT: *That's when you're twenty-one but when you're into your thirties, does that attitude change?*

DH: I suppose it changes piecemeal in any case, because there are always good things, good shows happening all the way along. *The Gigli Concert* was on while I was at College and Murphy is somebody I have been in awe of, really. He is the greatest dramatist writing now; terrific productions; when Garry Hynes worked at the Abbey; lots of things that you would have paid attention to. At the same time, I don't think anyone can argue that in the last 15 years the Abbey has really come a long way in terms of quality.

RT: *When you sit down to write – I know you had a play titled,* I Can't Get Started, *but does that terse expression say everything?*

DH: Yes, it does. The other night I was talking to a friend who is a novelist, with his first novel coming out in July, and we were talking about how each time you just start again from scratch. *I Can't Get Started* was my first play, and I wrote it about Dashiell Hammett, and about the thirty years of writer's block that he endured. It was a fairly unorthodox subject for a first time playwright. But each time you come again, you think well, it's going to be easier this time and I won't go through all that messy business. Why don't I just write it straight through this time, that'll be a good idea, 'cos I'll save time? Of course, you realize that, if anything, you seem to know even less this time than the last time, so that's no help. I think it's just a question of trusting that the germ of the idea that you have, is going to sustain itself and is going to grow and also the confidence you have, on a very simple level: "I've done it before and I can do it again."

RT: *Do you have a ceremony when it comes to writing? Do you write with a particular pen or do you always go into the computer?*

DH: I'm big on the idea that if you can hoodwink yourself into thinking you're not actually doing what you're supposed to be doing, then somehow it will get done.

RT: *You deceive yourself.*

DH: I deceive myself, I lie constantly, it's my job. So I will type straight onto a screen and sometimes that can be tricky because it looks like the official version and you think, "Oh well, that's it! But it's not right, is it?" So then I have to handwrite and then it will look very, very messy and I'll stay with handwriting for maybe a few days. Then it will occur to me that I have been doing nothing, because I just have a bunch of "stuff" written on pages that doesn't look like anything. So I'll type that up and see where I am and really it is a correspondence between those two things. I generally start off very brightly and there's a big surge of energy and then there's a kind of middle period that seems to last forever. That's a very dangerous period because that's when you can lose the play, where it can vanish on you, but you've just got to be patient and hang around for it. It can slip away very easily though.

RT: *As the father of a two year old, does a father need peace or does it help matters?*

DH: Well, yes it does. At a certain point, I try to get away for a week or ten days when I need that time to just go full out…

RT: *Like father, like son?*

DH: …a point where you can't actually pay attention to anything else, and if you live in a house with a two year old you can't pull that one off any more.

RT: *Do you have a study?*

DH: Yes, I have a separate room, a study and that's great. Generally speaking, I work during the day, say from 9.30-5.30 and that would be it but when you're heading for "home" it just gets longer and longer and you work into the evenings and you just need to get it finished.

RT: *You know when you're studying for exams or whatever – again this whole area of self-defeat – you find yourself studying a certain chapter, writing a certain scene or whatever and you might just go for that cup of coffee you don't want. Do you do that? Do you find yourself distracted unnecessarily just to get out, to unwind, or chill the head?*

DH: Oh yes. Until you're actually physically sick unless you do the work, I find you can find a hundred and one ways of avoiding it, but eventually there is a point where you realize that your sense of sanity and of actual physical well-being is going to be in question unless you get this done.

RT: *Do you find that there are dark moments when you are looking at that page and thinking "Oh why did I get into this business and not any other one?"*

DH: Oh yeah! Also on individual projects, you doubt. It makes you wary of starting something, because once you're starting you're going to have to go straight through. And there's a terror, because you always doubt. Sometimes it's not that the play gets away from you, but sometimes you think that maybe this is justified, maybe this one isn't going to work out and you re-draft and re-draft and just wonder if this is right.

RT: *Do you become difficult to live with then? Should we ask your wife that?*

DH: I couldn't possibly comment. I wouldn't like to live with me!

RT: *How do you deal with the whole area of criticism?*

DH: Badly.

RT: *If you read in the paper, "I went to see* I Can't Get Started *– I thought it was an absolute crud – I hated it", rather than the "I thought it was tremendous – Hughes is a genius, etc", how do you take the bad stuff?*

DH: Well, I don't think anyone takes it well – they're lying if they say they do. There are a lot of letters never sent and I think that's right because I don't think it does you any favours. If somebody is out of line and accuses you of ripping somebody else off, you should defend yourself but by and large opinions are opinions. Who was it said:"It's the dog to the lamppost?" – that's the relationship of the critic to the playwright and you're going to have to put up with it. Also, the good reviews sometimes don't quite capture what you intended either, so I don't think you can be precious about it.

RT: *But you do read them?*

DH: I try not to. If I know a review isn't good, I just don't read it. I avoid that. What is irritating mostly is that for a few days you carry it around in your head and you have this imaginary row with the person, when you correct them on all their grievous errors and misjudgements and that really is a waste of your time.

RT: *When you were drafting and writing away on* Digging for Fire, *your colleague you mentioned, Lynne Parker, turned around to you and described it as a second-rate Chekhov pastiche. When somebody close to you describes something you have been working your butt off for – obviously they want you to be better, but – how do you respond? It mustn't be that easy.*

DH: That was at the very, very early stages of drafting it. It was brutal but I think it was fair enough. I think you need somebody that you write for and at that stage you need to know where you both stand and what you're talking about. I wouldn't for a minute say that that's easy, that's a complicated relationship with occasional hostility or aggression, but you're working towards something and so it is hopefully a creative thing. It can sour and become injurious but in that instance, she was right. The very early drafts of some of that were not what they should have been.

RT: *Let's take that play for a moment,* Digging for Fire. *I get the impression that was hard for you to write because you described writing Acts 2, 3 and 4 as no problem to you. Obviously the juice was flowing, but it came to Act 1 and you were stumped. How did that happen?*

DH: I don't know. Often I find beginnings easy but in that case, there was a lot of rewriting of the early part of the first act and ... I honestly don't know. I don't remember it now as any more difficult than anything else but in a funny way, once you have a rehearsal draft of a play, it seems to shrink to the time it takes to read it. Which is why when you come to write another play, you have forgotten what you had to do to get the play. You think, oh there are seventy pages, it just seemed to flow, because your memory of the last play is in performance perhaps, so it is a curious thing.

RT: *What about the Ireland of today? Could we talk about that for a minute because that's what you do in many ways. For years people went to the theatre and it was "begob" and as you mentioned at one point, the Sacred Heart, the half-door and that sort of element of "gobbledegook shamrockery'. Then you come along and start projecting real life for so many people. That was middle-class. It wasn't O'Casey, it wasn't in a tenement, it was real, it was middle-class and it was now. But I get the impression that you don't like Ireland at the moment as a country, you don't like what we've become, with wealth. Would that be fair to say?*

DH: Yeah. I'd be uncomfortable with the way it is. Everyone says that it's suddenly happened but I think it's suddenly over twenty years. This has been evolving for quite a while and the Irish attitude to money is probably linked into some sort of post-colonial aping of our betters. We knew how to do it and we were resolved that once we got the opportunity, we were going to do it and do it better. The main focus I feel, in my own writing, and it's a focus that I like in general, is on the way we live now, whether it's in New York, or in Los Angeles or in County Wexford for that matter. But, capturing the way we live now is not something that people who go to the theatre are used to seeing. More often, they're given a version of the past, something that can be comfortably parsed and analysed and placed up there, for them to go: "Well, that's something else. That's not us." And that just doesn't provoke me in the way that I would like.

RT: *Declan, why are audiences reluctant to see the here and now, to, if you like, hold up the mirror?*

DH: They're not reluctant when its presented to them but often I think we all have a sense of: "How could that be the theatre, how could that be art when they look like a bunch of people I saw in the pub across the road. How could this be the story worth hearing?" But I think that has changed actually. I think there is a greater hunger for stories that talk about the world in which we live now.

RT: *Do you think it's a vulgar country now, do you think that people's approach to money is vulgar, a new vulgarity?*

DH: Well, I guess so. I think there is a great unease about. There's a truth that's peddled at the moment which is that the Celtic Tiger is a great thing and it's peddled by everybody in broadcasting and in journalism, you know: the partnership agreement has done so much for us! Then you start to count up the number of people who don't comprise "us', like nurses, teachers, junior doctors and guards and the very, very poor and many of the shopworkers and people who didn't vote for the partnership, people who can't afford to buy a house and people who can't afford to live close to the areas where they grew up. Suddenly, there are an extraordinary number of people. Yet you're told that everything is great, and "Thank God, we made those sacrifices." Meanwhile, the amount of money that capital has taken is much greater and the amount of money that labour is getting is much less than it was fifteen years ago.

RT: *You do really think there's a conspiracy.*

DH: Well, I would vote for a left-wing party if I could find one. I don't live in Dublin West and that's where there's the only left-wing politician in the country, as far as I can see. There's nothing to vote for in Ireland because the major parties all agree, there's a broad consensus on almost every issue so it's down to pub-fighting most of the time. That doesn't seem to me to have changed an awful lot.

RT: *When you were re-working* Tartuffe *recently, there was a sense of the brown-paper bag culture and all that went with it. I'm sure that was an assault on the senses for some, there could have been a few politicians in the audience who were sitting very uncomfortably.*

DH: Perhaps, but I remember when Rough Magic did *Serious Money*, about the depredations among the 1980s money markets in London, those guys went along and watched it when it was done in London originally. They loved it and cheered themselves being villainous. So, we were enabling *Tartuffe* to take place in the context of what is going on. I think the theatre can reflect those things but I'm not sure how uncomfortable you can make people like that, people whose belief in money and power is so absolute.

RT: *Would your interpretation of* Tartuffe *be the Socialist in you coming out?*

DH: In so far as it became a play about the state conspiring with the fraudulent individual, then it became a play about corrupt power rather than a more conventional interpretation which is, I think, that *Tartuffe* is the greatest imposter and the greatest con-man. I think you could set that in seventeenth century France and have exactly the same interpretation but, I suppose it is socialist, a left-wing way of viewing the world.

RT: *What makes you decide, "I'm going to write about this or that?" You might write about writer's block or you might decide to rework an old classic. How do you decide that? Is it very well thought out?*

DH: I can't remember who said it first but often it's the phone call. In *Tartuffe's* case, Ben Barnes rang me up and asked me to do it. Basically he liked what I'd done with *Love in a bottle*, a restoration play I re-wrote a few years ago. In other cases, I don't know. I'm writing a play at the moment and there are two couples living across from each other at the base of a quarry. That's the first thing I had and for a while, it was the only thing I had. It wouldn't go away. I couldn't tell you what that was all about.

RT: *So, you get a tune in your head but you can't quite put it on paper.*

DH: Yes, some of the tunes linger and some of them go away. With *Twenty Grand*, I had a scene, the one that opened the play, about a gangster and an apprentice gangster. The apprentice gangster comes in and the gangster says to him, "You're late" and he says "I got held up." He doesn't apologize, he just says, "I got held up." Immediately, I thought that will go somewhere. Why doesn't he apologize, who is he and what is going on, and I wrote about two pages while I was working on something else, then just left it there. About nine months later I came back and I wrote the rest.

RT: *You might be sitting on a bus or walking along the street and you turn around to whoever you're with and say, "It's like a scene from a film or a scene from a play." Does that happen to you?*

DH: I think everyone has those movie moments. I remember directing a play where a character needed to have a limp and we kept saying, "No, no, it's too much, bring it back, bring it back."

Then we broke for lunch and went out and this person with the most outrageous limp walked past. You think: "You couldn't do that on stage." You see two women fist-fighting in a pub and you think nobody would believe that. They'd think, "Oh that's degrading, his bleak vision is dragging us all down", but I just saw it. David Mamet has a great line in *Speed the Plow.* "I wouldn't believe this shit if it was true" and that occurs to me frequently, that sense that you're looking at something in real life and thinking that no one would believe it on stage.

RT: *So, you have to keep an eye on the believability factor, the credibility of the play even if you think, "Something has happened, but the audience won't buy it."*

DH: It's not the real world, it's an idea of the real world, it's a version of it. In a sense that comes back to what we were talking about; I would never want to be seen as somebody who is saying "Oh I want to show what is really going on." If you want to show what is really going on, make a documentary and even then, you're going to have only a version of something. When you're telling a story, you will automatically shape it to your own purposes or the purposes of the characters and through the beliefs and values that you have.

RT: *Whenever I ask a writer or somebody creative, "How much of you is in your work", they roll their eyes up to heaven, either physically or in their head, and think "Here we go again." So, how much of you is in your work?*

DH: There are two things interesting about that. Sometimes a lot and sometimes a little. In a way, perhaps you should ask someone who knows me.

RT: *I did. Somebody suggested that you were there in* Digging for Fire. *Would that be fair to say?*

DH: I don't know, but what is interesting about *Digging for Fire* in particular is the many people who were convinced that they were in it and they absolutely were not. Most characters are composites of people, usually of a couple of people and then a good dose of yourself. My best moment with that whole subject was in the pub after a performance in the first run. A woman came up to me and she said, "Thank you, I really enjoyed that. You know my friends, don't you?" I said, "No, I don't even know you." She said, "But, you just wrote about them all" and I thought that that was probably the best compliment I had been paid as a writer and it put into context how wrong people get it when they say, "I'm in that."

RT: *Do you find yourself plundering elements of people's personality and going, "That's what I need, I need a smart-ass loudmouth or whatever?"*

DH: I have to say, it never seems as conscious as that. You start off with a situation and you have people start to talk and you have some sense of what they want from each other. To be active at all, they need to want something, otherwise they're just chatting. Then, as they speak, you find out a little bit more about them and sometimes they'll be like three people in one and you've got to fillet that down and work out who is who. You are much more conscious of trying to work out a plot or story element, and characters, I find, grow more slowly. Really it is afterwards that you realize that that is a little bit like "so and so'.

RT: *If I could approach the delicate question of your age, which I am reluctant to do, but as you are settling down with wife and child, you are getting more mature, does that noticeably change your writing or do you sense a change?*

DH: I am 38. I guess it must change things, I don't know but as with all these things, wanting to analyse yourself is probably a bad idea. If you sit around going, "It's probably time to get a bit more mature now", I think that would be very foolish and forced. Equally, I guess I'm aware, as a person, that I'm not as anxious about the age I am as maybe I was five years ago. I don't feel as fazed by the idea that I'm not on the town every night of the week or that there are certain scenes that people in their late twenties are having that I don't know anything about. Maybe five years ago, I would have thought that I was losing touch and now I'm thinking, "Hey, you're welcome."

RT: *Is there anything theatrically that you haven't achieved that you want to achieve?*

DH: Oh, yeah. I feel there is lots more to come and I am really only getting started. Yes, absolutely.

RT: *I think we'll end on that note, a lovely ending.*

Declan Hughes was a founder member of Rough Magic, and worked closely with the company as director and writer-in-residence for fifteen years. His plays include *I Can't Get Started, Digging for Fire, New Morning, Halloween Night* and *Twenty Grand*. Adaptations include *Love and a Bottle* and *Tartuffe*. His work has won the Stewart Parker Award and a Time Out Theatre Award. *I Can't Get Started* is published in *Rough Magic: First Plays* (Methuen/New Island). *Declan Hughes, Plays: 1* is published by Methuen.

Ryan Tubridy is a graduate of History and Greek and Roman Civilization from University College, Dublin. In the summer of 1999 he presented *Morning Glory* on RTÉ Radio 1, which was extended from its original nine week run to continue throughout the year. *Morning Glory* was an eclectic mix of current affairs, potted histories and musical archive. In July 2000, Ryan Tubridy moved to the Sunday Show, on RTÉ Radio 1, which he continues to present in conjunction with his work as a reporter and stand-in presenter on the evening magazine programme Five Seven Live. When he was a youngster, Ryan's parents regularly took him to the theatre in Dublin where he remembers "watching *The Gigli Concert* at the Abbey followed by a drink across the road, matching cast with their programme photographs."

Garry Hynes in Conversation with Cathy Leeney

CL: *Garry, you founded the Druid Theatre Company in 1975 and so you've been one of the first professional theatre companies to come out of student work.*

GH: Yes, I would imagine so. The more relevant fact though is that we were the first professional theatre company outside Dublin. That's the marker!

CL: *For you as a director what was it brought you into theatre in the first place – was there a kind of epiphany?*

GH: I can't say there was. If I look for certain events that were life changing, it's only with hindsight that they were. So, I saw my first play when I was about ten or eleven or twelve. It was J.B. Keane's *Many Young Men of Twenty*. It was performed by an amateur company in Monaghan, where I lived then. To this day I have an image of the final scene when they marched out the door singing "Many young men of twenty." So somehow that stuck in my mind. At school as well, I got a play from somewhere, maybe an old French's edition. I did it with a couple of kids. This was in primary school. There was no such thing as drama or anything like that.

CL: *And was there anyone in your family …?*

GH: No. No. My parents would occasionally go to things like the amateur drama festivals in Loughrea, in the way that Irish people who didn't live in Dublin occasionally went to plays. That was very much in the context of the amateur theatre. That's where people got their theatre entertainment, at least when I was growing up, which was after the fit-ups and things like that. Then throughout my final years in secondary school I was involved backstage in doing a play that was a non-curricular part of school work and not regarded as particularly important. I was really looking forward to the non-academic side of university life because if you weren't terribly interested in sports, and I wasn't, then you had no extracurricular life in secondary school. I was really looking forward to things like debating societies and the philosophy society, and just thought it all sounded fantastic and I couldn't wait to get my teeth into it. One of the first societies I joined was Dramsoc, probably just because it was the first stall inside the archway or whatever. I went along to meetings there and at one of the first meetings they divided people into those who wanted to direct and those who wanted to act. Of course there was a huge number of people who wanted to act and very few who wanted to direct. But I knew I wasn't interested in acting. I wasn't quite sure what directing was, but it sounded better. So ...

CL: *It's extraordinary isn't it?*

GH: It is in a way, yes.

CL: *Did you have an instinct of what a director did?*

GH: I think I had an instinct towards organizing, towards groups of people and the organization of them – I think that was the instinct initially.

CL: *And you never wanted afterwards to do anything else except direct?*

GH: Absolutely not. No, I can't imagine what it's like to walk on a stage. I have done once or twice, twenty-five years ago in circumstances where there was nobody else, and I hated every moment of it.

CL: *And writing? You did some devised work with Druid.*

GH: Yes, I did, and writing was, I suppose, what I was about in cultural terms during my school years. I wrote a lot of poetry, I wrote some fiction. I was trying to write a book about sailing round the world. I was a complete magpie. I used to take out books that nobody else ever took out in the library and go from one crazy interest to another. I used the reference library in Galway an awful lot. Very few other people used it. I used to love the smell of the books. A few years later, in Druid, I became involved in writing a couple of pieces, but it was really a response to the fact that we didn't like any of the plays that were coming in to us; we didn't have any real interest in them. This notion came up about doing a play that matched two of my interests, because history was a huge interest of mine, particularly Gaelic history. That was *Island Protected by a Bridge of Glass*, which is from an eighth or ninth century poem.

CL: *Once you got started then were there other directors in the theatre that you had as mentors, or role models?*

GH: No, because I didn't see much theatre. The first sustained piece of theatre-going on my part was off-off-Broadway theatre in the early seventies in New York. I did see stuff there that really did influence me. Things like *Tooth of Crime* by Sam Shepard, the original production of which I saw in the Performing Garage where the audience moved round with the actors. That had a huge impact on me. I saw Joe Chaikin. That really was where the influences started. I came back then and did a play by David Rabe called *Sticks and Bones* – I did that in university [NUI Galway]. I was auditor of Dramsoc in my second year. My three years in university were dominated by my activities in Dramsoc. I did not begin to have any involvement with the professional theatre community until the late seventies, early eighties.

CL: *So you didn't have mentors as such in the theatre. You invented the thing for yourself?*

GH: Yeah. The biggest influences on me were my colleagues. Mick Lally and Marie Mullen and I forged a bond. I had worked with Marie all through college, but not Mick, who was then a teacher and acting in the Taibhdhearc [Irish language theatre in Galway]. In the first few months of Druid we realized we looked at the world in the same way, and we were going to go on with this.

CL: *Looking over your work you seem to have had an instinct for choosing brilliant actors.*

GH: I've been very lucky.

CL: *Do you think that casting is the major talent of the director?*

GH: I think if you don't cast well you may as well go home. Casting is *the* single greatest interpretive act. That and creating the environment in collaboration with the designer. It's such a fundamental relationship because you can have anything you like in your head but if it doesn't translate into what's there in front of you. Directing is really a response to a living thing in as much as theatre is a living thing; it's the audience watching it at the time. So if that living thing is in some way not living for you, it's like someone trying to ride a bicycle with no arms or legs – you just can't do it. I've been very fortunate. We in Druid have been very fortunate because there was a group of six or seven of us that came together in the early years and that was the creative force within Druid, these six or seven people, some resources, and a shared passion, that really was everything.

CL: *You've been working with some younger actors in* On Raftery's Hill *[Marina Carr] and it was a fascinating cast. Do you find it very different, now* *that you work so much on co-productions between Ireland and Britain for example, that wide openness, compared to working with a company of actors?*

GH: Things have changed so hugely. The original group of people in Druid created that first ten years, were the foundations of the company. That began to break up about the mid-eighties. Really when you're working in the Irish theatre, Irish actors are your company. It's a small group of people and everybody tends to know everybody else and when you've been twenty-five years in theatre, and have worked in most of the theatres, you tend to know all the major people. I've been working outside Druid since 1984/85 and I've had the opportunity of getting to know other actors. For instance, I did a production in New York earlier this year [2001] and there wasn't a single person in the entire team that I'd ever worked with before, which was very odd after twenty-five years and actually a wonderful experience. Some terrific actors. One of the frustrating things in the early years of Druid was the element of age. We were all in our twenties and thirties and we had no older actors. Older actors didn't work with young companies then. The first time I worked with an established older actor I found it very frightening. The fact that it was Godfrey Quigley [laughs] had nothing to do with it, but I was working with someone the right age for the role for the first time!

CL: *Do you need actors who are willing to work in a particular way? Is that an issue?*

GH: No. I don't think that's an issue. When you work with an actor you forge a personal relationship with them. And all personal relationships evolve and change and are significant or not in the way of all human relations. There are obvious things that are important to me as a director in relation to an actor, but they're so obvious as to not be very interesting. There has to be a connection between what the actors are doing themselves. The really exciting thing about an actor is not the skill – you take that as a given, that the skills are there, to a greater or lesser degree – what's exciting is the match of that particular personality and the role. I think that mixture is the combination of the skills of the person, the response to the role, the signifiers, the sound, and voice, and tone, and look. There's also the imagination of the actor in collision with the role. That's what's stunningly exiting really, and that's what creates real theatre. For me it has to be rooted. It has to be connected. And when it comes to actors who are connected to what they're doing in a real way, the impact of it is powerful. I've spent a lot of time in my life just stunned by what goes on in the rehearsal room. They, as well as what happens on stage, have been some of the greatest moments.

CL: *It's hard to describe what good acting is...*

GH: Yes, really good acting is transcendent.

CL: *When it comes to playwrights, are there qualities that you look for?*

GH: No. Anyone who reads plays for a living knows that ninety per cent of them are dead in your hands by page ten.

CL: *Are you looking for some quality of passion?*

GH: Oh, I think so. Theatre is an intensification of what we believe living to be. Passion is very much a given. I can't enumerate the qualities of what I respond to in a play – that's only to say what makes a good play: it's dialogue, story and so on and so forth.

CL: *When you say about the actor in collision with the role, does that have a naturalistic implication? Is it fundamentally a naturalistic interpretation of character that you're interested in as a director?*

GH: No, because one of the greatest collisions between the actor, who the actor was, and the role, was in something which was eventually a kind of artifice. I think all theatre is artifice; that's very much a passion of mine at the moment. This was with Siobhán McKenna and Mommo [in *Bailegangaire*]. Tom Murphy wrote this extraordinary play. It's so hugely ambitious. He creates a plot, if you like, which is an old woman in a bed endlessly telling a story, and eventually the object of the play becomes her grand-daughters' – that she's going to finish this story. It's so incredible. If someone took this idea to a playwriting workshop, they'd call the men in the white jackets. And then you have this actor who is first of all, as I discovered in rehearsal, an extraordinary actor. She is iconic in the theatre, and in relation to Ireland, and she's playing this iconic role.

CL: *Maud Gonne playing Cathleen ní Houlihan territory?*

GH: Yes, but then infused with the brilliance of the writing and the brilliance of the actor. It was extraordinary, and nothing to do with naturalism, neither the play, nor the actor, nor the eventual performance, nor the perception of it by the audience. That's not naturalism at all.

CL: *I remember your production of* Conversations on a Homecoming *[1985]. There was a naturalistic impact on the audience – they were in that pub with the characters. And yet the musicality of the rhythms you and the actors created...*

GH: To create something natural on stage is as boring as watching paint dry. It's not about naturalism, it's about intensification. *Conversations* is naturalistic and behaviour-oriented. It's in real time, in a pub, a group of people talking, no changes, no big things happening, just simply people talking. In fact, it's the most extraordinary condensation. It's not naturalism at all. Someone who doesn't understand English could nearly direct a Tom Murphy play in English because if you obey the writing in terms of the sound and shape and feel of it, you will get at the play. It's in there. It's actually in the form of the writing as well as in the content of the writing. It's a wonderful play and I had a wonderful cast. It's one of my benchmark productions. Indeed within all of us, we all carry something of ourselves in that play.

CL: *In your production of* Big Maggie *at the Abbey [2001] you seemed to be taking the play in a very different direction, resisting the idea of the play as a slice of Kerry life, and bringing it into something huge and symbolic.*

GH: Yes, it's right to say the production was pulling back from that up-close, "slice of life" stuff. I don't believe that at all. I think Keane is one of the least naturalistic writers we have. I'd a long time to think about Keane. That was the first play of his I ever did, and I'd wanted to do it. I'd like to do more in fact. Some of the responses that you saw in *Big Maggie* were responses to the play being one thing when it was done in 1969 [when written]; it's quite another thing done in 2001. So, for instance, a small specific issue was, if you populated the set with the objects that Maggie would have for sale in that shop, you could have walked into any pub anywhere in Galway now because the Bird's Custard, the Irel Coffee, it's all become iconic. It's all becoming something tourists walk into. It's all become part of this heritage business. No sooner have we something than we're reproducing it as art. Everyone in this country is involved in theatre. Everyone is out there selling a version of ourselves. [gesture towards Shop St.] I don't know what the real people are doing behind it.

CL: *Making computers probably?*

GH: Exactly. So that poses a problem straight away. If you go for some sort of realism you're suddenly part of the heritage industry. You'd find the stuff shipped off the Abbey stage down to Kerry or somewhere. I went to a bar museum in Kerry a few weeks ago. I never saw anything like it in my whole life! It seems to me in *Big Maggie*, and in *The Field* as well, that there's an incredible sparseness. He is just not going to make anything easy for us. He just sets it up: boom, buried a bastard, boom, I'm taking over, boom, I've a problem with this one, boom, I've a problem with that one. There's no decoration, there's no support, no softness, no lines. It's just relentless and it was the sense of relentlessness I was trying to get at. Watching the production and its revival [in 2001] I had further thoughts about it that go beyond what was there.

CL: *Did you consider using the coda that Keane wrote for the Abbey production in 1988?*

GH: No. It was a wonderful production. I loved it. But as soon as the coda started, I stopped. It meant nothing to me. We used most of Keane's original text as well, [rather than the edited version performed in 1988].

CL: *Regarding your earlier work, how do you look at it?*

GH: I don't know how to look at it. I've no idea what the meaning is now. I'm sure if I were to go to my earlier productions I would cringe and creep out of the hall. It's impossible to judge what that work was like.

CL: *What are the things you are fond of or proud of?*

GH: In my own development as a director, the discovery of Synge as a writer was an epiphany, one of the shock things. It completely influenced everything I've done since, and continues to do so. The discovery we made in 1975 that this was an extraordinary play, the commitment that *all of us made*, Marie, Mick and myself, that if we last, we will do this again. We did so in 1977 and started to begin to get at it.

CL: *This was* Playboy?

GH: We did it as one of our first productions in 1975 because we wanted to draw an audience. Halfway through we thought, "This is absolutely fantastic." And we said we'd do it again, which we did in 1977. That's the production I'd like to go back and see. And we did it again in the early 80s. And we did other work of Synge's. So Synge has been a constant companion. I haven't done any of Synge's work recently, and am about to embark now on this plan to do all of them. That's the major thing for me for the next few years. And then there are plays that are milestones in the development of the company. There was the Boucicault work, which I enjoyed enormously.

CL: *Would you like to do Boucicault again?*

GH: Yes. I love Boucicault. I love the showmanship. There's something quite extraordinary about this actor-manager – I'd love to do something about the whole world he portrayed. Also, the sense of Boucicault as a grandfather of the modern Irish drama movement is something I'm very conscious of. The line from Boucicault to Synge to Beckett is just fantastic.

CL: *And into O'Casey too?*

GH: Yes, O'Casey too, but I'm hopping off the big stones, d'you know what I mean. Just to see something as pure and extraordinary as the Beckett landscape and see that there's a direct track through – that's incredible. Although, any time I've done a Beckett play, I've done it badly. So. I think it's the inner landscape of Beckett for me, rather than the production thing itself.

CL: *What does it mean to you have been awarded honorary degrees [from the NCEA and NUI Galway] and the Tony Award?*

GH: It's nice, I'm proud of the degrees. They're an acknowledgement of some kind and it's nice for other people, for my parents. The Tony Award [for Best Direction, *The Beauty Queen of Leenane*, 1998] was great, no question.

CL: *You were the first woman director to win one?*

GH: Yes. I remember when I was nominated, people began to talk about the fact that no woman had won it. For weeks I said, "You've got to be wrong. These awards are nearly fifty years old." But in fact that was the case and I think it's something to do with the fact that Tony awards are for Broadway theatre, a theatre which has always been driven by money, rather than art, as such. This in spite of the fact that women in the U.S. have had an influence over and above the influence of women in Irish or British theatre. They founded the regional theatre movement in America. The great lighting and set designers in the early part of the twentieth century were women.

CL: *I suppose whether you like it or not, you're a role model for women in theatre. How do you feel about that?*

GH: I don't think about it. I meet people from time to time and they say, from their point of view, they're seeing me as somebody who's led a certain kind of life which offers some sort of ability to imagine to other people. But I'm not conscious of it myself, except where I come up against it from time to time.

CL: *You know how the world of theatre works by networking – are you conscious of operating differently as a woman or of creating new kinds of networking?*

GH: No, not at all. My life is effectively about the theatre, about the entertainment industry generally. The way I socialize tends to be very ordinary and informal, and networking as such is not something I particularly…

CL: So you keep your professional life separate?

GH: No, I wouldn't say that. I have a life and to me it's a very ordinary life. It might look extraordinary from the outside. To me it's about friendship and a sense of community with a range of people and all of us have grown up in the theatre at the same time, and it's just very ordinary. There is a response to women, and to what has been achieved there, and the sense that we are a generation – I mean my mother is only twenty-one years older than me, yet my life and hers could not be more different. So I am aware of that. But that comes out of a social, cultural thing of middle-class access – I grew up with an expectation that I was going to university and so on. That gap – it's just so different. I think an important influence for me was *when* I was born. I was born in 1953. And as a result, this came out in all the work with Druid. I have an incredibly strong sense of that rural, pre-city, pre-Lemass era kind of life. I was born in a small town in Roscommon. So I have a real sense of it. It wasn't really direct because I was only there for the first seven to ten years of my life, so it's a set of images and feelings. I'm very informed by and influenced by what I would have been told as I grew up. So having listened to that without being part of it, I think that has been very much a creative driving force in a lot of work I've done, including things like *Big Maggie*. The sense of understanding that [world] in some way, of knowing it from the inside and yet being completely distant from it, as my own life has been, that has been a very big influence.

CL: *Your work has been an interesting mixture of looking at canonical plays, and then working with new writers as well. Is there anything you'd like to say about the differences between those processes?*

GH: In terms of my own development, working with the canon was certainly something I wanted to do, and then gradually as you've done that quite a bit, you begin to go on to something new. I wanted desperately to work with new writers. I want to work with plays that have never been done before because it is very different, and because of the sense of collegiality and companionship with the writer; it's a great creative relationship. Well, it has been for me. I was fortunate in that the first writer I made a long-term relationship with was one of the best writers of twentieth century theatre, Tom Murphy. That was very important. The process is very different.

CL: *When you saw Martin McDonagh's work first, what was it that jumped out at you?*

GH: Well, when I read it first it was obvious that here was a man who could certainly write dialogue and certainly tell a story. That was clear. What was absolutely bewildering was what on earth these pieces were? Who wrote them? My mental image was of a fifty-year-old living out in Connemara. I couldn't imagine. I knew that couldn't be true as well. Then I saw his address was in London, and talking to him on the phone for the first time I realized that he was this twenty-four-year-old, south Londoner, pure bred with Irish parents. And suddenly it did start to make sense. But trying to make these plays work! I mean it was a long time since I had seriously read a play by a new writer that was set in a kitchen, with a Sacred Heart lamp and all the paraphernalia, and that opens with an old mother in a rocking chair, sparring with her forty year old virginal daughter. If Martin McDonagh had taken this idea to a writing workshop, he'd have been told "We don't write plays like that anymore." It was how to make these things work. There's this issue about Martin and authenticity – the response that his is not Irish life now and it's not Connemara life. Of course it isn't. It's an artifice. It's not authentic. It's not meant to be. It's a complete creation, and in that sense it's fascinating. The big challenge for us in doing *Beauty Queen* for the first time, well first of all the choice of the first play [to produce], because I read two plays initially, and then after I'd met Martin, read a third, and then optioned all three. At the time, the board said: "What! Three plays from a new writer who's never been produced!" There was the decision on which to do first, and then, the decision on how to make this work. How do you sit down with this dialogue and this situation and ask the audience to believe in it. How do *we* believe in it? How do we back it up? And that was fun.

CL: *So you are asking people to believe in it in a way, not to take it as an artifice?*

GH: No, no, I'm asking people to believe in it for the moment they're watching it. They never stop being watchers, and we never stop being performers. We all know we're in the same room. But we've done something much more exciting than being sucked into real life. What we've done is, we've agreed – I mean I always think it's incredible that a group of people actually pay to go into a room which they can't get out of very easily, and another group of people force their imaginations on them. It's incredibly powerful and that's what we've all agreed, "We'll sit quietly here, and you'll do this and we'll pay you." It's fantastic. Everybody knows it's artificial. Even if people think or say, "Oh God it was so marvellous. I felt I was there", it's still an imagined thing. It's the imagination. That is the really powerful thing in theatre. But you're asking them to find it credible to the degree, you know, that they won't respond with: "Ah come on! This is Synge-song type dialogue. Come on, who's he fooling?"

CL: *With Marina Carr's work, was that a very different kind of experience?*

GH: Yes, it is very different. Marina is one of those people who confidently walks down a road where other people are saying "Don't even think of going there." And Marina says "Of course. Let's go. Of course I'm going there." She's an extraordinary, beautiful, young, Irish woman, with extraordinary intelligence and this *incredible* darkness.

CL: *This darkness, which is also in McDonagh's work, is it characteristic of the end of the 1990s and the twenty-first century in Ireland? Is it all tied in with the economic boom, with the notion of the performance of Irishness?*

GH: I think it's characteristic culturally. I'm not so sure that it's of the 1990s. I think it's always been around. If you look at a play like *Lovers' Meeting* [Louis d'Alton], which was the last play I did for Druid before I went to the Abbey; that is a play of extraordinary darkness as well. *Playboy* is too, and all of Synge's work is teetering on the verge of the abyss.

CL: *And the cruelty? Do you see that as part of the Irish tradition in the same way?*

GH: I'm not quoting Marina, and it's out of context, but I imagine she may have said; "We're all pagans, we're all pagans really. We're all awful and terrible. There's a veneer of humanity and it is just skin deep. It can blow up in your face immediately if it's put under any pressure." That articulates something I feel, and Marina certainly feels it, and I think many other writers would not disagree with that. It seems to me a truism. It's what a lot of people believe. If you look at *The Lonesome West* – that McDonagh can make them argue violently over a packet of Tayto as if it's a hostage in some cowboy film! That's something about levels of human darkness.

CL: *You've been very instrumental in developing co-productions between Ireland and the UK, and the US. Is that an important change in Irish theatre?*

GH: It is an important change. It's part of globalization. From Druid's point of view we really didn't get any recognition from Dublin until we went and got Fringe Firsts in Edinburgh. That was very much why we went to Edinburgh as well. From then on, with Druid, it's always a search for new audiences. Now it's become so much easier to define your Irishness out of the fact that you don't actually have to be on the island all the time to be Irish. As somebody said, "I'm waiting for the Irish play that doesn't transfer to the West End or wherever." I think the fact that Irish theatre has been so celebrated internationally is important of course, and it's been great for the Irish theatre. Every person, regardless of the degree of their involvement in productions that have gone elsewhere, is part of what made that happen. So yes, I do think that's important.

CL: *Is there a downside to that market at all, especially that market in the United States?*

GH: I don't know if there's a downside other than *the degree* to which you think it's important. From our point of view it's great to get a Tony Award, but it's absolutely irrelevant really. It's great for people to have a success on Broadway, but other than the benefits that it brings in terms of acclaim and easier access to things and so on, other than that it's not at all relevant to what's going to be happening.

CL: *It doesn't influence your artistic choices then?*

GH: I don't think it does, other than connecting up with other cultures and connecting with other actors, so that things happen that wouldn't have otherwise. But that's life.

CL: *Do you think that the question of what it is to be Irish has to change hugely, when you look around you?*

GH: From a wider cultural perspective, and social perspective, I'm deeply concerned with what's happening, because I don't know what we're losing but I do think we're losing a lot. This town now seems to be a set for a version of Irishness. That's what it is. There's a gap between that and what we are. I don't know what's happening in that gap and I don't know how wide that gap is; but it's worrying. It worries me that the centre of Galway is effectively a tourist centre. It's not a living centre of a community. It's brought great wealth, great opportunity, but it seems to me we haven't even begun to think of the consequences of all this, and it's getting too late to be able to do anything about it. I do have great concerns. The degree to which it's my age – late forties, early fifties – the degree to which I'm beginning to think of something in the past as being better than something now... I've no idea.

CL: *It's hard to tease out those different influences?*

GH: It is yeah.

CL: *You mentioned workshopping a couple of times in such a way that makes me think you don't see it as a very useful process?*

GH: I've always been a little shy of the workshop process as absolutely being a valid way into things because, eventually in theatre, you have to get out there and do it in front of a group of people, and that puts a context on everything that's wholly different. When *I* don't have that live thing that goes out there, I'm not so sure the experience is the same. So I'm a little chary of it. Despite that fact, to put a bunch of actors into a room, and hear new work or any work aloud, whatever it is, yes of course, that's valuable and it helps.

CL: *Do you think the role of the dramaturg or script editor is one that needs more attention?*

GH: Yes, I think the dramaturg can be a great resource, within the rehearsal room, or to a production. As a director, it would be great to have a dramaturg who's coming at the script from a perspective that has nothing to do with the practicalities and has to do with the examination of the text in a wider context. And to say, for example, "This text fits into this context of prose writing", and so on. That's a resource I would dearly like to work with.

CL: *Looking at the National Theatre now, how do you think its role might change in relation to what we've been saying about the extraordinary changes in Ireland? Do you see a change in the way the Abbey represents the country?*

GH: If you think it represents the country, because I never thought that, whether I was Artistic Director or not. I've always thought that the stage of the Abbey is one of the hottest stages in the world, because of the link between it and the growth of the country. I think that the work that goes on on that stage has constantly to use that [quality] for the wonderful resource that it is.

CL: *Do you mean an awareness, a political awareness in the broadest sense?*

GH: Yes. It's an incredible connection. American theatre would kill for that . It doesn't have it and can't have it. That's the Abbey's single most important thing. It has two theatres to service. It has to produce somewhere between twelve and twenty productions per year. That's a powerful obligation and it's a powerful challenge as well. It does have to keep changing and evolving. As the whole notion of what it is to be Irish becomes more fragmented, the danger to the National Theatre is that it becomes hostage to one or other version of being Irish. It has to continue to be multiple and complex, and that's hard. That's hard when you're running a theatrical institution. It presents challenges to everybody, including the board. The person who meets the challenge head on is the artistic director, but the challenge is to the Board and the institution as a whole.

CL: *What do you think of the idea of moving the Abbey from its current site to the south of the river?*

GH: My first response to that is that the current building is completely insufficient for almost everything, so therefore it has to change. So that's a given. What has to drive the idea is to provide a terrifically exciting theatre, but theatres exist within communities. My concern about the move south-side would be that there's no community there, and nobody can know for certain what kind of community will grow up there. There is a community here [in Galway]. It may be, at the moment, in a very difficult context, but it's a context nonetheless. I think a theatre like the Abbey has got to stay in a living space, where there's multi-dimensional life going on around it. That would be my worry about a move south-side, that it would become a cultural breeze block.

CL: *What's your vision of the future of Druid as a company?*

GH: Druid's first runs were part of the personal drive on the part of a group of individuals. Then, in a very real sense, it was providing theatre entertainment for the people of Galway, who had none, only occasional visits from the Irish Theatre Company, and the amateur drama movement, which was never very big in Galway. So, gradually we grew up with the community; we did our growing up together and changing together. Now, Galway people are swamped by choice. I remember when the [Galway] *Advertiser* was two to four pages; now its thirty to forty pages and every single one of them yelling about something that's on tonight that you should come to. Therefore, I think the future of Druid is very different. What circumstance and fortune have brought us to is a situation where we are a mature theatre institution now, we're twenty six or twenty seven years old. We're in a fairly unique context. We're not a building, in the sense that we don't have to keep a theatre open. We have Chapel Lane [in Galway] which is our creative home. We have the ability to do things that other people can't do. What we have to do is find the uniqueness within ourselves and then be faithful to that. So, things like *The Leenane Trilogy* would be where I think the future is.

It's about theatre not as: "What's on tonight?", but as what theatre can be. It's about being able to gather a group of people together and do things that are simply not possible if you have to have a new play on every six weeks. Also, I think culturally we're unique. The theatre business is national. We're all a big group of people who live in Dublin, Galway, anywhere, but the history [of Druid], and the connection with the west of Ireland is a very important part of what we are. Druid has to justify itself on the basis of what's on now, not on what we did. So I think something like the Synge project is precisely what Druid should be doing. Regardless of whether it succeeds or not, for me it's theatre as an event that we need to restore to audiences. People always respond to an event. We have to feel: "Right now this is absolutely where we want to be." You have that sense of "We're both alive in this time and place." That moment is being made intense, not that you're sitting there as some sort of a receiver of something that's going to happen regardless of your involvement. The kind of responses and growth that you get when you put a group of people together over a period of time on a project that all of them feel is beyond them, can be very exciting.

CL: *That sounds like the kind of quality of experience that most people would aim for in their lives, no matter what work they do. As somebody who has to earn your living, how does the money aspect mesh with that?*

GH: Well, it doesn't, you know. [laughs] It just doesn't. In terms of provision, it's one thing to be doing plays when you come out of college. It's quite another thing when you're in your late forties and you begin to realize retirement is officially twenty years away. Theatre continues to be incredibly underfunded. Culture has unquestionably been one of the driving energies of prosperity in this town in particular, and in Ireland generally, yet there isn't a politician in the country that's not going to use that cultural beacon – "we're great." And then we actually reward those people so badly. It is an absolute disgrace. So you have actors, directors, people who've made an extraordinary contribution, and who are living hand-to-mouth. They're probably earning less than they did in their twenties and thirties. Yet they've given a lifetime to the theatre. It's so wrong. We should be insisting on some sort of pension process, and some way of looking after the people who have helped to create this wealth. I think that's very fundamental.

CL: *Do you have to choose to do certain work because of financial pressure?*

GH: No, I don't. I'm more fortunate than many others. I've been artistic director of an organization almost all my life. While the money is poor compared to what I might be earning had I gone into another job, or if I were teaching or something, it has always been there for me. I've had a regular salary. That's not the experience of most of my colleagues. For a lot of people in theatre it's almost impossible for them to make any provision for the future. A pension is a really important part of a financial package for people in almost every other profession and it doesn't even exist [in theatre]. Nobody even thinks to talk about it not existing in the arts. How are actors supposed to live when they can no longer work? It's so wrong.

CL: *Have you ever been tempted to do an Anthony Minghella, and make a film?*

GH: Yes, I'd love to make a film. But I've been talking about it for so long at this stage, I don't know. But yes, I still think I will, in some way, but how or why or what would it be…?

CL: *For your own future what's your fantasy project?*

GH: I'm hoping that we're about to do that, with the Synge cycle. That is a fantasy project. I had a notion at one time of leaving Druid and forming a Synge company for two years. It's been possible to conceive of that as a dream project within Druid. Otherwise there are notions in my head. There are things I want to express and I'm not quite sure how I'm going to express them, or through what play. There's a sense of wanting to say something, but I don't quite know what it is. It's revolving round in my head at the moment. What happens is there is a set of things in there, and you come across a script and you suddenly get a whiff of it again, and it's not quite that, it's not quite that! You become a lot more choosy really about what you do and what you don't do. Doing the Synge project is very important in terms of that. There are other things as well. I suppose I hope that what I do over the next five years will give me access to understand what those other things are.

CL: *Are you going to do that very early play of Synge's* When the Moon Has Set?

GH: That's one of the challenges. The play is generally regarded as being very unsatisfactory, and it's hard to believe that the play was written so close to when Synge was writing a play like *Riders to the Sea*. Certainly we will have an approach to it. It's not going to be a matter of just reading it, or publishing it. We will have an approach, but quite what that approach will be I don't know, but it will be within the context of all of the plays.

CL: *And are you just doing the plays? Or will you look at Synge's other work?*

GH: Oh yes, we will absolutely. It's a whole celebration of Synge's life and of his influence. One of the things people really respond to is how small the canon of Synge's work is. It's eight hours of drama. Eight hours of drama is all he wrote. He's still the dominant figure of twentieth century Irish dramatic literature, and a dominant figure in world dramatic literature. That's the frightening thing about doing this cycle. He influenced, effectively, everybody. I think doing the cycle will generate other kinds of responses in other media that will become part of the eventual performances in 2003. Doing the cycle is about the thing itself, but it's about its impact as well. We'll be premiering the cycle in 2003. There'll be an element of it in 2002 and then the full cycle of performances in 2003.

CL: *What's your ideal audience for the cycle?*

GH: Everyone. That's what it will be about. One of the theatre challenges is the connection with the landscape, both mental and geographical. With *Playboy*, one of the outstanding experiences was performing it on Inis Meain. One of the most important things for Druid has been the touring – playing to audiences outside the major urban centres. And that will very much inform the Synge work as well. What we're hoping is that the performances will be a set of responses to different circumstances: to performing on Inis Meain, where we'll premiere the entire cycle, and in Galway, and in other parts of Ireland associated with Synge, like Mayo and Wicklow, and internationally. So what I'm hoping is that we'll find a way for it to be a kind of communal experience, so that we're not just making this little box, and putting our production in and packing it in tight, and then we just plonk it down in Aran, plonk it down in America, but that it will be more protean than that.

CL: *Do you feel a bit haunted by Synge?*

GH: Yeah.

CL: *I see him over your shoulder.*

GH: [looking behind her] Where is he? That's a very good description. That's exactly the way I feel about it. I fantasize about him coming back to life. There's such an extraordinarily strong sense of a person in all of his work. I've an incredible sense of him. It's the power of the imagination, but I remember when we were doing *Playboy* on Inis Meain – we tried to get out on a boat all that day and had to turn back and turn back and turn back. We eventually got out hours late and couldn't unload the set. We just unloaded the door, and some black drapes. Radio na Gealteachta announced the performance was postponed for two hours because we weren't ready until then. And we were finally doing it with orange boxes, drapes, and two old-fashioned lights, and candles. There was darkness all around the hall by that time and we saw people coming with flashlights because there's no public lighting – we saw these pins of light coming. And then inside, and the hot buzz of the play being done. It was extraordinary when the door opened and Shawn Keogh stuck his head inside at his first entrance, you could see the door was covered in wet that looked like rain, but was actually sea spray from being lashed to the deck of a boat on the way out [from Galway]. The only place I could be to watch it was literally outside the door of the hall, so with the play going on inside, and the massive stillness outside – I saw John Synge that night. Definitely. [laughter]

Garry Hynes was co-founder of Druid Theatre Company in 1975, and has been its Artistic Director from 1975 to 1991, and from 1995 to the present. She was Artistic Director of the National Theatre from 1991 to 1994. She has directed at the Royal Shakespeare Company, at the Royal Exchange Theatre, Manchester, and at the Signature Theatre in New York. Her many productions include *The Playboy of the Western World*, *The Colleen Bawn*, *Conversations on a Homecoming*, *Bailegangaire*, *A Whistle in the Dark*, *The Plough and the Stars*, *Portia Coughlan*, *On Raftery's Hill*, and *The Leenane Trilogy*. She won a Tony Award for *The Beauty Queen of Leenane* in 1998, and has been received honorary doctorates from the National University of Ireland (1998), and the National Council for Education Awards (1998) for her contribution to Irish theatre.

Cathy Leeney is interested in twentieth century and contemporary Irish theatre, and in gender and performance, and directing. She is a lecturer at the Drama Studies Centre at NUI Dublin.

Marie Jones in Conversation with Pat Moylan

PM: *Marie, before we talk about your success with* Stones in his Pockets, *please tell me how and why you started writing for the theatre?*

MJ: I was working as an actress in Belfast, and at that time they really only had the Arts Theatre and the Lyric and they didn't do very many local plays. They produced many of the classics and constantly brought English actors over to perform in them. They probably thought we couldn't do an English accent or that if we were local and available, we were no good. Martin Lynch had started up a community theatre in West Belfast in the Turf Lodge area and I had seen some of his work. Then I heard that he had written a play called *Dockers* for the Lyric Theatre and I went to see it. On the opening night there were all dockers in the audience and I watched them relate to what was happening on stage. They were emotional because they recognized the characters and it was real for them.

At that stage there were about five of us – Eleanor Methven, Carol Moore (Scanlan), Brenda Winter, Maureen Macauley and myself – and we went to Martin and asked him if he would write some sketches for us. He said that if he could write then there was no reason why we couldn't, as we all came from the same background. So we started to meet in our front room every Sunday night. It was like being back at school, Martin would give us essays to write. We then explored our history and background and out of that came the realization that we were all connected to the Linen industry in some way. Given that it was, in the main, a female preserve, we all had aunts, mothers or sisters who at some time worked in the mills. We then set out to talk to some of the old workers in order to try to weave together a story that would make good theatre. In researching the newspapers in the library, we discovered that in 1907 there was a strike at the mills, and that a Sadie Patterson set up the first Textile Workers Union. Getting her story was really important, so we went to talk to her. She was in her eighties then, and she told us the most amazing facts about the difficulty of uniting women who were afraid of losing what, in many cases, was the only income coming into the house, and of the sectarian situation, as both Protestants and Catholics were employed there. As we left her, she said that if we didn't tell this story that it would never be told.

PM: *That was a hell of a responsibility.*

MJ: Well, we took ourselves down to Annaghmakerrig (the Tyrone Guthrie Centre for Artists) with all our notes and newspapers. Martin got us all to take a different situation and write a scene. I remember I wrote a scene between two women, and it was fourteen pages long as I had no idea of structure or craft, but Martin was brilliant and so patient with us. That was how *Lay up your Ends* was written.

PM: *So it was a collaboration?*

MJ: Yes, between us girls and Martin. We then needed to form a company to produce it, and that's how Charabanc came about. We all had our own strengths and weaknesses, so the organizers came into their own on the administration side, but I stuck to the writing and the acting. Martin Lynch said he would approach Pam Brighton to direct, and to our amazement she came to Belfast, even though we had no money and no facilities. Eventually we got some money from an ACE scheme, as we had been out of work for over a year. This was exceptional, as the criteria for the scheme was to produce something tangible. However, the woman we were dealing with was involved in amateur theatre and she made a case to her overseers to the effect that producing a piece of theatre was as important as any other product. Paddy Devlin was also a great supporter in the early days, as his Ma and Granny worked in the mills, so he got us the community centres to perform in.

PM: Lay up your Ends *was a great success.*

MJ: Absolutely, it was something that people had never seen before. Belfast women being funny, being bawdy and being strong. We played all over Ireland, we went to the Dublin Theatre Festival, we went to London with it and we even ended up in Russia. About two years after we wrote it, some American academics contacted us as they were doing their thesis on the play – isn't that amazing?

PM: *So where did that take you in terms of your writing career?*

MJ: Well, it was decided that I would be the sole writer for the group, even though it was still very much a collaborative situation. It was a wonderful time and we all worked really well together. We did about five or six more plays together, and although some were far more successful than others, they all got the same commitment, time and energy.

PM: *How did you publicize your plays?*

MJ: We went around from house to house with leaflets, and ended up going in for cups of tea with people, in the hope of getting them to go to the plays. One time we borrowed a loudspeaker from Sinn Fein and we lost it, so, when the election came up we had to keep our heads down.

PM: *What direction did your career take when you left Charabanc?*

MJ: In terms of recognition, I think *A Night in November* was the next highlight. It played all over the country and it ended up playing in New York in an off-Broadway theatre. But the thing that gave me most satisfaction was playing the Opera House in Belfast. The previous director of the theatre said that no local play could ever fill a house that size, but when Derek Nichols came along, his attitude was that the Opera House belonged to the people of Belfast and he was so encouraging. When my adaptation of *The Government Inspector* filled the theatre, I just walked out into the street outside the theatre and cried. I always believed that a local play would be supported, but the fact that it was my play made it a night I will always remember. Since then, many of my plays have been staged there, but that wouldn't have happened had Derek not taken the chance, I think he is great. I still get that same feeling every time we play the Opera House.

PM: *Having produced* Women on the Verge of HRT – *I know it was a terrific success, ending up in the West End and touring England on three occasions – I got great satisfaction from seeing large theatres in places like Sheffield and York filled to capacity with women. It was like going to the Chippendales – ninety per cent female, which must be a record for a play?*

MJ: The thing about that was that the men who went really enjoyed it. It wasn't anti-men but when it played in the Gaiety Theatre in Dublin, I loved seeing the buses pulling up outside the theatre as I knew they were all out to enjoy themselves. Being an actor in *Women on the Verge of HRT* was like a double bonus. A Cypriot barman in the Opera House "Marie, I hate your plays, as the women never want to go home, it's vodka, vodka, vodka all night."

PM: Stones in his Pockets *has been running in the West End since May 2000. It has played for 6 months on Broadway and I have no doubt that it would still be running there if it were not for the tragic events of September 11th 2001. The World Tour of the play starts in January 2002 and in February the North American tour. This obviously has been the highlight of your writing career. So, Marie, we all know that* Stones in his Pockets *is a major success, but when did it dawn on you that you had something special on your hands?*

MJ: It was into the second week in rehearsals and Ian McIlhinney, the director (who happens to be my husband), came home and said he was afraid to talk too soon, but that he felt that it could be a little gem. When I saw what the two actors, Conleth Hill and Sean Campion created around the work, I thought they were geniuses. They had so much flair and imagination and they worked so well with Ian, that by the end of the rehearsal period I was really happy. Then the reviews were terrific both at the Lyric and at Andrews Lane Theatre, and again when it went to the Edinburgh festival. They then went to the Tricycle in London, and from there things began to snowball, with talk of the West End and then Broadway.

PM: *You must feel very proud when you walk down St. Martin's Lane in London or 45th Street in New York, and see your name in lights over the theatres?*

MJ: It's like a dream!

PM: *What about all the awards – Oliviers, Tony nominations, the list is endless? When I suggested listing all the awards and nominations on the advertising for the show on its return to Dublin, I realized that I could not afford the amount of space it would take up, as the list is so extensive.*

MJ: I was truly overwhelmed by all of the awards – I still can't believe it.

PM: *What are the advantages and disadvantages of being married to the Director?*

MJ: The only disadvantage is that he is away a lot of the time and we have two young boys, but everything else is a joy. Ian, being an actor himself, is very caring and very patient with actors and he has a great appreciation of the work they do.

PM: *Tell me about the new play you have in rehearsal?*

MJ: It is called *Weddin's, Wee'ins and Wakes* and it is a re-working of a short play I wrote several years ago, and with Trevor Moore, a wonderful composer, we have turned it into a musical, so I am very excited about that. It opens at the Queen's Festival in Belfast this November.

PM: *Marie, why do you think there are so few women playwrights?*

MJ: Traditionally, I think women are very private and a play is very public. A novel is a one-to-one experience but if you have an audience looking at your work you are really exposing yourself. I have been very lucky as I have always had the support of a company to produce my plays and to encourage me along the way, but it is very lonely for someone writing a play at home and then sending it out in the hope that some company will produce it.

PM: *What advice would you give to new playwrights?*

MJ: Start small, there are little gems of theatre companies that produce plays in places like the Studio in Andrews Lane, and build from there. Make a reputation for yourself before you approach the Abbey or the National.

PM: *To what extent have Northern politics influenced your writing?*

MJ: *A Night in November* deals with the political situation head on but sometimes you are influenced by more personal political situations that effect you, for example, *Women on the Verge of HRT* deals with sexual politics, but growing up and living in Belfast has to colour your work.

PM: What playwrights do you admire?

MJ: Arthur Miller would be top of my list, as he does what I am trying to achieve. He takes a small section of the community and presents it to us warts and all, and although we accept the story on that level, we are also aware that underneath the small town politics we get a glimpse of a bigger picture – that leaves an audience thinking long after they see the play – this is what theatre is about.

PM: *I would describe you as more of an Irish Neil Simon.*

MJ: That's very flattering as he is a great craftsman and very funny.

PM: *You also fall into that category, because no matter how sad the subject matter of your work, and regardless of how emotionally involved you become with the characters, you are always guaranteed a great laugh.*

MJ: We also have some terrific Irish writers. I love a lot of Brian Friel's work but there are also some of his plays that I am not too keen on. Sometimes I have wanted to say " thank you" to a playwright at the end of the evening, when you see something that is so good you just don't want to leave the theatre. I remember having that experience when I saw *The Government Inspector* in

Hungarian. I didn't understand a word of the language, but I was so moved, that I sat on the steps of the theatre afterwards and cried.

PM: *In your experience, are audiences conservative?*

MJ: We get a lot of people who have never been to the theatre before and that is always great, as they tend to be so honest and are happy to give you their opinion. In the West End you don't get an opportunity of mixing with the audience as the bar is closed after the show and the audience just go their separate ways, so you never have a chance to get the same feedback. You learn a lot about your work by what people say immediately after seeing the play.

PM: *Were you pleased that so many stars of stage and screen went to see* Stones in His Pockets?

MJ: I'm sure the subject matter of the play has something to do with that, but I was awe-struck at the idea of some of the people I had really admired for years being so complimentary about my work. People like Donald Sutherland, Tom Hanks, Roger Moore and my favourite Dustin Hoffman, the list is so long, I can't remember them all. Even Prince Charles went.

PM: *Have you any ambition to write for films?*

MJ: Actually I was offered a major Hollywood movie! My agent was jumping up and down as the money was fantastic, and we were just about to sign the contracts, but I was unhappy about the idea. I thought that if this is going to make me miserable I wouldn't be doing anyone any favours. Mind you, if my children were hungry and I couldn't pay the mortgage, I would have done it, I'm not that stupid. It all seemed like really hard work for me. You see, plays are a pleasure and I don't ever see it as work.

PM: *Do you find writing a lonely job?*

MJ: Not at all, it is a wonderful job. You are never lonely, because you live with your characters and you get to know them and love them.

PM: *How do you feel about reviews and theatre criticism in general?*

MJ: Generally speaking, I think the standard of criticism is quite good, but I am affected by reviews, you wouldn't be human if you weren't. If someone says your play is great, you think they are brilliant and understand the work, but if they don't like it, it does hurt.

PM: *What does the future hold for you?*

MJ: My plan is to continue to enjoy myself, and that means writing plays.

Marie Jones, born in Belfast, is a playwright. She was Writer-in-Residence for Charabanc Theatre Company from 1983–1990. Marie's plays have toured extensively throughout the world including the former Soviet Union, Germany, coast to coast in America, Canada, Britain and Ireland. Her recent plays include an adaptation of *The Government Inspector, A Night in November, Women on the Verge of HRT, Eddie Bottom's Dream* and *Stones in his Pockets, which is currently running at the Duke of York's Theatre in the West End.*

Other dramas include *Lay up Your Ends* (co-written with Martin Lynch), *Oul Delph and False Teeth, Girls in the Big Picture, Somewhere Over the Balcony, The Hamster Wheel, The Terrible Twins, Under Napoleons Nose, Hiring Days, Don't Look Down, Yours Truly, The Cow the Ship and the Indian, Christmas Eve Can Kill You, It's a Waste of Time, Gold in the Streets, Now You're Talking, Hall All the Harpers* (co-written with Shane Connaughton) and *Ethel Workman is Innocent.*

She has written extensively for BBC Radio Four and BBC TV. As an actress, Marie has performed in most of the major theatres in Ireland with many Irish touring companies. She has worked extensively for BBC Radio Four in numerous productions playing a variety of characters from Natasha in Brian Friels adaptation of *The Three Sisters* to a cow in Gerry Stembridges *Daisy the Cow Who Talked.*

Pat Moylan was Artistic and Managing Director of Andrews Lane Theatre, Dublin. Pat co-produced *Women on the Verge of HRT* for London's West End and for its Irish tour.

Pat is also involved in publishing and has produced programmes for all the theatres in Dublin and the programme for Riverdance The Show in Ireland, England, the US and Canada to date. Prior to this, she edited and produced a theatre and film magazine *Irish Stage and Screen*. She is currently co-producing *Stones in his Pockets* by Marie Jones at The Duke of York's Theatre in London.

Pat produced an 18-minute short film *The Breakfast* which was written and directed by Peter Sheridan. Pat has now produced a feature film of *Borstal Boy*, also directed by Peter Sheridan and scheduled for cinema release in 2001.

John B. Keane in Conversation with Michael Scott

MS: *How many years is it since you wrote* The Matchmaker?

JBK: About forty years.

MS: *You have written a whole series of books of* Letters, *haven't you?* Letters of a Matchmaker, Letters of a Parish Priest, Letters of a Civic Guard, *etc.*

JBK: Yes, I wrote a series of nine books of *Letters* altogether but *The Matchmaker* was my favourite.

MS: The Matchmaker *was the only one of those books to be transferred to the stage and has always been a huge success as a play. To what do you attribute this?*

JBK: Yes, it was an awful success on stage and a great seller in the bookstores as well. You see, I grew up in the time when matchmaking was totally in decline and I was witness to travesties, tragedies and ferocious humour. To me, at least, it was ferociously humourous, but not so humourous to those who, if you like, fell down on the job!

MS: *How much matchmaking was there at the time you were writing about it?*

JBK: There was one matchmaker about twenty miles from me who claimed that he was responsible for four hundred marriages, with only one failure. Her blight was that she spoke too much, she never stopped talking. So, he placed a piece of sellotape over her mouth and sent her home. As far as I know, she is still there talking to herself and to the hearth.

MS: *Tell me about the language that you use throughout the play.*

JBK: The language was the spoken language of the people of the Blue Stack Mountains, Derrawest and other parishes that had, if you like, fallen behind the times a bit. Most of them had emigrated to England and what was left was pure – it was a language which had been spoken for over 150 years, during all the changes from Irish to English. It came across like a tunnel most of the time, because it was a language which was designed to shock, a language which is a cut above all other languages. I'll just give you a small example of how good this language was: A matchmaker called DanPaddyAndy was having his hair cut one day, not long before his death actually, by Sweeney a local barber. Now Sweeney observed that there were two black hairs after appearing on DanPaddyAndy's neck and he said, "Dan, I declare to God", he said, "there's two black hairs after appearing on your neck." "Ah", said Dan, he says, "I was after a gamey woman one time and I caught her in the finish" and he said, "It was those two black hairs that you see there on my neck that brought her down from her perch." That's an example!

MS: *How do you feel that the audiences react to your plays?*

JBK*:* They generally enjoy them and they generally come back again. I did discover when I had written *Sive* back in 1959 that a number of, what you might call, the new ascendancy classes didn't like them because they felt that they were crude and vulgar. What they were forgetting was that I was using a language which was used everywhere at the time. They had changed their language.

MS: *What do you feel about the current trend in Ireland of revivals of well-known plays? By comparison, there seems to be so little new writing being presented.*

JBK: When I started writing plays, it was a rather poor time for the Irish theatre. All the greats had gone, if you like, and what was left was a group of aspiring playwrights, so it was easy enough to achieve success.

MS: *Do you think that the theatre audience nowadays is very conservative?*

JBK: No. The theatre really has to be dodgy all the time. It has to be mad and dodgy, violent and obscene. It has to be full of shock if it is to get "bottoms on seats."

MS: *Do you think audiences for instance find that* Sive *is a very shocking play and also* Big Maggie? *I mean, love and violence are mixed so closely in those two plays.*

JBK: Yes, I wasn't surprised at the effect *Sive* had on people. They had never seen anything like it. A lot of them would be affected by it, deeply moved, because it was their own language that was being used. A language that they were being taught to be ashamed of.

MS: *Do you think that Irish theatre is changing now?*

JBK: Irish theatre is not changing sufficiently. In fact, I think theatre is a bit static at the moment. I think theatre-owners and producers are playing safe, which is fatal.

MS: *What has impressed you in the last ten years of theatre?*

JBK: Ten years, you'd have to go back further than that. I stopped going to the theatre because of illness and failing sight. I can't think of anything, offhand. Oh yes, of course there were Tom Murphy's plays, and Brian Friel's plays and many other writers. But, you see I am not a critic and I really lose interest when I am asked what I think of other people's plays. I am less interested when I am asked about my own plays.

MS: *What do you think about Irish theatre abroad?*

JBK: That's remarkable. The success of Irish theatre abroad is unbelievable, especially in the States, and in England indeed.

MS: *What do you think of the critics?*

JBK: I like them, by and large. They are entitled to their say and I have found them, for the most part, to be reasonable. You get the odd one who just might happen not to like you and that's too bad. That's tough on him, you know, that's his problem.

MS: *Women don't generally get good parts in Irish plays but so many of your plays like* Sive, Big Maggie *and* Moll, *are called after women.*

JBK: Well, I was always mad about women. I was mad about my mother, in the best sense of the word, and my wife, in every sense of the word. I would say that here, I was extremely lucky. All the women I knew, growing up through life, the women outside from Derrawest, the women of Lyracrompane, they were great women. They had to wrestle with shortages of cash and shortages of a lot of other things as well and a lot of hostility from a clergy who didn't know where they were going.

MS: *What else would you like to see happen in Irish theatre? The Abbey has finally started staging your plays, what else do you think the Abbey should be doing?*

JBK: I think the Abbey should be doing new plays, non-stop. Of course, you have to sometimes revive old plays, people have happy memories of plays they saw long ago and they would very much like to see a new Abbey group performing the plays. This is the most natural thing in the world. The one thing you've got to watch out for, in theatre, is the sweeping statement by a critic because he sweeps everything else away as well.

MS: *When you are writing plays, do you write for yourself or for your audiences?*

JBK: I write for myself. I'm the best judge of my own work, I suppose, because when I go back over it, I can see the flaws. Now, I'm going to make a move which is very common to the theatre, I'm going to exit gracefully.

> I will go now and I'll go to Inishfree,
> A small cabin build there
> And that's where I'll drink my tea.
> I'll have a bit of chicken there
> Because that agrees with me.

MS: *Thank you.*

John B. Keane has contributed greatly to both local and national theatrical life. His play's include *Sive*, *Sharon's Grave*, *Big Maggie*, *The Chastitute*, *The Field*, which was subsequently adapted for screen by Jim Sheridan and Noel Pearson in 1996. With *Letters of a Successful T.D.*, Keane began a series of epistolary novellas. In his mid-fifties, Keane wrote a series of best-selling works including *The Contractors*, *The Bodhrán Makers*, and *Durango*. J.B. Keane is president of Irish PEN, a member of Aosdána and the recipient of numerous awards and honours including honorary doctorates from Dublin University and Marymount Manhattan College New York.

Michael Scott received his theatre training in Europe and has been Theatre Director of the Project Arts Centre, Programme Director of the Dublin Theatre Festival and Director of the Tivoli Theatre, Dublin and the RHA Downstairs. Currently he is Artistic Director of the SFX City Theatre. His productions have been seen in Ireland, England, Germany, USA, Iceland, Wales, Scotland and France. Theatre productions include *Bent*, *The Morning After Optimism*, *The Woman in Black*, *The Antigone*, *Trafford Tanzi*, *The Normal Heart*, Thomas Kilroy's new version of *Ghosts* at the Abbey and a production of *The Hostage* (*An Giall*) with Niall Tobin. His production of John B. Keanes' *The Matchmaker* has broken box office records all over Ireland.

Raymond Keane in Conversation with Eric Weitz

EW: *I thought we'd begin the discussion of where you are, with some reference to where you've been and where you came from. The company being about eight years old now, was there any original brief, spoken or unspoken, when you mounted your introductory* Barabbas ... the Company *"season" in 1993?*

RK: There was a very definite one, in a way even more definite then than it is now. I suppose I will take you back a year previous to that, to answer that question, when we decided to get together. I'd known Veronica Coburn and Mikel Murfi over a number of years. We often give the reasons for starting up the company Barabbas as this reason alone: We always seemed to find ourselves in situations where we did the mad characters, and the "jumpy-up-and-down characters", as we like to refer to them which prompted one good reason for dedicating a company to eejiting. Veronica and Mikel had been friends for years. I really enjoyed the work of both of them and we had enjoyed working together when we did cross paths in revue shows and comedy things in, I suppose, the slightly alternative comedy scene at the time.

They had a plan back in 1992 or 1991, even. Just as a kind of exploration, they rented a studio and invited about thirty actors who they thought would be interested in this kind of physical theatre work, to use an overall phrase, and I happened to be one of them. So they rented a studio for a couple of weeks. At the end of three weeks, they approached me to see if I would be interested in doing a show with them. And I was, but I was actually more interested, at the time, in forming a company, because I had just done seven years in television and was really looking for something new. So we talked around that for a couple of days, drinking loads and loads of tea and talk and talk and talk which we still do a lot of and we decided we'd go for it.

We began to discuss what we were about, what kind of theatre we wanted to do, and we came down on a notion that we'd be based in or influenced by the traditions of clown, bouffon, and *commedia* dell'arte. I would throw mime, dance and puppetry in there, among other things. But these were sexier names.

Clown was very much at the core of all our beings. I had done a lot of clown work in my Grapevine Arts Centre days. So that was very much the core of all the work, and still is today. Whether we use red noses or not, it's still our heart and soul. Clown, bouffon and *commedia*, they were disciplines we were familiar with, not necessarily all three of us with all three of them, but we all had some history or involvement with one of the disciplines and they seemed to suit.

Now as time went by, of course, we dumped all those names, because in a way we weren't truthful to them. We weren't doing bouffon, we weren't doing *commedia*; clown, as I say, was still at the base of all our work. But we were exploring puppet theatre, lyricism, all sorts of physical theatres or image-based theatres. So over the years, those names have dropped off, and we now very cheekily describe ourselves as: "Barabbas is dedicated to its own form of theatre." It may sound cheeky, but, in a way, it's focused us terribly well because now we do the kind of theatre that we want to do. Which is "us."

EW: *Can you articulate how you might have diverged from these other classifications?*

RK: Maybe they didn't diverge. They're still there in the background because that's our training and our influence, I suppose. As I say, you can add a number of further disciplines to them. Like puppets, that's a background that I've had, both in television and in theatre. So that's an area that I love; manipulation of objects.

I would have studied an awful lot of mime before Barabbas. Mime was my first love. So that was my first discipline training, if you like. And then I went on to study with a guy called Kalichi at the Grapevine Arts Centre, who was more interested in the Eastern influence, everything from Japanese Noh theatre to Yoga, T'ai Chi. He used to call the workshops Liberation Dance Workshops and the company was called No Dance Performers, a play on Japanese Noh, of course, but also it was really physical theatre or movement theatre. There was sound in it, the notion that the voice is also a movement, and very experimental and very explorative. It was fantastic training to have.

However, back to Barabbas. First of all, we worked together for a year, the year of 1992. We borrowed a space from Dublin Youth Theatre, a tiny little room; the three of us used to go in there most days for at least half a day, for almost a year. And we'd just "kick space", get to know each other, get to know the kind of theatre that would tweak us. And we decided that we would put a show together and it would be a red-nose show, because that was the one discipline we knew we were very fond of.

We made a show called *Come Down from the Mountain John Clown, John Clown*, which we, in fact, showcased without launching the company. We played it at the Sligo Arts Festival of that year, just to see how it would go down. Around the same time we did a showcase in the Project Arts Centre to show our peers and contemporaries and Fiach Mac Conghail, who was running the Project at the time, the kind of work we might be poking at over the next few years. So Fiach saw it and our friends and colleagues, and they seemed to go, "Yup, you're onto something there."

Fiach gave us a time slot to play *John Clown* in the Project. He was offering us dates about six months later, so we decided we'd do two shows. We devised another show called, *Half Eight Mass of a Tuesday*, in which we wanted to use puppets, and as little language as possible. That's very much at the root of a lot of the work we've done: we always thought we'd do "theatre of few words." That was another way we would describe ourselves, as opposed to "silent theatre" or "theatre with no words," theatre with few words, because words were part of what we did, as well. Not necessarily text or dialogue, but words as part of a landscape, or as part of an image or a picture that a sound may accompany. Words served us just as well without us having to understand them as language, which is part of our artistic endeavour, I suppose. We could take Irish theatre abroad, to countries that wouldn't have the English or Irish language, let's say; we could take a breed of Irish work that could be understood without having our language.

So this second show, *Half Eight Mass of a Tuesday* brought a style of puppet into it that I had worked in with a guy called Roman Paska. He had done a Yeats piece at the Peacock here in Dublin, *Shadowy Waters*, several years previous to that. And he introduced me to a very beautiful staff marionette puppet. And I really fell in love with it because I thought there was a beautiful "life" in it, a beautiful control in it. This staff out of the back of the head gave me a real connection with the puppet. Then we added our own notions on top of that.

The show was a silent show bar whispers and wee words as you might hear in a small town in a very small congregation at mass at half eight of any Tuesday, wintertime. Our congregation was nine people, and you heard the mass in the background, so it was a little flip: When we're at mass, the altar is the stage in our show, if you like, the "congregation" was the audience.

And it was an ideal situation not to use words, because people don't speak, or when they do it's very whispery. And the mass offers you the perfect dramatic structure: beginning, middle and end. So all we had to do was gather around that format and we had a show. We chose that to say, "Take a congregation of nine people and have a peek into their minds, what they *might* be thinking about while at mass."

All three of us came from Catholic backgrounds; all went to mass as kids; all spaced out at mass, as I think most people do. And it was really that bit that really tweaked us which, I suppose, is very much in line with the way we see our theatre, or *what* we see our theatre accessing: the everyday, the absolutely mundane things that *we* find incredibly interesting.

The *third* show in our launch back in 1993 was a version of *Macbeth*. When it came to it there was a delay before we got the Project. We had more time on our hands; we had already devised two shows, and we thought, "What do we do now?" And Veronica, I think, piped up, "Gerry Stembridge has been talking about this show for years, which is a five-actor *Macbeth*.I wonder would he be interested in doing that?" Of course, the notion of doing a classic like *Macbeth*, was that we could sandwich it with the two brand-new shows.

We had worked with Gerry the previous year, in fact. We had done a one-act festival, which was produced by Passion Machine. He was an ideal person, and particularly with his notion of a five-actor *Macbeth*, which would be a very intense and physical interpretation.

What he did was cast "Mr and Mrs Macbeth" with two actors, and they were very much actors of a different style to us, Darragh Kelly and Ann Callanan, two very brilliant actors. Because what Gerry was asking them to do was play the play as it would be played "forever", let's say, and then we were the three witches. And as the witches we played all the other characters bar the Macbeths.

The interpretation Gerry gave it, I suppose, was this, "Is there evil out there? Is it in ourselves? How much do we access it?" And I suppose the way he was looking at Mr and Mrs Macbeth was that really *through* the witches he conjured up his world. And they helped, but they never pushed, they just assisted.

EW: *Gerry has been one of your throughlines. What, for your part, keeps that happening?*

RK: I suppose his enthusiasm for the company, and obviously he's a brilliant man, of course, and a wonderful director. And there seems to be that connection, you know. Anybody who's worked with Gerry over the years I'm sure will recognize this. You can't talk to Gerry about things, at *times*. Well, of course, you can, but sometimes when you ask, "Oh, should I do this Gerry, or shouldn't I?" He'll say, "Show me." And that's very much where we come from, as well, because we like to *do* things, rather than *talk*; even though we talk the hind legs off ourselves, never mind donkeys, over many cups of tea. But "doing" is what physical theatre is about, I suppose. That's always been a thing with Gerry over the years: "Don't talk, don't tell me about it; just show me, and then I'll tell you if it's any good." So I think that was the basis of the good working relationship. Also, he just likes what we do, and we seem to get on. He then became a board member and chairperson of our board.

Our festival of three shows was an absolute blinder. It was better than we ever expected. The whole notion of that festival was that, "We'll show the public and critics and practitioners, everybody, we'll show you three styles of work, so we can't be pigeon-holed." We showed people a landscape that was quite broad, three very different styles and works. And that worked for us.

Then we went back to devise a number of pieces like *Sick Dying Dead Buried Out*, which was another clown show, *Strokehauling*, and *Out the Back Door*. And they were all mostly non-verbal pieces. But when you're doing work like that, it's very hard to get an audience. Even though we always thought our work was "popular", when you're doing new work with mad names, like *Half Eight Mass of a Tuesday* – they're names that people don't recognize. I think every company will say this: if you do a show that is called *Macbeth* or *The Whiteheaded Boy*, people will come, because they know they're on familiar territory and they'll be interested to see that play again or see it for the first time. If you're doing new works with new names, it's harder to attract an audience.

In fact, it was our board who kept sort of prodding us, saying, "What you should do is do something popular. Show what you can do, and use that to build your audience." So eventually we took that on board and, again, in discussion with our board, said, "Yeah, we should do something really Irish, a crackin' Irish comedy, because what we do has a lot of comedy in it, it's what we are."

So: comedy, popular Irish, classic play, and do your interpretation of it. That was the brief. We then asked Gerry would he like to be involved, would he direct it? And he said, "yeah", he'd be up for that. We were all supposed to go off and read loads of plays which we promptly didn't do, except for Gerry. The first one he picked up was *The Whiteheaded Boy* by Lennox Robinson. We were in rehearsal for *Out the Back Door*, at that stage. Gerry called us and he said, "I'm after reading this play, will you come out and have a look at it?" So we said, "Grand"; jumped in a bus out to Gerry's house. Read the play.

There were twelve characters in the play and Gerry divided the characters, dished them out to all three of us. And, in fact, that first reading was how it stood in performance. He read "the whiteheaded boy' character, and we had a crackin' time, just really enjoying it, because it's such familiar territory for us all. You know, the notion of "the golden son."

Of course, its brief was, as I said, a popular Irish comedy that people would be more willing to come to, and satisfy our artistic remit and expand our audience in doing so. And it was a runaway success for us. It did much more than we ever thought it would do.

This year, 2001, we intend to mirror that very first festival, when we did three shows back to back. But now we look to the future, as well. The format it will take is exactly the same: three shows back to back. But now we've cast a new company of actors for this festival, five actors whom we'll devise two shows with. I will devize and direct the five actors in one show, and Veronica will devise and direct a show with the same cast. And then both myself and Veronica will devise a show with Gerry. And so it will be like we have the old Barabbas on crutches or zimmer frames, nearly, at this stage to give it a centre. And this newness, which also gives us a chance to extend the work we do. Mikel Murfi, now, has left us as of a couple of months ago. He may return in the future, as well as not. We didn't have a big row or anything. He just needed to go and do his own thing. He had been doing some directing with Macnas, which I'm sure he'll return to, as well.

EW: *Would you say that there's anything that fired you at the start, or that you talked about at the start, that you still haven't gotten around to?*

RK: Oh, yes. We had fantastic notions over the first couple of years … The reason, for instance, why we called ourselves *Barabbas* … *the company*, was that in the bigger scheme of things we thought we'd be a production company that could produce anything. We thought, if we call ourselves *Barabbas* … *the company*, then we could call

everything we did *Barabbas* ... the "something." We launched
ourselves as *Barabbas* ... *the Festival*. It could be *Barabbas* ... *the
Festival II*, this year; *Barabbas* ... *the TV programme, Barabbas* ... *the
Film, Barabbas* ... *the Book, Barabbas* ... *the Workshop, Barabbas* ... *the
whatever we wanted it to be.*

Every year, if possible, we do at least one set of workshops, let's say
a two-week workshop for fellow practitioners, people who are
interested in this kind of work or are interested in the kind of stuff
that we've been getting up to over the years. They've proved very
successful, and also very enhancing, in fact, because we get to share
the things we've accessed with a bunch of people for two weeks
and we get to rob all their ideas in the end, as well. But also it's
good training. It focuses us terribly on what exactly we're chasing.

So we did make a little jump into television because we received a
commission from Telefís na Gaeilge [TV4] to make ninety one-
minute films, based on the characters from our very first show, *John
Clown*. We shot the ninety on film, which meant that it had a very
good quality, and TnaG loved it and put it out for a number of
years, at all different time slots, repeating it over a few years, and
they sold it abroad, as well, as far as Korea and parts of Spain.

EW: *You wouldn't stand still in your life for eight years, so your travels or
what's going on in Irish theatre and culture around you must somehow be
affecting your work. Can you see anything that wouldn't have occurred to you
when you started that now seems very natural in terms of topics or theatrical
techniques?*

RK: I would hope we're refining them as time goes by, getting
better. I think at the beginning a lot of our shows were terribly
flawed, but people were so generous in the way they reacted to
them. And that sort of brought me to think in a way, "Well what is
it we're getting right, as well? Sure, the shows are all right, but
they're not great masterpieces." But people were responding almost
over-positively at times, so it began to make you think, "Well, what
is it that we do that people like?" Sure, it's gentle, it's naïve,
truthful, I hope, respectful, the characters that we would portray.

What we, by default, ended up accessing was a way of presentation,
about *how* we present theatre. And maybe that's the thing that's
excited me, in a way, something I never realized. I suppose it began
with things like *Half Eight Mass of a Tuesday*, where you almost saw
us wandering around the stage as ourselves. Then you saw us jump
into characters, then you saw us jump back out again, sometimes
even watching other things that were happening. That seemed to
show up again in our version of *The Whiteheaded Boy*, where the

initial impulse for that was, if you like, "Hello, everybody", you know, talking to the audience before the show, walking around the auditorium, chatting away. I suppose the conceit was, "We're going to do a play here, a great Irish play." We took Lennox Robinson's stage directions and used them as narrative, speaking to the audience, "*The Whiteheaded Boy*, by Lennox Robinson, a well-made play in three acts. Mrs Geoghegan's house is at the end of the street", which is the actual first line in the stage directions. That was another area where we used this "presentational" form, which I think has the potential to actually invite your audience in a bit more.

I would relate it to puppets, as well: When I worked in television on *Pajo's Junkbox*, doing puppets, obviously you didn't see the puppeteers in television, we were hidden so they only shot the puppet. And it was a kids' programme, and we used to invite kids in from time to time to see the studio. I did the main puppet, called Pajo. When the kids came in I would not hide myself, so I'd have Pajo on my knee, and the kids would be in absolute horror, shock, when they'd first see that. They'd look at *him* and say to *me*, "You're working him, aren't you?" And then look at the puppet and say, "Isn't he?" And that was, for me, the most magical thing.

EW: *I remember that from* Out the Back Door. *When you were manipulating all the undersea creatures, it was great to watch the sort of dance that you did while working the puppets. You could see both puppets and performers at the same time, and it didn't spoil whatever illusion there was, it just made a beautiful counterpoint to it.*

RK: Again, I see puppets like masks. I see red-nose clown as mask, as well, it's a very tiny mask. And there's something magical about putting on a mask. Whether it be neutral mask or the biggest character mask. Maybe that's the whole magic of theatre: it *is* "makey-uppy." It's essential to the whole way I see theatre: All I have to do is fifty percent of the show. The other fifty percent is the audience's. But my job and service is, if you like, to keep the magic bubble "unburst", so to speak. To *create* the bubble for the audience to come into and keep it from bursting.

EW: *I suppose there's a school of thought that thinks the magic bubble is the fact that we can't see who's pulling the strings of theatricality. But maybe that's not always the case.*

RK: I think, when we've been most successful with keeping that bubble alive and it's odd now that I say that it is sometimes about piercing it. Though while piercing it, we're actually strengthening it. In a way, this theatre bubble ... If I say at any time to anybody,

"Once upon a time ..." we have attention, story. And in a funny way theatre is like that, isn't it? The way you'd say, "We're going to do a play", in our case, let's say, "We're gonna do a play called *The Whiteheaded Boy*, and it goes like this ..."

And that's the basis. So sometimes, I think exposing that bubble draws us in even more, because we're now asked, as the audience, to make that extra leap; basically we've signed that contract, and now we've bought even further into the contract. And that, for me over the years, is the most exciting thing that I've learned about theatre, about this contract we have with our audience.

EW: *Has there been any conscious dedication to things Irish?*

RK: Yes, very much. We always said that. We *are* Irish so that whatever we make will be Irish. But we were also obsessed with this Irish psyche. Maybe that's the clown factor within us all, as well, that we're all interested in the "small" character, the mundane, the naive, maybe because that's what we are ourselves.

EW: *Can you talk a little bit about "clown?"*

RK: I find clown work sometimes very difficult to talk about because it's such a rich area to be in. It's a bit like physical theatre. How can you talk about physical theatre when it's physical? At the basis, I suppose, for me, it's a mask to begin with whether I use a red nose or not, there's still a mask involved in clown. Clown is a remove from reality, except that, particularly in Barabbas clown we love to mix it with absolute reality and keep that mask of clown, which is somewhat unreal.

Our clowns aren't big colourful garish clowns. In fact, as I say, they're based on real people; with one red sphere on the nose, a small red sphere, this little mask. Interestingly, this red nose thing can often be somewhat scary for children which raises some questions around its suitability for children. Clown is an adult theatre. It's a sophisticated form of theatre. *Or* is it that we have freaked the hell out of our kids with nasty clowns over the years? Like that circus thing, where they come and dump the bucket of water, which ends up being confetti, on top of you. That standard clown gag, is that too much for a young child? Or a car exploding and wheels falling off of it. It certainly scared the hell out of me when I was a kid. And a lot of clowns are still like that.

Sometimes when I see big, garish clowns it doesn't work, unless they're exquisitely well done, like Slava, in *Snowshow*. He's a master clown, and quite a big, garish clown. But a lot of big, garish clowns still turn me off. Maybe it's my memory as a child of being scared.

But I find their attack on the audience is a little too much for me. And what clown has taught me over the years is the exact opposite: It has trained me, as an actor to "wait" for my audience to *come with me*, and give my audience the choice to come with me, as opposed to me imposing myself.

EW: Is there a sense that the mask can force you or allow you to find something inside yourself that you didn't know was there?

RK: Perhaps deeper, yes. The difference, for instance, with neutral mask, is that neutral mask allows us the capacity to learn how we speak with our bodies. You add character mask on top of that, and then you must now be truthful to that character. When theatre is at its best, is when it's at its most truthful. That you absolutely buy what you see: you buy the characters and you buy the actor playing it. So you're not watching the actor playing it, you're actually experiencing the character.

EW: *Isn't that what makes people laugh, often, seeing something that's exceedingly true and surprising?*

RK: Absolutely. You're familiar with it: "I know that. That's happened to me. I can experience that." The thing that we've been accessing over the years is that you take off the mask and then go back into the mask. People are willing to make that trip with you. We talk to the audience, now we play the play by taking off the mask. And they still come with you, as long as you're truthful. Which has another little echo in physical theatre, I suppose.

One of the reasons we went down that road is that, for instance, human beings are great liars with words. We can lie brilliantly. If I call you on the phone, I can say things, and you'd probably believe them because we're good liars. But if you're sitting in front of me, my body will give me away. We'll have a little twitch; and even if we don't recognize the lie, something deep in your subconscious will not have bought it.

And I think if you transpose that into the theatre: Why is it that sometimes when we go to the theatre and see the most brilliant work, brilliant actors performing beautiful language and you still come away slightly not having gone the whole hog? I almost guarantee it has something to do with physicality that you haven't bought into.

Because actors are liars; that's what we are. We tell fibs, we makeup; that's what we do. And we're good at it. Sometimes we fail and sometimes it's through words and sometimes through physicality.

So if you take that notion of truth into theatre, obsessed with physicality, you begin everything with physicality. You find your character with physicality: pure shape – form you begin with. Does the character bend over? Does he or she have a limp or twitch? And then you add and add more truth. And of course the psychology comes into it, because you have nothing if you *only* have the physical structure.

But I suppose what has really excited us over the years is accessing character; once you put down the physicality of a character, it just seems everything else flows from it. It becomes easier, even the way the person behaves or the way the person speaks seems to come much more easily. That's our practice, that's what works for us.

EW: *One of the things about* The Whiteheaded Boy, *was that it seemed like the characterizations were so essentially Irish, yet you toured to many different countries, and it seemed to provoke a response in each case. So in a way it seemed like you had tapped into something that those bodies could recognize as their own.*

RK: It's amazing, I suppose, isn't that the brilliance of it all? When you get your theatre right, we'll watch a Polish company, and we won't speak Polish, but if it's good, we'll be riveted. If it's truthful, it works. Beckett was at it years ago, trying to find truth in absolutely mundane things. Beckett is brilliant. People think that he's dense and difficult, but he's very simple. I'm not interested in making theatre for people who are the intellectuals or the "theatre people." I want them to like my work, of course, and enjoy it when they do. But I'm much more interested in making theatre for people like myself ... where I come from, a small-town background, where I never had any access to theatre. Our show *Half Eight Mass of a Tuesday* went to France. Catholicism is big in France. And then we went to Denmark, which is Lutheran. And it was lovely, there, actually, because a lot of people who came, said, "God, it's just like our church."

EW: *It obviously worked.*

RK: One of the instances, which maybe proves this point as well: when we were researching *Half Eight Mass on a Tuesday*, we set it in a very small town, literally we're talking a street and pub or two and a grocery shop and a church. We decided, "Yes, let's go down the country and research, again, what we've grown up with." Of course we never got around to it and we went across the road to Gardiner Street church. And spent a couple of hours, the odd day, here and there and, of course, it's exactly the same there as we remembered it growing up, because people are people are people, in a funny way.

EW: *I wonder if we could just change perspective, and look at the company from the administrative side, which you've had to take a hand in. Veronica was the Artistic Director for a while and then you took over. What effect has that had on the working of the company, the kind of work that the company does? Will this continue, and will you be looking for a new set of actors to carry forth a Barabbas tradition?*

RK: That's an interesting question because we're right in the middle of it now. What we did first, and what I would say to *any* company starting out, is to put your administration in place, if you want to access funding, particularly through the main funding partners that are around, which is the Arts Council, nowadays. It is very much a partnership for us and the Arts Council; we have built a very good relationship. It's no longer "the funders" and "us", it is actually a dialogue. So luckily, wherever we had that foresight, we put that administration in place, which freed us up to be the creators, if you like. Even though we were very close to our company, and wanted to manage everything it did.

As the company grew, we saw, "Well, if we're *really* going to make a go of this, an artistic director or a full-time person would be of benefit to the company." We had put in place an administrator and an assistant administrator, and then we brought in an artistic director. The question we had was, "Well, who would be the artistic director?" Obviously it had to be one of the core trio, either myself, Veronica or Mikel. Now we sat and talked, had lots of cups of tea about that. What would be the best scenario? It was very obvious that both myself and Mikel were just assuming that Veronica might take on the role, because we thought her to be the most qualified; she has a good head. It just seemed that it would suit her. Now, the brief of the Artistic Director, of course, was to act as the figurehead for the threesome. Because, if you like, it's a threesome of Artistic Directors, but we would put one person in place that would drive our dream, so to speak. It would be a full-time employment, as well, for a year; and a wage, which is a nice thing, because we worked for years without any wages, bar when in production. In fact the first three years, we paid everybody else, bar ourselves, because we had this notion that we didn't want to ask people to work for nothing, whether it was a very small fee or whatever, at the beginning. But we insisted that we wouldn't ask people to do things for nothing.

So it was an opportunity, I suppose, as well, to build up the company, have a full-time person thinking about and applying themselves to the artistic direction of the company which would be dreamed up by the threesome and drive the bigger picture of the company, as well. Marry the administration to the artistic, and create a better structure that we could move and grow with.

Luckily, Veronica accepted the position for the first year and the system we put in place was that we would rotate it. So come the end of the year, one of us would take over; and we'd decide as the year went by, who would take over next. Veronica did a year. Half-way through the year, she said, "Yep. I'll do one year, but I don't want to spend my time doing this." So, it was up to myself and Mikel. At the time, I remember we said, "Really the way we should be looking at this is that if you're interested put your hand up", as opposed to *having* to do the job. So I went off and thought about it; and I was quite surprised with myself, actually, that I wanted to do it. So I put my hand up and Mikel was greatly relieved.

And then it came to the middle of *my* year as Artistic Director, and it was up for grabs again. And we did the same thing: "Does Veronica want to come back? Does Mikel want to come in? Do I want to stay?" I put my hand up for staying, and both were absolutely relieved with that, because neither Veronica wanted to come back nor Mikel wanted to step in. And I was delighted, because I found there was a really big learning curve for me; it made me think of the bigger picture, and made me operate in a different way. And also, I suppose, I just loved working with the company and being the representative or the figurehead. This is my second year, as we speak.

There's a broad core of people from management and administration – Audrey Behan and Amy O'Hanlon – to designers Sean Hillen, Paki Smith, Laurent Mellet, Carole Betera, Mark Galione, and soundscapers like Roger Gregg. Stage managers, makers, doers, inventors, Marie Tierney, Miriam Duffy, Emer Murphy. A team of people that we've been so lucky to access, and who have influenced Barabbas' theatre in no small way. Because their invention has allowed us to go, "Oh, wow, let's use that."

EW: *You have been drawing on a variety of other people for the past few years. Will there be a Barabbas … The Next Generation?*

RK: In the long term, I suppose since I've been Artistic Director, that has been our dream. You've used the perfect phrase, there, "The Next Generation Barabbas." That's what we would love to see happen. Because it's time now for us to be influenced by new blood.

EW: *The show you auditioned last year, it seemed like you went out of your way to see anybody in Dublin who was interested.*

RK: Well, it's absolutely delightful, but also you feel like one of those documentaries at the moment, casting for a pop band.

EW: *Popstars.*

RK: Honestly, when I saw that, I thought, "God, are we like that?" We have this policy about opening our gates. People send you their CV's. They at least deserve a postcard back or a letter back. When we can, and it's a style of casting that suits us, we do auditions in workshop format. So you don't come in and just do your audition piece, because, to be totally honest, I couldn't. I'm sure Veronica and Mikel could but I couldn't tell you whether you were any good after an audition piece, you know what I mean? But what I would be able to say, by the end of a day with you, is, "Do you like the work? Are you tweaked by it? Do you have skills towards it? Do I like working with you?" And for you to make those same decisions.

It seems that there's a whole heap of people out there who would love the chance to kick space with us. And our casting workshops are delightful in that way, as well, because people do leave at the end of the day, going, "Look, best of luck with everything, it's been a great day." And actually it's been a workshop, as well, because they've gotten to see the way we work, a little like a free workshop, as they would say themselves. We wouldn't view it like that; we'd love to be paying you for your time, to come along and spend the day with us.

For *Brilliant Day's Blue*, some years back, we saw 130 women over two weeks, with callbacks. We were casting 15 women then. This time around, we cast five people, we'd intended doing that again, but we couldn't see that amount of people for five places. But as soon as word got out, people we're going, "Ahh, I'd love the chance to show you", and then you go, "Well, this is our function, as well, open the gates." Let people have a look at us; we can have a look at people, and if it doesn't happen today, there may be something down the line. And also it gives us a lovely look at the broader community: what's out there, who's out there. And what kind of trainings are out there.

EW: *Are you excited by all that?*

RK: Hugely. We get such a buzz when we invite people in for those day workshops, those casting workshops, I think people don't feel the pressure as much. After the first half hour, they don't feel like they're on display or have to prove themselves. They enter into the fun which is actually the core of the way we work. Barabbas is about fun, quite a lot. Of course it isn't always fun; there's a lot of hard work, a lot of struggle to put a piece together. But we do really try to keep a lightness of being in the way we access our work.

EW: *Is there any kind of unlikely dream, or unlikely notion that you might have on the back burner, but would like to see the company go towards at some time?*

RK: Right now, this notion of the next generation is really tweakin' me. In the event of that happening, what will that do to us if we're to be influenced by a small or big bunch of new performers and theatre makers?

We used to have dreams, years ago, about what we would do with a hundred actors, and how you could just blow people away. An area we've touched on over the years is outdoor spectacle. Again, from a very Barabbas perspective, as opposed to, I'll just choose one, a Macnas perspective, as this big pageant thing. Macnas are brilliant, but we have another way of accessing things, like a little clown exhibit a few years ago for May Day and for St. Patrick's Day, which was basically three clowns living out their lives in a room in the back of a truck, in fact, for the parade.

And we had Barabbas … the Cube, last year, which was a very interesting thing for Expo 2000. And that's something that both myself and Veronica have been talking about of late, as well. An area we could develop over the years, maybe bigger: civic events, if you like, rather than outdoor. And it may not be theatre. It could be a visual. Like for instance when we were in Chicago with *The Whiteheaded Boy*, we saw this fantastic thing, a street exhibition of cows. The Cow Parade, it was called. Basically what they did was put 5,000 cows out there, made from fiberglass. And you got your basic cow as an artist and you got to do with it what you would like to do. You could recut it, reshape it, two ends of a cow back to back; the "cow jumped over the moon" theme… every street corner, sometimes up the sides of buildings, sometimes jumping over a bridge. We were close to going into it, the notion of importing it back to Dublin.

EW: *I'm going to stop, now, but I just wanted to know where the name, Barabbas came from?*

RK: Basically, at the time, Mikel had a short story on the go, called, "Barabbas Banana, the Fastest Banana in the World." We were going through suggestions for names, and Barabbas Banana was one that Mikel suggested. Both myself and Veronica dropped Banana and Veronica added …the company.

EW: *Is there any religious connection?*

RK In Mikel's story, his notions about Barabbas were that he hasn't been treated terribly fairly. He's just "the one that got away." And every Easter, who do we condemn? Who's the baddy? I was looking it up lately and Barabbas actually means, "son of the father." So was it a wee word play? I just like the name, full stop and the fact that he got away. And we might get away with murder. Then I found out he wasn't a murderer at all, he was a robber. So maybe we'll get away with robbing other people's ideas.

Raymond Keane is a founding member of Barabbas and is currently Artistic Director. He has devised and appeared in all their work to date except *Strokehauling, Barabbas the CUBE* and *Hupnouse*, written for the company by Charlie O'Neill, which he directed. Outside Barabbas he has worked with Grapevine, Wet Paint, Copol, Horizon, Macnas, Passion Machine, The Crack '90's, No Dance Performers, the Oscar Mime Co., Throwin' Shapes, CoisCéim Dance Theatre, the Abbey and the Gaiety. He also directed *Pam Ella* written and performed by Alice Barry. Before Barabbas, Raymond worked for several years in television as writer/actor/puppeteer on programmes including Pajo's Junkbox, The Whole Shebang, Pajo and the Salty Frog, Pajo and the Salty Frog in Space, Scratch Saturday, J.M.T.V., The Morbegs, Nighthawks, The Basement and Fair City. In film he appears in *The Boy From Mercury, St. Patrick, The Last Mango in Dublin* and *Sweety Barrett*.

Eric Weitz teaches practical and academic classes in theatre at the Gaiety School of Acting, Trinity College Dublin, and University College Dublin. A former actor, director, and journalist in the U.S., he has directed several shows in Dublin, where he founded his own company, called Tricksters. He holds an M.A. in Modern Drama Studies from UCD, and a Ph.D. in Theatre Studies from TCD.

Tom Kilroy in Conversation with Gerry Dukes

GD: *To begin, a small piece of background. Your first play to be produced on stage was* The Death and Resurrection of Mr Roche *[Dublin Theatre Festival, 1968]. In May of the following year an earlier play of yours,* The O'Neill, *was produced at the Peacock theatre. And then in 1971 your novel,* The Big Chapel, *was published in London. In certain respects* The O'Neill *and* The Big Chapel *are cognate stories.*

TK: Yes, I had not thought of them in that way before. I started out writing by submitting a radio play to the BBC in Belfast, for a competition. The play was called *The Door* and it won first prize in the competition. The BBC then did a production of it with Cyril Cusack and Godfrey Quigley. That play was one of the sparks towards writing for the theatre.

GD: *You were working as a full-time academic at the time.*

TK: That's right. I was teaching in the English Department at UCD in Earlsfort Terrace. I was writing *The Big Chapel* at the time. The novel really comes out of my childhood and the folk memory of Callan in Co. Kilkenny where I had grown up. Before I started the novel I had been reading a great deal of Faulkner and my novel is quite Faulknerian. *The O'Neill* comes almost directly out of Sean Ó Faoláin's *The Great O'Neill*, a book which unlocked in me an interest – one I continue to have – in the Anglicization of Ireland and of the Irish character and temper which I see as much more than merely linguistic but as a profound mind shift. This shift is very subtle and various and impacts on the "Irish Story" in many fascinating ways. One of the things Ó Faoláin tried to argue in his book, and this was very much in keeping with the temper of the 1950s, was that O'Neill was one of the first Irishmen who was also consciously a European. He was bringing to the tribal warfare in Ireland a distinctively European consciousness, one that was informed by certain European attitudes towards politics.

GD: *You must have had a certain uneasiness about these matters because in* The O'Neill *your character Master Mountfort, an English preacher on the Irish side, a man who could be described as an agent of the Roman counter-reformation, does not get a good press. In your play O'Neill is not in sympathy with the notion of a pan-European version of the Holy Roman Empire led by the Roman Catholic and Apostolic Church.*

TK: True. If you think of O'Neill as attempting to lift Irish civilization out of the backwater and into, ideally, some European mainstream then Mountfort in the play represents the way the Roman Catholic Church latches on to what is really a secular notion and makes it into a platform for religious advancement and empowerment.

GD: *And this is where the play actually intersects directly with* The Big Chapel.

TK: Yes, that's right. It also intersects with *Talbot's Box*. One of the things that fascinates me about the church and about religion is the way in which religion, as it were, adheres almost like a mollusc to political idealism, and it manages to convert that political idealism into something which empowers the church, so that the whole European idea would be in fact something which the church adopted for its own ends. For me, on the other hand, the whole European idea is something much more secular. I was fascinated by O'Neill because I saw him as a figure who tries to find himself through authority, who tries to have a personal fulfilment or make a personal journey through the whole business of power and authority. In the play I was trying to dramatize the way in which personal mission or commitment in some respects clashes with the public role. I have always been fascinated by the way in which private qualities, maybe even private weaknesses, become hugely important when the figure is a figure of authority. And, yes, you are right. This is certainly one of the main things I tried to work on in *The Big Chapel*.

GD: *You maintain that interest or focus right across your work. For example,* The Secret Fall of Constance Wilde *moves towards an ambiguous and ambivalent moment at the end of the play where the truth is finally going to be revealed, where Constance Wilde's "private secret" is made public but the audience's view is obscured by a large puppet and its attendants. The audience has to "read" the secret from Oscar Wilde's distress at its revelation.*

TK: The clash between public and private life shines a light on the individual involved. It's a strange kind of highlighting because it tends to distort the personal and I think great leaders become monstrous in that regard. Their skill is in fact a skill of massive simplification of personality, so that the complex personality that we ordinarily expect to exist seems to be clarified into a single, potent and essentially non-human simplicity.

GD: *It strikes me that somebody interested in those kind of ideas and interested in excavating those kind of experiences would find theatre an enormously congenial medium in which to work.*

TK: Yes. I think that most playwrights are actors *manqué* and that in a sense what distinguishes the writing of plays from other forms of fiction is that the playwright is listening to not just simply the voice of character, but in some mysterious, simultaneous way, listening to the voice and to the voice of the actor playing that character. So what we have is a voice which is being performed and being performed in the act of writing. Already implicit in playwriting you have this transition from the private to the public – playwriting is a histrionic art form. It's an art form that has to do with role-playing, with acting, with pretence, with artifice at the level of revelation and concealment, with illusion. Writing plays and the theatre itself are ways of, inevitably, giving public exposure to privacies.

GD: *You have exploited this in your* Double Cross *and have eloquently "theorized" this aspect of playwriting in the introduction you published with the play text in 1994. There you note that* Double Cross *"is a play which moves along the line from role-playing at one end to treachery at the other, from fiction-making to political treason." You go on to note that the act of deception is common to theatricality and criminality. This is underscored in the play itself by having the parts of Brendan Bracken and William Joyce played by the same actor. You even provide for an electronic contrivance to present the actor playing both parts simultaneously. There can be few finer demonstrations of the "dual voice" of playwriting of which you have spoken.*

TK: I think theatre invites that kind of manipulation or trickery. At least the theatre I'm interested in invites it. I'm not interested in naturalistic theatre and in the theatre of conventional narrative and conventional storytelling. I think that is a very rich theatre but it is not one that attracts me. Perhaps I am not up to meeting the demands of that kind of theatre. I'm fascinated by the theatre that offers multiple illusion. The kind of theatre that interests me is one that invites you in and never for one moment pretends to be anything else but theatre, that celebrates itself and celebrates the theatricality of action and movement and the rest of it.

GD: *This then goes some way to explaining or illuminating a play like* Tea and Sex and Shakespeare *which opens in a naturalistic mode. We see a room with a wardrobe, a typewriter, a door to a landing and a telephone. In fact the very furniture of a real world. Then all hell breaks loose until the end when* *some kind of normality is restored. By then, of course, the play has established a kind of collusive relationship between the audience and the character Brian, the writer, a relationship cemented by Brian who, as the final stage direction prescribes, raises an eyebrow. That small gesture invites the audience to regard the events they have just witnessed as a kind of surreal overlay, a temporary hijacking of the real by the febrile imagination of the writer. You have played with the naturalistic theatre – you have torn the tripes out of it – you have done all kinds of extraordinarily comic things but, as I recall, the first production at the Abbey with the late Donal McCann in 1977 was an unsatisfactory production.*

TK: Well, it was also an unsatisfactory text. It was a play that gave me enormous difficulty and it came out of a personal passage which could only be described as a kind of breakdown and it had to do with personal, domestic circumstances. It also had to do with the first real serious prospect of total silence from me as a writer, where I felt I could never write again. This comic play, and comedy always comes out of great distress, comes out of that kind of personal trauma so that the writing of it was like cutting through immense, tangled undergrowth and it meant numerous wrong directions. I could never quite see the way in which this might end so that the first version I produced, which was directed by Max Stafford-Clarke, was, as you say, unsatisfactory. Max responded to the play as a great lark, which was absolutely right, and Donal [McCann] went for it in the same way. He found the language of the play very exciting and interesting to an actor but what I had not given the play was a workable shape. I had not provided a structure which would house the thing on a stage for two hours. So there were endless problems in rehearsal. I recall the late May Cluskey, whom you will remember as an extraordinary comic actress, had no problem whatsoever delivering individual lines but every so often she'd turn to me and say: "What in the name of Jaysus is going on in this thing at all?" I couldn't answer her. Therefore I jumped at the chance to re-work the script when Rough Magic wanted to do it [in 1988]. It was the most major reworking I have ever undertaken. I worked with Declan Hughes [the revised text is dedicated to Declan Hughes] and Stanley Townsend and the company and we did actually find a shape and that shape is exactly what you described. It started out in some sort of pedestrian normality and re-entered that pedestrian normality at the end. As soon as we saw that this had to happen the thing went right, found its coherence. There is one problem in the printed text of the play – it suggests that the setting should be a kind of surreal version of this house of flats and I think that is wrong and I'd like to correct it if I could in some future edition. I think that it should be absolutely naturalistic, as normal as possible. There was a recent production by a young Cork company, Brown Penny, and they did in fact create a kind of surreal set and it caused a lot of problems at the beginning of the play because the audience did not know where it was. What is required is a grounding in, say, Dublin flat-land, then the thing just explodes.

GD: *Your experience with* Tea and Sex and Shakespeare *prompts the question, or rather, three questions. When is a play finished: when do you let it go and is it possible to generalize about these matters?*

TK: The first thing to be said is that the practice of playwrights differs, it is as individual as the playwrights themselves. There is a huge range of attitudes among playwrights towards the whole process of production and the role of a director. My good friend Brian Friel will come to the first rehearsal with an absolutely finished text and will look for, and rightly look for, a loyal and faithful rendition of that text. I'm completely different. I actually enjoy the uncertainty of rehearsal and I enjoy the subversion of the text in rehearsal. I also have a great belief in the responses of actors to a text. They may not articulate quite what their worries are but when they do express a worry or a modest suggestion for change then you listen to them. Actors are at the sharp end and I have always found it rewarding to listen to their views and suggestions. Actors have very different perceptions of what is going on in a text to those of the writer. I have always found collaboration to be useful and exciting. I've had very happy working relationships with directors, by and large. We have had difficulties and collapses but I have enjoyed good relationships with directors here and in the UK. Patrick Mason directed the first production of *Talbot's Box* and the true, the physical nature of that play really only emerged for me in rehearsal. It was Patrick who "discovered" the strong, almost frontal physicality and imagery in the play. I like to think all of that was there in the text but Patrick was wonderful in bringing it out and showing the possibilities. This is the great value of the collaborative approach; once a set of possibilities has been identified you can then work on those which need to be, ought to be, realized. So, my relationship with Patrick is a very dear one, both professionally and personally. He brought the same sense of physical theatre to *The Secret Fall of Constance Wilde*. What I wanted to do was to go into the fraught environment of three people in crisis, to show that the world they occupy as they tear one another apart is in some way inhuman, it has gone beyond easy feeling. I wanted a style which would actually allow the audience access to that. Some of the audience, perhaps a significant amount, found this intimidating and cold. Naturally, I disagree. The play was simply asking the audience to abandon the very obvious and very basic emotional responses that you get in theatre and to try to reach the feeling of the play in another way, by another route.

GD: *Hence the large puppets. These require attendants, manipulators if you will. You've always been interested in the notion of character, on stage, being manipulated. Talbot's Box is very much in this mode. Tea and Sex and Shakespeare is a manic version if you like, because there is something in Brian that is causing all this mayhem, and he is a writer. So there is a dark presence behind the stage and it is that of the author.*

TK: Yes, that is one way of putting it. Or perhaps it is theatre itself or that performative dimension that theatre has in common with life. A kind of diminution of human power and human capacity to be in control. My sense of theatre is now increasingly pictorial and the kind of analogy I think of in relation to theatre is that of painting. I love Yeats's notion of the painted stage and I really enjoy being able to paint large scale images which act as a theatrical and informing backdrop to the human dilemmas out front, so to speak. That seems to me a very rich way of using the stage. For me the stage is this very potent place. An empty stage is a very desolate place but it has within it the seeds of this potentiality and when you have human beings moving and acting and creating a dynamic up there, there's nothing quite like it.

GD: *I remember you talking at a conference some years ago and you responded memorably to a questioner. The question was direct, as I recall: "How do you write a play?" Your response was equally direct: "I hear voices in my head and when they get too insistent I begin to write them down." Would you care to elaborate on that?*

TK: Playwriting is all about voice – in the initial stage at any rate – because voice is what you are going to hear if and when the play makes it to the stage. You are going to hear voices speaking. For me though, in the writing, I hear the voice but I also hear the possibility of an actor playing that voice so that the language, the speech in a play is fundamentally different to speech spoken on the street and speech written in prose fiction. You are not allowed the degree of, I don't know what it is, perhaps it's some kind of relaxation in the writing of speech for prose-fiction. You are limited in the theatre to producing speech which can be spoken by an actor, which is actable, in the strict sense of that term. Until the voices become fully formed and fully authentic in character I cannot begin to write the play. But as soon as they have that authenticity I can begin to write and then the only problem is how to shut them up. It is at this point that the real problem arises, the problem of containing the voices within an efficient shape. Without that there is nothing.

GD: *The play is at an advanced stage before you write it down, or up. We will not quibble about prepositions.*

TK: We should do so. As I intimated earlier, I bring what I have written down to rehearsal and then discover, in conjunction with the cast and the director, how it must be written up. It is a salutary and grounding experience to discover the mistakes one has made and to try to rectify them before public performance. Rehearsals test the private theatre of the mind in a space that soon, sometimes too soon, will become public.

GD: *You talk about an actable speech and yet in* The Seagull *[1981, a version of Chekhov's play] you give an odd dialect, if I can call it that, to the characters; to Aston particularly and even more so to Constantine, the young writer with his Moytura play. You were quite cruel to the young Yeats.*

TK: I was thinking of all of those awful nineteenth century melodramas and pageants that were being written before Yeats came along. If Yeats had not gone east of a line drawn from Sligo to Coole he might have sounded like Constantine.

GD: *On reflection, the stiltedness of the language is entirely appropriate for a version of Chekhov. The characters seem to be locked into a language that is gradually losing its purchase on the real world, a language gone beyond its sell-by date. The country house where the play is set is encircled by the flux of history – ribbon-men, Land League agitation, rent strikes. Was there a particular difficulty for you as a writer making that odd, stilted language?*

TK: The thing arose through Max Stafford-Clarke, and Max asked me to do the job of work and literally it was offered as a job of work and of course it became something entirely personal, fortunately. Max's father was a distinguished psychiatrist, in fact one of the early exponents of Freudianism in Britain, in Edinburgh as it happened. He was an advisor to John Huston in the making of *Freud.* When Max was a student in Trinity, Huston invited him down to Galway where he was living the life of an Anglo-Irish squire. Max was fascinated by the area and by the wonderful house. When he came to do *The Seagull,* he had the idea of making it into an Anglo-Irish play and the reason for this was that he felt that the typical English production of Chekhov made it sound as though it were set in the Home Counties and that you had this kind of genteel polish put on top of Chekhov. Max's instinct was that Chekhov was much rougher and his characters lived in a world having its share of chaos and brutality. So he asked me for a version because he had liked *The Big Chapel* and the fact that we had worked together before. When I started to work on it I was thinking in terms of the 1870s but then I realized that I couldn't be specific, that I had to allow a wider, more flexible time-scale. So I was very loose in my use of theatrical and literary references, and with history too. My version shuttles across a much wider range than Chekhov's original play. But what I did want to do was to create a theatre language for, say, Aston, a language which would imitate the mechanistic, stilted kind of language of late Victorian prose-fiction, a language of domination and authority at odds with a world no longer content with being coerced. I was very fortunate in that Alan Rickman played Aston in the first production in London and he caught the fact that I had produced a kind of a pastiche. He immediately caught what I was trying to get at so that he had this very English, almost mechanistic tone in that big long speech he has with the girl. This was exactly the kind of thing I was hearing while writing the play.

GD: *You had an association, a fruitful association with Field Day, for some years. Was this a significant interlude in your life as a playwright?*

TK: Yes. I got involved with Field Day largely out of friendship. I was very close to Brian Friel, and Seamus Heaney, and Seamus Deane, and Stephen Rea. I didn't know Tom Paulin or Davy Hammond as well but I knew the others very well and we were constantly in and out of each others' houses so that when Field Day started I was on the side-lines, interrogating, and being told, and arguing about what Field Day was. The fact that Field Day was a theatre company meant that I was passionately interested so I was in Derry for the famous first production of *Translations*. And I was up there a lot with Deane, experiencing at first hand some of the trauma of the North. I was quite surprised when I was asked to join because I had this very clear sense of Field Day as being a northern enterprise and here they were looking for somebody from the south to join it. I think it had partly to do with the fact that both Brian and Stephen felt that there should be another playwright involved. Seamus Deane had asked me for a pamphlet but I regret to say I never got around to producing one.

When I joined Field Day, and I'm not betraying any secrets at this point, there was a general perception that it was a single-minded group moved by a certain idea of nationalism and republicanism. Those who were hostile seemed to think that Field Day was the cultural wing of the Provisional IRA, to put it mildly. Of course, there were as many political views in the group as there were individuals. I think it is fair to say that they were all trying to get behind or cut through the clichéd versions of politics that were then on offer. They were certainly trying to restore some of the lost voices of the common people of Ireland. Oddly enough I found myself becoming one of the strong political voices on the board and I eventually left Field Day because I felt it wasn't actually coming to a sense of political definition in the way that it should be. I felt that Field Day should be trying to free politics of sectarianism, making large statements about a possible, a feasible non-sectarian future for the island that would be hospitable and accommodating for everybody.

GD: *Nevertheless, as a theatre company Field Day was a great success. From it came your* Double Cross *and Derek Mahon's* High Time, *which was a marvellously liberating play. Tom Paulin's version of* Antigone – The Riot Act – *was courageous and provocative.*

TK: Field Day was in fact open to all kinds of possibilities in terms of theatre. It has since gone silent but there are stirrings still, signs of possible revival. But the Field Day enterprise as such ran its course. There is one aspect of the achievement of Field Day which has not yet received due recognition or acknowledgement from theatre historians and that is the fact that Friel and Field Day opened up the London stage for Irish writers. When I started out in the fifties and sixties with Hugh Leonard and Tom Murphy and others there was a hostility, a palpable resistance to Irish plays among London managements. I think Field Day did an enormous amount to turn that round, particularly with the touring productions of Brien Friel's plays. Field Day unlocked that scene for other writers.

GD: *So Conor McPherson, Martin McDonagh and Mark O'Rowe are all by Field Day, out of the Royal Court?*

TK: That is one way of putting it. I imagine that younger writers would probably find the whole notion ridiculous but they wouldn't have been aware of how serious the blockage was and the sheer disdain that existed in London theatre for Irish work. We all had plays performed there but it was practically impossible to have the work regarded as in any way serious or substantial.

GD: *Am I to infer from what you say that Irish writers could not have entered on the coat-tails of Beckett, perhaps because he was a luxury French import?*

TK: Beckett is *sui generis*. In many ways he is outside the whole modern Irish theatre experience.

GD: *Given the commitment to non-naturalist theatre that is evident in your work, almost from the beginning but particularly from the seventies onwards, and given your close working relationship with Patrick Mason [the published* *text of* The Secret Fall of Constance Wilde *is dedicated to Mason] would you care to comment on Mason's other collaborative theatre venture with Tom MacIntyre? I would have thought that collaboration between MacIntyre and Mason radically altered the shape of theatre in Ireland in ways that are still not appreciated. Would you care to comment on that?*

TK: Yes, I would say that it should have. It should have had a much more electric influence than in fact it had and MacIntyre is a key figure in it. The dominant mode in Irish theatre has been the naturalistic. There is that old joke about the Abbey theatre's commitment to the naturalist play being predicated on using the same set, a kitchen, again and again.

GD: *Behan's famous quip about putting down a pan of rashers for the "dacent man."*

TK: Exactly. MacIntyre's work and Mason's work was an attempt to bring in a very non-Irish sense of theatre into Ireland. MacIntyre was very interested in modern dance and mime. He was also very interested in the inarticulate. Giving the inarticulate a voice. You surely recall that astonishing last speech in *Rise Up Lovely Sweeney.* Irish theatre generally aims for perfect articulation. It prizes the ability to articulate things exactly and completely realistically. The naturalistic play claims to complete everything – to offer the absolutely perfect, contained solution. MacIntyre was working against that. Remember that his stage adaptation of Kavanagh's *The Great Hunger* was virtually wordless. But naturalism has proven to be pervasive and powerful. We have to bear in mind that before the 1890s we had no indigenous Irish theatre and what we had was an indigenous histrionic art form of story-telling and *scéalaíocht.* This was profoundly influential on the plays that followed, shaping the whole theatrical enterprise for generations of writers and performers. It has been the dominant mode throughout the twentieth century. Plays have to be set up to enable the efficient telling of a story, or in the case of the wonderful *Bailegangaire,* the non-telling of a story. You also have it in Beckett, the notion of a voice telling or trying to tell a story or an anecdote. This in itself is inherently dramatic. There are great richnesses in this mode of drama but there are also great weaknesses. It's remarkable how pervasive story-telling has been in shaping the work of writers like Murphy and Friel, down to Conor McPherson. The naturalistic mode of drama has a huge hold on Irish theatre in itself because of its own innate appeal but also because of the influence of television. The contemporary audience is conditioned by television, conditioned by factuality, conditioned by so-called real images. Mac Intyre and Mason were working against all that but their impact was not that great. The work never commanded a mass audience. It's almost now as if they had never existed. Naturalism has had an enormous impact, not just on playwriting but on production and on acting. It is exceptional to find a company which is willing or able to explore theatre languages other than the verbal.

GD: *Given the regrettable persistence of naturalism and the rarity of companies willing to explore other theatrical modes, would it be fair to conclude that there has been an absence of critical and theoretical thinking in Ireland about the multiform nature of theatre? What needs to be done to open up Irish theatre and make it hospitable to the kinds of theatre you would like to see develop?*

TK: Serious writing on theatre in Ireland is a rarity and there has been very little attention to theatre, by and large, from the intellectual community in the country. Nevertheless, there are encouraging signs but it might take some time yet before the range of initiatives undertaken by academic institutions and others come to fruition and begin to feed into the mainstream theatre. There are always waves in the theatre, waves of enthusiasm, waves of experimentation and so forth and I would hope to see a young theatre movement developing which would, for instance, draw on cinema. There are certain things that theatre cannot do as well as cinema and there are things that theatre cannot do as well as fiction writing but there are things that theatre can do uniquely well. Perhaps we should go back to the empty stage again and begin again at the beginning. If you look at the history of theatre, it is in fact a series of cycles and these cycles begin with a naturalistic stage and work towards a high degree of stage artifice. This is usually followed by a reaction against artifice and a restoration of naturalism again. There is a reaction at the moment against elaborate stage artifice and I think it has to do with the influence of television and with the televisual moulding of people's expectations, their imaginations and their hungers.

Many of the successful plays in London and New York at the moment are television plays. You're looking at a square box up there and you're watching something that could just as easily be on a television screen. There are things that can only be done on a stage and that is where they should be done. If they can be done elsewhere, then that is where they should be done. I hope that coming out of the schools you would have young people who would want to go back to the primitive appeal of the stage and to start using the full resources of training which are now becoming available. Young actors are coming through from the schools who are immensely better equipped, physically and professionally, than anyone I would have seen in my generation. The old Irish acting was wonderful but it was a kind of acting from the waist up. The most fundamental resource of the theatre is the body in space.

My ideal theatre is one in which the author is merely a cog in a bigger machine and the text is merely an available medium. The text may have its own integrity and uniqueness apart from performance but it is, foremost, offered in service, an occasion for something else. I recently saw a revival of *Double Cross* by Impact, a young company from Limerick. It was a minimalist, non-costume production and the amazing thing was that the text came through with great clarity. They stripped the play down to essentials so that it was almost a presentation of the text. The production was a lesson in how effective an elementary use of the stage can be, that you don't need those heavily embossed naturalistic settings, décor and the slavish imitation of what we think is real life and which is finally very dull. The hope is that we will go through a cycle and rediscover the very small number of instruments that the stage offers, and that, when used with skill and purity, they are very effective.

Tom Kilroy was born in 1934 in County Kilkenny and now lives in County Mayo. He concluded his career as an academic as Professor of English at NUI Galway. His novel, *The Big Chapel*, was shortlisted for the Booker Prize and won the Guardian Fiction Prize and the Heinemann Award. His plays include *The Death and Resurrection of Mr Roche, Tea and Sex and Shakespeare, Ghosts* (after Ibsen), *The Madam MacAdam Travelling Theatre, Six Characters in Search of an Author* (after Pirandello), *The O'Neill, The Seagull* (after Chekhov), *Double Cross* and *The Secret Fall of Constance Wilde*.

Gerry Dukes lectures in literature at the English Department, Mary Immaculate College, the University of Limerick. With the actor Barry McGovern he scripted the stage show *I'll go on* (based on Beckett's post-war trilogy of novels) which has toured the world. His reviews, articles and essays on writing and on the visual arts have been published in Europe and the United States. His most recent book publication was an annotated edition of Beckett's novellas and his biography of the writer is forthcoming in the *Penguin Illustrated Lives* series in January 2002.

Hugh Leonard in Conversation with Pat Donlon

PD: *Okay Jack [Hugh], what brought you into theatre? How did you start?*

HL: There's a fanciful story – put about by me! – that I discovered that I belonged not in front of a stage but rather on it. I think I described in my book *Home before Night* how I went to see *Plough and the Stars* with F. J. McCormick in the Abbey and this sparked something. I went back to take my mother the following evening, I think it was the only time I ever took her anywhere, and went to see it again. I wanted to write, but didn't know how and I didn't find out for a good many years. By then I was in the Civil Service, in the Land Commission, and I got involved in amateur dramatics. That was the first step and then I began to write for that particular amateur company, and the first play I ever wrote turned out to be my first play at the Abbey. Years later, I sent it in at my wife's suggestion and they accepted it and that was that.

PD: *That was starting at the top in a way, wasn't it?*

HL: Well, there was no place else to go – the Gate didn't do really original plays. You know the old joke, that the Abbey and the Gate were known as Sodom and Begorrah, and the Gate was the Sodom part of it. It did original plays that were sort of clique-ish; I don't mean "camp" or "gay", but they came from a charmed circle of people, the sort of Protestant theatre you would call it. So, other than the Abbey, there was really no other theatre. The Gaiety and the Olympia – they were doing repertory but it was usually touring companies from Britain, very well established plays that were sure of an audience. So the Abbey was the one you shot for, really. All you did was try to please Ernest Blythe and if you pleased Ernest, you were in. He liked political plays and he liked plays dealing with the Troubles and things like that. I remember he turned down *Madigan's Lock* because he said he didn't like plays with a ghost in them and I told him, "In that case, there goes *Hamlet*." There wasn't any bitterness but for about ten years afterwards I realized I was not writing the Abbey's kind of plays and it was a long time before I went back. Ernest was dead by then.

PD: *And your first play in the Abbey was?*

HL: It was *The Big Birthday*. This is a play that was first of all done by amateurs under the title of *Nightingale in the Branches*. The first play I wrote explicitly for the Abbey was for a play competition – it was called *The Italian Road*. It wasn't a bad play, I thought. But the Abbey said the standard was awful, that they weren't going to give an award that year so I decided that perhaps I wasn't God's gift to the theatre. Then I got married and my wife suggested that we send in *Nightingale in the Branches* which was really an apprentice play, but such was Ernest's weird sense of humour that he thought it was good. He put it on and it later became Barry Fitzgerald's last play and I'm not surprised. I'd be very embarrassed to see it today but anyway I can remember Barry Fitzgerald being in it, but I never met him.

PD: *It must have been an extraordinary experience seeing your play produced by the National Theatre, with somebody like Barry Fitzgerald acting in it. What was the moment like?*

HL: I soon came down to earth. I had no reputation – I was a new voice. The critics really came after me and they demolished the play – possibly quite rightly. Seamus Kelly from *The Irish Times* – I think he had a sadistic streak, but the others were a lot of old women, old women of either sex – Seamus was something else. A journalist named Sam Edgard read an interview he did with me and said "He's going to give it to you; he's going to lambaste that play of yours." And so he did, and that was the start of a beautiful hatred, as they say.

PD: *You were starting to write for theatre and there must have been people up there that you admired, whose work you aspired to in some way. Who were your mentors?*

HL: Well I evolved from one to the other. I liked the irreverence of Denis Johnson. There's a kind of a story about me and Denis Johnson that I met him in later years and because I was adopted I suggested very jocosely that he may have been my father. If he had heard me say it he would have been furious, but to this day whenever I meet Jennifer, we address each other as "Bud" and "Sis." So I admired Denis Johnson because of his irreverence, although I felt that his plays were a bit broken-backed. I liked Lennox Robinson – I liked his little evocations of an age that is gone, the *Church Street* era, with its staid provincialism and gentleness. I used to act in amateur theatre and I loved playing Harold Mahony in *The Far Off Hills* – that's the man whose wife went mad on honeymoon and he hasn't smiled since. You know, he'd look up into the clouds and somebody would say "It's a beautiful day" and he'd say "Yes but the evenings are drawing in, it's getting very near the winter." Everything had a downbeat for Harold and I loved playing that, I had them rolling in the aisles with that one!

PD: *Did you start as an actor and then write a play or did you write a play and then act in it?*

HL: No, I was only an amateur actor. I suppose it was a way of getting over shyness. Maggie Smith once said that she was very shy and she went on the stage to hide, and I suppose that was true of me. But I was writing on the side. Basically I was always a playwright but the acting was something to do in the evenings. It was a social activity and I enjoyed it.

PD: *And did that actual experience of acting give you insights into the production of plays, into the writing of plays? Did it alter your writing in any way, do you think?*

HL: It didn't alter it because I don't think I was writing. Somebody said of William Burroughs, "That's not writing, that's typing" and I was sort of "only typing" at this stage. But then as an actor you learn your lines, you learn the play for maybe five or six weeks and you begin to analyse it and find out what makes it tick. You ask why are these lines in here and you realize they're not in to be said, they're only punctuation, things like that. You learn not the tricks but the components of a play and it's very handy. You're in an amateur company and they say "Come on, do us a set" so I go to an old stage manager, say in the Bernadette Hall in Rathmines, and I ask him "How do you paint a set?" And this old chap would say "with your back to it" which is absolutely right because if you do it small-scale the people are so far away they won't see the details. So you're painting large scale, you're like an impressionist, you're slapping on the paint, and so you learn about sets. You learn how to put up a set, how quickly it can be taken down, stuff like that, you learn bits and pieces. I just this week reviewed a book about Alan Ayckbourn, who was a stage manager for many years, so he knew everything the stage was capable of and he was able to write these plays that played great tricks with the audience's imagination, you could say. He couldn't have done that without working in the theatre, he couldn't have written those plays.

PD: *You've had a life-long love affair with film and you're enormously informed about the history and the whole development of cinema. In a way you have also experienced a generation that has moved from the experience of theatre and small local theatres to this phenomenon of cinema in your own front room. Has it influenced how you write or how do you see the cross-cultures?*

HL: Cinema is something you look at, a play is something you listen to. I'm trying to use cinema as much as I can, and if a play is going a bit sour I say "Wait a minute. What can the people on the stage hear at this moment, are there external sounds, what can they smell, what can they taste, what can they touch?" And if you can answer these questions then suddenly it creates an entire world, it sweeps different things in and it makes writing that much easier. You can integrate film and theatre very easily and very rewardingly. I mean, in my play *Da*, there is a man alone on the stage, because all the other characters are ghosts. They just come on. The father is dead, the younger Charlie is dead, the mother ditto, and so on. And there are only a very few living people at the beginning and the end of the play so you're using a filming thing to step from the past into the future.

I was fascinated I think by J. B. Priestley's *Time* plays, particularly the concept he would have that if you were off in space with a telescope you could see a man travelling from say Birmingham to London. The fact that he has left Birmingham does not mean Birmingham no longer exists. And although you're not in London yet, it's still there, waiting for you. Priestley said this is the way we travel through time. It's the whole thing – the present, future and the past, as part of the same landscape. You don't know where you're going or what's going to become of you. I find in that sense my work is filmic.

PD: *You've done many adaptations of novels, of classics like Dickens and of various authors like that. How do you decide what to leave out and what to put in?*

HL: Well the first question is to ask oneself "Do you wish you'd written that?" If you can say that, then it's a "contender." I won't touch anything otherwise. My approach is to read the book very quickly, and the bits you remember are the skeleton of what will go on the stage. Then I do it a second time and this time I'm working on the skeleton. I think I know what is going to be boring for an audience. I think I have an instinct for what I can leave out and keep in, you know, it's as simple as that.

Dickens now, he had a wonderful sense of dialogue and basically all you do with Dickens is you cut him, because if he was alive today he'd be working for television. He had a terrific sense of dialogue, of colours. My favourite has always been *Great Expectations*. I've adapted it a few times for television and for the theatre and it's been done very well. I've done *A Tale of Two Cities*, *Dombey and Son*. I did *Bleak House*, and *Nicholas Nickleby* was another one I enjoyed. Wilkie Collins' The *Moonstone* was another favourite. I've done a lot of stories. Maugham I enjoy because I've always thought that at his best he was a superb writer. And we did a series of stories called *The Sinners*, by Ó Faoláin and O'Connor.

PD: *Was that televised?*

HL: Yes.

PD: *Am I right in thinking that Des Keogh acted in one of them?*

HL: Probably. I did some comedy scripts as well but they weren't adaptations. They were just things for fun for Milo O'Shea and to see if I could do a comedy sitcom. I like to break new ground with everything I do.

PD: *Comedy is extremely difficult, is it not? Tragedy is actually much easier.*

HL: There used to be an actor called Edmund Gwenn and when he was on his deathbed somebody asked "Is dying hard?" and he said "Yes but not as hard as playing comedy." It's quite difficult writing comedy for television, a sit-com, where you've got an audience in front of you and you're expected to make the buggers laugh maybe once every two minutes. So that's difficult. You find a lot of material and a lot of ingenuity is being pumped into that.

PD: *Do you think Irish audiences have changed since you started writing and since your very first play? Are audiences more sophisticated?*

HL: They are much more sophisticated. They get the shorthand quicker, you know. It's funny, the reversal has happened in cinema. If you look at a movie from about 1932 or '33, you'll find they galloped through at enormous speed and packed everything into 65 or 70 minutes. They move like lightning. Part of the reason is the writing style but the other part is that they have all these actors who are typecast. The same actor, maybe someone like Frank Jenks, would play a taxi-driver and Charles Coleman specialized in butlers, and they just went into different films but played the same part. Now of course there's no such animal as a comic actor, no such thing as comic relief, and the film has a running time of two, two and a half hours. It's much more leisurely, much more self-indulgent. So it's a different ball game.

PD: *Your most recent production has been a radio play and radio is always rather special, is it not?*

HL: Well, yeah, I wrote *The Kennedys of Castleross* and all that kind of thing. It was a wonder in its time, you know. Every three or four months, we'd have somebody reading a will and whole villages would stop. I heard the account of people from a certain locality who were in a local farmhouse listening to one of these battery radio sets and suddenly it dried up, it expired as they were all listening to the reading of the will. Next thing, there was a mass stampede down the hill to the next house that had a "wireless." I write very little for radio now. It's a good medium but it just doesn't occur to me. I find it's sort of a little bit easy. That's not puffing myself up, it's simply the people in charge of radio stations have a contempt for their job.

PD: *You say that's a bit easy. So do you set yourself a challenge then for everything you do?*

HL: I like to. I like to stretch myself. They got me to do this programme, this play *You and the Night and the Wireless* and I really think that when they came to putting it on they didn't know that the title came from a song called *You and the Night and the Music*, otherwise they could have played it as theme music. And then they got me starting late, they didn't send a contract for months and months after the writing was due to start. And so when I sat down I hadn't the faintest idea what I was going to write about and so I just went on battering on and a play came out the other end of the sausage machine. I don't really know if it's any good or not.

PD: *Is that a scary thing? In some ways, you're only as good as your last production and that must be slightly frightening. Where do you get your inspiration? Where do the ideas come from?*

HL: That was a bit frightening because it was the 75th anniversary of radio in this country, and in fact the 75th anniversary was last January 1st so RTE was late as usual, and it was my 75th birthday so they decided they were going to combine the two things. And I wanted to write something about wireless, radio, so I got dates and things from the Internet and basically a few facts and then started to write the play. But I had no idea where it was going till I was about half way through which is always a bit scary when that happens. You wonder if there's a play in there at all.

PD: *Looking back over your career which covered film scripts, the classic theatre, radio and adaptations of novels what, for you, are the highlights?*

HL: Well, the occasional play I think. Paule, my late wife, she was a great judge of plays. It's very strange. English was not her first language but she was one of the very few people who could read a play, and most of all she loved my own favourite *Summer*. I liked it too but it's strange that it's called *Summer*, because it's a very autumnal kind of play and I think it's the best thing I've done. It's a very difficult play: It can't be done as a piece of acting, it's got to be performed as if it's overheard conversation. And it's hard to get a producer who sees it as such. The Abbey is doing *Da* next year. *Da* is actor-proof and director-proof and while I like it – you don't say "No" to four Tony awards – I've done better work than that.

PD: *So* Summer *is the one that you'd put up there as one of your fondest memories of theatre?*

HL: *Summer* and *A Life* and I also have a warm space for a little play called *Love in the Title* which has parts for three actresses. Usually I get very bored watching my own work but with *Love in the Title* if the girls are well cast, I can sit and enjoy them because they're three very nice people, the girls in that play.

PD: *And the other side of that coin – what are the things you wish you'd never written?*

HL: Lots of things, there were a few television plays that didn't work and there's the occasional stage play that I wish I hadn't done. They all had their appeal; I gave them all plenty of attention when it came to writing them but by and large there's just a few that…. (A pause). You know I'd really need a list of all my plays. I got a book *The Twentieth Century Companion to Writing* or something like that and there was a complete playography or whatever you call it of mine and I went through this and there were some plays I can't remember writing. I remember saying "Well these were television works you know." *The Au-pair Man* I think was a failure but it was an honourable failure – I needed to write it. I just had an idea for a two-hander, two people, and so I took off on it but at the same time I don't think it worked.

PD: *Do you think maybe it was a failure because it was at the wrong time? Is timing everything because so many plays slot into our needs, our perceptions at a particular period?*

HL: I was working on this in a stylized kind of dialogue – it was a send-up of the monarchy really, the monarchy and Ireland and all that. I disobeyed one of my own rules – I stuck in a lot of symbolism and I don't think the symbols worked at all. So Danielle (my daughter) and my wife, they were very loyal about it but I just felt, "No I shouldn't have done it" and I didn't want to do it again.

PD: *You have had considerable experience in not just writing plays but in programming. Talk to me a little about your years in the Dublin Theatre Festival.*

HL: Well, my first was *A Walk on the Water* which was done in 1959 and then I tried to do a play a year but I wasn't able, because I think after a year one has to lie fallow and that's where the adaptations came in. You aren't using the same juices to write a play as with adapting, so I would do a *Dalkey Archive* or the like every second year. Also, I was working with Phyllis Ryan as an impresario, and I broke away. I needed a change and I don't think I was forgiven for that, ever. So I did *Stephen D* which was a kind of a breakthrough but really it was a very easy thing to write because it was editing more than anything else – there was hardly a word of my own in there, it was all Joyce. And I did *Dublin 1* which was, as Brendan Smith would have called it, the first part of a "triology" – he did call it that. And I don't think that worked very well either, I think I took on too much. But I did plays like *The Poker Session* and *A Walk on the Water* and stuff like that and I enjoyed doing it. Then I took on the job of being Programme Director and I had to quit after two years, because I wasn't doing it very well. I was trying to write my own play, *A Life*, at the time and I think I was skimping the job a bit. So I wasn't successful. Basically I'm only a writer, the other things I've taken on haven't worked very well.

PD: *Was it an interesting experience?*

HL: Oh yeah, it was interesting. I remember Brendan Smith, of whom I was very fond, Brendan gave me a car at the time of the Festival. It was a beat-up old Merc so I could be driven around town and see as much of every play as I could, maybe 15 minutes of each. And I remember going in to see a play called *Prayers for my Daughter* with Donal McCann and Anthony Sher, at the Project, and it was packed. I walked in and I was just about to leave when a young man took his clothes off on the stage, all his clothes, and I thought if I go now they'll think I came in to see him without any clothes on. So I waited and waited and after about 15 minutes he put his clothes back on and I went out and I was outside and in the street, when I realized now they'll think I only came in to see him with his clothes off.

PD: *Which brings me to the thorny topic of critics. What do you think of the standard of theatre criticism in Ireland? And what about those who say that critics have gone soft.*

HL: Well, I don't know about going soft. It's very difficult to go and see a play and sit down afterwards and write a review. Now they skip a night, they don't do it until a day later, and that hasn't improved them. You've got to be able to write well. Take for example Fintan O'Toole, he has taken over as Senior Critic of *The Irish Times*, and he kicked off with an analysis of Tom Murphy's work. He was explaining Murphy to Murphy and I found that he was giving cold analysis to what needs to be done with zest and spontaneity. He will never say, "This was a rotten play but I had great fun at it." I think that part of him is missing as a critic, which means I don't think there's much hope for him.

PD: *Are people influenced by critics? Are people going to theatre on the basis of a review?*

HL: The speed with which they would go, or not, I think can be sort of helped or hindered by a review but by and large, ours is rather small town and the play-going population is a minority. If, as we do now, you have previews, everyone goes to them, because they're cheap, and the word-of-mouth spreads around town, so that before the play opens, it's usually beyond the power of a critic to make or break it. I think if all the critics get on and say "This is terrible, take it off" then I think you could be in trouble but by and large, if the opinions aren't too polarized you can be sure that it's word-of-mouth that will keep it running or not, you know.

PD: *You raised a very interesting topic when you said that this is a small town. Ireland is a small country and you have a very strong personality – you don't take hostages. Has that made life difficult for you?*

HL: It hasn't made life difficult. It's made working slightly difficult. It's created an attitude towards me. I mean, there might be a critic out there who says, "If I give him a bad notice he's going to come back and crucify me, so we'd better leave him alone and not give him any notice at all" which is the downside of it. But I never hit out at a bad notice. You know, as Kingsley Amis said, "You can let a bad review spoil your breakfast, don't let it spoil your lunch." But I think if a critic is wrong on a matter of fact or if he is glaringly incompetent, you should say so.

PD: *What do you say about the future of theatre in Ireland? Are you hopeful about it? In the last ten years, what has really excited you in Irish theatre?*

HL: Well, a few faces are coming up. For economic reasons, most new plays are little more than monologues. Or one gets *The Weir*, say, which is a brilliant play but three or four people sit down and each person embarks on a very, very long talk-jag, and they're speaking virtually alone, which throws the dramatic tension out the window. There are young writers who will imitate this kind of thing and they don't have the author's stamina or his style or whatever.

Terrific actors coming up, I don't know half of them. I meet someone like Ben Barnes and he says "What about so-and-so for your play?" and I have to say I've never heard of him and then when I see him I find that he's absolutely brilliant, so that's happening. For myself, I sort of felt I'd like to do a novel, so I wrote one, and now they want a second and I find novel-writing is much easier than playwriting, because you don't have the same disciplines. You don't have to look at the clock and think you've got to get an audience out of their seats by 10.45. You don't have that but my home is basically the theatre and I wish I were back in it.

PD: *Your heart is obviously back there in theatre with capturing people and keeping them enthralled for a very small period of time.*

HL: It's lovely to see a play working like when I saw *A Life* at the Abbey last summer, and watch it working with an audience after twenty years, and know that the play will go on a while longer anyway. And now the Abbey is planning to do *Da* next year. I'm fed up looking at it – I don't want to see it again.

PD: *Will you go?*

HL: The first night, and maybe the last night. But it would be because, now and again, you get a great performance as one did from Donal McCann or as one still does from Pauline Flanagan, and you'd go for that rather than the play.

PD: *So have actors taught you something about your own plays? Do you ever come back from a performance thinking "there was something in there that even I didn't know."*

HL: Oh yeah, now and again. Not that often, but Donal could do that to you. I always remember, this is a very basic story, but I remember he came in, in the second act of *A Life* and he was playing the good-for-nothing Lar, the husband. He was wearing a watch-chain, sort of a fob, which went from his belt down in a loop and back up to his pocket. And I wondered why, because this character would never have a watch, he'd have pawned it. I said "What's he up to?" and then I forgot all about it. Then, later on, he asks somebody what they are going to drink and he reaches into his pocket and you see that there's a bottle opener on the end of the chain. I said, "Well I wish I'd thought of that." That teaches me so much more.

When Cyril Cusack did the play, there's a bit where Lar takes his coat, which is one of these gabardine raincoats, and he just hangs it up on the hook behind the door, just roughly and puts it over the hook. Whereupon Cyril snatched it down and hung it again – but by its tab. That in a moment said everything, first of all about the character, that he was pedantic and fussy, and also said a lot about his relationship with Lar. And I thought now that was good, that I should really seriously have done myself. So now and again you get little surprises.

PD: *If money were no object, if staging and casting were no object, is there something you want to do – is there a play you want to put on?*

HL: I've always wanted to do a kind of an *Our Town* which would be set in Dalkey but *Our Town* has been done twice, once by Thornton Wilder, and later as *Under Milk Wood* which was poetry and I'm not a poet. One can hardly do it again without using one voice or the other, Thornton Wilder's or Dylan Thomas's . In my own case, it segued into a play called *Fillums* in which the people of an Irish town in the early 1940's begin to live their lives according to the rules of the movies: happy endings, villainy punished, lovers reunited. In other words, the whole town bases its existence on cliches, and they are enjoying it no end! I was going to do that at the Abbey, but Ben Barnes wasn't sitting still for long enough to let the idea take fire.

PD: *So you're saying that you've got this idea, this plot, this whole vision of a play, but yet you find yourself being constrained by the physical realities of theatre in Ireland?*

HL: Maybe I'm out of touch but you see I'm a writer for the Abbey. I had a run-in with the Gate – I sound a terrible person but I had a run-in with the Gate and Michael Colgan is not likely to want to do anything of mine – and that leaves me with the Abbey. So I'm steering *Fillums* into the shape of a novel. It's lost as a play, I think.

PD: *Are you sad about that?*

HL: I am, of course I'm sad. I like to have a play commissioned, most of my life I've had plays commissioned and I find this is a great stimulus to me to sit down and do work. There's been a deposit paid, there's a company waiting for the play, there's a provisional date – this is all a great help to me. You know when you're upstairs, alone, at the machine, you're very vulnerable and you don't like writing into a vacuum so it's very nice for me to say, "Oh, so-and-so is going to do my play if I make a good job of it." So then you do a good job!

PD: *Well Jack, may you long continue to do so.*

HL: Thank you.

Hugh Leonard has written thirty-two stage plays, including *Stephen D*, *The Patrick Pearse Motel*, *Da* (Tony Award; New York Critics' Circle Award), *A Life* (Harvey Award), *Time Was*, *The Mask of Moriarty*, *Moving*, *The Lily Lally Show* and *Love in the Title*. He has written extensively for film and television and has won the Prix Italia and the Writers' Guild Award. His books include *Home Before Night*, *Out After Dark*, and *Rover and Other Cats*. He has a weekly column in *The Sunday Independent*.

Pat Donlon was Director of the National Library of Ireland from 1989-1998, during which time Hugh Leonard's archive was acquired by the Library. A former Chairperson of the Irish Museums' Association she served for many years as a Judge for the Gulbenkian Museum's Award and is currently Chair of the Irish Press Photographer's Association Awards. Pat has also chaired *The Irish Times* Literary Award and is a member of the Heritage Council. She is currently Arnold Graves Scholar at the Faculty of Applied Arts, Dublin Institute of Technology working on a Dictionary of Irish Illustrators. Married to Phelim Donlon, former Drama and Opera Officer of the Arts Council, she shares his passion for theatre, music and literature.

Tim Loane in Conversation with David Grant

DG: *Tim Loane, as an actor and director and latterly as a writer you have been very closely associated with Tinderbox Theatre Company from its beginnings. As I recall that started in 1988 with a lunch-time production of Edward Bond's* Stone.

TL: The best thing that came out of that production was the profile it got because critics and pundits seemed to be crying out for something new and different. Tinderbox grew out of a necessity for a few of us as individuals. We had no altruistic plans to start with at all, we wanted to work. And as actors who were not officially trained and had not been through any official process and wanted to be professional, we found that to do it ourselves was the most realistic route. The core of Tinderbox at the outset was Lalor Roddy and myself. We decided to give it a go for a year and see what we could achieve, and we found we had a reason to continue and develop. Our first shows were all twenty or thirty-year old English plays – Bond, Brenton, Pinter – but the idea of local writers was something that came to us very quickly, within a year of the company's existence. We realized very quickly there were very many writers who just wanted their stuff read by somebody who just wasn't the Abbey and wasn't the Lyric.

DG: *Apart from Charabanc, who had the woman's issue to drive them on, you were the first people I remember in Belfast to provide an independent alternative to what was happening at the Lyric. But were there other models?*

TL: The university set-up most definitely had an input. [Apart from Lalor] myself, Stephen Wright, Mark Carruthers, Chris Glover and Jules Maxwell – what became the larger core of Tinderbox within eighteen months of its inception – had come from Queen's Drama Society. Working together at Queen's, we'd already I suppose lost our fear of just doing things because we wanted to do them and we felt they needed doing.

DG: *You were director of the ISDA [Irish Students' Drama Association] Festival held in Queen's in March 1988. Was that an influential force in terms of galvanizing you all?*

TL: ISDA proved to us, especially in 1988 – a bloody awful year it was in Belfast – that you could actually achieve things by simple determination. A lot of the Southern groups either came with great reluctance or didn't come that year, there was a genuine fear around that alright. But it got us in contact with other people – the Paul Hickeys, the Jim Culletons, who then went on to start Pigsback [Theatre Company]. Druid from Galway, and Rough Magic from Dublin and other similar notable cases were also inspirational models. We got to understand that there are other people who are doing this and have not just *done* it, they've made it massively successful. In a very early radio interview I remember saying "Rough Magic can do it in Dublin and Druid can do it in Galway, so why can't we?" and being *hammered* for doing that, for being so arrogant. Well, there may have been a certain amount of arrogance.

DG: *And they all grew out of university origins, too, didn't they? The comparison with Rough Magic seems less precocious because there was that proximity in age. But you did later collaborate with Pigsback.*

TL: We had a lot in common, Pigsback and Tinderbox. It's ironic that the writer and the play we chose to go with had nothing whatsoever to do with two communities, two different locations or two different companies. It was a play called *This Love Thing* [Marina Carr] which was basically a piece of theatrical fun.

DG: *Was that the first new play Tinderbox did?*

TL: No. I think *Fingertips* by Thomas McLaughlin may have been the first full production of a new play [but] by then we'd already done seven or eight rehearsed readings. We did a festival of new writing where we spent a week working intensively on a script with a writer and director and really, really testing the script and the idea at the core of it and presenting it as a developed reading at the end of the week. And the first time we did that, 1989, we realized we had something special because at the very first reading, where we wondered if ten people would turn up, it was standing room only in the Old Museum. We knew almost everybody in that audience because they worked in theatre and were desperate to find out what new writing was out there and to see what new energy was coming from a new company. So we committed ourselves to develop writing and writers. From then onward we became a serious company I suppose, a company who knew what we wanted to do.

DG: *You also did first Irish productions of plays that had been seen first elsewhere* – Donny Boy *and* Catchpenny Twist, *the Stewart Parker play. Was that for want of new writing or was it a distinctive policy?*

TL: It was a distinctive policy. It was a mixture of two or three things to be honest. These were plays we wanted to do, plays Belfast needed. The development of writers and new plays takes so long it's impossible to only do new work so we also felt we needed to do stuff – and wanted to do stuff – we could tour. *Catchpenny Twist* was our first successful one. Since then we've balanced on a fine line between doing plays from the canon, and we've toured them, and new work, some of which has also toured. New work has so many inherent risks but touring a new play has even more risks.

DG: *You went through a tricky phase, I remember, when the Arts Council was practically obliging you to do mainstream work. I remember you doing a Dario Fo under a certain duress.*

TL: They didn't know what to do with us at first – I'm convinced of that. Charabanc fitted in, they had a particular agenda which justified their funding. Field Day a different one, but they were all professional with a big P. Whereas some of us didn't have our Equity cards. The Arts Council was aware that there was a gap – a number of gaps – but they didn't know how to fill it. I think Denis [Smith, Arts Council] wanted to support Tinderbox but the Arts Council itself didn't know how.

DG: *So the key was getting them off the regional touring hook?*

TL: I think so. Touring was a problem and the gaps were becoming more obvious. When they started giving us proper money they did say you need to tour. But we wanted to. The company went through a difficult phase at that point because you were obliged to create accessible popular stuff. And I suppose part of the company's growing pains were that we went down that route before we came back a bit.

DG: *A lot has changed since then. You've made a name with film and television writing and you're now chair of the Tinderbox board. The company has started to pioneer big spectacular events like* Northern Star *at Rosemary Street Church,* Convictions *at the Court House, and your current project which involves taking over the old Assembly Rooms with a new play. How does the clear commitment to new writing connect with this latest phase in the company's development?*

TL: It's to do with tenacity in the face of adversity. We have no venue. Belfast does not have adequate facilities for theatre companies like us. There's us, there's Prime Cut, there's Kabosh ...

DG: *All of which emerged from the Old Museum. If that hadn't been there would you have simply done it somewhere else?*

TL: I don't think we would have been able to. The Old Museum was there just at the right time for Tinderbox, also for Prime Cut, and Replay – perfect for the nurturing of new companies.

DG: *Clearly the Old Museum then became inappropriate. Why was that?*

TL: Companies work the way they want to work. Tinderbox's needs became bigger than the Old Museum could provide. There also was, however, a distinct change in programming policy in the Old Museum. We were performing our plays for production for three weeks, for instance, which we had to do, especially with only 90 seats. And we were selling it out. The Old Museum will not now take a local production for that length of time so it's not a viable option at all for a company like Tinderbox.

DG: *The Arts Council could not countenance the venue only being open to the public for a certain proportion of the year. That does seem to me to have been very short-sighted because effectively it did inhibit the development of indigenous theatre projects.*

TL: Independent theatre has had to look for other ways and find other means. It has given Tinderbox greater resilience in that we are prepared to put our plays on in remarkable places.

DG: *Do you go to Rosemary Street Church and the Court House because you have nowhere else to perform or is a site-specific approach a positive option?*

TL: For quite a while we have known that there is not a venue available for the kind of work we want to do. From the very outset when we discussed *Northern Star* with Stephen Rea it was immediately obvious that it was a priority not to do it in a straightforward theatre. We wanted to make it more than just that, so Rosemary Street came up as a real suggestion, and it worked very well for us. Likewise the courthouse. Not that we had this play that was ready to go somewhere, it was that we became aware that the Courthouse was there, and empty, and we did *Convictions*.

DG: *And after the success of* Northern Star, *which won Belfast Arts Awards and so on, did you find yourself saying the star should be the building?*

TL: Absolutely not, no. It was just a very fortunate circumstance that made us aware that the Courthouse was empty and just by visiting the building it cried out to us that it needed a performance within it. And that was just ideal for us. So that production was our response to the building at that time. *Convictions* entailed seven separate pieces, all about ten minutes long, all written by local writers. Each piece was performed in a different location within the building. The Courthouse is a massive building, like any municipal edifice, and each piece of theatre was intended in some sense to articulate that writer's reaction to that aspect of the building so it was seriously high-risk. It was a very short production schedule, they were the very finest of theatre writers, and it ended up being a very extraordinary experience for the audience, which was always what we wanted. It was more than we ever could have dreamed of.

DG: *To me as a spectator, it seemed some of the pieces of writing were less satisfactory than others but the fact was the extraordinary nature of the whole thing. Mark Lawson chose it as one of his highlights of the year.*

TL: This was not "going to see a show," it was an *experience*. You could not go to that performance and leave with a half-assed response.

DG: *One of the fascinating things was the subjectivity of the experience, and the logistics. You had eighty people in four groups and you managed to get them around a building in a strict timetable that allowed them to come together three times and see the other four plays separately. Will that kind of planning be necessary in the Assembly Rooms project or is that more conventional?*

TL: It's going to be more manageable rather than conventional I think. There's not an awful lot I can say about that project at the moment except that the project has been developed with the building in mind and is going to use everything that comes out of that building. We're doing productions that are reactions to those buildings because the buildings we're choosing have immense significance to the town through their location and history and all of that. Our dream would be to be in one of these places and to stay there for a while, because it is sapping the resources consistently, and staff energies.

DG: *It's like the Druid warehouse, in the end.*

TL: That would be our dream and it's something the company has been looking for, for the last number of years. It's a home – just somewhere that we know we can plan to be. The building in Waring Street is not that, it's far too big. But the dream and the long term goal has to be for us to find a base.

DG: *We've obviously seen a huge change in Belfast since the company started. According to Stephen Rea, when they started Field Day they couldn't have cast* *a play like* Northern Star *from local actors. It seems to me that's one major change. How would you assess the changes in Northern theatre in that time?*

TL: The thing seems to have gone in waves. It seems to me that five or six years ago there was a larger and stronger community of locally-based actors.

DG: *Certainly many more local companies, anyway. There was Scarecrow, Out and Out, Point Field. I can think of at least half a dozen companies who have come and gone.*

TL: Some of those companies were short-lived because that's what they were intended to be, but there was definitely a time when there were more of them. What worries me most is that over the last five years it seems to have waned and that there are pressures upon professional theatre in the city that are stronger than they ever were before, the pressure to create more quality. And they're doing so I believe but they are so starved of resources compared to other artforms.

DG: *Perhaps what keeps them going is pragmatism rather than quality?*

TL: It's desperation I suppose. We have never been anywhere near well supported financially in order to show what we can do, so you're constantly watching an industry in crisis. I suppose if there's a change, there are a number of people who believe in it [theatre] as an industry and are prepared to organize it and mobilize and fight. But it really does feel to me at present that this is a make or break time. The professional independent theatre in Belfast is at a point where it is having to state its case to the Arts Council and to local government that its future is in jeopardy. So it gives me optimism to know that the industry is organized but it's hard to get excited when you consider that we're up against a wall in many ways, in a way we never were before.

DG: *Your world of work now is more for the camera than live events.* Dance Lexy Dance *got an Oscar nomination – an extraordinary thing early in your directorial career. And with the success of* Teachers *[TV series] writing for television seems to be your principal livelihood. Does that reflect a disenchantment at the undernourishment of the live theatre or is there a symbiosis between television, film and live theatre?*

TL: It's not a disenchantment, it's personal circumstances, personal choices and all of that. I still am committed to working in the theatre in Belfast. I do believe there's a symbiosis between them – between stage and screen – and I do believe that one of the problems with the screen industry in the North and in the South is that professional practitioners are not supported enough to enable them to become good enough, skilled enough to branch into screen. Not that screen should be the be-all – not at all – but it's a healthy thing for it to be an option.

DG: *Your route was basically to win a competition for a short screen play.*

TL: Yes, that was because I was so fed up with auditioning for films where I'd end up with two lines and a gun in the back of the head.

DG: *You wrote yourself a part*

TL: I wrote myself a part. I didn't expect anybody to make it, but the director read it and the first thing he said to me was "I don't see you in this part." But it WAS me. It was written for me. Thank god Conleth Hill played it because he did it much better than I ever could. Personally I wanted to move on from acting. I focussed on acting for many years, then directing and then writing seemed a natural progression. I still do a bit of everything, and I want to carry on doing a bit of everything.

DG: *And you're writing a play for Tinderbox at the moment?*

TL: Yeah, but there's not an awful lot to say except that I'm writing it.

DG: *With your success in television, clearly it's not the money that's drawing you back to theatre, so what would actually revive your enthusiasm for the live stage?*

TL: The location where I live. That's what makes Tinderbox important to the town and Tinderbox important to me: as time goes by it has become more and more about where it is. When I write for television I write about God knows what, in God knows where, but writing for Tinderbox is something that's very rooted in its location. When you talk about the changes from 1988 to now, that is something I definitely see in Tinderbox, a definite focusing on the location, a focusing on the reality of where we live. Not that we have any easier answers for anybody, but I think we're becoming better at syphoning influences from the city in which we live and firing out things onto the stage that reflect, question, interrogate, challenge those. That's something that's taken us a long time to learn. And we're still learning.

DG: *I'm greatly in sympathy with that. It's all very well knowing the world's round, but sometimes you also need to know it's flat. The world of film is very enticing but there is something about theatre that can speak within its own horizons.*

TL: Because it's so close to our hearts at Tinderbox, it's something that surprises me that I don't see more of in the country – and I don't mean Belfast at all. I was amazed at the Irish Theatre Awards this year down in Dublin – at which we won Best Production award for *Convictions* – the number of times people referred to the success of Irish theatre in terms of the West End and Broadway. Now, those are valid achievements, but they are *not* the definition of the success of Irish theatre. This was something that went right through [the occasion]: productions that were built in Dublin but made for London audiences it seems. And then also there's such a significance attached to European influence, which is fine, but if you make that your priority – to get European influence, rather than to contact your audience or say something that's important? It's something that really shocked me how much they were looking to London, how much they were looking to other European capitals instead of looking at *themselves*.

DG: *That was before* Stones in his Pockets *went on to win all those awards, so they were referring back to McDonagh in particular. It's hard not to be taken with the superficial glamour of all of that.*

TL: I understand that. All of those are important achievements and all of those productions have made real inroads.

DG: *They've made real money*

TL: Have they made money! They are very important exports and all of that. And of course many of those productions define what we are ourselves. But I believe there's a danger if those plays, those productions, are created specifically for an audience that *isn't here*. And I think some of them are.

DG: *And yet* Convictions *took the key award in a context where usually there's just a token gesture towards the North.*

TL: And the year before the same award was won by *Stones in His Pockets*. So two years running Northern productions won Best Production. I think there's something in that. The theatre that's happening here – it's so small, the actual community that's doing it is so small – everything is under such scrutiny that we have to be very careful that we do the right things for the right reasons. So there's very little flab. We're lean and mean.

DG: *The broader context of this discussion is the issue of infrastructural developments and possibilities – in the North and in Ireland as a whole. Having been on the other side of the fence at the Lyric, I know the biggest struggle is a fifty-weeks-a-year operation, checking every day to see how many people were in the seats that night. Given those pressures, if you had the* *resources of the Abbey what would you do with them? How does the big theatre institution relate to the independent activity you've been associated with?*

TL: I'm not sure how it *does*, but how it *should*? I'll talk about the Lyric and I'm sure it's the same in the Abbey. What these major institutions need to do is *not* have everything rest on one person's shoulders. One person cannot represent the artistic vision of a nation, that's ridiculous. Their job is to collate artistic visions and present various things from various people. Any National Theatre should pull together all the independent initiatives and all the individuals and allow them access to creating or contributing to the creation of the work that goes on in the National Theatre. Does that make sense?

DG: *Does that connect then to Ben Barnes's approaches to the work of Blue Raincoat, Barabbas, — y'know there seem to be some constructive collaborations there which tie in with that theory.*

TL: Yes. In Belfast there's too clear a demarcation. "The Lyric does *that*, and there's the line and you don't get over the line; Tinderbox does that; Prime Cut does that." There needs to be a cross-fertilization that allows the companies to retain their own identity.

DG: *In a way the Abbey seems removed from our sphere of operation.*

TL: Well it shouldn't do, we're not that far away. There should be a clear infrastructure which entitles people who work here to contribute in some sense to the Abbey. It's a long time I think since the Abbey auditioned actors in Belfast. When I used to work as an actor that was a consistent bone of contention.

DG: *Especially for Northern plays.*

TL: Oh God yes. And let's face it, we've always been better at doing Southern accents than they are at doing Northern ones. [Laughs] But that didn't stop the buggers taking our work. The other thing is, I was speaking not long ago to an actress from Dublin who was up doing a show with an independent company in Belfast who was going "fantastic! why don't you employ us more — us Dubs or us Southerners?" And we're going "we're just glad that you wanted to come up because you often give the impression that you don't." She was being deliberately generous but it's hard enough to get tourists to come up from Dublin so I suppose it's just as difficult to get actors.

DG: *Perhaps it should be said that the Abbey has a touring policy of coming to the Lyric now, and the Lyric itself had quite a good record of bringing in Tinderbox to perform there and I do remember the concerns about a dilution of* *identity. You said you cannot expect one person to be the custodian of a whole nation, I would say the same about one company. In many ways the Lyric was at its healthiest when it was mixing its own product with the independents and with the Abbey coming in.*

TL: Two things. I think one person and one person only can be the *custodian* of that – but it's not just one artistic vision. And in the case of the Lyric, yes there was a time when it was a healthy mixture. The problem [is] the Lyric relying on other companies to fill gaps in its programme, as opposed to discussing with companies what their work is, and making their work something that the Lyric really wants because it helps the Lyric's identity or helps the Lyric do something that it wants to achieve. But – like so many other aspects of theatre in the North – the necessity has been to fill gaps and save cash and cut corners in the Lyric: "Christ! we've got a few weeks empty, get a show in, no matter what it is, just get it in." And that does not allow for an identity that represents a region.

DG: *So what would your hopes be for Tinderbox and theatre in the North of Ireland?*

TL: Very simple, more money! Independent theatre should have a home but it can only have that if the Lyric is stable and if the Lyric becomes a centrepiece of the theatre in the North so that the other independent companies are *with* it. Not below it, *with* it, so that the companies themselves are all able to stand on an equal footing. So much rests on the shoulders of the Lyric. It needs to be given the space to succeed, to reinvent itself and redefine itself.

DG: *The Lyric was forced to become something it wasn't. So there's four or five hundred thousand pounds of public money – a huge proportion of the total available – going to maintain a building which isn't really adequate. Is there not an argument for doing away with a building-based producer altogether, selling that space, putting the money into a trust that will allow the Lyric to produce periodically and tour and take advantage of these new venues in Armagh, Derry, and so on? This would allow the subsidy to be spread between the imaginative producers of theatre.*

TL: My problem is I don't trust those who decide where the money goes. So I think we as the creative community in this city need a building we can call our own because, without that, we are cap-in-hand to whoever is doling out the money for productions and I really believe that administratively we have been shafted for many years and continue to be. The other thing is the situation in this country is so precarious isn't it? In this part of this country?

DG: *Politically?*

TL: Politically yeah. I have a present concern for the professional theatre when I see the funding round that came from the Arts Council this year where all professional theatre was on stand-still, some even got cut, while community theatre all got massive, *massive* increases. Now they *should* get increases, yes, but not at the expense of professional theatre. This is an industry; this is a profession; this is creating something that is an export; this is something that tourists come to; this is something that gets nominated for Tony's in New York! Community theatre, community arts are vital for the future of this place but *not* at the expense of the professional arts. That plan you had outlined, my fear is that that's what the Arts Council would love to do because that's where the money would go. That is the populist vote and that is the fear here: we have our local politicians now deciding arts policy and these guys are not informed. That's why I would react very strongly against that notion.

DG: *We've really only touched on the writers tangentially. What's your feeling about the actual writing situation at the moment?*

TL: Owen McCafferty is a very bright, shining light for the future and the present. I think we have some very strong voices that are now being heard, or are about to be heard. Owen and Daragh Carville for instance, that have had one, two, three productions, none of which have hit the big time profile-wise, but Owen and Daragh have been commissioned by the National Theatre now.

DG: *Still, they're fairly mature. I'm just concerned that we don't seem to have a new wave.*

TL: We don't. It's the same with actors, right across the board. Five years ago it was me and my generation who were doing it – becoming writers and all of that. No, there are not fresh young voices that are easy to find. And worst of all, or hardest of all, women writers. Maybe because all women who are interested in theatre get out of Belfast fast. But Marie Jones's is a magnificent achievement. There is no other female writer [for theatre] who lives here.

DG: *Well, at one event in the Linen Hall last year we had seven women writers all sitting in the same room. Not all based here, mind you.*

TL: But new and young? And those who have something new to say? I would count Nicola McCartney who is a fresh voice and has a new angle on things – she's great.

DG: *Tinderbox actually gave Gary Mitchell his first stage production didn't they?*

TL: I directed that. It was called *Independent Voice*. Gary had worked on radio plays up until that point and gave me the script. We worked it through and we turned it into his first theatre show which was an outstanding experience because all of us were flying by the seat of our pants. It was a very low budget and very hasty affair in every way, but it worked.

DG: *Would you single out a particular highlight? What has been the most memorable part of it from your point of view?*

TL: From my personal point of view it would probably be *Language Roulette* because I directed it, and I loved it. But I can remember going in to see that – the show had been running for a week and every ticket was sold. And I went into the foyer, and it was packed. And I didn't recognize a single face there. And I didn't see a single face that was over twenty-five. And I was stunned. Because I thought "fuckin hell actually we got something that's for the ordinary punters on the street – the *young* ordinary punters on the street, it is a piece of theatre in the conventional sense, but this is a fresh audience. And they loved it. And it was a high quality piece of theatre I think in the end. That's a personal one. As well as that I would also go for ... *Northern Star* was a play we wanted to do for five, six, seven years. Stephen Wright and myself, the first time we ever read it really wanted to do that show, so it was a real dream to see it done and to see Stephen Rea directing it. And it was a massive experience. And then, I suppose *Convictions* is the other, which represents a new era for Tinderbox. Things are becoming very very different for us, and the scale of *Convictions*, not the physical scale, was something that deeply affected us all, those who worked on it. You know that's a good thing to do, that's good therapy.

DG: *Tim Loane, thank you very much.*

Tim Loane is a founder and former Artistic Director of Tinderbox Theatre Company. He has also acted with Druid, Lyric, Dubbeljoint and been a guest director with Prime Cut. He has recently become a writer for stage and screen. His theatre direction includes *Language Roulette* (Daragh Carville), *Independent Voice*, *Dealer's Choice* (Patrick Marber). Film work includes directing *Dance Lexie Dance*, a short film which won numerous awards. More recently he has written for television, including the original series Teachers. His first stage play, *Caught Red-handed* is due for production by Tinderbox in 2002.

David Grant is a theatre director and critic who teaches Drama & Theatre Studies at Queens University Belfast. He was one of the founders of the Old Museum Arts Centre, Belfast; he worked as managing editor of Theatre Ireland; he was a Programme Director of Dublin Theatre Festival; and he spent a period as Artistic Director of the Lyric Theatre, Belfast. He has also had a long association with the youth theatre movement in Ireland.

Tomás Mac Anna in Conversation with Karen Carleton

KC: *What brought you into the theatre? How did you start?*

TMacA: When I was about six or seven I found out I could draw and that I could draw in perspective. I have no idea where the gift came from but one of my uncles and a cousin of mine were both very good painters, so I suppose it was in the family from the beginning. Anyway, I could draw and thought in terms of something like that but what brought me into the theatre? As I explained in my book *Fallaing Aonghusa (The Mantle of Aonghus)* – Anew McMaster used to come pretty regularly to Dundalk, which was my hometown, with a selection of mostly Shakespearian plays. In school we were taught Shakespeare of course and we learned reams of stuff but the textbooks we had were very dull. There were no illustrations as such and we just had to learn them off by heart but it was hard work, nothing artistic about it. We were brought along by an artistic Christian Brother to see a matinee of Anew McMaster's company doing *Julius Caesar* and all at once it became a beautiful masterpiece before our eyes. The lines we had been learning off by heart suddenly came alive. McMaster of course was playing Brutus and he was magnificent.

KC: *I come from Carrickmacross and my earliest memory was of him in a tent playing "the moor".*

TMacA: He would have played Othello and Oedipus the King but it was the magic of it all , the curtain going up, the way the scenery changed, the way the lights changed and possibly because I had an eye for drawing and so on, it intrigued me immensely. Later on in my life, I was to meet McMaster and we became quite friendly and when I told him it was he who started me off, he said, "Oh my Lord, don't tell me I started you off on the wrong road." As well as the McMaster Company, there were other companies who came along with thrillers like *Night Must Fall* and *Someone Waiting*, up-to-date West End thrillers – this would be the late 1930s, early 1940s. Louis d'Alton came with the Abbey plays of O'Casey and his own plays and I realized that apart from Shakespeare which was very rhetorical, here were the ordinary speeches of ordinary people. For the most part they were Dubliners on the stage, marvellous stories, marvellous characters, coming before our eyes, very beautifully done by the d'Alton company. And I thought to myself – "This is the life for me!" I wanted to write and just before I left school in the mid-1940s, I wrote a play which was accepted and produced by Radio Eireann. It was about local history.

KC: *You were quite a young man at that stage.*

TMacA: I was about nineteen and it was a great thrill to get it accepted and get the princely sum of three guineas, which was something in those days. It was about Redmond O'Hanlon, the local Raparee. I went on to write other plays and sent them to the BBC and Radio Eireann and made a kind of name for myself as a playwright. But I had to earn my living and I joined the Customs and Excise and sat an exam in Dublin for it. When I was in Dublin the first stop I made was to the Abbey Theatre where I went in and saw Mr. Blythe. He very kindly saw me. I was a nonentity from nowhere but I had a letter in my pocket from Lennox Robinson, whom I had met at the Dundalk Drama Festival. I had told him that I wanted to paint scenery. So I had this letter for Ernest Blythe and I went in and we spoke in Irish. I was a Gaelic speaker from the Dundalk College of the Christian Brothers and he said I could come in and help the lady who was designing scenery in the Abbey at the time. Her name was Elisha Sweetman. He didn't intend to pay me. So I came in at three in the afternoon, because there was a morning call and a night call for the boats in the Custom and Excise – and helped her mix paint and lay it on. But then I was transferred to Ballyshannon in Donegal. I was still interested in the theatre and joined a local group and performed with them there. We did, for instance, O'Casey's *Juno and the Paycock* in northern accents (*Laughs*). I also kept on writing plays and managed to get a play of mine accepted by the BBC and in the main kept up that part of my career. I also kept in touch with Ernest Blythe and with Radio Eireann.

At that particular time, we are talking about 1946/47, things were opening up in the artistic world. There was an advert in the paper for various officers in the radio station – producers of plays, outside broadcast officers. I applied for the whole lot and went up for interview. I had kept up my connection with Ernest Blythe and he heard one of my bi-lingual plays on the radio and he wrote and asked me if I would think of helping to write a pantomime. So I wrote back and said: "Of course I would" and then almost immediately he wrote back and said "Look, there's a vacancy in the theatre very soon. Will you come up and see me?" So of course, the wind of the word and off I went and saw him. Again we spoke in Irish and he offered me the position producer of Gaelic plays. It was a new position that he was introducing, not exactly that he wanted all the actors to speak Irish, no, he asked young actors coming in to have a good knowledge of Irish so that he could put on Gaelic plays from time to time. So I found myself appointed and resigned from the Customs and Excise and headed for Dublin. This was in 1947 when I arrived to take up the position of producer of plays in the Irish language. I asked him if I could also design and he said "No. Better to stick to one thing at a time!" He gave me very good advice actually; one was not to go looking for publicity. It's better to quietly go into a job and do it – learn about it than to come with a great big fanfare. So quietly, I went about my work and didn't look for publicity.

He told me to study Freud, which I thought a bit daft at the time, but what he was saying to me was that a director must know human motivation above everything else. You can learn movement on the stage, you can learn about setting, you can learn about lighting, but the motivation, what makes a play really grab an audience has everything to do with psychology.

I did the plays in Irish, mostly one-act plays and then I found myself involved in the Christmas Pantomime, again in Irish. I didn't know I had a flair for pantomimes. I will say at once that I had a sense of humour and possibly it worked into the pantomimes but I found myself year after year, not exactly looking forward, but advancing, towards the dreaded St. Stephen's Night when I had to open a brand new pantomime. I did twenty-one of them in all between the Abbey, the Queens and the new Abbey Theatre. I must say I enjoyed doing them. It was a young company and they could dance and they could sing and it was a break for them from doing the ordinary plays where farmers were ruined in the third act and all that sort of thing. Anyway in the meantime, the Abbey burned down. We have never known why the Abbey burned down; we suspect an electrical fault. There was a rumour that it might have been the butt of a cigarette in the dressing rooms as the fire started at the backstage area. There was the old Abbey gone, very sadly, but we moved to the Queens theatre and continued on with the same policy. Ernest Blythe became ill for a while, and when he was ill our set designer disappeared –well, he resigned, he had other work to do – so Blythe sent me a letter saying "Take over set design till I get back." So I took over set design, doing it for years and years so eventually when we left the Queens and moved to the new Abbey I was designing sets, producing pantomimes, producing plays in Irish and indeed substituting or taking over from Ria Mooney and Frank Dermody with plays in English.

KC: *So would you say Ernest Blythe was your mentor?*

TMacA: To a great extent. I got on very well with him. I was his whiteheaded boy in a way. Somebody asked how he came to appoint me and he said "Leimt sa dorchadas" (a jump in the dark). In any event, I landed safely with the jump. Of course we had rows from time to time but he was very good in that respect: a row could be over and forgotten the next day. You could talk to him and even if you didn't agree with his policy, your business was to carry it out.

After the Queens we opened the new theatre in 1966. He was in his late sixties. He managed to manoeuvre, coax, in a way, blackmail the Government to build the new theatre. It has been in the news recently – the acoustics are very bad in it and its appearance is strictly functional. There's some talk about moving it somewhere else, but no, I think we are going to stay there. It was the first new theatre built in Dublin for over 100 years. It took some time to get it organized and then we opened the Peacock. Ernest was resigning or at least he was retiring, but not yet. The Government appointed Walter Macken, the playwright, as a member of the Board and then he took over. His position was Assistant Manager and Artistic Advisor, but he resigned almost immediately. I'm not quite sure why but I don't think he was all that well. I think he was making up his mind about whether to be a writer or run a theatre. So it was decided to split: there would be a manager, an administrator looking after the front of house and there would be an Artistic Director. Much to my surprise, I was called in to Ernest Blythe and he told me in a sort of roundabout way that I was appointed. What he said to me was, "What was Walter Macken doing, or what was he not doing?" I hadn't the faintest idea of what he had been doing or not doing. So he said: "Well, whatever he was doing or not doing, you do it from now on." So I was appointed. Nobody knew about it, there was no fanfare in the newspaper. Phil O'Reilly was appointed as Administrator. I wasn't called Artistic Director but Artistic Advisor, possibly because there was a Board of four or five directors and they begrudged anyone else to be called a director, but anyway I was doing all that an artistic director does. I had made a certain name for myself in the Queens with a sort of Brechtian production of *Galileo*. They said it was Brechtian, but it wasn't

Brechtian. It was exactly the thing I was doing in the Gaelic plays for years and years. In the meantime in 1966, I found myself in Croke Park doing the commemoration pageant for 1916. The Government put up quite a lot of money and I had the army, the boy scouts, the F.C.A. and every actor in Dublin. I went to town, had a ball – damn it all, Croke Park! It rained on us at dress rehearsal and it rained on us some nights. But to have Croke Park, such a vast area to work in, I felt like Orson Welles when he was told he had RKO studios as his toy. That I regard as an achievement. It was called *Aiséirí* and it was the story of Irish Republicanism from 1798 right onto the rioting of 1916.

KC: *You mentioned Brecht – Is he one of the playwrights you admire?*

TMacA: I managed to get across to the Berliner Ensemble, stayed in West Berlin and got over the wall. I went through Checkpoint Charlie every morning where there was a soldier who'd say, "Hello, see you're back again. How are Shamrock Rovers doing?" He was from Dublin, in the British Army. I found the Berliner Ensemble absolutely magnificent but I didn't quite agree with some of their plays. They were very naïve, very simple, some of the plays – not exactly propaganda but very close to it. I admired the lighting; I admired the way the plays were done. There was some talk of a thing called the "alienation effect" but they didn't know anything about it. It had been invented by an American professor! Oh, the academics – keep them away from the theatre for God's sake! I helped them design and put on *Purple Dust* and found myself also over in the State Theatre where they were doing a one-act of O'Casey's. I was received with great courtesy and I can say the Berliner Ensemble made the best beer, not alone in East Germany, but in Germany. Brecht was dead at that time but I met his wife Helene Weigel and stayed with them and saw a very fine production of *The Threepenny Opera*, with Wolf Kaiser playing Mac the Knife. That sort of thing stimulated me. Basically, I can take Brecht or leave him alone. All I know is that I like to think of theatre as something revolutionary. Remember I was coming from a theatre where every play seemed the same; either about a ruined farmer or a priest who had lost his vocation.

KC: *Do you think Irish theatre is still like that today?*

TMacA: No. Things have changed in many, many ways. I looked forward to having a good play, well written – a good play by M .J. Molloy, a play by Walter Macken or the plays of John McCann. Before there was TV and the soaps, McCann was there to show ordinary Dublin life. They were very popular. Some of the runs in the Queens went on for twenty-four, twenty-five or twenty-six weeks. It was a difficult theatre to keep going without going bankrupt and Blythe did very well in that respect. He did manage to bring us into the new theatre. My interest was in Meyerhold, a Russian director, who put his actors up on scaffolding and did all sorts of daft things. I managed to follow his ideas when I did *Ulysses in Nighttown* in the Peacock and I put all the actors up on scaffolding. A few times in the new theatre, I hung the actors from the flies.

KC: *I didn't realize you were interested in Meyerhold. I thought you were interested in Brecht.*

TMacA: No – I got the name of being interested in Brecht and when I did productions in the Damer Hall – I did *An Triail* by Mairéad Ní Ghráda which was lauded to the skies – people said it was very Brechtian. If it was Brechtian, it was a thing I was doing for years and years myself. I admired the way Brecht revolutionized certain ideas in the theatre but my man is Meyerhold and in another sense Max Reinhardt.

KC: *Did you see the Schaubühne's* Mann ist Mann *this summer?*

TMacA: I saw it. Believe it or not, I helped paint it in a little theatre in East Berlin. I think it's a crushing bore! Looking back at Brecht, there are some very good things. *Galileo* is a very fine play. *Mother Courage* is a very fine play if you've got a good Mother Courage. I said to Helene Weigel "Do I have to do what Brecht has written?" She said: " No, Bertolt wrote a lot of these things with his tongue firmly in his cheek!" I did my own thing with anything like that. One of the best productions I've done was in the Peacock with the young Joe Dowling playing Brecht. The title of the play was *The Plebians Rehearse the Uprising* by Günter Grass. It's about Brecht during the revolution in 1953. When he was asked if he would lead it, he sat on the fence. They said: "Well, you're sitting on the fence." He said: "Show me a better seat." That was typical Brecht! I like spectacle. I like to fill the stage. I like colour and that brought me to the later O'Casey plays because he looked for total theatre, song, dance, colour, music, as he said himself "glittering words." I did *Cock A Doodle Dandy, Red Roses for Me,* and one of the best *A Star Turns Red* –the play that the academics said wouldn't work on the stage because: "It's just communist propaganda." To my amazement I found it did work on the stage. It had great power and it was based on the Sermon on the Mount. It's about Jim Larkin who O'Casey calls Red Jim.

KC: *What do you think of* The Silver Tassie?

TMacA: I like *The Silver Tassie* very much. I don't think Yeats should have rejected it. It has faults of course. O'Casey was going a different way altogether. Yeats always wanted the poet in the theatre. Here was O'Casey coming along and he was becoming the poet in the theatre. He was doing something different. Why Yeats should have thrown it out, I do not know. He never really got on with Sean O'Casey and tended to call him "Casey."

Lady Gregory did get on with him, very much so indeed. Anyway, it lost Sean O'Casey to the Abbey. I was the first person to write to Sean O'Casey for new work, just before he died. The Abbey had never looked for new work from him.

KC: *Do you think the National Theatre should have more of a European dimension?*

TMacA: That is the idea of the National Theatre. It was very narrow at one time – plays about Irish life. It was founded to, frankly, kill the stage Irishman stone dead. It didn't quite do that but it came close. It was to show Ireland to itself as it really was. Remember what Cromwell said to his portrait painter "Show me as I am, warts and all." That was the idea, Synge, O'Casey, they all followed through on that effect.

KC: *How do you regard Martin McDonagh?*

TMacA: I think Martin McDonagh is an excellent playwright, a first-class playwright indeed. There are more plays being written now. I remember in the old Abbey, we'd have a revival and another revival and then a new play would come, M. J. Molloy or T. C. Murray. You'd look forward to a new play. But now all the young people seem to want to write a play, even without a certain amount of technique because we've broken through the Act One and Act Two and all that and they've broken through a lot of phobias and inhibitions. I think about 200 – 250 new plays reach the Abbey every year. Of them, you'd only look at thirty to forty a second time. If ten of them make it, it's a very good year. In the old days, we used to say if we got five new plays a year we'd be doing all right, but nowadays the new plays are coming, not alone to the Abbey but to other theatres as well.

KC: *You've talked about* Aiséirí, *the 1916 Commemoration Pageant – do you think the place of history is changing in Irish plays?*

TMacA: Yes! At one time when you had a play about Ireland, it tended to be a hagiography in a way. Nowadays playwrights are becoming more critical and that is by no means a bad thing. It can go to extremes in other ways – like the portrait of O'Casey that

Augustus John painted. O'Casey is looking askance at things. There's an element of that about playwriting at the present time. The old sentimental, farcical, anything for a laugh sort of play has disappeared. In its place comes a play dealing with social conditions, life as it is, the lower depths, the higher depths. What we do need is a good comedy writer, a successor to Hugh Leonard and Bernard Farrell.

KC: *Over the last number of years, what have you seen that has excited you?*

TMacA: Friel's play – *Translations*. Another play that the critics didn't like but I thought superb, was his *Volunteers*. I put it on during my time at the Abbey. I've been intrigued also by Tom Murphy's experimentation – notably in *The Gigli Concert* and also in *The Sanctuary Lamp* that went on during a festival when I was there. He has a very original point of view, outlook on life. I often looked for interesting Gaelic plays. Apart from inventing story theatre with Eamonn Kelly in the Peacock, I was disappointed in the new plays coming. There was a fine writer, a poet, Eugene Waters who wrote as Eoin O Tuairisc, and Chroistoir O'Floinn also used to provide a play. But I was disappointed that the Gaelic writers didn't come forward. It was the business of the National Theatre to put on Gaelic plays as well as English – not to force them. Ernest Blythe made one mistake. He tried to use the theatre as a sort of medium for reviving Irish. That wasn't a good idea and he probably knew it himself. We should be able to produce a good Irish play side-by-side with a good play in English with the same technique and the same attention.

With regard to the European Theatre, I have always felt that the Abbey should be true to itself in putting Irish life on stage, but it should also bring the classics on to the stage with an Irish point of view, a particular point of view of the Abbey. One of the highlights of my own career as Artistic Director was when I brought over Madame Kneval, from the Red Army Theatre – originally from the Moscow Art Theatre – to do *The Cherry Orchard* with Siobhán McKenna, Cyril Cusack, and the Abbey Company. That was a superb production. Looking back on my own work, as one of the actors said "Give him a daft play that nobody else wants to do, a set of actors and a bare stage and away he goes." I also did *The Borstal Boy* in 1970.

KC: *What did you think of the production of* The Plough and The Stars *in which they had their heads shaved?*

TMacA: Bloody awful! One of the tendencies of directors (at one time in the European Theatre, the set designer decided things) is to look at a script and say "What can I make of this?" not "What did the writer intend in the first place?" At a recent Synge School, we were talking about the *Playboy* and someone said to me: "Now what's your approach to this." I said, "I always trust the author, whether it's Synge, O'Casey, Friel or Leonard; they've done their homework. Your business is to get the spirit of the play and to inspire the actors with that spirit." That's the whole point of directing and that is my attitude towards it. What is the point of shaving people's heads for God's sake and in fact, the citizen's army came in with so much ammunition and so much military hardware that nobody could have possibly got them out of the GPO (*Laughs*). There are one or two others…there's a tendency in young directors to take a classic, let's say *Juno* and say "Now, where did O'Casey go wrong – and what can I do to improve that?" It's absolute nonsense. Trust the author. There's a play by George Bernard Shaw called *Fanny's First Play* and he brings all these things to it– the director arrives and causes terrible trouble but he hadn't read the play.

KC: *Do you think that plays written in the 1940s, 50s or 60s are relevant to nineteen and twenty year olds now?*

TMacA: A good play is relevant at any time. O'Casey's plays are relevant all the time. A Shaw play, with the exception of the later ones, where he was preaching his head off, is relevant.

KC: *Would you say that what happens in the National Theatre and in the other commercial theatres at the moment is conservative theatre?*

TMacA: No harm in being conservative. The Peacock was given to us as an experimental theatre and to put on Yeats' plays and to a great extent it has followed that. The Abbey has a big stage, too big, and bad acoustics and very little rapport with the audience. Even in the third seat from the stage, there is an alienation effect (*chuckles*). Brecht would like it in that respect. We hope with the help of Síle De Valera and a few pounds, that those things, which we knew all about all along, will be rectified. We were thinking of moving but I understand from the Chairman of the Board that the Board of Works descended on the theatre and environs (to quote Joyce) and they put up some propositions about taking over the property on either side. It'll take some time but I hope it will come to pass.

KC: *Would you consider today's audiences conservative?*

TMacA: Most audiences are conservative. The plays I like reflect life. No preaching, no desire to send out the audience better informed than when it came in. Audiences have a habit of not being better informed after a play but have a habit of just enjoying the play.

KC: *How would you regard Paul Mercier?*

TMacA: Paul Mercier is excellent. He is from the community. From his own environment he writes his plays. There are one or two playwrights in Belfast, inevitably writing about the Troubles, bringing the life of Belfast to the stage, even though audiences tend to stay away from plays about the Troubles.

KC: *At one time training for the actor wasn't considered necessary, talent was all. What do you think of the plethora of training institutes there are now?*

TMacA: I think it's good. The fact of the matter is that there are things you can learn. If you want to act, the best thing is to go and find out all about it. You can do that in a school of acting. We had an Abbey School of Acting several times. It was to train people for the Abbey Company. We had a permanent ensemble then. Unfortunately, it's been done away with. The old repertory company idea has long disappeared. Things are different now. The Abbey Company was an excellent company. Unfortunately over some years they were neglected. They were drawing full salaries but were seldom cast, which was a scandal. At shareholders meetings, it was pointed out again and again to the directors. Of course, it is the Artistic Director who has the authority to cast or not to cast but it was a scandal at the time.

Young actors will not learn their business until they go on stage in front of an audience and that's when they need a school of acting. That is the paradox of it; time and time again I've found it. I was criticized for putting youngsters on the stage before they were ready but an actor must know if he is getting through to an audience and if he is not, then he must find out why he is not getting through. I think it's good to have schools of acting. Damn it all, in Dundalk when I joined the Abbey Theatre, the next-door neighbour came in to my mother and said " Mrs McCann, what's your eldest boy doing now? I see he's in the Abbey Theatre but what is *his job?*." The fact of the matter is that there's plenty of work – theatre in Ireland is thriving. Even in Dundalk they are thinking of a playhouse, a 250 seater. Clonmel has a theatre, Derry, Sligo, Monaghan. Smaller towns now have theatres and that's a most marvellous thing. They used to rely on community theatre, that's the amateur movement. That's a very strong movement.

KC: *You adjudicate. Do you enjoy that?*

TMacA: My God! I adjudicated nearly every Theatre Festival in Ireland until very recently. I am still asked to adjudicate but my concentration, in my seventies, is not the same as it was and I prefer not to. I have adjudicated and was accused as an adjudicator of giving a one-man show – partly true – but I always made sure to find something positive to say and to say: "Go ahead and do better work." I would never attack a company. Funny enough, in an amateur performance, even if you know the play – and as an adjudicator, I always made sure I knew the play – you might see something and say: "I never realized that about the play" or "That is most extraordinary, that point had never occurred to me" or you might see some little touch that the director put in that was marvellous.

KC: *You were saying that the amateur movement is quite strong.*

TMacA: It is quite strong, not only in English but in Irish as well. In Irish, at one time, it was awful. Walter Macken as an adjudicator at Feis Sligeach, awarded a play five marks out of a hundred: two marks for knowing where the stage was, two marks for getting the curtain up and one mark for mercifully getting it down again. Things have however gone on marvelously since then and amateur theatre, in Irish, is alive and well.

KC: *How would you improve the amateur sector?*

TMacA: I wouldn't. I'd leave it alone. It improves itself. The amateurs today, the people directing now, will make sure they have done their work, will have read the books, seen the plays, have their own ideas and sometimes there's very little between the amateur and the professional. It's not true what James Ague said: "The professionals can do a job when they don't feel like it and the amateurs can't do a job when they do feel like it." It's untrue and a bit cruel. Amateurs have done some really excellent work – the thing to remember is that the Abbey was an amateur company when it started first. Amateurs kept theatre alive when there was nothing else. I remember adjudicating plays down in Scarriff, in New Ross, where bus loads of people would be coming in to see the plays. Listowel Players when they travelled with *Sive* had bus loads of people, like a football match, wonderful!

KC: *Looking back on your earlier work from your current perspective, what is your most satisfying memory?*

TMacA: *The Plebians Rehearse the Uprising* in the Peacock; *The Borstal Boy* – it was difficult to stage but when I saw it on Broadway, I realized how absolutely it worked – and to hear the critics on the radio afterwards… One of them said: "*Borstal Boy* was like an old

75rpm record and I loved every minute of it"; O'Casey's *The Star Turned Red* I was told wouldn't work and it did– and the Gaelic plays, the story-telling with Eamonn Kelly in which we had mime, song, story and dance. At the moment, I am writing a script for Radio Eireann about a production that took place in October of 1901 at the Gaiety. The Irish Literary Theatre was run by Yeats, Lady Gregory and Edward Martyn – three who hadn't the remotest idea how to run a theatre, for God's sake. Anyhow, they put on a play by George Moore and WB Yeats called *Diarmaid and Gráinne* with an English Company – The Frank Benson Company. With it went a little Irish play called *Casadh an tSugain* by Douglas Hyde, with Willie Fay directing, at the invitation of George Moore, a group of amateur actors from the Keating Branch of the Gaelic League in Parnell Square and they romped home and stole the laurels. The English language play wasn't a success, there were hisses and boos for Yeats and Moore, but anyway it brought Willie and Frank Fay into the orbit of Yeats and Gregory and the result was the Abbey Theatre. The Fays went out on their own and formed their own company. They didn't ask Yeats to be their President, they asked the poet, George Russell. George, who had an enormous beard and great deep voice, said "Wait a Moment" and went into another room, came back out and said " I've just been communing with *Mananan MacLir*, the Sea God and he says, "No, I must not do it – ask Willie Yeats." That's how the whole thing came together.

KC: *Audiences are very quiet now, considering they used to hiss and boo!*

TMacA: I was responsible for the last riot in the Abbey in 1970. It was a revue about the North, called *A State of Chassis*. All sorts of things were happening then. I thought I'd put on a political Brechtian revue – for satirical purposes. It was originally to be called *Ian Paisley is very un aysey and living in Drimnagh*. On the first night, some factions came in. The audience laughed – I hadn't expected them to laugh – and there was a disruption, the audience were shouting and yelling. Eamonn McCann, who may be a distant cousin of mine, took to the stage and made an impassioned speech followed by Lelia Doolan, and it was the only time in my life that I said a bad word in public. I said " Will you f*** off, Lelia, for God's Sake." Anyway, we quelled it down and I was inspired to quote from Byron, "And if I laugh at any mortal thing, "tis that I may not weep."

Tomás Mac Anna joined the Abbey Theatre in 1947 and was in turn Director of Gaelic Plays, Setting Designer and on the opening of the new Abbey in 1966 was appointed Artistic Director, a position he occupied three times in all over twenty years. He has written plays and revues, has produced plays in all the Dublin theatres, as well as in England, Europe and America, where his production of Brendan Behan's *Borstal Boy* won a Tony Award on Broadway in 1970. He also wrote and directed the State-sponsored 1916 Commemoration Pagent, *Aiséirí*, in Croke Park in 1966 and is at present a member of the share-holders' Council at the Abbey. He is married to Caroline, has a grown-up family and lives in Bray. He published, this year, his memoirs in Gaelic, *Fallaing Aonghusa*.

Karen Carleton is the recent past Chairperson of the Drama League of Ireland, the umbrella body for amateur drama groups, societies and individuals. Currently, she is Development Officer with the D.L.I., involved in supporting workshops through professional tutors to the voluntary Arts sector. Karen is a director of B.P. Productions and is a member of the Board of the Pavilion Theatre, Dun Laoghaire.

Barry McGovern in Conversation with Michael Ross

MR: *How do you explain the affinity you seem to have with Samuel Beckett's work?*

BMcG: Joyce and Beckett are my literary gods; I go back to their work again and again and enjoy it. I suppose it goes back to the time I first encountered Beckett, in 1961, when I was 12. I saw a production of *Waiting for Godot*, on BBC TV, with Jack MacGowran as Vladimir, a production Beckett disliked. It struck a chord with me, like hearing a certain piece of music or seeing a certain girl for the first time. I bought some of Beckett's work when I was a teenager, then saw a UCD Dramsoc production of Godot at the Gate in 1966, which was directed by a girl I knew very well, Máirín Cassidy. Colm Ó Briain played Vladimir, John O'Conor, the pianist, played the boy, Chris O'Neill played Lucky. The first Beckett play in which I performed was Endgame, which I did in 1970, in my last year at UCD. At this stage I was pretty hooked on Beckett.

The Beckett Actor mantle seemed to descend on me like the Holy Ghost after I did the one-man show in 1985. I can only assume it was because it was a one-man show. The same thing happened to Jack MacGowran after he did his one-man Beckett show. Do you know how many Beckett plays he performed in, on stage? Three. I've done four. I've done more Shakespeare plays on stage than Beckett plays. It used to irritate me terribly to be called a 'Beckett actor.' Others such as Johnny Murphy have done just as much Beckett as I have. Maybe I have done more than others – I don't know, I don't care. I'm an actor. I happen to love Beckett but I'd be quite happy for the Beckett mantle to descend on someone else for a change. I must have an affinity with Beckett's work, because people keep telling me I have. Perhaps it's true. I certainly like reading it, and I think I can perform it reasonably well, in the sense that there is a lot of irony and black humour in it, and when you hear some people do Beckett – especially outside Ireland – they don't get much of the humour, which is not just Irish but Dublin.

MR: *Why, do you think, are certain actors particularly well suited to performing Beckett?*

BMcG: If there is something that distinguishes some actors from others when it comes to Beckett it may be a quality of insight into Beckett's vision, which is bleak but tinged with humour. It's a tone of voice, it's an attitude, its something that is a mixture of the spiritual and the corporeal. Most 'Beckett actors' tend to be thin people, for example. You don't associate Beckett actors with fat people, maybe because he wrote about emaciated wayfarers. When I read Beckett I hear a voice that is common to his work from *Belacqua* on. Certainly from *Molloy* on, all his characters are essentially the same character, even down to *How It Is* and the narrator of the short prose. It's all the same I. It was third person in *Murphy* and *Watt*, but you can see it happening even in *Watt*, the first person is approaching. Beckett's experience in the war, and afterwards with the Red Cross in St.-Lô, changed everything for him, and you can see the war and post-war experience coming out in *Waiting for Godot* and *Endgame*.

MR: *It sometimes seems that entire countries don't get Beckett. You see American or British productions that camp up the slapstick –* Waiting for Godot *on Broadway, for example. Is that something you've noticed?*

BMcG: It's an odd thing but it does seem to be the case. I've seen a lot of British productions, in particular, that just didn't get it. I've seen Irish productions that didn't get it either of course, and doubtless I've been in some, but there's something about the humour in Beckett that seems not to come across well on stage in some countries.

In America, particularly in Broadway productions, there is the danger of the inevitable star unbalancing the production. You can't do a star turn in Beckett. In some plays you can add your own flourishes if you want, they're more jazz than classical music. But not Beckett.

MR: *You were a professional actor, doing Beckett plays, for a long time before you met him for the first time. Had you wanted to meet him at an earlier juncture?*

BMcG: At the risk of sounding like somebody from Beckett, I never went out of my way to meet anybody. I wouldn't want to have met on him on the wrong basis, because I knew of his need for privacy, particularly after he got the Nobel Prize in 1969. After that, everybody wanted a piece of the action. Students slept in his doorway, waiting to get him as he came out. One of the reasons he loved living in Paris was that people left him alone. He got on well with people in pubs, chatting to people who didn't know who he was. He had a tremendous interest in – and I mean this in the best possible way – low life. He liked ordinary working people, real people who were not attached to the artificiality of the literary world.

For years, had anybody asked me who in the world I would most like to meet, of course it would have been Beckett. When I got the chance to meet him, in 1986, it was a great thrill and a little daunting. When Michael Colgan took over the Gate, he asked me if I would consider doing a one-man show on Beckett. I was reluctant because it had been done by MacGowran and by others. Eventually he persuaded me to do it, and so we based it on *Molloy, Malone Dies* and *The Unnameable* – which Beckett hated being called a trilogy.

So eventually Gerry Dukes and I put the texts together, Colm Ó Briain directed it, Robert Ballagh designed his first stage set for it and we put it on as a late night show in the Dublin theatre festival in 1985. I thought it would last six performances, hopefully some people would like it and that that would be it! But it took on a life of its own that was unexpected. When we went to Paris in 1986 to perform *I'll Go On* as part of the celebrations for Beckett's eightieth birthday, he did not want to celebrate what Krapp calls 'the awful occasion' in any way. He couldn't stand any fuss about his birthday, so the celebrations went ahead without his blessing.

Michael wrote to Beckett for permission to do the show. Originally there was talk of us reviving the MacGowran show, but some difficulties arose. Beckett said that if there was a problem reviving the MacGowran show, "There remains the possibility of another one-man show with a different title and a different choice of texts." A nod was as good as a wink to a blind horse, so we went ahead and did our own show. When we went to Paris with the show, Michael wrote to Beckett to ask if he would meet us. He agreed to meet us, and said he would ring the hotel when we got there. We got there late because of the traffic, and when we arrived there was a message to say Mr Beckett had rung and would ring back at seven o'clock.

Exactly on the dot of seven, the phone rang in Michael's room, which was next door to mine. An arrangement was made to meet the next day at the PLM hotel across the road from his flat at 38 Boulevard St.-Jacques in Montparnasse. We were there with half an hour to spare, because we didn't want to be late for Beckett. We were hanging around in the foyer, and just as it came up to the appointed time, he appeared. We hadn't seen him come in. It was as if he had materialised near us. Beckett was thinner than I had expected, and ever so slightly stooped.

MR: *How many times did you meet him?*

BMcG: I met him on six occasions in all. I used to send a card to his home address asking to meet, and then he'd send a card back saying he would meet me at a specified time and place, and not to reply unless I was unable to make it. He'd say: "I'll meet you at 3pm in the PLM. If you're not there I'll know that you wanted to be."

He replied on plain postcards with his name printed on them. On one, he mentioned that he was toying with a new ending for *Dante and the Lobster*, which had been published 50 years earlier. "Thought of a new ending ... Instead of: 'It is not.' 'Like hell it is.' Better? Worse? Can't decide. Yours, Sam." I met him three times in 1986, once in 1987 and then finally twice in 1989. The last time I met him in 1986 I met him on my own, the only time I did so, and we had a great chat about Joyce. I was a relatively young actor, and I was fortunate and privileged to meet him. He was very kind to me, but probably in the same way he was kind to lots of other people. He never saw me perform but he heard tapes of pieces of his that I performed and he wrote me nice notes in relation to them.

He was a kind man, and you felt always that you were in the presence of somebody very special, but there was nothing in particular he did to make it special – he just had enormous integrity, enormous intelligence, his mind was crystal clear, and you sensed that to try to hoodwink this man, or to spoof him in any way – or tape him under the table, or film him secretly, which was done – would be terribly wrong.

He was an enigmatic man; he had a severe need for privacy, which he didn't make a big deal about. We knew he simply didn't go to see his plays on stage, so Michael invited him to a dress rehearsal of *I'll Go On*, assuring him that it would be utterly private. He took his cheroot box and wrote down the details, but we knew there was little chance of him coming; it was like expecting Shakespeare to turn up at a rehearsal of *Hamlet*. In the heel of the hunt, like Godot, he didn't come. We got a message, relayed by Seán Ó Mórdha, to say that Mr. Beckett couldn't make it and sent his apologies. I was relieved in a way; it would have been too much to try to do it with Samuel Beckett as your audience.

MR: *You were one of the last people to visit him in the Tier Temps retirement home before he died. What was he like at the end of his life?*

BMcG: When he moved into the Tier Temps the year before he died, I used to ring him there when I was in Paris. I never rang him at his flat – I didn't have the number but even if I did I wouldn't have rung him there – but by the time he moved into the home I felt I knew him well enough to ring. The last time I met him was about four weeks before he died. He was weak, suffering from emphysema, and was extremely thin.

In that last meeting I mentioned to him that *Endgame* was my favourite play of his. "Mine too" he said, and then he quoted the speech in which Nell says "Nothing is funnier than unhappiness". He gave me a copy of *Le Monde et le Pantalon*, a critique of the work of his friend, the painter Bram van Velde, then he quoted Nagg's speech about the world and the trousers, and he did it fantastically well. He would have made a wonderful Nagg. I remember being aware that my wife, Medb, and I were here in a room with Beckett, just the three of us, and he was performing part of Endgame for us beautifully and there was no way of sharing that with the rest of the world. It would have been nice had it been a few years earlier and I had got to work with him, which I never did. On the other hand, a few years later and I would never have met him at all!

MR: *What effect, if any, did getting to know Beckett personally have on your performances of his work?*

BMcG: Not very much, quite honestly. I don't think it would have made any difference to the work had I never met him. I asked him some specific things, and it was a help to get answers from the 'horse's mouth'. For example I asked him the pronunciation of Clov. [Hamm's servant in *Endgame*.] I liked the idea of it being pronounced 'clove', with a long vowel, rather than a short as I had often heard it. You put cloves in ham, so there seemed to be a pun on that in the play. Beckett said it was pronounced 'clove', so that was that. He said too that Godot was pronounced with the stress on the first syllable, not the second, as Americans tend to pronounce it.

I wish I had asked him more about the work. There are a couple of things in *Godot* and *Endgame*, in particular, I wish I'd asked him about. And as an actor puzzling out the texts I always found him ready to help when he could. There were always these stories that you couldn't talk to him about his work. I found that was rubbish. He was very much a practical man of the theatre. He was always willing to change things in texts when he was directing, if he felt there was a better way of doing it.

MR: *Why did you choose acting in the first place?*

BMcG: It wasn't like the Cusacks or the Brennans, where there was a family tradition of acting to follow. My parents had performed in an amateur capacity but there was no professional involvement with performing. I also remember, at home, my mother playing the piano and my father singing, so that sort of performance was in my consciousness from an early age.

I was in boarding school for five years in Castleknock and was in the choir. We used to do a musical every year. Music is without doubt the art form that I love the most. I could do without theatre long before I could do without music. I was in the musicals and began to get leading roles, and that was something I enjoyed doing a lot.

My father was a trained barrister and after I left school I toyed with the idea of doing law. I thought of becoming a journalist at one stage, and a priest at another stage. There's an element of performing in all those occupations. I knew that to work in banking, insurance or something along those lines would be for me a living death. Acting is said to be the shy man's revenge, and although I wouldn't say I'm shy now, I was fairly shy as a young man. When I went to UCD I joined Dramsoc, and while doing my B.A., I answered an ad for the Abbey School of Acting, got in and things went from there. I wasn't one of those people who from the age of ten wanted to be on the stage. In retrospect it's the only thing I could imagine myself having done, but it came about because I got an audition and little by little it crept up on me from there.

MR: *Does the ephemeral nature of acting, particularly stage acting, bother you?*

BMcG: No, it doesn't. I quite like it. With stage acting there is no 'product' in the way there is with film acting, but the ephemeral nature of theatre is not unlike sport. You train and then perform and it's done. There are nights when it simply doesn't happen on stage, for reasons that can be hard to pin down. But if you're well rehearsed, no matter how bad it is, it's never going to go below a certain level. On nights it can soar, when the actors and the audience fuse, and that is exhilarating. But if the play is well rehearsed, the difference between the best night and the worst should be small.

Theatre is the most bastard-like of all arts. I sometimes think it's the easiest discipline in which to get away with something substandard. If you're a long-jumper, a jump of eight metres is measurably and unambiguously a great jump. A great clarinet player is a great clarinet player. But acting is highly individual in the way it is perceived. Stage acting is a bit like jazz. You can play the same notes in successive performances, but there can be a slightly different energy from one night to the next, a different relationship with the audience, a slightly different tuning between the actors, so every night is like a first night on stage.

MR: *As an audience member, how often have you experienced magical nights in the theatre?*

BMcG: I've been around a while and seen a lot of shows. There have been magical nights but they have been relatively few. That elation, the hairs standing up on the back of the neck; I've experienced that more at concerts than in the theatre. The first performance in Ireland of Brian Friel's *Faith Healer*, in 1980, was one of those nights. The first time I saw Micheál MacLiammóir's *The Importance of Being Oscar* was another. I watched a performance of it on television recently and it's strange to watch it now, it's so camp, but wonderful in its own way. I'm not normally a fan of the one-man show but that was one of three that had that effect on me, the others being Jack MacGowran's Beckett show *Beginning to End*, and Eamon Morrissey's *The Brother* [based on the work of Flann O'Brien], which was a great marriage of man and material.

MR: *How do you recognise genius in acting?*

BMcG: It's hard to talk about genius in acting. It's much easier in those arts where there is something concrete to examine: a score, a painting, a piece of sculpture. Acting is so ephemeral. There's a mysterious quality to any talent and certainly to any genius. People who try to analyse it kill it. There's a dimension to it that cannot be quantified or described, that mystery is part of art and spirituality, and I think to analyse it is dangerous.

MR: *What type of temperament does it help to have as an actor?*

BMcG: If you're insensitive, you're not likely to be an outstanding success in the performing arts. You need a certain sensitivity. On the other hand, if you're too sensitive it can be a liability. I've never found actors to be the bitchy people that the stereotype might suggest, but there's a lot of competition for parts, it's a cut-throat world and inevitably you have to put up with a lot of disappointment. Sometimes you have no work for months on end, sometimes you are offered something that you don't particularly want to do; other times you are offered two great parts at the same time and have to make a choice. You need to have the temperament to cope with that.

MR: *What remains in acting that you wish to do?*

BMcG: Lots. At fifty-three I'm just coming into the right age for a lot of roles I want to play. There's lots of Shakespeare I'd love to do. Half of his plays, at least, are wonderful, and I haven't done as much Shakespeare as I'd like. Over the past forty years we've lived though a golden period in Irish writing and there are a lot of great plays by contemporary Irish writers that I'd love to do. There's still a lot of Beckett that I haven't done and would still like to do. In the Gate's various Beckett Festivals I was in all three of the longer Beckett plays – *Waiting for Godot, Endgame and Happy Days*, but there are lovely chamber pieces, like *Play, A Piece of Monologue* and *Ohio Impromptu* that I'd still love to do.

I'd like to do more film work. As an actor you don't get much opportunity to do film work in Ireland, and while my family was young I was reluctant to travel in the way film sometimes demands. Now that my children have got older, I'd like to do more film. I've no ambitions to decamp to America, but it would be nice to do something decent occasionally in that medium.

But overall I am lucky to earn a living doing something I enjoy. It has its ups and downs but what business hasn't? All I ever really wanted to do was good work with good people.

Barry McGovern has been an actor for over thirty years. He has been a member of both RTE Players and the Abbey Theatre Company playing many leading roles with both. He has written music for many plays and two musicals with Byran Murray. He has occasionally directed plays and opera. He has worked frequently on Radio and Television and has appeared in a number of films. He is perhaps best known for his work in Beckett, mostly with the Gate Theatre. His award-winning one-man show *I'll Go On* has toured all over the world. In 1998 he was awarded a honorary Doctorate in Letters from Trinity College, Dublin.

Michael Ross is Editor of Culture & Arts for *The Sunday Times*.

Frank McGuinness in Conversation with Joseph Long*

Frank McGuinness' play *Mutabilitie* received its Irish premiere in September 2000 at the Samuel Beckett Theatre, Dublin, in a production directed by Michael Caven. *Mutabilitie* explores the relationship between two cultures, the Irish and the English, and presents a highly personal view of how the history and the identity of the two countries are intertwined.

Historically, the play is set in Ireland, in 1598, amidst the violence of the Munster Wars, at a critical, defining moment of Irish history. After the failure of the Reformation in Ireland, a new order is being imposed. The English crown will no longer accommodate itself to the loose, fragmented control of medieval feudalism. The imperialism of Queen Elizabeth is no longer content to seize lands: souls must now be seized, for their own betterment and salvation. The struggle is interiorized: it can no longer be a matter of territorial conquest, it has become ideological and religious, a struggle for identity. Lord Grey is appointed Lord Deputy of Ireland, to be the agent of this new imperialism. Before he sets out in 1580, he recruits, as his secretary, a young intellectual by the name of Edmund Spenser (1552-1599), destined to become the greatest poet of his generation, who will serve the Crown in Ireland for seven years and receive, as his reward, the Castle of Kilcolman, set amidst the wild forests of west Cork, where the disinherited Irish are plotting their resistance. In this perilous and implausible situation, more an enforced exile than a sinecure, Spenser writes much of his work, including the *Mutabilitie Cantos* and a section of his famous allegorical poem, *The Fairie Queen*. In 1598, the castle is destroyed by fire. Spenser and his family escape and return to London, where he dies the following year.

Into this historical framework, Frank McGuinness introduces, with a characteristically provocative humour, the fantasy that the young William Shakespeare might well have travelled across Ireland with a group of players and be rescued from destitution and drowning by the dutiful hospitality of Edmund Spenser. I asked Frank what was the significance, within the fiction of his play, of this strange encounter between the poet and the younger playwright.

FMcG: I think that they represent two very different types of the English imagination. I think that Spenser is, on the surface, an untroubled creative artist, very much in the service of the imperial power. When you go beneath that surface, you discover raging terrors and disturbances, which are very clearly present when you do start to probe beneath. I think he was a man who had a desperate struggle with his own psyche, with his own soul. But he had to keep a firm grip, he had to regulate his conscience in order to carry out the policies of the Crown that he served, the policies of Elizabeth's government. Then with Shakespeare, I think you get a much more diverse, a much more liberated consciousness, a much more challenging, invigorating imagination, because he was in the process of inventing the theatre. And at the same time, in Shakespeare there are desperate contradictions, all the way through the work, and these contradictions resolve themselves quite helpfully in characters that he creates. But when I was trying to create him, I had, very deliberately, an idea that he would practically change character in every scene he was in. He moves from a man who was, through force of circumstances, absolutely helpless ...

JL: *He's fished out of the river early in the play and saved by Edmund, he has a fever ...*

FMcG: He's out of self-control by reason of his illness. He moves, in the end, to being a man absolutely in command of himself and of his destiny and of his art, in a way that Edmund in the end loses all that control. It's a very basic medieval idea, the Wheel of Fortune: the man at the top at the beginning, goes to the bottom, the man at the bottom at the beginning, goes to the top. And that was, again, a recognition of how deeply the Middle Ages did influence the Renaissance in England especially. It wasn't a clean break by any means. They still had this idea of *Fortuna*.

JL: *The third party in the play is the group of the native Irish, living in the woods. There's Sweney, the King, there's Queen Maeve, there's the remnants of a court, and in the centre of all that, the woman-poet, the File, whose name, of course, is the Irish for "poet.*"..

FMcG: She makes her journey as well. She makes her artistic journey. At the beginning of the play, when she starts to recite, when she starts to create poetry, it is very much a bardic tradition, a very fixed, inherited literature, and by the end of the play she has travelled a journey in her own literary aspirations, in her own literary achievement, where she is writing a personal poetry, she is becoming much more her own voice. It is William, it is the character of William who gives her a confidence to speak for herself, rather than for her tribe or for her tradition. She is now managing to articulate what she herself is, in artistic terms.

JL: *Do you see these different journeys of identity as symbolizing, in a way, the relationship between the two cultures, the Irish and the British?*

FMcG: Yes, I do, actually. I do very much see it as an articulation, on the part of the Irish, but in the English language, of their own Irish identity and of their own independence, while at the same time acknowledging the debt to both traditions and to both inheritances – the Gaelic and the English-speaking.

JL: *The Gaelic group are represented by a strange mix. There are legendary heroes, King Sweeny, whose name suggests King Sweeney of Dal Arie, the hero of a seventh-century tale, who was defeated at the Battle of Moira, goes mad and is changed into a bird; and Queen Maeve of the* Táin Bó Cuailgne, *the warrior queen of Connaught. In legend, these two have no connection. There are suggestions of historical leaders of the time, Hugh, whose name evokes Hugh O'Neill. It's a strange composite. They're living in the woods, and even that suggests, perhaps, a mythological space, or else it can be read as an historical fact, a reference to the conditions of the Irish Rising and the wars in Munster at the end of the sixteenth century. Why did you choose such a mixture of references and identities for that group?*

FMcG: Largely because I wanted them to have enormous resonance, enormous stories to tell about themselves, stories that were effectively censored both by the art form of the theatre and also by their own refusal to recognize any longer what they were. They know, in the play, that they run the threat of their own extinction and of their own silencing and they choose, Sweney and Maeve, they choose at the end to extinguish themselves rather than have others do it for them.

JL: *Queen Maeve orders her two sons, Hugh and Niall, to slay them, to slay their own parents.*

FMcG: They choose their own to kill them. This is their act of defiance and, in doing that, they will live forever. That's what I was trying to get at there, that they are not put under by the occupying forces, they choose rather to go themselves and to believe in a new order that will come after them. New stories to be told.

JL: *They assert their identity, they will become truly themselves, in the new order that will be brought into being through the File ... ?*

FMcG: Through the File and Hugh, that marriage.

JL: *In Trevor Nunn's production in 1997, at the National Theatre, the closing tableau was made optimistic. Spenser's child escapes from the burning castle and is taken in by the Irish. In that production, the child became the centre of a gesture of giving, there is an exchange of food. But as you wrote it, the ending is ambiguous, even negative.*

FMcG: More ambiguous than negative, I think. The weapons are still on stage. When the Irish lay down their weapons, the weapons still remain there, on the stage. Michael Caven's ending was closer to what I wrote. It's up to the production to choose what way they want to view that reality.

JL: *That's a fairly clear reference, isn't it, to the present-day situation in Northern Ireland?*

FMcG: Yes. There is a flicker of hope, but that's all. It can be very easily extinguished. But it's still there. There is a flicker of hope.

JL: *This is the third play you've written which examines, quite explicitly, but in very different ways, the relationship between the two cultures, the two islands. There was* Mary and Lizzie, *which was first performed by the Royal Shakespeare Company in 1989, and there was* Someone Who'll Watch Over Me, *performed at the Hampstead Theatre, London, in 1992. How conscious were you of following out a design, through these three plays?*

FMcG: I certainly didn't set out with a conscious design to write three plays about the two cultures. It's more a retrospective thing, that I see it now as fulfilling. But there was certainly a conscious design, in terms of structural ambitions. I wanted to write a great, big folk play in *Mary and Lizzie*, which was deeply influenced by *Peer Gynt*, coming from the Norwegian folk tradition, as Ibsen drew on there. That gave it its – for want of a better term – its *sprawling* nature, its ability to cross continents, its ability to go anywhere that it wanted to go...

JL: *You had been working, at the time, on a version of* Peer Gynt, *which was performed in 1988 at the Gate Theatre, Dublin. So then, when you moved on to* Someone Who'll Watch Over Me, *you gave yourself entirely different parameters. You set the play indoors, in a prison cell in Beirut, with only three characters, three hostages, an Englishman, an Irishman, an American. You were consciously exercising yourself in a radically different dramatic genre.*

FMcG: I was very consciously writing a chamber piece, a very enclosed, extremely stark prison piece. I wanted to go into nothing there but character and the self, the explorations of the self. And at the same time, a very close examination of the three main dialects of the English language as I understand them to be, the Irish, the English and the American. Then in *Mutabilitie*, it was very much an epic, but I was setting out write a five-act Elizabethan play which would contain within it, of course, the sense of disturbance, the sense of stretching itself to breaking point. There are two occasions in the play when the breaking point is reached and explodes. The first is at the end of the third act, when you have eleven voices speaking to you, which is deliberately doing ultimate violence to the consecutiveness of the English language ...

JL: *Yes, at the start of the third act, the discourse is perfectly consecutive, there is a sermon from Edmund and there are long, coherent speeches from him and from Elizabeth, his wife. The tone is analytical and rational. But after Edmund leaves, the discourse becomes fragmented, the lines are single, short sentences, and in the end there are four different locations represented simultaneously on stage, with four dialogues intercut. It creates the effect of a polyphonic chorus with, as you say, eleven voices. You had done something similar, in 1985, in the third part of* Observe the Sons of Ulster Marching Towards the Somme, *but there the effect was different, it suggested a coming together, a regrouping, a shared fate. Whereas here, you were setting out to do violence, as you say, to the rationality of the English language, the language of a governing class ...*

FMcG: Deliberately setting out to upset an audience as to what the hell is happening, what is coming at it, to make the English language sound, particularly to English people, something foreign, something that they don't know what is coming next. Then the second breaking point comes in the play within the play, when the Irish appear and start their chant of Troy.

JL: *That's in the fourth act, where, as it seems to me, you do pull out all the stops. There's a storm, William conjures spirits and the Irish appear and chant the story of Hecuba and Cassandra. You place your main theme, the change of Fortune, inevitable change, at the heart of it: "Chaos of change that none can flee, / This earth is Mutabilitie." Of course, the play within the play is clearly political, the British Empire will fall as Troy fell. But was that the only reason you chose to place the story of Troy at this point of the play?*

FMcG: Here you have a reduction of the whole basis of Western civilization, the story of Troy, told by the Irish, who are taking control of it and presenting it in their own particular voice. That is why it had to be accompanied by music, belted out, sung. These are the two breaking points, two linguistic threats to an audience.

JL: *So the Irish re-appropriate the story of Troy, which is a story of origins, of European origins, they make it their own, the expression of their own identity, they wrest it back from the dominant discourse of the occupier. In almost every play of yours, Frank, there is a sense of language being pushed to the limit, almost beyond the limit, certainly pushed beyond its daily use. There is a central importance given to song. In* Observe the Sons of Ulster Marching Towards the Somme, *there is a critical moment, when the eight Ulster men assert their collective identity, and they do it through a hymn they sing; it's a hymn written by Martin Luther, "From depths of woe we raise to thee / The voice of lamentation ... " They go back to the very source of their Protestantism, to their origins, to sing their identity, what they see as their essence.*

FMcG: The thing about the songs is, especially in *Mutabilitie*, but also in *Someone Who'll Watch Over Me* and in *Sons of Ulster*, when they sing, they say what they mean. If you want to understand where *Mutabilitie* is going, what is really at the heart of it, look at the songs, at the poems, that is where the cards are on the table, where the characters put their cards on the table, anyway. In *Mutabilitie*, the File's song about losing her child, which comes when she is singing to Annas, that is the heart of the woman, that is when she is coming to terms with herself.

JL: *Women are often at the heart of your plays. Your very first play,* The Factory Girls, *in 1982, was about the protest of women, their attempt to assert themselves in the factory which they occupy, to claim their place in history and in society.* Mary and Lizzie, *then, presents two very marginal women, who set out from Ireland on a picaresque kind of journey and wind up being housekeepers for Friedrich Engels, when he was in Manchester ...*

FMcG: They did more than keep house for him. Let's not be polite ...

JL: *What brought you to these two women, originally?*

FMcG: There is a note in Edmond Wilson's *To the Finland Station*, where he mentions that Engels lived with two Irish women, Mary and Lizzie Burns, and that they gave him safe passage through Manchester, when he was researching for the *Conditions of the Working Class* – which is a book that changed the world. I felt that they were ideal for my kind of investigations, because they were absolutely excluded, written out of history. There are very few references to them. Yet they were responsible, ultimately, for the writing of that book and they did allow him to tell the truth. Engels" idea of the truth does contain some deeply racial stereotypes about the Irish people, which can be excused by reason of his compassion for the suffering of the Irish in Manchester, and can be excused by saying that he did write it in the middle of the nineteenth century. But there are other truths in it that go beyond excuses, and I think that it has been a terrible failing, particularly of the socialist imagination. They share in a terrible condescension to the Irish people, a terrible predictability in what they think of the Irish. And that is basically what I was trying to attack in the play, in the scene – the Dinner Party scene – where Jenny Marx reads out, from Engel's book, the particularly offensive parts about the Irish, and Mary and Lizzie meet it by singing *She moved through the Fair*, which is their absolute answer to any accusation of inferiority, cultural inferiority. They meet these attacks with their own art, which is song.

JL: *It's a song about love, about sorrow and innocence, an old folk song. The play has a serious intent, at the same time it's a very playful piece. It plays with theatrical forms and is very funny, at times. The dinner scene – Dinner with Karl and Jenny – is a caricature of Noel Coward, of a theatre of social manners. You parody a whole gamut of theatrical forms. The final scene is epic in its vision, a tableau outside of real time, where you evoke the collective experience of women through history, their marginalization, their repression.*

FMcG: The intention there, with *Mary and Lizzie*, was to write a big play. It's as simple as that. I think the expectation was that I would follow up the *Sons of Ulster* with a big commercial success. I had no intention of doing that, actually. I wanted to write an extremely large play, with a very big cast. I still remember with delight the look of shock on preview audiences when they were confronted, at the Royal Shakespeare Company, with six near-naked women up trees, singing in Gaelic. I think the words "this will not move to the West End" were immediately voiced.

JL: *Your play was provocative in its form and in its themes, but also in the circumstances of its presentation – because, in the first instance, you were putting it on with the Royal Shakespeare Company, the most respectable institution of British theatre.*

FMcG: It's part of the pleasure of putting plays on in England that you do not give the English audience what they believe they're going to get, when they go to "an Irish play." Even with *Someone Who'll Watch Over Me*, which was very successful, even there I think they were quite taken aback by something I personally do believe in, which is a very deep love of the English language, going right back to Old English, and the celebration of it and of *their* literature. Again, that didn't give them what they wanted, but they liked that image of themselves. They don't like the image of themselves in *Mary and Lizzie* and in *Mutabilitie*. I'm not in the business of, all the time, flattering them.

JL: *You mentioned* Peer Gynt, *which was a strong influence on* Mary and Lizzie, *a formal influence at any rate.* Peer Gynt *is one of a number of adaptations you've done. There is a major part of your work, over the past twenty years, which is comprised of translations or adaptations of European plays. I think you see this as an intrinsic part of your own writing, as part of your function as an Irish dramatist, to re-appropriate these texts, and not just as a service of translation.*

FMcG: Absolutely. It's also a liberation. Irish literature has always been far too much defined in terms of its relationship with English literature. It's been a part of the taming of the Irish by the English to do that. But in fact if you look at our major authors of this century, O'Casey has much more in common with Brecht than he would with any other playwright, particularly in English. Joyce and Beckett looked to the continent. Joyce was deeply in touch with Dante and the Greeks, and Beckett with both French and Italian literature. I remain at home and try to make these great European playwrights part of our vocabulary. That is definitely a cultural ambition. But the private ambition is there too, which is to learn more about writing plays, really. Because these authors, Ibsen more than anybody, and Lorca, Strindberg, Chekhov, they teach you more about your craft. We are dealing with an art form, unapologetically dealing with an art form, and we need to know more about it. A painter has to go and look at other traditions, you have to go and look at other theatres and know at least what you're rejecting.

JL: *So it's partly an apprenticeship to your own craft...* DBS Arts Library

FMcG: Absolutely.

JL: *... and then there is the wider agenda that both Tom Kilroy and Brian Friel seem to have pursued, and consciously pursued, through the eighties, and which has to do with giving an Irish voice to these plays, which were certainly not written in English, but which have been, in a way, appropriated and are treated in Britain almost as part of the canon of British theatre, of a British theatre tradition, Chekhov and Ibsen especially. Both Kilroy and Friel have been quite explicit about their ambition to reclaim these authors from that anglicized tradition, to restate them in an Irish voice. That was part of your ambition too, wasn't it?*

FMcG: That is certainly the case for *Three Sisters* and for *Peer Gynt*. But what is significant is that I am now being invited by companies outside Ireland to do versions. And I do them as I hear them, and they do them as they want to speak them. That was the case with *The Caucasian Chalk Circle*, with Brecht, which was a multi-cultural cast ...

JL: *That was the Théâtre de Complicité, wasn't it, who performed it in April 1997, at the National ...*

FMcG: They have a policy of working with actors from all over the world. They're an English company, but they're multi-national. We had actors from France, from Vietnam, from Spain, from Bosnia, Sarajevo, from Ireland, from Scotland, from England, and they took my text as their multi-language. They spoke English with this text – which was a great liberation for me. *A Doll's House* was done with Celtic speakers, Scots, Irish, Welsh, as well as English. I think it is the mark of a new confidence in Irish theatre that we are not frightened of that. We no longer need to assert that we have a right to do these plays, we take it for granted, of course we do it. And this is because, especially, of Tom Kilroy's *The Seagull*. That was the beginning.

JL: *That was back in 1981. In fact, Tom Kilroy's version of* The Seagull *had been commissioned by the Royal Court London. Max Stafford-Clark shared Kilroy's view of how received British versions had "neutered" Chekhov, casting him in a genteel, Home Counties diction. Whereas he wanted to stage Chekhov in a rougher, more immediate, more comic mode. Is that kind of work behind you now? Is writing versions, for you, now, as dramatist, a thing of the past?*

FMcG: No, not at all. I've just finished two Ibsens, *The Wild Duck* for the Abbey, and *Ghosts* for Thelma Holt Productions. I still very much enjoy doing them. They still are enormous help for teaching. They've always been the bridge between teaching and writing – and, you know, I'm still learning, still very happy to learn from those who stretch the boundaries, who still stretch the boundaries, when they're properly realized.

JL: *Your most recent adaptation was Valle-Inclan's* Barbaric Comedies, *which was co-produced by the Edinburgh Festival in August 2000 and by the Abbey Theatre, Dublin. I thought that was an extraordinary theatrical moment, both your text and the staging, in Calixto Bietto's athletic, open-stage production. It disappeared into a welter of anecdote. How do you feel, as a dramatist, about that project? What impelled you to go for that, in the first place?*

FMcG: It was an enormous task, but I tend to take on enormous tasks. I hope it will feed the writing. Weirdly enough, it did feed the poetry, working on that text. It was a full-time job for a substantial amount of time – there was a good year's work in it. I don't know if I would commit myself to that length of time, to that scale of involvement again, for a version. I felt that I would have made changes, if it had been me, involved deeply with the production, I would have asked for changes, but I wasn't. That's another story. It was a great thing to do. I'm very glad I did it. I'm very glad I got to know Valle-Inclan's work. He's a truly mighty writer that I didn't have a clue about. At least now I can say, well, I know three of his plays. I've worked on those.

JL: *How about writing for the screen?*

FMcG: No plans. That's a different world — not just a different skill, but a different world financially, a different world in terms of responsibility, in terms of control. You're at the mercy of so many people in the film world. I don't like that at all.

JL: *How healthy is Irish theatre now, Frank? Can I quote you on that, to close with?*

FMcG: Seeing the emergence of Marina Carr — that has been, I think, the development of a major new voice, a fearless voice, a woman who will take on enormous challenges. I think, when there's that strength, I think it's in pretty good shape.

Frank McGuinness was born in Buncrana, Co. Donegal, and now lives in Dublin and lectures in English at the National University of Ireland Dublin. He is best known for *The Factory Girls, Observe the Sons of Ulster Marching Towards the Somme, Innocence, Carthaginians, Someone Who'll Watch Over Me, Mutabilitie* and *Dolly West's Kitchen*. His adaptations of Sophocles, Ibsen, Chekhov, Strindberg, Lorca and Brecht have been internationally acclaimed. His work for film and television includes *Scout, Henhouse* and *Dancing at Lughnasa*. He has published two volumes of poetry with Gallery Press, *Booterstown* and *The Sea with No Ships*.

Joseph Long is a Senior Lecturer in the Department of French, NUI Dublin, and Director of the UCD Drama Studies Centre. He was Chairman of Project Arts Centre from 1989 to 2000. He has lectured at universities in France, Germany and the UK, notably on modern European dramatists such as Beckett, Gatti, Genet, Ionesco, McGuinness. He has directed productions professionally in France and the UK. He has a specialist interest in the translation of dramatic texts, and his edition of Armand Gatti, *Three Plays* was published last year by Sheffield Academic Press.

*The above interview reproduces in part material published in Joseph Long, "New Voices in Irish Theatre", *Etudes irlandaises* CCXLIV, Spring 1999, pp. 9-19.

Tom Mac Intyre in Conversation with Fiach McConghail

FMacC: *Tom, I know your work as a playwright, but I also know your work as a short-story writer and also as a poet, a fine poet, in both Irish and English, so how would you describe yourself and your craft?*

TMacI: I'm a storyteller, working in a variety of forms, because simply put, that's my nature. More precisely, I guess there's an adventurer in me. Put it another way, there's material that can be dealt with beautifully on the stage, there's material that cries out for the lyric, there's material that cries out for fictional treatment. The fun is to identify the material properly in reference to the form and then go and play – and play is the central word for me. Play, to be playing – otherwise you might as well be at home minding the tongs from the fire.

FMacC: *In terms of playing, do you visualize a structure from the outset, is it the short-story, is it the poem, is it the three-act play; and do you decide on it, before you begin to play?*

TMacI: Not to be contrary, I'd approach the question from a different angle. The play element is contingent on interior weather and a particular kind of interior weather that it seems to me is largely lacking in the Irish soul at the moment. Just to stick to Ireland, our theatre, for example, seems to me to be a "daddy-theatre." There's little room for play, there's little room for the sensual, and the erotic is almost entirely missing.

FMacC: *But it's not missing in poetry, so is it just particular to theatre?*

TMacI: I'm not sure at all that it's easily to be found in contemporary Irish poetry – perhaps in contemporary Irish poetry, *in Irish* – from Nuala Ní Dhomhnaill, and Biddy Jenkinson, mar shampla, but it's missing from the writing – *en général* – because it's missing from the society. That's what I mean when I say it's a "daddy-society." If the event of the last century was, as I believe it to have been, the opening up of the unconscious, giving males such as Picasso, Balanchine, Mizoguchi, Kawabata, notably among the women Pina Bausch, a road into the unconscious, where you cannot, and here we come back to the play, get the play quality without having gained permission to frolic in the unconscious.

FMacC: *So therefore is it in the realm of the unconscious that you feel most comfortable?*

TMacI: Writing that isn't dripping from the unconscious bores me very quickly – that's what I call "daddy-writing." As we all recognize by this hour, the desperate need in the contemporary psyche is for the grip of the patriarchal goosestep if you like, to be marvellously mitigated and for the males who run the show to bring up, way, way up, the female energy. Now when that happens, the possibility of beautiful play is there and the fun begins as in Picasso, as in Balanchine, as in Pina Bausch. A lot of the writing in this country proceeds as if these major artists never happened.

FMacC: *You have recently returned from seeing Pina Bausch's work in Germany, would you consider her to be a seminal influence on you? How would you describe her work and why do you still go and see Pina Bausch's work?*

TMacI: I'd certainly consider Pina Bausch to be a huge influence, the kind of theatre or dance theatre she's into is marvellously adventurous, it's sensual, it's erotic, it has a dangerous contemporary edge. It's theatre that's no longer "daddy-theatre." It's theatre with wild surges of the female energy and that's what's needed and that's what makes it a marvel. When I say female energy, implicit in that is access to the unconscious and I'd always make a point of seeing the Pina Bausch work in Wuppertal or wherever on a regular basis.

FMacC: *If we return to the early 1970s when you began to write for theatre, can you perhaps describe that initial discovery, was it a discovery? Was it a deliberate attempt to open up that unconsciousness through theatre?*

TMacI: I was brought up in East Cavan, a Presbyterian stronghold, clamorous, evangelical, always somebody in the tub announcing a new gospel and protesting, protesting current circumstances. My colleagues in the writing business said to me "Mac Intyre, you're a Protestant" and I agree, I must take the adversarial stance. I had to take that starting out. I was surrounded by tame, boring, verbal theatre. A play is three or four people standing on a stage talking platitudes to each other. It took me a long time, being badly brought up, to decide to do something about that but when I did, I had done a certain amount of homework. I had read Meyerhold and Appia and Grotowski and the whole bunch. I came on a wonderful sentence in Meyerhold in the long ago, I was living, not unexpectedly, on a remote island off the west coast of Ireland and Meyerhold says "look if you want to learn how to write plays, write a play without words." Ah, I said this is wonderful and I did that and the Peacock Theatre produced it and in a sense then I was on my way.

FMacC: *Was this Jack Be Nimble?*

TMacI: Yes, it was Jack Be Nimble, about 1975. Then that opened a door. I began to get very interested in contemporary dance, and dance theatre, and modern cinema, and to try and get hold of the variety of languages available to the playwright, languages beyond the verbal – the language of gesture, the language of movement, the language of the image. At the long latter end, it is no harm to say I came to recognize that if theatre is action and of course it is action, the verbal score, if you get it right, if you give it the intensity of incantation, that is also action. So finally my position now would be to have a blend of incantatory language and the other marvellous languages of the body and various modes of the imagistic.

FMacC: *So in writing a play, you describe scenarios to allow for that non-verbal to permeate through in the rehearsal process. Would that be rough structure so that by the time you enter into the rehearsal process the script or the writing is permeable – it can be permeated by the director, the actor, the performer, and the designer?*

TMacI: The script is there to play with, that is axiomatic. Nothing is written in marble. So I'd have thought, "that is probably at odds with conventional verbal-score theatre, here's a play, now go and put it on the stage for me." But there you're back to the element of play, to have fun playing. I got a marvellous glimpse of the crucial importance of play in the theatre, and indeed in literature, one night in the 1970s. I was in the middle of the USA. It was winter, it was always winter in the 1970s in the middle of the USA, Vietnam was in full swing, and there was considerable unease. Word came up the turnpike; Grotowski is speaking in Room 207 of Kent State Campus tonight. We all piled into a car and set out. We arrived there to find Grotowski looking exactly as one anticipates a Polish prophet would look, dressed entirely in black, chain-smoking and speaking only French. This is a great start, this is a mighty start, so he has an interpreter alongside him. And I'll always remember the key sentence from that expedition that Grotowski gave us, and we come back here to what is already a motif in our conversation, he said: "We speak of going to a play, never lose sight of *a play*, never lose sight of the noun to play, to play, to play." That rose the hair on my head. It seems to me the challenge for the writer now and always is to somehow get into that space where the magic of play is readily accessible.

FMacC: *And yet what I find fascinating and most interesting in your work is that you locate it in an Irish idiom, you locate it in key historical figures, I'm thinking of Swift, Kavanagh, Kitty O'Shea; I'm thinking of the work that I'm reading at the moment about Grace O'Malley and Queen Elizabeth. For me, you root it in Irish legends, in a sense of the myths that occupy our unconscious here in this island.*

TMacI: Well that's my oxygen. And what an extraordinary oxygen to have available. Irish folklore, Irish mythology, Irish history, the contemporary scene. I would be inclined to add, there you are talking about the containers but what's inside the container? For me what I'd say consistently that I am seeking to have swirling, dancing inside the container is the desperate contemporary male need to make contact with the female magic, which I mentioned before and that's where it's at, it seems to me.

FMacC: *Okay we then — nice link — move into the discussion. Having travelled the States and met Grotowski, you began an important theatrical journey; and I mean that word important also in terms of Irish theatrical history, an important journey in the 1980s with your fellow collaborators, Patrick Mason the director and Tom Hickey the actor and indeed the Abbey Theatre Company. Can you describe the genesis of that and how that evolved into what I would consider an important landmark in Irish theatrical history?*

TMacI: Well by the early 1980s I'd gotten hold of a kind of basic idiom, the constituents being incantatory verbal score, dance, movement, a degree of mime, the images stick. Now the problem was to find players who could handle that idiom. No, I guess, first put it into a theatre space then find players. Now in the early 1970s and I guess through the late 1960s there was a delicious question exercising the minds of theatre folk in this country —"How could you put *The Great Hunger* on the stage" and it exercised me also. I knew only one thing: that it couldn't possibly be done except in electrifying poetic terms. I was wandering in Boston and in a major Boston museum, sometime around about 1980 or 1981, and there was a Pissarro exhibition and I was looking up at a Pissarro drawing of men and women making hay and suddenly the picture, my head, the gallery, exploded and I said, "I have it, I can sit down and script *The Great Hunger.*" That's obviously a blast from the unconscious — you can't explain that rationally. But great, I went home and wrote it and everybody said, "Well you needn't be giving it to the Abbey because the Abbey would have nothing to do with that." And then somebody else said: "Put it up to them, put it up to them." I gave it to the Abbey and Joe Dowling instantly said: "We must do this." But at the same time I was asking my friends: "Who in the hell can I find, where do we get a company, where do we get a player to carry Paddy Maguire?" and everybody said, "There's only one player in Ireland to do that and it's Hickey." And I said, "Who's that now?" (because I had been living a lot abroad and on remote islands) and they said: "That's Tom Hickey – you've got to meet him." I met Hickey and next thing we had Patrick Mason in on the gig and away we went for the next five years and that was, I can tell you, one hell of an education, to be working with artists of the calibre of Mason and Hickey. An extraordinary adventure.

FMacC: *Tell me about that adventure, I'm picking up on the word of education. I find that fascinating. I presume you're inputting into this project but also you're getting additional skills from it.*

TMacI: Well, as I've said before, I was very badly brought up and I was brought up at a remove from theatres and in fiercely constricted society. Now I was suddenly being given an opportunity over a five/six year period from 1983-89 say, in a series of shows travelling here there and everywhere, to work consistently in the theatre and learn the ropes. Now the mode of work that declared itself to us was as follows: it was, let's say, spontaneously agreed, that the writer could also be quasi-director and quasi-actor, the director could be quasi-writer and quasi-actor and the actor could be quasi-writer and quasi-director. And I think it's probably extraordinarily rare in the theatre for that conjunction to occur.

FMacC: *There are words that are bandied around rather loosely in today's theatre making: one is "collaboration" and the other one is "devising." How would you respond to those two words in describing what was occurring in the 1980s?*

TMacI: Devising should be banned from the vocabulary, I think. Well, you would expect a writer to say that perhaps. I guess the mode was: I had leave to pick the themes and provide the basic script and then – let's play. Here we have a way into *The Great Hunger*, let's play with it. We have a way into Swift; let's play with it. Play with it, play with it. That's the real fun. I'd go crazy in a theatre experience that didn't have that dimension where every day in rehearsal the exploration and quality of the play is an exhilarating dominant element.

FMacC: *Do you think the work that you produced with Tom Hickey and Patrick Mason had an influence or has continued to have an influence in theatre making in Ireland?*

TMacI: Not the slightest influence ever, not the slightest, so the question of us continuing to have an influence doesn't arise. Not a bit of it, I don't believe it for a moment. No. I think it occurred, I think by definition that kind of conjunction has a short life. I think it's magical that it occurs. Well magic doesn't stay around for long, it arrives, it goes and if you're saying your prayers to the right powers, you'll be able to bring it back for another adventure. But that it lasted five years, six years, and then was no more makes not just sense but even exhilarating sense to me.

FMacC: *As an episode in your work as a writer, it appears to me that you're kind of content at the fact that it had a limited life, that it did perhaps cause ripples at the time. Are you disappointed, are you agitated that it hasn't caused more ripples?*

TMacI: I'm only disappointed if I get out of bed on the wrong side in the morning. No, no, I'm not into disappointment, that's a bad drug to play with. It was thrilling, it was over, and it was an extraordinary education, basic education in the kind of theatre that interests me. And then you lie down at the end of it, in a kind of exhaustion actually, and that's a real test because now you've got to gather your resources and find the next move, not just the next move but also a move that ups the ante.

FMacC: *I think that every single work and every single script that you write is a development. I see you pushing the boundaries, I see you challenging yourself and indeed not being cosy about your own work; but how important is a linear narrative to you in your work as a writer?*

TMacI: Look, with regard to linear narrative, there is no linear narrative to the story of the woman I love, my relationship with her, a central part of my life, there's no linear narrative to my relationship with the powers. Au contraire, you're into a zone where the action is the antithesis of the linear, it's probably spiral, you know. Spiral up, spiral down, and spiral back up.

FMacC: *Like life?*

TMacI: Precisely, so I'd be inclined to say linear narrative comes under suspicion invariably for me.

FMacC: *After the important work that you achieved in the Abbey Theatre with Tom Hickey and Patrick Mason, how would you describe your next stage? There was a gap in terms of your writing in theatre, then came* Kitty

O'Shea, *then came* Foggy Hair, Green Eyes, *then* Sheep's Milk on the Boil, The Chirpaun *and other works were commissioned that weren't produced* ......

TMacI: After that wonderful romp with Mason and Hickey, I was staggering around with little sense of who I was or where I was for two or three years anyway. It's worth perhaps saying – maybe it's necessary to say – that if you're an apostle of the unconscious, you're playing with a dangerous fire all the time and you're liable to suffer severe burns and that means you're invalided; and there was a period, that period I'm speaking of say 1988/89, for two or three years, I'd have said I was staggering around directionless. Okay, learn from that, find your bearings and seek to discover a new mode. Well for a start, I'd call *Kitty O'Shea*, early 1990s, that piece, maybe 1992/93, finding my way back into the room. Fun aspects to it but for Tom Mac Intyre incomprehensibly conservative, I'd have said. A suspicion the next piece might have been *Sheep's Milk on the Boil* where I had great fun because now I was, I felt, developing the mode. Suddenly here was a verbal score of wild crazy colours; the zone was quite simply the world of the unconscious.

FMacC: *Was it your own unconscious or ...*

TMacI: Tom Mac Intyre's unconscious, don't have any doubt about that.

FMacC: *So it was biographical?*

TMacI: Sure thing, it was the only story that Mac Intyre is interested in telling. How do you come to an understanding, a fecund understanding with the female inside you and the female beside you? This seems to me to be the crucial contemporary question for the male writer, as I keep saying. *Sheep's Milk on the Boil*, I had wonderful crazy fun with that show. It does have to be said not a show for the urban audience, for the lazy urban audience. It should really have toured the wilds of Ireland where I believe the population would have been wide open to it since as you are aware it's a free for all folk play.

FMacC: *During that period as well in the early 1990s you published a collection of short stories* The Word for Yes.

TMacI: Right, *The Word for Yes* is dominated by that theme I've referred to again and again. What's to say about that? I guess since I started out writing short stories, when I started writing in Ireland several hundred years ago, the mode was the short story. It was O'Connor, O'Flaherty, Ó Faoláin, Mary Lavin, Joyce, George Moore, and there was a strange obsessive focus on the short story.

So I kind of fell in love with the short story and if you're a storyteller anyway it's an irresistible form. And it was fun to get together some old stories and write a batch of new stories, exploring my obsessive theme. I guess a writer is always looking for not merely the next story but the right container for the next story and maybe it was a quiet theatre space for a little and I was free to concentrate on fiction.

FMacC: *So we move from the* Sheep's Milk on the Boil *to* The Chirpaun. *Again* The Chirpaun *was a container, which had several layers in it as far as I can see that somehow also predicted certain tensions in Irish society about the outsider, about the ageing male, about certain myths as well.*

TMacI: Well *The Chirpaun* was a fun exploration and I'm not sure we made it work. At the centre of it, as usual with this writer, is the male desperation for contact with the female, in that instance the wounded female. But the wounded female in a large sense is inside the afflicted male and that's always the story that I'll be telling. Now Tom Hickey approached me not too long after the run of *The Chirpaun* and said: "Wouldn't it be fun to script that for one actor and concentrate on John Joe?" And I eventually got around to that and it's been one of the great adventures, working closely with Hickey over a protracted period. Something about the material invited deeper and deeper and deeper exploration on a number of levels. For one, that theme of a demented male howling for the salvation touch of the healing female. Well, alongside that I want to talk about language here for a moment. I'd have said that after *Sheep's Milk on the Boil*, which was a verbal extravaganza in what you might call a jump ahead from Synge. One critic described *Sheep's Milk on the Boil* as Synge on speed. Naturally I was delighted with that but another side, the lazy side, of me would have said there isn't any more to be done with the rural Irish idiom after the fun you had with *Sheep's Milk on the Boil* and to a lesser degree with *The Chirpaun*. But in John Joe, with Hickey's encouragement, even Hickey holding a whip, I discovered to my joy that that is an inexhaustible well.

FMacC: *It seems to have coincided with your residing back in the county of your birth, the well of both your family folklore and the county folklore and for me it also sparked great playing with memory in terms of important events such as Gaelic football but also the rural male, ageing male, and his conflicts with the female . . .*

TMacI: Well being back in Cavan, many would say – and I would say – that the road back to Cavan was scripted for Tom Mac Intyre. I had to go back to Cavan. I love rural Ireland and I love my own part of rural Ireland. I love the storytelling in it and the folklore and the mythology. Now, to concentrate on the language for a moment: for a writer to have that still vivid language around him or her every day of the week is thrilling. It was still a delicious shock for me to discover that inexhaustible quality in Irish rural idiom and here we come again to my focus on the unconscious as the crucial element, as the well, as the font. You cannot possibly get the language effects to be found in *The Gallant John Joe*, unless you're working from the unconscious. That is to say, for the five-hundredth time perhaps, you don't write it, it writes you.

FMacC: *But it writes you with a dependency on the writer – Mac Intyre – being permeable, being open to it, and also in terms of a context, a geographical context in terms of Cavan, but also in terms perhaps of your continued collaboration with Tom Hickey.*

TMacI: Oh for sure. All of those ingredients. My lazy side needs Hickey with a whip in the vicinity. It might be worth mentioning a colour of the collaboration. We were in the house where I live in East Cavan and we were in session about the script and Hickey would say: "Now I think between that moment and this we could do with a development of such and such" ... And I would say, "Ok, take it easy for a minute," and I would write, comme ça, a page and a half whatever it is, and as the script I like to think testifies, it came off a fair amount of the time. But that kind of writing, for the writer, for this writer, is the ultimate frisson, because I call it writing on the hoof. Again I emphasize that is total, humble, venturesome, a reliance on the well of the unconscious.

FMacC: *In terms of your future work or the forthcoming work moment, I think that you're in a parallel track with current writing in Irish theatre. How do you currently – or do you – locate your work within an Irish idiom, an Irish genre in terms of theatre or do you still consider yourself to be looking towards world movements, the Pina Bausch movements or whatever?*

TMacI: I'd be inclined to say both. With regard to Irish theatre, to refer again to something I said earlier, Irish theatre is "daddy-theatre." "Daddy-theatre" is "front of the head" writing; writing which makes minimal deference to the unconscious – male writing which is reluctant, on the evidence before me, to allow much if any of the sensual, the erotic, the sexual, on stage. That's the central challenge for me, dramatically speaking. I write to resolve that contemporary nightmare question for the male. In terms of technique and style, I find our contemporary theatre wearisomely conservative.

FMacC: *In terms of the genealogy of theatre writing in this country, do you consider any Irish writer, be it a playwright or no, to have had an influence on* *you, unconsciously or subconsciously, and do you consider there are any current writers that perhaps you would have a* báidh *with, or (how would you say it in English) ... have an empathy with?*

TMacI: In terms of influences in the Irish theatre, and this answer will surprise you: the early one-act fantasy plays of George Fitzmaurice – *The Dandy Dolls* for example, *The Magic Glasses*. These seem to me to be absolutely extraordinary, lunatic pieces, and roaring from the unconscious, and using the idiom that I'm using in *The Gallant John Joe*, loosely speaking a hundred years afterwards. Those plays raised the hair on my head when I read them first, and when I saw them performed, and they still do. I guess, to be honest, they excite me far more than Willie Yeats' plays, or even John Synge's plays, or O'Casey's plays. All right, the impact of contemporary cinema, Mizoguchi, Herzog, Fellini, that whole bunch, huge, of modern dance, Pina Bausch, that's where I'd be pulling energy from. In terms of contemporary writers in our theatre, there are three writers coming up, waiting to explode, and their work interests me a great deal, one is Marina Carr, the other is Tara Lovett, and the third is Michael Harding. Now they're all, it seems to me, at a moment in their writing development where everything seems to me about to happen and I'm fascinated to watch and see what does happen.

FMacC: *Finally, Tom, have you fully explored your unconscious in terms of playwriting?*

TMacI: I've scarcely started, I should imagine, and also I'd be inclined to say in the matter of writing, I started yesterday morning.

Tom Mac Intyre was born in Cavan in 1931 and still lives there. He has written many plays for the Abbey Theatre, most notably *The Great Hunger*, which toured internationally. Other Abbey productions include *Sheep's Milk On The Boil, Good-Evening, Mr. Collins, The Chirpaun, Jack Be Nimble*, and *Find The Lady*. Recently, his *The Gallant John-Joe* – written specially for Tom Hickey – toured Irish theatres successfully. His selected stories – titled *The Word For Yes* – are available from Gallery Books. He has also published several volumes of poetry – including two in the Irish language. The most recent collection – *Stories of the Wandering Moon* – is available from Lilliput Press. Tom Mac Intyre is a member of Aosdána.

Fiach Mac Conghail is a producer of theatre, film and visual arts. He was Director of Project Arts Centre, Dublin from 1992–1999 and was appointed Ireland's Cultural Director at EXPO 2000 in Germany. He was Irish commissioner at the Venice Biennale (1997) and Sao Paolo Bienniale

(1998) and is currently Programme Manager of the Irish College in Paris, which is due to open in the Autumn of 2002.

Patrick Mason in Conversation with Colm Ó Briain

CÓB: *Patrick, over three decades of professional practice as a Director, has there been any significant shift in your understanding of the role of Director, has your approach to your work deepened significantly over that time?*

PM: I think I am only just beginning to really understand what it's about. It is so multifaceted, the whole business of directing. I often have problems with the word itself and I prefer the old word "producing" used in the English speaking theatre up until the Second World War, when the director was known as the producer. In fact, it's only since the rise of Hollywood and the American influence that the word "director" comes in. I think producing/production is a kind of richer word really and more descriptive of the process, because you are leading something out or bringing through a group of very disparate talents from writer to actor to designer to lighting designer. There are indeed moments when you direct, when you are that "man in the jodhpurs with the loudhailer and the whip", but there are more moments when you are not directing, when you are producing or enabling others to function fully.

There are two broad aspects of that process of production, one is organization and the other is inspiration. We are generally split between the two and I think some of us are more organizers and others more inspirational. In fact, you need to be very strong in both areas. I suppose one of the ways in which I would hope my work has deepened is that I always had a very strongly organizational mind and I was always someone able to keep to budgets and schedules, to see patterns and shapes very easily in ways in which the work might be managed. I think probably in the early years, I lacked something of the inspiration. As my own imagination has grown and been enriched and so my own understanding of theatre has grown and been enriched by practice, I hope that I have worked hardest on developing the inspirational side.

So, having said that, I feel, particularly in recent years, that I am far more confident in one way about my experience and my skills. Like every job, there is a lot of skill involved and, talking to young directors, I always tell them that there are basic skills involved and you must learn them; you must learn your stagecraft, you must learn about the dynamics of theatre, how theatre works, the nuts and bolts. However, you then have to have this space to fill with imagination and the key to imagining, to using your imagination is the old E.M Forster thing about "only connect." It is about making those connections and we all tend to panic about our ability or inability to make those connections, those vital fresh insightful connections, those leaps, that arc of imagination that suddenly connects two disparate points and creates this extraordinary intense light, a light that reveals, quite frankly, the essence of character, of action, of being in the theatre in performance. That is the mysterious part.

CÓB: *Has your work in trying to make these connections, manifested itself in any particular style that you can detect?*

PM: Yes, I think it has. I hesitate to call it a method, but I think a key influence in my work and key moments for me were the years in the eighties, between 1982 and 1989 when I was working consistently with Tom Mac Intyre and Tom Hickey on a range of productions. Mac Intyre is a great poet for the theatre, an extraordinary theatrical imagination, poetic imagination, non-realistic imagination. I think it was the intensity and energy of that contact that really jolted me out of a more literal, realist kind of reading of text into a far more emblematic, symbolic reading of text and action. Since then, the work I did was trying to find some kind of synthesis between these two aspects of the work.

In many ways, all a director's work is about reading the intensity (and the levels) of a text and then animating it. There is a strange tension between the more literal, musical even, technical reading of a text and the reading of its subtext, not just in terms of the basic psychology of character, but the deep structure of metaphor, of symbol, of emblem, of the theatre action. It tends to be either one or the other but how do you hold both? You either get the Eastern European utterly emblematic, metaphorical, approach where the text collapses and disappears in literal ways, or you get the very studied, literal, mostly

English-speaking, text-based "realist" approach. How do you achieve a synthesis of the two, so that you can hold the precision and detail of literalness in one sense and yet let it resonate, let it open out into a far more extensive network of metaphor and multiple meaning? It is balancing the sound and the word and the picture, the sound and the image, picture into image, image into imagination.

This is, I suppose, grasping for some kind of methodology of the thing. But how to do it, that is the question. I think that was what was behind a lot of my work in the nineties, what I was constantly trying to do. One of the things there, of course, is developing the whole physical and visual language of the stage. It's been a very challenging pursuit and one in which I feel I am only just beginning to find a language that convinces me, whatever about anyone else.

CÓB: *From your focus on the visual language, it seems to me that the design concept is central to your work on a production, that you engage on a very fundamental level with your designer. How does that process begin?*

PM: It used to be a bit hit and miss! I used to talk with a designer about the images that arose in and around the piece, in a very loose way without trying to impose any shape, until we had built up quite a store of images, pertinent or totally impertinent, but which seemed in some way to be connected. Then we would start on another process or run that process in parallel with a very pragmatic hard-headed finding of a ground plan, just that, a ground plan. These people have to move in the space; certain actions take place in proximity or with distance, inside or outside; how do we achieve this in terms of a ground plan, where are these people, where are we, where are they, how does this go? You go from one process to the other and gradually a shape begins to emerge and from that choreography a structure begins to emerge.

A lot of my work is done with the designer Joe Vanek He is very structural, very architectural as a designer, he likes solidity and he likes defining space. Indeed, so do I. A synthesis of these ideas then would involve structure and image and space. Another designer who I have been working with quite recently is Francis O'Connor. I suppose because of my own shift in emphasis I find that I am going for a less structured and less architectural sense of design and a far more open, fluid sense of space and light. The extraordinary developments in lighting technology that have occurred increasingly in the last ten years for me aremost exciting. It really is. I sometimes think I would love actually just to work with a lighting designer and do this whole thing in terms of space and light.

CÓB: *How would you compare your creativity as a director in the pre-production phase and in the rehearsal phase?*

PM: Well, both are crucial. When I was in drama school and coming into the theatre in the late 1960s and early 1970s, there was this great thing about "you let it all happen" spontaneously. There was no such thing as technique, you had months of rehearsal and you could forget the whole thing and re-do it. Unfortunately, the economics of theatre have gotten no better and in many ways they have got worse and there are very, very definite limitations, certainly in the English-speaking theatre, to the amount of production work and the amount of pre-production work. That puts a huge onus on pre-production work, because quite frankly there are things you have to try to solve creatively before you ever go into the rehearsal room because you will simply not have the opportunity to even think about them once you are in rehearsal. I think all directors regret this, but in thirty years, English-speaking theatre has not got any better. Even in German and French theatre, where they did have this enormous bonus of being able to work for months in pre-rehearsal and then from the fruits of pre-rehearsal to put together some ideas for rehearsal and then from rehearsal to performance take another transformative step. Even in the German and French theatres, the wherewithal to do that is being eroded. I think pre-production has to be enormously creative, between designer and lighting designer, because you are already limiting your choices. You must limit to be free.

CÓB: *When you encounter your actors, your principal deliverers of the play to the audience...*

PM: Key decisions have been made.

CÓB: *... the process is somewhat inflexible?*

PM: No. There are limitations in terms of the potential of space, of physical staging. You have set those boundaries but you try to keep them as open as possible. You have also made decisions about the "style" of presentation, the way in which you are going to ask an audience to see and hear and participate in this performance. Having said that, you should have based decisions on a very intensive and multi-layered reading of the text. The text is crucial, because it is that text that has also inspired your choice of cast and it is those multiple readings that have actually guided you in the casting of the play. So all the major physical limitations and possibilities of performance have been set and the one thread that goes from that process into the rehearsal process is the text. It is that text then, with those actors in that space that you then seek to animate. There is that extraordinary thing that in rehearsal you start with limitations and yet the spirit of rehearsal is that anything is possible. And that is the great fun of rehearsal. Then of course as the weeks go by and the performance date approaches, you have to start closing down again. Day to day, you test the findings of the previous day in the most practical and immediate way.

Let's go back to what I call the physical/spatial limitations. What are those limitations? They are hopefully limitations that in themselves paradoxically release a physical and imaginative potential. This is a crucial paradox in all creativity or inventiveness, it seems to me. We need closure to actually achieve some kind of opening. That is just how it is and to question it is like questioning the weather. That's how it is, that's how we work!

I notice that young directors, in particular, get terribly upset when you start talking about limitations because they believe in this romantic nonsense about total freedom. There is no such thing. You have got to be incredibly skilful about the definitions, to ensure that the limitations you use are creative limitations, so that by pressuring your imagination, they actually release something. There is this enormous thing in theatre that through a compression of meaning, of sense, of feeling, of experience into this crucible and on through that extraordinary technique of reduction to essence, out comes that experience of thoughts, a huge internal opening of the imagination. That to me is a crucial dynamic. So, that's the link between the pre-production and the rehearsal.

CÓB: *You said on a number of occasions that the play is disappearing. Is this particularly true of the Irish play?*

PM: There is a wilful neglect of some of the basic techniques of language in the theatre and form in the theatre. This is not to say that everyone has to write three-act plays, or two-act plays, or there must be a middle, end and interval. This is a crude parody of what I want to say. It is something that comes up over and over again. There is an experienced difference between a flabby, loose meaningless line and a taut, tensile packed line of language. This is why we have playwrights.

Most people can write lines of dialogue, actors are brilliant at improvising lines, but you know the more improvisation I see, the more improvisational things I see, the more I find them loose and flabby. They and the acting are generalized and in the end, indulgent. Form is there for a very specific reason, to produce this intensity of performance, the specificity of performance.

CÓB: *We continuously hear it bemoaned that the Irish play is too language focused.*

PM: This is not just a matter of language, but let it be said, "Why are we so against language?" I was enormously struck, in the wake of the World Trade Centre disaster. What is the one thing that kept on coming up? – our need for words, our need for language. We wanted President Bush to make the speech, we wanted the rhetoric, partly for the comfort of rhetoric but actually there was this deep need to find a word. It was extraordinary to watch the struggle of the very expert speechmakers to find that word, whether they managed or not is questionable. It is the need that struck me. Again, it has been very fashionable, promoted in the academy and in the media (and they both have their own agendas) to attack the word because frankly they wish to dominate the word and they wish it to be the word *they* say. Words are crucial to our experience, not just in terms of the language animal, but also in terms of a major doorway to our imagination. If we lack words of power, it is because what has been done to words in, say, the last hundred years or even the last fifty has been so horrific that I think we are rightly hurt and suspicious of words and their power. Having said that, we cannot remain in this defensive mode, denying language and the power of language. Substituting what? A kind of non-language, de-potentiated journalese, which is there because we will not face up to the fact that there are words of power and we are really frightened of their power. I'm sorry, but this has to be met head-on.

CÓB: *Your passion for language has obviously been a critical force in your engagement with Irish writers.*

PM: Absolutely. That is absolutely right. I suppose it also explains my presence in Irish theatre. Looking back, though these decisions are never clear-cut at the time, in many ways my coming to Ireland to work in Irish theatre was a happy accident. I didn't then have the intention of dedicating twenty-five years of my adult life to the Irish theatre. It was just a job, I had never been to Dublin and it seemed quite a nice job. Over the years, I realized that that was a passion that I had and that I shared and I think I still have that thing about the word of power and the power of the word. But, to write it and then to speak it, that is the thing.

I do not want to be misunderstood here. I am all for new forms, I am all for the visual and the physical in theatre, but I am also for the specificity and intensity of theatre. Look at physicality: you can mess around, you can swing upside down, you can fall off things and roll over things and God knows you cannot go to the theatre nowadays without someone doing one or all of those things, but you know there is a certain sensationalism about it, it's got a certain energy and energy is very seductive. Sometimes it is done very brilliantly but you know, like patriotism, energy is not enough. There is potential for more to come out of this bizarre art-form that we have and in the end I want words of power, movements of power, gestures of power, I want presence. I want not only to hear and to see, I want to feel that extraordinary thing of presence, that presence of the live performer. That does not necessitate being upside down on a trapeze in a tree. I have been in theatres when certain actors have simply stood on stage and said words of power and have incarnated them, have made them vibrate in that space and it is breathtaking. It is extraordinary when it happens and it happens unfortunately so rarely but when it happens, my God, it is extraordinary. These words happen in you. There is the external sensory pleasure but they explode inside you, that gateway into the imagination.

CÓB: *So therefore is it logical to conclude that your view is that the Irish play is in a very healthy dynamic state?*

PM: No. I think that the standard of writing, of word use, is very, very mixed indeed, just as it is everywhere. Where we do still have that lingering tradition of the word and we are still more obsessed with the word than other cultures, we have a very mixed bag of writing.

CÓB: *Do you feel that you have developed a particular empathy with one playwright out of the many that you have brought forward on to the stage for us?*

PM: I think that they brought me forward actually! I have always said this: that one of the great privileges of my work has been to work with some extraordinary, extraordinary talents like Brian Friel, Tom Kilroy and Frank McGuinness. These are challenging talents to work with. I am not in the business of hero-worship and they are just as capable of blotting a line as anyone else but, you know, it is this combination of sheer intelligence and a deep musical understanding of language, their ability to pinpoint a word, a sound, a phrase and then craft it into this extraordinary, precise, tensile unit. The way that that supports an actor in performance is, at its best, the greatest! Of course, it is connected into a great mainstream tradition of western theatre and they are acutely aware of it and they too are pushed to the limit in the knowledge of that. They have loomed very large.

Equally, I mention Mac Intyre who is no mean user of the word but his wonderful sense of the visual, physical possibilities of theatre, the poetry of the body, the performance actor's body. I will always remember one of my key moments which was in *The Great Hunger* – the moment when Tom Hickey was sitting on top of the five-bar gate and he just turned himself around and put his head down and his feet up, until he was hanging upside down, looking through the gate with his boots in the air and it was an extraordinary image of the poet – this strange creature suddenly swinging round on the gate and becoming the poet! Words could not have done that as succinctly and as intensely and even as I am talking about it I can still see him, hanging upside down, looking at us through the bars of that gate.

CÓB: *You have described your presence in Irish theatre as an accident, how has Hugh Hunt influenced your response to the accidents in your life?**

PM: I'm glad you mentioned Hugh because in his gentle, reticent way he was something of a mentor. In a way it's easy to romanticize these things: I don't know whether he knew what he was doing or whether he just did it out of the kindness of his heart, but he set me on a path and he identified something in me that connected to Irish theatre in particular. I suppose if you look at Hugh's own life (I often think of the parallels), his early involvement with Yeats at the Abbey, his career in the British theatre and then his move back to Ireland towards the end of his life. I remember him saying to me, "If you are not careful, you can find yourself caught between two countries and then you are a man of no country."

CÓB: *Do you feel that?*

PM: Actually, no I don't. I feel Irish. I put it off for many years because I didn't think it was perhaps appropriate but I did take Irish nationality. My life is here now and I feel deeply, whatever others may feel, that it is a territory of the soul, not so much just a homeland. The danger of that is, of course, that it may be a romantic view and blind you to the

political and social realities of what is going on around you. I think
there was a bit of that in me in the seventies and eighties but I don't
think there is much of that in me now! At the same time, I have the
deepest sense of belonging and that's all I can say about it.

CÓB: *Did your sense of the work and achievement of Hugh Hunt loom in your
mind when the opportunity to become Artistic Director of the Abbey Theatre
presented itself?*

PM: Yes, very much so. Hugh loved the Abbey because of the Yeatsian
vision of what theatre should be and he had been hurt and rejected by
it and then adopted by it, then hurt and rejected by it again. Yet, at a
crucial phase in the history of the Abbey in the sixties, he had been
instrumental in doing two things: reconnecting the Abbey, after the
disastrous years of Ernest Blythe, to Yeats its founder and to the values
that were articulated for the theatre by the founder; and attempting to
give it a modern structure, the structure that I inherited and I think
tried to push on. I think I feel a very strong line from Hugh and from
Hugh to Yeats. I know I am always being parodied about my obsession
with Yeats, but he was not only a genius but a key figure – he is the
conscience of that theatre. That is what gives what he says a peculiar
intensity and vitality in terms of that theatre. You must listen to that
conscience. If you take issue with it, fair enough, but know what you
are taking issue with, understand deeply what you are taking issue with
and whenever the theatre has not done that, it has ended up in a mess.

CÓB: *You have said that going into that job actually confronted you with some
political realities, which you have already said you did not want to avoid. Were you
comfortable in the political role of Artistic Director of the National Theatre?*

PM: In terms of the actual work of theatre, I was comfortable. In terms
of the public role, I was deeply uncomfortable, deeply ill at ease. I find
the necessary "doublespeak" of public life extremely difficult, but again,
you might as well complain about the weather because that's how it is.
You learn very fast that there are certain things that belong in the
private register and certain things that belong in the public register and
the two things do not equate. I think I found that the hardest. I also
found it extremely difficult – I suppose because I am who I am and
also because of my own passion and intensity for theatre and for the
work – to be patient with bureaucracy. Not the bureaucracy of the
Abbey but the bureaucracy of Arts Councils and Departments and all
that. I suppose I was a bit of a bull in the china-shop.

Though I understand the necessity of it, I have problems with the way in which theatre is subsidized. There is a necessity for public subsidy of the performance arts in particular, because they are so labour intensive and require such commitment. There has always been patronage, be it private or public, and the democratic state in Europe takes on that patronage, through subsidy, but the price of that subsidy increasingly in the society that we are living in, for good or ill, is to see the art form described more and more in terms of its political and sociological benefits. I am all for politics and sociology and an ethical consciousness of the artist towards the community that feeds and inspires that artist, the individual and the collective. There is a necessary ethical link and again the events of the thirties cannot reinforce this strongly enough. It is no good simply claiming total artistic freedom: there is an inherent responsibility, political and social, in every word and in every gesture. That is there. But, there are also the demands of the imagination – the needs of the soul. The art form has its own integrity.

CÓB: *Did your role as Artistic Director not give you a unique opportunity to express that responsibility and to engage in public dialogue on the public role of both the artist and the theatre?*

PM: It did and that was an aspect of the role that I tried to fulfil, not only in the spoken word in meetings and talks but also in the policy documents that I produced in the years I was there. As someone working in the theatre, I am deeply uneasy about that sort of public interface. I have to say that I share, like a lot of people who work with the public, a deep paranoia about the public, "The people" of whom of course we are part and yet from whom we stand apart. "The people" are a troublesome entity, fickle and potentially very aggressive, very demanding and sometimes downright mendacious and hypocritical.

CÓB: *You have spoken about a stridency of consumerism in audiences. What did you mean by that?*

PM: From my understanding, when you come to the theatre, you come to participate fundamentally in an act of imagination. That is a traditional and well-founded description of the compact, the deal made between the audience and the performer. For their investment of time and attention and through the performers' investment of talent and inventiveness, they will together create an act of imagination. They will share in this act. Sometimes it works, sometimes it doesn't. If you reduce that to a fundamental consumerist bargain of "I get what I want because I pay", you are in big trouble, because that essential participation is not there. There is a tyranny of the consumer, you can see that most clearly and spectacularly in the Hollywood film industry. The danger of that is it becomes a sort of demagoguery; it becomes in fact the collective consciously fighting the vision of the individual. Sometimes that is a necessary thing to do and there will always be that power struggle. George Bernard Shaw was big on that, saying that the whole thing is a power struggle, "My vision against yours. Who the hell are you to come here telling me this?" That has always been there. Nor does one want the indulgence of the individual, the megalomaniac ego kind of tendency that says: "My vision is the only vision." It is a very subtle compact that has to be made between collective and individual. That's what theatre is about, making that relationship. The whole horror of the crude Thatcherite movement, global monetarism and all that, has been to say that all human transactions can be described by the basic consumer compact of "I get what I want because I pay." I don't think we have even begun to understand the reduction of that, how deeply this has eroded all civil and personal values.

CÓB: *How destructive has it been of artistic values in the theatre?*

PM: I think it has been enormously destructive, even more so because the one area that should have been resisting this monstrous spread of the paradigm of the reductive global catalyst has been the Arts Council and the Government. Who can blame them? The one thing that politicians want, of course, is value for public money. It is a huge responsibility. But if you try to describe the responsibility of value for money, it becomes that incredibly crass and utterly revealing phrase, "Bums on seats."

Did anyone ever think you would rehearse a play for an empty theatre? Do people really think that that is what we do in theatre – that we seek to empty theatres by the work we do? That is sometimes the price of the work we do, because the intensity and specificity of our vision is not one shared by the great mass of people, but that has always been the case. If you take that one simple expression, "Bums on seats", so appealing to politicians and arts administrators, I want to say that I don't do plays for bums. I do them for hearts, heads and imaginations.

* **Hugh Hunt** was producer at the Abbey Theatre from 1934 to 1938. He founded the Bristol Old Vic and was director of London's Old Vic. A former

director of the Australian Theatre Trust, he was Professor of Drama at Manchester University where Patrick Mason was a student. He was Artistic Director of the Abbey from 1969 to 1971.

Patrick Mason is a freelance director of theatre and opera. He has had a long association with the Abbey Theatre which culminated in his tenure as Artistic Director from 1993 – 1999. He has worked extensively with writers such as Brian Friel, Hugh Leonard, Tom Murphy, Tom Kilroy and Tom MacIntyre. His production of Friel's *Dancing at Lughnasa* won him a Tony Award for Best Director. He is also closely associated with the work of Frank McGuinness and directed the premieres of *Observe the Sons of Ulster Marching Towards the Somme* and *Dolly West's Kitchen*. He has directed extensively in the U.K. and the U.S.

Colm Ó Briain served as Policy Advisor to the Minister for Arts, Culture and the Gaeltacht from 1993 to 1997. A former Director of the Arts Council/An Chomhairle Ealaíon he is currently a freelance theatre and television producer/director and most recently produced the RTE books programme "UnderCOVER", and Samuel Beckett's *Happy Days* at the Civic Theatre and on national tour.

Paul Mercier in Conversation with Jim Culleton

JC: *In the 1980s, the independent theatre companies that were an influence and really inspired people to set up their own companies were Passion Machine, Druid, Red Kettle, Rough Magic and companies like that. What was it that made you set up a company back then?*

PM: If you think about it, though, you started off with Pigsback in 1988 – we started in 1984, so there's only four years in the difference. I've always wondered was there some sort of movement waiting to happen at that time, do you know what I mean? In terms of Irish theatre, was there a sort of a general consciousness – or a general feeling – that enough was enough and it was time to start changing things. It grew out of this, I think. Some things can have a knock-on effect and the birth of one theatre company can stimulate something else or give people the confidence to go and do it themselves. The thinking at the time was "Look – no one else is going to do it for you, you'd better do it yourselves." What I find lately is that there is a bigger emphasis now on getting others to do it for you again. There has been a shift in emphasis.

JC: *But many people are coming out of training courses and setting up their own companies now and creating work for themselves, aren't they?*

PM: Some are, but I find myself saying to people – actors in particular that you see in auditions – I say: "Go and make the work" and I find sometimes that they look at you as if to say "No that's not what we do; we're trained to be actors" and I say "no, no, no, you have to think more laterally. At the end of the day, you're going to find that – no matter how good you are – you're going to have to start thinking about doing your own work." There was a big movement in the 1980s, definitely, because there was a huge birth in companies. I don't think there has been the same recently.

JC: *But it's harder in some ways for companies to start now because there are so many trying to do it. The development of the independent theatre sector really* *started with Druid and then other companies came along in the 80s and 90s. Even though it was a time when there was little or no money around to fund these companies, there were also fewer of them looking for support and recognition.*

PM: That's true. I don't know how the Passion Machine came about, in terms of what I was feeling at the time. It's one thing doing the work, doing the plays, getting something off the ground. Then to set up a company that is going to commit itself to a particular artistic policy or type of work – that obviously grew out of something: a sense of despair that the work wasn't happening. I know, for one thing, I didn't set up the Passion Machine so that I could work in theatre. It wasn't that I wanted a job in theatre. It was never the case that I wanted to use it as a route into the mainstream. It was to do – in a hugely naïve way – with saying "the only way you're going to do this kind of work is to do it yourself." I know if some of the work we did in the past had gone through the system, it may never have seen the light. Or it would have gone through a process that would have changed it. Perhaps for the better, but it would have lost its initial quality. So you have to do it yourself – it's the same for every company that grew up.

JC: *Yes – and the artistic control you have over work you do is so important and exciting.*

PM: Oh, that's essential. It is absolutely important. It's the same with you in the original Pigsback and now Fishamble. All independent companies are interested in doing a certain type of work, they're all contributing to the canon of work that is being produced, they are all reflecting on the society in which we live and they are all trying to do things in such a way that makes artistic life and creative life in theatre and to say something about the world and to come to some point where you feel you've changed things for the better. We're not in it so that we can become involved in a commercial, West End kind of world. If you want to go that direction, you can go and do it.

JC: *You'd hardly set up your own company if that is really your goal.*

PM: No. And you wouldn't be working in this city if that was what you wanted. You wouldn't be committed to touring and new work. Yourselves and many other companies are committed to new writing and are bringing new talent into the theatre. It's been the only route really for the last 25 years, although that's changing now.

JC: *How do you feel the Passion Machine has changed during its life so far? All companies do alter and develop, don't they?*

PM: Yes – and I think it's par for the course.

JC: *You need to evolve and grow.*

PM: It's all part of growing up and a company has to grow up. It has to go through its own experiences, its own phases, its own watersheds, its own falling away and coming back together: reinterpreting itself and what it's all about. Reinventing itself – you know that with Fishamble growing out of Pigsback – it's all part of the process. And I think that's part of the creative process in itself. Because that will be reflected in the work.

JC: *And I suppose an energy comes from finding a way to grow through moments of change.*

PM: Yes. It's necessary for all companies to go through internal difficulties that do arise because people have made commitments to a company and have visions for it. There will always be artistic struggles and career struggles and various agendas but any artistic grouping will go through this. You are going into the unknown with a company. But you know, Jim, that the company's essential philosophy and policy is going to grow with whoever is running that company. Especially if the company is committed to new writing which, in itself, is such an important act. Particularly in theatre, because it's a collaborative exercise. It's vital that subsidy is there – that the value of the work is recognized – that's why the Arts Council funds companies. But coming back to what you asked about how the company has changed. You put in place a plan of action that you hope you can fulfil over time but you know that as you develop artistically, it's going to change. It's a living thing and it will change. And the fact that it exists in the first place and continues to exist is very, very important.

JC: *And your ambitions change with time too.*

PM: Yes, and there are times when you question everything that you do.

JC: *Well that's very necessary as well.*

PM: Of course.

JC: *How about the way the company is funded and can plan at the moment – is that something you are happy with?*

PM: Yes and no. I have to say, we are very grateful for the funding we get and wouldn't survive otherwise. We just wouldn't exist. Without Arts Council subsidy, the whole thing would collapse – unless you were doing commercial hits but there's no guarantee of that. The whole scene is very fickle in one respect – it can change very quickly – so without Arts Council support, you could not operate properly with confidence. On the other hand, we'd like to have greater subsidy than we're getting at the moment. It's very, very tight. We have to be very resourceful and we would be recognized as a mainstream, independent company that should be paying top rates. So there's no way we can go back to the old ways of saying "we'll pay you what we can."

JC: *I know what you mean. I remember thinking "when we are funded more reasonably, we'll be able to produce so much more work" because – like every company really – we all spent years working for nothing and you are driven to do that by your belief in what the company is about. But then when you receive more substantial funding, you are also ambitious to respect people's creativity by paying them properly and are acutely aware of your responsibilities. So you end up doing the same amount – or less – of work in order to run the company in a business – like way.*

PM: Absolutely – it's like an entity enters your company that dictates that you cannot function unless you have a standard rate of pay and pay certain amounts towards publicity and rental. There's no way you can just say "come on, let's get this together."

JC: *And that's a good thing in many ways. Do you think though that the spontaneity and freedom that was there at the beginning of a company's life is in danger of disappearing as companies become more formally structured and institutionalized, really? How do you think you still ensure that new, exciting work can develop in the company?*

PM: You have to restructure. You find yourself reorganizing the timetabling of artistic activity. I always get very nervous when I realize we're doing this from 9 to 5 now. Things have to be structured to accommodate how people need to work. And that can be difficult. But, of course, I would never tolerate exploitation of anyone working for the company, and you wouldn't, and I don't think any company working in the sector does. I think we're generally very fair to the people we work with. You have to create fair working conditions and have respect for people so that everyone can benefit from it. I think the independent sector has been good at that with limited resources and limited funding for the last 25 years. You have to try and give everyone a fair chance and to be creative and help sustain livelihoods. Restrictions and limitations to do with working conditions are in people's best interests but they can have a detrimental effect on companies that are getting on their feet. That's a very delicate period that all companies go through. And the whole nature of theatre dictates that the first performance is hugely important, so there's enormous pressure on everyone. And people will sacrifice anything to ensure the show is done well. There's no negotiation in the latter stages of that process. And the show goes on and it's a collaborative effort. And if it works, it works. But it's the process that's important. The fact that it went on. It was worked through, discussed, interrogated. There's a lot of emotional investment and intellectual investment and investment of time and energy that go into a production. And it can be hard for a young company to handle and come through that. But you have to deal with that and it is part of the learning process. And loyalty is a big thing with me, you know. Particularly after the process we've been through. I think it's important.

JC: *In terms of the work of the Passion Machine — one of the most exciting and exhilarating aspects of the company's work has been the productions of your own plays. The word "dramaturgy" is being used a lot at the moment — I wonder how do you deal with the development of your own plays. Obviously there is huge artistic freedom and control when you're directing them yourself for your own company, but is there a worry that you might lose a sense of objectivity with your work? Or how does the process differ when someone else directs your work?*

PM: Well, I'm a really hands-on man, you know! It took me a long time to get my head around separating the process of directing from writing. *Down the Line* at the Peacock was my first experience of only writing the play. Lynne Parker directed and I came away wanting to do it that way again. But, in the work that I do for the Passion Machine, its one and the same thing for me. That's the way I work. It's not that I want to be a director or to have my hands on every aspect of the production. In the past, it sometimes was a case of "well, if no one else is going to do it, I may as well…." You have to do whatever is necessary. It was the same for you, Jim. Are you telling me you haven't been up a ladder with a paintbrush in your hand, or proofing the programme until all hours in the morning or writing funding applications while you're in rehearsals? Of course you have.

JC: *Sure.*

PM: I'm not just a writer who sits in there chewing fags and lets it out of his control. Fair enough, that's one way to do it. But it is not my way. I like to be involved.

JC: *Maybe that's because we came through student drama societies in TCD and UCD where you made the sandwiches for the audience before acting or stage-managing a production. And you enjoy the total hands-on involvement so much that you wonder if it might be possible to make a living from continuing to engage with it all.*

PM: And in a way that was a crucible or workshop where you learnt so much because you were so devoted to it. In fact, I was more involved with Cumann Drámaíochta, which really stimulated me. That had the extra dimension of being an Irish language society with all the baggage connected with that. There was a strong belief that we were doing something important and worthwhile – in our own small way – for the Irish language and trying to get it to work in a theatrical manner. So that fired me a lot at the time.

JC: *You worked recently with TG4 – is working in the Irish language something you intend doing more in the future?*

PM: Well, I got to the stage that I had to ask myself "what the hell am I doing?" I don't even come from the Gaeltacht – it's not my native tongue! So I was questioning my motives and my original interest in it. Whether it had to do with some romanticism or belief in some idealistic system or whether it was about a leaning towards the minority view or a threatened way of life – a threatened culture. Or maybe I saw the Irish language as a way of saying something about the establishment at the time. But I never lost my love for the language and have since tried to – in some way – articulate my feelings on the language. But at the time I was involved with a lot of people who were committed to – I hate to use the word "cause" because it's a dangerous word – but committed to the language and its survival and development. It wasn't just theatre, it was more than that. So in that sense, Jim, you never questioned the effort or the time you put into it. What you found was that others questioned the effort or the time you put into it.

JC: *That's interesting what you say about an association with minorities and people under threat. Is that a theme that drives a lot of your writing? It seems that a lot of your plays deal with intimate relationships, people on the edge of society, the effects of time passing, living in Dublin… What do you feel are the issues that fire you to write plays?*

PM: It's all that kind of thing. It's a sense of trying to give voice to the weaker sections of society. And, at the same time, reminding myself "you live in Dublin, this is the city that you live in, this is where you're from – why even attempt to write about other experiences." You write about what you know and where you live, essentially. All that is there and then a moment can trigger an idea or feeling. A feeling can become something greater and, before you know it, you have a play on your hands. And what happens then is that all the other feelings start finding their way into that play as well. You start off with one simple idea – and you may not know why you're writing it to be honest – and then it takes on a whole life of its own. And it gets to a stage where, as it goes into production, there are other concerns. I mean, I never knew the word "dramaturgy" until the 90s.

JC: *Have you ever used someone in that capacity yourself?*

PM: No, not really, but I wouldn't mind having someone like that. But that doesn't mean I haven't called on others to do something similar for me. People that wouldn't like to be described as a dramaturg – don't call them that, whatever you do! A cold, critical, analytical eye that understands the nature of storytelling in theatre and the theatrical process can be useful. Someone who can see problems coming, or suggest why things are not working – to help fix things that are wrong with the narrative, to trigger debate or provoke other ways of doing something. It's hard to keep your peripheral vision working when you're directing. Perhaps talking about things working or not working is wrong – it's about looking at something and realizing it hasn't reached its full potential. That there's a process where you can look at a play and say "there's more to it than that – something you maybe never thought of – there's another direction that it can go in."

JC: *And sometimes in an early draft of a play, you can realize that what a play is really about might be buried under a lot of other things.*

PM: And you might start off saying "but that's the reason why I wrote it, I can't cut that out" but sometimes you have to cut out lines that were your first lines because a greater force is at work. If you're engaging with an audience and you're telling a story, there are guidelines to follow – and you can make up your own rules as well. You write a play that adheres to conventional rules or a play that breaks those rules but sets up its own system.

JC: *And it has to be consistent within that.*

PM: Yes – and that's crazy territory because there's a new relationship with your audience. You need the audience to will the play to happen and to invest in it.

JC: *In terms of your own plays, the approach often seems to be an exuberant and boisterous one – in plays like* Studs *or* Home *or more recently* Buddleia *– within which to explore relationships. Other plays are more intimate, perhaps, like* Pilgrims *or a play like* Kitchensink *which is small in terms of cast size but epic and theatrical in theme and style. How do you think they've progressed in terms of finding a way to present work or – as you were saying – creating a new set of rules?*

PM: Well you get fixed on an idea and, as you work it through, you realize you are creating your own rules. And people go with it or not. So you find you come up against restrictions. Sometimes you'd love to just do something which breaks all the rules, just say "fuck it" and do it. Every play I do, in terms of narrative and characterization, it's like I'm starting from scratch. I really feel that.

JC: *And do you have a favourite play of your own?*

PM: Not really, no.

JC: *Is it a matter of loyalty, again?*

PM: Well each play belongs to its time and its circumstances. It belongs to a moment. And one play sometimes brings about another. For example, when I did *Buddleia*, I had no idea I was going to be doing *Kitchensink* but in the process of *Buddleia*, *Kitchensink* came about. And in the process of *Kitchensink*, *Native City* came about.

JC: *So you didn't set out to write a trilogy?*

PM: No, I just realized I was writing about Dublin – about a bigger picture. It was a bigger canvas and I wanted to say all these things. There were loads of things I wanted to say in the first one that I got to say in the third one. There were loads of feelings I couldn't do in one that I got to do in another. And it all became about life in the city. One view of the city that was given expression as an act of theatre. Things change from starting to write a play to the final production.

JC: *So – in terms of how a play develops and is analysed – what do you think is the value of theatre criticism? What do you think of theatre criticism in Ireland?*

PM: Iffy, to say the least. I suppose critics have been good to the work, even when they haven't written favourable reviews. There has been a sense of "this one is unfavourable because we expected other things of you. We expected you to do better – even if you think what you did was your best."

JC: *So do you feel generally that, even if critics don't like some of your work, they are bringing an open mind to it – or do you think they have their own agendas?*

PM: Oh the only critics I like are those who want to engage with it. They might not like it, but they still see the worth in what you do. But there have been critics – oh mark my words – who just mean ill or have no understanding of what's going on. There are critics who think if they don't like it, that the rest of the world shouldn't like it. That's terribly wrong – you know yourself.

JC: *Yes, or it can be frustrating when a critic assumes he or she knows better what way everything should have been done.*

PM: Well they're either frustrated writers or they have very sad lives. I mean, no theatre company sets out to do a bad production. And especially in the area of new work, I think the level of criticism out there – generally – has been atrocious. With the development of new work, it's almost as if you feel they want to nip it in the bud and not give it time. I think this has made the scene very cautious. And that's the biggest change – coming back to what you were saying earlier – from the 80s. In the 80s, I didn't give two shites about the reviewers. It didn't matter. We got some great support from critics, but it wasn't the reason we did the work. And flawed and naïve and rough as it all was, it wasn't going to happen any other way. And I have to say the critics at that stage were good to us and allowed us to grow. And that still exists now but there are certain critics out there now who are not taking in the bigger picture. The tone of a review is often "how dare you put this on – who the hell do you think you are – this is an effrontery!" and people who write those types of reviews don't seem to realize the damage they can be doing. At the end of the day, the act of putting it on is such an important act. It's a cultural act. It's a social act. It's a spiritual act, as far as I'm concerned, because of what has gone into it. No one went out of their way to do a bad show – everyone went out of their way to do their fucking best. With limited resources and in ridiculous circumstances. And then some prick walks in and sits down and dismisses it and walks away. Those people are not being challenged enough. I don't mind critics saying to me "that's a load of shite" – fair enough. But I do have a problem with other types of reviews where there is something else at work. And everyone becomes cautious then when doing new work because you don't want to be slated. The reality is that less and less people are taking chances. There has been a huge growth in readings because of that. It's too risky to put on a production.

JC: *Yes – readings can be helpful in the development process of new work but it can become a vicious circle as well with work never getting produced fully.*

PM: It is dangerous that way. They're great for getting feedback to a play but there have been lots of readings where the script goes no further – particularly by companies that have no intention of doing new work. It's a safe option and no one gets hit critically. Some critics say "well it's our duty to the public" and I say "well I think you've missed the point there."

JC: *Critics have a responsibility surely to new work too.*

PM: Yes – well that's how I feel about it anyway.

JC: *Do you have any playwrights you admire particularly?*

PM: I love them all! I have respect and admiration for anybody who puts a play together. Particularly anybody dealing with the Irish experience. I have a big hang-up about the huge imbalance between indigenous writing and theatre being done at home and work that comes from abroad and has nothing to do with our experience. It comes back to criticism again, Jim. An American or British playwright can be done here and it might get hit critically or it might be lauded critically. But at the end of the day it will have no impact whatsoever on the play or the writer. It'll just be the Irish critics having their say on the matter. But the Irish critics having their say on indigenous work is a different thing altogether. The damage that can get done is huge and it can retard the new writing process. You know yourself, Fishamble is committed to new writing – you've been doing new work and developing new writers solidly for years. No one is saying you should make allowances for the work. No one is saying "this is a new Irish play and we want you to reduce your standards."

JC: *No, of course not.*

PM: But just recognize what it is that's being done. Most of it is better than what gets done around the rest of the world anyway. And a lot of work – if it got a chance to get outside this jurisdiction – would probably make a bigger impact than it does at home. I do feel that. And I feel that the scene is still looking elsewhere for its validation – it's still looking to London, New York, Australia for its validation. And I think Irish theatre needs a kick up the arse for that. It's unbelievable. I hate that – it worries me.

JC: *Do you not think that it's enriching to bring work elsewhere and to engage with other audiences though?*

PM: Oh don't get me wrong. I think so. I want every Irish writer to do well and for that work to thrive. And if that means success abroad – that's great. It might wake people up a bit here. But it shouldn't change things fundamentally. There is a perception abroad about Irish theatre and it is a certain type of Irish theatre. It's not contemporary theatre. It's that we live in the twilight zone here. We do things differently. There is a danger that we'll start to play to that kind of constituency to the detriment of developing our own voice – our own unique way of seeing the world – through work of our own making, rather than being dictated to by what tastes are outside the country. And there's a danger as well that – for a small scene – Irish theatre has its class system. In terms of what is considered literary or not; what is considered high theatre or not. It's not a good way. Attitudes like "if you're not on the main stage – if you're in a small space – it can't be worthy."

JC: *Do you really think that exists?*

PM: Oh yes. In the bigger constituency it does. And that's a problem. It doesn't matter where the play goes on. That's why Arts Council funding and a strong supportive structure to support all artistic activity is vital.

JC: *So what sort of criteria should there be to assess and make decisions about supporting work?*

PM: Well I'm not sure what they are at the moment. How can you define what should be supported? It's a difficult one. I wouldn't like that job – to judge who gets what. But there are many attitudes and agendas which can differ a lot and impact on funding.

JC: *So what's next for you, Paul? I heard a rumour you're devising something!*

PM: A dangerous word "devising." I used it with someone the other day and he ran away! It's all about making it up. I'm doing a treatment – that's another dangerous word – of the Diarmuid and Gráinne story. Reinterpret, reinvent, rework, transpose, translate, explore – there are so many words. But I just want to tell the story. I did a treatment of it in the Cumann Drámaíochta as a rock musical, so it'll be different from that! It might spark something else, I don't know. Years ago I'd have been able to tell you exactly. I'm just going to tell the story, really, that's it.

Paul Mercier, born in Dublin in 1958, is the Artistic Director of Passion Machine Theatre Company, for whom he has written and directed ten plays to date: *Drowning, Wasters, Studs, Spacers, Home, Pilgrims, Buddleia, Kitchensink, Native City* and *We Ourselves*. His most recent work for the company is his own adaptation of *Diarmuid And Gráinne*. He also wrote *Down The Line*, commissioned by the Abbey Theatre, directed by Lynne Parker and staged at the Peacock. He has written and directed three short films for Brother Films; *Before I Sleep, Lipservice* and *Tubberware*.

Jim Culleton is the Artistic Director of Fishamble Theatre Company for which he has directed new plays by Mark O'Rowe, Pat Kinevane, Joe O'Connor, Dermot Bolger, Maeve Binchy and Ian Kilroy. He has also directed for Pigsback, 7:84 (Scotland), Project Arts Centre, Ambarclann de hÍde, Tinderbox, Passion Machine, the Ark, Second Age, TNL Canada, Scotland's Ensemble @ Dundee Rep and Draíocht. He co-edited *Contemporary Irish Monologues* for New Island Books.

Eleanor Methven and Carol Moore (Scanlan) in Conversation with Helen Lojek

[In 1983 Eleanor Methven, Carol Moore (Scanlan), and three other women actors (Marie Jones, Brenda Winter, and Maureen Macauley) from Northern Ireland founded Belfast's Charabanc Theatre Company, which operated to public and critical acclaim until 1995. In the later years, Methven and Moore served as the company's Artistic Directors. Today Methven is a stage and film actor based in Dublin. Moore is a stage, film, and television director based in Belfast. In separate interviews in December 2000 they reflected on Charabanc Theatre Company's history and its lasting impact. They responded to questions from Helen Lojek.]

HL: *You've often told the story of how five out-of-work Belfast women actors founded a theatre company and began to develop their own scripts. Now that you have a perspective of almost eighteen years, how would you summarize the company's origins and script development methods?*

CM: Impulse. Unemployment. Little or no Irish material, and particularly no Northern Irish work for female actors of our age. When we approached playwright Martin Lynch it was to do some of his sketches. He suggested we all write something weekly. Anything. We decided we might do three plays looking at Belfast over 100 years. From some initial newspaper research came the mill girls' strike of 1911, which was the focus of our first play, *Lay Up Your Ends*. But the newspaper research wasn't enough. We also wanted actual anecdotal stories of life in the mills – so the method of research became mostly oral interviewing.

The plays were creative interpretations of real life situations, characters, and times. We hoped we reflected an authenticity of the times, but art isn't documentary – there was creative license. As a result, we spoke as much about ourselves as anyone else. Oral interview is about memory, so I suppose the plays might very well have been different without those memory experiences. I think the Charabanc methodology still holds in my current work, since the material I've chosen to deal with in my films [*Gort na gCnámh* (*Field of Bones*) and *Room*] is material that emotionally engages me.

EM: We were angry. We were very, very angry. I'd been an actress for five years before Charabanc, and I'd pretty much worked consistently. But the Lyric Theatre would not employ Irish women actors. Instead, they brought over English actresses to do four lines. It was an absolute confidence thing: "I'm so bad I can't even do this." It was a reaction. We said "How dare you?" But what also drove us was a desire to examine the place we were in. It's not just being an actor. It's the kind of person you are. We were political beings, and it was very important to us to write political work, to examine where we came from. But a lot of it was reactive anger. We were extremely, extremely angry. When I was eighteen and joined the profession I remember thinking, "At least I'll never be sexually discriminated against, because no man can ever take my job." What I didn't realize for about a year was that there just weren't any jobs for women

Martin Lynch got us going. Sunday nights we'd spend together, and he'd go, "Okay, write a wee scene about something." He was enormously encouraging. His support was absolutely fundamental. He was brilliant. And then it became very obvious that Marie Jones had a real talent for writing dialogue, and it just went from there. There were two enormously influential men. Martin and Ian McElhinney. Ian put money into the company without knowing he would get it back. He was just great. We were angry about male advantage, but we had a lot of good support from men as well. The night we opened our first play the audience queued from the door of Belfast Arts Theatre down Botanic Avenue and around the corner to Laverty's Pub. We were still inside hammering the set together, so we had no idea until we walked out for the first song and saw them hanging from the rafters. Ian was there, his voice going up six registers, saying "You've made me a lot of money," because until then he'd no idea he'd get his money back at all, much less on the first night. It was a phenomenal success in part because Martin was writing a weekly *Irish News* column, so the whole time we were developing the script he wrote his column about being out with these girls talking to mill women. We just picked exactly the right subject at exactly the right time.

HL: *The company was founded by five women. Was it a feminist company?*

EM: When we were first interviewed in the early eighties, particularly in rural Ireland, all the males would go, "Well, are you

feminists then?" And the only thing I could ever say back was "You
define it and I'll hum it. You tell me what it is." All they ever came
out with was "Well, you don't like men." I'd think, "Well, yes, I
do." The questions were a bit accusatory, but mainly roguish, you
know – "Oh, I know a bit about this "Women's Lib', and you're
obviously all like that." The other thing they'd say was, "My God,
there are five of you in the dressing room, you must fight like cats."
Actually, we got on perfectly well together, but there was this
automatic thing of if it's feminist you must laugh at it because that's
the best way to do, just to put them down. Extremely and literally
patronizing. Coincidentally the company was fairly solidly
heterosexual, yet there was also the implication that we must be
lesbians and all lesbians hate men. Feminism was defined in very
narrow terms. In the early years we spent a lot of time back-
peddling – going "No, no, no, we're just a theatre company, and we
want to be known as a theatre company. It just happens that we're
mainly women and focus on women's work." At the end of the day
we did not get referred to continuously as the women's theatre
company. It was just Charabanc Theatre Company, one of our
leading theatre companies. That was a huge victory.

HL: *Is there such a thing as "Northern Irish Drama?" If so how would you
define the term?*

CM: I do believe there is such a thing as Northern Irish drama.
While Irish identity has been a theme running in all Irish drama,
Northern Irish writers, including Charabanc, possibly offer two
particular styles. The first is the deliberate political intent of the
drama discourse; the second is those plays that, in Michael
Etherton's words, "describe Irish politics, but … are not plays
which commit their audiences to any political meaning for them."
Both suggest a rugged, robust and unsentimental view of the world
(possibly because that view has traditionally been more urban than
rural) and depicting the sensibilities of ordinary people in Northern
Ireland with whatever political or religious views and in particular
political times and scenarios. Charabanc mostly fits into the second
category, but early collaborations with Martin Lynch and Pam
Brighton leaned more to agit-prop. *Now You're Talkin'*, directed by
Pam Brighton, for example, suffered in my view from being overly
polemic and because the Protestant characters' mindset was of little
interest to the director. What it does highlight, though, is the
collective spirit of Charabanc's work at a time when all company
members participated in the writing process. But it also exposes a
working methodology which was open to being politically high-
jacked.

Everyone involved with the company came from Northern Ireland, and all of us grew up accepting and/or rejecting some or all of the views of that community. All those experiences were fed into our work, as were rural/urban and middle-class/working class dimensions. The Troubles kept Northern Ireland very much a mono-culture, apart from the growing Chinese and Indian communities. But scratch a sectarian, and I believe you'll probably find a racist. An influx of East European immigrants to Dublin over the last few years has seen an upsurge in racist name-calling and attacks. As more ethnic minorities settle in Northern Ireland, traditional sectarian attacks familiar to Northern Ireland could very well shift towards ethnic attacks.

EM: Northern Irish theatre is theatre that addresses the issues that are particular to the Six Counties – political issues. We did it with a female gaze and a female voice, and nobody else did that as a project. The three people mainly associated with Charabanc – Marie Jones, Carol Moore and I – were all Protestants. I think that's interesting, because continuously we were dealing with all sections of the community. Mainly we were dealing with working class, but all sections of the religious community. We would get an initial idea of the kind of subject matter we wanted to look at. Then we'd go and interview people. We'd do it in their houses and their living rooms and it wasn't just what people said, it was the things they chose to put on their walls, the ornaments they had on their mantle-pieces, the way they related to their husbands and their children – all of that informs a character. Charabanc's writing definitely came from an actor base; we looked continuously from a character outwards to inform the subject, as opposed to looking at an issue and developing around it. The characters were important – the way people spoke and felt and expressed themselves. I think we managed to have politics at the heart, but to portray politics not from a paramilitary or military base, which I think a lot of male writing comes from. Our characters could have been IRA wives or IRA mothers or UDA wives or UDA mothers, etc., but first and foremost it was a very human and domestic point of view, radiating outward to the universal from a domestic place. That's what politics was about for us.

CM: Initially we just wanted to work, and we tackled subjects that personally and politically interested us. In retrospect, we certainly were politicizing ourselves through the research and playwriting process. We didn't use interviews as biographies, though. The plays gave voice to the voiceless, so the research material and tapes are historical documents in some sense. We never directly translated people's stories into plays. The interviews added insight and richness to characters, content, themes. They were a background resource for performance, though occasionally some aspects of an interviewee's personality or story would be filtered into a script. The universality of the characters made the work very accessible to foreign audiences despite the specific Northern Irish political context.

EM: We were not writing propaganda. We were in an exercise to try and understand our own cultures, where we came from – and to try and understand ourselves. That was one of the prime motivations behind Charabanc. Right from the start, when there were four Protestant women and one Catholic, and then increasingly as the company came to depend on three Protestant women, there was a Protestant domination. Yet right from the start Charabanc wasn't insular but reached out to non-Protestant segments of the community. I can't actually say where that impulse came from. I suppose it's because we were all in theatre before we were in Charabanc, and when you work in theatre it's a non-sectarian profession. Theatre's a place where you don't have to belong to a tribe. Or rather, you belong to a tribe in theatre anyway, so you can actually cut loose from your childhood tribe.

HL: Somewhere Over the Balcony, *set in the largely Catholic and nationalist Divis Flats, is the clearest example of Charabanc's ability to cross stereotypical community boundaries. Where did that play come from?*

CM: The play came from a surreal dream Eleanor had about the Troubles. We asked ourselves where was the maddest place to live. Of course it had to be Divis Flats, Belfast. We did a lot of interviews with a group of women from Divis and decided the themes in the play should be tackled through a black comedy. We were in a very privileged position, gaining access to people's homes and discussing sensitive personal and political issues with them. The play, set in the nationalist/Republican Divis flats, is a good example of a community that we personally knew little about before the research. We always promised that the interview tapes would be confidential, and that was an essential component to gaining the confidence of people. For me the play signalled the scale of emotional, psychological, physical and economic damage suffered by individuals during the Troubles. I think we grew up politically from that experience.

EM: I suppose the three of us in particular were interested in trying to understand. If you live in this place you think, "Well, we can't go on. We've got to try to understand what motivates other people with different upbringings." It was a continuous questioning. That's what Charabanc was, a questioning all the time. It let us into hugely privileged positions such as working in Divis for the summer. For three Protestant women it was quite extraordinary. Lots of journalists were there at the time – Americans, Germans, and others – but there wasn't anybody from Northern Ireland. I think we were some of the first people who had come with a recognizable accent. We weren't other. We weren't journalists. We weren't going to be printing it in a newspaper. We made it very clear we were going to be writing the play, but we kept on taking it back to them, saying "We're thinking about writing this bit." It was important a) that we were very much of an age with these women, and b) that we spoke with a recognizable accent. The thing that was different about us – and we made no bones about it – was that we were Protestant, all three of us. That's probably one of the most interesting dialogues I've had in my life or ever will have. A huge privilege.

HL: *How would you describe the balance of urban and rural in Charabanc's work?*

EM: There has always been a heavy bias in Northern Irish drama toward Belfast imagery. It's always little back streets, helicopters overhead and so on. We were a Belfast-based company, so there was an urban focus in our plays as well.

CM: Most of the company came from Belfast, and Marie Jones' ear as the writer was very urban, so we tended to focus on urban stories.

EM: But we found, even in researching our first play, *Lay Up Your Ends*, that the language of the older Belfast mill women we were interviewing (nearly all of them since dead), while richly Belfast, was a very old fashioned Belfast. If you looked at their idiom and their means of expressing themselves verbally, it was very influenced by the rural places they'd come from. There are very few people in Belfast more than two generations removed from the soil, from that real, rural Scots-Irish dialect. I was the only rural one in the company, but there was always a rural character. Even in *Lay Up Your Ends* I played a girl who came into town from the country.

The first play we did that actually concentrated on rural Ireland was *The Girls in the Big Picture*, and that was quite deliberate. Our first three plays – *Lay Up Your Ends, Old Delf and False Teeth, Now You're Talking* – took us from 1911 to contemporary Northern Ireland in 1985. After that *Gold in the Streets* was an amalgamation of three one-acts that covered the same period. Then we thought, "Oh, we can't think of anything else to say about the situation at the moment, so let's just take a break from it and look up the position of women who were thirty-something in rural Ulster." We deliberately set the play in 1960. My point was that if we set it in rural Ulster after that we'd have to put a lot of men in the UDR. Having grown up in rural County Derry during the seventies, I know that we had the same war as Belfast, though the battles were very different. People in rural, isolated areas are very interdependent, helping each other with calfing, lending tractors, and so on. Suddenly all that broke down into suspicion. You had big dark country roads, and the UDR was hugely active, and the sons of local Protestant farmers would join the UDR and could stop the sons of local Catholic farmers coming home from the dance and intimidate them because they had a uniform on and a gun. That creates a very, very different atmosphere. You knew these people, but they hid behind masks and guns on both sides, and that was very odd.

Setting *The Girls in the Big Picture* before this particular conflict allowed us to examine the possession and dispossession of land, which is the root of everything that's happened in the last 40 years. All those things come in from rural culture, and they are much more barely seen in rural culture. We all came from these places that were part of the Plantation where Catholics were put into the bad land and Protestants into the good, and you cannot just start with Belfast in 1964 or Derry in 1969. You've got to start way back. We were setting the play only ten years before it all blew up.

CM: I don't think there was a rural/urban balance at all. *The Girls in the Big Picture* was a quirk of fate. While on tour Marie Jones and Eleanor and I would create characters to amuse ourselves. We would become those characters at any time – out shopping for example. When it came time to come up with a new play idea I suggested that we should look at a rural theme based on these characters. Our research (as usual) was by oral interview. My family comes from the Glens of Antrim, so my relatives were a good starting point. My aunt Jean described the "basket tea," where unattached women would bake goodies for baskets that would then be auctioned to the highest bidders (male, of course). It became a pivotal scene in Act 2. Set in rural Ulster in 1959 the play examined the sexual politics of a community on the cusp of a new decade, as well as exploring subtle rural sectarianism built around the ownership of land.

EM: Audiences and reviewers often responded differently to *The Girls in the Big Picture* than they had to our earlier work – not just because it was rural, but because it did not deal specifically and immediately with the politics of contemporary Northern Ireland (with Protestants and Catholics) even though there were Protestant and Catholic characters who were clearly delineated. Of the three main female protagonists, two were Protestant and one (their friend) was a Catholic, and it was quite obvious that she lived on a poor farm. She didn't have as much money as everyone else. I think we were sexy in the first few years. People wanted to know about the Troubles, that sort of thing. Then we came along with this other play that said, "But this is where it comes from. This is the culture and understanding of what we're dealing with now. Be it Belfast or Derry we all came from this rural root." The women from the Drill Hall in London, a place that we played a lot, came to Enniskillen to see the opening of *The Girls in the Big Picture* and they just didn't get it at all. They were expecting the fast Belfast crack and all the rest of it. They were also cutting edge British feminists, and they thought surely these women characters should dominate in the end, should win. Our thing was that the women didn't win and we were trying to tell the truth.

HL: *Were such responses to* Girls in the Big Picture *an isolated phenomenon, or are there difficulties in general with theatre criticism in Northern Ireland?*

CM: Some people didn't want the work to change. They wanted the same style with different stories – stick to what you are good at. A fair enough criticism, but as an individual artist I certainly wanted to try other things – extant work, for example, which we went on to do later. Theoretical critical analysis at that time was and still is generally very poor. Plays were "reviewed" and at no time was serious attention paid to the development of a company's work. Theatre critics in Northern Ireland will only be pushed into some sort of training when newspaper editors take seriously the role of arts and culture in our society. You only have to open a Northern Irish newspaper to see that sports coverage dominates any other cultural event. You have to search for "reviews," and when you find them, critiques they are not. Well, not unless you simply want to know the story. Government departments on both sides of the border should also be working towards an all Ireland "arts training" facility. Why can't theatre criticism, like arts management, be part of the curriculum? I avoid the term "drama school" because I feel it doesn't encompass the staggering range of arts disciplines in Ireland.

HL: *Only one Charabanc script,* The Hampster Wheel, *has been published. Why do you think it has been difficult to get them into print?*

EM: People saw the plays as written by committee, which is very unfair. Marie Jones sat there and slaved over those plays. But they were written in a very strange way. Everybody was involved in the early days, certainly, but then Carol and Marie and I later. There are bits of those plays that we penned. All the characters come from collective work, all the plot lines come from collective work, and I think people just couldn't get a handle on that. While we were doing them people thought they were very specific to Charabanc, very Northern. It's only now, with hindsight, that people are saying, "Oh, we should do these plays again." I think Charabanc's work will come into its own in the next couple of years.

HL: *Charabanc played in a lot of non-traditional venues – community centres, parish halls, and the like. How did those venues relate to the company's sense of purpose and style?*

EM: One of the main political thrusts behind the company was to take theatre into venues where it wasn't normally done. We were lucky in a way because there had been a huge growth in community and leisure centres in the seventies, as a response by the British government to the Troubles. It was very important to us to play in those venues. That was a prime motivation.

CM: Martin Lynch's agit-prop style of writing, Pam Brighton's direction, and financial necessity motivated us towards a "rough theatre" presentation style and made community venues an obvious choice, but the plays worked equally well in purpose-built theatres. Music-hall and agit-prop influenced the treatment of our work and made it easier for the cast to play multiple roles which became something of a "house style." The audiences we attracted depended on the venue, but content and style seemed challenging and/or entertaining across the board. We called ourselves a "community" theatre company because our research was from the community and we were reflecting it back as theatre. Today "community art" is vibrant all over Ireland, but its focus is access to the arts for and by the community.

EM: Once the Anglo-Irish Agreement was signed, Belfast City Council just decided not to talk to each other, and all funding went and we couldn't actually tour. At the time Martin Lynch was saying "I don't care, let's go and do it for nothing." But one of the other badges of Charabanc was to say "No, no, no. This work must be respected as professional and we must get paid for it." That was difficult because nobody would give us any money to tour community centres. Fortunately we had been going for about four years by that stage, and if we played, for instance, in the Belfast Arts Theatre people would come in from the outlying areas to see us. That's even more interesting, because then audiences were mixed, as they were not in the community and leisure centres. In the Arts Theatre there were Catholics and Protestants who didn't know each other sitting side by side watching political argument and debate on stage. We tried to keep our prices down, and as a result nobody in the company got paid very much, though we always had union rate. But we didn't reach as many people. We just didn't. You could go back into community centres now and people wouldn't come out either. There's been a huge shift. People now would be used to going out for the night. When we were first operating Belfast city centre was still underused, and people were wary about coming in at night. Those things have changed. You now have huge social clubs built, with absolutely great theatre facilities. Things have changed enormously.

CM: In challenging ourselves creatively, a move away from agit-prop possibly meant we were perceived by some as appealing less to community venues and more to theatrical touring. Martin Lynch was very critical of this apparent and conscious switch, but the fact was that funding in the community sector was drying up and the company on its own could not subsidize community touring. I was disappointed that Martin, who had been so inspirational and encouraging to a group of out of work actresses, later criticized us for pursuing our creative goals, albeit in different directions to himself. I also regret that I didn't start directing in Charabanc much earlier. As our work began to diversify I think people's changed perceptions of the company might have been cushioned had we directed within the company more.

EM: Going into it at a young age – I was 23 and totally committed – means that you will sacrifice yourself completely to this other thing. I suppose now I'm at the age everybody gets to when I have to have time for me. And increasingly it got to the point where dealing with the arts bureaucrats became a job in itself – trying to remind them that they wouldn't actually have a job if there weren't any arts to manage. Sometimes we ran a tighter ship than they did, and that made it very difficult to have them lecturing us about what we should do when they didn't actually understand what it means to be self-employed and not have any pension plan. Official people – they were a nuisance.

HL: *What do you think the future holds for theatre in Ireland?*

EM: I love Marina Carr's work, and I think Tom Murphy is wonderful and has not got the respect he deserves. There aren't so many writers in Northern Ireland. But it is now possible in Irish theatre to be taken seriously as a career actor. When I was doing it actors just weren't taken seriously, but now it's a perfectly valid job.

CM: Playwrights north and south will continue to look forward by reflecting on their past. In Northern Ireland hindsight, dramatic and otherwise, helps us reflect on a savage and troubled past. Plays like Stewart Parker's *Pentecost* articulated the need for healing during the dark days of the seventies. Younger writers like Nicola McCartney, Owen McCafferty, Darragh Carville, Damian Gorman and Gary Mitchell will continue to do the same. What excites me the most at the moment, though, are companies who choose not to be necessarily text-led in style. Barabbas is a breath of fresh air. But the situation for actresses in the theatre hasn't really changed. Yes, more of them are writing for themselves or creating companies, but until more female Irish playwrights start writing leading roles for women we will continue to have the situation Charabanc found itself in. Perhaps it's time for Charabanc 2. What form that might take is for a new generation of young female actresses to answer.

EM: Another theatre company full of young men should go and do something about another culture that's dying – it's called work. Light industry. It's what built Northern Ireland, and it's just gone. The manufacturing base is just completely gone. That male intensive labour is gone. It's not tangible any more. Work. Nobody actually sees what they do. It's been particularly affecting for the Protestant working class, the whole of the Shankill Road and East Belfast. They were plumbers, carpenters, riveters. Those were trades, respectable trades. That's completely gone. Maybe a young men's company should investigate that the way we investigated women's work?

HL: *What has been the lasting effect of Charabanc on Irish theatre and on you as individuals?*

CM: Charabanc's contributions may be more easily defined by others than by those who were in it. However there is no doubt that the emergence of other independent theatre companies became a reality because we demonstrated that it was possible to create your own work, company and power base with nothing but creative ideas and energy. I don't think any other theatre company at that time, outside of the Abbey, had the international touring experience that we had. There is no doubt Charabanc put Northern Irish theatre and the agenda of Northern Ireland into the hearts and minds of international audiences. Charabanc was a major contribution to Northern Irish theatre – that was the community we served, although the work had an impact all over Ireland and further afield. Charabanc reflected the lives of people back to them, gave them a voice, and illustrated that their stories were culturally valuable. It also reflected and/or challenged their political worlds and entertained them in troubled times. Working with Charabanc politicized me and gave me a sound theatrical/business training base. It gave me confidence in my own capabilities and offered me many opportunities to travel and extend my life experiences. Directing now gives me the freedom that Charabanc gave me as a collaborator and performer. Ideas, characters, images were what I offered Charabanc. I still collaborate with writers in the theatre and work on dramatic ideas for film and television.

EM: When you're in the middle of it you don't really see it. Since Charabanc stopped people have started paying tribute, and that's obviously immensely pleasing. In some ways people want you to be a revisionist, to say you knew you were starting this theatre movement. We didn't. We started it for the reasons that have been recorded many times – we wanted work. But now that I look at it I think, Yeah, it was really important. Young academics coming over from America or Australia or wherever, particularly if they're female and interested in Irish theatre, will have an interest in Irish women's theatre, and Charabanc is like a gift, particularly since it's well-archived at the Linen Hall Library. It has that place. It has a place in Irish theatre as a women's theatre company and as a Northern Irish theatre company. During the Linen Hall celebration of Charabanc [in September 2000] it was lovely to hear people pay tribute to the work. Peter Sheridan also said his two young daughters found role models in Charabanc. I was blown away by that – that was such a nice personal tribute. Lynne Parker does that as well. She's always very conscious of paying tribute. You don't always realize what you've meant to people until they tell you. Directing a theatre company gave me enormous confidence. Carol and Marie and I realized early on that if we did not go in there and fight for what we wanted we would not get it. We learned to do that and it gave us confidence. I get some respect now, and I like that.

Eleanor Methven was a founding member of Charabanc Theatre Company and later served as Artistic Director, a position she held until the company closed in 1995. Now a Dublin-based stage and film actor, she recently appeared in *Pentecost* (Rough Magic), *Barbaric Comedies* (Abbey), and *Weddin's, Weeins, and Wakes* (Lyric). Her film credits include *The Snapper*, *The Boxer*, and *Disco Pigs*.

Carol Moore (Scanlan) was a founding member of Charabanc Theatre Company and later served as Artistic Director, a position she held until the company closed in 1995. Based in Belfast, she has produced two original short films, *Field of Bones* and *Room,* and works as a stage, television, and video director. Recent stage appearances include *Pentecost* (Rough Magic) and *Weddin's, Weeins, and Wakes* (Lyric).

Helen Lojek is Professor of English at Boise State University (Idaho). She has published work on Brian Friel, Frank McGuinness, and Charabanc Theatre Company, in *Modern Drama, Contemporary Literature, Irish University Review,* and *Politics and Performance in Contemporary Northern Ireland* (1999). She spent 2000-2001 on sabbatical leave and as a Fulbright Scholar, completing research for a book-length study of Frank McGuinness.

*Belfast's Linen Hall Library (www.linenhall.com), which has an extensive Charabanc Theatre Company archive, may be contacted at outreach@linenhall.com.

Tom Murphy in Conversation with Anne Fogarty

AF: *I'll begin with what is an obvious question and one that I know you have been asked thousands of times. Why were you attracted to writing plays in particular because to me it seems to be the most difficult form of writing? What led you in that direction?*

TM: I thought that play-writing was the most accessible to me. I agree with you that it is the most difficult but I didn't know that at the time. The idea of prose frightened me. The nature of the education that I had, the peak of writing prose had to do with Hazlitt and Francis Bacon and I knew that I could never even dream of writing in that form. A kind of writing indeed, now that I can be more objective about it, where there is absolutely no personality behind the writer. But also it was, I suppose, syntactically etc. perfect, whereas the form for writing a play is dialogue, and grammar or syntax have very little to do with it as far as I am concerned and as far as my aspiration for what I want to do is concerned. I had become involved with the local amateur group and it's an oft-told story now that a friend of mine said, "Why don't we write a play?" – and we wrote a play.

AF: *Do you think it's possible to define or pin-point what makes theatre different from any other kind of art form, for example, cinema or opera? Or does it just remain elusive?*

TM: It's elusive to me and I hadn't thought of that question. As you imply opera is live also. But again with the limited, or what I felt were the limited opportunities for me to express myself the idea of opera or indeed being a classical singer was a world away and similarly film seemed too remote. I find that my instinct is for the stage even though there may be other reasons pushing me into that form of art. Also, I suppose like many other playwrights I'm very interested in sound *per se*, the individual sounds that people make, the sound that powers the words they use. The sound that demands certain rhythms of people – that excites me and I try to make a kind of music of my own out of the spoken word.

AF: *I was struck by one of the comments that you made about what you want to do in writing a play. You said that what you were attempting to do was to create or re-create the feeling of life. Isn't this quite a paradoxical summing up of what theatre does?*

TM: Well, for a long, long time, certainly in my own case, I felt that there has been an incredible amount of snobbery about emotion or emotionalism. A lot of that has come from academics. In fairness, it's very, very difficult to write about emotion, let alone try to recreate emotion. And, I think that life is about feeling, it's not about thought processes. Religion is feeling. In William James's *Varieties of Religious Experience,* at one stage he said that the menu is not the dinner – he was referring to the liturgy of the church. Religion is feeling and, although I hadn't articulated it in any way for myself, that confirmed to me to some degree what I was trying to do. I used to say: "Recreate the feeling of life", now I'm saying: "Create the feeling of life", because the feelings and emotions that we express are quite inhibited in life or at least they are repressed. They don't get out, we suppress them ourselves. I feel that the stage is a place – as far as living artists like actors can be true to themselves – to achieve some sort of pure form of emotion. I'm sure that it is impossible, but on stage you get closer to the human condition in terms of what the human feels and what he or she is longing for, without even being able to intellectualize it.

AF: *It seems to me that you bring your characters to a point which reaches beyond language. You talked about trying to create a particular sound or acoustic but very often you lead your characters to a place where they express themselves through silence or just, as you were saying, through emotion or through music or something that is nearly beyond words. That kind of deep level that you are reaching for isn't even within language sometimes, even though you get at it through words like in the singing of the aria in* The Gigli Concert.

TM: I've said to a number of actors who have played the Irishman in *The Gigli Concert* that perhaps the biggest aria in the play is the one where he breaks down and he is on hands and knees. There is no way that I could write the score for what sounds should emanate. But, I think there is a stage direction that starts with a scream and then goes into a roar and then into sobs, and the sobs become drier, and then into laughter and tears. I agree, I don't know that the words are there at times. Obviously, it's a playwright's business to combine words in certain ways that don't necessarily have a literal meaning. But again the emotion generated by the structuring of words can go some way towards producing the goal that I'm after.

AF: *There is much self-conscious talk now about Irish theatre and about the new generation of Irish playwrights. Do you think there is such a thing as an Irish play and/or a tradition that gets in the way of, or helps, writing?*

TM: I really don't know. That question has been around for a long time. Thirty years ago I wouldn't know what to say and I still don't. The influences on me aren't solely Irish ones or a background in a small town in the West of Ireland. I'm influenced by everything, by wherever I've been geographically, the people from different races that I've met, plays I've seen, other forms of art that I might be interested in. I suppose a lot of my plays are set here as I don't see any reason really for setting them in a foreign location, let alone in outer space.

AF: *Do you think perhaps that the notion of the Irish tradition and the Irish play is something foisted on writers by critics?*

TM: I think so, yes. In the generation after me, an extraordinary crop of writers has emerged and it seems to me that when the celebration happens it seems to be because they are Irish rather than a more weighed, objective look at the content of what is being written.

AF: *Still connected to that topic, do you think there is a point to having a national theatre in Ireland? There is even a debate about where the Abbey should physically be located for its centenary in 2004. Is that part of the problem that the Yeatsian ideal of a national theatre is always hovering there and no one seems to know quite what to do with it? The Abbey always seems to fall short of something or other.*

TM: I'm probably the worst one to ask, because my life has become inseparable from the National Theatre. Again, it's fairly well documented that I had my rejections first, but I was very surprised recently when an interviewer was talking about the rejections I had had and said: "Now you've joined the establishment." Maybe it's the ageing process that one becomes the establishment without knowing it. But I've never considered the people I've worked with in there for the last thirty years as establishment people. I don't consider actors, directors, designers to be establishment people. Yeats as a playwright doesn't mean anything to me. Perhaps in the tradition that you're talking about there might be something of Synge. Synge would be someone I admire greatly. I admire him, not because of his Irishness, but because of the outrageous premises that he uses whether it's *The Well of the Saints* or whether it's *The Playboy*. I very much like that big, brave, bold, extravagant notion – rather than say the current affairs ideas of something that would approach the Pinter-type of play – and the broad strokes that Synge used. Of course, he was I'm sure very influenced by his time in Europe and in Paris. Like *The Lame Man and the Blind Man,* for instance, a medieval French morality tale, that I'm sure led to *The Well of the Saints.* The way he turned a type of so-called accepted status quo on its head – a guy arrives and he's killed his father and he's celebrated as a hero. I love that kind of stuff, which I wouldn't call subversive or if it is subversion, it's a badly needed subversion of accepted standards of artistic goals.

AF: *In a way, hasn't Irish theatre had a very short history? Synge was inventing things from scratch, inventing a tradition.*

TM: I suppose. We go back to Farquhar and Goldsmith and people like that but they were almost another race of people. I don't like calling them Anglo-Irish but it was a kind of Anglo-culture that they came out of. We had the mummers, I suppose, and the strawboys, types of superstition ... Halloween. At home in my parents' house I can remember the grotesque business of having a cake and candles, one for each child. And whichever candle went out first was going to be the first one to die. I was fascinated by this kind of natural, primitive kind of ritual.

AF: *How different do you think the theatre traditions in Britain and Ireland are? We seem to be symbiotically connected and yet diverge all the time.*

TM: I must acknowledge a gratitude to London theatre because I served my time there but then it wasn't all English theatre. There were the world seasons that Peter Daubeny used to do. I saw the Greek National Theatre, *Hedda Gabler* directed by Ingmar Bergman. I must say I now find English theatre boring. Maybe I'm back to Syngean stuff, but I like big strokes in theatre and not the sit-com nature of so much British theatre and indeed of our own theatre. I arrived in London in 1962 to stay permanently there and you still had an excitement from *Look Back in Anger* days. You had great writers like John Arden, who lives here now, and David Storey. There was a lot more experimentation I think. I'm not one for censorship but sometimes I think that the boredom element in things should be censored in some way.

AF: *Do you think that commercial forces are taking over theatre in London and in Ireland? Writers get packaged now very, very fast.*

TM: I don't go to that much theatre in England any more. I did my apprenticeship there which lasted for the best part of ten years. And since then there was the occasional visit doing what a lot of other people do, getting in seven shows in five days and perhaps I sickened myself with the theatre I was seeing. There's this other business about writers being political. I think that there is obviously a place for the playwright as political commentator, just purely that, like Brecht. But it's very facile I find when these days people throw words like Thatcherism into something and they are taken very seriously when I think that they are saying fuck all.

AF: *It happens in Ireland too, doesn't it? – writers are always found to be saying something about the current state of the country and to be acting as barometers.*

TM: I don't know that it is as self-conscious here. I've denied on a few occasions that I'm in any shape or form political but, of course, I'm political. But if a writer says anything about a political aspect in a play that he or she has written, that is the easiest one for a commentator, critic or academic to focus on. The play is reduced to that. Whereas for me the play is some sort of fabric or tapestry in a way. There are motifs running through it and one dominant one perhaps. In the way that one's life is such a fascinating, complex business, for me personally, I like to bring a lot of threads together and I'm reluctant – since we are talking about a type of politics – to mention the political.

AF: *I'd like to ask you a little bit about what must be the entirely peculiar process of writing a play and seeing it staged and produced. Again, I think that this adds to the difficulty of writing plays as they seem to go through a double birth process. To what extent do you like to be involved in the beginnings of the staging of a play? And to what extent can you think ahead to that process or does that come much later?*

TM: I think I do but it isn't to the forefront of the mind, the staging of the play. I know whether the character is standing up or sitting down. I would know the proximity of the characters to each other. If I go down to the end of this room here now, I think that certainly the delivery of question and answer will alter and perhaps even the content. They are almost faceless people – I know whether they are male or female, obviously, tall or short. Generally, I work out things like that in the writing. In the business of the ritualistic, first reading, it's always a shock on the first day but I think maybe even a bigger shock for me because I am thinking in terms of sound, the words creating, heading towards pools of mood where words might even be distorted. But, at this stage, I know that it's going to be a shock and I know that I mustn't be a pest in the rehearsal room. The actors and the director have their processes too and there is a degree of compromise that has to happen. Occasionally, actors and director will exceed any expectation that I've had of a piece.

With my second or third play at the Abbey I was trying to make a point on the first or second day of rehearsal and the director whispered, "Too soon love", and then the weeks went by and we were into dress rehearsal and I was trying to make the same point and he said: "Too late love." In rough terms, the ritual first reading is done, then the second reading starts, usually the afternoon of the first day and it's a stop/start situation particularly for the writer. I try to explain what I'm getting at, point out things about punctuation, and it is stop/start for everybody else – it's a kind of open forum. The second reading could go on for possibly a week. But then I could leave the rehearsal room, come back after ten days and gradually then it would cease to be an open forum. But I would feed most of what I had to say to the director, because actors can get very confused if looking to the writer and then to the director. The director at that stage has formed a kind of rapport with the actors.

AF: *Do you think that your plays make certain demands of actors?*

TM: I do. Again, we're back to recreating or creating the feeling of life. I'm not trying to short-sell the intellectual side of things. There has to be a motivating power that is intellectually understood by me as I progress. Play writing to me is discovering the process of doing the play. But, as I discover that, then the structuring of the play has to be thought out very carefully – the time sequence of the play and indeed the ideas in the play. It can't be a willy-nilly, whimsical sort of thing that I've induced in myself. In the writing process I'm aware that I'm a playwright and that it's going to be a collaboration between me and the actors and the director. And, indeed, the first thing I say to actors and director on that first day is that the script is a theory and that they have to make that incarnate. But it is a very carefully worked out theory and, if we change anything in it, there has to be a very good reason for doing that. I am very willing to change, emend because, as I say, it is a theory that is worked out on paper and the practical demands of theatre can be beneficial, bonuses, that can improve on the original theory.

AF: *Do you think that the urge of your plays to recreate feeling is somehow connected with life as it is lived or has been lived in Ireland? You mentioned earlier the way in which emotion gets repressed as we live our everyday lives. Are there particular forces in Ireland that repress things so that Irish theatre has to leave even more out of the box as a result?*

TM: I don't know. Tuam people come up to see my plays – they would say, "But, of course you were writing about that person." Other people – and it's gossip really they're looking for – want to know autobiographical details. The autobiography in the plays is frequently a mood in myself, but I've found just trying to get the mood that I am experiencing is boring for me. I may start with that but, as the play progresses and the breakthrough happens, that time comes of watching the autobiographical mood transcend itself and move to art. This is also rather similar to walking down the street out there and recognizing on other people's faces a longing, a yearning, a dreaming, a depression, an elation. It moves out of the purely personal and the merely local.

AF: *Music is very important in your plays. Do you think again that it is linked with creating the feeling of life and moving beyond the personal?*

TM: I don't know whether I cut the line or whether it's still in *The Gigli Concert* but one of the characters says, "When I listen to music, I don't know whether it's keeping me sane or driving me crazy." A mood, one of elation, one of depression, music can feed that either way – in a manic way or in a depressive way – as if the thing is a disease. But also when I listen to music I'm very jealous of the musical notation. I'm jealous of music because so much can be achieved in a phrase of music as against the limitation that is inherent in the linear aspect of a sentence, words.

AF: *Getting back to the politics of theatre, there is a lot of talk nowadays about having or creating an audience. Do you think that for you as a playwright it is important to have an audience in mind or is that something much further down along the road that you can't really think about when you're writing?*

TM: That's down the road. I know, not necessarily in the forefront of my mind, that I'm a playwright. Obviously one knows that the thing is being written to be performed but I don't think that I'm thinking of a particular audience. But I would like to see the build-up of a substantial audience through the idea of doing seasons of plays rather than the conveyor belt, month after month. There's a punctuation mark from the beginning of a season to the end of a season. I think that the standard and quality of the work, indeed the standard and the quality of the work that fails, are important; but that if a theatre deals in the slight I think that there will never be a significant, permanent audience or the change from generation to generation won't happen because the quality isn't there for them. I would think of audiences in those terms.

If theatre becomes sensational or slight, the audience is going to be as fickle as the ideas. I do see theatre as a religious kind of thing and I don't mean that's necessarily unentertaining. Archbishop Richard Whately of Dublin said – he's in *The Penguin Dictionary of Quotations* – that "happiness is no laughing matter." I can apply that to the theatre because the great moments I've had in theatre have not been the ones where I was laughing. I've had great times laughing out loud, which is a rare occurrence for me, and it's wonderful when it happens. But the true theatre for me is when the lights come down at the end of the show and I just want to sit there and let nobody talk to me. I don't want to get a bus home or a taxi; I just want to be on my own for a while because I feel cleansed in some way and as a playwright I would say I must do better the next time. It encourages a greater aspiration. Something holy has happened.

I'm not making claims for *Bailegangaire,* but in the set we had for our first preview (which we had to look on as an opening night because there was going to be an eight-day lapse before our official opening night), the three actresses and myself just walked out onto the stage with the pre-set lights and it was as holy as any church that any of us had been in. We tried in the collaboration to make it as clean as possible but the drama increasingly dirtied it again. But we managed to make it as clean as possible again at the end. Part of the idea was that maybe something holy could happen in life. We were working on a theory which was the play with three characters going crazy and all sorts of threats of killings and murder and killing babies in fields and so on. We did discuss this: "Is the reality that is theatre impossible in life?"

AF: *The family and the past are two of the big themes that you keep reworking in various ways. Do you think that you write about those themes differently now in comparison with your earlier work?*

TM: I know that with my last full-length play, *The House,* I hoped to Christ that that would be the end of the family stuff. I don't know that I have much choice in that. I seem to be coming at the subject of the search for home, doing different takes on it, sometimes more sophisticated, sometimes more complex. The word that seems to apply to humankind is longing. My attempt to write a play is the search for home whether that is home in the usual way that we understand home or whether we're talking about harmony or whether we're talking about God or whether we're talking about the grave. It's a very big subject – this is a universal condition applying to all of humanity this thing of longing, the flight from one's own home. Again, I've said elsewhere I find the idea of the family so sanctified in our culture but it's perhaps the most undemocratic institution that exists. It's made up of individuals who would like to declare their individuality or who succumb to the tyranny of forced membership. Goldsmith called it – he was talking about exile of course but it's the same thing – "the lengthening of the chain", which is a very good description.

AF: *I was struck by the similarities between Pinter's* The Homecoming *and* A Whistle in the Dark. *I hadn't realized until I saw both plays this year how indebted to you Pinter actually was. However, one of the major differences was the treatment of the female figure. In your play the woman gets away, whereas the woman in Pinter is trapped. This seems to me symbolic of the way women operate in all of your plays – they can be victims but they also can move in whatever direction. Do you find it a particular challenge to invent female figures?*

TM: I've been writing so many female characters in the last ten or twelve years that I think it's time for me to go back ... but I certainly did. This again is a documented fact: on my first, first night ever a woman came up to me – this was to do with *A Whistle in the Dark* – and said, "Very good but if you don't mind my saying so you know nothing about women." That stuck in my mind. I think that like everybody else of my generation there was abysmal ignorance – enforced ignorance – which the culture put on us. I looked on women as a race apart and, in the way that I've written English characters in my plays, for a long time I was looking at women as if I had to cross some sort of national boundaries to write them. I thought I was getting somewhere with Rosie in *The Morning After Optimism*. Then, in *Famine*, which I suppose veers towards the intellectual in the way that the characters were evolving, the mother figure has to face reality. It seems to me that women more than men have to face reality. I'm not trying to elevate them – it's part of the make-up, I think.

A man can get lost in abstracts – like John Connor does in *Famine*. When I came on to *Bailegangaire*, in the second or third last draft, there were three women and a male character, called John. He was a very good character and we did a good reading in Galway with Sean McGinley reading this character. I wouldn't call the play pure – it's a very baroque piece – but these Aristotelian unities of time, action, and place took over. I think it did occur to me consciously that I would try for a unity of gender in it. And I think that it's much more interesting that the three women arrive at whatever the conclusion is in that play, rather than having a man intrude. There's also another aspect to a man writing female characters. It both frees me to go further into that and indeed maybe to conceal the autobiographical in it. I found particularly in *Bailgangaire*, and then, *The House*, that I was fascinated by the mother figure. It is a much more interesting thing for me to do. But the line of least resistance, of course, is to go for the male character.

AF: *Tom Murphy, thank you.*

Tom Murphy was born in Tuam in 1935 where he became involved with local acting groups. He wrote his first play, *On the Outside*, with Noel O'Donoghue in 1959. His second play, *A Whistle in the Dark*, was staged to great acclaim in London in 1961. In 1962, he emigrated to London and turned to writing full-time. His plays include *Famine*, *A Crucial Week in the Life of a Grocer's Assistant*, *The Morning after Optimism*, *The Sanctuary Lamp*, *The Blue Machusla*, *Conversations on a Homecoming*, *Too Late for Logic*, *The Gigli Concert*, *Bailegangaire*, *The Wake* and *The House*. He has been writer-in-association with both the Druid Theatre Company, Galway, and with the Abbey Theatre in Dublin. A Tom Murphy season of six plays was held at the Abbey Theatre during the Dublin Theatre Festival in October 2001 to celebrate his achievement and to honour his contribution to the canon of Irish dramatic literature.

Anne Fogarty lectures in English at NUI Dublin and is Director of the James Joyce Summer School. She has published essays on Joyce, Kate O'Brien, Denis Devlin and Maria Edgeworth and on many aspects of Irish Women's poetry and fiction. She is currently working on a study of Spenser and early modern colonial representations of Ireland.

Paddy O'Dwyer in Conversation with Geraldine O'Neill

GO'N: *Paddy, you are most closely associated with the development of youth theatre but how did you first get involved in theatre yourself?*

PO'D: To be honest, I didn't get involved in youth theatre but I think I had an experience very similar to many young people involved in youth theatre now in that my sense of theatre was mostly through film. My mother was a great theatre-goer. A woman I thought of as very exotic, Phyllis Ryan, lived down the road. I never knew her or spoke to her, because my mother was pretty much in awe of this woman as someone very important and I had seen lots of performances in the Eblana and so on. So I did have an exposure to the theatre, but at the same time the influence on me was film really. At College I did a little bit, but nothing spectacular. Actually my first major performance was in Cork. I was in College in Cork and John O'Shea, who's very famous in Everyman productions, was doing a play called *Hamp* – the film was called *King and Country* with Tom Courtenay and Dirk Bogarde. He put an ad in the College: I went down for the auditions and got it, to my own surprise. Some of the people in that were semi-professional, as many of the people in theatre in Cork would have been. Anyway, I left Cork almost immediately afterwards. I worked in England for a few years and got involved in am-dram over there.

When I came back after a few years in England I saw there were auditions for the Abbey School so I went and auditioned and got it – again to my surprise at that particular time. Well I suppose I had the fantasy about being an actor but I don't think in the final analysis I would have had the courage or theatrically the balls to go ahead. I left the Abbey after a year. When I'd say to people that time I was in the Abbey School, they'd go, "Oh my goodness, fantastic!" But it was very *ad hoc* the way it was run. I was used to academia I suppose – not in the sense of being very academic, but – I was used to structure. Everything was unstructured and you were constantly being asked to join the crowd scenes and I was too important and too high and mighty.

GO'N: *Was the School run as full time?*

PO'D: No, it was part-time. It started at about five in the evening and finished about ten at night. A really long evening – I might be exaggerating that a bit but it was quite long. After a year I got fed up with it and I made certain career choices and I suppose I really didn't have the courage of my convictions – I didn't see myself as the matinee idol – and decided this isn't for me. After that I got involved in amateur drama in Strand Players but I got fed up with that as well – somehow it was unfulfilling. So that's how I got involved in theatre in the first place.

GO'N: *So how did you actually encounter youth theatre then?*

PO'D: I was very involved through my professional work in youth work and children and so on. I woke up one day – and this is not an exaggeration – and said, "How come there isn't a youth theatre or a children's theatre?" I knew nothing about it, I have to say. I knew about the schools of speech and drama and so on and I had respect for those places but, well, there were fees involved and at that time of my life I felt people should have access to these things and not have to pay for them. So I said to myself, "Maybe I'll start a youth theatre." I had no idea! So I thought I'd better do some research. I read a few books and things – there was quite a developed youth theatre scene in Britain at that time, in 1977. So, one weekend during the old B & I days, I took the old boat to Liverpool on a Friday night. There was a theatre there – a link again with Cork – called Everyman Theatre run by Ken Campbell. I'd read about him and theatre-in-education and all that kind of stuff. They had a youth theatre attached – very like Activate attached to Graffiti. They were in theatre-in-education but they were also in agit-prop and street performance as well.

Anyway I went over and met this very strange guy who was in charge of the youth theatre – a skinhead, a little bit older than myself, because I was about twenty-six at the time. So Saturday morning the youth theatre opened at eleven o'clock, I met a few people, had lunch there, said "Thank you very much", went and looked at the two cathedrals in Liverpool and said to myself "I could do that, really" I went back then and I wrote a letter to the papers. Ten people turned up to the first auditions, but two of them – two girls – were very involved in the basketball team in school and they had basketball on a Saturday and they had to make choices. So that's really how I started.

GO'N: *Where?*

PO'D: I happened at that time to be on the board of the Catholic Youth Council. The Catholic Youth Council had an office on Aran Quay in Dublin so I asked if we could use one of the offices. And there wereall sorts of complaints on a Monday morning about desks not being in the same place and someone had interfered with a typewriter or whatever so that couldn't last forever. But it did last for a year, thanks largely to the generosity of the people who let me invade their offices every Saturday morning.

GO'N: *And that was the bones of Dublin Youth Theatre?*

PO'D: That was the bones of DYT. I actually looked out the door one Saturday and said "What do we call this? There's probably a Dublin Youth Theatre somewhere" – I was very naive at the time. And I discovered to my surprise there wasn't a Dublin Youth Theatre, so why not call it that?

GO'N: *At what stage did you think up that movement? There wasn't such a thing at the time.*

PO'D: If there was, I wasn't aware of it. I was very involved in the mainstream education system myself, but I didn't see it as the place to develop ... . For me youth theatre was part of the non-formal education system. That's the way I wanted to view it: a certain amount of freedom and release. But to go back to your question, was there another youth theatre? I don't think there was. I'm informed reliably that there's a youth theatre in Carrick-on-Suir called Brewery Lane – a fantastic name – that started about three months after me. That was in the context of amateur theatre. But because of my involvement in amateur theatre later – I joined a working party on amateur theatre about setting up a national association – I quickly formed the view that amateur theatre was not going to support youth theatre. Effectively the people involved in amateur theatre were busy doing their own thing, and to sustain more time to do somebody else's thing wasn't on. Then we formed the national association.

GO'N: *You formed the National Association for Youth Drama?*

PO'D: That wasn't until 1980.

GO'N: *And how many people were in the National Association?*

PO'D: Dublin Youth Theatre essentially *was* the National Association but I got to know a few people in professional theatre-in-education and some people in amateur theatre – notably Gerry and Patricia King in Tuam and Joe Donoghue. They were very friendly with Tom Murphy and did a lot of his plays. I often wonder whether the English guy King in *The Gigli Concert* (the play is based in Dublin I know, but I often suspected the builder guy came from Tuam) – I wonder whether he picked that name deliberately. I knew Tommy McArdle through drama-in-education and theatre, Martin Drury I got to know because Martin Drury was like a force ten gale that time [and] Eithne Healy and Gaye Tanham, and the Wards in Cootehill. So that was the circle and we got together and started the National Association – an *ad hoc* group – who got together in a hotel in Mullingar. It happened by happenstance. I didn't plan it but the combination of people from amateur theatre, from education, from drama-in-education and from professional theatre was a nice mix from the very beginning.

GO'N: *What were you aiming for with that? Did you feel the need for a support system?*

PO'D: I think one of the reasons I didn't continue with acting [is] I like a lot of structure in my life. I'm not a very structured person myself, I'm all over the place, but I like structure in my life and if I don't have a structured base I think I fall apart. Essentially I was a Civil Servant by that time too, so I understood "strucshures." If you wanted money you must have "a strucshure." DYT for example, looking for money, went to the Arts Council. They laughed. They *laughed*. But if you have a structure and you have a Board you can go back to these people and keep an eye on them, then they give you stuff. And the same with NAYD – if you had a structure and an organization people would respect you.

GO'N: *What were the most crucial moments during that time? The highs and lows?*

PO'D: The high point came in my second year in DYT. In the first year we had eight kids and we put on two plays. One was a terrible thing I had got about some kids who had run away from home – it was an awful yoke altogether – and the other was *Lovers* [Brian Friel] which I directed myself. Because of my contacts in the youth world I happened to meet the famous – well he's famous in the youth world anyway – Peter McLoughlin – and he helped me put up the set and all those things. Peter has been, I think I'll call him, my gift to the struggling professional theatre because he has moved sets in every part of the country and brought them to France and everything over the years. Anyway, Peter knew of a youth club that was disused, so we went over and looked at the premises. And it was an Old Boys – literally an Old Boys – past pupils' union which had this premises that had been designed for the past pupils of Artane. But they had shut down Artane and so there were no more youths. We knew about this premises. So we started in the basement and infiltrated our way up until we persuaded the owners to let Peter move in as a caretaker. And eventually we bought that premises with an Arts Council grant.

GO'N: *That was Gardiner Street?*

PO'D: Yes. And again it's my hankering after structure. You can't do anything unless you have a premises. But the second year was very seminal for me. I sent another letter to the papers and instead of eight we got approximately a hundred people applying. I had no notion about what you should do. Because only eight people had arrived first time I just met them all and I interviewed them. The second year I had a friend of mine "doing the door," as they say, and I was interviewing all these one by one. After about half an hour he came into me and said "What the hell are you doing? We got a hundred people outside the door, you won't be finished here until *tomorrow*!" So the group interview was born on the spot and you had to do a little workshop – that was the only thing I could do to decide. And one young man was leaving the room and he said to me "I'll do anything – I'll sweep the floor or anything." And I said "Yeah, that's fine, thank you very much." And you could see he was having a problem with his own sense of identification and he was ... he was somebody else basically. On the basis of his insistence – I thought he looked a bit strange – I took him. He played a bit of music – he wasn't a great musician by any means – but we took his songs one day and devised a kind of play around them. And then I wrote to somewhere in Europe that there was a festival and we travelled to it with this improvised piece. To Europe! It was a high point for me. The work was probably very naive and lacking in dramatic structure and so on but, looking back on it, I think it was very important for me and also very important for this young man. Because I think it changed his life. He didn't go on to professional theatre but I think it changed his life.

Obviously I'm a psychologist, I'm interested in people, and their problems, but not just the problems. But this was drama *as* therapy, not drama therapy. I think it changed his life, and that was an important lesson for me because it's part of what we're about. These international festivals were high points. We had kids playing in the aisle of a Viennese theatre, playing ball games – they were being kids in a street in Dublin. And this woman came over to me and said "We do not behave like this." This was the pre-curtain and the kid was trying to explain to her "We're not in Vienna. We're in Dublin!" which she didn't understand at all. But in fairness to her, at the end of the play she apologized because she didn't understand. She had never seen a pre-set like that.

GO'N: *Was there anyone who influenced you in that kind of work?*

PO'D: No, because I'd never seen it, more's the pity. I wouldn't call myself educated in terms of teaching in this area but I was very influenced by Brecht. I liked the notion of the *ensemble*, even in its socialistic sense but, more importantly, in terms of the acting everyone was important. And even in terms of alienation, I liked the idea of young people stating who they are and doing it as young people. We would have seen that in terms of this production of *The Old Lady Says 'No!'* with the National Youth Theatre. The most stunning moment of that production was the end of the show when they went back into their own clothes and said "This was a play. This was us doing it. But this is us now, this is what we look like." So the notion of taking a young person and putting make-up on them to make them look like an old woman, all that kind of stuff would have been totally alien to me. I was also influenced in terms of what I liked in theatre by American plays, I like the American theatre – [laughing] which is probably very Stanislavski influenced – but I like Arthur Miller and have done a few productions of Lanford Wilson.

GO'N: *I shouldn't be getting my tuppence worth here, but it is the sort of Brechtian thrust of Stanislavski – that switching between two styles – that can happen with young people. It doesn't happen with older actors so easily.*

PO'D: I think Stanislavski is great, of course I do. But I wonder sometimes: the exercises might be great but it's not a great technique for young people because they have so little experience to draw on. At my age you have all sorts of terrible experience to draw on in the emotional moment but young people are very much focused in the here and now. That's what I like about Brecht.

GO'N: *I like the ability to switch between styles.*

PO'D: Yeah, that switch is great. Maybe Brecht is sorry he did it. He wanted alienation but then he goes and creates one of the greatest characters in modern theatre – Mother Courage – and maybe he wasn't satisfied that that happened. I don't know.

GO'N: *Let's move on. How do you see your work in relation to the Irish theatre scene at the moment.*

PO'D: That would have been an easier question for me to answer ten years ago. This sounds really grandiose on my part but, at the time DYT started, Paul Mercier was in college I think, doing wonderful work out there, you had the Druid theatre, and there was a zeitgeist generally in Ireland. I think we were emerging. Okay, we were going into recession – the terrible recession of the eighties I remember very well in the youth theatre with the unemployment levels of the members and so on – but there was a cultural identity-change happening in Ireland at that time. And I'm glad to say that we were part of that – changing values, changing understanding of ourselves in relation to Europe. I'm a bit of a Europhile and I was deeply committed to the notion of us having a bigger stage; I loved the notion of DYT representing Dublin. And I also was fed up with people talking about disadvantaged communities and community work. I wanted people to reach *beyond* their communities in order to actualize themselves, which is not to denigrate all the wonderful work people do in communities. But you reach beyond it and that was what I wanted to achieve. So I wanted to think European. So we did make a contribution to theatre in general in terms of freshness, lack of inhibition, some people would say lack of technique.

GO'N: *And lack of reverence.*

PO'D: Of course, lack of reverence. We can illustrate that with that production by Eilis Mullan which was totally irreverential – her production of *A Midsummer Night's Dream* took place in a disco, and had a rock band and kids absolutely adored it, packed it out. That lack of reverence! Of course Eilis knows her Shakespeare, that was also important, but "at this point in time" is the question you're asking and I don't know the answer to that. I think the youth theatre has had its influence. That's come through. I'm not saying every young actor has come through youth theatre ...

GO'N: *A huge range of theatre people have come though, when you think of names like David Parnell, Aidan Gillen, Veronica Coburn, Brian Brady, Julie Hale, Enda Walsh, Emer McGowan, Fionnuala Murphy, Eana MacLiam, Peter Hanley, Eileen Walsh, Janet Moran, Eamonn Fox, Darren Thornton – loads of them.*

PO'D: But even those who haven't have been influenced by it by association. Loads of people out there now have so much courage, such willingness to risk – I suppose that is the job of an actor or anyone in theatre – I think that's come through. But now? What's the influence now? I don't know. Well we're almost establishment I suppose, in a way, and I think we have to re-invent ourselves now a little bit.

GO'N: *There's new writing as well.*

PO'D: Yeah we've tried to foster that in DYT with playwrights like Mark O'Rowe and Nick Kelly and Loughlin Deegan coming up through that. And indeed Gerry Stembridge himself would be the first to admit that [while] youth theatre wasn't a seminal influence for him, it informed his work a great deal.

GO'N: *So what do you think of the Irish theatre scene now?*

PO'D: Well, I always leave it to my betters to explain to me what the movements are and where we're going. Actually I feel we're at a bit of a crisis at the moment. I suppose theatre's always in a bit of a crisis.

GO'N: *What sort of crisis? In what way a crisis?*

PO'D: Irish theatre always relied on writing – that sounds as if it shouldn't rely on writing, but compared to Eastern European theatre and so on. Writers are the backbone of every theatre in every country in the world, but especially in Ireland. And we have great writers and the writers continue to come through. But, if I go back to the NAYD experience again, our young writers are more influenced by film. Take Mark O'Rowe, he's influenced not by David Mamet the playwright but by David Mamet the screen writer. And Irish film has blossomed in the past few years. I don't know the future for that, we obviously have the famous names but we also have those who are making the smaller films like *Disco Pigs* and *On the Edge* and all those. Very, very well-crafted movies. And even if you look at *Bachelors' Walk* now, it's so well crafted as a piece of film. So that's where the buzz is at the moment. That's where you feel things happening. I don't feel things happening in theatre at the moment.

GO'N: *And it's cheap to make a film. Sometimes it's cheaper to make a film than to put on a play.*

PO'D: Well it's certainly cheaper to go to the movies.

GO'N: *It is, but it's also cheaper to make one. If you're a digital movie maker you're not renting a theatre for two thousand pounds a week.*

PO'D: That's interesting because I think that we – I certainly don't want to eliminate the writer by any manner or means – we really haven't embraced the new technologies in theatre. We are waiting for something exciting to happen there. I still love going to the theatre. I love new writing. But I don't see the same excitement. The fact that I don't see the same excitement could be just that I'm a lot older and I prefer the old, reliable stage productions.

GO'N: *There are probably far more film makers being produced than there are new theatre people.*

PO'D: And a lot of those film people would have been directors in Dramsoc or UCC Dramat, or Players.

GO'N: *People who also have the technology. They can write, produce, direct.*

PO'D: But you never will replace the writer – even a good movie has to have a good writer – I'm not saying that. But there is a place for the visual and writers will emerge to embrace that.

GO'N: *It's a cross-over.*

PO'D: It is. Theatre isn't theatre unless it is staged, and so you have the meeting of the forms with the writer and the director and the actor.

GO'N: *The Abbey is also one of the big forces in Irish theatre. If you were given charge of it tomorrow what would you do with it?*

PO'D: This is a difficult question because I have a vested interest in the Abbey at this point in time because I am actually the chair of the Advisory Committee of the Education and Outreach programme there. Now I'm not going to say that's the major development in the Abbey in the last few years, but it certainly is a significant one and I think they're doing fantastic work and I would like to see them with a bigger budget and more of an influence in the Abbey. And indeed one of the things we wish to do with the National Association is involve people in the Aquis Project* [a project involving youth theatres and established professional venues such as the Abbey and the Royal National in London], developing people's technical skills and so on – it was a wonderful success. The Abbey has to reach out to the community.

GO'N: *The national community?*

PO'D: The national community. The Abbey means an awful lot to me as a citizen. Now unfortunately I don't think it means an awful lot to a lot of other people. But to me it's part of the Gaelic Revival, part of the nationalist movement, all of those things, the first state-subsidized theatre in the world. We can be very proud of so many things about it. But most of the controversy around the Abbey now is where is it going to go. The building doesn't much matter, it's really about what it's going to do. I think it needs to foster new writing a lot more.

Even the present regime in the Abbey, with the appointment of Ali Curran, would agree that it needs to foster new writing. I suppose a big theatre like that costs a lot of money, maybe at this stage they can't afford to take too many risks with the main stage, but they have been developing new writing and the arrival of Ali is a very important development for the Abbey. I'd be reasonably optimistic about the Abbey. It's place in Irish history is obviously secure but it has to continue to earn that place and we have to continue to challenge it. But I don't have any suggestions ... . Except I think it should *stay where it is*. Obviously the theatre is a disgrace in physical terms, it's a joke. I don't understand. Here you have an architect who designed a theatre that's totally hopeless when you come to the technical end, backstage.

GO'N: *What would you do with it?*

PO'D: I wouldn't be on for total revolution in the Abbey but I would have as a policy far more access. People can deconstruct things. Kids can deconstruct a television programme for me now. They know the camera angles and so on. And yet they don't get an opportunity to meet actors, or directors or ...

GO'N: *That was one of the major things about the Aquis Project for the group coming up from Cork. It was access to the Abbey, demystifying the Abbey.*

PO'D: It's important. Kids can electronically, through the internet, deconstruct everything. And yet we have this edifice that cannot be accessed and I think it needs to reach out.

GO'N: *Who do you see as the most exciting talents currently on the Irish scene in writing, directing, acting or whatever? Where are these people coming from?*

PO'D: There are lots of them around. I like Conor McPherson. I find his work a bit unvaried but he's okay. And there are lots of directors around, and they have such technical skill. The thing anyone of us would notice would be such an improvement in design. Design is fantastic in Ireland – really brilliant.

GO'N: *Are there any policy changes you would like in Irish theatre? Do policiies matter? If there was one thing you would like to improve, what would it be?*

PO'D: I think policy does matter an awful lot. If I have a regret in the past few years – I understand where it's coming from because life is more complicated, so the Arts Council is now more complicated. I miss the sense that you could lobby the Arts Council, not like a political organization, but that you could state your case. Now you have to go through so many layers. I understand the need for this because of the way the place is constructed, the way the world is constructed, much bigger budgets, they're understaffed, all this sort of thing. But I always had the feeling – even when you were getting very little money – that you had access to the Council. I feel now that you have no access to the Arts Council. It's a reality, not just a perception. There was a drama subcommittee – there probably still is – but you can't actually meet these people and expostulate on your passion, that you're not a fly-by-night and that you do want to do things and so on. I think the Council has to find a way that people feel they have access and I feel an awful lot of people in theatre now – it's not just about funding – feel they have no access. I know the Arts Council must organize itself bureaucratically but I think we've lost something in that.

GO'N: *Do you see any development in the Arts Council's attitude to youth theatre?*

PO'D: It would be true to say with regard to lobbying and meeting people – I feel it's necessary because they don't understand what we're on about. By coming in, by bringing a young person with you, and explaining what it's all about – you have to try to show to them the whole range, the whole holistic nature of the work we're trying to do. And that those of us really involved know our art form. Sometimes I feel that they think we don't really know the art. And they're very much mistaken. And we don't get the opportunity now to explain that. So there's a lot of commitment to children and so on but it's not translated into policies. I think they're trying to do that but I feel they don't really understand. In the Arts Plan they promised this ten percent or fifteen percent but they didn't even know how to implement that, or they never succeeded, and you wonder was the will there or was there a lack of understanding about how to do it? I feel in a sense that, although youth policy should permeate across the board, if there's nobody responsible for it it's in danger of getting lost. In a way, we've been well treated by the Arts Council – they've always been very courteous and so on – but they have not really engaged with our section.

GO'N: *Paddy O'Dwyer, many thanks.*

Paddy O'Dwyer in 1977 founded Dublin Youth Theatre, the first youth theatre in Ireland. He was a key figure in the founding in 1980 of the National Association for Youth Drama, of which he is currently Chair, and in 1985 helped to found EDRED, European Drama Encounters. He is Chair of the Advisory Committee of the Outreach and Education programme of the Abbey Theatre and is co-ordinator for the Children and

Youth section of the International Amateur Theatre Association. In that capacity he has acted on selection committees for the World Festivals of Children's Theatre. He works as a Regional Director in the National Educational Psychological Service Agency.

Geraldine O'Neill is Outreach Director of Graffiti Educational Theatre Company and Artistic Director of its attached youth theatres, Activate and Physically Phishy. She is a member of the executive committee of the National Association for Youth Drama. She is one of the Irish representatives on the Aquis Project. Recent work includes co-directing *Cliona's Wave* for the National Festival of Youth Theatres in Galway and directing *More Light* (Bryony Lavery) and *After Juliet* (Sharman MacDonald).

Fintan O'Toole in Conversation with Redmond O'Hanlon

RO'H: *Fintan, as a critic in a small community, have you experienced personal backlash from friends and theatre people you've criticised?*

FO'T: This is a problem and you do write on regardless. But I take absolutely no pleasure in annoying people or making anybody feel upset and I would try to operate an absolutely consistent rule which is that you never criticise an individual unless what that individual has done or not done is essential to the reasons why you liked or didn't like the play. You know that sometimes there is such a thing as completely gratuitous personal insult which passes itself off as critical appraisal, but equally there is also such a thing as opting out. I mean, if someone in a principal role is miscast or is not up to the job or is simply not performing with any kind of force, it's negligent for you not to deal with that and to say what you see. The critical thing here is, I think, that the function of a newspaper critic is primarily directed towards the audience, towards the readers of the newspaper; it's called journalism. It is not primarily directed towards theatre professionals or towards the people whom you are writing about. Now obviously you would hope to have some kind of creative and symbiotic relationship with those people because critics are only as good or as bad as the work they review, but it is not primarily intended either to flatter or to teach the people who are directly engaged in the performance. It is primarily intended as a view which is magnified by print and which is there in order to serve the audience or the wider theatre-going community.

But I have had the experience of people ringing me up on Sunday mornings to complain. It was never about themselves, it was always about what I did to somebody else in the cast: "X was extremely upset by your review and do you not realise what a great old trooper he is and how much he's done for the theatre?" and all that sort of stuff, and that's very unpleasant. I instinctively shy away from either inflicting those kinds of things on people at all or suffering the response; I don't want either of them. But I would also feel I was negligent if it was relevant and I didn't say it. I have to point out that I get an awful lot more abuse in print than any actor or any playwright. I do know directly what it is like to be criticised. I am not some kind of pathological person who takes pleasure out of inflicting this on someone. I know what it's like and therefore I try to use the power, which you undoubtedly have when you're writing, responsibly. But I think responsibility is two-sided. One of the things that always amazes me is how often you get a different kind of response. I sometimes get private letters from people who are in a poor production saying: "Thank you very much for saying that because we all thought it as well, but we're stuck in the middle of it."

RO'H: *Really, that's interesting. So, basically, there's the consolation that you have some function, even in relation to the trade.*

FO'T: Well, very often people in the trade are the first people to recognise when something isn't working and it's a nightmare for them. I've had some direct experience, through being in the Abbey, of the whole process of rehearsal and the whole process of failure. It is a nightmarish thing and I don't blame anybody for feeling desperately hurt by it or for wanting to find some kind of focus for that hurt. Very often when something isn't working at all, it may be the fault of the director, for example, but many actors feel that they can't criticise the director because they're in a very unstable profession. There's a sort of "code of silence" but also there's a very real, tangible, economic thing; they depend on directors to hire them so they're often very glad when somebody else says: "The reason this doesn't work is because there's not a coherent approach to the piece of theatre, which in turn makes it very difficult for the actors to do what it is they ought to be doing". Like everybody else they want praise. If I write a book, I want it to be praised. I don't want somebody pointing out, even very intelligently, all the things I haven't done or all the flaws in it. On the other hand, if somebody writes a review that is full of empty praise, you've got absolute contempt for that person. Actors are exactly the same, they actually can have complete contempt for critics who just pat them on the back and tell them how wonderful they are. Because, at some core level, they take what they do very seriously and they understand that that seriousness involves a possibility of failure. I don't think they really like it when people say they're wonderful.

RO'H: *I'd love to believe you.*

FO'T: What I'm saying is they like it at some level, an immediate human level, but at some deeper professional level they find it gross.

RO'H: *I would feel, in my experience, that it's only the pretty good ones that have that point of view. For those in the middle, anything is grist to the mill. It's my feeling that they're not as contemptuous; it's only the good ones.*

FO'T: I think you're probably right that generally serious-minded people don't mind serious-minded criticism if they think it is motivated by a genuine concern for what they do, rather than by malice. But there's never going to be a time when actors don't resent criticism.

RO'H: *No, it has to be a difficult relationship, hasn't it? If it is not difficult and thorny, there's something wrong.*

FO'T: On Broadway, for example, somebody calculated that a good review in the *Daily News* was worth an average of $1.5 million at the box-office! So even where you're dealing with absolutely enormous amounts of money, the critic is protected to some extent by the scale of it, the number of theatres, the size of the city, all that kind of stuff, so you remain a relatively distant figure. You almost never have direct contact with the people you write about. Dublin is not like that, Ireland is not like that. If you're around as long as I am you probably know a lot of these people, you meet them walking down the street, you probably admire and respect them, you went to college with them or whatever. The natural tendency of the system is to move towards cosiness, not just in theatre but in politics, economics and everything else. That's the way society tends to work. It's just not your job to tell politicians how wonderful they are. It's not your job to tell actors, playwrights or directors how wonderful they are, unless you have made an honest judgement that they are wonderful. And you can't control an honest judgement, but you have an obligation to explain why you don't like something, because otherwise it's just abuse. In the course of explaining why you don't like it, you do sometimes have to say that the role was miscast, that the actor just didn't give what was needed. I perfectly understand when people say: "What gives you the right to say this or that"? The answer is nothing, absolutely nothing, and they're quite right about that. There's nothing that qualifies you to be a critic. So the desire for cosiness comes from a notion that the critics aren't serious, you know, that they're just well-meaning amateurs and therefore they should act like amateurs.

RO'H: *The question of your credentials as a theatre critic are sometimes raised. How do you respond to accusations about your 'lack of training' or suitability for the task?*

FO'T: I have no answer in relation to why me rather than somebody else. But in relation to professional qualification or expertise in some aspect of the theatre, I would say that I have very considerable experience and expertise in being a member of the audience. There's a fundamental misconception which is that the critic must come from within the profession, which would not be applied to any other area. It is not said that nobody should write about politics except politicians or former politicians. Quite the contrary: it's generally regarded as a difficulty for somebody to become a political correspondent if they have already been a T.D. It seems to me that what we should remember is that what's distinctive about the theatre is that it does not exist in the absence of an audience. It's not like other forms. I think it's probably true that the best reviewers of novels are very often novelists. Not necessarily, but very often the best reviewers of poetry are poets. The best reviewers of painting at least paint themselves. But there's a fundamental distinction between those forms and theatre, which is that a painting exists independently, whereas the audience is an integral part of the active theatre and the function of the critic is derived from membership of the audience and not from membership of the profession. I was maybe slightly sensitive to these criticisms and deliberately spent a year working in the Abbey, and people then said to me: "Well, you must look at it all very differently now", and the answer was: "Not at all". You simply change roles in that when you're at a rehearsal looking at how the play develops, chipping in your tuppence-ha'pennyworth, you have one view of what the intention is. But the difficulty that theatre practitioners often have is that their intention makes not the slightest bit of difference unless it is communicated, and the enormous difficulty of theatre is the communication of the intention. So when people say to me you didn't understand what we were trying to do, I tend to say: "Well, whose fault is that? I tried, I was open-minded, I sat there, I watched, I tried to get on your level, I want to enjoy myself, I really want to be engaged by this piece of work and if I didn't it is absolutely possible that it is to do with my limitations, intellectual or emotional or spiritual or whatever. But at least I am honestly trying to receive what it is you are trying to communicate. It is also possible if you fail to communicate that it might also be your fault". It doesn't help, regardless of how much time you spent functioning in the theatre. It may well be a hindrance because you're not functioning like a member of the audience. You're thinking about it in a completely different way, which is not relevant to the nature of the work you're doing.

RO'H: *How did you end up at the Abbey?*

FO'T: When Garry Hynes was appointed Artistic Director, she asked me if I would go in for the first year with her. I was there really to advise in terms of repertoire, in terms of different productions, and it was a terrific experience, but for better or worse I don't think it has fundamentally changed me.

RO'H: *Occasionally, I have been at a play and realised that I have nothing to bring to it, I'm exhausted or perhaps distressed about something else. It is not a positive experience and it may have had nothing to do with the play itself. If that happens when you have to review something, what do you do?*

FO'T: It's an absolutely valid question in that it's a one-off experience and it's quite possible that very untypical things happen on certain nights in the theatre. What I would say is, that's where the professionalism comes in, not a professional training in the theatre but in journalism. It is my job to be engaged in what's going on.

RO'H: *Does it not happen? Have you never nodded off? Surely there has been a night when you are just not up to it and yet you have to be there.*

FO'T: I can't honestly remember it happening. I find it's very, very different for me to go a piece of theatre when I'm not working. Basically, when you are reviewing, you are working and you have an obligation. It does annoy me when people say that it's not really work. It is very hard work, I find it absolutely exhausting, particularly now during the Theatre Festival and you need to be receptive to the work.

When I first saw *The Gigli Concert*, I'd been up nearly all of the previous night and I was so tired. I sat down and thought: "Look, I'm not going to review this on the basis of this production, I'll come again tomorrow night". I have to say that within 30 seconds of that play beginning, I was absolutely alive because the play made me so and that was when it was in its famously long version, which went on until after 11 o'clock. I do think a good piece of theatre breaks down all the banal daily cares, it does take you to a different state and it makes time pass in a very different kind of way. Nothing moves more slowly in life than a bad piece of theatre and nothing moves quicker than a functioning piece of theatre. One of the interesting things with this current Festival, which has had a number of very short shows, and some quite long ones, is that you realise that theatre time is different from real time, absolutely different. Look at Friel's play, *The Yalta Game*, which is only about 50 minutes. It's a much longer play than some things that go on for 3 or 4 hours because it's denser, there's more happening and you don't feel short-changed. I actually thought they should have presented that on its own because it's a full evening's theatre – it just works.

RO'H: *Do you have you any internal test to tell you that the play is not working?*

FO'T: Well, I suppose if I start being tempted to look at my watch! Of course you're aware of a general sense of time unfolding and passing but even reasonably good theatre transcends that and creates its own time. I suppose that's my basic test. The way I would tend to operate would be quite unreflectively while I'm watching, so I would try not to be reflecting on what I'm seeing while I'm watching it because I think that distorts the process. I think the key filter is the night's sleep.

RO'H: *See what is decanted the next day, is it?*

FO'T: Absolutely, what comes back, what stays in the mind, a feeling or a texture or something special, which is why the one thing I have never done, and never will do on principle, is an overnight review. I will never, ever do that. If I was ever asked, I argued strongly against it because I think it is disrespectful. It distorts the nature of the process because the process is one which needs some kind of filter.

RO'H: *Some critics, like Nathan, have been known to say that it's not their business if they empty every theatre in the country. Would you go that far?*

FO'T: I think you have to be prepared to go that far, in a psychological sense, in that it is not part of your job to think about the amount of money they have spent on the production, the livelihoods of the people involved, how sad it would be if there was no theatre going on at this time. That's actually not part of your job. Obviously at a broader level I would deeply regret if what I wrote actually did all that, partly for selfish reasons in that if there are no theatres, there are no critics and no people going to the theatre. People tend to forget that critics have a vested interest in theatre being good and lively and something that people talk about.

RO'H: *Peter Brook is very good on that relationship, on theatre's essential need of critics.*

FO'T: Absolutely. To some extent, criticism is a parasitic function. I don't mean that in a nasty sense but parasitic in that it is utterly dependent on the vibrancy of the body to which it is linked. You can't write good criticism of universally bad plays. You just get fed up. One of the awful, most depressing things about Broadway was that very often you would go to three or four shows in a week and not one of them would be any good at all. Apart from being just an excruciating experience, you also think: "Why am I doing this? What is the point?" I am in a fortunate position in that I don't have to be a theatre critic in order to make a living. A lot of my colleagues in political journalism would think of it as a kind of affectation, a strange aberration. I simply wouldn't do it if there weren't something in it that continually changed the way I think about things or challenged me or had some kind of grip on who I am and where I'm going and what I'm thinking about.

RO'H: *When I was referring to emptying the theatres I particularly remember someone complaining bitterly to me that your negative review of a play starring his wife had emptied the theatre. And I remember doing a critique of Sebastian Barry's* Prayers of Sherkin *for* The Arts Show. *It was never broadcast due to a strike at R.T.E but several people associated with that wonderful play felt that a good Arts Show review would have make all the difference. Now, you said that you weren't sure that you had any real influence on how a play went or on its reputation or on its continuation in the box office. What would you say about that?*

FO'T: I've huge sympathy with theatre professionals from that point of view, which is that in a way they lose both ways. I think bad reviews do tend to empty the theatres but good reviews don't necessarily fill them, and that's what's really unfair about the process. They don't even have an each-way bet.

RO'H: *I thought you had always felt that even bad reviews didn't do much either way, that it was word of mouth?*

FO'T: I probably used to think that, but I've since thought about this quite carefully. I suppose my general view would be that theatre is, for the majority of even the middle-class population, a completely optional extra. There is a core of people who want to see everything, who will go and they will be your 20% or 30% of the house who will always be there, but the others are sometimes looking for reasons not to go, if you know what I mean. They're almost relieved if they see something in *The Irish Times* saying that it's terrible. On the other hand, the power of even good reviews to shift that doesn't equal the negative power and that's where I completely sympathise with people who are directly involved. Let's face it, bad reviews can be bad reviews in both senses, sometimes they're negative reviews but sometimes they're also poorly written and there's nothing worse for anybody than to be dismissed without feeling that at least there was some kind of honesty...

RO'H: *Or that the idea might have been thrown off late at night after a few drinks?*

FO'T: ...and that is a very unfair business. It's very difficult to find an alternative because it's not as if the media, in general, are clamouring for more theatre reviews, better theatre reviews. It's increasingly treated within the media as a relatively unimportant thing and there are now relatively few reviews in the mainstream newspapers. It's very difficult in that context not to sympathise with people who say: "Look, these people have power over us but it's not a power which is exercised seriously or responsibly."

RO'H: *I have the feeling that it's easier to get a preview page with a big picture on a play rather than to get a decent amount of space for the actual criticism of the play. In other words, a theatre with a good PR machine might bypass real criticism. Is this so?*

FO'T: I think that's absolutely true and two things should be said about that. To a large extent, theatrical institutions are responsible for the turn in theatre culture, about fifteen years ago, which fostered the idea that the best way to deal with critics is to make them irrelevant. "Let's get the photograph. Let's get the feature about the leading actress and her love life". If you do that well enough, you create a sense of an event, which not only by-passes the critics but to some extent intimidates them because you make an opening night into a gala occasion which has already been hyped up. It's much easier for people who are supposedly taking an objective view of that event to go along with the hype rather than to pull out and say: "Well actually it doesn't live up to the hype, or it's not working or whatever". So it's a very good strategy, but it is a strategy which has primarily come from theatrical institutions themselves, essentially from Michael Colgan.

RO'H: *Surely the problem is when you have two PR geniuses, himself and Mary Finan. They have to do their PR job brilliantly, and they do, but the other side of it is maybe it's so well done it's scary, isn't it?*

FO'T: Yes it is, and the second point about this is that there's also a huge ambivalence on their part which is that they still want to use critics, they want the quotes for the ad, and they want the quotes to be as banal as possible. If the quote says: "Absolutely marvellous", they will put it up in big letters. They complain about the power of critics but they also add to it enormously by giving massive coverage and massive boosts to what they see as favourable. Again, I know why they do that, it's because they're trying to survive in a very tough business and desperately trying to get attention, but it doesn't help in terms of trying to say that the right to an independent view is also important. Critics, if they're worth paying for, must have some sense of integrity and some sense of honesty.

RO'H: *With regard to your own background in relation to theatre, what turned you on to theatre, what grabs you, when and where did the bug bite?*

FO'T: My father was a bus conductor and there was a wonderful woman, Lily Shanley, the front-of-house manager of the Abbey, who was one of his regular passengers. He was a nice man and knew the regulars on his route and if she wasn't at the bus-stop, he'd hold the bus for her. So sometimes he would get free tickets and when I was 13 I started going to the theatre with my Dad. So it was the Abbey first, but then he also used to get tickets for the

Gate. I vividly remember going to the Abbey for the first time, it was Hugh Hunt's production of *Macbeth*. Frank Grimes was Malcolm, Ray McAnally was Macbeth and Angela Newman was Lady Macbeth.

RO'H: *I saw that and she acted him off the stage. He was brought back at great expense and she was just stunning.*

FO'T: It was amazing. It was that big Celtic production. That was the very first thing I saw. I thought that was absolutely stunning. My father was an interesting kind of working-class intellectual, he told me that everyone had read the entire works of Shakespeare by the time they were 14 so I spent the summer feverishly reading through the stuff without understanding a word of it, but I loved the strangeness of Shakespeare. Then I saw some minor Shaw plays in the Gate, I think the first one was *Fanny's First Play* which is a thing I've never seen since, it's a small little odd Shaw play, but I thought it was absolutely wonderful. I suppose for 3 or 4 years I was just completely uncritical and I thought everything was great.

RO'H: *Any other things that come to mind from those early days which made you say: "This is where I want to be, this is what I want to be around"?*

FO'T: Well, the other thing I really remember very strongly was MacLiammóir in *The Good-Natured Man* and it was absolutely extraordinary because MacLiammóir was very, very old. He subsequently did a few performances of *Oscar* but it was the last actual play he did and he was very old, very blind, and very doddery. Yet, it was extraordinary. It was a bizarre production because they had to almost hold him up, so every actor around him had to literally stop him from falling over as he moved across the stage, and, as he couldn't see, they obviously led him through it. But that actually made it; in it's own way it had its own drama.

RO'H: *Kind of historic, really.*

FO'T: But of course I wasn't aware of that, I didn't really know about MacLiammóir, it was just this old man with this incredible presence and I was trying to figure out how can he do that to you when his voice is nearly gone and he obviously can't see, he can't move properly round the stage. How is it possible that it's still incredibly moving? If you ask me to say what *The Good-Natured Man* is about, I haven't a clue but there was just that presence. I certainly wasn't aware of this at the time but I think it was a kind of substitute, that sense of a communal event and it coincided with my stopping going to Mass. I think what I liked was the act of theatre itself rather than necessarily what I was seeing and I haven't a clue whether those productions were any good or not. I really couldn't tell you now, but I just loved the notion of it. I suppose I didn't really become conscious of what I was seeing in theatre until I was at college.

RO'H: *In UCD what interested you theatrically? Was it what was going on in DramSoc?*

FO'T: Shall we say, I was a very poor attender as a student, but one DramSoc production that I really liked, and I saw a lot of DramSoc productions that weren't very good, was Gerry Stembridge in *The Morning After Optimism*. I had vaguely heard of Murphy and I had thought: "Oh well, an Irish playwright of that age, it's probably all about people standing around in kitchens". I was absolutely stunned by it.

Other productions at that time, though in An Cumann Drámaíochta not in Dramsoc, (and in Irish) that really impressed me were by Paul Mercier who was aware of form, from the very beginning. He was really interested in how you could make a theatre piece without a play, how you could get songs and people moving around the stage and all of that into a form that would be interesting. And he was very good at it from early on! I found that the dialectic of theory and practice actually very profoundly changed me as a person.

RO'H: *Really? In what way?*

FO'T: Well, I would have been quite a dogmatic individual because I was coming very much from a working-class background, in the 1970s. I mean I was involved in student politics from the time I was 15, running international seminars, doing all that kind of stuff. I was highly politically motivated but also politically active in that sense and I would have had a relatively dogmatic view of the world in terms of what was right and what was wrong, what was good and what was bad. I was never entirely convinced by revolution, I couldn't quite see that happening, but I was certainly very interested in agitation. I was very interested in Marx's early writings about aesthetics and all that kind of stuff, but the person who really influenced me the most was Ernst Bloch.

The wonderful thing about theatre was that it always provoked interesting arguments with my father. He was a working-class man trapped in a terribly boring job and deeply resentful of having to work 60, 70 hours a week to make a living. Say we went to see something by Chekhov, he would say: "I can't stand this stuff, I don't care about these people", and I would say: "I am really moved by them, I know you're right but it's really moving and there's something else going on there". So even in terms of my relationship with him, in terms of accepting the notion of the complexity of contradiction, accepting the notion that people are people first before they are members of classes, it would have changed the way I saw the world. It lightened me up a lot in terms of my own development. A lot of people are probably saying: "Jesus, I wouldn't like to have seen you before you were lightened up!"

RO'H: *Are you saying the fundamental change was that it put you much more in touch with the practice of both theatre and what it is to be human, made you more complex and subtle and not too ideologically hard-line?*

FO'T: Much more flexible and much more open-minded, I think. But there's a fundamental mystery about theatre which is: how does that act of communication happen? It remains absolutely mysterious on some level, but at what point does that bond between the actors and the audience begin? It's utterly unscientific and utterly non-rational. I'm not saying it's anti-rational, but it's non-rational and if you're an atheist, if you're someone whose early experience is about becoming an atheist, then it's very difficult to acknowledge the supra-rational, to acknowledge the mysteries.

RO'H: *I'm very glad to hear this because I've been thinking a lot about the question of mystery. If mystery is not acknowledged, at some level, I think you can't really stay in theatre. And the naturalists had a real problem with it, as did the 19th century positivists; mystery was an embarrassment and then tragedy goes unless there's some sort of level of mystery at the heart of things; and science hasn't understood all those demons in the psyche; and if you don't acknowledge that I think maybe theatre's not for you.*

FO'T: And possibly theatre's completely irrelevant. Yet one thing theatre can do is somehow to create that mystery. In order to be a critic you have to have very clear views and yet hold them absolutely lightly in the moments when you go into the theatre. You need the clear views in order to be coherent, in order to have some sense of consistency in terms of how you judge things, but you also need to be absolutely and genuinely open to have a completely contradictory view on the night. That's not an intellectual process, it's an adventure.

RO'H: *It's a total process and you have to become totally human I suppose. Your eyes have to be working, your inner ear has to be working, your musical sense, it's all calling on you to be extraordinarily human and open.*

FO'T: And utterly contingent.

RO'H: *And non-judgmental, I suppose, for those few hours.*

FO'T: Absolutely, because the conditions for your response are created by what's happening on stage, not by what you brought in. That is not to say that it's a one-way process. Clearly your capacity to respond is determined by who you are, by your experiences, by what you've read. If that was only about an academic process, an analytic process, it wouldn't really hold a huge amount of interest for me, because I have enough scope to analyse all sorts of things if I want to. What I don't get anywhere else is the openness of it, you have to put your own experience, the sum parts of yourself, on the line.

RO'H: *I love that phrase Peter Brook uses when he asks: "How often is a play a 'scorching event'"? It's great, the idea of "when did it scorch you and what scorched you?" By the way, who were the critics that scorched you — my feeling is probably Kenneth Tynan, and from the past, I would suspect John Lahr? Who scorched you in that sense of saying: "Jesus, criticism too can be extraordinarily alive, an extraordinarily powerful thing to be involved in".*

FO'T: John Lahr would have been much more important early on to me because he would have been the only critic I had read much of and I loved Lahr's way of trying to interpret events and of trying to relate them to society. The first book I read of his was a small book called *Acting Out America*, a collection of essays, but he could create quite complex essays on the basis of single events. It didn't influence me directly in the sense of "I can do this" but it influenced me in the sense of feeling that this is a bigger project, a bigger canvas, it's actually about how does this event, which is incredibly complex, relate to who we are, where we are in relation to time and space, the nature of society and all of those things?

Tynan I wouldn't have read until quite late — I was probably in my early twenties before I read him at all. Tynan was such a legendary figure, I remember being incredibly disappointed when I read his stuff first in the sense that there are almost no ideas in Tynan. I remember wondering what he wrote about *Waiting for Godot* when he saw it first as he doesn't actually tell you about the nature of the play or what's going on or anything else. And then of course I got over that prejudice, because my primary interest was ideas, and just looked at what Tynan did, which was to say a critic is not the key, he's the lock. Your function as a critic is not to pretend that you can provide the answer to what this piece of work is, it's to talk about whether or not that key, which is the piece of work, opens your lock and how that might have happened. In a way there's a fundamental honesty to Tynan's writing, because his style acts as a kind of moral limit; it says: "This is me".

RO'H: *And it was fearless in a certain way; he cut through a lot of crap.*

FO'T: But also he implicitly says to his readers all the time: "This is who I am and this is how it affected me and I'm not saying that it might affect you in the same way, or I'm not saying that I'm here to interpret this work for you, you can go and bloody-well do the work yourself. But what I will just tell you is if you get a sense of how I work and how my mind works, you can also get some sense of what this thing was like by judging its effect on me." That's a very liberating notion for someone who's practising criticism because it simply says: "Yes, these are the limitations of what it is, yes there is no particular reason why it should be me doing this rather than you. But the fact is I am doing it and the least thing I can do for you is to honestly try to show you, through the way I write about it, what my response was." All I think I'm ever doing is trying to reconstruct my response and one of the problems with this is that it has no external guarantor. If I write about a political event, it's open to everybody to say: "Actually, that's not what happened." It either happened or it didn't happen. But why should how it affected you be important for anybody else? And all you can say is that I am someone who is professionally used to trying to decipher my own response and to translate that.... It is my experience as a member of the audience but also my professional integrity which helps me, I hope, to genuinely reconstruct my response. There's no control on that, I could be lying, I could actually have enormously enjoyed this piece of work and then say I didn't. My editor can't come back and say you've told lies, the people in the play can't come back and say: "That's not how it really affected you, I saw you were really happy going out of the theatre"; that doesn't happen. So it is a terrifying responsibility in one sense, but what Tynan gives you is the sense that it is a responsibility which can be carried out ethically through a certain consistency of styles, through actually saying: "This is me, this is who I am, this is the way I operate, this is what I like, this is what I don't like, this is the kind of stuff that has this kind of effect on me"; and if you read Tynan week to week, you know the nature of his responses. You know at least the way his mind is working and it may be sometimes intellectually inconsistent, but beneath that there is a fundamental consistency, emotional consistency or stylistic consistency or a consistency of presence.

RO'H: *But he did something else. You might feel it's a rather old-fashioned virtue, but in a lot of Tynan's criticism I got an extraordinary sense of the event, the particularity of the event and even of certain particularities of an acting style. I think it's very hard for a critic to talk about acting but I have great memories of his critiques of Wolfit: that was the only access I had to that sort of performance and how it was carried out. Would you have been aware of his strength in bringing out that sense of the actual, the present power of the event and of the actor?*

FO'T: Completely. I think what he does better than anybody else is to recreate a sense of the event and, you're right, that is an old-fashioned virtue in that it's almost a kind of reporting but he does it with such style that it lives on the page completely. I agree it's old-fashioned, but I don't think it's an unnecessary virtue. I think it's a fantastic thing if you can do that in relation to a form that is so evanescent; that you're at least fulfilling some kind of function by saying: "This is what remains of this performance so let's make it as evocative as we possibly can." There are two things I would say about that, one is that I'm not nearly as good as Tynan at doing it and the other is that I've been trying to do it more because I do think it is a relevant part of what we should do. You need to find a forum in which it works. Part of the problem is it doesn't work for everything.

RO'H: *Exactly. Talking about the detail of the actor's work – it's very difficult and not many critics seem to risk themselves on that description, yet sometimes you're forced into it. For instance, let's talk about say three or four great performances. I remember you writing about Donal McCann's performances in* Steward of Christendom *and* Faith Healer, *and Siobhán McKenna's in* Bailegangaire *as among the great performances: you gave a great sense of their presence. Also I found Rosaleen Linehan's playing of Feste one of the most unforgettable and disturbing things I have ever seen.*

FO'T: I suppose you always ask the same question at incredibly complex events like that, which is: "What can I communicate to people that is most germane to the event"? Now sometimes what is most germane to the event is the fact that this is the way the play works, this is what it says, that is what you should mostly talk about. In other cases where the most germane thing is the performance, (and this is not to the exclusion of the play at all), when we're really lucky the play comes into being through the creation of a performance. I think that was absolutely true of *Faith Healer* and it was true of *Bailegangaire* completely.

RO'H: *I remember your review of* Steward of Christendom. *I was slightly underwhelmed about that precisely because it was McCann 9, and the rest 0; and maybe even the other characterisations and the writing 0; and that was a bit of a problem for me. So when people say it was the best play for the last 15 years, for me it was "yes, but"!*

FO'T: I would say you're absolutely right in the sense that clearly McCann's performance in that overwhelmed everything else that was happening on stage and if you read the play it is actually much better because it does open up other possibilities. But your immediate duty there is to report that extraordinary event, that meeting of minds between Barry and McCann. And I suppose this goes back to what I was saying about negative criticism; I would never on principle criticise somebody in a play where I think their failings were not germane to explaining to a reader why a thing worked or didn't work. Now the other side of that is that if someone is so absolutely central to the event in terms of what it does to you, I think you are just obliged to actually say that is what has happened here.

RO'H: *Are you saying that such events happen once in a decade, so you go for it?*

FO'T: Your function there is just to go for it. I would say the same things about McCann again and John Kavanagh in Joe Dowling's production of *The Plough and the Stars* – they're just the kinds of thing that don't happen to you very often and you may as well just go after it. I'm quite proud retrospectively of my review of *The Gigli Concert* when it was first done, in the sense that I think I got it broadly right in terms of the nature of the event. Now, objectively, you could say it was overlong, there were some things wrong with it, which improved over time as Murphy has cut it down. The performance now in the Abbey is probably three-quarters of an hour shorter than the original production, but it is very tight now compared to what it used to be. When the Abbey was announcing this recently, I remember seeing a press release – "*The Gigli Concert* was put on in 1983 to universal acclaim." It wasn't. I think every single review except mine said: "It's kind of good, but it's very long and would you not cut this stuff"? I remember the thing that most tempted me to give up criticism was the final line in *The Irish Press* review, by Michael Sheridan, which ended with: "Take out the scissors Tom and you will have the masterpiece you so obviously desire." Now to me it is absolutely wrong to place yourself in a position of superiority saying: "You obviously desire this masterpiece", as if that's some kind of futile obsession on the part of this weird fellow and I didn't like the patronising tone of "take out the scissors Tom." I remember making a conscious decision at the time to say, while I was as aware as everybody else that it went on till quarter past eleven: "Look, that's not actually germane to the event that happened." No matter how you would write it, you would seem to be balancing incredibly minor things against an absolutely extraordinary event, with magnificent performances by Hickey and Quigley and a play that to me was just astonishing. There was no safety net, there was a high wind, it was an incredible height, the risk that was taken was immense. I suppose that I'm saying in some ways your duty as a critic is not to say everything you think but it is to communicate broadly-speaking on a register of seismic shocks; is it a little tremble or is it a volcano? For me, that is the essence.

Fintan O'Toole is one of Ireland's leading political and cultural commentators. Born in Dublin in 1958, he has been drama critic of *In Dublin* magazine, *The Sunday Tribune* and the *New York Daily News*, and Literary Adviser to the Abbey Theatre. He edited *Magill* magazine and since 1988, has been a columnist with *The Irish Times*. His work has appeared in many international newspapers and magazines, including the *New Yorker*, the *New York Review of Books*, *Granta*, the *Guardian*, the *New York Times* and the *Washington Post*. Awards include the AT Cross Award for Supreme Contribution to Irish Journalism (1993), the Justice Award of the Incorporated Law Society (1994) and the Millennium Social Inclusion Award (2000). He has also broadcast extensively in Ireland and the UK, including a period as presenter of BBC's The Late Show. Books include *The Irish Times Book of the Century* (1999); *A Traitor's Kiss: The Life of Richard Brinsley Sheridan* (1997); *The Lie of the Land: Selected Essays* (1997); *The Ex-Isle of Erin* (1996); *Black Hole, Green Card* (1994); *Meanwhile Back at the Ranch* (1995); *A Mass for Jesse James* (1990) *and The Politics of Magic (1987)*.

Redmond O'Hanlon lectures in Drama at the Centre for Drama Studies, NUI Dublin. He has published internationally on modern drama and on the novel and he has broadcast internationally on the novel, drama and cultural affairs. He is a translator of modern poetry and drama.

Lynne Parker in Conversation with Loughlin Deegan

LD: *As you and your work are so obviously associated with* Rough Magic *Theatre Company, you might begin by talking a little about how* Rough Magic *came to be, who the key personnel were and why you all decided to undertake the perilous journey of establishing a professional company together?*

LP: Well, the first key personnel, I suppose, were Declan Hughes and myself. We had the notion while we were at college, because we'd had such a wonderful time doing plays in Players Theatre in Trinity, that we wanted to continue working this way. I suppose the other important thing was that there was no other option if you wanted to work in theatre. The Abbey had just sort of closed down its director training programme and there was no opening at all at the Gate. That wasn't even under any kind of fixed management at that time. I suppose that's why there was such a proliferation of independent companies in the early 1980s, because people were really thrown on their own resources. We did our first season in Players and co-opted the other members of the company. There were eventually four core actors, Hélène Montague, Ann Byrne, Stan Townsend and Arthur Riordan. The other vital and key person in the organization was Siobhán Bourke, who came in as a sort of stage manager and production manager to begin with, but then decided to stay on with us at the end of the summer season and that made all the difference to us. We were one of the few companies around who actually had a designated administrator, who didn't want to be doing anything else but was devoted to the management of the company.

LD: *So many independent companies, from Druid who were arguably the first, to yourselves, Pigsback, Tinderbox and Passion Machine, all came out of university drama societies. What impact do you think this had on the independent scene? I'm talking particularly about the kind of work that was produced and the audiences for whom it was produced.*

LP: Well, even though we were all university educated you're still looking at a very broad spectrum of people. We were all children of an era when anybody, more or less, could go to college, whereas maybe ten years before it had been people from rather more wealthy backgrounds. So I think that that provides a very interesting panorama of views and experiences and backgrounds. I mean Rough Magic would be an example of that. There are companies who didn't come from that tradition, i.e. Charabanc, maybe Wet Paint and Co-motion, but it's true to say that the kind of company that still exists, if you look at the Bedrocks and all of that, were people who had found some kind of common denominator, their tastes and what drew them to theatre, the kind of work they wanted to do.

LD: *It seems amazing now to think that Rough Magic, in those early days, presented the Irish premieres of the work of such important writers as Caryl Churchill, Howard Brenton and even David Mamet and that those writers hadn't been produced at all in Ireland until that time. Why do you think that was the case? It just seems so unusual now.*

LP: Well, I suppose Irish theatre, when we started off, was quite inward looking in that there was the posh stuff being done at the Gate, and there were the Irish classics being done at the Abbey. The Abbey did have a tradition of new writing but it wasn't really hot when we came onto the scene. And we felt very strongly that we were of a generation whose main influences were British and American television and American film as well, and that we were definitely being influenced by other cultures and I suppose we were also looking to similar kinds of companies in the UK and elsewhere. We would count Druid as one of our big influences, and Steppenwolf, and we were very aware of those companies as undergraduates. It seemed obvious that what was turning on audiences in London, for instance, was something that we would want to bring to Dublin, and in those days you could get the rights to those plays.

LD: *And do you take any credit now for the fact that so much international work is being done in Dublin?*

LP: I don't know that we would take credit although perhaps we introduced the notion of presenting such work to Dublin audiences, but I don't think that we were the only people looking in that direction.

LD: *Obviously, presenting new international work is still an integral part of the company's artistic policy. How do you think that's changed, given the* *proliferation of young independent companies who are also covering that territory in Dublin, and throughout Ireland, indeed?*

LP: Absolutely, and not just them, because the Abbey is starting to do that kind of work as well, so we can't claim that that's the one thing we have to offer that's different to anybody else, but because of our connections, because of our history, we are in a position to make the acquaintance of a writer like, for instance, Michael Frayn. A lot of young companies wouldn't be able to get anywhere near Michael Frayn, although he is, I have to say, extremely approachable. But because he has known of our reputation, because we do have connections to places like the Bush, the Almeida, the Donmar, the Hampstead, we would be the first to know about work of that kind and we would have possibly more access to the writers of that calibre.

LD: *In the early days of Rough Magic the company was made up of a company of actors and two directors, essentially working together all the time, resulting in strong ensemble work. I'd be interested to hear your opinion of that form of theatre making. Did you enjoy working in that way? Was it beneficial?*

LP: It was possibly one of the most exciting times of my life, and all credit to the actors. I mean, the input of those four actors, and the other people who worked with us on a regular basis, was huge. And Declan and myself gained a lot from that and we all knew initially, without having to argue too much about it, the kind of work we wanted to do. Of course that changes over the years, because people's tastes begin to develop and grow further apart. But I think it would be true to say that there is a recognizable Rough Magic show, even though I find it very hard to define, and that was largely put together by the sensibilities of the people who started the company.

LD: *I know that all of the original members of the company are still involved with Rough Magic in one way or another and continue to work for the company on an ongoing basis. I'm also aware that the company has established an artistic advisory panel comprising of the original members and other artists who have a long association with the company. But essentially the individuals have moved on and the permanent company has ended. Do you think that was inevitable? Was it acrimonious in any way? And how do you think Rough Magic has dealt with that process of change?*

LP: It was inevitable because no company that's funded to the level that companies like us are, is going to be able to sustain a full, fully-paid ensemble. When we started nobody got paid anything. You did the shows on shares, and all of that. But you can't continue like that. I suppose it was down to market forces to some extent. An ensemble which is very rich and very ambitious when it's young, can do things that in a way you can't in your more mature years. I mean, you can tackle things that you're far too young to do, and because you're that kind of company, you get away with it, whereas fifteen years down the line, you have to be a lot more specific about how you cast shows and what kind of work you take on. So eventually of course, the company had to restructure itself in terms of management and how it processed the work. That was difficult for the actors, to some extent, because they felt they no longer had a permanent place. But it has to be said that they were all working freelance, they were developing their own careers and I think in the long run, it's healthier that that was the way because they were able to bring experiences back into the company and they all worked with us over the years from time to time, and they do all feel some kind of ownership of the company. The actors are still very keen to express their opinions about what's going on.

LD: *Given the process of change that has taken place and the way Rough Magic now operates, how would you position the company in terms of the entire map of Irish theatre?*

LP: We are one of the leading independent companies and it's hard to be more specific than that. I think it's interesting for instance that we are doing our most recent show as part of the Dublin Fringe Festival. Now, when we started off we were undeniably "fringe" but we very quickly became quite established and much more part of the "legit" scene, as it were. But in Dublin those things are completely mixed up and, I mean, it's true of the Edinburgh Festival, where the Fringe is now more dynamic, I suppose, and more prestigious, than the official festival, in many ways. These things are changing here as well, but because Dublin is so small, the actors in Rough Magic have been working in the Abbey and the Gate and vice versa for years. There's much greater cross fertilization. I suppose what you could say is that we're not building-based, we are a touring company. We feel that we have a fairly flexible format, and hopefully, have some kind of pulling power over a young audience, as well as the one that we've taken with us.

LD: *Out of the original core company new writing seemed to flow naturally, whereby actors, and directors (obviously Declan Hughes, in particular) began to write original scripts for the other members of the company to direct and perform in. This was arguably quite a unique and original approach to producing new writing, and one that the company has been complimented and criticized for, almost in equal measure. What is your opinion now of that process, with the benefit of hindsight?*

LP: I'm interested that you say "criticized", I don't know that people necessarily criticized us. Do you mean in that it was regarded as something of a clique?

LD: *Indeed, or that people regarded the company as some sort of a closed shop.*

LP: Well, you can only produce so many new plays, so it seemed fairly natural for us to invite people whose work we knew and who we knew had another string to their bow. For instance, Pom (Boyd) and Gina (Moxley) had both worked as sketch writers. They'd done a lot of comedy and stuff like that. Now, it's not an automatic transition from that to writing a play, but our guess was that they had that in them, and they were both quite serious about that, as indeed was Morna Regan, who's written our more recent play (*Midden*). With Declan, I mean, I'd known for years that he was interested in writing. He had done several adaptations for the company including a very successful adaptation of the *Woman in White*. He's also adapted *Caucasian Chalk Circle*. You just felt that here was someone with a skill, who needed to put it to the test. Now if your own company can't do that for you, then what's it for? I think we were providing that service and of course we're first going to go to people who were working for us, because that's the way life is, that's the way it works.

LD: *And did you actually approach people directly and say, "I think you should write a play," or did they come to you?*

LP: Well first we ran some workshops. We were five years down the line and we were looking at the work we'd done and we reckoned that it was time we started to engender our own stuff, so we approached a couple of writers and did some workshops. Declan's work emerged from that process. He wrote his first play *I Can't Get Started*, as a result of that. And after that we just thought, this is the way to go because it was such an exciting process for all of us. Also, he was writing specifically for the company, so it's a perfect system, as a process, because the actors are having things sculpted around them.

LD: *So he was writing with those particular actors in mind.*

LP: Exactly, yes. That's not true obviously when you come to *Danti Dan*, because then we were looking for very young actors. But I don't think there's any reason to feel guilty for going to people who have a proven record with the company, and whose skills you want to foster.

LD: *Sure. In terms of my own appointment here at Rough Magic as Literary Manager, and the Seeds Initiative that's just been launched with the Dublin*

Fringe Festival, it could be argued that there are, in fact, more conventional structures for developing new writing. Do you think that the company's approach still echoes some of the earlier ethos however?

LP: Well, what we realized was that, although we'd had great success with new writing, it was slightly ad hoc, and that what we needed was some kind of formal structure, and a means of testing the work at every stage. It had happened that we'd gone into production without a script being completely ready, and I knew that this kind of system worked really well in theatres in the UK, where there would be a literary manager and a panel of readers, and it seemed to me that it would be safer to have a number of heads working on this rather than just mine. As you well know, I didn't really have the time to devote to painstakingly going through all the scripts, and that certainly needed to be done. As a result, the volume of work that we're taking in and processing has gone up hugely, and that's great because it means that nothing is going to slip through the net.

LD: *It's also a fact of course, that two of the debut plays that Rough Magic has produced in the last two years have also been from actors. Personally I think this is because Rough Magic exists so much within the theatre community in Dublin and because of that tradition of allowing people who work in other aspects of the business to try their hand at writing.*

LP: Something I feel is of great benefit to any writer is a knowledge of the manner of performance. Actors who write are very aware of how other actors are going to feel standing up there saying those lines. Someone like Pom, for example, also has a great sense of how to handle an audience as well. That experience of knowing when an audience's interest is beginning to wane or what they need to happen next or how to tell a story through performance is actually very useful. It doesn't mean only actors can do this, of course not, but I think it's a great help.

LD: *Moving away from your role as Artistic Director now to talk more specifically about your role as an actual director of plays, I'd like to start by asking if you agree that they are, in many ways, very different and particular disciplines?*

LP: They are, there's no question about that, and it's always surprised me that people viewed the two jobs as parallel. Well, they are parallel actually, it's that they view them as the same thing. If you take for example someone like Jenny Topper who is a very successful Artistic Director of the Hampstead Theatre, she doesn't direct at all...

LD: *And indeed Michael Colgan here and Richard Cooke at Bickerstaffe.*

LP: Yes, that's true. I like being able to do the two things because I love rehearsing. I love being in the rehearsal room. I miss it terribly when I'm not there. But I also love the strategic planning, and the building of a company and the management that goes with being Artistic Director of Rough Magic. But I have to say I've always worked in tandem with a producer, and as part of a team, and I get a huge kick out of that as well, I don't know how I would feel about being a solo entity, I can't envisage that at all.

LD: *I know in college you acted a little; there's photographic evidence to prove it. But you also designed the posters for most of Rough Magic's earlier shows…*

LP: I designed the sets for a lot of Rough Magic's earlier shows as well because there was nobody else to do it. We couldn't afford anyone else.

LD: *Did you enjoy it? Did you have aspirations to possibly become a set designer instead at that time?*

LP: Before I went to university, I did. But that fell away very quickly. I mean, I realized that every so often I was able to have a good idea but that I couldn't produce the good stuff on a daily basis, that my skills lay in other directions. I did enjoy doing it, but it was an incredible work load as well, so I was very glad to let the professionals take over.

LD: *At what point did you realize that you wanted to direct? Or come to the realization that making theatre was what you wanted to do with your life? Was that in college as well?*

LP: It was really. I went in not knowing how to get into Players, but just that I wanted to be there and I wasn't going to be told "no." And then Pauline Mc Lynn and I directed the Fresher's Co-op, and I got a bit of a taste for it. I then did another show a year later, which was Wycherley's *The Country Wife*, which I subsequently did with Rough Magic. On the opening night, nobody knew their lines and the set fell down. But I was undeterred, and that was when I knew I had the bug.

LD: *In the rehearsal room for* The Country Wife*?*

LP: Well, it wasn't so much the rehearsal room, it was a nightmare, but I just knew when I saw it on stage that I wanted to go on, that I wanted to get it right, and there was the narcotic effect of the audience coming in and actually watching it. I think in a way, directing actually uses what I can do best. I've always been quite good at a selection of things, and not good enough at any one of them to make a career of it. But with directing, you have to be that jack-of-all-trades. You have to have a visual sense. You have to have musical sense. You have to have a sense for literature and language, so …

LD: *…you have to be able to communicate with people…*

LP: Yeah, you're middle management really, because you're the liaison between the writer and the audience, via the acting ensemble.

LD: *You say that you were driven by a need to make sure that it worked, and to get it working, but at what point did you think you had a talent for it? At what point did you go "I can communicate this play to the audience and I can lead the audience through this play and I know I'm good at it?"*

LP: Oh, that was very late in the day, I'm not even one hundred percent sure of it now.

LD: *Would you consider yourself a good director?*

LP: I would be out of my mind to give a straight answer to that. I think that is for other people to say. I am a passionate director and I'm a sane director, I think. Then again, that's for other people to say as well. But that's as far as that goes.

LD: *Do you see yourself as fitting into any particular style or school or directing?*

LP: No.

LD: *Well do you think there is an Irish style then? Do you think that we have a way of directing plays here that's very different to the more visual or expressionistic theatre in Europe?*

LP: That's possible. But there's plenty of visual and expressionistic stuff being done here by Irish practitioners as well. I mean, I think I'm interested in plays, I'm interested in speech and language and storytelling, and that would be my approach to it. Operating Theatre for example is doing work that has a very different look to it. I suppose, in a way, I'm old fashioned enough to like the "well made play." But that can take you many and varied places. If you look at the work of O'Casey, for instance, *The Silver Tassie* is an extremely expressionistic play in the best European tradition. Rough Magic did a production of that play some years ago, so the style of work we do is not limited to merely text-based stuff.

LD: *What directors would you list as your great influences?*

LP: Well, Garry (Hynes) obviously. There's just no one to touch her when she's on form. She can get performances out of people that simply blow your mind. And as a woman and as a theatre practitioner, she's pretty much at the top of the tree here. Other influences: there's a choreographer called Christopher Bruce who's influenced me a lot. My uncle (Stewart Parker) influenced me a lot in terms of how you get across a story, which he had a very practical approach to. Also Max Stafford-Clarke. When you're directing you're drawing from such a range of influences and then you watch a Billy Wilder film and you think that's the sense of humour I want to bring to my work.

LD: *You mentioned your uncle Stewart there. Knowing you as I do, I'm aware that he was a major influence on your life; not only your decision to work in theatre but also professionally and even personally. Would you like to say anything about that?*

LP: Yes, he was one of the most important people in my life ever. His plays speak for themselves; I won't go into that. His philosophy, his vision, is an even greater influence on me personally than he was as a theatre practitioner, because you've got to carve your own way. I can't simply ape the things that he did. And he was a writer: I'm a director. We come from different disciplines. But his whole approach to life is something that influenced me greatly. And in terms of his plays; the breadth of vision, the playfulness, the sense of fun, the erudition, the intellectual force, …

LD: … *the fearlessness…*

LP: Absolutely, the courage that he had has been a great guide to me.

LD: *You've obviously produced quite significant and critically acclaimed productions of his work. How has that been; being so close to the man, and then directing the plays?*

LP: When I did *Spokesong*, just after he died, it was actually too close to his death. I wasn't able to be objective enough. The most successful production we've done of one of his plays was *Pentecost*. While he was alive I'd done *Nightshade*. We were really too young at the time to be doing that play, but he was extremely pleased with the results. I think I can now bring a clarity to his work which is reasonably objective no matter how passionate I am about the plays themselves and I think that's increasing as I get older. I'm looking forward to doing some more.

LD: *Apart from the original Rough Magic actors, you've developed very close working relationships with a number of specific actors that you work with again and again. How important are those relationships to your work as a director?*

LP: They're vital. One of the reasons I went into theatre is because it's an extremely social profession. I can't work with people I don't get on with. Well, I have done once or twice, but it makes the load a lot lighter if you've got people who you can have a bit of a laugh with. It's very important because it's really hard to get plays right and people have to have a sense of humour, and that lightness of touch is part of the creativity. People can't work, in my opinion, unless they're relaxed, unless they're clear. That doesn't mean you just fall around laughing all the time, but with a good sense of humour and a sense of proportion you can overcome problems. That's what you're there to do. That relationship is what ensemble work really means.

LD: *Indeed you are renowned for your ensemble work with actors. I think immediately of the most recent show,* Midden, *and of* Pentecost. *Would you consider yourself to be an actors' director? Do you think actors enjoy working with you in the rehearsal room?*

LP: Well, I hope that they do enjoy working with me. What I feel foremost is that I am the audience's director. I think that's my first responsibility. Once you employ actors with brains, which are the very, very best kind, they themselves take on much of the responsibility for their performance. And of course, there's interaction with me and the other actors. But what I feel I'm there to do is to say to them; "If you intend to do this, then something else is coming across." That to me is the director's most important job. What it basically comes down to is that what the audience sees is what the actor really wants them to see.

LD: *It's quite similar to the way I view the work of a literary manager actually, only the literary manager is obviously working with the writer. I believe that the literary manager must act as an educated and informed audience member, in advance of putting the play in front of an actual audience. It sounds like a very similar process. And speaking of writers, where do you see the writer fitting into the equation? I mean particularly in terms of new writing and how the writer relates to the actors and the director and the rehearsal process?*

LP: I think it's quite important that the writer's work is done before you get into the rehearsal room. I mean the main bulk of the work. Because that's the template, that's what we're all there to work with and represent. Once the writer is involved in massive changes within the rehearsal process, it becomes a different process altogether, and it creates all sorts of pressures. I think that the writer's vision should be kept very clear, and subject only to them. The process of getting that vision to the audience is what myself and the actors do. If that vision is complete and strong, then what we do is simply mould it in various ways so that it's clear, and it has the correct pace and correct narrative. I haven't worked in a situation where the writer would be within the rehearsal process, making changes according to the dictates of the rehearsal room. I'm sure that can work but it wouldn't be my way.

LD: *So your approach to a new play would be quite similar to an existing text, or do you approach them in different ways?*

LP: I think it comes down to the same thing. You simply have to look at what works. Sometimes with an old play, things that worked in the eighteenth century simply won't work anymore, or they have to be translated. That's the job of the director, and the imagination of the company. But the rule I would put down is that you don't cut until you're absolutely sure that you've tried everything else. Whereas with a new play, with the writer on call, you've got that authority to rely on. You can make those changes quite quickly.

LD: *And when it comes to working with designers, do you find that your earlier forays into that area benefit you now? Do you enjoy the process of conceiving a design with a designer?*

LP: Yes, I do. I like the interaction with the whole production team. The stage management and technicians and all of that. I love working with lighting designers. That's one of the great pleasures for me. That's why I love the technical rehearsal. Then you get to play with a big paint box. That's part of the fun for me. Whereas a lot of people regard it as quite stressful.

LD: *You mentioned eighteenth century plays earlier. Everyone who knows your work is aware that you have a particular passion for these plays.*

LP: That comes, I suppose, from loving really dark comedy and comedy of manners; that whole presentation of a society. That is why I love the work of Wycherley and Congreve and Sheridan and then up past the eighteenth century, to Wilde and Coward, (whom I'd love to attempt at some point), because I think they render the human condition with incredible style and wit, and that's fantastically entertaining for me.

LD: *You're on record as saying that some of your more inventive productions, like the cross-dressing version of* Lady Windermere's Fan *for example, were born out of economic necessity. Would you consider that that economic situation fuelled you creatively?*

LP: Absolutely. Because you're looking at a practical solution. But I would hope it was also a very entertaining one. Wilde had been very relegated to a drawing room atmosphere for a while and I wanted to get him out into the theatre again and put a bit of rumbustionness back into the performance. He's an immensely classy and polished writer but he's also got an enormous sense of mischief. He loved cross-dressing himself. There's a wonderful portrait of him as Salome. It's just divine. We didn't cut a word of the play, we kept the rhythms very true and we kept the central character as a woman. The rest of it was a little bit of a circus, I suppose.

LD: *Rough Magic has done less of that type of work in recent years. Why is that?*

LP: Well, it's very expensive for one thing. And we also felt we wanted to concentrate on the international work. It doesn't mean to say we'll never do another eighteenth century play again. I'd hate to think that. Also, one of our recent plays, *The Whisperers*, was both new writing and eighteenth century, because it came from two writers (Frances Sheridan and Elizabeth Kuti). That work will be done again, but not in the immediate future. You just can't do everything at once.

LD: *A lot of the theatrical references you made throughout this interview were to theatres and individuals in the UK. This obviously reflects the fact that you have worked a lot in Britain, particularly at the Bush, the Almeida and most recently on the main stage at the RSC. Are you proud of these achievements?*

LP: Yes, absolutely. It is always great to be invited to do work elsewhere. It's good for the ego, good for your creativity and it also exposes you to different systems, structures and ways of working. It was particularly interesting to work at the RSC and to see what an impressive machine it is, the level of support that is available and the facilities. It is also good to be invited to work on Shakespeare and other English plays and not just Irish work all the time.

LD: *Is this because you would have previously been invited to direct only "Irish" plays?*

LP: Initially, yes. Which is to be expected of course. What is exciting for me, however, is that there are so many different styles or types of the English language, each with its own rhythms and challenges. I am obviously used to working with plays written in "Irish" English. Working in the UK, however, gives me the opportunity to work with plays written in Shakespearean English and the many different dialects of modern English that are now spoken.

LD: *Does your work in Britain also give you the opportunity to work with designers and actors who you wouldn't have worked with before?*

LP: Well yes, even though I usually do bring Irish designers and many Irish actors with me. It gives me the opportunity, however, to work with really wonderful British actors such as David Troughton and Sheila Gish, whom I wouldn't have access to otherwise.

LD: *And you are now also an Associate Director of the National Theatre here in Ireland. Do you subscribe to the argument, however, that the Abbey failed to support young directors from the independent sector at a time when that support was most needed?*

LP: Yes I do think that for a certain period both the Abbey and the Gate failed to provide that support. The reason why Declan and I formed the company in the first place was because there was quite simply nowhere for us to go to direct plays when we left College unless we established our own company. The Abbey had abandoned its directors' training programme and in many ways that very lack of support created the proliferation of independent companies that sprang up in the 1980s. There are now, of course, many, many more companies claiming a right to public subsidy for their work, which may ultimately be to the disadvantage of the Abbey and the Gate. The lesson to be learned, in fact, is that the established theatres ignore the independent sector at their peril.

LD: *Do you think that many directors may have been lost to Irish theatre during that time because they didn't manage to hang in there long enough for those new structures to be put in place.*

LP: No, I'm not sure that I agree with that. One of the many characteristics required of a director is pugnacity and a refusal to give up. I think if a director really wants to make work they will find a way to do so.

LD: *And do you think that situation has changed now?*

LP: Oh yes, most certainly. Since Garry (Hynes) became Artistic Director in fact there has been a very real change. The doors have opened quite literally and I think that attitude has prevailed through Patrick Mason and now Ben Barnes. Patrick obviously brought in young directors like Jimmy Fay and Conall Morrison and what we have now is a much healthier situation whereby there is now cross-fertilization of directors in the same way that there has always been a cross-fertilization of actors and designers.

LD: *Does the opportunity to work at the Abbey allow you to work on projects that wouldn't fall within Rough Magic's brief? Are you less limited now, in a sense?*

LP: Well firstly, I wouldn't like to think that Rough Magic's artistic brief is in anyway limited, in fact I like to think that we are now in a situation whereby Rough Magic can respond to any artistic challenge and I don't think the company's policies are set in stones in anyway. Having said that I do believe that Ben Barnes is doing some very exciting things at the Abbey and I am delighted to have a chance to be a part of that. Take the Murphy festival for example. That is a project that Rough Magic would possibly never undertake, even though we obviously have a long and deep respect for Tom Murphy, so it's great to be able to be a part of that at the Abbey.

LD: *And what about Rough Magic's future? Would you agree that the company has now re-established itself firmly after a few rocky years?*

LP: Yes. The company has recently gone through a very significant process of change and had come out the other end strengthened and enhanced. There is now a new management structure in place, a new board and although a theatre company never sails on completely blue water all the time there is a sense of "company" again. We have a new Producer, Deborah Aydon, who came to the company from the Bush Theatre in London where Rough Magic performed many times. Deborah is such an important part of the company now. It is still very much about a collection of individuals creating work together as opposed to an institution of any kind. The establishment of the Literary Department was a very significant development in that process, the need to bring on a new stable of writers and to be in a position to respond to changes in international theatre as they happen.

LD: *The company previously identified the need for its own performance space as a priority for the company. This seems to be less of a priority recently, what with the company's growing relationship with the new Project. What are your feelings now about a permanent home for Rough Magic, and do you think the work of the company has been hampered by the lack of suitable performance spaces in Dublin?*

LP: Yes I do think our work has been hampered, and not only our work, but many other independent companies as well. This is something that I've spoken to Paul Mercier about for example, and I know that he is completely in agreement with me in relation to Passion Machine. There is an enormous need for a dedicated theatre venue in Dublin, as opposed to an arts centre, that is about good theatre one hundred percent. It is impossible to build up an audience and develop a unique performance style without a permanent base.

LD: *So Rough Magic would still hope to have its own space some day.*

LP: Absolutely.

LD: *And would you like to give any indication of when that might happen, I mean are we talking in the short term or medium term or…*

LP: It'll happen.

LD: *And what about theatre in Ireland in general: do you think Irish theatre is in a strong position as we face into the Twenty-first century?*

LP: Well yes I do. Take Dublin, for example, in comparison to other cities of its size like Edinburgh or Glasgow. People in Edinburgh and Glasgow are envious of the proliferation of theatre that is happening in Dublin. This is due to many things like the expansion of the Fringe Festival for example. But I think there are major problems as well, particularly in terms of funding. Companies are being starved of the hard currency that they need to develop professionally.

LD: *And again it appears to be the independent sector that is suffering. In fact, it is probably more difficult for a younger company to get off the ground now than it was when Rough Magic started.*

LP: Absolutely. There is no shortage of people entering the industry now, but they have to work so much harder in order to survive in this city. Dublin is a much more expensive city to live in now than when we started when you could survive on the dole and produce plays all the time. People now have to have two or three other jobs in order to remain in the theatre, and the danger is that the theatre work will become marginalized. I don't envy them at all.

LD: *And what about the future for Lynne Parker? How would you like to see your own career developing in the future?*

LP: Well, for a start I want to do less work. I've been doing shows back to back now for a couple of years and I need to slow down a bit. I want to be able to pick the plays that I really want to do and be a position to spend more time concentrating on projects in Rough Magic.

LD: *So your future is very much with Rough Magic.*

LP: Absolutely.

LD: *And Rough Magic is here for the long haul?*

LP: Yes, of course. As long as the company is doing good work and we are still enjoying ourselves. Of course.

LD: *That's certainly good to hear.*

Lynne Parker is co-founder and Artistic Director of Rough Magic Theatre Company and an Associate Director of the Abbey Theatre. She has directed over thirty productions for Rough Magic, including plays by Stewart Parker (*Pentecost*), Declan Hughes (*Digging for Fire*), and Gina Moxley (*Danti-Dan*). Recent shows include *Three Days Of Rain* by Richard

Greenberg, *Dead Funny* by Terry Johnson and *Midden* by Morna Regan. She was an associate artist of Charabanc, and has worked with a number of companies in Ireland including the National Theatre, the Gate, Druid, Tinderbox, Opera Theatre Company, and The Corn Exchange. Work in the UK includes shows for the Bush Theatre, 7:84 Scotland, the Almeida Theatre, the Peter Hall Company at the Old Vic, the West Yorkshire Playhouse, Traverse Theatre, Edinburgh, and the Royal Shakespeare Company.

Loughlin Deegan is Literary Manager with Rough Magic Theatre Company. For the Theatre Shop he has edited the *Irish Theatre Handbook*, a comprehensive guide to drama and dance in Ireland, North and South, now in its second edition. For the same organization he is currently compiling the Irish Playography, a catalogue of new plays produced by professional theatre companies in Ireland between 1897 and the present. Loughlin is also the new writing editor for *Irish Theatre Magazine*. Loughlin's playwriting credits include *The Stomping Ground* (1997) and *The Queen and Peacock* (2000 and 2001), both produced by Red Kettle Theatre Company.

Billy Roche in Conversation with Conor McPherson

CMcP: *I think a good place to start would be to tell us about your new play, what's it called?*

BR: Well, the new play is called *On Such As We*, the line was stolen from a song which goes something like this: "We are poor little lambs who have lost our way, Ba, Ba, Ba, little black sheep, who have gone astray, Ba, Ba, Ba. Gentlemen, songsters, out on a spree, doomed from here to eternity, may the Lord have mercy on such as we, Ba, Ba, Ba." So you can see there is the line and also the line "from here to eternity" is in there somewhere as well; the film, *From Here to Eternity* comes from that as well. Strangely enough I was doing a show in Wexford recently, a one-man-show and I realized that this song had actually appeared in my first novel, *Tumbling Down*. Everything I have written actually stems from that little book. I realized that all of my themes are in there, in an innocent kind of a way.

CMcP: *Yeah, I think that if there is a recurring theme in your work, you can tell me if it is in this new play as well, it is this idea of being lost. Have mercy on such as we, it is kind of looking for some kind of help or looking for some kind of comfort. It seems to be a very universal theme and I think it is probably what people relate to in your work. I think that people take your plays quite personally and remember them.*

BR: I think redemption, forgiveness and understanding are prominent. I do get surprised at how judgmental people can be about little things, about other people's misdemeanors and sexual adventures, and they take it all so personally, "but what has it got to do with you?" People live their own lives and the person that doesn't go astray, is a person that I don't particularly want to meet. When I wrote *Tumbling Down* I wouldn't have had any notion of metaphors or allegories or themes, I was just literally writing a novel. As I went to do this one-man-show everything pointed back to that novel. Actually I was on stage when I realized it.

CMcP: *I think that when you look at a writer there does tend to be the same refrain going through the work; if you are inspired to write, it is probably going to be the powerful thing that is going to drive you.*

BR: That's interesting because I have been reading John Banville a lot, an amazing writer, and if you trace back through his books, you find a linking story that he always knew right from the word go. At a reading recently in Enniscorthy, somebody said to him "why do you keep writing the same book all of the time?" And it is beautiful that the story is one he just keeps telling all the time, just from a different perspective. And always at the heart of it there is always an extremely articulate lost soul, who is desperately trying to be stoic against the world. I have to say that I admire him and envy the fact that he has discovered this personal myth. I know that Ted Hughes reckoned that Shakespeare also had an equation that he was trying to work out and that it ran through all of his plays, even the comedies, with the male trying to come to terms with the feminine aspect of life. He wouldn't have written so many plays had he not got some kind of – formula is the wrong word – equation into the work.

CMcP: *It's a kind of an engine, that's always kind of motoring away. You're never quite right, so you try again and again. So how do you think that such a theme manifests itself in* On Such As We? *What's the story?*

BR: Well, it's set in a Wexford barber shop and Oweney, who at forty is separated from his wife and family, has been around the block a few times and as one character says "Why did you leave your wife?" and he says "Well I didn't leave her, she put me out," and he asks "Well what did you do?" He replies "Well rambling and gambling and staying out late at night." Living above the shop is a young artist and there is a hotel porter that comes straight from the orphanage into the hotel and the hotel has closed down, he now goes out into the world and he is alone. So really the shop is buzzing with orphans of every description, not necessarily literally, but they are all lost and alone and Oweney is kind of a lonely angel who guides them all into a safe harbour. That is the theme really of the piece.

CMcP: *I relate very much to your work and I think that it is what my plays are about as well, it's about that search for comfort and I wonder if it is because you feel out of step with everything? Have you always felt that you need to somehow explore your place in the world?*

BR: Well absolutely, I was reared in a small town. Lucky enough, it was a town that looked out rather than in, we were not a ceilí town, we looked out to pop music and Hollywood and everyone went to the cinema and everyone listened to pop music as opposed to listening to Radio Eireann. I always said that the quintessential Wexford man has no idea that he belongs to a small town. He thinks that he comes from a big cosmopolitan place with the Opera Festival and things like that. We were born into this world daring to dream. Nevertheless it was a rather small town and you can imagine having these dreams in your head. Very often small town people think that having gone into theatre you might have joined an amateur dramatic group. But that was never for me because I was thinking more of Broadway and the West-End. When I first began writing my first play, *A Handful of Stars*, it had loads of locations in it: it was the snooker hall, the factory and the street. I remember Patrick Mason desperately trying to guide me into the one spot and at the time I was thinking, no the set is going to be coming down out of the ceiling and up out of the ground. And I knew nothing about the mechanics of theatre. I learned that lesson, as it was, it wasn't going to be feasible to put this play on, so I re-worked it. But I think that that's right for a new writer to dream like that.

CMcP: *This theme that you come back to of someone staring at a handful of stars and people who are out of step, the dynamic that really seems to drive your work is the difference of those who know it and those who don't, essentially. Everybody seems to be out of step but there are then ones who are sort of cowboys who cover that insecurity with a lot of talk and a lot of boasting and putting people down and setting themselves up as some sort of judge and jury and then there are the characters who are watching really from the sidelines. And it is those kinds of characters who always emerge quietly as the heroes of your plays. I am just wondering personally what your own sense of morality would be? There seems to be a lot of sympathy for characters who are dysfunctional or unhappy in your work. In* A Handful of Stars, *the character Jimmy is a lawbreaker, but the play does essentially seem to be on his side in the sense that we hear his story and in the sense that somebody has to fulfill that role in the community. Do you have that sort of ambiguous sense that you wouldn't judge somebody?*

BR: Certainly for Jimmy Brady his destiny lies in what happened. That is his destiny. His destiny is also to give other people wings in some way. Without somebody like that, nothing would have happened. We would be stuck in a doldrum. Really you shouldn't like him; the audience shouldn't have sympathy for Jimmy Brady because he is a pain in the neck. So I do like to challenge the actor and myself as a writer. For instance I am writing a screenplay at the moment about a hurling hero – an Irish version of *This Sporting Life* or a *Raging Bull*, if you like. This guy is just impossible, but somehow as a writer I have to learn to love him and I have to hope that you love him too, in spite of all of the things that he does.

CMcP: *Do you think that a production which works on that level and has managed to bring those seemingly conflicting things together, do you think that it serves a kind of function in the community?*

BR: Yes I do. I don't write it from a social point of view. But it was interesting at *A Handful of Stars*, so many older women would come and say "that poor chap" and in real life I am sure they'd say "it serves him right." Stephen in *Poor Beast in the Rain* is a very morose and sad creature. People say it is because his wife left him. No, I say, Stephen is like that anyway. If she had stayed, he probably would have been like that anyway. He'd probably feel more control but that is the way he always was. That's why he lost her.

CMcP: *The response to your plays is always very warm: it is very emotional, human. I would say a very open and lovely response to your work which is heartfelt and I think it is because people identify with the fundamentals because I think that you are writing about very primal instincts that people have, which probably aren't even very articulatable, for instance, love in* Poor Beast in the Rain. *Georgie is completely besotted with Eileen and you know just the way the play is structured that it is never to be. He really drinks her in every time that he looks at her. I think that because you are unashamed to write about that stuff in a very direct and honest way it allows people to identify and I think probably take away something from your plays which you really are not even aware of.*

BR: On the good days at the office you do see it, that thing, and then it disappears and you just get on with making the work and it is always a lovely surprise when you can feel that certain something in the audience and you know you have everyone connected. Because it is a risky thing that we do. Nothing might happen, if an audience is not tuned in. I have been very lucky with actors. The acting has to be impeccable. There is just no way that you can fake this stuff at all. So if you get all of the elements right and everybody is tuned in, then it can be a beautiful feeling. Plays have to work on the off-nights too and maybe they don't work so well if everybody is not tuned in or if you happen to have a cynical audience for example.

CMcP: *I think that your plays are different from what might be deemed fashionable work, which comes with some stamp of academic approval. In Ireland, the plays that are regarded as very good plays always seem to be intellectually challenging in the sense that I think that people like Frank McGuinness, who is an academic, writes about major themes, historical themes.*

Tom Murphy, for example, with his best play, The Gigli Concert, *is really exploring a whole notion, but on a very rational level. I think that your work is really much more than that. If you have got a big play, which is a play of ideas, the actors on an off-night still convey that, whereas I think that your plays always need a 110% commitment from the actors because it is about much more than what you can talk about.*

BR: One of my favourite books is *The White Goddess.* One little secret in there is that you hide it in the long grass. It is difficult to do. As a writer I usually sit down to write a scene and decide what I have to say in that scene and then I have to proceed not to say it. How does an audience figure out what it is, without me saying it? The first draft is always quite vulgar, if you can be brave enough to take it out, you are playing to the best minds, you imagine a very imaginative audience.

CMcP: *The thing about your work as well is that it needs that essential credibility, it needs that someone isn't suddenly saying "listen to me." Your plays tend to have a strong realistic basis. I know that you never would do something that was banal and just capturing life, for capturing something very accurately could be very boring. You have a great craft in that you make it seem as though these people are saying these things for the first time because they are inarticulate: and that is the trick. Most people, if they have a problem, don't really express it and it is how you convey that…*

BR: They say everything except that. I just want to say something about the things I learned growing up in my father's waterfront bar in Wexford. People say to me you must have listened to a lot of talk. Yeah I did. But nobody ever said anything. No man ever divulged a single secret out loud. They never spoke about sex, never spoke about marriage, about love. So I wonder what really happened in the five or six years that I was behind the counter. I think I learned what we don't say to one another basically, what's lying in the middle of it all really. But it is a theatrical trick really isn't it? If you look back through many plays you will find an exceptionally articulate character who is, by accident, able to use every word in the English dictionary if he has to. He is a professor or something. Therefore the world is your oyster. It is a beautiful theatrical trick that you could use if you wanted to.

CMcP: *I think that there is that tradition in Tom Murphy's play* Too late for Logic: *to have the central character as an academic suddenly does free the writer up to go anywhere that he wants.*

BR: Yes, it is a brilliant device. And Tom has an amazing mind anyway.

CMcP: *He is very brave.*

BR: Very, very brave. He would be one of my heroes and one of the reasons why I became a writer. You see one of his plays, and you think that you have the measure of it and then he goes "bing" and it's somewhere else.

CMcP: *It is like good music, suddenly when you think that it cannot go anywhere...*

BR: It changes key and it moves into a minor or something; it is a diminished cord or an augmented cord you did not expect. He is very operatic, a very musical writer.

CMcP: *He is a great mixture of head and heart and his instinct is very strong in his plays and as you say his mind is...*

BR: He writes from the libido really. When I was first thinking about theatre as a young actor and eventually as a young writer, there were only four or five playwrights in this country, Murphy, Brian Friel, Hugh Leonard, Tom Kilroy and John B Keane, that we could look to. We were all suffering from a severe inferiority complex, because Irish people couldn't direct, they couldn't be the boss. It takes a fair amount of ego to write a play and the country didn't have that. And now it is amazing, you throw a stone out your backdoor and you hit a playwright in the back of the neck.

CMcP: *Do you feel that it is mostly good work?*

BR: I feel some of it is very exciting work. Cinema has played a big influence and that is not a bad thing. I think traditionalists would say that it is a bad thing, but I don't think that it is. I think that what we learn from cinema is that audiences are not stupid, that they don't have to be told something three times, they just have to see it, you might not even have to say it at all. Until recently it was almost unheard of to see a scene without any words being spoken. If an audience get it without you saying, it is much more beautiful.

CMcP: *I don't know if you know that film* Big Night *and the final scene of that when these two brothers had this terrible fight on the beach and the final scene is that one of them just makes an omelet and we just watch this for 5 minutes while the other one just sits there and they just divide it up, and he puts his arm on his brother's shoulder. I remember talking to one of the actresses who was in that film and I remember asking her about that. She was saying that Stanley Tucci and Campbell Scott knew from being actors that the whole system of filmmaking was that they would be asked by the financiers, "Why can't we cut in here?" What they did was just shoot it from an angle and just leave it, and that was the only ending. They couldn't do a thing about it. But they knew that if they had alternatives, then alternatives would have been used. What you have is a much more powerful ending.*

BR: A film that did the same thing for me was a re-make of *The Browning Version* with Albert Finney, a gentle, beautiful film.

CMcP: *I would imagine the type of writer you are, you probably have had a hard time working in the film business, I am not sure how much you worked in it, but I would imagine that it would be very difficult.*

BR: Yeah, I got lucky with *Trojan Eddie*. I had this idea and a producer brought me over and we got lucky straight away. We got the go-ahead to write it anyway and it seemed to get made without too many problems and they didn't change a line. Since then, I thought that was going to be the norm that I would write every time I wanted to and it would be made. But it is a problem area, because reading my stuff is tricky for them. I don't think the cinema world in general is big into subtext. Everything I do is hidden in subtext.

CMcP: *I think the problem is that there are an awful lot of people who work in the film business who really want to work in the film business for the sake of it, they don't necessarily have a story to tell. The way that they protect their job is to give a film which people can exhibit in cinemas and they know that people will come and buy the popcorn. That usually means bankable stars.*

BR: If the story can be told quickly.

CMcP: *That's it, and that it can be told in a couple of lines because the big stars' agents will pass it on. That struck me when I went out to Los Angeles and I was working with a studio. That place is the story-telling capital of the world and no one has a story to tell out there, nobody has one. They just have ideas, and if a studio likes them, that suddenly becomes their story. They don't really have an instinctive need to communicate.*

BR: I get calls from people all the time, it is diminishing now, "Would I adapt this story? They don't understand. I am not a journeyman. I could do it, but I couldn't guarantee that I would pull the job off but when I write it comes from somewhere inside me. I suppose if I had to do it to make a living, I could apply myself. I don't want to and it wouldn't be right and right now I don't need to. But they don't understand that obviously.

CMcP: *To adapt a novel…*

BR: Or something like that.

CMcP: *It is a funny story. The screenwriter, Robert Towne, best known for writing* Chinatown, *said he was asked when they were going to make a film of* The Great Gatsby *would he adapt it and he said that he refused because he said that it is a great book and he loves the book, but he said that it is a mirage and he said that he felt that there really isn't a character of Gatsby in* *the book. It is just so beautifully written that there is a nobody at the centre and he didn't understand how he could show that cinematically and he said that he decided not to do it because he would be famous for being the nobody who fucked up a great book. "Who do you think you are, that's a great book it should have just been an easy film?" I think that he was right, everything isn't necessarily a film…*

BR: That's right, sometimes they say the better the book the worse the film, bad books make good films. One of my favourite films of all time is *Cool Hand Luke*, I don't know if it is a novel or not, maybe it is, and if it is, it is probably a fairly mediocre one.

CMcP: *Because it is plot driven. A brilliant film. The directors that you have worked with, just to get back to your theatre work, Robin Lefevre, who has been a longtime collaborator and now it seems that you have a relationship with Wilson Milam. This will be the fourth of your plays that he will have directed? What do you look for in a director of your work?*

BR: Music.

CMcP: *Music?*

BR: Because if he picks the wrong track he's gone.

CMcP: *That's it?*

BR: Yeah, absolutely. If I have a drink with someone and I can see that they are musical, and on the right wave-length. When we did *A Handful of Stars*, my first play, I was unaware of Robin's previous work. And during rehearsals, when we came to the end of the play I suggested Johnny Rotten from the band Pill, doing "I should be right, I should be wrong." So I gave him the tape and asked him to have a listen overnight to it. Next morning he came in and said, "yeah, you are right about that." So he heard it, knew it. On one of the nights during the previews I was sitting beside this young couple, and when that song came on at the end, the guy lit up. It was one of those things you never forget that you see in small theatres, when they don't know who you are. A less musical director would not have seen that effect.

CMcP: *Robin makes decisions very quickly and he sticks to them.*

BR: Absolutely.

CMcP: *Once they are made, I think that he is someone who would suit your work very well because he trusts his instinct implicitly and I have worked with directors who talk around an issue for a very long time, until reaching some sort of agreement with the actor which may last and may not last. Robin is always very strong…*

BR: Very strong, he has a brilliant directorial mind. He makes that decision and lives with it. When we did *Belfry* for the first time, there was one line that neither of us was sure about. Artie, at the end of the play, says that he has been seeing another woman, a young widow called Rita. He claims that he met her at the bacon factory re-union. Robin was unsure and he kept pushing me. "Maybe it is vulgar." The fact is that Artie found love in the strangest of places. It was decided just to leave it in for a preview and see what happens. On the line, that first night, there was a great response from the audience. He was sitting behind me and just tapped me on the shoulder. We never spoke about it ever again. That line is there for life now and I would have taken it out had he pushed me, as I was unsure too. The audience got the exact message that someone could find love at a bacon factory re-union. Unbelievable really, even to go to a bacon factory re-union. Robin has those wonderful decisive powers really.

CMcP: *There are always those small things in your plays, like where you say "the bacon factory" and suddenly the whole thing resonates, because everybody has this idea of a place, and it probably slightly jars and you have to start thinking about it for a second and that makes it all the more real. There is the priest in* Belfry, *who is terribly lonely and there is a whole play in him and at the beginning of Act Two, we get his story and it is really left as a whole sort of open book to be explored and it is very sad really. Robin is a good collaborator in a sense that he will allow it to breathe and just to leave it, where another director would probably try to drive you to resolve it.*

BR: And do a little more. When I started to write Father Pat in *Belfry*, I was as riddled with prejudice as any young man would be in this country. He was going to be a typical priest and he just refused to be. I learned so much from that. I know a young man who had become a priest and had left the priesthood. After he saw that play many times, he went back in again and I am not saying because of the play. He was going through a really hard time. He must have thought that you can be a priest and be human at the same time.

CMcP: *The play helped him to crystalize what he was thinking about.*

BR: I hope so. It is a very hard life.

CMcP: *Fr. Pat, he is a young man and it is a dying breed. You don't get the young bucks going into the priesthood. So he really is a very isolated character.*

BR: He clearly believes. For Fr. Pat, the Mass is not just symbolism. God is coming down onto that altar. It is an amazing mystery, when you take it apart. I was in New York for St Patrick's Day and we went into Mass, and to hear a priest with a New York accent celebrate "the mystery of the mass." It put a whole new spin on it. The mystery of the Mass, I had forgotten about those words. Taking it from that ritualistic, almost pagan origin, it is almost incredible.

CMcP: *Particularly when Fr. Pat describes himself seeing a woman on the other side of the road with a small family, the details of when he was studying in Rome and his description of the swish of the girl's skirt that he befriended. It is in those tiny details that the devastating recognition comes to your work. I think that you have almost a painter's eye for what will register with people. Do you think that you have a good visual sense?*

BR: Always for me it starts with the visual. It will never be a kitchen sink. I think that there is an aesthetic that we owe to our audience that when they come in and the lights go out, it is a painting in itself. The new play at the Abbey has a painter who lives upstairs, every scene is one of his paintings. The director has that clear vision of a visual aesthetic. That is essential.

CMcP: *In a way it stems from the fact that all of your life you have worked as a showman in one way and you know how important it is not to let your audience down.*

BR: Absolutely. My job as a singer – and I couldn't do it now, you lose the power – I played all over Ireland and I played in some of the roughest bars. My job as a front man of that band was to make them look at me. And they did. They might not necessarily like me, but they were going to look at me.

CMcP: *And your job was to make them forget about everything else.*

BR: There for an hour and a half, whatever it takes. There was quite a theatrical quality to the Roche band. There was a kind of a Chaplinesque quality to the character I played. I would put that suit on me and forget that two hours previously I had just come out of a factory somewhere.

CMcP: *Where do you think that confidence came from with you? Is it a feeling or restlessness that you want to shake things up a bit or do you think that it is more an ego thing?*

BR: Ego certainly drives you out there. But I always was attracted to performance. I think in a strange way that the character I played in the band, is not unlike many of the characters in the plays: Oweney, in my new play, and Artie and Joe from *Poor Beast in the Rain*. Everyman. There was a hidden depth to Artie that he didn't know about. In fact *Belfry* was supposed to be about the barber. I set out to write this play, I didn't know what this story was going to be, maybe they met every Thursday in the Barber shop and played poker. Men that came over were going to tell me about Oweney.

There was a women involved who ran a boutique across the street, she was going to be the beautiful aspect to the play. The first one I elected to talk was a lonely mammy's boy, middle-aged sacristan. When he started to talk he said, I know what they think of me, I know what they say about me behind me back. "There he goes, Artie O'Leary." And this was complete news to me. I went with *Belfry* and saw where it took me.

CMcP: *So now your new play has come back to the barber. Tell me about your journey towards production, how has it ended up at the Abbey?*

BR: Well it was a long haul, the story first emerged way back in *Belfry*. Then I was asked to write a six-part love story for the BBC and Oweney became one of the characters in there, as did the hurling hero that I am now writing a film about. There were going to be six stories, the first one was concentrated on the hurler and the last one was going to end with the hurler, and minor characters in one episode became major characters in the next episode. Oweney and his barber shop, and his love story were in there. The love story refused to die really. When all of that fell through eventually, it simply wasn't going to be made, I decided to turn it into a stage play and it happened quite organically. I married a few stories together to make the play.

CMcP: *Where do you think that it should go if you have a new play, do you have a theatre that you would ideally like it to happen in?*

BR: After you write it, that's the hard part of it isn't it, "who" and "when." In some ways, who will mind it the best. Who will take care of it? One of the things that would make me go back to novel writing is all those problems. Who directs? Who acts? Who lights? Where? When? At that stage you are at someone else's mercy. Will it go on at all? And if it goes on, will the rest of the world see it? When it slots into place, then it is beautiful of course. I won't take commissions anymore. I just can't deal with it anymore, because you are writing, you are working for somebody. If you can afford it, it is much better not to. It is hard to afford it. My house is falling down with plays that somebody said didn't work. Maybe they do work, but you lose heart and faith. And then you put them in a drawer somewhere. It has taken me about eight or nine years to write a play after *The Cavalcaders*. I have written about three other plays in that time. To write three plays, that nobody ever sees, is a lot of work. I just get absolutely exhausted from trying to make stuff work and maybe not getting feedback. Positive responses are much more important than criticism. I remember talking to a writer who had sent something out and they were going to make this film or whatever it was going to be and they were saying that this is wrong and that is wrong. Eventually he wrote a letter to the producer asking, "Is there anything about my play that you like?" "We love it." "Will you please tell me?" Some of them take that for granted.

CMcP: *These plays that you wrote that you haven't produced, were they commissioned?*

BR: Yes, some of them were commissioned. I tried a few times to write for the Royal Court. Might even be three that went by the board.

CMcP: *I remember reading in Nick Hern's book catalogue that you had a forthcoming play to be published called* Haberdashery *but it never seemed to appear anywhere?*

BR: No. I have been struggling with it for a long time. People have been showing interest in the play, maybe it is slightly flawed or something. I turned it into a short story, which I do on stage now and that lasts about 20 minutes. I condensed all of it down. I am really in love with the story and I am delighted to have found it. I don't know if the play will ever see the light of day. I don't know if it should actually. My mother was dying, and I began working on this short story *Haberdashery*. It was like all hell was breaking loose around me, and I was obsessed with this short story. It was like as if the Gods were giving me something to take my mind off it. So I created it and tried it out on stage a few times actually. I was toying with the idea of going on the road and doing an evening's performance, a kind of modern... *seanachaí* is the wrong word. I don't want it to be a theatrical piece. I don't want it to be a reading, because I do actually perform them. I don't need it to be regarded as a play. I have been trying to write this series of short stories, or tales might be a better word, that are centred around this place called Rainwater Pond. All of them have this mystical place at the centre. One is called *Maggie Angre*. She makes a pilgrimage once a year to the place where her brother Stephen had drowned when she was very young. Ironically, now she is a brilliant swimmer. And she is fat, ugly, chilblained, all the things that a woman is not supposed to be and this is the way that she sees herself. In some ways she comes to this place looking for redemption and forgiveness, of course. She swims out to the spot. *Haberdashery* ended up being another story. I have written about three or four of them now.

CMcP: *How many do you think you would need to publish them?*

BR: I think it might almost be a lifetime's work. I've got to slow down, because I've been panicking on it. I think it might be a ten –

year job. Maybe publish them in magazines in the meantime, to keep them alive. When that panic comes on you...

CMcP: *You are best to leave it. It will come back to you. You cannot go chasing it.*

BR: Some of the themes of those plays that may be in the drawer may end up coming back. I am pretty sure that that will happen. One of them certainly.

CMcP: *What would your relationship be with the theatre administrations in this country, in terms of the people who have the power to produce your play or not?*

BR: I think it is pretty good. I deliberately stay out of the centre of things. I am glad to be living where I live. I don't attend many opening nights. I like to slip in and see a play in my own time, later on, when the fuss has died down. I am not on committees and I don't join boards. Maybe people like us should? Maybe it is a cop-out. I am just not interested in politics of any description. I'd like to go a gentle Sam Shepard route, just plough my own furrow. It will happen. If it doesn't happen, as it didn't with *Amphibians*, I will get up and make it happen.

CMcP: *You directed that yourself and it became a success. The Irish production was a great critical success.*

BR: Yes it was. It broke me, of course. It was not just money, I lost a year's work. I also produced it. I am glad I did. I got on the phone for the first time. I thought three days on the phone and I would sort all the problems out. A year later, I was still on that phone. I acted in it also of course. It may have been a mistake, but I didn't have to pay myself. Also I always wanted to play that part, so I think we should always treat ourselves to stuff we want to do. I don't ever want to say I am sorry I didn't do something.

CMcP: *It seems to me that you have a healthy self-belief. You are quite comfortable with being in an ambiguous place, because you know who you are.*

BR: Most of the time. It is better if you are a little more financially secure. I have to say that it wasn't good when *Amphibians* was over and I was broke. I was trying to fight back up again. That is not easy. I wouldn't want to go there again.

CMcP: *Did you come close to thinking that you might have to do something else for a living?*

BR: Oh no. Never. I could always act.

CMcP: *Or take one of those writing jobs?*

BR: Yes. That is always an option.

CMcP: *I have talked to people about your work and the success of your work. In my opinion, I still think that your work has not hit the audience it deserves. I remember talking to the people at the Bush Theatre, who originally produced* The Wexford Trilogy. *I remember saying to them that I could not really understand why it was not still running at the West-End or Broadway. And maybe that is just my taste. Maybe you and me are wrong. Their reaction was that really nothing like that had ever happened to them before, and they didn't know what to do. Suddenly to have this success, which everybody was vying for and looking at, and wondering would it transfer from a small place to a bigger place. Then I remember talking to them a few years on from that success and their attitude then was that they should have gone on further with it, that it was a missed opportunity. Again, when* The Wexford Trilogy *was done again, brilliantly, by Wilson Milam, it didn't transfer. Do you think that one day* The Trilogy *will hit that* The Steward of Christendom-*type of success?*

BR: There are still talks of that production going out to New York. Maybe it is a tall order to bring three plays to New York. I'd love to go with *The Trilogy*. And I would like New York to begin at the beginning and slowly work all the other plays out there. It is out of my hands. I walk away from productions in America all the time, because I don't like the sound of it or something. I want that first one to go out there to be special.

CMcP: *It is very important that the first one is done right, because it will prolong the life of the play, because people will know how to do it.*

BR: We had Peter McDonald, Michael McIllhatton, Gary Lydon again, Hugh O'Connor, Michael O'Hagan, Rebecca Egan, Elaine Symons, a brilliant team. That cast would be fabulous to send out, as a little band going to New York.

CMcP: *Do you think that the standard of acting in Ireland is as good as it could be?*

BR: It is amazing. We are doing auditions for the upcoming Abbey production and the acting is of an amazing high standard. People that may not have suited the parts, still they gave incredible performances.

CMcP: *Billy Roche. Thanks.*

Billy Roche began his career as a singer/musician, forming The Roach Band in the 1970s. His first novel, *Tumbling Down*, was published by Wolfhound Press in 1986. His first stage play, *A Handful of Stars* was staged at the Bush Theatre in 1988. This was followed by *Poor Beast in the*

Rain. Belfry completed this powerful trilogy at the Bush. All three plays became known as *The Wexford Trilogy* and were performed in their entirety at the Bush, the Peacock, Dublin and the Theatre Royal, Wexford. His fourth play, *Amphibians* was commissioned by the RSC and performed in the Barbican. This was followed by *The Cavalcaders* at the Peacock, Dublin and the Royal Court, London. His latest play *On Such As We* opens at the Abbey in December 2001, directed by Wilson Milam. He wrote the screenplay *Trojan Eddie*. Billy has been Writer-in-Residence at the Bush, writer in Association with Druid and with the Abbey Theatre. As an actor, Billy has appeared in numerous theatre, television and film productions.

Conor McPherson was born in Dublin. He attended University College Dublin where he began to write and direct. He co-founded the Fly by Night Theatre Company, which performed new plays in Dublin's fringe venues. His plays include *Rum and Vodka, The Good Thief, This Lime Tree Bower, St. Nicholas, The Weir, Dublin Carol* and *Port Authority*. He wrote the screenplays for *I Went Down* and *Saltwater*, which he also directed. He directed *Endgame* as part of the *Beckett on Film* series. Recently, he directed Eugene O'Brien's play *Eden* for the Abbey and for BBC Radio 4.

Annie Ryan and Michael West in Conversation with Luke Clancy

LC: *Why did you start to work together?*

AR: Well I came to Dublin in 1989 to escape method acting in New York and I saw Michael's *A Play on Two Chairs* in ISDA, which I was performing in too that year. When I saw Michael's play it really struck me because it looked like it was straight out of the Chicago training that I'd had in improvisation and story theatre and theatre games. In fact, it looked like a piss-take of that work. So I thought, "Here's someone I'd like to work with." So we started to work together that summer and I started telling Michael how to do it. [laughter]

MW: I suppose we started working together and then we stopped all that nonsense to get married. And then once we got married, we sort of settled down and started working together again. In 1999, I did a version of *The Seagull*, which Annie directed, and then *Foley*.

LC: *What was your idea of Irish theatre when you moved to Ireland?*

AR: Well, I didn't really know much about it. I had been here for a year in Trinity, but I didn't really go to the theatre. I mean I never went to the Abbey for the entire year I was here. I just did Players and had a ball. But I sort of knew that I would get a certain amount of respect as a practitioner of what I did, for bringing *commedia* and so forth, whereas people with my training were a dime a dozen in Chicago. Well, perhaps not quite. But there were plenty of people there who knew what I knew. Before I started directing, when we were working together, I was just so on fire to direct that I couldn't stop coming up with ideas. I did a version of *Sexual Perversity in Chicago* that David Parnell directed. I just kept butting in. We ended up using a lot of these ideas, but I suspect he would never work with me again because I just couldn't stop myself coming up with the big picture thing instead of just doing my job.

LC: *What theatrical traditions are you most interested in?*

AR: I was trained in a Chicago style of improvisation, theatre games which led to *commedia*. There is really no method to learning the *commedia* thing. It's a very renegade style from Chicago: it's not really anything to do with the Italians. An actor that was in [Ariane] Mnouchkine's company taught a crowd that was in LA. Actually Tim Robbins' Actors' Gang formed from that. And then John Cusack took that form into Chicago and started up New Crime [Theatre Company], where I was working. So the tradition I learned it from was really these football-playing suburban boys who thought "this company is about "fuck the president," maaan." They were these ridiculous Chicago boys. They had no sense of how you would bring a performer into it, like maybe Mnouchkine does. It was all trial by fire kind of stuff. You literally arrive that day, you get up in makeup that day – in full image with wigs and shoes and whatever you could find – and you get up and do it, with mirrors and lights and drummers. And that way you find character images that work. So that's the way I do it.

MW: What's really great about *commedia* is that you don't worry about motivation, just as long as you're in the present tense. A character comes in and if you have a Pantalone, a high status power-grabber, and you have a stupid servant, well, that's the story already. If you play the emotions, you've already got a scenario. So you don't have to come in with anything other than who you are.

AR: It is a little more difficult to practice that in Ireland, because people are not so versed in improvisation. Whereas in Chicago, everybody grows up improvising all their lives. That doesn't mean that all of us were good at it – I'm not a particularly great improviser. But here, the whole notion of having to improvise is very new for people. So it makes it doubly scary.

LC: *What performance style are you happiest with?*

AR: I would really love the *commedia* work to be the backbone of the company. But two things really set us back from that. One was that we started with *Streetcar* and *Big Bad Woolf* which were illegal shows. We didn't have the rights for them and we did things that we discovered were expressly forbidden.

MW: Williams left a specific prohibition against doing *A Streetcar Named Desire* in drag, believe it or not.

AR: We can't tour them and we can't continue on in that kind of vein. So I've been looking for the perfect *commedia* show to do which would be as exciting as something like *Streetcar*. But the more important thing is that we haven't got the funding to do it. *Foley* was very much a case of we can only afford to do a show with one guy if we are going to get an administrator and pay the actors more than a hundred quid a week. And if we have a hope in hell of building an organization that has any kind of solidity to it. But I'd love to get back to the *commedia* work, because that's the sort of work I want to do.

MW: It's very curious for me, because I felt very involved in those productions [*Streetcar* and *Big Bad Woolf*] but I had no involvement. I was just watching great classics of American literature and theatre being transformed into this lurid, camp, fly-by-night style. But part of what led us away from that was rights. We had to get shows that we could get permission to work with. So we had to choose somebody who was dead, or somebody who was married to the company. So we tried both with Chekhov and me.

LC: *So does* commedia *play a part in an ostensibly naturalistic production like* Foley?

MW: Yes, because Andrew Bennett would have been there from the earlier days, from the first time Annie began working with *commedia* in Dublin, which I think was at a workshop organized by Barabbas when they were starting up. At the time, I think the only other person who had really seen *commedia* was Mikel Murfi, who had worked in that clown style in Paris. But Bennett was there. And worked in the early show. And I think all that informs things like *Foley*, even if it is not always obvious. Though I think sometimes it is very obvious.

AR: The point is really that the *commedia* work is, at the end of the day, a really good tool for naturalism, even though it doesn't look naturalistic. What it does is it breaks every moment down. It makes you see every moment as it happens. If someone is going to pick up a cup, you see how they feel about that. You break the whole thing up into little movements. In naturalism, because you don't have that tight structure of what to do, people "burn their steps" as they say in *commedia*. They leap from one thing to the next, and they miss out all the stuff in between the lines. I mean you still see it a lot in Dublin, in naturalistic productions. People are just saying the lines and jumping to the next bit. Missing out everything that is between the lines. And that is what *commedia* is great at curing, making things seem more naturalistic. After all, what could be more extreme and grotesque than the way we are.

People use their faces and their bodies in a much more extreme way in life than you often see on the stage. Irish actors still stand with their arms stock still – I've really seen actors who don't move their arms in a whole performance. It's really hard to do that; it's kind of impressive. But we move all the time in life, there are all sorts of things going on physically all the time. And the *commedia* work really brings that out. So to bring it back to something as kinda low-key and protestant as *Foley*, there was still all that kind of language going on in the rehearsals, to find the humanity. And I suppose that would be our starting point in working on anything.

LC: *Given how central the performance style is to the company, how much do you think about the style in which things are performed when you are trying to write a piece?*

MW: My interest in writing is kind of two-fold. I started off doing adaptations and translations of European classics, which is concerned very much with the text and old-fashioned unities. That kind of world. But at the same time, I was interested in wordless physical theatre, and in how you could possibly write for that. So I've always been very interested in performance vocabularies and performance styles. But for me, the job in the last two years has been to try and mix those two ideas. And for me, it is usually a warning sign if I start worrying about how this is going to be performed, what physical style should be used. If I'm thinking about that, it usually means I am not paying attention to what I should be doing.

LC: *How do you see yourself in theatre in the future?*

AR: Well the idea is to build a company. What I would really like to do is build a company of actors. Not even so much a formal company, but more a small group of people who are actually versed in the style. The way we have done everything so far is completely backwards. We have done productions in order to teach people *commedia*, whereas what you should have is a troupe who know the style and then do a play. But how do you do that if you are not twenty-one and willing to work for free? So if we can cast maybe four to six people and start there, start workshopping characters and ideas and coming up with something from that group.

LC: *Does it matter what critics write about your work?*

AR: It does matter what the critics say. I mean, we'd never had a bad review in our lives as a company before *The Seagull*. We were used to being terribly popular with critics and the reception we got there was just fantastic!

MW: You have a very small spot in your RAM cache of your brain for what critics say and you usually flush it out quite often. But there was one that just really stuck. "This is a production which robs the word travesty of any meaning." I'll never get a worse review than that.

AR: It was so great. It was fantastic.

MW: I would be interested in talking to members of an anonymous public about how much a critic's opinion influences them. I don't know whether critics actually create opinions or whether they reflect general opinions. I remember going to the Gate and seeing a production of *Arcadia*, which was a play I had read and was interested in. And a guy beside me actually fell asleep in the first act. And then at the interval, he woke up when the lights came back on and said "Isn't the Gate marvellous?" And he was right. He seemed to be having a marvellous time. One of the fallacies about criticism is that you are all supposed to agree with it.

AR: But in a way, the company's only communication with the public is through this person, the critic. You can have your flyers or your posters around the town, or maybe you get a feature page. But reviews are still the most important link.

MW: But there are different types of critics. I mean, the Arts Council are a type of critic because they give you money for what you do. It is impossible not to take that as some sort of criticism too.

LC: *Do you agree that theatre audiences are naturally conservative?*

AR: I think people get excited by exciting things. The whole shape of Dublin has changed so that you have to think about if people are so busy buying nice cars and nice shoes, how do you attract their attention in the first place? Because what is happening in the theatre is not fast or high-tech. It is trying to do something theatrically true or beautiful.

MW: But it is an issue of community really. Which is sort of a separate issue. How do you create a community where people talk about theatre? I mean things like aftershow discussion don't happen here ...

AR: ... they do happen here. They're starting to happen here ...

MW: So where do people find the language to discuss work, to make it or to talk about it? Where do they find the language?

AR: But it is tricky, because it is all so small time. Take any of our shows. I mean, how many people get to see them? *Foley* has toured Ireland. And we would get small, happy audiences and they would be saying "bring it back and this time we'll get everybody to come." But we're never going to tour *Foley* nationwide again. That's it, man. *The Seagull?* That was three weeks in Project. I mean how many hundred people get to see you work? So the work never becomes something that people talk about, like say movies or television shows do.

LC: *What, in Irish theatre, has excited you over the last 10 years?*

AR: Productions always seem to remind you of times. Thinking of something like [Corcadorca's] *Disco Pigs*, in 1996 the boom was really kicking in and it was very exciting.

MW: It is easier to be excited by a visiting show: people you have no preconceptions about; people you have never met; you've never hated their other work. Those are still the experiences that make you say "Oh thank god for festivals." And that is true for most of my favourite experiences. *The Great Hunger* in the Peacock, I suppose. It wasn't my first time in there, but it felt like it.

AR: Something like the [Théâtre de Complicité's] *Street of Crocodiles*, I know it is not an Irish show, but it had such a strong impact when it came here. It made me think "I'm not crazy." "That kind of theatre can work!" "People like it!" "People will go see it!" And when Desperate Optimists first came, you had all the actors in the Clarence Bar giving out about how that sort of work should not be put on stage. The idea that even so recently anything could have such an impact is amazing. And I really liked [Fiona Shaw/Deborah Warner's] *Medea*. I got really excited that something like that could even happen in the Abbey. That was really exciting to see that kind of kickass, fuck off performance. She was so funny and ballsy.

MW: [Eugene O'Brien's] *Eden* was one of the best things I've seen in years. I loved the simplicity of it. It was so totally unembarrassing just to watch two totally fantastic actors be fantastic for the full length of time. I found that such a relief.

LC: *Isn't that sort of the problem with the theatre, in that there are so few ancillary rewards? If you are not enjoying the main thrust of what is going on, then you are just having a bad time. There is no way you can just go, like you might in the cinema, "hmm nice aerial photography of that waterfall, there."*

MW: But the thing is that even when there are a few ancillary rewards, there is no way that they are ever going to make up, in something like the *Barbaric Comedies*, for however many hours of sitting there thinking "that's kind of cool side lighting" and "I never knew the Abbey stage went back that far."

LC: *Is money an issue in relation to your work?*

AR: The way I'd like to work, with a kind of mobile hit squad of people versed in the style, well, that can be very expensive. You can't just rehearse in four weeks and throw something up. We'd be looking at maybe eight weeks, but even that is not nearly enough to become good at the style, to feel that you really know it. With *The Seagull*, for instance, we worked with it for seven weeks. But in the end seven weeks wasn't nearly enough time to explore the kind of things I wanted to explore with it. Eight weeks is only really long enough to start opening up interesting stuff. It is not enough to actually do anything with it. The really great thing is that we have secured the funding to start this up. It took us over a year of hearbreaking applications, but we got it.

MW: One of the things that we thought after *The Seagull* was that we need to do a show that was flexible and viable. In *The Seagull*, all that effort went into a three-week run. We needed to do a show that was cheap to do and could last for more than three weeks. And that is one of the reasons why *Foley* came about.

AR: We actually broke even with our tour of *Foley*, which is actually very hard to do, especially as a legitimate company, with tax, insurance and marketing.

MW: The subsidy on theatre here is enormous. And usually it is subsidized by people working for free or for almost nothing. I mean I can remember working out how much it was costing us to do *The Seagull*, and it was something like £25 a punter if you included the admin costs with tiny wages and the rent. But the price of the tickets was £7. And you think "That's crazy."

AR: But it is a cultural thing too. When I first came here trying to get the *commedia* thing going, I found that you really had to pay people to work, or you had to make them pay. But this thing of "it's free" just did not work. People just did not show up. If there was some exchange of cash, they were either getting something out of it that they were paying for, or it was a job. There was no middle ground. I suppose it is a controversial thing, but if you did have a show where the tickets were much more expensive, maybe people would value the show more. Having said that, there is so much crap theatre, you'd have a lot of irate people on your hands that way.

Annie Ryan was born in Chicago where she learnt *commedia* as well as training with the Piven Theatre Workshop; she also received a BFA from NYU. In 1995 she founded the award-winning Corn Exchange, for whom she has directed *Streetcar, Big Bad Woolf, Baby Jane, Car Show, The Seagull,* and *Foley.*

Michael West: Work for Corn Exchange includes *The Seagull, A Play On Two Chairs,* and *Foley* (which has toured Ireland, the Edinburgh Festival and played at the Hampstead in November 2001). Other recent work includes a translation, *Death and the Ploughman,* a radio play, *The Death Of Naturalism,* and a new piece for theatre, *Another Country.*

Luke Clancy writes about theatre, technology and culture. His work has been seen or heard in various media, including *The Times* (London), *The Evening Herald, The Independent* (London), *The Irish Times, The New York Times, The Boston Globe, The Sydney Morning, Circa, The Guardian, The Face, Art Review, Meridian* (BBC World Service) *The World Tonight* (BBC Radio 4) and *Rattlebag* (RTE Radio 1).

Phyllis Ryan in Conversation with John P. Kelly

JPK: *Phyllis Ryan, let's start at the beginning and for all of us the beginning is now. Tell me what's happening for you in theatre, right now?*

PR: At the moment, I'm in the middle of a production of John B. Keane's *The Matchmaker* which has run since January and has taken us to Edinburgh. We are contemplating a further tour. I am also half-way through another book, which should be the second part of my memoirs, but is turning into something else altogether! I have done a couple of film parts and hope to do a couple more before Christmas. I am very busy. That's the way it should be and that's the way I like it.

JPK: *Looking around you, what do you think of the present state of theatre in Ireland?*

PR: I think it is extremely healthy, I think it's exciting. There are wonderful new young people coming up, young men as well as women, it used to be mostly young men. There is amazing talent in young playwrights. I think theatre is healthier now than I've seen it in many, many years.

JPK: *No complaints at all?*

PR: Well, I think the funding for theatre is a bit haphazard. I do see groups that need money, are doing great work but they are not being funded. I see ridiculous things like the Gate for example, where the standards are extraordinarily high, possibly the highest in the country, and they are being kept short of money. I have no idea why. I don't care what the reasons are, but when you are achieving that kind of excellence, you should be funded properly. Small companies that are showing real talent should be funded properly too. Those who are not pulling their weight shouldn't be getting huge subsidies. I think it is all very unbalanced.

JPK: *Looking back over the last fifteen or twenty years, talk to me about what you see as some of the highlights of theatre in Ireland during that time.*

PR: Last Christmas, we celebrated forty years of Gemini Productions, while Gemini and The Machine Productions were presenting *The Matchmaker* as a tribute to John B. Keane. During that time, there would have been many, many highlights including firsts from Hugh Leonard, John B. and one from Tom Murphy, which he now thinks shouldn't have been done, called *The Orphans*. I thought it contained some brilliant writing. There was a Brian Friel play that was the beginning and maybe a blueprint for some of his greater works. A lot of younger playwrights that we tried to encourage would have been highlights for us, also the amazing number of talented young artistes that we helped to develop and are now famous.

For one of the biggest highlights for other companies I should go back to the sixties and say that Micheál MacLiammóir's first performance in *The Importance of Being Oscar* was a highlight that should not be forgotten. I have seen it many times since but I remember how people were moved, that first time, because the character of Wilde seemed to merge with Micheál, though he wasn't trying to do an impersonation. It was beautiful theatre. Also, Donal McCann's unforgettable *Steward of Christendom*, Sebastian Barry's beautiful play which seemed to be made for Donal. There were many others, like Conor McPherson's play *Port Authority*, which I saw at the Gate Theatre, and his even better play, *The Weir*, and when I went to the Edinburgh Festival recently I saw Conor's one-man show, *Saint Nicholas*, a superb piece of work. I think he is exceptional and as there have been many other up and coming young writers, it really is very exciting. Every time you see a new young writer or a young performer suddenly turning a trick that you don't expect, that's a highlight, isn't it?

JPK: *Can you give us a list of playwrights whom you personally regard as the great playwrights, on a world stage.*

PR: I assume we are leaving Shakespeare behind us here? In the last ten, twenty years, you have to think about Arthur Miller who comes to mind with a *thump* and, of course, I love Brian Friel's works. I have always been a supporter of Hugh Leonard and he has contributed greatly to our lives in Gemini. Tom Murphy is very, very special and Frank McGuinness, Bernard Farrell who is an entertainer, unashamedly so, and hasn't plumbed any great depths and seemingly doesn't want to... yet... but what he has done is very much worth doing and we need that kind of flair for comedy that touches on social issues, which is what Ayckbourn also has. I think that Alan Ayckbourn should be mentioned here. The list is almost endless: Sebastian Barry, Paul Mercier, Roddy Doyle and many others I have seen in the last year. I really can't have favourites.

JPK: *Playwrights need theatres. What do you think of the state of the National Theatre in Ireland?*

PR: Well, to start off with, I was a shareholder there for many, many years. Indeed I grew up there as a child actress and I have a sort of healthy affection for it. I have seen some wonderful eras in the Abbey particularly when Tomás Mac Anna was the Artistic Director. There was extraordinary theatre going on there then. I don't really know what the problem may be now. I think the Board may not be making itself felt enough or maybe it is making itself felt too much but we have had so many Artistic Directors come and go over the last few years, I don't know what all that is about. But I do know that standards tend to slip in between and then rise up again. Sometimes you don't know where you are in the Abbey, you might go in and feel that a production should not be on in the National Theatre, that it's not up to standard and then you go in again and see something brilliant. I don't think they maintain a steady level of excellence and I think that they should. I think they should have their own school of acting and not be bringing us back to academia and having the training done in Trinity. I think that was a bad move. We should have a National Theatre School, where kids who don't have the money or opportunity to go to Trinity can train and as, nowadays, we don't have repertory companies to give them a chance, the Abbey should be providing a school which would not just feed the Abbey with actors, but the world. I know that people from all over the world would go to the National Theatre school of acting.

The Gate theatre has a standard of excellence which it seems able to maintain under Michael Colgan (a very controversial figure but one I happen to be very fond of). Probably the only quibble you might have had would be that they do so many revivals, though they are beginning to break ground more and more with new plays. Mind you, in the old days Micheál MacLiammóir and Hilton Edwards did revivals till the cows came home, restoration comedies, Wilde, Shakespeare and everything else. They don't seem to have been blamed for that. The Gate however was thought culpable because it chose to follow the same path, while the Abbey were trying out all the new plays. The Abbey should get great credit for this. Now the Gate is beginning to challenge them on that ground, which is wonderful.

JPK: *A critic recently asked the question, "Why are there so many revivals" and the answer was "because they work!"*

PR: That must be one of the best things I have heard from a critic.

JPK: *What do you think of the state of theatrical criticism in Ireland?*

PR: Well, I don't think it is any worse today than it has ever been. The problem is that we get people who use theatre, not knowing a great deal about it themselves, to give themselves an importance that they normally wouldn't have. They are not particularly good writers, our critics, though I suppose there are one or two I should exempt from that. In other countries, certainly in Russia, the critics do have to have some training in Ballet or Theatre or Opera, before they are allowed to go and cut their teeth on the performers. Here, you can just be given the job, "Why don't you go out and do a play?" Certainly during a Festival five or six new names will appear who are not normally seen and who may not even be theatregoers. Reading their reviews, one would assume that they were not! I think our critics are not well trained. Often if something is wrong, they don't know why it is wrong. They don't know if it is the play, the director or the acting. They should know these things. The one who gives me a pain in the ….. neck, is the one who tries to be smart at everybody's expense and I think there are far too many of those. I feel better now that I've got that off my chest.

JPK: *Who were the great directors with whom you have had the pleasure to work?*

PR: I think Hilton Edwards was a great theatrical director. Apart from his technical skills, Hilton had to rely on his own imagination a lot. There weren't all the gimmicks around then like memory boards, huge sets, lighting gimmicks and also he didn't have any money. That means you have to use your imagination and Hilton was a creative artist and a very fine actor himself. He was an innovator who brought things into theatre, with no resources. Considering that they had so little money and so little technical wizardry available at the Gate in those days, it was quite incredible what Micheál MacLiammóir did with the sets and what Hilton did with lighting. He was a great director.

I also think that Patrick Mason is a great visual director. However there are directors today who will use huge sets, full of beauty and light behind actors who are sometimes dwarfed by this. You can put a group of talented actors on a bare stage and they will do it for you. Of course, they can be assisted by a well-designed set but they don't need to be dwarfed by it. They don't need to have your eye drawn outside. The playwright wants his words heard. I don't want to look at leaves or lights or stars or clouds moving across skies. That is distracting to me and I want to hear the beauty and poetry of the words. I think there are very few actors' directors nowadays.

I do think that Tomás Mac Anna was one of the great spectacle directors who had a good ear for actors. I don't know who today would be noted as an actors' director, from what I hear from the acting community! I think that Michael Scott has endless creative imagination and again, not being grant-aided very much, uses the sort of imagination that Hilton brought to bear on a production. What actors are crying out for is a director who can turn a key for them; they don't want someone to show them how to do it they just want someone to say "If you are in difficulty, here's a way to open that door."

JPK: *You recently worked with Deborah Warner on* Medea. *Had you worked with a female director before?*

PR: No, that was a first and I must say one of the most exhilarating experiences of my career. Ben Barnes had mentioned to me that although I had been so much associated with the old Abbey I had never performed in the new Abbey and I was thrilled to be offered a part as one of these Corinthian ladies, all individual characters, in the chorus of *Medea*. I must say here that Fiona Shaw was a wonderful Medea. She is a fantastic performer, in an international context. She and Deborah are an extremely strong working combination.

Of course, I had heard about the casualties that usually occur when Deborah is directing a show and so I was looking for the dragon in her, but I honestly didn't find it. I got on very well with her and I liked her. She had an interesting approach to rehearsals and in the early days we played lots of theatre games which I hugely enjoyed and they helped to create a unity within the chorus. We studied Medea's lifetime and interchanged parts with people reading each other's lines which was very stimulating. When the run began, we still got notes every single night and sometimes had to make very late changes. It kept the actors sharp, I can tell you! But Deborah's ways are not for every actor, she can be exhausting and autocratic.

JPK: *Speaking of actors, you must have met so many great ones, good ones, bad ones, tell us about some of them.*

PR: Well, the list is endless as I had the great good fortune to work with the old Abbey company and one of the greatest actors we ever produced was F. J. McCormick. Then of course we had Cyril Cusack whom I worked and acted with a lot and who taught me so much about the business and about the work. We can't forget

Donal McCann but I don't want to shame myself by leaving out some of our other superb actors. We have had so many. We have very fertile soil here and there is a rich imagination in the average person and it breeds the sort of creative ability that acting requires. I have been talking to younger actors and they have a capacity to take on huge creative responsibilities that I don't believe we could have done in our day, at the same age. I think they are further on in some way.

JPK: *What is the central talent that makes a good actor great?*

PR: That's a question that I try to deal with in a chapter in my book, the nature of creativity. I don't know what it is but I would like to know what it is. I am talking to various people at the moment and saying, "Don't tell me that you got this inspiration from a teacher in school or a godmother or something, how did this ability come to you?" John Hurt made a very interesting comment in a radio interview the other day when he said, "All children can act" and I think that is true, though not all children grow up to be actors. He said "You can watch a group of children playing games and one will not be pretending to be the Master of the Universe, or whatever, he will believe that he *is* the Master and he is the one who will go on to be the actor. He really believes it." I thought that was a very apt comment. By the way, anybody who misses John Hurt in *Krapp's Last Tape* is missing a performance of hypnotic brilliance.

JPK: *Whilst I am not going to ask a lady her age, I would like to ask you about your earliest theatrical memories.*

PR: As a senior actor, you are usually asked your age. As Anna Manahan and Des Keogh were so busy with rehearsals for our recent run of John B. Keane's *The Matchmaker*, I had to do most of the publicity interviews for the show. A young man who was conducting a telephone interview for a radio programme talked about the work I had done with my company, Gemini Productions and my late partner, Norman Rodway, and then he asked me my age. I said I would tell him my age if he told me his. He said that he was twenty-three and I said "Aren't you wonderful to be able to conduct an interview, ask intelligent questions and present a programme when you are only twenty-three? It's really amazing." He got the message and said he would never ask anyone their age again. I knew that if I had told him my age, he would have said things like, "Aren't you wonderful at your age to be still working?" The point is, either you are able to do it or you're not. It doesn't matter at all what age you are.

JPK: *Take me back to the days when you started in theatre.*

PR: I was in the Abbey in the late forties and fifties and was lucky enough to be in the School of Acting and at age twelve I was the only one under the age of eighteen. The actresses who were then playing schoolgirls in the Abbey were getting a bit long in the tooth, many of them were over thirty and to me of course they seemed to be really old. I was there for pageboys and all the younger roles. In a way I came to acting accidentally as until I was eleven, I thought I was going to be a great musician, having learned piano from the age of five. Hilton Edwards once said to me, "You and I are failed musicians but look at what we did instead!" I was doing an exam once and the English examiner told me that though I had got the best marks overall, I was not the best performer. Some of the others had better interpretative skills, but he told me "Don't be too upset as you will do something very creative, I just don't think it will be music." I was heartbroken. I remember telling Micheál MacLiammóir, who was very good with children, what had happened and he said, "Darling, I think you are being a bit over the top about being a failed musician at eleven. I think you will become an actress so why don't you think about that and become one of us?" I felt it was the next best thing and went for it.

JPK: *What sort of roles did you play?*

PR: Well, I played child roles – sometimes little boys and I played the little girl in that lovely play of Denis Johnston's, *The Moon in the Yellow River*. At sixteen, I got my big break – Bridget in *Shadow and Substance*. That was amazing. A few years later, I had a run-in with Ernest Blythe who wanted us all to be Gaelic speakers as well and I hadn't had any school emphasis on that, though I would love to have been fluent in Irish and still would. I couldn't see the point for a once-a-year play and refused to go to the Gaeltacht. I really didn't like Ernest Blythe and decided it was time to move on.

I then played almost everywhere as I was very well known as a young actress and almost any theatre you could name that had a play on, I was in there somewhere. I played in *Happy as Larry* and other plays in England and I toured with the late Ronnie and Maureen Ibbs and their company, The Irish Theatre Company, on an American tour. That was when I thought I might like to do what they were doing, producing plays and finding new writers. In 1958 I found a little premises in Ely Place, the old Pocket Theatre and brought in artistes like Anna Manahan and my own daughter, Jacqueline, who had starred on TV and film. Micheál MacLiammóir in the Gate lent me costumes. They all thought it was a fun thing I was doing. It was called *Guided Mistletoe* because of the guided missiles during the war and was a huge success. When the late Godfrey Quigley left the Globe Theatre in Dun Laoghaire where I had seen so many wonderful things, I moved in there.

JPK: *Tell us about some of the memorable people you knew at that time.*

PR: Well, there was the Globe Theatre and Norman Rodway, a leading actor of the time, who subsequently became my partner. My company name was Orion Productions and was named after a star belt, in a play on my name. When Norman joined us about a year later he said we should stick with the star name, which had been lucky for me, and we became Gemini. We did all the plays other managements wouldn't do, like Tennessee Williams' *Cat on a Hot Tin Roof,* which was banned even in England. We were asked to leave the theatre or take the play off, but we dug in until it became dangerous. We didn't want to lose the Gas Company Theatre as we had nowhere else to go. In the meantime, the Eblana Theatre opened and we took it over. I knew Pauline Delaney and Genevieve Lyons, who is now a great novelist, and Milo O'Shea and they all worked with us. There was Maurice Good who went on to do great work in America; Maureen Toal and Anna Manahan, there was huge talent around at that time.

JPK: *Take me through the development of Gemini Productions, from its creation to the present day.*

PR: We moved into the Eblana soon after it opened because they were beginning to censor our plays in the Gas Company and we knew we couldn't stay there. We put on a lot of new American and English plays which weren't being seen and any new Irish plays that we could get hold of. Hugh Leonard was one of our writers, he stayed with us for eleven years and he gave us a play for every festival. John B. Keane became a Gemini writer in the sixties! We had no money, the audience subsidized all of us actors playing for £8.00 a week, but we loved every minute of it. The other day, I was talking to my great friend, Anna Manahan, and she said, "We don't have the fun now that we used to have. Actors are all too worried about billing and money and "Would my agent like this, is this right for me?"" We feel that young people miss out on the joy of it all. Maybe it has become too competitive. I'd love to think that they can still have the level of enjoyment that we had. Mind you, when you go out and get the applause at the end of a play, whatever age you are, it's a feeling like no other.

JPK: *Imagine I'm a twenty-two year old (I'm not) and I come to you and say "I'm going to throw in the day job and become an actor." What do you say to me, now?*

PR: If someone wants to do it, they will do it and more power to them. Every year there are students pouring out with certificates and diplomas from the schools of acting, Trinity, the Gaiety and wherever. There are no repertory companies and so there are no places for most of them. You have to think about that. What you have to say to them is, "These are the disadvantages and these are the rewards." You have to tell them that this is a tough road and that they may never make it, in the way they want, and may never feel fulfilled; that they may have long periods when they may not work for maybe a year, even though they may have just had three star parts in a row. They have to be able to face all that. You could say that until the cows come home and they will still do it, if they really want to.

JPK: *Well, Noel Coward tried to say that before us, didn't he? Considering you have done so much work outside of Ireland, tell me what you think about Irish audiences. How do they compare?*

PR: I honestly think they are the best. To a certain extent, they haven't become too sophisticated. In a wonderful way, if they like something, they can still let themselves go. They want to tell you how good you are and they are full of the desire to say, "That was wonderful" and they will give a standing ovation. They are not conservative, they don't hold back. I have seen wonderful productions in other theatres and they just don't get that reaction. Irish audiences are totally uninhibited and it just isn't like that anywhere else.

JPK: *Earlier you mentioned some views about funding. There is a lot of development going on with the Arts Council at the moment in terms of Arts Plan 1, 2 and 3. It appears that their intent is to move from being a funding agency to being a development authority, an aid to the development of theatre. Do you think that the Arts Council should move in this direction or is it your feeling that people just want money?*

PR: I think people want money! There have been some wonderful officers in the Arts Council and I know some of them personally. (I seem to know all those at retiring age and don't really know any of the new appointments.) I think money should be given where it is needed as I think you could knock a really wonderful young company on the head because they are just too weary to go on any longer, on the dole or whatever. I don't think a talented young company should be allowed to go down the drain for lack of a few bob, just give them the money! Who from the Arts Council is watching the work being done? Why continue to give money to companies where the work isn't good any more, companies who are not making the advancement they should, considering their level of funding. Then, I see young struggling companies working miracles and I think, "C'mon, give them some funding." I make it my business to see as many plays as I can, so I can make a fair assessment of where the quality productions are to be found.

JPK: *In your business, you are always looking for new plays. How do you know when you have a winner?*

PR: I have often been asked that question. I think I am an instinctive audience. I think I read a play almost as though I am seeing it. To an extent, I may be limited, in that I do not think that unnecessary crudity and violence are good ways of making points. I feel that a few passages of good writing would make the point even better. I think that beauty has gone out of plays and while some would say that this is the world we live in, I don't agree. The world is beautiful, as well. It is not all four-letter words and violence; there are many beautiful things in the world. I am getting tired of downbeat, black scripts and I think at this stage of my life I would go for the uplift play.

JPK: *A theatre manager told me recently that he/she has to read a hundred plays to get perhaps one that is worth looking at.*

PR: There would have been a time when that was also true of me but I wouldn't be getting that many scripts now. I would maybe get three or four a week and it is only occasionally that I would say, "Hooray."

JPK: *Phyllis Ryan, what of the future? What do you see from here on?*

PR: I want to work on, hopefully getting around to my book. If I stop acting and producing and all the other things I do, I will sit down some day and say "Go away everybody, I am now writing my book." As I said, it has turned into a very different exercise than I expected. However, every week something new happens and I hope to continue! Theatre is such an exhilarating chain – one link leads to another – and one is involved regardless of one's previous plans or wishes.

JPK: *Perhaps I can ask you again in twenty years time! For now, thank you, Phyllis.*

Phyllis Ryan started her career in the Abbey School of Acting while still a schoolgirl, becoming a member of the company when she was seventeen. In 1958 she founded Gemini Productions with the actor Norman Rodway. Gemini has played in every Dublin theatre, presenting new Irish plays, classics and revues, and has also presented plays in the West End and the U.S.A. Phyllis has won awards in America and was honoured in a

Gala Celebration by the acting profession in 1981 and presented with life membership of Equity. She was awarded the Harvey Trophy for services to Irish Theatre in 1986, the Kilkenny Cream of Irish Award for Lifetime Achievement in 1997 and the Oscar Wilde Literary Recognition Award for 2001. Her acclaimed memoir, *The Company I Kept* was published in 1996. She is a regular lecturer at the annual Boston College Drama and Literature Course in association with the Abbey Theatre. She is currently working on *The Matchmaker* by John B. Keane.

John P. Kelly is now a freelance theatre director, having spent many years working for RTE. He began there as a Radio Drama producer, before moving into management as Managing Editor of Features and Arts. He moved to Switzerland in 1994, where he worked for four years with the European Broadcasting Union. On his return to RTE, he operated as editor for Digital Audio Broadcasting and as Editor for New Media. In his earlier days, John trained as a theatre director with the Abbey Theatre on an Arts Council bursary. He recently directed the successful production of *How the Other Half Loves* at Andrews Lane Theatre. He has worked at the Gate, the Gaiety, the Cork Opera House, the Project Arts Centre and the Taibhdhearc in Galway.

Peter Sheridan in Conversation with Deirdre Mulrooney

DM: *Peter Sheridan – what brought you into theatre in the first place?*

PS: Well it wasn't particularly a family tradition or anything like that, but when I was fifteen my father started a local amateur drama society in the Seville Place area called the Saint Laurence O'Toole Dramatic Society – which we shortened to SLOT players later on. And we started off by reading the plays of Sean O'Casey, Lady Gregory, J.M. Synge – the whole Abbey revival plays – and then we staged a production of *Shadow of a Gunman*. I played Tommy Owens and my father played Seamus Shiels, Jim directed and we had a gang of people from around the area in it. And from the moment we started working on this I was in love with it. I just thought this is the most incredible way to tell a story. The idea of dialogue and characters in a specific place, at a specific time – everything about it appealed to me. And the play felt like an extension of our house. Because our house was a pretty flamboyant place to grow up. As well as us children, there were these lodgers that my mother took in. And there were discussions and rows every night with my father acting as head honcho at the table. So there was always activity going on. There were always stories with the lodgers. Like one lodger had a woman staying in his room. And that was strictly forbidden. Just crazy stuff. Anything you could imagine. Another lodger who used to take down his trousers and show me a thirty inch scar on his leg that he got in the Congo when he was an Irish soldier out there.

DM: *So you had to work it all out on stage?*

PS: Yeah. It felt like I was away working out all this stuff. So that really was the start and from there we progressed and we did *Juno and the Paycock* in which I played Joxer. Then we did a famous production of *Waiting for Godot* where my dad played Pozzo, I played Vladimir, my brother Johnny was Lucky and Vinnie McCabe played Estragon. Jim directed. We toured it around some of the amateur festivals. People stood up and shouted at us, and walked out, storming out saying "this is not a play." It's amazing when you think in 1970 *Waiting for Godot* hadn't been seen in rural Ireland. It was still regarded as almost Satanic. It was "anti-theatre." So this was all part of my theatrical/dramatic education from 1967–1970. Then my father faded into the background and Jim and myself really took the reins of the group. We brought in other people from outside the area, and we staged a production of Christopher Marlowe's *Dr. Faustus* in which the music was Pink Floyd.

DM: *You were groovy guys.*

PS: Yeah! We combined that with Johann Sebastian Bach for example, and original songs. Neil Jordan and myself played Valdes and Cornelius. We were like two roving singers, throughout the play. Vinnie McCabe played Faustus. We staged it in the Oriel Hall and in amateur drama festivals. We got to the All-Ireland finals in Athlone in 1971.

DM: *Did you have any theatrical influences?*

PS: Well our influences would have been much more music when we were cutting our teeth on getting into theatre and drama. I saw the Rolling Stones in 1965, The Animals in 1966 and The Pretty Things. I saw The Who smash up their instruments in the National Stadium. We watched a documentary about The Doors when The Doors came out in America. I always remember seeing the early Jim Morrison and thinking "what a guy, what a performer." So our influences were much more in the music area than they would have been in the theatrical area. The one big theatrical influence was The Living Theatre of New York when they came to Dublin in the late 1960s. And after the show we marched from the theatre to the Bridewell and held a protest about how prisons were run, with Julian Beck and his wife. That was amazing. I began to see shows in the Abbey. I saw the original *Borstal Boy* with Niall Tóibín. That blew me away I had never seen anything like that. I saw MacLiammóir do his one-man show in the Gate, Ray MacNally in *The Field*. So I certainly did go to stuff. But we weren't coming out of theatrical tradition and continuing that. We were coming out of an experience of being in Dublin in the 1960s, my father introducing us to theatre and the combination of those elements. Music was always really important. It's probably not a much understood thing about Jim and myself, but music was a huge part of what we were doing in the theatre.

DM: *You mentioned a protest – that's quite interesting, because your theatre is quite "social" – is it social realism?*

PS: It certainly was in the early days. But we moved out of social realism pretty quickly. The production we did of *Oedipus Rex* in UCD in 1971 was anything but social realism. It was very expressionistic. The centre piece was "The End" by The Doors. I played Oedipus Rex, Neil Jordan played Tiresias, Des Hogan, the novelist, played King Laius. Deirdre Nunan played Jocasta. We had an amazing crew of people in that show. It was very music-based. A lot of original music. We built a courtyard with scaffolding on three sides. We put the audience up three levels on the scaffolding and we played the play down on the courtyard in the middle of them.

DM: *Was that influenced by anybody?*

PS: That would have been The Living Theatre of New York. They were very much into scaffolding-type sets, where the set was very basic, very primitive and just – it was like Sheriff Street. It was like being in the flats in Sheriff Street. Where you've got the flats up there and you've a courtyard in the middle. So it was an extension of that. In a way DramSoc was never the same after that – I don't think.

DM: *Then when you went on to the Project, did you bring those principles on?*

PS: That's what we brought. We brought all of what we'd been learning for those years. Before the Project there was the Children's T Company, which came out of the UCD experience. Neil, myself, Jim, Susie Kennedy, Garret Keogh, David McKenna, Ruth McCabe, they were all members of the Children's T Company. We did children's theatre. It was a way of earning money. We brought the plays around to schools. We did the beaches in the summertime and brought the plays around to parks. And again – the plays were not naturalistic. We did a version of *Ulysses* on Stephen's Green in 1973. Again very heavily music-based. *The Unhappy Birthday* was a fairly traditional kid's show that we did. I played a character called Tatty Mattie. I always remember that. That went on for a couple of years. And then, out of the experience of SLOT Players and the Children's T Company when the Project moved from South King Street in 1975 to the disused factory in Essex Street, Jim and I made moves to get involved there. In early 1976 we did our first show, my play *No Entry*. It was very much social realism, set in Sean MacDermott Street about a couple who couldn't afford a house and were squatting. They had to break into a house to squat and found a dead body in the bed. And then from 1976 to 1980 Jim and I ran the Project, did shows that we wrote ourselves and a lot of original work by other Irish writers. So the Project became this breeding ground for new talent, both acting and writing. It became a focus for a lot of the energy that was around at that time. Ex-punks say that the seminal event of the 1970s was the Dark Space Event which was a punk celebration in 1978. We ran thirty-six hours non-stop punk music. There were side-shows. We had all kinds of things going on: visual art, a bit of theatre, the Virgin Prunes, U2, The Undertones. The Project was the place that people naturally gravitated to because it had the feeling of a garage space. But one of the great things we did of course was that we bought the building.

DM: *You did?*

PS: Yeah, that's how the Project is still there. The board bought the building – at our instigation. We learned that from Sheriff Street too!

DM: *To buy a building, and rent it?*

PS: (*Laughs*) Well, to own something.

DM: *What about funding?*

PS: We went from virtually zero funding – the first big grant we got from the Arts Council was £3,500 and that was in 1976 – to £32,000 in three years. And then there was a big row about the money because when we brought over the Gay Sweatshop from London in 1978 that caused such a furore.

DM: *What was that?*

PS: They were a gay company that I had seen in a show in the ICA in London. I brought over a play of mine to the ICA, and met the Gay Sweatshop people there. I thought this would go down so well in Dublin. The idea of people getting up and being proud to be gay. There was a debate in the Dail about it and a leader in *The Irish Times*. There was a lesbian play and a gay play.

My mother was great with them. They had a kid with them – my mother used to give out hell about the way they used to leave the child to go off and rehearse. But I was saying, "Look Ma, you know you have to rehearse when you're doing theatre." So my Ma would be minding the baby for them when they were off rehearsing. Then when the row erupted, my Ma went up to the local Fianna Fail councillor saying: "What's going on here? These are lovely people staying in my house. How dare you be saying things about them." But they did the show in 1978 and it caused a lot of controversy. There were pickets outside and Dublin Corporation withdrew their grant. The Arts Council suspended their grant and we were left with no money and survived on box office for about six months.

We revived *Waiting for Godot* as a result, because Godot is an easy show to stage. It's just four actors and a child actor. It was a new production we did in 1979, but we did it because we had no money. We eventually got the money back. We won the war. Famously Ned Brennan, a famous Fianna Fail politician from up the road here [Clontarf] described the Gay Sweatshop as "funny bunnies from across the water."

DM: *As a joke?*

PS: No in all seriousness.

DM: *Condemning it?*

PS: Yeah. "Why should Dublin Corporation be funding the funny bunnies from across the water?"

DM: *Were you happy about it?*

PS: Delighted. Wasn't the controversy what it was all about? The era of the beginning of gay rights and gay consciousness and gay pride. And the Project was right in there at the forefront of the debate. So when you say "social, political", yeah we were right in there at the cutting edge. My play *The Liberty Suit* based on Mannix Flynn's experiences were very much an attack on the juvenile prison system. So a lot of the stuff we did had an edge. When we did a show called *The Ha'penny Place*, which was a loose working of *The Beggar's Opera* set in Dublin. The central character was based on Haughey. The opening scene was all these crates with "Libya Handle With Care" marked on them, because of the arms coming in, in 1970. The whole thing was set around the idea of Ireland at that time in 1969/70 being like the Weimar Republic, where the crooks were very close to the centre of power. The people bringing in the arms were very close to the government. There was this duality in Irish life at that time which the play explored. So a lot of the work that we did had a definite political cutting edge to it.

DM: *How did that go down?*

PS: Great. Mannix played the lead, Jeananne Crowley was in it, Peter Caffrey, Agnes Bernelle doing a wonderful Madame dressed up all in black – in black leather with a whip with which she whipped her customers –

DM: *Type-casting.*

PS: And boots up to here (points to his thighs) with Agnes just strutting her stuff. It was wonderful. Pirate Jenny was the character she played.

DM: *For you, then, is theatre to provoke?*

PS: Well I think it has to be relevant. For me it's a way of addressing the world I'm in, of being engaged in the world I'm in. It's not a retreat or an escape. That's not to say you can't have good escapist theatre. But the best theatre is the one that is pulsating right now in this second, in this moment in time. And of course you can take a thirty year-old text and make it vibrate. Shakespeare is great like that. Shakespeare just seems to be capable of resonating in all sorts of different ages – because he's such a great writer. You can take the Greek legends and make them have a relevance to today. It doesn't necessarily mean that the play has to be written yesterday, but it means that there's a consciousness about what you're doing, that you're engaging with the world as you see it. That's why I write books now, because I can write freely about the world as Peter experiences it. I'm talking about my family, I'm talking about my family and society and how I experienced it as a kid, and as an adult, and why it interests me, why I'm intrigued, and why I'm involved.

DM: *And who are you writing for?*

PS: Myself. I always have been. I am the audience for my work. And then if it translates to other people that's great. That's the bonus. But I'm never thinking of a person that's reading a book or seeing a play except myself. I've always been working for me. I don't work for a specific audience. I want everybody to see the play, to read my book.

DM: *Why?*

PS: Because I think that ultimately the people I have loved best in the performing world have been the people that are the most popular. So I regard Shakespeare as the ultimate dramatist. He was also the most popular. I regard the Beatles as the best rock band of the twentieth century, they were also the most popular. So it doesn't necessarily follow that you have to be obscurantist or elitist or in a corner or a minority interest. I'm not interested in being a minority interest. I'm interested in reaching a huge audience. I believe that really good art can reach a really wide audience and move them and affect them.

DM: *So are you thinking about entertaining?*

PS: Yeah but entertaining is my lifeblood. I don't have to think "Am I entertaining?", that isn't ever a discussion for me. I'm an entertainer. That's what I do. I grew up in a house where it was entertainment twenty-four hours a day. I know how to do plays. I know where the drama is. One of the problems I see a lot of the time when I go to the theatre is you watch stuff and neither the director nor the actor knows where the drama is. The drama is a very specific thing – you have to find it. And then you explore it and you present it. But you have to know where it is. And very often you see stuff and – it has no point of view. They get up and they say the lines but they don't have a point of view. Art must have a point of view. Art to me is about getting really clear about those things. Really specific.

DM: *Are you trying to educate people?*

PS: That sounds like a grandiose idea of "I'm an educator and you should be very grateful that I'm going to give you my pearls of wisdom." By definition it does educate. But it doesn't educate necessarily on the level that we think of school as an education. Because education can be an emotional thing. Like when we're moved to tears by something. When we're brought to the point where something engages and makes us laugh or makes us cry, makes us experience those big emotions – we're in a learning situation automatically.

What makes *A Whistle in the Dark* a great production is – here's a play that was set in 1961 that is resonating today as if it was written yesterday. It's about the tribe of the Irish in Coventry, still at war. We've moved the war, i.e. from the war of independence in Ireland. It's now happening in Britain, and we're looking for recognition. We don't want to be Paddies any more. So we've brought the war to England, and we're fighting among ourselves. We're looking to be accepted, we don't want to be patted on the head and put down. And that's why Murphy's play is so brilliant and so brief. It has that feeling of a tribe pulling itself apart, looking for an identity in this foreign place. It's a war play, a *casus belli*. It's powerful stuff. It feels like it's on the point of war. It has huge resonance today because the world is on the point of war right now. We're hearing the war drums. We're seeing the manipulation of the forces, the cranking up of the machine, the having to buy into stuff that makes it OK to kill people. And that's what *A Whistle in the Dark* does. The death at the end of that play is so inevitable. And we accept it, because it's about war. Because that's what happens in a war situation.

DM: *And this is obviously from a Greek model – I wonder in your own work does it always go back to a well-made-play structure? In terms of theatrical form do you consciously do that?*

PS: No. I wouldn't in my own writing. I haven't written for the theatre in ten years. Though I have just finished a first draft of a new play for a young audience. And the reason why I've written for the theatre again is I think we are losing the young audience in the theatre. I don't think people under twenty-five really go, and the audiences seem to be getting older and older. Which is a real tragedy because I think the theatre is fantastic. When it works there is nothing like it. I mean the cinema is great but it doesn't compare.

DM: *Why? Is it something about having people physically together in a room?*

PS: It's just that you are part of it. When you're an audience you are part of the performance in a theatre. You are not neutral. You are part of something. It's like a great spiritual experience. The kind of thing you would get at a great mass, or Mecca, or being with 7,000 or 700,000 other people in the Ganges. There is a sense of community, of a shared purpose. It doesn't happen very often in the theatre but when it happens it is special. It happened the other night at *A Whistle in the Dark*. It's electric. But I still hanker for that. I still love that feeling.

DM: *So you've moved into film.*

PS: Yeah.

DM: *What do you think the relationship is between those two media?*

PS: I think it's been a logical move for both Jim and me. Because I think that our upbringing, and the kind of theatre that we did, was always very filmic, in essence.

DM: *In a narrative sense?*

PS: Yeah. So I think that film comes natural to us. We think film. We think "story." And story is very important to film. The narrative structure of film is actually much more locked off than theatre in many ways. A classic three-act structure and that's what you stick to. And film is also more encompassing. Theatre is expensive; it's a place where people are intimidated to go into. In America no one would have the thought of "should I or shouldn't I go into the cinema?" Going to a cinema is a part of the culture. And it's part of the culture here too.

DM: *Or you get them on television.*

PS: Yeah. So it doesn't feel like you're having a cultural experience. It feels like you are doing something that is entirely natural. Whereas going to the theatre feels like you are paying to have a cultural experience. And it's expensive. It has all of those trappings with it. So by definition it's less encompassing. The cinema is much more embracing.

DM: *So you reach more people.*

PS: Yeah and it feels much more comfortable to where Jim and I are coming from. We were always trying to break down that sense of the theatre being an elitist space. Which is why I've always worked so hard at the idea that creative expression should be available to everybody. There's nothing about it that says to me you have to be born into a certain class, or you have to have a special kind of training, or you have to have a special eye or any of that nonsense which other people foist for their own reasons. There are a lot of people that are very, very happy with the idea of theatre as an elitist tool.

DM: *What do you think of training in Ireland? Do people need training?*

PS: Well it's come a long way. Of course people need training. The training for us was that we did it in situ – by actually doing it. But I've met the people who've come out the other end of the Gaiety Schools and the Samuel Beckett Centres and some of them are very, very good. So what can you say? Obviously the training is working to some extent. I'd prefer to see it much more based and involved in community than engaging with itself.

DM: *How do you mean?*

PS: Go into the north inner city, and have a drama school there. Operate in that environment. Do shows about the drugs. Come on, immerse yourself in it. That's where I come from. I've done the community-based work. It was probably the most exciting time of my life when I did the city workshop from 1982 to 1984. I developed the trilogy of plays with that group in the north inner city.

DM: *What were they about?*

PS: They were about Dublin. The first one was about the Monto [Montgomery Street, a red-light district at the time]. The second one was about the collapse of the docks, the third one was about the start of the heroin scourge. So I've been engaged in that debate in a community context and I just don't think there's enough of it being done.

DM: *What about Northern Ireland? You did* Diary of a Hunger Strike, *and you worked with Charabanc...*

PS: In a break from working with Jim I went up to Belfast in 1970 because I was really interested in what was happening there. The Troubles were a year old. And I had a girlfriend from Derry in 1969. I had spent time in Derry in September 1969 just after the whole thing blew up. And you just knew that "this is going to go on and be so important in terms of our history, and in terms of who we are and where we're going." Northern Ireland felt to me like the most important political issue, not just in Ireland, but probably in Europe. In Derry at that time you could feel it. The sense of anger, the sense of "we're not going to let them walk on us again." The sense of "this time it's going to be different. We're going to really take control of the situation." The Provos were beginning to get organized. And there was tremendous energy around. So I got hooked into the whole thing in 1969/1970. I went to Belfast in 1970, and got a job in the Lyric. I just happened to be walking by the door and I saw "forthcoming production *Shadow of a Gunman*. So I just went in, auditioned on the spot for Tommy Owens and got the job. I spent the next six months in the Lyric doing shows in Belfast. It was a really important time for me. So that cemented the connection. And my mother had been raised there, so she always told us stories about Belfast. I always wanted to write about it. When the hunger strikes happened I thought "I've got to do something now, I really really have to write something about this." So I lived in Belfast for three months, commuted up and down, just absorbed the atmosphere and then wrote *Diary of a Hunger Strike*. And again there was more furore over that in 1982 at the Edinburgh Festival.

DM: *What happened?*

PS: Well just the fact that the two guys were naked, and the set was a cell with shit all over the walls. It upset a lot of people. There was a furore about bringing the show to Dublin. And Michael Colgan, who was the head of the Dublin Theatre Festival at the time, said he didn't want a H-Block image in the Dublin Theatre Festival. Imagine, a play about Ireland – about something as seminal as the hunger strikes – could not find a home in Dublin.

DM: *So what did you do?*

PS: We got into Limerick for a week. It just did astonishing business. I remember being on the radio with Jim Kemmy and Bernadette McAliskey debating the play, and debating the issues. So again it was like art, politics and current affairs.

DM: *What was your point in doing it? Were you trying to open it up to discussion?*

PS: Yeah, absolutely. The basic proposition was "are these guys criminals or are they politically motivated?" To me there was no argument that they were politically motivated. These were young guys who'd come out of the experience of 1969-70: Bloody Sunday, 1972 and the whole birth of the republican movement. These people were trying to change the society in which they found themselves. And they found themselves in prison with no option left but to go on a hunger strike. And we've a British Prime Minister telling us that these people are criminals. And you go and live in Belfast, and everybody to a man on the nationalist side is saying these people are political. You've got the essence of Greek Tragedy right there. Two immovable objects. And I just wanted to write something that explored and showed these people in the light in which they found themselves. The horror of finding yourself in that situation where you feel you've no option left but to actually starve yourself to death. By definition, someone who is prepared to make that sacrifice is politically motivated. Criminals don't do that. So Thatcher's argument was defeated. And while she may have won the battle, she lost the war because within two years they had all the demands they were looking for on the hunger strikes. And also, they had given birth to a political movement that now fifteen to twenty years later is at the centre of political life in Ireland. It was the hunger strikes that taught them the lesson. When Sands got elected they realized that they had a political way forward. Obviously America [the events of 11th of September] has changed it to an extent. But there is no question about it that the hunger strikers taught Sinn Fein that the strategy they had been adopting of indiscriminate bombing was doomed to failure and that the political way was the way forward.

DM: *And do you think that theatre somehow parallels the political?*

PS: I think it better be talking about it or else it's not going to be relevant. I think it better be in there. Otherwise what is it?

DM: *Did that get shown in Belfast?*

PS: No, but I was up at a twentieth anniversary production of it about four months ago. It was a very moving experience, particularly in Belfast, in the Waterfront Hall. The families of some of the men who died were in the audience.

DM: *How about your work with Charabanc?*

PS: Well that was a logical extension to the work I had done on the hunger strikes, and the work I had done in the north inner-city. Charabanc was a women's community group. The issues they were addressing were "there are no roles for women." They were addressing a very important question – what is the role of women in contemporary Irish theatre? They set about devising and writing plays about women's issues. They had seen my work – I had toured my community work to Belfast. And I had seen their early work in Dublin and we became friends. They asked me to come and work with them in 1987 and I directed *Somewhere Over the Balcony* for them. It was absurd. Three women, in the Divis flats which is this high-rise block of flats in the centre of Belfast, who basically spend the day watching helicopters landing on the tops of the buildings, and their imaginings – this fantasy world they create about what's going on in the middle of this absolute horror. It's a completely funny play – a black, black comedy. And it was just the three girls, the three Charabanc women. I worked with them on five shows between 1987 and 1992.

DM: *What about the importance of writing – is it going by the wayside?*

PS: I think there has been a total resurgence on the writing front. I was on an interviewing panel for writer-in-residence at the Project which they've just introduced. It gives a writer two years, and a good stipend – I think it's £30,000 over two years to concentrate on writing. I think we saw fourteen people and I was so impressed by the standard of the people we interviewed. Nick Kelly got it. So there are talents coming through. There are definitely people writing for the theatre. I think probably what's lacking is a little bit what the Project provided. There are plenty of theatre spaces – but do they have a vision, I wonder. People relate to something that has a vision, has an analysis of what it's trying to do, of its way forward. I think good plays come out of a fairly radical analysis of society. I think the Abbey came out of a radical fairly nationalistic view of Ireland and where Ireland was at, at the turn of the century. And you've got the twin pillars of Synge and O'Casey, one being a rural poetic voice, and the other being an urban working-class political voice. But they were all about a fundamental analysis of Ireland.

DM: *Say you were going to be Artistic Director of the Abbey, what would your agenda be?*

PS: Well I think you've got to combine the bums on seats part of the policy – which is difficult. You've got to do a certain level of business. You've two theatres to run. They say there are fourteen plays you can do in the Irish canon that will do business. And that's probably about right. Take four classical Dublin plays. Take an

O'Casey. Take Behan. Take Jim Plunkett. Take maybe even Seamus Byrne's *Design for a Headstone*. But you take a number of classic plays about Dublin and you present them over a two-year period as well as a series of plays about the contemporary thing that's happening in Dublin. So you'd have something about the refugee situation. Maybe something coming out of the experience of what's happening in terms of the whole revolutionization of the docks. That community is gone. There's the financial services centre and the whole thing has changed.

DM: *And the Abbey moving…*

PS: I think that would be a fatal mistake for them. They are in a community where they are. Do you want to move them somewhere they are…

DM: *They're part of a shopping mall?*

PS: Yeah, what's that? Most people would give their right arm to have a theatre in the city that's fifty yards from the centre; fifty yards from O'Connell street and fifty yards from the centre of the Irish rebellion, the GPO. Almost on the river, and they could extend to the river. You want to put them in a car park down on the south quays somewhere? Please!

DM: *Do you think it still has a function, as it originally started out "to forge the national identity?"*

PS: There is no question about that. The question of Irish identity and what is the nation is still a pivotal question in Ireland right now. We have the machinations of what has been going on in the North, and that movement that I would fully support – the peace process and so on. The Abbey or any arts institution that doesn't see that it has a role in that isn't worth its salt as far as I'm concerned.

DM: *And how would you see the Project in the same light – say you were Artistic Director again?*

PS: It's a different thing because the Project has a different remit. And I think the remit of the Project has changed since the time that Jim and I were there in the mid-70s. I think probably what the Project is moving towards is much more showcasing alternative art and alternative art-forms. So dance has become very strong – which I think is great. There's always been a real lack of a venue that showcases real, professional dance work in Dublin. Much more avant-garde type work – like Desperate Optimists. It might be good for Project to engage with some of the acting schools to develop some kind of a policy in relation to some of the work that they might do. I think the Project is in a different world than the world that we found ourselves in.

DM: *Well with the new building it has a whole new vibe off of it – a little sterile…*

PS: Yeah. It is a bit. But it seems to be moving in that direction. Much more specialized. Fairly avant-garde contemporary music. And that's great, I think that there is a need for that kind of stuff. It seems that's the home of it now. It wouldn't suit me. It wouldn't be somewhere I would want to run. It's not my thing. My thing is much more populist than that. I'm a populist at heart.

DM: *Do you think critics can show the path theatre should be going?*

PS: There have been very few critics who have been able to do that. But Fintan O'Toole would be up there without question as one of the best drama critics in the world.

DM: *What do you think is the role of a critic?*

PS: The role is to be able to relate to the play as you see it and to be able to relate to it in a broader context. And see Irish theatre and its relevance to Britain, and to New York, Broadway, or wherever. To be able to go beyond just a very narrow insular view and to inform. I think good critics inform. I think you need those voices.

DM: *Now we're here talking about theatre and you actually haven't done theatre since …*

PS: *(laughs) Brighton Beach Memoirs* in Andrew's Lane.

DM: *So why is that?*

PS: I love the theatre. It's my first love. It's my home. I just got to a point in the late 1980s where I made a decision to resign from two or three different boards of community-based arts projects. And I said I'm going to spend the next ten years on Peter's work. I'd been doing everybody else's work, facilitating a lot of other people. I'd been involved in the coal-face in helping other people's creativity. And it's great and it's really rewarding but I really, really needed to take time to develop some of my own stories. I'm glad I did because I gave myself the time to develop. I now have a book career, which was unimaginable to me ten years ago. And the books are about family, and relation to society, and society in relation to the arts, and the arts in relation to society. Obviously, *Forty-four* deals with the creation of the drama group in Seville Place. I'm going to finish the third book and then in between times I've written a show for young people, *The North Wall Witches*, for the Draíocht Arts centre which will probably go on in the Spring. It's been a hoot going back to write for a young audience again. I'm a big Harry Potter fan.

DM: *They are very entertaining, and very imaginative.*

PS: But they're dark as well. I love the darkness in them. The Harry Potter books were inspirational to me. Because I thought I'd really like to do something for the audience that reads those books. I'd like to write a theatre show.

DM: *With their fresh imagination.*

PS: Yeah. So I've written a thing about friendship between two boys. It's about friendship and morality, but essentially it's about having a great pal in your life. And this is about two pals.

DM: *Have you plans for more plays?*

PS: Yeah. I'd have plays in my head that I want to someday write.

DM: *And what about how difficult it is to do theatre? To make ends meet, to fund it?*

PS: It's really difficult. It's really, really difficult. I didn't make any money until I wrote books.

DM: *Do you think that people should take the initiative and secure corporate sponsorship or private funding? Where is the responsibility?*

PS: The responsibility is at the state end of it rather than at the corporate end of it. But the Abbey has been very fortunate with that Ansbacher Writer-in-Residence scheme. I don't know what the commission is now for a play in the Abbey. I'd imagine it's about £7,500. I could be wrong. A play is a year's work. So what value do you put on a year's work? I would say for me to be able to concentrate on writing a play for the next year I'd want £20,000-£25,000. That's what a commission should be. If you want to seriously engage and really take the time and have the freedom and the space to do it, that's the kind of money you'd need to be putting up. And it's about a third or a quarter of that. It's ludicrous.

DM: *So why would anybody do it?*

PS: Love. Vocation. In your blood. Can't stop doing it. That's why it needs to be supported.

Peter Sheridan was born in Dublin in 1952 and has spent most of his adult life writing, directing and collaborating in the theatre. His plays have been seen in the major theatres in Ireland and in London, Montreal, New

York and Los Angeles. He is a founder member of the community arts movement and believes in access to the arts for all. His short film *The Breakfast* has won several European awards and his first feature, *Borstal Boy* was released in the autumn of 2000. He was awarded the Rooney Prize for literature in 1977 and was Writer in Residence at the Abbey Theatre in 1980. He has written two novels, *44: A Dublin Memoir*, and most recently *Forty-Seven Roses*. He lives on Dublin's North Side with his wife Sheila and their family.

Deirdre Mulrooney is a freelance writer, director and lecturer. Her book *Orientalism, Orientation and the Nomadic Work of Pina Bausch* is published by Peter Lang. After directing Jennifer Johnston's *The Nightingale and Not the Lark* in 1998 Deirdre was invited to participate in the Lincoln Center NYC's Director's Lab. Earlier this year she produced, co-directed and adapted *ShesaWhore*, based on Angela Carter's concept for John Ford's *'Tis Pity She's a Whore*, at Project Cube. She has lectured in Drama at UCD Drama Studies Centre, The Samuel Beckett Centre, The National College of Art and Design, and NUI Maynooth. She was awarded an annual *DAAD* scholarship for her Ph.D. research in German dance theatre, and continues to write on contemporary dance. Among many other newspapers and magazines Deirdre has contributed to *The Irish Times*, *The Irish Independent*, *Liveart Magazine* and *Dance Europe*. She contributed an essay on Tom Mac Intyre to *Theatre Stuff: Critical Essays on Contemporary Irish Theatre* and has reported on the Arts for Lyric FM's *Artszone* and for *Rattlebag* on RTE Radio One.

Gerard Stembridge in Conversation with Hugh Linehan

HL: *When you look at your own work, are there certain other people who have influenced you, or do you find yourself working in a particular tradition?*

GS: I am a very definite non-joiner and non-follower. I can never remember a time when I went around saying "We must do Brecht. It's so important." Shakespeare is the only one. I've directed about ten Shakespeare plays, and the thing about Shakespeare is that it's a kind of alternative to writing your own thing. You can reflect something you're going on about by doing a Shakespeare. If I think about the Irish tradition, I've enjoyed and liked plays by nearly every single one of the pantheon of Irish writers. Some more than others – Tom Murphy is more my style than Brian Friel, which doesn't mean I don't like Brian Friel. But I'm unaware of following in any particular tradition. I do believe that we should not be slaves to a certain kind of literary theatre, or to the adulation of a particular text or writer. I think that if someone's total work is to mean anything, they should be dead before we all start looking at their work and wondering what it meant.

HL: *How do you feel about the Irish fondness for revivals?*

GS: I have to admit I find it odd when the same director revives the same work again and again, because I feel that there are so many other plays to be done.

HL: *But there's a logical commercial imperative, isn't there, in doing something which an audience will find familiar?*

GS: Very often there is. And often it's just someone saying "I can do that very easily and there's a handy slot available." The other thing I'd feel is that there aren't enough revivals undertaken with a sense of re-interpreting the play, of tackling it anew. There are good examples of people who have done that, principally Garry Hynes who has done marvellous work with revivals, giving them a new slant, but never doing anything mad or stupid with them. Most of her stuff, apart from the Martin McDonagh plays, has been revivals, and they always have a wonderful freshness about them, even when they don't work. Her *Plough and the Stars* probably didn't entirely work, but it was still such a relief to see it at least being tackled in a new way.

That would be where I come from on the theatreometer, that's my interest in theatre. I think the fact that I have never depended totally on it for my living has given me what some might call a dilettante-ish attitude to theatre. But the other side of that is that I can actually approach it without those commercial pressures you're talking about, and really go for what interests me. Even when I choose to move back into it from some other form, I'm doing it because I like the idea of theatre itself, of deliberately choosing the medium in order to explore something.

HL: *Do you think the conservatism of audiences is at least partly to blame for this return again and again to the same small group of plays?*

GS: Well, if you have to do five or six plays a year, and you have to put your mind and imagination into creating that, then pretty soon, within a few years and with the best will in the world, you're going to end up recycling stuff, or you're going to take a rest with a very ordinary play. It's perfectly respectable to do that kind of work, and audiences love it. After all, it's not always going to be about reinventing the wheel. But I do think that at the moment in Irish theatre the balance is wrong. We're losing out on a lot. We talk about the great classics of Irish theatre, but we don't look at them enough and take them on.

HL: *What sort of plays are you thinking of?*

GS: There's a list of writers, most of whom I haven't had the chance to do. There's Lennox Robinson, whom I *have* done (*The Whiteheaded Boy*). There's George Shiels from the 1940s, M.J. Molloy, Louis d'Alton, Denis Johnson … That's five off the top of my head who not only aren't revived very much, but when they are revived it's done in a very straightforward way. With the exception of Garry Hynes, who's done brilliant work there. But I do think the Abbey has a particular responsibility. When I did *The Whiteheaded Boy*, one of the reasons I chose that play at that time was because of a memory I had from about five years previously of seeing an amateur production of it. I remember thinking that it wasn't a very good production but that there was something very interesting in the play that still emerged. That brought me to look at the text again. So it has to be sparked by something, and it would be good if directors were encouraged to take a look at that. Patrick Mason, the previous Artistic Director, was always going on about revisiting the great tradition of Abbey plays, but in the end it didn't happen. I wouldn't remotely say it's my mission in life, but it's something worth looking at.

HL: *Is the world of Irish theatre divided into mutually suspicious camps?*

GS: Actually, I hope so. Now that I'm over forty, I hope that there are people in their early twenties somewhere in Dublin right now who hate me and my kind and all we represent and believe that we are the death of theatre. I don't know them, but I hope they're there. Just as when I was in my early twenties, those who were directing plays in the Abbey and the Gate were equally the death of theatre. It's a natural progression that you must have.

HL: *Are you aware of those people in their twenties, and whether they're actually out there?*

GS: Sadly not. I hope they are. I should be more aware of it. This may partly be the prejudice of the old, but I think there is some evidence for the argument that in the early 1980s there was far more vibrant activity at the fringe level. There were new companies coming up with all sorts of ideas, ranging from companies like Rough Magic that focused on acting and on bringing English plays onto the Irish stage, to Passion Machine trying to find a new way to write and produce Irish drama. There was Wet Paint… if I thought long enough about it I could easily come up with half a dozen examples. There was a level of activity always happening – I never felt in the early eighties that I had to get a job in the Abbey or the Gate, even though times were harder. There were plenty of places to get plays put on. I wonder whether, as with so much in our happy and healthy economy, there's now a greater premium put on doing well commercially in the theatre than on doing something new or different. With the Gaiety School and the acting course in Trinity, actors are focused more and more on the idea of a career progression, of being successful.

HL: *Presumably with more opportunities around, an increasing number of Irish actors think of film and television ahead of theatre work?*

GS: Oh God, yes. At the simple financial level, it's a problem which has grown over the last ten years. It's harder to cast a theatre play now. And theatre is much more likely to compromise now than it used to. They will take on somebody for a show, knowing that they have a commitment to some film or TV thing and that they won't be available for half the rehearsals. All those things that theatre used to be able, to some extent, to adopt a lofty disdain about, they now have to accept. Especially with the younger actors. If you think about it, there's been a lot of television activity this summer, as it happens, which is a great change – suddenly RTE has come to life. So, coming back to theatre recently, I have encountered television and film as difficulties to be dealt with.

HL: *Surely that's a good thing for actors, that maybe they're finally moving towards that British system, where they can subsidize the miserable pittances they get for theatre work with remuneration from the occasional screen role?*

GS: Absolutely, there's nothing wrong with that at all. It's great. Where I have a problem with it is not with theatre having to compromise on these things. It's more to do with a reluctance on the part of a new generation of people who might make the theatre interesting, a reluctance to sit down and think about what should make it interesting. A reluctance to put themselves in the way of saying "Let's start a theatre company and give our commitment to that company. Let's make interesting theatre." Instead it's "Oh it's a very interesting job and you might become a star somewhere down the line – who knows?" The simple fact was that in the eighties, when there was no choice, there was much more freedom to do that sort of thing, because you were going to be broke anyway, so you might as well do something interesting and exciting with your life. And even your parents might think you might as well do this since you were going to be on the dole anyway. Whereas now I suspect parents would think that if you're going to be an actor, it should be a successful actor, on TV.

HL: *I think we'd both agree, though, that misery and poverty are not necessary conditions for producing good work?*

GS: What I would be saying to people, if I was in there teaching in acting schools or wherever these ideas ferment, would be that I've always felt that to a large degree artistic integrity and self-interest go hand in hand. I've no interest in being poor, or in just doing something for the sake of it. I've always found that the people I like to work with are not only good at what they do but serious about it. It's very easy to spot those people who really aren't that interested unless it's going to do their career prospects some good in the future. But there's no reason why you should starve in an attic just because you take your work seriously. I firmly believe that talented people who have integrity and treat their work seriously also get their rewards.

HL: *Do you think then that theatre reflects the fact that we're living in what some have called a post-ideological age?*

GS: I first noticed that when I was doing workshops with youth theatres. These were young people who were interested in drama, and I was interested through workshops in finding out what was important to them. And – this was over a period in the early nineties – I discovered that politics never came into it. In the workshops I'd be giving them subjects, encouraging them to improvise, and it was all interpersonal stuff, all sex and drugs and rock 'n roll. It never occurred to them that they might even give a nod to the idea that they ought to be doing things with a social or political twist. That's when I first began to see what you describe as a post-ideological age at work as a daily reality. You see it more and more with writers as well. There are very few writers who, even if they do have politics in their work, would trumpet the fact that it's there.

HL: *Like Mark O'Rowe, for example.*

GS: He'd be a very good example of that. Or indeed, Conor McPherson. It's there if you look for it, in the texture of their writing. But they would die rather than tell you that that was their intention, to make some kind of socio-political statement. At least I think they would – I must ask.

HL: *But the consequences of that shift are not all bad. There was a time when it could be argued that there was too much simplistic polemic.*

GS: The weird thing for me, personally speaking, is that I was less polemical myself back when theatre was much more polemical, when I was in college in the seventies. Then I was deliberately against that, but now I've become more polemical in my own thinking with the absence of it.

HL: *Is that just contrariness on your part?*

GS: Partly, yes, but it also came from a growing understanding that, whereas I'm nervous on one level about agit-prop, I'm also nervous when it's not there. I'm thinking of the Philip Larkin poem, *Churchgoing*, where he poses the question of what happens when not only is religion gone, but we forget that it ever existed. It was actually towards the end of the Thatcher era that I began to think about the way she had almost succeeded in eliminating the history of social democracy from people's minds. It's as if people growing up had no idea even of what a union had represented a hundred years ago. All they knew was that unions were bad. In theatre terms or drama terms, we could be going down a road where people forget that those types of theatre or drama ever existed and then forget how to make it. So that, whenever the wheel turns, you'd have to start again from the beginning. There is a danger that the political edge to drama is in danger of disappearing altogether.

HL: *It can't be kept on a life-support system for the sake of it.*

GS: No of course not, but one of the things I like about theatre is the rapid turn-over time, so with the principal things I've done in that regard, which are *Love Child* in 1993 and *The Gay Detective* in 1995, and also in an odder kind of way, *Ceauşescu's Ear*, which was a Romanian co-production set during the fall of Communism. I didn't do those to keep political drama on a life-support system, but in each case the timing was appropriate, and it could be done within that time. So now, for example, I think that anybody who makes theatre which hits the nail on the head at the right moment will keep the idea of political theatre alive, but also produce something which is entertaining, on its own terms.

This is another problem we have with the development of traditional theatre, because we concentrate so much on the whole idea of the writer's theatre, the text-based "Great Plays", and the tradition they represent. Of course, the academics love that, so they enshrine a list of authors, which rules out what I would call disposable theatre, which I would have done. It would be a great surprise to me if someone were to decide to do a revival of *Love Child* in twenty years' time. I don't know why they would, although maybe that moment will arise. But it was perfect for the moment in time which it captured. That's very important in theatre, and people shouldn't be afraid to do it.

I do notice something, particularly with the main theatres. When you go to an opening night of a new play at the Abbey or the Peacock or the Gate, you sit there and there's a strange aura of tension and reverence that relates, not to the fact that you're going to see a play, but to some question of whether this is a new person to be beatified as part of the great tradition of theatre. Or, if it's one of the playwrights who are currently in the pantheon, will they maintain their status or will they fall short? So, what chance had Brian Friel after *Dancing at Lughnasa*? I think he'd have been better off to write some silly one-acter and put it on in Bewleys, just to make a break, to say "Look, I don't have to do this. It doesn't have to have that weight of Tonys on Broadway." The more we make space for the idea of simply making theatre because it's right to do it right now – and it doesn't have to be political – the better. The other thing I'd be interested in as a viewer is the other stuff, like Tom Mac Intyre's work. The non-text-based stuff, where the text on its own gives you nothing of the sense of what the theatre production does.

HL: *Speaking of Tonys, it does seem as if Irish theatre defines itself more and more by overseas reaction.*

GS: As someone who hasn't achieved that, my answer would of course be bitter and twisted. But I do find it interesting. The Americans, oddly enough, are more open, I think. I feel that the British still unconsciously want something from Irish theatre which, if they get it, gets the tick in the "correct" box, and if they don't get it, gets nothing at all. So they're not interested in Irish theatre, as such, but they're interested in that thing, which is usually some preconceived notion of what Irish theatre can or should be.

I was watching Richard Eyre's television series about the theatre. Irish theatre does fantastically well out of it, but in exactly the way you would expect. He centres an entire programme around *The Playboy of the Western World*, and why it's one of the great plays of the twentieth century. And then Shaw gets pretty much a whole programme to himself as well, and O'Casey. So they're constantly looking for an update on that tradition. The other thread which is constantly running through all that, from Oscar Wilde and Brendan Behan, probably up to Martin McDonagh, is the idea of the mad Irish genius. That somehow we of the Irish theatre have a spark that is missing from British theatre. An interesting aspect of this is that, if you look at British theatre, there are lots of Irish actors and writers there. Directors also do well. But nobody who's Irish runs theatre or produces theatre. I've never heard an Irish person being mentioned as a possible Artistic Director of the National Theatre or the RSC or any of those institutions. I'm not suggesting there's any dissimulation going on there, but I am suggesting that what they see and like in Irish theatre is something to do with a mad seed of creativity…

HL: *A lot of critical and academic writing, as much from Scotland as from Ireland, has suggested that sort of attitude is rooted in notions of the metropolitan centre versus the "untamed" or "primitive" fringes.*

GS: … and the same with Northern Ireland and theatre about the Troubles as well. I think it's very true. To mention my most recent failure in Britain, *About Adam*, which was received with a resounding lack of interest. That may reflect a number of things, but it got a much better response in America. Even those who liked it in Britain were just saying "Yeah, it's fine, so what?" It wasn't what they wanted from an "Irish" film or play.

HL: *Does that mean that stories rooted in the realities of the contemporary, urban society that you and I live in here, are not going to travel across the Irish Sea?*

GS: Yes. We might partly see it as some kind of slight, that Paddy isn't supposed to be as sophisticated as the rest of us, but the other way of looking at that is very simple. It's them saying "We have that over here. We don't need to see an Irish version of that." Irish people have only succeeded with that when they've gone to England and written about England.

HL: *What about Northern Ireland and the conflict there, which, it seems, hasn't interested you directly as a subject for your work, although it's had a direct or indirect effect on a lot of other Irish theatre?*

GS: That really was a post-colonial thing, where the British for a while were only interested in stories that reflected the Troubles in some way.

HL: *Whereas people in the Republic didn't really want to know.*

GS: To be perfectly honest, what does sadden me is that we didn't reflect that lack of interest in a positive way. I've never seen a drama that has depicted that point of view, and projected it as an attitude which it's alright to have. Instead, the lack of interest has been expressed by not putting on very many productions of Troubles plays. Or if we have put them on, we've imported them from Northern writers. We haven't generated many of our own plays about it. I would love to have done one myself. It's a hard enough one to pull off, but something about how uninterested people down here were by what was going on.

HL: *It's always tricky to write an interesting play about people's lack of interest.*

GS: It does mean we've never put our finger on that very important truth about people in the south. The only time it's ever arisen is in some Northern plays when Southerners are berated for leaving them in the lurch.

HL: *What about the still surprisingly low proportion of Irish women writing for theatre?*

GS: It's a curious thing, when there are so many women novelists. I had an interesting experience a few years ago, when the National Association of Youth Drama asked me to chair the panel of judges on a first-time playwrights competition. One of the things we decided straight away was not to have positive discrimination, but for every play to be submitted to us anonymously. Of course, as you read a play you tend to make a fairly accurate guess of whether the writer is male or female, and most of the time you're right. Anyway, we got well over one hundred entries, knocked them down to thirty. We decided that there would be no winner, but there would be public readings of the four best in the Peacock. And of course all four were male. But even within the thirty, only three or four were female. And I should say that three of the five panellists were women.

The whole point about novels is that they're something which can be done at home, and finished and then sent off. Even if theatre was a very masculine environment, that should affect the directors rather than the writers, and there are plenty of good female directors. I can't give a reason for it, but it's certainly the case that there are fewer good women writers.

HL: *How well do you think Irish theatre is served by the media and by critics?*

GS: I notice that I'm changing with the years, especially because of the way I work in theatre, which means that my life doesn't depend on it. It's interesting to me if there's a bad reaction, but I rarely get myself into a spin about it. I do find them less useful than I used to. Because theatre criticism is largely review-based, the likelihood of getting some new insight into the work, which you hadn't thought of before, is much less. Whereas I might accept that somebody could write a very good think-piece about a production they've seen, that's unlikely to happen in a daily newspaper. But, to date, I don't find anything malicious or vindictive or consciously unhelpful. Most reviewers are decent theatre-lovers who say what they have to say.

HL: *What about the other side of that argument, which I've often heard articulated, that Irish critics are too close to the people they're critiqueing, and that as a result there's too much soft reviewing?*

GS: That's certainly true, and many people in theatre would agree with that, because it creates divisions in theatre. There are people who would feel very strongly that certain reviewers are more likely to kow-tow to the mainstream theatre, and would be loathe to attack it, however true or untrue that is. And that they're quite happy to take the guns out on the little people. Largely, however, we are lucky in Ireland that theatre criticism cannot make or break people's careers or force theatre practitioners to change their belief in what they are doing.

HL: *What's your experience of the difference between working as a writer-director in theatre and in film?*

GS: Obviously, on one level they're both about working with actors, but on another level the two are entirely different. What's important to me is that because of doing other stuff, I've never had to be a working director to pay the bills, so that's given me a certain kind of freedom. On another level, it's also meant that I've particularly enjoyed doing theatre at its most theatrical. It has allowed me to be more extreme, and has given me a slightly different view of theatre. You know the way distinguished British actors appear on TV chat-shows and say, "Of course, theatre is what I really love, theatre is what lasts." But in an odd kind of way, without meaning any insult, I enjoy theatre because it's ephemeral, and I'd be inclined to think that film is the thing that lasts. There's a significance in that moment when you have to say, "That's the final cut, that's the finished film." It probably won't ever change and you know that, in a hundred years time, somebody will wipe the dust off it to have a look and it'll be exactly the same. So I love the passing excitement of theatre and related to that is the excitement I get from the way it can change. When you make a film, you find yourself looking at the same performances over and over again, until you reach a point where you wish the actors would do something different. That's an element of the theatre director coming out in me; it's something you'd think directors would hate, the notion that the work you've shaped might change. But actually, in theatre, that's almost always a positive thing. I love the idea that you can go back to the theatre to see the same play a week later and it might have subtly changed. Of course, you always hate it when it develops too much away from your intentions, but I've even grown more mellow about that. Obviously, if something's got to the point where it's just not good any more, then you want to fix it.

HL: *I think the real reason actors prefer theatre is because of the greater level of control or input they have in the process.*

GS: That's true and I think it's what really lies behind those sorts of comments I talked about. They pretend it's because theatre is a higher art form and more permanent but I tend to think it's because they know that ultimately they control it – particularly leading actors. It you have a production of a major Shakespeare play, it's more likely to bear the stamp of the leading actor than the director.

HL: *By contrast, in film the director-as-auteur is seen as the real creator of the work, which obviously isn't the same in theatre, although you're an exception as a writer-director.*

GS: It's interesting that the writer-director in film is pretty well encouraged, whereas not so in theatre. For example, I already mentioned Mark O'Rowe and there's no doubt in my mind that he would be capable of directing his own work but, he probably hasn't had an opportunity yet because of that general suspicion in theatre of people doing that. Equally there are writers whom you would advise to keep well away from directing, but you get that in film as well. The one danger, I think, in playwriting of the last thirty or forty years, not just in Ireland but in Britain and America, is of a sort of writing which is just a variation of a certain type of screenwriting – more television actually than film – that kind of thing drives me insane.

HL: *In the Irish context, it always seemed to me, especially during the 1980s, that RTE's failure to produce any TV drama had a positive impact on Irish theatre, in that you had writers like Paul Mercier who in the UK would have been snapped up for TV but here kept writing for the stage.*

GS: Certainly Paul is somebody who I've always thought could transfer very well to film and has actually done so, although only to short films so far. It was too long in coming. But it's interesting that, while you're right about the subject matter, and some of the Passion Machine plays were natural telly material, it's often not noticed that there's fantastic poetry in Paul's writing and that it's very lyrical.

HL: *But surely lyricism and poetry can be just as much a part of cinema as of theatre?*

GS: I'm talking more about television when I say naturalism. If you were to look at the two films I've made (*Guiltrip* and *About Adam*) and ask whether I think of myself as a naturalistic film-maker, the answer clearly would be "No." It's one of the things that annoys me when people comment on my films in such a way as to suggest they're meant to be taken literally. They're missing the point entirely. But I suppose what I'm talking about is that wonderful trick in film, where you think you're watching something real but you're not. Although, to contradict myself entirely, theatre can achieve that same thing. But when film tries to become more theatrical, it seems to me to become tiresome.

HL: *Gerry Stembridge, thank you.*

Gerard Stembridge has been writing and directing professionally since 1984, has written 12 plays for theatre, *Leaving, The Young Europeans, 1992, Betrayals, The Girls of Summer, Goodnight Strabane, Lovechild, Ceauşescu's Ear, The Gay Detective, Daniel's Hands, Nightmare on Essex Street* and *Denis And Rose*. He wrote a radio series *Scrap Saturday* with the late Dermot Morgan and several radio plays, including *Daisy the Cow Who Talked*, and *Daylight Robbery*. He has also written and directed two TV series, *Nothing To It* and *Commonplaces*, two TV dramas *The Truth About Claire* and *Black Day at Black Rock* and two feature films *Guiltrip* and *About Adam*. He has also occasionally directed other theatre including   *The Comedy of Errors* (Shakespeare), *The Whiteheaded Boy* (Lennox Robinson), *Massive Damages* (Declan Lynch), *Made In China* (Mark O'Rowe) and *The Morning After Optimism* (Tom Murphy).

Hugh Linehan is Entertainment Editor of *The Irish Times*, for which he writes on film, television, the arts and popular culture, as well as editing its weekly entertainment supplement, The Ticket. He is a former editor of *Film Ireland* magazine and has contributed to publications including *Variety* and *Cineaste*. Prior to taking up journalism, he worked as an assistant director on films including *The Dead*, *December Bride* and *The Commitments*.

Enda Walsh in Conversation with Emelie FitzGibbon

EF: *Enda, you started out with Dublin Youth Theatre, you've worked with Graffiti, and Corcadorca and the Abbey, you've worked as an actor and a director and a writer in a number of different sectors within the Irish theatre. Do you feel there are divisions in Irish theatre, differences in terms of prestige?*

EW: Without a doubt and it really infuriates me when I see it because of my experience with Graffiti and writing a children's play. I'm still actually very proud of that play. In a previous Dublin Theatre Festival I went to see some of the children's shows and they were incredibly weak, they were obviously shows that were on the circuit and exhausted. That really infuriated me. It was like because it was for children or for family it wasn't important theatre and that's complete bullshit because from my point of view there isn't a division. There is good and bad theatre. What happens a lot of the time, and what has happened, is you had people who aren't experts, producing work and starting companies, and they're like a group of mates together and the work has been substandard. And they're the ones who are actually making it shit for everyone else.

EF: *In fact there's good work and there's bad work, and good writing and bad writing in every sector.*

EW: Yeah. But there is without a doubt an inherent snobbery among people who say "Yeah, I've made it. I'm working in the National Theatre. This is fantastic." But good community work – some of the stuff that Peter Sheridan did – was absolutely fantastic. That's stuff the National Theatre should be doing, more of that sort of thing as opposed to doing the oul' rep.

EF: *As you raise the issue, what function do you think a National Theatre should have. Is it needed at all?*

EW: I think it is. But the work has to be vigorous and strong. I understand that they do have to do the repertoire and that's fair enough, but I think the presentation of them ... some of it has been very, very dull. So far, I think what Ben Barnes [Artistic Director of the Abbey] is doing is good and is right. I think the changes he wants to bring to the Peacock are right and hopefully it will become a good studio theatre. The big problem that I basically have with the bloody National Theatre is that their spaces are so ugly, their theatres are ugly and actors hate performing on the stages because they're just dead stages. But I'm very heartened by the fact that he's brought over people like the Schaubühne in Germany.

EF: *You feel having visiting companies in there is a good thing?*

EW: In a Festival situation you're reminded of what they're doing with theatre in different countries and we do need to be reminded of that: that our work is very text based, and quite dull at times, and it does need an enormous kick up the backside. I think there's a lot of work and it's all monologue based and that's fine, but I don't find that theatre. I don't find it very theatrical. It's not using the medium to its full capabilities.

EF: *If you compare some of our monologue theatre at the moment with some of the physical theatre that's being done in Europe, we do need to see that, don't we?*

EW: Absolutely. I've been lucky enough now to do a lot of work in Germany and the style of performance, the actors, are really really *committed* over there. Of course they've a lot of rehearsal period and everybody wants that, but just the risk's there. And it's good to have risks and to fail. We can all fall back into "Oh yeah that's definitely going to work" – that style of stuff. "It's worked in the past and it'll work again." But to throw it out there and to trust that an audience will warm to it? If there's *conviction*...

EF: *Do you think that is an important factor for the Abbey? Conviction?*

EW: What you have to do is *have conviction* in the building and that hasn't been there in the past. My brief experience was that I thought it was a bloody awful, dead building and very dysfunctional. But I really hope that Ben and the Peacock get it right and get interesting work there. What's happening in Dublin at the moment is there is no centre. In the seventies and the eighties there was the Project and there was a bit of a buzz. Dublin theatre needed something that was important or pivotal or reacting to what the National Theatre was. But there isn't anything at the moment. The National Theatre – and rightly so – wants a new Artistic Director for the Peacock and that's *right*. I think they should kick ass with it, and push the work much, much further.

EF: *And your experience of working there – which I know was not particularly happy – wouldn't put you off working with the National Theatre again in given circumstances?*

EW: It certainly wouldn't be a priority.

EF: *Is that mainly because of the spaces?*

EW: The spaces, yeah. I'm very fond of what actors can do, and I know from talking with actors they feel uncomfortable there. I think the Peacock is a very difficult place. I have been asked to work there, but I wouldn't.

EF: *What's your favourite theatre space in Ireland? Is the quality of the space terribly important to you?*

EW: Absolutely. I must say I had a great experience in the New Theatre in Dublin doing *Bedbound*, because everyone had forgotten it as a venue. And it was all small companies in there, doing worthy work and all the rest. I was really glad we did it in there because it was very raw and very dirty and smelly but then it became this lovely place over the time we were there and I was very happy with that. I was really glad that I could do it because there aren't places like that now. The new Project and all these new venues – it does take them a couple of years to weather, to become real spaces. No one actually *likes* working in these concrete blocks and I think an audience don't like that either. I mean, in the New Theatre we had the audience coming through a bookshop and through the back of the bookshop and into the theatre and it was all sort of sweet and very special and you want to keep that. In the past *Disco Pigs* played bloody everywhere, but everyone says the *best* it played was in the International Bar, above the pub – as opposed to the West End where it was crap.

EF: *Do you like site-specific work, or where the space is fitted to the play or there's some sort of synchronization or harmony between the place and the play? Does that make a difference?*

EW: Absolutely. I think you can get lost in that though. I think you can actually get obsessed by the site and the work gets lost. But I think it does make it special.

EF: *Your own writing – I'm thinking of* Ginger Ale Boy, Misterman *and* Bedbound *as much as* Disco Pigs *– seems very distinctive. A very particular style and a focus on characters who seem trapped, although some of them are now moving towards the possibility of some kind of redemption within themselves. How do you see your work in the context of contemporary Irish theatre? Is that a very large question?*

EW: It is really. All writers and all creators will see themselves as being separate. But there are a group of us of a similar age who are going through classic themes of men in their early thirties. Conor McPherson is dealing with a real bundle of anxieties. It's similar to what I'm doing but in a completely different stylistic way. He is dealing with characters who are really lonesome, and not aware of where they're actually going, and afraid of that, but really carrying on because they have to. But this is general. Many people in their thirties – particularly men of our generation – just maybe look at their fathers and look at their fathers' failings as fathers and as people and go "well I don't want to be that, but what do I want to be?" It's all that. Not "new men."

EF: *Unreconstructed?*

EW: But for every generation there is that need to get better. You revolt against the previous generation – sometimes a tiny little revolution – but to improve things, to get better. You do don't you?

EF: *I don't know. I'm still trying to get better. Whatever about men in the thirties, just over the last two years I've noticed university productions and young writers favouring a style similar to* Disco Pigs *or influenced by it. Do you find that flattering?*

EW: It is very flattering. But I would say if I was to ape somebody I wouldn't ape S Club 7 or a pop group. I would ape someone like The Beatles. I think *Disco Pigs* linguistically was good but I think it's a flawed play in many ways. However it sort of captured a moment and there was a little bit of Irish theatre that was just right. So in many ways it was very fortunate, the success that it had. It was just a moment in Irish theatre and it was so unusual at the time.

EF: *And it went across audiences too, which was interesting – even segmented audiences.*

EW: Yeah, absolutely. In many ways I look back at *The Ginger Ale Boy* and I think there are passages of *The Ginger Ale Boy* that are a hell of a lot stronger. I know it's a flawed play – what play isn't – but I still look at that play and think there's definitely another life in that play. The landscape of it is much, much bigger. Probably that's why it's flawed; it's trying to capture too much.

EF: *Do you think you might come back to it?*

EW: I think so, yeah. There's a production of it at the moment in Germany and I'd love to go and see it. It just sounds hilarious. You remember there's this scene – for no particular reason – in *The*

Ginger Ale Boy, this ice-cream man comes on and paints this whole picture ...

EF: *A monologue, isn't it?*

EW: Yeah. And in Germany – I've just seen the photographs – and it is an ice-cream van that comes down from the flies in clouds – that'd be quite funny to see.

EF: *I'd love to have the capacity to do that, as a director. If that kind of thing were possible here would it make a difference to your work? If you could have your ice-cream van coming down from the flies, would you go for it?*

EW: I probably wouldn't go for it. I probably wouldn't. I know that because I've just finished a play recently and the work is becoming much, much smaller.

EF: *Smaller than* Bedbound, *which is just a box?*

EW: Yeah, just a box. But *Bedbound* is all ... it's so *fast* and then it stops and someone says "I'm sorry" and then they go "Okay, I accept your apology and we can carry on." That's basically the play. I'm trying to push the work much more abstract but it is difficult. I'm very, very interested – as we all are – in an audience learning the language of the play, *having* to learn it and then getting lost in it and coming out the other side having experienced a different world. I'm pretty good at developing worlds – that's probably my one big strength – but I need to push it in a much more abstract way. I like it when an audience doesn't like a character – I'm pretty decent like that – but I want to push it so they don't like the play, but then they begin to learn the *form* of the play and how the characters are. So the actual payoff – the emotional payoff – is a hell of a lot bigger because you're disliking something; you're not liking the characters, but then you begin to care about it and you learn the form of the play. So really, I'm trying to make the work smaller and more abstract and difficult for people and for me. I've just finished something and I don't know whether I like it yet but I know it's got a really big emotional punch and that's the one big thing that's important to me.

EF: *That's another thing that characterizes your plays – there is a lot of emotional punch in them. It obviously distinguishes your work from the rather distant writing of some of your contemporaries. You force the audience into emotional engagement ...*

EW: I love that. I want that in theatre. I love crying – I *love* it and I think it's wonderful – and feeling, being part of an audience. Everyone is laughing and when everyone's upset, everyone's upset. It's wonderful. I'm not a religious person but it is the closest I've got to a religious experience, sitting in an audience, crying, watching something and everyone is just held together as a group. Yeah, definitely!

EF: *What about the wider question – something that could be done in Irish theatre that would improve your capacity. If somebody could wave a wand in the morning and say – Enda you may have whatever you want for Irish theatre. What would that be?*

EW: This is difficult but it comes from my experience and it's something that I've formed the last few years. I think writers need to write alone and they should write outside of companies. What happened to me in the past – and I'm very grateful for it – was that I ended up for a long time working with one company. I learned so much. But then writers get sort of locked into writing for a particular style and they need to move on. So writers need to be alone but they also need producers and directors and actors so it's difficult. I was lucky with *Bedbound.* Dublin Theatre Festival produced the work and asked me to direct it – not that at the time I wanted to direct it. But we brought different people together out of companies and worked on it, freelance people. And really you want that set-up all the time, because a lot of the time you're dealing with – unfortunately – egos and the history of a company. And you're also dealing with audiences who are getting used to how you write for a company or how the company produces your work. You can get locked into just doing the same thing and that's wrong. Obviously in the ideal world you want producers floating around there with loads of money and going "great, let's bring in the people that we really, really want, but let's *not* get locked into the idea of working with those people again."

EF: *The Enda Walsh style with the Enda Walsh company?*

EW: I've *never* liked that. I've been asked now, since *Bedbound,* whether I want to direct the thing I've just written and I don't even know whether I want to because maybe it isn't right for me. That was right for me, it was right for that specific time. Each project should have its own ... there should be enough *care* to it. I don't want to get locked into dealing with just the same people. Being a writer in a company is just ridiculous and difficult. I talked to John McArdle about this recently and he was going "You're dead right. You do work alone." That's when you become creative and you're able to push your work much, much further. I know I'm very fortunate in that I feel that my work now – I can get it produced. But I think there are many writers out there – better than me – who are too locked into writing for a particular company and their work is just samey, year after year ...

EF: *So directors should just go and crawl into a shell – particularly directors who have worked with Enda Walsh.*

EW: Jesus, no. I'm so thankful. I wouldn't be the writer I am now if it wasn't for my brilliant experience with Pat Kiernan and with Corcadorca. But he would be as honest as I am to say we just grew apart. And then you can't work with those people any more.

EF: *I was referring back another step to when Graffiti did your children's play* Fishy Tales. *But that leads me to wonder what you think of the training available for theatre in Ireland. You yourself came into the profession through DYT but is there anything you see in the actors you work with in Ireland, or techies or directors that you think could be better?*

EW: I love what actors can do. But there is *one* school in Ireland and whenever I see them I *know* there is a particular sort of way of acting and I find it incredibly pompous. They're producing little pomp-ass sort of actors and I think it actually comes from the people who are training them. It does infuriate me. I think in training you want to have practitioners, you want to have teachers who make you really aspire to be that person and they have a real *love* of theatre and they want to shake it up. And it isn't about "my *job* is training people to be an actor," it's their whole bloody *life*! They're really energizing people; they're not bloody administrators who happen to know a few theatre games. You know what I mean? That annoys me.

EF: *I find you still see some of the best actors coming out of youth theatres and universities.*

EW: Still, you do, without a doubt.

EF: *Although you do get good people coming out of the acting schools as well.*

EW: You do. But people need to be told that there are so many things that you have to *undo* in actors when they've got that particular type of training. It's *important*. You want them to have an *energy*. I hate getting into a dialogue with actors about acting. You just do it, and believe in it, and do it one hundred percent. Do not over-analyse. An actor has to take on this particular sort of character in a play, but actors need big hearts and good minds. Ultimately they need big fucking hearts: they need to be able to understand the *life* of these characters. It's not something that can be taught through little games.

EF: *I know* Disco Pigs *has just been released on film, but in terms of theatre, what do you see as the relationship between theatre and other media? Is there a temptation to use videos and multimedia and so on …*

EW: For me, no. I actually quite like it – if it feels right, it's dead right. But for me? No. I did it in *The Ginger Ale Boy*, but briefly, and it wasn't integral and could've been done in many other ways.

EF: *So you don't feel the influence of television?*

EW: No. I feel the emotions of characters or of people are so fascinating for me and so big that if you can manage to actually create a character and make it whole and make their emotional journey whole, that's big enough.

EF: *What's your own taste in theatre? Have you seen anything in Irish theatre that's really excited you in the last ten years?*

EW: There are writers I love. Donal O'Kelly's *Catalpa* I thought was just fantastic. I like his stuff that he does himself, I love all his work. I think Paul Mercier's work is at times just brilliant and really touching. And I find his work really interesting. I love *Kitchensink*. I brought my Mom to it and she got very upset at the way the play is structured from these young characters and they get older and older, and telling the lives of these people, of a whole life in a short period of time. It was really brilliant and really touching. He handles big, big issues; he handles Ireland and society better than any writer I can think of at the moment.

EF: *And in a deceptively simple way, very accessible ...*

EW: Absolutely.

EF: *You were talking earlier about productions of your own plays in Germany. Why do you think Irish theatre is so successful abroad?*

EW: I know. There've been something like fifty productions of *Disco Pigs* in Germany already and I know that *Bedbound* has sold all over it already. And you think "Why?" I think the Germans in particular are interested in characters who are very troubled, who are dangerous. But they do like the simplicity of the kind of stuff that I am writing. I think my work is very simplistic in its themes. But the characters are very hard and have a real struggle about them. I think my work has been largely successful because it's small.

EF: *Two actors.*

EW: And people see it and they go, "bloody hell." It's just about actors, about performing, about developing these characters. And there's always full throttle behind anything that I've written. And these moments where their emotions just begin to reveal themselves to us and then we understand them, we understand why they have this anxiety.

EF: *And in a sense they are not particularly Irish, or with Irish concerns. Even though your vocabulary is very much set in Cork. You always write in a very patterned style. Almost poetic, prose-poetry. Does that translate? Do you have good translators?*

EW: I do. My work hasn't been produced in France, although it's been done in French translation. I know that obviously it's a bad translation and I know that Ian Galbraith, my German translator is very good. He's a Scottish guy. But largely it's because I know that my work is ... the root of all my work is obviously Cork but in Germany it's Bavaria, so it's similar and they've really looked after that. But it has been hilarious. My first experience going over to see the very first *Disco Pigs* was a big event in Germany and I went into the foyer and there were pictures of Bernie Murphy [a well-known Cork character] all over the place, and of Cork. And now people in theatre over there know Cork and they know the city and I'm very very proud of that.

EF: *Last question. If you had one gift to give Irish theatre what would it be?*

EW: I think, another Enda Walsh? No! God, I don't know. There's loads of things. A lot of the time I think theatre is very, very important and we're all in it and we love it and we want it to be bigger than it is. And yet I don't think it's had the exposure it's had in other countries. I don't think it's taken as seriously. Bar *The Irish Times*, their one Arts Page, what is there? You have these critics, say, in *The Independent* – okay, I'm saying that because they've hated everything I've done, but that's fine – but it's the way they go about criticizing things. I think Irish theatre criticism is appalling. I would like better critics. I would like larger space given over to theatre. I would like theatre practitioners to try harder, to take bigger risks. I would like actors to train harder, to work harder.

EF: *Put their heart and their guts into it.*

EW: Exactly. Because ultimately that's what we want. We want an audience to walk away completely shocked and moved and we can only do that if we give our own hearts to our work, ourselves and all of that.

Enda Walsh is a playwright. He worked for some years with Corcadorca theatre company who premiered many of his earlier plays, including *The Ginger Ale Boy* (1995), *Disco Pigs*, which was a winner of the Stewart Parker award in 1997, and *Misterman* (1999). His most recent stage plays are *Bedbound* (2001) and *Sucking Dublin* (1998) which was written for the Abbey Outreach Department. In addition to mainstage work, Enda has written

Fishy Tales (1993) for Graffiti Theatre-in-Education company and a number of radio plays. His short film *Not a Bad Christmas* (2001) and the feature-length *Disco Pigs*, for which he wrote the screenplay, were released this year. He has just completed a new play, *Pondlife*, and is currently under commission for two feature length films, *Being Ugly* and *The Rose of Tralee*.

Emelie FitzGibbon is Artistic Director of Graffiti Educational Theatre Company, Cork. She served ten years as Chair of the National Association for Youth Drama and is Course Director of New York University's Educational Theatre Department Graduate Study Abroad programme in Ireland. Her many productions for Graffiti include premieres of *Infidel* (Roger Gregg); *Jackie's Day* (Sarah FitzGibbon); *Teanga* and *Forget-Me-Not* (company devised); *The Riddle-Keeper*, *Tangled Web* and *Deadly Weapons* (Laurie Brooks); and *Striking Distance* (Raymond Scannell).

Vincent Woods in Conversation with Kevin Barry

KB: *Vincent, you started in the theatre after another kind of life, what brought you to the theatre?*

VW: Sometimes I think it was sheer accident. I always loved the theatre since I was small.

KB: *Did you go to it?*

VW: I did as far as one could, growing up in a poor rural part of Leitrim. It is the same way as I remember discovering a love for books, almost from the moment that somebody began to read to me. I think that I discovered a love for theatre almost when I saw my first – probably very badly produced – play in the local hall, where I later, when I was about fourteen, put on a play of my own. I wrote, directed and starred in a very bad play, which was attempting extraordinary things like showing hell, which was attempting to have few realities going on, this life and the after-life.

KB: *And there wasn't just a hole in the stage with hell underneath? Hell was in the open? That would have been wonderful.*

VW: We had great difficulty in trying to conceptualize hell. About the best we could come up with at the time was wonderful tails, made from rubber tyres and little points on the end and horns.

KB: *What age are we talking about now?*

VW: Fourteen or fifteen.

KB: *What was the name of that play? Did you give it a name?*

VW: I did, but I can't remember what it was. It was slightly influenced by Noel Coward. I had seen Margaret Rutherford in a comedy of his with a séance. So I had grey hair, a stammer and a limp and somebody said to me afterwards you really were being ambitious, never having acted before to attempt all these things.

There was a very significant kiss towards the end. It was a happy ending.

KB: *And then years went by and other ways of life, you were still writing?*

VW: I always wanted to write from the time I was very small. When people asked me what I wanted to do, I always said that "I want to be a writer." And I had no idea really what that might involve, so that when it came to practicalities, when it came to college and taking options, somewhere along the line I confused journalism and writing, in a creative sense. I went on that career path and really enjoyed it. I was living in Dublin from 1978-1989, and I went to theatre quite a lot and I think that it is again where I began to feel that this was something I could do; it was not even an ambition, it was not as if I felt this was something I wanted to do, it was more like an innate feeling of it being the possibility of something I could turn to.

KB: *We won't talk about the journalism, we'll stick on the line of the theatre you are going to in late 1970s, early 80s Dublin. Are there plays from that time, theatres from that time, writers from that time that influenced?*

VW: I will never forget seeing Tom Murphy's *Bailegangaire*. That was a moment of absolute revelation.

KB: *After it had come to Dublin from Galway with Siobhán McKenna?*

VW: It was a most extraordinary moment of theatre.

KB: *Why?*

VW: I don't quite know why. I think it was partly that here was an exploration of language as well as an exploration of place, people, history and story. It was that melding of all those things, and somehow, the absolutely truthful theatricality of it, – and of course, Siobhán McKenna's incredible performance.

KB: *I sometimes felt after seeing that play that I had seen something that I had never seen before. There was equal force, there were energies in the play saying tell the story and then there was against that, another equal force, saying don't.*

VW: Yes.

KB: *And that was in some ways the drama. The play is almost a monologue that doesn't want to be spoken.*

VW: Yes.

KB: *How did you feel that for you it was an extraordinary kind of event?*

VW: It was quite personal in some ways, curiously, my parents were visiting me at the time and so I took them to the play and, as so often, here was art mirroring life, because when I was a child, my grandmother, my mother's mother lived with us. She was a wonderful woman, but at times she was domineering as well. So to an extent there was a mirroring of some of my own realities in the play. It was interesting to observe the reactions of my parents, because my mother loved the play, but my father was deeply uncomfortable with it, and he was shuffling in the seat beside me and I remember saying "sit down" to him. He was also quite horrified at the sight of Siobhán McKenna sitting on a pot and afterwards, we had a drink in the bar and my mother said you can go now and tell the people that you saw Siobhán McKenna in a theatre in Dublin and my father said: "Indeed I will not go and say I saw her pissing in a pot." That was his reaction. I was the only person in the audience that night who stood up, so I gave it a kind of solo standing ovation and will never forget catching Siobhán McKenna's eye, seeing her, and resolving to go back before the end of the run to give her flowers and I didn't. And then, a few months later she was dead. I was working as a radio journalist at the time and I was in a newsroom on the Sunday when the news of her death came in and it was so shocking. I was deeply upset about it and deeply upset about the lack of response within a news organization to what I saw as the significance of this death. And I suppose that was the measure of the gap between the life I was living as a journalist and the reality I felt to be much stronger for me, the reality of the theatre.

KB: *That is a tough play and it is a tough moment when an actress, in a way, brings her life as an actress to a crisis in a play like that and everything falls together. Were there lighter moments? Was there anything in the theatre of the day in Dublin, which seemed to you to be witty, humorous, sharp and playful? Was it a darker kind of period in Dublin theatre?*

VW: I suppose it had at that time the collaboration between Tom Mac Intyre and Patrick Mason, it was also the era of *The Great Hunger* and that was wonderfully witty. What was so interesting in that for me was the deconstruction of language (as opposed to Tom Murphy in *Bailegangaire*), which is dismantling the poem and creating this vivid and vibrant piece of theatre. Sebastian Barry's *Boss Grady's Boys* I remember with great affection.

KB: *So there were different kinds of moods on the stage and different kinds of experiments?*

VW: At the time I went to London quite often and I was and am very interested in dance. So I went as often as possible to see dance companies in London because it was an area I felt where there was a terrible absence in Dublin.

KB: *With that kind of use of the stage, as it were, more spectacular or musical or choreographed forms which were the opposite to a fairly verbal Irish theatre. Anything coming in to the Dublin Theatre Festivals that made an impact?*

VW: I don't remember that so clearly, actually. Another play that stands out in my memory, from the late 1980s, was a production in the Gate Theatre of a play based on a Jewish legend, *Dybuk*. It was I think done by two actors. It was a very simple telling of this legend of a spirit returning to take over the body of a living person in order to fulfil something that has been unfulfilled in their own life. It was the most wonderful piece of theatre. Again, I saw it the night before I left Ireland in 1989. I had resigned from RTE. That play certainly influenced what I subsequently wrote in my first play, *John Hughdy, Tom John*, especially in its confronting of the audience, because I was sitting in the Gate Theatre and maybe it was the first time and the last time in the Gate where you felt confronted. There was this marvellous moment when the actor put on a scarf, bent over, became an old woman looking into a graveyard, looking into a cemetery. There was this very simple gesture where he/she said: "Look at them all, they are all dead." And sitting in the audience you began to feel like you were dead and it was a shock, the sort of shock theatre should provide. And somehow that stayed with me and in me and in writing *John Hughdy* and *Tom John*, about a year later in New Zealand, something of that feeling came back, especially that notion of confrontation.

KB: *So the night before you left, in the sense that you were going away, you had thrown in the job in RTE and so forth, this play impacted on* John Hughdy *and* Tom John *that you then wrote, which was your first mature play?*

VW: Yes.

KB: *Did you feel because of what you had already learned from the theatre that you knew what you were doing?*

VW: No. I think it was absolutely instinctive. I had a feeling somewhere that writing for theatre was something I could do. *Translations* was very important for me when I first saw it, and Druid's production of *Wood of the Whispering*, all of those and all of the other plays that I had seen over the years were all present in a sense. But it was instinctive. When I sat down with the space and the time to do nothing except write, in other words to do what I wanted to do and had set out to do, I didn't know what I would write so I didn't sit down to write a play. I sat down, and the play began to write itself.

KB: *Was that a slow process?*

VW: No. It was quite fast. I wrote the First Act of *John Hughdy* in a couple of days and I remember then thinking how do I stretch this, how do I make it last longer. And the shape emerging and deciding I was going to make one parallel another. Then the feeling of astonishment that this was being written. I realized subsequently that the voices were in my head all my life. And it is the usual story: how long did it take to write a play. Well it actually took me twenty-nine years and a few days.

KB: *And then the play goes through a process. You have the text, but on the other hand you have the event of working in the theatre with the play. That play, what happened when it was brought to the theatre?*

VW: I was still in Australia when Maelíosa Stafford came back and I had given him the text in Sydney. So he rang me to say that Druid wanted to put on the play during the 1991 Arts Festival in Galway. He asked me to come back for that, which I did. Rehearsals had already been on for about three weeks. So I came back to seeing something very close to being the finished play and that was very interesting. I remember the first morning in the rehearsal room seeing Des Braiden become John Hughdy, and it is the first moment of transformation of my words becoming his.

KB: *The voices had been in your head for a number of years and now they were being spoken and they were no longer in your head.*

VW: Yes, they had a life of their own; they were separate. This character came to life. It was my first real engagement with professional acting, taking a text with that whole level of the professional world of theatre and it was very exciting.

KB: *So there was this meeting between the playwright and text and the professional world of the theatre. How do you feel about those two worlds? In other words, is the text paramount, central or the interaction that then occurs from designer, director actors all that kind of area? Because when I saw* At the Black Pig's Dyke, *your second play, I had the experience of seeing the play, but I could not tell where the act of writing left off and the act of direction, choreography and design had begun. I could not separate text from performance.*

VW: I suppose for me that is when theatre is at its most successful, when that kind of seamlessness is present, and as regards which is most important, which is at the centre, I think they are both at the centre of successful theatre. Usually, nothing can happen without a script. But equally a script remains flat and remains only a script without the involvement of director, designer and actors. For me, I hope that I would always be open to the input of other people and, out of respect for their work, I hope that I would always be open to looking at my own work in the light of what they would say. For me, text is not sacrosanct. If I see something in rehearsal that isn't working, then out it goes.

KB: *In the rehearsal and production process of* At the Black Pig's Dyke *what happened?*

VW: Something extraordinary happened. I had been working on the text for about nine months. I began to write it in October/November of 1990. It was a very strange time. My mother was ill. She had cancer. She was dying over that period of me writing. I was travelling quite a lot between Leitrim, Sligo and Dublin, where I was working. So the play was written in these intense bursts, moments, and sometimes it was written on trains and buses here and there. But we did have a complete finished text by the time we went into rehearsals in July of 1992. At that stage, because I had been through so much in the previous six months, emotionally, I didn't really know any more what the play was going to be like. But I felt that it had a power and I felt that it could work very successfully. It was like one of these moments when everything is right and I suppose because Maelíosa Stafford was so passionate about the play and about the whole project involving mumming.

KB: *The play is about a group of mummers and those mummers are, in terms of design and spectacle of the play, always present.*

VW: That is central. Maelíosa Stafford first mentioned the idea of a play involving mummers when we met in Sydney. I had written a couple of programmes on Irish poetry for ABC radio and Maelíosa read, and we did a programme on Austin Clarke. And he mentioned this about the idea of a play on mumming and I said, which is true, I know quite a lot about mumming, so out of this, in a sense, a chance meeting in Australia, *At the Black Pig's Dyke* came to be. Actually, I often think about this, the title was one of the last things to emerge in the writing.

KB: *What does the title mean?*

VW: I suppose for me it is also deeply personal. Because the story of the *At the Black Pig's Dyke* was a story I had heard time and again as a child, I heard it from my mother who had heard it from my grandmother. And it was somehow towards the end of the writing process, when almost everything was there, somehow the image of the black pig, of this endless cycle of violence and retribution, with the faintest glimmer of redemption seemed utterly appropriate and I know as well that it is somehow something to do with the death of my mother, with her dying at that time. And I remember saying to her before she died that I had come up with a name for the play and I told her what it was and she said: "I think that is a very good name." And, again, I believe all that is personal does run into one's work. It has to.

KB: *That play is also a very public play, in so far that it was a historical play of a kind. I remember reading a book by Gramsci in which he speaks about mummers and clearly that book informs your play, yet you took, it seemed to me, a much more sceptical or a much less benign sense of what mumming might have been in a community, that a community in holding itself together through mumming could also be tearing itself apart and Gramsci seems to me to only have allowed for the first of those options. Was that part of your thinking?*

VW: I suppose it was. I have never had any illusions about folk tradition's ability to hide as well as reveal, so what may seem to be benign tradition, on closer examination may have a very different face indeed. The last Strawboys at a wedding in the area where I grew up, were present at a wedding in 1960 which is the year I was born, and my father and my brother would have been Strawboys on that occasion and I had heard stories more to do with Strawboys, people to use masking and disguise as an excuse and an opportunity to wreak a bit of havoc. It was hell. I saw it happen in different ways, with established traditions such as Halloween where people could go and fling rotten vegetables at people's houses and it was also used as an opportunity to settle scores, and inevitably in any society, no matter how small, there are going to be divisions, conflicts and enmities beneath the surface.

KB: *So the devices, the theatre of carnival isn't just a joke?*

VW: It is very much a reality.

KB: *And when subsequently with* At Black Pig's Dyke *there was considerable conflict between the stage and the audience and there were intense feelings about the play being politically unaccepted by certain audiences, did you anticipate that happening or were you surprised by that outcome?*

VW: I didn't anticipate it, which was possibly naïve of me, but I suppose I also feel that I did not set out with an agenda, I simply told things as I perceived them. And most of the stories in *At the Black Pig's Dyke* are based on real events. I suppose I am not surprised that some people found them unpalatable. I'm not sorry that they found them unpalatable. I think that one of the functions of theatre and of writing in general is at times to confront us with what we might like to have buried, what we might like to keep buried and unseen. And I had on a personal level, politically, moved from being a young republican. When I was eighteen I campaigned for Sinn Féin and I was involved in the campaigns around the hunger strikes of 1981 and had always felt very strongly about the republican agenda, about nationalism, about the desirability of unity. Growing up in the 1960s in Leitrim, you could not but be aware of the injustices that were being perpetrated in the Six Counties. As the years went on, and as I saw this cycle of horrific violence seeming to have no end, and working as a journalist, observing the brutality, the futility and the brutalization of people, I just began to feel more and more dubious about the worth of all of this. Really for me it called into question the use and the justification of violence for any political end.

KB: *And did you know when you were writing the play that it was in many respects an allegory for the world that you had been spectator to as a journalist in Ireland during the 1970s and 1980s?*

VW: Yes I did. Again, it was probably more unconsciously or sub-consciously so. I did not set out to mirror that, but certainly the instincts built up from all those years of observation, from all that experience are at the heart of it.

KB: *A great deal happened at the same time in that play. The personal, the professional work that you had been doing, the events that were beyond your own life, the death of your mother, many things coming together – and then after that play you wrote again. Would you tell us about that play?*

VW: *Song of the Yellow Bittern* was again a story I had been wanting to tell for a long time – partly, a meditation on family and on community and history and how stories are told and again on the truthfulness of stories. It was inspired partly by a real set of characters, real people in Leitrim in the 1820s and by a very controversial priest, of whom we heard a lot as kids.

KB: *The story is still told?*

VW: Yes, the story is still told. Mixing that with a family story of a widow who went to jail in place of her son, who was sentenced – jailed for poteen making. It was very potent ground, again, looking into folk tradition and attitudes to women in traditional society. It is something I always felt very strongly about. All of those impulses went towards creating what I suppose is a very big play, big in the sense of a spanning of time, maybe the telling of several stories. And it was deliberately and more consciously theatrical even than *At the Black Pig's Dyke* and some of that conscious theatricality came from the experience of having been involved in the previous two plays, so there is perhaps a greater sense of the structure of theatre.

KB: *If we turn sideways a little bit from your work as writer and as participant in theatre to the context you find yourself in, for example, the context of theatre criticism. I don't mean only with regard to your own plays,* *because obviously the critics are available to us as some kind of measure of the intelligence that is there discussing theatre or not. How do you see the context of criticism about theatre in Ireland?*

VW: I always read the critics. As a child in Leitrim I read *The Sunday Independent* and *The Sunday Press*, they were the only papers we got. And I read the reviews when I didn't have the remotest possibility of seeing the plays. That was an education in itself. I think there has been a very slap-dash attitude towards criticism in Ireland in that I know from working as a journalist quite often a paper would send out, in the past, any rookie to review a play. It was always like: "You can do this."

KB: *Have the major critics, nevertheless, lost the plot, lost their authority? Is there a serious level of discussion available?*

VW: I don't think there is. I think all you should do is look at the amount of space, the amount of words given to the reviewing of theatre in the newspapers to realize that it is utterly inadequate. And if you compare it to coverage of popular music, for instance, or film, the disparity between coverage of film here and of theatre is terrible.

KB: *The reviewer has more access to information and argument about film than about Irish theatre.*

VW: Definitely.

KB: *So this world doesn't have a structure of discussion around it? There are different kinds of playwrights; is there an interest in conflict or complementarity or whatever? Is there an interesting dynamic going on at the moment in Irish theatre, different kinds of writing?*

VW: I think it is beginning to happen. And I think that the slow development of professional theatre courses in Universities will have a knock-on effect and I hope and believe they will have a very positive knock-on effect. It's striking that, in the latest wave of successful theatre people like Conor McPherson, the notion that their work was rejected is very telling. I think that Irish theatre had become quite safe in a way.

KB: *McPherson made his reputation with some successes in London, before his popularity in Ireland.*

VW: Yes. I suppose I'd say that can be a mixed blessing. Billy Roche the same thing. There certainly has been a feeling that the people reading scripts were missing many fine plays and that is a separate issue to criticism, but it is part of the same thing, and I think that the emergence of stronger voices at all levels of criticism, of dramaturgy, even of new theatre groups, can only be beneficial to theatre in the long run.

KB: *So that even though perhaps there are certain dominant successful forms of theatre in Ireland over the last five to six years, you see that new theatre groups are perhaps not visible always, because criticism in reviews doesn't tell us enough of what is going on. But do you see a lot of activity that is there through new theatre groups, with new kinds of theatre and new approaches?*

VW: Yes. For instance, the Yew Theatre group in Ballina, their production of the rugby play (*Alone it Stands*), as I call it, was astonishing.

KB: *Is this the one where the baby is born from the scrum?*

VW: Yes, the sheer joyous theatricality of that was so encouraging – the vibrancy of that. It depresses me: too often, when I go to mainstream – I hate that word, but I'll use it – theatre here, I think, why, why is this going on? Why are people here? What are we doing? And it is very depressing when you feel that. And I sometimes feel like a "cynical bastard." I don't like that feeling, but I can't help it. I think we all have to ask ourselves questions about why we are involved in theatre, what we want to achieve and is it justified to say that we are going to put on this play because we have to put on this play? Is it not more honest to say, there is nothing worth putting on, so we are shutting down for six months?

KB: *Certainly in my experience, it is the small, very active theatre groups that are doing new work. Barabbas would be an example, there are several others – Blue Raincoat – there are many: some of the most exciting and unusual events that occur and they are almost homeless and they are fantastically alert and interesting. But with that then I think there is an issue for theatre. Who is its audience?*

VW: Yes.

KB: *Who is your audience?*

VW: I don't know. I hope my audience is anyone with an open mind, anyone who has even an instinctive interest in the possibility in theatre, and who will be open to any form, any form that emerges. I am sure that there are other plays that I want to write, I am not sure what they are yet, but they will be different to what I have done before.

KB: *Would you be optimistic that audiences are out there for that? Or do you feel that there is a kind of conservative tendency amongst audiences not to want new work?*

VW: Quite often, people will hope for or expect a new play by any playwright to mirror something of their favourite work by them, so maybe there is conservatism in that regard. People may want the same voice the same tone, the same dramas.

KB: *And the big theatres want revivals to fill the houses?*

VW: They do. Inevitably, there is the hugely commercial side of theatre and I again often find that depressing. Even in the midst of all of that you hope that glimmers of light come through. Even recently, *Eden* (by Eugene O'Brien) is fresh, it's taut and it's good. And those moments make it all worthwhile really.

KB: *And create their own audience?*

VW: Yes. I think that quite often, but not always, strong original work will get through, will be recognized.

KB: *Does the main stream sometimes have a difficulty in locating an audience? There is an audience in Ireland, yes, but does it also have a very strong eye on audiences in London or New York so that Irish plays sometimes seem to retain the stereotypical view of Ireland that is enjoyed at home and abroad, which is oddly stultifying?*

VW: I was working with a group of students recently on very short versions of six Classical Irish plays and seeing these being done – they were about ten minutes long – I was thinking my God the image of Ireland to emerge from all of these is pretty scarifying. It also oddly, at times, feels almost archaic. I think there is certainly an absence of new work reflecting the huge changes that have occurred and are occurring in this country. I think that that work will come. I think it must come. One of the things I found exciting about the changing face of Ireland is the notion that some of the so-called "refugees", some of the people coming in to Ireland, will perhaps see us as we are and tell it as they see and experience it.

KB: *So there maybe all kinds of unexpected mirrors?*

VW: I think that there will.

KB: *So instead of perhaps the hope that we would find by having more women playwrights than having men playwrights, those kinds of aspirations to build a different Irish theatre, perhaps a different Irish theatre might arrive from being seen in others' eyes?*

VW: I really believe that. I think that there is an enormous insularity here. I feel I don't see nearly enough theatre from other countries; we are starved of it. There is an arrogance; there is a belief that Irish theatre is at the centre of the world in a way. It is not. It is one aspect of theatre. And we miss so much. I always think about around 1996 the Irish Festival Imaginaire d'Irlande in France and there was to be a reciprocal festival of French culture in the theatre and in writing. It never happened.

KB: *We are more concerned to export than import?*

VW: Yes. I think that there is an unwarranted belief in our own culture.

KB: *If we imagine a national theatre, you might see its brief as quite a different thing from being a national theatre that is pre-occupied with national representations?*

VW: Yes.

KB: *You might prefer to see a National theatre, which threw open its doors in a quite different way to foreign product?*

VW: Yes, we should see that. I think it is beginning to happen more in the Abbey now and I really welcome that.

KB: *So how would you put its priorities? If you were to propose priorities, for a national theatre?*

VW: A few of the primary functions of a national theatre is what the Abbey has been doing for a long time, which is to present the canon of classic/modern Irish theatre, while fostering new writing. And I would put that as a huge priority and think it has been neglected. There is something of an attempt to rectify that. But also, I think, to bring to the national theatre of this country, work from other countries, from around the world. Not only some of the classics that we get, but new work and new voices.

KB: *And to inform audiences?*

VW: Yes.

KB: *And have critics serve in that process?*

VW: Yes. There is a terrible lack of new international work in Ireland.

KB: *There is the financial side to that kind of proposal. How do you view the financial infrastructure that is there, not just for playwrights, but also for theatres? It seems a very complex area that has been much argued and disputed over in recent years. How do you as a practitioner in the field judge the structure of financing for theatre that is available?*

VW: In complete honesty, I don't think about it very much. Many playwrights, many writers generally struggle to make a living.

KB: *And they don't?*

VW: They just about do. Obviously the odd one will have a hit and can become very wealthy, that's terrific, but I often think about that first two one-act plays –*John Hughdy* and *Tom John* – I was broke when that went on, On the last day of performance somebody turned up from the bank chasing me for money I owed on a credit card. And there was this lovely ironic and theatrical moment in the lobby of Druid theatre, where there were champagne corks popping inside, at the end of a very successful run for the play. I owed a couple of thousand of pounds and I had this image of the writer as a prop, being carried out and being thrown out. I look at it very much from that point of view. Clearly, there is an onus on the government of any civilized society to make adequate funding available for theatre and I suppose I am not enough of an economist to know what that might come down to in financial terms, but there are people who know that, the government should know that and should be doing it.

KB: *Does that lead to any judgement on your part as to the role of Aosdána, which clearly supports playwrights, but does not support theatre or indeed other arts, in so far as those other arts are fundamentally always linked to practitioners of other kinds; designers, directors and so on, who have no representation of any kind, whereas the writer has something at Aosdána?*

VW: Yes, I think it is a defect of Aosdána and think it is something that will be addressed. I think there should be great room for interpretative artists to be recognized as well. There are people who have made enormous contributions to the arts in Ireland, in terms of interpretation. We writers for theatre would not have plays without the work of directors, designers and actors. I think they should be given due recognition.

KB: *So you think there is a world of wonders that we are not giving recognition to because we don't see the possibilities that can be achieved through the work of directors and designers and lighting people. Is it something that we are almost blind to, that we have blurred vision on?*

VW: Yes, it is a failure of the imagination, a failure of understanding. Theatre perhaps more than any other of the arts is so much about collaboration. I think that sometimes the cult of the writer in Ireland really annoys me.

KB: *Would you put the writer slightly aside and let others take centre stage here?*

VW: I think it might not be any harm to shift the writer slightly. I still hold that the writer, the text, is central to theatre, but we should not be glorified either.

KB: *You mentioned before the impact of new programmes in four or five universities here in Ireland. Are some of the things you are saying here to be distributed out to audiences and those who could enjoy theatre, but don't yet know what is there to be enjoyed?*

VW: I sincerely hope that there will be a flowering out of the various courses. And I think that the Arts Plan for the country is again attempting to address some of this. I still come back to the notion of that small parochial hall where I saw my first play. You can build magnificent theatres all around the country; unless you put on the plays and unless you maintain a certain standard within that, then these buildings could become white elephants. I believe in the potential of theatre within different places, it doesn't matter at times where something happens. I think about Fiona Shaw's production of *Hamlet*, which was staged in ruins, old factory spaces and warehouses. That was the most extraordinary version of *Hamlet* that I had ever seen. I think that sometimes to take theatre out of the theatre can be a very positive thing and I think that it can shape people a bit, because I think that we can become complacent in our nice comfortable seats where we go and expect to be entertained. Maybe sometimes we need to be put on benches or made to stand and have something happen out of life, out of reality, rather than within the confines of a new theatre.

KB: *You moved away from the theatre in the last several years in that you have been writing poetry and you also have been working on an anthology of Irish-Australian poetry, and you must be looking forward to going back at the theatre again.*

VW: I think I am. I don't know. The two things are so closely linked for me – poetry and theatre – that I find it hard to separate them. Sometimes my poetry runs into the theatre and vice-versa. I know what I am at in terms of the poetry, and I have a notion of where it may lead me in terms of theatre, but I am not absolutely sure. I think because I work a great deal by instinct, I don't necessarily plan ahead.

KB: *You work by instinct, you may not plan ahead, but you certainly in all your work, both poetry and theatre work, aim towards a work that is highly finished and effective, and as it were, disturbing, but not disturbing through being vague or ambiguous, disturbing in the form of having the wit of black humour. You force the thing to a point.*

VW: Well I hope I force myself to a point of grappling again with theatre, which is this extraordinary animal. I feel very strongly that there is no point in saying something unless you really have something to say. I am not going to write plays simply for the sake of having written plays, I want to write plays that mean something, say something, that engage with those forces of life and those workings out why the hell we're here. There are several themes that I have, if I can mix metaphors – on the long finger in my mind, but I'll know there will be a right time to tackle those and I think it is probably not very far away. I want to write a play out of Irish-Australia, for instance, and it is curiously apt that I should, given that that is where I met Maelíosa Safford, who was very important for me. There are extraordinary voices, extraordinary stories and histories in what I have been working on for the last number of years, in terms of the poetry of Irish-Australia, and there are people whose lives I want to explore, somehow theatrically.

KB: *Things are coming together?*

VW: Yes.

KB: *I hope so. The best of luck with that Vincent. I look forward to seeing the anthology when it appears, a book of verse and a new play at another time.*

Vincent Woods's two one-act plays *John Hughdy* and *Tom John* were produced by Druid Theatre Company and performed during the Galway Arts Festival of 1991. *At the Black Pig's Dyke* was produced by Druid in 1992 and won a Steward Parker award. *Song of the Yellow Bittern* followed in 1994 and his radio play *The Leitrim Hotel* won a P. J. O'Connor Award. He adapted Ignazio Silone's *Fontamarra* for stage in 1997. Collections of poetry include *The Colour of Language* published in 1995, *The Turning Wave, Poems and Songs of Irish-Australia* published 2001, and a new collection *Lives and Miracles* is due out early 2002.

Kevin Barry is Professor of English at the National University of Ireland, Galway. His most recent publication is *The Dead* (Cork U. P., 2001), a study of film versions of Joyce's story by John Huston and Roberto Rossellini.

Editors:

Lilian Chambers has always been passionate about theatre. She was active for many years on the amateur drama circuit and was an award-winning actor and director. She holds an M.A. in Modern Drama Studies from NUI Dublin.

Dan Farrelly was born in Melbourne, Australia. He studied in Melbourne, Frankfurt am Main and Strasbourg and lectured at University College Dublin as a Goethe specialist. He has published several books on Goethe. For four years he was Director of the UCD Drama Studies Centre and is currently active as a translator of German classical works, including Goethe's *Urfaust, Iphigenie auf Tauris*, Act One of *Claudine von Villa Bella*, and Büchner's *Woyzeck*.

Ger FitzGibbon lectures in the English Department, NUI Cork and is Chair of the University's Board of Drama and Theatre Studies. He has lectured and published on the work of Brian Friel, Tom Murphy, Frank McGuinness and Sebastian Barry. He is a former board-member and director with Cork Theatre Company and a founder of Graffiti Theatre Company, of which he is currently Chair. He has written a number of plays, including *The Rock Station* (1992) and *Sca* (1999). His stage-directing includes *The Birthday Party* (Harold Pinter), *The Shadow of a Gunman* (Sean O'Casey), *Accidental Death of an Anarchist* (Dario Fo) and *Scenes from an Execution* (Howard Barker).

Eamonn Jordan is a lecturer in Performing Arts at the Institute of Technology, Sligo. He is the editor of *Theatre Stuff: Critical Essays on Contemporary Irish Theatre*. His book *The Feast of Famine: The Plays of Frank McGuinness* was published in 1997. He has also written two critical commentaries for the Leaving Certificate: the first on Frank McGuinness's *Someone Who'll Watch Over Me* and the second on Arthur Miller's *Death of a Salesman*.

Cathy Leeney is interested in twentieth century and contemporary Irish theatre, and in gender and performance, and directing. She is lecturer at the Drama Studies Centre at University College Dublin.

Publications by Carysfort Press

Theatre Stuff

Critical Essays on Contemporary Irish Theatre
edited by Eamonn Jordan

Best selling essays on the successes and debates of contemporary
Irish theatre at home and abroad.

Contributors include: Thomas Kilroy, Declan Hughes, Anna
McMullan, Declan Kiberd, Deirdre Mulrooney, Fintan O'Toole,
Christopher Murray, Caoimhe McAvinchey and Terry Eagleton.

ISBN 0-9534-2571-1   €19.00/Ir£14.99/$18 *

The Starving and October Song

Two Contemporary Irish Plays
by Andrew Hinds

The Starving, set during and after the siege of Derry in 1689, is a
moving and engrossing drama of the emotional journey of two men.

October Song, a superbly written family drama set in real time in
pre-ceasefire Derry.

ISBN 0-9534-2574-6   €10.15/Ir£7.99/$9.50*

Seen and Heard

Six New Plays by Irish Women
edited with an introduction by Cathy Leeney

A rich and funny, moving and theatrically exciting collection of plays
by Mary Elizabeth Burke-Kennedy, Síofra Campbell, Emma
Donoghue, Anne Le Marquand Hartigan, Michelle Read and Dolores
Walshe.

ISBN 0-9534-2573-8   €19.00/Ir£14.99/$18 *

Theatre of Sound

Radio and the Dramatic Imagination
by Dermot Rattigan

An innovative study of the challenges that radio drama poses to the
creative imagination of the writer, the production team, and the
listener..

ISBN 0-9534-2572-4   €19.00/Ir£14.99/$18 *

Publications by Carysfort Press

Urfaust

A new version of Goethe's early "Faust"
in Brechtian mode, by Dan Farrelly

This version is based on Brecht's irreverent and daring re-interpretation of the German classic.

ISBN 0-9534257-0-3 €7.60/Ir£6.00/$7*

Under the Curse

Goethe's "Iphigenie auf Tauris",
in a new version by Dan Farrelly

The Greek myth of Iphigenie grappling with the curse on the house of Atreus is brought vividly to life. This version is currently being used in Johannesburg to explore problems of ancestry, religion, and Black African women's spirituality.

ISBN 0-9534-2572-X €8.15/Ir£6.50/$7.50*

The Theatre of Marina Carr

"before rules was made",
edited by Anna McMullan and Cathy Leeney

Essays by leading commentators and practitioners in theatre, placing Marina Carr's work in the context of the current Irish and international theatre scene. This book will examine the creative dialogue between theatre professionals, Carr's powerful plays, and their audiences.

2002

* Plus post and packing

General Editor: Dan Farrelly

Carysfort Press, 58 Woodfield, Scholarstown Road, Rathfarnham, Dublin 16, Republic of Ireland.

t: (01) 4937383 f: (01) 4069815
e: info@carysfortpress.com **www.carysfortpress.com**